Search Engine Optimization
ALL-IN-ONE
FOR DUMMIES®

by Bruce Clay and Susan Esparza

Foreword by Danny Sullivan
Editor-in-chief, *Search Engine Land*

WILEY

Wiley Publishing, Inc.

Search Engine Optimization All-in-One For Dummies®

Published by
Wiley Publishing, Inc.
111 River Street
Hoboken, NJ 07030-5774

www.wiley.com

WILEY

About the Authors

Bruce Clay is president and founder of Bruce Clay, Inc., which specializes in Internet marketing. Bruce has worked as an executive for several high-technology businesses and comes from a long career as a technical executive with leading Silicon Valley firms, since 1996 in the Internet business consulting arena. Bruce holds a BS in math and computer science and an MBA from Pepperdine University and has written many articles. He has been a speaker at more than one hundred sessions, including Search Engine Strategies, WebmasterWorld, ad:tech, Search Marketing Expo, and many more, and has been quoted in the *Wall Street Journal, USA Today, PC Week, Wired, SmartMoney,* several books, and many other publications. He has also been featured on many podcasts and WebmasterRadio.fm shows, as well as appearing on the NHK one-hour TV special, "Google's Deep Impact." Bruce is a principal editor and speaker for *SEMJ (Search Engine Marketing Journal),* a scholarly research journal for search engine marketing. He has personally authored many of the advanced search engine optimization tools that are available from www.bruceclay.com.

Susan Esparza is senior editor for Bruce Clay, Inc. She joined Bruce Clay, Inc. in November 2004 and has written extensively for clients and industry publications, including the *SEO Newsletter, The Bruce Clay Blog,* and *Search Engine Guide.* Susan is an editor for *SEMJ,* a peer-reviewed research journal in the search engine marketing field and co-hosts *SEM Synergy,* a weekly half-hour radio show on WebmasterRadio.fm. Her goal is to have a longer author biography in the future.

Dedication

To Cindy, for supporting me through thick and thin; to my coauthor, Susan, for helping with this endeavor. And to the entire SEM community that I've been privileged to be a part of for more than a decade.

— Bruce Clay

To my family, for being excited about the book when I wasn't — particularly to my brother, Robert, who made me quit my previous job to join Bruce Clay, Inc. And to Bruce himself for being an awesome boss and coauthor.

— Susan Esparza

Authors' Acknowledgments

Special thanks to Kyle Looper, who had the idea for this project and who has displayed unending patience no matter the setback. Also, thanks to Linda Morris, our editor, who answered a hundred questions as we figured out the process of writing this. Many thanks go to Paula Allen, Johnny Lin, Scott Polk, Katherine Wertz, and the rest of the Bruce Clay, Inc. staff, for their input, expertise, and support. And not least, we'd like to thank the entire search marketing community, without whom this book could not exist — it's truly a measure of this industry's willingness to share knowledge that this book was possible.

Publisher's Acknowledgments

We're proud of this book; please send us your comments through our online registration form located at http://dummies.custhelp.com. For other comments, please contact our Customer Care Department within the U.S. at 877-762-2974, outside the U.S. at 317-572-3993, or fax 317-572-4002.

Some of the people who helped bring this book to market include the following:

Acquisitions and Editorial

Project Editor: Linda Morris

Acquisitions Editor: Kyle Looper

Copy Editor: Linda Morris

Technical Editor: Paul Chaney

Editorial Manager: Jodi Jensen

Media Development Project Manager:
Laura Moss-Hollister

Media Development Assistant Project Manager:
Jenny Swisher

Media Development Assistant Producers:
Angela Denny, Josh Frank, Shawn Patrick,
and Kit Malone

Editorial Assistant: Amanda Foxworth

Sr. Editorial Assistant: Cherie Case

Cartoons: Rich Tennant
(www.the5thwave.com)

Composition Services

Project Coordinator: Katherine Key

Layout and Graphics: Sarah Philippart,
Christin Swinford

Proofreaders: Evelyn W. Gibson,
Jessica Kramer

Indexer: Sherry Massey

Publishing and Editorial for Technology Dummies

    Richard Swadley, Vice President and Executive Group Publisher

    Andy Cummings, Vice President and Publisher

    Mary Bednarek, Executive Acquisitions Director

    Mary C. Corder, Editorial Director

Publishing for Consumer Dummies

    Diane Graves Steele, Vice President and Publisher

Composition Services

    Gerry Fahey, Vice President of Production Services

    Debbie Stailey, Director of Composition Services

Contents at a Glance

Foreword .... *xxii*

Introduction 1

Book 1: How Search Engines Work 7
Chapter 1: Putting Search Engines in Context 9
Chapter 2: Meeting the Search Engines 25
Chapter 3: Recognizing and Reading Search Results 39
Chapter 4: Getting Your Site in the Right Results 47
Chapter 5: Knowing What Drives Search Results 65
Chapter 6: Spam Issues: When Search Engines Get Fooled 75

Book 11: Keyword Stragegy 85
Chapter 1: Employing Keyword Research Techniques and Tools 87
Chapter 2: Selecting Keywords 97
Chapter 3: Exploiting Pay Per Click Lessons Learned 109
Chapter 4: Assigning Keywords to Pages 117
Chapter 5: Adding and Maintaining Keywords 129

Book 111: Competitive Positioning 141
Chapter 1: Identifying Your Competitors 143
Chapter 2: Competitive Research Techniques and Tools 153
Chapter 3: Applying Collected Data 179

Book 1V: SEO Web Design 193
Chapter 1: The Basics of SEO Web Design 195
Chapter 2: Building an SEO-Friendly Site 215
Chapter 3: Making Your Page Search Engine-Compatible 241
Chapter 4: Perfecting Navigation and Linking Techniques 275

Book V: Creating Content 291
Chapter 1: Selecting a Style for Your Audience 293
Chapter 2: Establishing Content Depth and Page Length 307
Chapter 3: Adding Keyword-Specific Content 327
Chapter 4: Dealing with Duplicate Content 341
Chapter 5: Adapting and Crediting Your Content 355

Book VI: Linking 365

Chapter 1: Employing Linking Strategies 367
Chapter 2: Obtaining Links 389
Chapter 3: Structuring Internal Links 405
Chapter 4: Vetting External Links 421
Chapter 5: Connecting with Social Networks 435

Book VII: Optimizing the Foundations 449

Chapter 1: Server Issues: Why Your Server Matters 451
Chapter 2: Domain Names: What Your URL Says About You............ 471
Chapter 3: Using Redirects for SEO 487
Chapter 4: Implementing 301 Redirects 495
Chapter 5: Watching Your Backend: Content Management System Troubles....... 509
Chapter 6: Solving SEO Roadblocks 523

Book VIII: Analyzing Results 553

Chapter 1: Employing Site Analytics 535
Chapter 2: Tracking Behavior with Web Analytics........................ 557
Chapter 3: Mastering SEO Tools and Reports.............................. 571

Book IX: International SEO 591

Chapter 1: Discovering International Search Engines.................... 593
Chapter 2: Tailoring Your Marketing Message for Asia 609
Chapter 3: Staking a Claim in Europe 621
Chapter 4: Getting Started in Latin America 633

Book X: Search Marketing 641

Chapter 1: Discovering Paid Search Marketing............................ 643
Chapter 2: Using SEO to Build Your Brand................................. 669
Chapter 3: Identifying and Reporting Spam 691

Appendix 707

Index 725

Table of Contents

Foreword..*xxii*

Introduction *1*

About This Book 1
Foolish Assumptions...2
How This Book Is Organized 2
    Book I: How Search Engines Work......................2
    Book II: Keyword Strategy 2
    Book III: Competitive Positioning.......................3
    Book IV: SEO Web Design 3
    Book V: Creating Content....................................3
    Book VI: Linking 3
    Book VII: Optimizing the Foundations 3
    Book VIII: Analyzing Results 3
    Book IX: International SEO..................................4
    Book X: Search Marketing...................................4
Icons Used in This Book 4
Conventions Used in This Book............................4
Where to Go from Here..5

Book 1: How Search Engines Work *7*

Chapter 1: Putting Search Engines in Context *9*

Identifying Search Engine Users 10
    Figuring out how much people spend.............10
    Knowing your demographics 11
Figuring Out Why People Use Search Engines.....13
    Research 13
    Shopping 13
    Entertainment...14
Discovering the Necessary Elements for
Getting High Keyword Rankings 16
    The advantage of an SEO-compliant site 16
    Defining a clear subject theme.......................17
    Focusing on consistency.................................18
    Building for the long term 18
Understanding the Search Engines: They're a Community....18
    Looking at search results: Apples and oranges 20
    How do they get all of that data?...................22

Chapter 2: Meeting the Search Engines...........25

Finding the Common Threads among the Engines 25
Getting to Know the Major Engines...........................26
    Organic versus paid results................................27
    Directories 27
    Yahoo!..28
    Google..30
    Microsoft Live Search.....................................32
Checking Out the Rest of the Field: AOL and Ask.com............33
    AOL..33
    Ask.com..33
Finding Your Niche: Vertical Engines 34
    Industry-specific..34
    Local..34
    Behavioral...35
Discovering Internal Site Search.............................35
Understanding Metasearch Engines 36

Chapter 3: Recognizing and Reading Search Results 39

Reading the Search Engine Results Page.......................39
Understanding the Golden Triangle............................41
Discovering Blended Search 43
    Results of the blended search on the Golden Triangle.......43
    Understanding the effect of Blended Search................46

Chapter 4: Getting Your Site in the Right Results.............47

Seeking Traffic, Not Ranking 47
Avoiding Spam 48
Understanding Behavioral Search Impact on Ranking 48
    Personalizing results by location.........................49
    Personalizing results by Web history 50
    Personalizing results by demographics.....................50
    Opting out of personalized results 50
Using Verticals to Rank....................................52
    Video..52
    Images 53
    News 54
    Shopping...54
    Blogs and RSS 55
Showing Up in Local Search Results 55
    Getting into Google Local 56
    Getting into Yahoo! Local 57
    Getting into MSN Local (local.msn.com) 57
Making the Most of Paid Search Results 58
    Google AdWords 58
    Yahoo!..60
    Microsoft Live Search.....................................62

Chapter 5: Knowing What Drives Search Results **65**

    Using Advanced Search Operators 66

        Combining operators for turbo-powered searching 68

        Searching for images 69

        Searching for videos 69

        Searching for news 69

        Searching through blogs 70

        Searching with maps 71

    Distinguishing between High Traffic and High Conversion Search 71

Chapter 6: Spam Issues: When Search Engines Get Fooled **75**

    Understanding What Spam Is 75

    Discovering the Types of Spam 76

        Hidden text/links 76

        Doorway pages 77

        Deceptive redirection 78

        Cloaking 79

        Unrelated keywords 79

        Keyword stuffing 79

        Link farms 80

    Avoiding Being Evil: Ethical Search Marketing 80

    Realizing That There Are No Promises or Guarantees 81

    Following the SEO Code of Ethics 82

Book II: Keyword Stragegy **85**

Chapter 1: Employing Keyword Research Techniques and Tools **87**

    Discovering Your Site Theme 88

        Brainstorming for keywords 88

        Building a subject outline 89

        Choosing theme-related keywords 91

    Doing Your Industry and Competitor Research 92

    Researching Client Niche Keywords 93

    Checking Out Seasonal Keyword Trends 93

    Evaluating Keyword Research 95

Chapter 2: Selecting Keywords **97**

    Selecting the Proper Keyword Phrases 97

    Reinforcing versus Diluting Your Theme 99

    Picking Keywords Based on Subject Categories 104

        High traffic keywords 104

        High conversion keywords 106

Chapter 3: Exploiting Pay Per Click Lessons Learned............109
Analyzing Your Pay Per Click Campaigns for Clues About Your Site ...110
    Brand building..111
    Identifying keywords with low click-through rates 112
Reducing Costs by Overlapping Pay Per Click
    with Natural Keyword Rankings................................114

Chapter 4: Assigning Keywords to Pages 117
Understanding What a Search Engine Sees as Keywords 117
Planning Subject Theme Categories..................................118
Choosing Landing Pages for Subject Categories 121
Organizing Your Primary and Secondary Subjects 121
Understanding Siloing "Under the Hood"..............................122
Consolidating Themes to Help Search Engines See Your Relevance....124

Chapter 5: Adding and Maintaining Keywords.....................129
Understanding Keyword Densities, Frequency, and Prominence.........130
Adjusting Keywords 133
Updating Keywords 134
Using Tools to Aid Keyword Placement 134

Book III: Competitive Positioning................... 141

Chapter 1: Identifying Your Competitors 143
Getting to Know the Competition....................................143
Figuring Out the Real Competition.................................145
Knowing Thyself: Recognizing Your Business Advantages.............147
Looking at Conversion as a Competitive Measure 148
Recognizing the Difference Between Traffic and Conversion.........149
Determining True Competitors by Their Measures 151
Sweating the Small Stuff..152

Chapter 2: Competitive Research Techniques and Tools..........153
Realizing That High Rankings Are Achievable.......................153
Getting All the Facts on Your Competitors 154
Calculating the Requirements for Rankings.........................155
    Grasping the tools for competitive research:
      The Page Analyzer..156
    Discovering more tools for competitive research....................161
    Mining the source code...162
    Seeing why server setup makes a difference 164
    Tracking down competitor links.....................................168
    Sizing up your opponent..169
    Comparing your content...170

Penetrating the Veil of Search Engine Secrecy 171
Diving into SERP Research 172
Doing More SERP Research, Yahoo! and Microsoft Style.................... 174
Increasing your Web Savvy with the SEMToolBar 175

Chapter 3: Applying Collected Data **179**

Sizing Up Your Page Construction 180
Landing page construction 180
Content.. 184
Engagement objects 185
Learning from Your Competitors' Links.. 187
Taking Cues from Your Competitors' Content Structure.................... 190

Book 1V: SEO Web Design 193

Chapter 1: The Basics of SEO Web Design **195**

Deciding on the Type of Content for Your Site.................................... 196
Choosing Keywords 197
Running a ranking monitor to discover
what's already working 197
Matching `Meta` tags and keywords to page content.................... 200
Using Keywords in the Heading Tags 201
Keeping the Code Clean... 203
Organizing Your Assets 205
Naming Your Files 206
Keeping Design Simple... 208
Making a Site Dynamic 211
Develop a Design Procedure... 212

Chapter 2: Building an SEO-Friendly Site **215**

Preplanning and Organizing your Site 215
Designing Spider-Friendly Code.. 216
Creating a Theme and Style 218
Writing Rich Text Content... 219
Planning Your Navigation Elements.. 220
Top navigation 222
Footer navigation 223
Side navigation 224
Implementing a Site Search 224
Incorporating Engagement Objects into Your Site............................ 226
Embedding interactive files the SEO-friendly way.................... 227
Allowing for Expansion 230
Developing an Update Procedure.. 231
Balancing Usability and Conversion 232
Usability and SEO working together... 232
Creating pages that sell/convert.. 236
Creating a strong call to action.. 238

Chapter 3: Making Your Page Search Engine-Compatible........241

Optimizing HTML Constructs for Search Engines...............................242
    The Head section 242
    Body section...248
Using Clean Code..256
Making Your Site WC3–Compliant...257
Designing with sIFR 261
Externalizing the Code 268
Choosing the Right Navigation 269
    Image maps..269
    Flash 270
    JavaScript..270
    Text-based navigation 270
    A word about using frames 270
Making Use of HTML Content Stacking..271
    Implementing the table trick 271
    Div tag positioning...272

Chapter 4: Perfecting Navigation and Linking Techniques 275

Formulating a Category Structure..276
Selecting Landing Pages 281
Absolute versus relative linking 283
Dealing with Less-Than-Ideal Types of Navigation.........................284
    Images 284
    JavaScript...285
    Flash 286
Naming Links 288

Book V: Creating Content **291**

Chapter 1: Selecting a Style for Your Audience.................293

Knowing Your Demographic 294
    Finding out customer goals 294
    Looking at current customer data......................................295
    Researching to find out more...296
    Interviewing customers..297
    Using server logs and analytics 299
Creating a Dynamic Tone 299
Choosing a Content Style..301
Using Personas to Define Your Audience 301
    Creating personas...302
    Using personas..303
    Benefits of using personas...305
    Drawbacks of using personas..305

Chapter 2: Establishing Content Depth and Page Length 307

Building Enough Content to Rank Well...308
Developing Ideas for Content...309
    Brainstorming to get ideas 310
    Looking at competitors for content ideas 310
    Utilizing your offline materials...311
    Listening to customers...312
Using Various Types of Content 312
Optimizing Images 313
    Naming images 313
    Size matters 314
Mixing in Video 315
    Placing videos where they count most.....................................316
    Saving videos, and a word about formats 316
    Sizing videos appropriately for your audience........................317
    Choosing the "best" video quality...317
    Choosing the right video length...318
    Posting your videos to increase traffic 318
Making the Text Readable 318
Allowing User Input..322
Creating User Engagement 323
Writing a Call to Action 325

Chapter 3: Adding Keyword-Specific Content 327

Creating Your Keyword List..327
Developing Content Using Your Keywords 329
    Beginning to write..330
    Keeping it relevant...331
    Including clarifying words 331
    Including synonyms to widen your appeal................................332
    Dealing with stop words 333
    Freshness of the content 333
    Dynamically adding content to a page......................................334
Optimizing the Content..334
    Digging deeper by running Page Analyzer................................336
Finding Tools for Keyword Integration..338

Chapter 4: Dealing with Duplicate Content. .341

Sources of Duplicate Content and How to Resolve Them....................342
    Multiple URLs with the same content 342
    Finding out how many duplicates the
        search engine thinks you have...343
    Avoiding duplicate content on your own site.............................344
    Avoiding duplications between your different domains 345
    Printer-friendly pages...346
    Dynamic pages with session IDs 347
    Content syndication 348
    Localization 349

Mirrors 349
CMS duplication 350
Archives 351
Intentional Spam 351
Scrapers 352
Clueless newbies 353
Stolen content 353

Chapter 5: Adapting and Crediting Your Content **355**
Optimizing for Local Searches 356
Creating region-specific content 357
Maximizing local visibility 358
Factoring in Intellectual Property Considerations 359
What to do when your content is stolen 359
Filing for copyright 360
Using content from other sites 361
Crediting original authors 362

Book VI: Linking **365**

Chapter 1: Employing Linking Strategies **367**
Theming Your Site by Subject 367
Web analytics evaluation 372
PPC programs 372
Tracked keyword phrases 372
Keyword research 372
Using search engine operators for discovery 374
Implementing Clear Subject Themes 375
Siloing 377
Doing Physical Siloing 378
Doing Virtual Siloing 380
Anchor text 381
Backlinks 381
Keyword-rich anchor text 381
Relevant Web sites link to relevant categories 382
Natural link acquisition 382
Ethical site relationships 382
Purchased links 382
External links 383
External link anchor text 383
Internal linking structure 383
Excessive navigation or cross linking 385
Building Links 385
Link magnets 386
Link bait 386
Link requests 387
Link buying 387

Chapter 2: Obtaining Links **389**

Researching Links...389
Soliciting Links 393
Requesting unpaid backlinks 393
Soliciting a paid link 396
Making Use of Link Magnets and Link Bait........................397
Articles 398
Videos 398
How Not to Obtain Links 399
Evaluating Paid Links 400
Working with RSS Feeds and Syndication 401
Creating a press release...402
Spreading the word 403

Chapter 3: Structuring Internal Links **405**

Subject Theming Structure...405
Optimizing Link Equity 407
Creating and Maintaining Silos 408
Building a Silo: An Illustrated Guide...................................410
Maintaining Your Silos 414
Including Traditional Site Maps...415
Using an XML Site Map 418

Chapter 4: Vetting External Links **421**

Identifying Inbound Links...421
Avoiding Poor Quality Links 422
Reciprocal links...422
Incestuous links 423
Link farms 424
Web rings 424
Bad neighborhoods 424
Identifying Quality Links..426
Complementary subject relevance...............................426
Expert relevance reinforcement 427
Quality testimonial links 428
Finding Other Ways of Gaining Link Equity 429
Making the Most of Outbound Links....................................430
Handling Advertising Links 431
Dealing with Search Engine Spam 432

Chapter 5: Connecting with Social Networks **435**

Making Use of Blogs 435
Discovering Social News Sites 437
Promoting Media on Social Networking Sites.....................438
Social Media Optimization..440
Community Building..442
Incorporating Web 2.0 Functioning Tools...........................445

Book VII: Optimizing the Foundations 449

Chapter 1: Server Issues: Why Your Server Matters. 451

Meeting the Servers...452
    Using the Apache server..452
    Using the Microsoft IIS server 452
    Using other server options..453
Making Sure Your Server Is Healthy, Happy, and Fast 453
    Running a Check Server tool 454
    Indulging the need for speed..457
Excluding Pages and Sites from the Search Engines...........................458
    Using a robots text file 458
    Using Meta Robots tags...461
    Being wise to different search engine robots..........................462
Creating Custom 404 Pages 464
    Designing a 404 error page 464
    Customizing your 404 error page for your server 466
    Monitoring your 404 error logs to spot problems....................467
Fixing Dirty IPs and Other "Bad Neighborhood" Issues......................468
    Diagnosing your IP address's health 468

Chapter 2: Domain Names: What Your URL Says About You 471

Selecting Your Domain Name...471
Registering Your Domain Name...474
Covering All Your Bases 475
    Country-code TLDs...475
    Generic TLDs 477
    Vanity domains 478
    Misspellings 479
Pointing Multiple Domains to a Single Site Correctly 480
Choosing the Right Hosting Provider 481
Understanding Subdomains...484
    Why people set up subdomains..484
    How search engines view subdomains 485

Chapter 3: Using Redirects for SEO. 487

Discovering the Types of Redirects 487
    301 (permanent) redirects..488
    302 (temporary) redirects 489
    Meta refreshes...490
    JavaScript redirects...491
Reconciling Your WWW and Non-WWW URLs 492

Chapter 4: Implementing 301 Redirects 495

Getting the Details on How 301 Redirects Work...................................495
Implementing a 301 Redirect in Apache .htaccess Files......................496
    To add a 301 redirect to a specific page in Apache....................498
    To 301 redirect an entire domain in Apache............................498

Implementing a 301 Redirect on a Microsoft IIS Server 499
    To 301 redirect pages in IIS 5.0 and 6.0 499
    To 301 redirect an entire domain in IIS 5.0 and 6.0 500
    To implement a 301 redirect in IIS 7.0 502
    Implementing a 301 redirect with
      ISAPI_Rewrite on an IIS server 503
    To 301 redirect an old page to a new page in ISAPI_Rewrite 503
    To 301 redirect a non-www domain to
      the www domain in ISAPI_Rewrite 504
Using Header Inserts as an Alternate Way to Redirect a Page 504
    PHP 301 redirect 505
    ASP 301 redirect 505
    ASP.NET 301 redirect 506
    JSP 301 redirect 506
    ColdFusion 301 redirect 507
    CGI Perl 301 redirect 507
    Ruby on Rails 301 redirect 508

Chapter 5: Watching Your Backend: Content Management System Troubles **509**
Avoiding SEO Problems Caused by Content Management Systems 510
    Understanding why dynamically generated
      pages can be friend or foe 510
    Dealing with dynamic URLs and session IDs 511
    Rewriting URLs 513
Choosing the Right Content Management System 515
Customizing Your CMS for SEO 517
Optimizing Your Yahoo! Store 519

Chapter 6: Solving SEO Roadblocks **523**
Inviting Spiders to Your Site 524
Avoiding 302 Hijacks 528
Handling Secure Server Problems 530

Book VIII: Analyzing Results *553*

Chapter 1: Employing Site Analytics **535**
Discovering Web Analytics Basics 535
    Web metrics 536
    Web analytics 537
Measuring Your Success 538
    Identifying what you are tracking 539
    Choosing key performance indicators 541
    Measuring reach 542
    Acquisition 543
    Response metrics 544

Conversions 544
Retention 545
Examining Analytics Packages 546
Google...546
Omniture Site Catalyst 548
Others..550
Getting Started: Log Files Analysis 551
Log file analysis tools 554
Check out traffic numbers 555

Chapter 2: Tracking Behavior with Web Analytics 557
Measuring Web Site Usability 557
Personas...558
A/B testing 558
Multivariate testing...559
Cookies...560
Session IDs 562
Tracking Conversions 562
Measuring marketing campaign effectiveness 563
Building conversion funnels.......................................564
Preventing conversion funnel drop-off 566
Analyzing your conversion funnel.............................566
Making site improvements 567
Assigning Web page objectives...................................567
Tracking the Success of Your SEO Project............................568
Analyzing Rankings 569

Chapter 3: Mastering SEO Tools and Reports 571
Getting Started with A/B Testing...571
Getting ready to run an A/B test 573
Doing an A/B test with Website Optimizer.................577
Viewing your results..583
Discovering Page and Site Analysis Tools............................584
Understanding Abandonment Rates 585
Measuring Traffic and Conversion from Organic Search 586
Click maps...587
Pathing 587
Using Link Analysis Tools..588

Book IX: International SEO 591

Chapter 1: Discovering International Search Engines 593
Understanding International Copyright Issues.......................593
Targeting International Users 595
Domains and geolocating..598
Site architecture tips 599

Identifying Opportunities for Your International Site.............................600
    Single sites 600
    Multiple sites 601
    The blended approach 602
Realizing How People Search 602

Chapter 2: Tailoring Your Marketing Message for Asia...........609

Succeeding in Asia..609
    Assessing your site's chances.......................................609
    Sizing up the competition and sounding out the market 610
    Determining your plan of attack 611
Discovering Japan 612
Succeeding in China 613
Finding Out About South Korea..618
Operating in Russia 619

Chapter 3: Staking a Claim in Europe...........................621

Succeeding in the European Union 621
Knowing the Legal Issues in the EU..622
Working within the United Kingdom.......................................623
Discovering France..625
Operating in Germany...627
Understanding the Netherlands 629

Chapter 4: Getting Started in Latin America..................633

Succeeding in Latin America..633
Geotargeting with Google Webmaster Tools 635
Working in Mexico...635
Operating in Brazil..637
Discovering Argentina..638

Book X: Search Marketing................................. 641

Chapter 1: Discovering Paid Search Marketing................643

Harnessing the Value of Paid Search 644
    Writing and testing the ad 653
    Preparing the landing page..654
    Figuring out ad pricing 655
Making SEO and Pay Per Click Work Together........................658
    Complete market coverage with SEO and PPC 659
    Reinforcing your brand with PPC 662
Supplementing Traffic with PPC 662
Making Smart Use of Geotargeting 663
Starting Your Seasonal Campaigns 664
    Principle #1: Start your seasonal campaign in advance 665

Principle #2: Adjust your spending levels as
the buying season progresses 665
Principle #3: Use some of the same keywords
your site already ranks for 666

Chapter 2: Using SEO to Build Your Brand 669

Selecting Keywords for Branding Purposes 670
Using Keywords to Connect with People 670
How to Build Your Brand Through Search 672
Writing press releases 673
Optimizing for blended search 674
Using Engagement Objects to Promote Your Brand 676
Building a Community 677
Being who you are online 678
Blogging to build community 680
Using other social media to build community 682
Connecting to your audience with social networking 683
Spreading the word with social bookmarking 685

Chapter 3: Identifying and Reporting Spam 691

How to Identify Spam and What to Do About It 691
Hidden text or links 692
Doorway pages 693
Frames 693
Deceptive redirection 693
Cloaking 694
Unrelated keywords 695
Keyword stuffing 695
Link farms 696
How to Report Spam to the Major Search Engines 696
Google 697
Yahoo! 698
Microsoft Live Search 698
Ask.com 699
Reporting Paid Links 700
Reducing the Impact of Click Fraud 704

Appendix 707

Index 725

Foreword

*I*n the search marketing industry, Bruce Clay is a legend. Those who sailed the largely uncharted waters of the Great Search Engine Ocean back in 2000 remember fondly his first Search Engine Relationship Chart. It plotted out the relationships between more than 20 different search engines, explaining which search engines generated their original own results versus those that simply white-labeled results they got from others — the "powered by" search engines, as they used to be called. In such a confusing space, Bruce endeavored to bring order, guidance, and education.

But Bruce has been more than a chart-maker, of course. As early search marketers struggled to understand which practices were acceptable to search engines and which weren't, Bruce was among the few leading the calls for standardized best practices and a code of conduct. From the early years, he's also been a leading educator for others coming into the space. Whether writing about search marketing, participating in forums, or speaking in conferences, Bruce has been a consistent font of wisdom. He has freely shared knowledge and helped hundreds, if not thousands, of people successfully tap into the power of search marketing.

Finally, we get Bruce's wisdom distilled into book form. And it's no surprise that he's plotted out a comprehensive guide to the still-vast Great Search Engine Ocean that exists out there. There might be fewer players these days, but that doesn't mean search marketing has gotten simpler. If anything, it has become more complex. Rather than the world of the 1990s, where there was one type of search results — unpaid results that listed Web pages — today's search engine world encompasses paid results, local results, video results, "blended" or "universal" search pages, and more. There are social sites that serve to build links. An entire economy revolves around the buying and selling of links, along with penalties that can hit those who do. We also have more ways to analyze the traffic we receive, as well as ways to test different types of pages that people "land" upon to convert.

Don't be scared. Although the world is more complex, it's a complexity that can be mastered — and to great gain. Search engines remain one of the top ways Web sites gain traffic. Moreover, they drive visitors who are poised to convert. Millions turn to them asking questions each day. The smart marketer who understands search engines positions her content to answer those questions. It's a perfect match-up.

In the spirit of his original relationship charts, Bruce has once again plotted out a path for others to follow. So read on, and I wish you the best in your search marketing success.

— Danny Sullivan

Editor-in-chief, *Search Engine Land*

Introduction

Since the late 1990s, Internet marketing has taken off as a dynamic marketing channel because of its accuracy and ease of tracking. The Internet has come a long way in a short time: As it grew, finding the sites you were looking for with a directory became impossible. Search engines appeared as the way forward, offering a way to have the Web come to you. Savvy marketers began to realize that search engine results pages were the place to be for any business that wanted to take advantage of the Web. Search engine optimization grew out of the need to develop pages in a way that tells search engines that your site is the best for a particular topic.

Search engine optimization is not a difficult discipline, but it's a complex one with many different parts that need to be tweaked and adjusted to work in harmony. It's not a game of chasing search engine algorithms. Instead, the goal of search engine optimization is simply to present your pages as the most relevant for a given search query. Resist the urge to assume that one part is more important than another. All the various aspects of SEO need to work together in order to succeed.

About This Book

Throughout the book, we reference tools and other experts in the field. Search engine marketing (SEM), as an industry, is very active and excels at knowledge sharing. Although we cover the basics here, we strongly urge you to take advantage of the community that has developed since search engine marketing began. Truly, without the SEM community, this book could not have been written.

We hope that you keep this book at hand, picking it up when you need to check for answers. For that reason, we attempt to make each minibook stand on its own. If something is outside the scope of a particular minibook, we refer you to the correct chapter or minibook for more information.

Search engine optimization has grown and changed over the years, along with the search engines themselves, and it will continue to grow for years to come. Although we call this an "All in One" guide, we have to stress that it is a guide built of the moment with an eye on the future.

Foolish Assumptions

We wrote this book for a particular sort of person. We assume that you, the one holding this book, are a small business owner who is pretty new to Internet marketing. You might have a Web site or you might just be thinking about getting into this online thing, but either way, we presume that you have already figured out how to turn on your computer and connect to the Internet.

A second assumption is that you're either somewhat familiar with the technologies that power Web sites or that you have access to someone who is. HTML, JavaScript, Flash, and other technologies are broad topics on their own. We don't expect you to know everything there is to know about JavaScript programming or Flash, but we don't spend time teaching you them. If you aren't familiar with how to program in these technologies, we recommend that you find a super-smart programmer and treat her like she's made of gold. For a primer, you may also wish to seek out the other *For Dummies* (Wiley) titles devoted to these topics.

How This Book Is Organized

Like most books in the *For Dummies* series, *Search Engine Optimization All-in-One For Dummies* is structured as a reference that you can turn to again and again. You should be able to go to the Table of Contents or the Index and jump straight to the topic you're interested in. Of course, if you're completely new to search engine optimization and Internet marketing, you can read the book from cover to cover. In the next several sections, we outline what each minibook is all about.

Book 1: How Search Engines Work

The first book is pretty much exactly what its title says it is. It focuses on how search engines developed and how they work, and introduces the basics of search engine optimization. For a little spice, we also throw in a brief introduction to spam and set out some ethical guidelines that we follow when working on our clients' sites.

Book 11: Keyword Strategy

This chapter focuses on how to research which keywords are going to bring the most valuable traffic to your site. It gives you the tools and tactics to build a keyword list and themes. These keywords serve as the basis for almost every other element in search engine optimization.

Book III: Competitive Positioning

Chances are there are hundreds of thousands, if not millions, of Web pages that are relevant to the keywords that you want. The top ten sites for those keywords are your competitors, and you have a lot to learn from them. This book focuses on how to identify and analyze competitors in order to use their successes to make your own site soar.

Book IV: SEO Web Design

You're not going to get very far in search engine marketing without a Web site. It's simply a must. The most successful search engine optimization campaigns begin before a single Web page is uploaded to your server. This book starts with a very high-level analysis of a search engine–friendly site structure and then goes a level down in specificity with each subsequent chapter to help you build the very best site you can.

Book V: Creating Content

Search engines can't rank your site for something that it doesn't have related content for. Content is one of the cornerstones of ranking, but it's also the least understood element. This book focuses on developing content ideas, identifying different kinds of content, and explains the best ways to implement various types of engagement objects to enhance your site for your users.

Book VI: Linking

The humble hypertext link forms another of the cornerstones in SEO. Whether you're linking to yourself (internal linking), others are linking to you (inbound links), or you're linking to other sites (outbound links), this book covers them all and explains why each is vital and important. In addition, we give you firm guidelines to help you in your link building efforts.

Book VII: Optimizing the Foundations

The environment that your Web site lives in is critical to your SEO success. A slow server, badly written robots text file, or mishandled redirect can tank your rankings. In order to give your site the best place to live, check out this minibook.

Book VIII: Analyzing Results

You can't know for sure if your SEO campaign is really working until you track the results. Web analytics packages are a must for any online business. This chapter covers basic methodology, implementation of one of the most common analytics tools, Google Analytics, and how to apply the findings to improve your business.

Book IX: International SEO

Most companies never look beyond the borders of their home country, but some companies like to dream big. For those businesses, we take a trip around the world and give some pointers on how to get started overseas. From Europe, to Asia, to Latin and South America, this book introduces the online culture of several nations and takes a look at the cultural and legal concerns that await an international business.

Book X: Search Marketing

There's more to search engine marketing than just search engine optimization, and each of the chapters in this minibook could be a book in themselves. This minibook is simply intended to be a very basic introduction to this subject and how search marketing can work together with SEO to deliver stellar results. Hopefully, it whets your appetite for more.

Icons Used in This Book

This icon calls out suggestions that help you work more effectively and save time.

You should try to keep items marked with this icon in mind while doing your Web site optimization. Sometimes it's a random tidbit of information, but more often than not, it's something that you'll run into repeatedly and is therefore worth remembering.

SEO can get pretty technical pretty fast. If you're not familiar with the terminology, it can start to sound like gibberish. We marked the sections where we get extra-nerdy with this icon so that you can be prepared. If these sections go over your head, don't worry: You can move on without understanding every nuance.

We were sparing with this icon. If you see a Warning, take extra care. This icon denotes the times when getting something wrong can nuke your site, tank your rankings, and just generally devastate your online marketing campaign.

Conventions Used in This Book

When we talk about doing searches, which we do a lot, we need a way to differentiate them from the rest of the text. Enclosing search terms in quotation marks doesn't work because quotation marks have a special meaning when you type them into a search engine, so throughout the book, you see search queries surrounded by square brackets, like this: [search query]. All the text inside the brackets is what you type into the search engine.

In most cases, we refer to the authority passed by links as *link equity*; however, in your travels through the wide world of Internet marketing, you're bound to come across several other terms like *link popularity*, *link juice*, and *PageRank*. (The latter is a Google proprietary term and using it generically for all search engines is sort of like calling all facial tissue *Kleenex*.) They all mean the same thing; we picked *link equity* for clarity's sake.

Where to Go from Here

The best thing about this book is that you can go anywhere from here. Although we've written it like a regular instruction manual that can be read from beginning to end, we also want you to be able to use it as a reference or a go-to guide for tricky problems. So start anywhere you want. Jump into link building or take a crack at creating great content.

Our recommendation, if you're brand new to SEO, is to start at the beginning. After that, it's up to you. Good luck and have fun. Just because this is serious business doesn't mean you can't enjoy the rollercoaster ride.

Book I
How Search Engines Work

The 5th Wave   By Rich Tennant

Contents at a Glance

Chapter 1: Putting Search Engines in Context .9

Identifying Search Engine Users 10
Figuring Out Why People Use Search Engines.. 13
Discovering the Necessary Elements
    for Getting High Keyword Rankings 16
Understanding the Search Engines: They're a Community.................... 18

Chapter 2: Meeting the Search Engines. 25

Finding the Common Threads among the Engines 25
Getting to Know the Major Engines.. 26
Checking Out the Rest of the Field: AOL and Ask.com.......................... 33
Finding Your Niche: Vertical Engines 34
Discovering Internal Site Search... 35
Understanding Metasearch Engines 36

Chapter 3: Recognizing and Reading Search Results 39

Reading the Search Engine Results Page.. 39
Understanding the Golden Triangle 41
Discovering Blended Search 43

Chapter 4: Getting Your Site in the Right Results. 47

Seeking Traffic, Not Ranking 47
Avoiding Spam 48
Understanding Behavioral Search Impact on Ranking 48
Using Verticals to Rank... 52
Showing Up in Local Search Results 55
Making the Most of Paid Search Results 58

Chapter 5: Knowing What Drives Search Results 65

Using Advanced Search Operators 66
Distinguishing between High Traffic and High Conversion Search 71

Chapter 6: Spam Issues: When Search Engines Get Fooled 75

Understanding What Spam Is.. 75
Discovering the Types of Spam 76
Avoiding Being Evil: Ethical Search Marketing.................................... 80
Realizing That There Are No Promises or Guarantees 81
Following the SEO Code of Ethics... 82

Chapter 1: Putting Search Engines in Context

In This Chapter

✔ **Identifying search engine users**

✔ **Discovering why people use search engines**

✔ **Pinpointing elements for getting high keyword rankings**

✔ **Defining relationships between search engines**

The Internet offers a world of information, both good and bad. Almost anything a person could want is merely a few taps on the keyboard and a couple clicks of a mouse away. A good rule of thumb for the Internet is if you want to know about something or purchase something, there's probably already a Web site just for that. The catch is actually *finding* it. This is what brings you to this book. You have a Web site. You have hired what you hope is a crack team of designers and have unleashed your slick, shiny new site upon the Web, ready to start making money. However, there is a bit of a problem: Nobody knows that your site exists. How will people find your Web site?

The most common way that new visitors will find your site is through a search engine. A *search engine* is a Web application designed to hunt for specific keywords and group them according to relevance. It used to be, in the stone age of the 1990s, that most Web sites were found via directories or word-of-mouth. Somebody linked to your Web site from their Web site, or maybe somebody posted about it on one of their newsgroups, and people found their way to you. Search engines such as Google, Yahoo!, and Microsoft Live were created to cut out the middleman and bring your user to you with little hassle and fuss.

In this chapter, we show you how to find your audience by giving you the tools to differentiate between types of users, teaching you to sort out search engines, identifying the necessary elements for being prominent in those engines, and giving you an insider look at how all the search engines work together.

Identifying Search Engine Users

Who is using search engines? Well, everyone. A significant amount of all Web traffic to Web sites comes from search engines. Unless you are a household name like eBay or Amazon, chances are people won't know where you are unless they turn to a search engine and hunt you down. In fact, even the big brands get most of their traffic from search engines. Search engines are the biggest driver of traffic on the Web and their influence only continues to grow.

But although search engines drive traffic to Web sites, you have to remember that your Web site is only one of several and a half trillion other Web sites out there. Chances are, if someone does a search, even for a product that you sell, your Web site won't automatically pop up in the first page of results. If you're lucky and the query is targeted enough, you might end up somewhere in the top 100 of the millions of results returned. That might be okay if you're only trying to share your vacation photos with your family, but if you need to sell a product, you need to appear higher in the results. In most cases, you want the number one spot on the first page because that's the site everyone looks at and that most people click.

In this section, you find out a bit more about the audience available to you and how to narrow down how to reach them.

Figuring out how much people spend

The fact of the matter is that people spend money on the Internet. It's frightfully easy: All you need is a credit card, a computer with an Internet connection, and something that you've been thinking about buying. E-commerce in the United States reached $34.7 billion in the third quarter of 2007 alone. Some project that e-commerce could reach $1 trillion a year by 2012. Combine that with the fact that most Americans spend an average of 24 minutes a day shopping online, not including the time they spend actually getting to the Web site (19 minutes), and you're looking at a viable means of moving your product. To put it simply, "There's gold in them thar hills!"

So, now you need to get people to your Web site. In real estate, the most important thing is location, location, location, and the same is true of the Internet. On the Web, however, instead of having a prime piece of property, you need a high listing on the *search engine results page (SERP)*. Your placement in these results is referred to as your *ranking*. You have a few options when it comes to achieving that. One, you can make your page the best it can be and hope that people will find you, or two, you can pay for one of the few advertising slots. More than $12 billion was spent in 2007 on the North American search marketing industry alone. Eighty-eight percent of that was spent on *pay per click (PPC)* advertising, in which you pay to have search engines display your ad. The other 12 percent goes to *search engine optimization (SEO). SEO,* when properly done, helps you to design your Web site in such a way that when a user is doing a search, your pages appear on the first page of returned results, hopefully in the top spot. Your main focus in this book is finding out about SEO, but because they overlap somewhat, you pick up a bit of PPC knowledge here and there along the way.

Knowing your demographics

In order to get the most bang for your SEO buck, you need to know the demographics for your Web visitors. You need to know who's looking for you, because you'll need to know where best to advertise. For example, if you're selling dog sweaters, it's probably not a great idea to advertise in biker bars. Sure, there might be a few Billy Bob Skullcrushers with a cute little Chihuahua in need of a cashmere shrug, but statistically, your ad would probably do much better in a beauty salon. The same goes for your Web site in a search engine. Gender, age, and income are just a few of the metrics that you'll want to track in terms of identifying your audience. Search engine users are pretty evenly split between male and female search engine users, with a few slight differences: 50.2 percent of Yahoo! users are female, whereas 53.6 percent of Google users are male. In terms of age brackets, the older set leans more towards using Ask.com, and the younger users wind up on Yahoo! and MSN.com most often. In fact, Ask.com is changing their focus in order to cater specifically to married women. Google reaps the highest number of users with an income of $100,000 a year or more. Search engines even feed their results into other search engines, as you can in see our handy-dandy Search Engine Relationship Chart later in this chapter. Table 1-1 breaks down user demographics across the search engines for your reference.

Table 1-1	User Demographics Across Major Search Engines		
	Google	*Yahoo! Search*	*MSN Search*
Female	46.58%	50.76%	54.26%
Male	53.42%	49.24%	45.74%
18-34	43.57%	48.23%	39.53%
35-54	42.85%	39.83%	44.49%
55+	13.57%	11.94%	15.99%
Under $30K/year	20.00%	21.87%	21.01%
$30K-100K/year	57.05%	57.69%	58.84%
Over $100K/year	22.95%	20.44%	20.16%

For the 12-week period ending May 15, 2004

You need to know who your search engine visitors are because this demographic data helps you effectively target your market. This demographic distribution is often associated with search query *keywords*, the words that search engine visitors use to search for your products. For an in-depth look at choosing keywords, you can check out Book II, Chapter 2, but a brief summary is that *keywords* are what a search engine looks for when figuring out what sites to show in the SERP. Basically your keywords are the words you used in your *search query* — or what you typed into the little search window. If you are searching for something like information on customizing classic cars, for example, you would type [custom classic cars] into the search field. (When we discuss search queries through the book, we use square brackets to show the keywords. You wouldn't actually type the brackets into the search field.) Figure 1-1 displays a typical search engine results page for the query [custom classic cars].

Figure 1-1: Keywords in a search engine window: [custom classic cars].

The search engine goes to work combing its index for Web pages containing these specific keywords and returns to you with your results. That way, if you have a product that's geared towards a certain age bracket, or towards women more than men, you can tailor your keywords accordingly. It may seem inconsequential, but trust me, this is important if you want to be ranked well for targeted searches.

Figuring Out Why People Use Search Engines

We've already established that a *lot* of people use search engines. But what are people looking for when they use them? Are they doing research for restoring their classic car? Do people use them to look for a place that sells parts for classic cars? Or are they just looking to kill time with video that shows custom cars racing? The answer is yes to all of the above. A search engine is there to scour the billions on billions of Web sites out there in order to get you where you need to go, whether it's doing research, going shopping, or just plain wasting time.

Research

Most people who are using a search engine are doing it for research purposes. They are generally looking for answers or at least to data with which to make a decision. They're looking to find a site to fulfill a specific purpose. Someone doing a term paper on classic cars for their Automotive History 101 class would use it to find statistics on the number of cars sold in the United States, instructions for restoring and customizing old cars, and possibly communities of classic car fanatics out there. Companies would use it in order to find where their clients are, and who their competition is.

Search engines are naturally drawn to research-oriented sites and usually consider them more relevant than shopping-oriented sites, which is why, a lot of the time, the highest listing for the average query is a Wikipedia page. *Wikipedia* is an open-source online reference site that has a lot of searchable information, tightly cross-linked with millions of back links. *Open source* means that anyone can have access to the text and edit it. Wikipedia is practically guaranteed to have a high listing on the strength of its site architecture alone. (We go over site architecture in much more depth later on in Book IV.) Wikipedia is an open-source project, thus information should be taken with a grain of salt as there is no guarantee of accuracy. This brings us to an important lesson of search engines — they base "authority" on perceived expertise. Accuracy of information is not one of their criteria: Notability is.

In order to take advantage of research queries, you need to gear your site content toward things that would be of interest to a researcher. "How to" articles, product comparisons, reviews, and free information are all things that attract researchers to your site.

Shopping

A smaller percentage of people, but still very many, use a search engine in order to shop. After the research cycle is over, search queries change to terms that reflect a buying mindset. Terms like "best price" and "free shipping" signal a searcher in need of a point of purchase. Optimizing a page to meet the needs of that type of visitor results in higher *conversions* (actions taken by a user that meet a sales or business goal) for your site. As we mentioned, global search engines such as Google tend to reward research oriented sites, so your pages have to strike a balance between sales-oriented terms and research-oriented terms.

This is where specialized engines come into the picture. Although you can use a regular search engine to find what it is you're shopping for, some people find it more efficient to use a search engine geared directly towards buying products. Some Web sites out there are actually search engines just for shopping. Amazon, eBay, and Shopping.com are all examples of shopping-only engines. The mainstream engines have their own shopping products such as Google Product Search (formerly called Froogle) and Yahoo! Shopping, where you type in the search term for the particular item you are looking for and the engines return the actual item listed in the results instead of the Web site where the item is sold. For example, say you're buying a book on Amazon.com. You type the title into the search bar, and it returns a page of results. Now, you also have the option of either buying it directly from Amazon, or, if you're on a budget, you can click over to the used book section. Booksellers provide Amazon.com with a list of their used stock and Amazon handles all of the purchasing, shipping, and ordering info. The same is true of Yahoo! Shopping and Google Product Search. And like all things with the Internet, odds are that somebody, somewhere, has exactly what you're looking for. Figure 1-2 displays a results page from Google Product Search.

Entertainment

Research and shopping aren't the only reasons to visit a search engine. The Internet is a vast, addictive, reliable resource for consuming your entire afternoon, and there are users out there who use the search engines as a means of entertaining themselves. They look up things like videos, movie trailers, games, and social networking sites. Technically, it's also research, but it's research used strictly for entertainment purposes. A child of the 80s might want to download an old-school version of the *Oregon Trail* video game onto her computer so she can recall the heady days of third grade. It's a quest made easy with a quick search on Google. Or if you want to find out what those wacky young Hollywood starlets are up to, you can to turn to a search engine to bring you what you need.

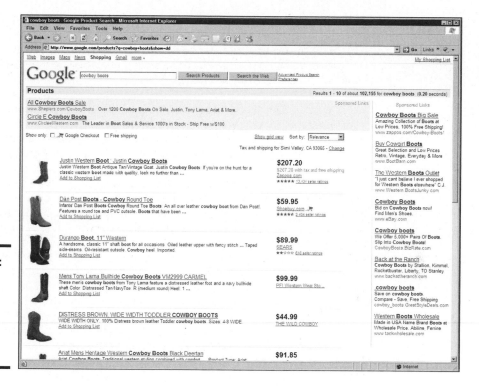

Figure 1-2:
A typical
Google
Product
Search
results
page.

If you're looking for a video, odds are it's going to be something from
YouTube, much like your research results are going to come up with a
Wikipedia page. YouTube is another excellent example that achieves a high
listing on results pages. They're an immensely popular video-sharing Web
site where anyone with a camera and a working e-mail address can upload
videos of themselves doing just about anything from talking about their
day to shaving their cats. But the videos themselves have keyword-rich
listings in order to be easily located, plus they have an option that also displays other videos. Many major companies have jumped on the YouTube
bandwagon, creating channels for their companies (a YouTube *channel* is
a specific account). Record companies use channels to promote bands,
and production companies use them to unleash the official trailer for their
upcoming movie.

Discovering the Necessary Elements for Getting High Keyword Rankings

If the mantra of real estate is location, location, location, and the very best location on the Web is on the search engines, the mantra of SEO should be keywords, keywords, keywords. Search engines use a process to categorize and grade keywords in order to bring you the Web pages you're looking for. The more relevant your keywords are to the user's query, the higher ranking your page has in a search engine's results. Keeping the keywords clear, precise, and simple helps the search engines do their job a whole lot faster. If you're selling something like customized classic cars, you should probably make sure your text includes keywords like classic cars, customized cars, customized classic Mustangs, and so forth, as well as clarifying words like antique, vintage, and restored. You can read more about how to choose your keywords in Book II.

In this section, you get a broad, brief overview on how you get a higher rank than the other guy who's selling macadamia nut butter. You need to know the basics, or you can't do targeted SEO.

The advantage of an SEO-compliant site

Having an SEO-compliant Web site entails tailoring your Web site to have the highest SERP ranking for a keyword search. This includes optimizing your metadata and `Title` tag (for more on metadata, refer to Book IV, Chapter 3) so they are chock full (but not *too* full) of relevant keywords for your industry. Also, make sure that your Web page contains searchable text as opposed to lots of pretty Flash animations and images (search engines have limited ability to understand non-text content), that all of your images contain an `Alt` *attribute* (an alternative description of an image) with text that describes the content of the image, and that you have keywords embedded in your hyperlinks. You also need to be sure that all of your internal content as well as your links are siloed. You want to be sure to optimize every single one of these elements. Use this checklist to get yourself organized:

✦ `Title` tag

✦ `Meta` description tag

✦ `Meta` keywords tag

✦ Heading tag(s)

✦ Textual content

✦ `Alt` attributes on all images

✦ Strong/bold tags

✦ Fully-qualified links

✦ Site map

✦ Text navigation

✦ JavaScript/CSS externalized

✦ Robots text (.txt) file

✦ Web analytics

✦ Keyword research (technically a process — See Book II)

✦ Link development

✦ Image names

✦ Privacy statement

✦ Contact information

✦ Dedicated IP address

Defining a clear subject theme

Another way of getting a high keyword ranking is having a clear subject *theme*. If you're selling kits to customize classic cars, keeping your Web site streamlined and keeping all topics on the Web site relating exactly to classic car customization not only makes it easier for users to navigate your site and research or purchase what they need, but it also increases your chances of having a high page rank when those search engine spiders come by. The more similarly themed keywords you have on your pages, the better. It's the nature of a search engine to break up a site into subjects that add up to an overall theme for easy categorization, and the more obvious your site theme is, the higher your results will be.

It's kind of like going to an all-you-can-eat buffet and deciding you want to get a salad. You, the search engine, immediately go to the salad corner of the buffet because it's been clearly labeled, and from there, you can do your breakdowns. You want romaine lettuce, croutons, parmesan cheese, and Caesar dressing, so you go to where they keep the lettuce, the trimmings, and the dressings in the salad bar section. It's easy to find what you want if everything is grouped accordingly. But if the restaurant stuck the dressing over with the mashed potatoes, you'll have trouble finding it because salad dressing and mashed potatoes don't normally go together. Similarly, when you keep your Web site content organized with everything in its proper place, the search engine views your content with clarity, understanding what you're about — which in turn increases your page ranking. *Siloing* is a way of structuring your site and links in order to present a clear subject theme to the search engines. For more on this technique, refer to Book II, Chapter 4 as well as the entirety of Book VI.

Focusing on consistency

Methodical consistent implementation is the principle that, when you update your Web site, you should do it the same way every time. Your site should have a consistent look and feel over time without massive reorganizations at every update. In order for a search engine to maintain efficiency, you need to keep related content all placed in the same area. You also need to keep all of your updating processes consistent. That way, if something goes wrong during your next update, you can pinpoint what went wrong where without too much hassle since you update things the same way every time. It is confusing to customers to have things constantly changing around. Search engines and visitors to your Web site face the same challenge as a restaurant patron. Getting back to our salad bar analogy, the restaurant owner shouldn't scatter the salad dressings according to the whims of his salad bar designer, and randomly change things every time he gets in a new dressing or someone discontinues one of the old dressings.

Building for the long term

You need to consider your persistence for the long term. How long will your Web site be sticking around? Ideally, like with any business, you want to build it to last without letting it fall behind and look dated. Relevancy to the current market is a big part of this, and if you are behind the times, you are probably behind your competitors. The technology that you use to build your Web site is inevitably going to change as the Internet advances, but your approach to relevancy should remain the same, incorporating new technologies as they arise. This is also a process you should develop over time. In the early days of the Web, frames were used to build sites, but that looks very outdated now. A few years ago, *splash pages* (introductory pages, mostly built in Flash, that provided no content or value to the user) were very popular. Today, they are discouraged. The Internet is an ever-changing entity, and if you're not persistent about keeping up with the times, you might fall by the wayside.

Understanding the Search Engines: They're a Community

Although dozens of search engines dot the Internet landscape, you'll be happy to hear there are really only a few you'll need to consider in your SEO planning. Each search engine appears to be a unique company with its own unique service. When people choose to run a search using Google, Yahoo!, Microsoft Live Search, Ask.com, or any of the others, they might think they've made a choice between competing services and expect to get varying results. But they'd be surprised to find out that under the surface, these seeming competitors are actually working together — at least on the data level.

Google's stated purpose is to "organize the world's information." When you think about the trillions of Web pages and multiple trillion words that exist, multiplying and morphing every day, it's hard to imagine a more ambitious undertaking. It makes sense, then, that not every search engine attempts such a daunting task themselves. Instead, the different search engines share the wealth when it comes to indexed data, much like a community.

You can see at a glance how this community works. Figure 1-3 shows how the major players in the search-engine field interact.

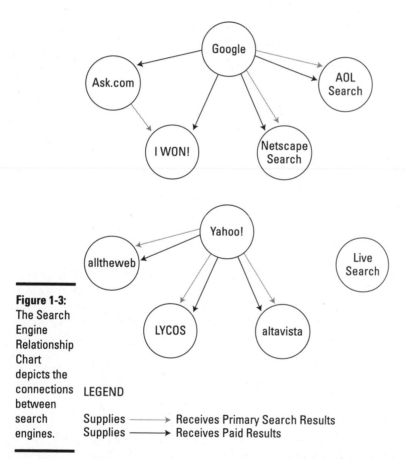

Figure 1-3:
The Search
Engine
Relationship
Chart
depicts the
connections
between
search
engines.

LEGEND

Supplies ------> Receives Primary Search Results
Supplies ------> Receives Paid Results

Chart courtesy of Bruce Clay, Inc.

This search engine relationship chart includes all the major players. The arrows depict search results data flowing from supplying sites to receiving sites. Only four players, whose shapes are outlined — Google, Yahoo!, Microsoft Live Search, and Ask.com — are suppliers. They actually gather and provide search results data themselves. All of the non-outlined search engines on the chart, including AltaVista, AOL, and the like, receive their search results data from some other source. The chart makes it clear that when you do a search on Netscape, for instance, the order of the results is determined by Netscape, but the indexed results are supplied by Google.

Bruce Clay's Search Engine Relationship Chart is also available online in an interactive Flash applet at

`http://www.bruceclay.com/serc/`

As the arrows depict, most of the search engines receive their data from one of these four sources. To further reduce the field, you can tell from the number of arrows coming from Google and Yahoo! that they feed the vast majority of other search sites. So in the world of SEO, you can feel pretty comfortable that if you're indexed in just two sites, Google and Yahoo!, you have a chance at ranking in most other search engines.

Looking at search results: Apples and oranges

One more thing to know about search results — there are two types. Figure 1-4 points out that a search engine can show these two different types of results simultaneously:

✦ Organic search results are the Web page listings that most closely match the user's search query based on relevance. Also called "natural" search results, ranking high in the organic results is what SEO is all about.

✦ Paid results are basically advertisements — the Web site owners have paid to have their Web pages display for certain keywords, so these listings show up when someone runs a search query containing those keywords. (For more on the whys and hows of paid results in greater detail, you can read about pay per click, in Chapter 5.)

A look back: Search engines a decade ago

Bruce Clay first published his Search Engine Relationship Chart in 2000. Back then, there were more major players in the search game and things were, to say the least, somewhat cluttered. The chart had 26 companies on it: everyone from Yahoo! to Magellan to that upstart Google. Fifteen of those companies took their primary results from their own indexes; five of those supplied secondary results to other engines. Without a roadmap, it was an impossible task to keep it all straight. But over the years, things changed. What was once a cluttered mess is now a tidy interplay of a select group of companies. Here is an example of what the very first search engine relationship chart looked like:

Note: To view an interactive version of this chart online, check out `www.bruceclay.com/serc_histogram/histogram.htm`.

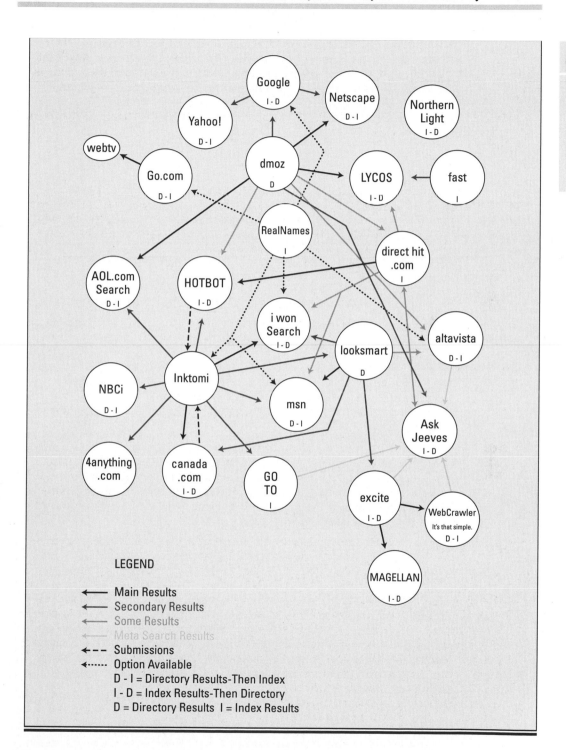

LEGEND

⬅ Main Results
⬅ Secondary Results
⬅ Some Results
⬅ Meta Search Results
◄--- Submissions
◄······ Option Available
D - I = Directory Results-Then Index
I - D = Index Results-Then Directory
D = Directory Results   I = Index Results

On a search results page, you can tell paid results from primary ones because search engines set apart the paid listings, putting them above or to the right of the primary results, or giving them a shaded background, border lines, or other visual clues. Figure 1-4 shows the difference between paid listings and organic results.

Paid result   Paid result

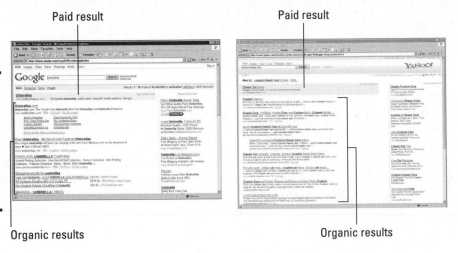

Figure 1-4: A results page from Google and Yahoo! with organic and paid results highlighted.

Organic results   Organic results

The typical Web user might not realize they're looking at apples and oranges when they get their search results. Knowing the difference enables a searcher to make a better informed decision about the relevancy of a result. Additionally, because the paid results are advertising, they may actually be more useful to a shopping searcher than a researcher (remembering that search engines favor research results).

How do they get all of that data?

Okay, so how do they do it? How do Google, Yahoo!, Ask.com, and Microsoft Live Search keep track of everything and pop up results so fast? Behold the wonder of technology!

Gathering the data is the first step. An automated process (known as *spidering*) constantly crawls the Internet, gathering Web-page data into servers. Google calls their spider the *Googlebot*; you could refer to them as *spiders*, *robots*, *bots*, or *crawlers*, but they're all the same thing. Whatever you call the process, it pulls in masses of raw data and does so continuously. This is why changes to your Web site might be seen within a day, or may take up to a few weeks to be reflected in search engine results.

In the second step, search engines have to index the data to make it usable. *Indexing* is the process of taking the raw data and categorizing it, removing duplicate information, and generally organizing it all into an accessible structure (think filing cabinet versus paper pile).

For each query performed by a user, the search engines apply an *algorithm* — basically a math equation (formula) that weighs various criteria and generates a result — to decide which listings to display and in what order. The algorithms might be fairly simple or multi-layered and complex.

At industry conferences, Google representatives have said that their algorithm analyzes more than 200 variables to determine search ranking to a given query. You're probably thinking, "What are their variables?" Google won't say exactly, and that's what makes SEO a challenge. But we can make educated guesses. (Same for Yahoo! and the others.)

So can you design a Web site that gets the attention of *all* the search engines, no matter which algorithm they use? The answer is yes, to an extent, but it's a bit of an art. This is the nuts and bolts of SEO, and what we attempt to explain in this book.

Chapter 2: Meeting the Search Engines

In This Chapter

✔ Finding common threads among the engines

✔ Meeting the major and minor search engines

✔ Finding your niche in the vertical engines

✔ Understanding metasearch engines

All search engines try to make their results the most relevant. They want to make you happy, because when you get what you want, you're more likely to use their site again. The more you use them, the more money they make. It's a win/win situation. So when you do your search on classic car customization and find what you're looking for right away instead of having to click through ten different pages, you'll probably come back and use the same search engine again.

In this chapter, you meet the major search engines and discover their similarities and differences, find out what makes a directory work, get familiar with the difference between organic and paid results, and how the search engines get their organic results. Plus, you find out about the search engine's paid search programs and decide if metasearch engines are important to your SEO campaign.

Finding the Common Threads among the Engines

To keep their results relevant, all search engines need to understand the main subject of a Web site. You can help the search engines find your Web site by keeping in mind the three major factors they're looking for:

✦ **Content:** Content is the meat and bones of your Web site. It's all the information your Web site contains, not just the words but also the *Engagement Objects* (the images, videos, audio, interactive technologies, and so on that make up the visual space). Your page's relevancy increases based upon your perceived expertise. And expertise is based on useful, keyword-containing content. The *spiders,* the robots the search engine uses to read you Web site, also measure whether you have enough content that suggests you know what it is you're talking about. A Web site with ten pages of content is going to rank worse than a Web site with ten thousand pages of content.

✦ **Popularity:** The Internet is a little like high school in that you are popular as long as a lot of people know you exist and are talking about you. Search engine spiders are looking for how many people are linking to your Web site, along with the number of outgoing links you have on your own site. Google really loves this factor.

✦ **Architecture:** If you walk into a grocery store and find everything stacked haphazardly on the shelves, it's going to be harder to find things, and you might just give up and go to another store that's better organized. Spiders do the same thing. As we mentioned earlier, search engines love Wikipedia because of how it's built. It's full of searchable text, `Alt` attribute text, and keyword-containing hyperlinks that support terms used on the page.

You also have some control over two variables that search engines are looking at when they set the spiders on you. One is your site's *response time*, which is how fast your server is and how long it takes for them to load a page. If you're on a server that loads one page per second, the bots request pages at a very slow rate. A second seems fast to us, but it's an eternity for a bot that wants five to seven pages per second. If the server can't handle one page per second, imagine how long it would take the bots to go through 10,000 pages. In order not to crash the server, spiders request fewer pages; this puts a slow site at a disadvantage of sites with faster load times. Chances are, bots will index sites on a fast server more frequently and thoroughly.

The second variable is somewhat contested. Some SEOs believe that your rank could be affected by something called *bounce rate*, which measures whether someone has clicked on a page and immediately hit the back button. The search engines can detect it when a user clicks on a result and then clicks on another result in a short time. If a Web site constantly has people loading the first page for only a few seconds before hitting the back button to return to the search results, it's a good bet that the Web site is probably not very relevant. Remember, engines strive for relevancy in their results so this could very likely be a factor in how they're determining rankings.

So if all search engines are looking at these things, does it matter if you're looking at Yahoo! versus Google? Yes, it does, because all search engines evaluate subject relevance differently. All of the Big Players have their own algorithms that measure things in a different way than their competition. So something that Google thinks belongs on page 1 of listings might not pop up in the top ten over on Yahoo!

Getting to Know the Major Engines

It's time to meet the major search engines. Like we said before, they all measure relevancy a bit differently. Google might rank a page as more relevant than Yahoo! does, so their results pages would look quite different for the same search query. One engine is not necessarily better at search than another. For this reason, deciding which search engine is best is often subjective. It all depends on whether you find what you're looking for.

Organic versus paid results

One of the major ways search engines are differentiated is how they handle their organic versus paid results. *Organic results* are the Web pages that the search engines find on their own using their spiders. *Paid results* (also called *sponsored listings*) are the listings that the site owners have paid for. Usually paid results appear as ads along the side of the window, or in a series of *sponsored links* above the organic results. Paid results don't necessarily equal your search query either. Here's how this happens.

Companies can bid on almost any keyword that they want to get traffic for (with some legal exceptions). The *minimum bid price* is based on many factors, including competition for the keyword, traffic on the keyword, and in Google's case, on the quality of the *landing page*. The better-constructed the *landing page* (the Web page that a visitor receives when clicking on an ad) is, the lower the minimum bid price is. This doesn't have to be an exact match. Businesses often bid on keywords that are related to their products in hopes of catching more visitors. For example, if a visitor searches for tickets to Popular Musical A, a *sponsored* (paid or advertising) link might show up advertising Popular Musical B. This is what's happening below in Figure 2-1. Ticketmaster has bid on Musical A as a keyword in order to advertise Musical B, so that's the musical you see when you click the sponsored link. The organic links, however, should all take you to sites related to Musical A.

Paid results are quite different than organic results. Generally, people click on organic results rather than paid. You can't buy your way to the top of organic results. You can only earn your way there through effective search engine optimization.

Directories

Some search engines use a directory from which to pull information. A *directory* is a list of Web sites the engine can search through that's typically compiled by people, rather than by computer programs. The greatest distinction between a directory and an index involves how the data is arranged: Whereas indexes use algorithms on a database gathered through spidering, directories simply structure the items by theme, like in a phone book. (Note that directories offer their own searches, but sometimes directory content influences regular search results as well.)

Table 2-1 lists all the major search-engine players and the attributes of each, for comparison. Below the table, we introduce you to each search engine in more detail, and talk about organic results, paid advertising (including pay per click), and directory services for each engine.

Figure 2-1:
The search result for [mamma mia musical] includes an advertisement for *Anne of Green Gables* tickets.

Table 2-1   **Search Engine Comparison Table**

Engine Name	Organic	Pay Per Click	Directory	Paid Inclusion
Yahoo! Spider name: Slurp	Yes.	Yes. Yahoo! Search Marketing.	Yes. Yahoo! Directory.	Yes. Search Submit Pro.
Google Spider name: Googlebot	Yes.	Yes. Google AdWords.	Yes. Google Directory (data drawn from DMOZ).	No.
Microsoft Live Search Spider name: MSNbot	Yes.	Yes. Microsoft adCenter.	No.	No.

Yahoo!

In 1994, two electrical engineering graduate students at Stanford University, David Filo and Jerry Yang, created Yahoo! as a list of Web sites (later broken into categories and subcategories as it grew, making it into a directory). This directory became one of the most authoritative on the Web. If a site wasn't listed in Yahoo's directory, it just couldn't be found, much like having an unlisted number keeps your name out of the phone book. For many years, Yahoo! outsourced their search function to other providers (like Google).

Organic results

By the end of 2002, Yahoo! realized how important search was, and they started aggressively acquiring search companies. Yahoo! purchased Inktomi in December of 2002, and then acquired the pay per click company, Overture, in July of 2003 (Overture owned search sites AllTheWeb and AltaVista). Yahoo! then combined the technologies from these various search companies they had bought to make a new search engine, dropping Google's engine in favor of their own in-house technology on February 17, 2004. So now all of Yahoo!'s results come from its own index and directories instead of from Google.

Paid results

Yahoo! Search Marketing (YSM) was formerly Overture, and before that, GoTo !— the original PPC engine. The difference between YSM and Google AdWords is that YSM's editorial process takes longer for ads to go live, and your ranking is primarily based on your bid. Therefore, the top bidder gets the top position, even if it's a different company (like when you search for Musical A but see a paid result taking you to tickets for Musical B instead). That policy is now starting to change, however.

Yahoo! Search Marketing offers two sign-up options:

✦ **Fast Track:** Provides assistance with campaign setup, keyword selection, ad copy, budget advice, and strategy.

✦ **Self Service:** Advertisers create their own bidding strategy, with ads subject to review.

The Yahoo! distribution network also includes AltaVista, Excite, Go2Net, InfoSpace, and Microsoft Live Search. The content partners include Cool Savings, CNN, Consumer Review Network, Knight Ridder, and more.

Search Submit Pro

In addition to paid results, Yahoo! is now offering something called Search Submit Pro. The Search Submit Pro (SSP) Trusted Feed (sometimes called Paid Inclusion) option allows you to submit your Web pages and content to the search engine. Participation in SSP guarantees inclusion in Yahoo's index, bypassing the need to be spidered because you're feeding the pages directly to the engine. This theoretically gives your site a greater chance to be ranked because your whole site is known by Yahoo!. Your Web site listings are displayed based on the relevancy of your site content to search terms, so no keyword bidding is required. Search Submit Pro allows you to tailor your titles and information provided in search-results listings and make content that is not normally seen by a spider visible. It's a paid service for people with search marketing budgets of at least $5,000 per month, or advertisers who have more than 1,000 Web pages to submit to the program. Like we said before, you can't pay your way into the top organic results, but there are systems out there that can help increase your page rank.

The criteria for acceptance are that your site must be high quality and worthwhile, and it must offer your own product or service, not simply be a lead generation or affiliate site. A self-service SSP program that caters to smaller firms is available at a lower price point. This is definitely worth considering if you're having a hard time getting into Yahoo!.

Yahoo! Directory

The Yahoo! Directory is Yahoo!'s personal phone book of Web sites. It's both a free and fee-based directory that's human-reviewed. This means that actual people go through these Web sites and rank them according to popularity and relevance. You can search directly in Yahoo! Directory, and the results are ordered based on their own Yahoo! Search Technology. If it's a big category, the listings display over multiple pages. Since the launch of Yahoo!'s search index, the traffic received from directory listings has fallen off dramatically as fewer people use the directory on a regular basis.

Google

Google began as a research project by two other Stanford University students, Larry Page and Sergey Brin, in January 1996. They hypothesized that a search engine that analyzed the relationships between Web sites would produce better ranking of results than the existing techniques, which ranked results according to the number of times the search term appeared on a page. They originally called it BackRub, because the system checked backlinks in order to estimate a site's relevance. (A *backlink* is an incoming link to a Web page from another site.) They officially incorporated as Google in September 1998.

Organic results

Over time, Google has developed into the powerhouse of the search engine medium. Here are just some of the reasons why Google is the king of search engines and shows no signs of giving up the crown:

+ **Highly relevant:** Google's relevancy is one of its strongest suits thanks to its reliance on site popularity (links) and content searches.

+ **Research-oriented:** Most Internet searches are research-based in nature, making Google's research-friendly results highly attractive to users.

+ **PageRank:** PR is a famous (though somewhat minor in practice) part of Google's search algorithm, which assigns a numerical weight to a set of hyperlinked documents in order to measure their importance.

✦ **Enormous index:** Google has indexed an estimated trillion pages on the Internet and still counting.

✦ **Brand recognition:** The Google brand is used as a verb and listed in dictionaries (as in, "I just Googled something on Yahoo! the other day . . . ").

✦ **Most-visited Web property:** Google has more of the search market than all of the other search engines combined. They net more than 60 percent of all of the search engine traffic (see Table 2-2).

Table 2-2	comScore Core Search Report (November 2008 versus December 2008)*		
	Share of Searches by Percentage		
Core Search Entity	*November 2008*	*December 2008*	*Point Change November 2008 versus December 2008*
Total Core Search	100.0%	100.0%	NA
Google Sites	63.5	63.5	0.0
Yahoo! Sites	20.4	20.5	-0.1
Microsoft Sites	8.3	8.3	0.0
Ask Network	4.0	3.9	-0.1
AOL LLC	3.8	3.8	0.0

*Based on the five major search engines, including partner searches and cross-channel searches. Searches for mapping, local directory, and user-generated video sites that are not on the core domain of the five search engines are not included in the core search numbers.

Paid results

Google has a service called Google AdWords for its paid results. It's a pay per click service that lets you create your own ads, choose your keyword phrases, and set your maximum bid price and a budget. Google ranks its ads based on the maximum bid price and their *click-through rate,* or how many times the ad is clicked on. Google AdWords can also help you create your ads if you're stuck on how to do so. Google then matches your ads to the right audience within its network, and you pay only when your ad is clicked on. Google has also recently introduced limited demographic targeting, allowing you to select the gender, age group, annual household income, ethnicity, and number of children in the household you wish to target. They've also added location-based targeting, *day-parting,* which is advertising only at certain times of the day.

You can potentially get a lot of exposure for your paid ads. The Google AdWords distribution network includes Google sites and affiliates like America Online, HowStuffWorks, Ask (US and UK), T-Online (Europe), News Interactive (Australia), Tencent (China), and thousands of others worldwide.

Google also offers the ability to publish ads on their content network of sites called AdSense. These are the same familiar ads that you can find on the search page fed to regular Web sites. AdSense offers a larger variety of ad types as well.

Google Directory

Google offers a directory based on the Open Directory Project. The *Open Directory Project* is an open-source directory maintained by an army of human volunteers. It's a widely distributed, human-maintained directory. Google applies *PageRank* to sequence the results in their directory. PageRank is Google's own patented algorithm that, in a nutshell, assigns weight to a page based on the number, quality, and authority of links to and from the page (and other factors).

Microsoft Live Search

Microsoft Live Search (previously named "MSN Search") is a search engine designed by Microsoft in order to compete with Yahoo! and Google. It's currently the fourth-most-used search engine in the United States behind Google and Yahoo!. Live Search differentiates itself through new features, like the ability to view additional search results on the same Web page instead of having to click through to subsequent search results pages. It also has the ability to adjust the amount of information displayed for each search result (for example, just the title, a short summary, or a longer summary).

Organic results

Microsoft Live Search has had many incarnations, but previous versions used outside search engine results from companies like Inktomi and Looksmart. After Yahoo! bought Inktomi and Overture, Microsoft realized that they needed to develop their own search product. They launched the preview of their search engine technology on July 1, 2004, and formally switched from Yahoo! organic search results to their own in-house technology on January 31, 2005. Microsoft then announced they were dumping Yahoo!'s search ads program on May 4, 2006. Since then, Microsoft Live Search has been almost exclusively powered by its own search algorithms.

Paid results

Microsoft's paid program is called adCenter. It's the newest pay per click platform available on the Web right now and reports are that it offers extremely good *return on investment* (ROI). Like Google, Microsoft Live Search ranks its ads based on the maximum bid price and their *click-through rate,* or how many times the ad is clicked on. Microsoft also allows you to place adjustable bids based on demographic details. For example, a mortgage lead from an older person with a higher income might be worth more than an equivalent search by someone who is young and still in college.

Checking Out the Rest of the Field: AOL and Ask.com

The four biggest search engines worldwide right now are Yahoo!, Microsoft Live Search, Baidu (a Chinese search engine — see Book IX, Chapter 3 for more information on Baidu), and Google, with Google taking home the lion's share. But other smaller engines operating that do draw a pretty respectable number of hits are still operating.

AOL

AOL has been around in some form or another since 1983. It has grown from a company that provided a service through which users could temporarily download video games through modems that connected their computers to the phone line, to a company that provided a link to other computers using software that provided a "gateway" to the rest of the Internet. Although not as big as it once was, it still provides some services such as e-mail, chat, and its own search engine. But AOL gets all of its search engine results from Google, both organic and paid.

If you want to appear in AOL search, you must focus on Google.

Ask.com

Ask.com was originally created as Ask Jeeves, and was founded by Garrett Gruener and David Warthen in 1996, launching in April of 1997. It set itself apart from Yahoo! and AOL by using editors to match common search queries, and then compiling results using several other search engines. (See metasearch engines later in this chapter for a more in-depth analysis.)

As competition mounted, Ask Jeeves went through several search engine technologies before acquiring Teoma in 2001, which is the core search technology they still use today. In March 2005, InterActive Corp. announced they were buying Ask Jeeves, and, by March of 2006, they changed the name to simply Ask.com. After pioneering *blended search* (the integration of different content types onto the search results page, such as images, videos, news, blogs, books, maps, and so on) but failing to gain any significant market share from the larger three engines, Ask.com is now changing its market strategy and targeting what it sees as its core demographic: married women.

Ask.com gets most of their paid search ads from Google AdWords. Ask.com does have its own internal ad service, but they place their internal ads above the Google AdWords ads only if they feel the internal ads will bring in more revenue.

Finding Your Niche: Vertical Engines

We've been talking mostly about *general search engines*, whose specific purpose is to scour everyone and everything and return results to you. But there's also another type of search engine known as a vertical search engine. *Vertical search engines* are search engines that restrict their search either by industry, geographic area, or file type. Google has several vertical search engines listed in the upper left-hand corner on its home page, for images, maps, and so forth. So when you type [jam] into Google's images search, it only returns images of jam instead of Web pages devoted to jam products and jam-making. The three main types of vertical search engines are detailed in the next sections.

Industry-specific

Industry-specific vertical search engines serve particular types of businesses. The real estate industry has its own search engines like Zillow.com, Roost.com, and Realtor.com that provide housing listings, and companion sites like ServiceMagic.com, which is for home improvement contractors. For the medical industry, there's WebMD, a search engine devoted entirely to medical questions and services. If you are searching for legal services, Findlaw.com and Lawyers.com can help you search for an attorney by location and practice.

Niche engines like these deliver a lower traffic volume but make up for it in quality of traffic. Visitors from niche engines are prequalified because they're looking for exactly your type of site.

Local

A *local search engine* is an engine specializing in Web sites that are tied to a limited physical area also known as a *geo-targeted* area. Basically, it's looking for things in your general neck of the woods. In addition to their main index, each of the major search engines has a local-only engine that they can integrate into their main results, like Google Local and Yahoo! Local. In submitting a page to a search engine, you have an option of listing up to five different criteria you can be searched under, including address, telephone number, city, and so on. That means if a site is submitted with information stating that it's a local business, it'll pop up if someone's looking for that location and product. If you live in Milwaukee and you're looking for a chiropractor, you would have to type in [Milwaukee chiropractor] into the search box: If you don't, you would end up with listings of hundreds of different chiropractors in places that are a little out of your range, like Grand Rapids. Adding a city or a ZIP code to your search automatically narrows the focus.

In late 2008, Google began attempting to determine the intent of the search and automatically started to geo-target search results based on the location of the searcher, even if the user did not specify a city or ZIP code in the query. Not every search gets these modifications automatically, but as Google's algorithm gets more accurate, Google will certainly seek to customize results further.

Less than one percent of searches in the major search engines include local search criteria, however. That's why many large cities have their own local search engines. TrueLocal.com and Local.com are the most well known local-only engines. Internet yellow pages like YellowPages.com, SuperPages.com, DexKnows.com, and YellowBook.com are also out there clamoring for your local search queries.

Behavioral

A *behavioral search engine* is a little bit trickier. *Behaviorals* look for searches by prior history. In other words, these search engines try to guess what exactly you're looking for based upon your previous search inquiries. If you're a coffee-drinker, and you're always searching for some good java, a general search engine might turn up results about coffee beans and the computer programming language. By contrast, if you search using a behavioral engine, over time, it's going to figure out by your user history that you're only looking for coffee, and drop out the technology results completely the next time you run a search for [java].

A good example of a behavioral search engine is Collarity (`www.collarity.com`), which sends you results and advertising based upon your search and browser history. The engines keep track of your history by using *cookies*, tiny innocuous text files automatically stored on your computer that can be easily referenced by these external programs. You're basically leaving an electronic breadcrumb trail as you browse, and the behavioral search engine uses it to give you the most relevant results possible.

Discovering Internal Site Search

Say you're writing an article and you need to reference something in the *New York Times*. NYTimes.com keeps an archive of online articles, but because you can't remember the date the article was published, you'd have a long trek through the online archives. Luckily, they have their own internal site search engine that enables you to look up articles using keywords. Any search engine that's site specific, or searches just that Web site, is an *internal site search engine*.

Larger Web sites with thousands of pages employ these as an easy way of browsing their archives. A very small site probably doesn't need an internal search, but most e-commerce sites with more than a few products should consider implementing one.

Techniques that help you rank in general search engines also help your users when they need to find something on your site using an internal search. A good internal search can be the difference between making a sale and visitors leaving in frustration. To get started quickly, Google offers a hosted internal search solution as well as an enterprise level solution. See `www.google.com/enterprise/public_search.html` for more information.

Understanding Metasearch Engines

Another breed of search engine you should be aware of is a *metasearch engine*. Metasearch engines do not maintain a database of their own, but instead combine results from multiple search engines. The advantage they tout is a twist on "bigger is better" — the more results you see in one fell swoop, the better. The sites Dogpile.com and Metacrawler.com top the list of metasearch engines. When you run a search on Metacrawler.com, it pulls and displays results from the four largest global engines (Google, Yahoo!, Microsoft Live Search, and Ask.com) in one place.

A brief history of metasearch

Metasearch engines have passed their heyday. In the old days (1996, if you're curious, which is approximately 10,000 BC in Internet years), there were dozens of different search engines still in their growth stages. None had indexes that encompassed the whole Internet. Because every search engine had only a piece of the pie, metasearch engines that could dish up the whole thing at once served a real purpose. Now, however, the big search engines all have fairly exhaustive indexes with billions of listings with usable and relevant results, and as we covered in Chapter 1 of this minibook, there's already a lot of indexed-data sharing going on. When you run a search in any of today's four major search engines, you can be sure that you're seeing most of the applicable organic results, and many of the paid ones.

The metasearch engines today rank very low in total market share compared to the four big players. According to ComScore statistics (at the time of writing), Google has more than 63 percent of all search market share in the U.S., and a majority of Web searches globally. That means that six out of ten searches performed in the U.S. are done using Google.com. In the United States, the four big guys combined (Google plus Yahoo!, Microsoft Live Search, and Ask.com) make up more than 90 percent market share. AOL takes a big chunk of the remaining few percentage points, leaving little left over for the metasearch engines to claim.

After pulling results from multiple search engines, the metasearch engines filter those results to determine what the user sees. This is different than applying an algorithm as the indexed search engines do (an *algorithm* is a mathematical equation that weighs many specific criteria about each Web page to generate its "rank" result, as discussed in Chapter 1). Metasearch engines take more of a filtering approach to all of the indexed data gathered from the other search engines. They display organic and paid results mixed up on the page, according to the order they think is most relevant, based on your search terms.

Can metasearch engines help you at all in your quest for great traffic from search engines? Well, possibly. You might enjoy using metasearch engines to help monitor your search engine optimization efforts because the results page tells you exactly where each listing comes from. We've found them especially helpful for keeping track of which competitors buy paid results for which key-words (you can read more about paid search in Book I, Chapter 4). Figure 2-2 shows you a results page from Metacrawler (`www.metacrawler.com`).

You can see the source of each result in small, bracketed text at the end of each listing. Notice that you can only tell which results are paid ads by this source information (such as, "Found on Ads by Yahoo!"). Is it necessary to use a metasearch engine for this type of information? Not really, because it doesn't take too long to run a search in several sites to find their paid results. However, running it in a metasearch engine could, theoretically at least, save you time.

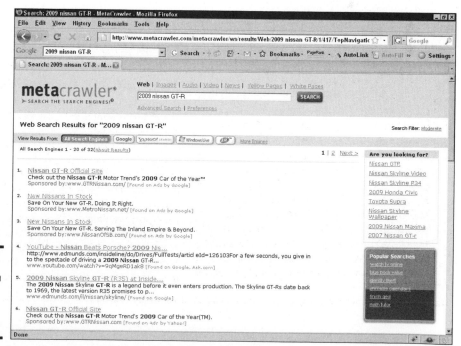

Figure 2-2:
Metasearch
engine
results
page.

Chapter 3: Recognizing and Reading Search Results

In This Chapter

↙ **Reading the search engine results page**

↙ **Understanding the Golden Triangle and its impact on rank position**

↙ **Introducing blended search into the equation**

↙ **Discovering the impact of blended search on the Golden Triangle**

In Chapter 2 of this minibook, we discuss organic versus paid results: *organic results* being the listings that are ranked by perceived merit by a search engine, and *paid results* (also called sponsored results or sponsored links) being purchased links and ads that appear along with your organic results. In this chapter, you discover what the rest of the results page means, find out about the Golden Triangle, are introduced to blended search results, and discover how blended search is changing the game.

Reading the Search Engine Results Page

Say Mother's Day is coming up, and you want to buy your mother a nice bouquet of roses. (Good for you! No wonder Mom always liked you best.) After going to Google and typing your [roses] search query into the box, you're presented with a results page. The results page contains many different listings containing the *keyword,* or search word, [roses], sorted according to what Google thinks is most relevant to you. Figure 3-1 shows a Google results page for the query [roses].

We labeled the different parts in Figure 3-1 so that we can explain them one by one. (Note that we're using a Google results page because they get the lion's share of traffic. Plus, there isn't much difference between their results-page layout and those of Yahoo! and Microsoft Live Search.)

✦ **Search Box:** The box where you type your *search query,* or whatever it is that you're looking for. In this case, it's roses.

✦ **Search Verticals:** Links to the *vertical search engines,* the specialized ones that narrow your search into a specific type of result, such as images or news. Clicking one of these links takes you to a results page with only news or only images.

News results   Search box   Time search took

Search verticals   Related searches   Page count   Sponsored links

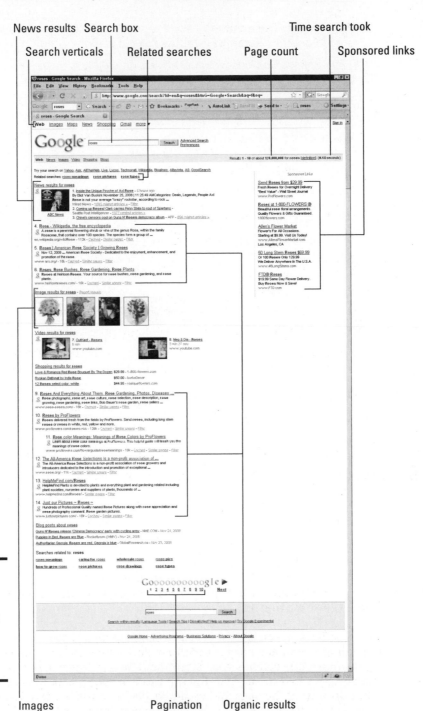

Images   Pagination   Organic results

Figure 3-1:
Things to
notice in
this typical
Google
search
page.

✦ **Page Count:** The number of Web pages Google found that match your search query in some way. In this case, it's a lot.

✦ **Time Search Took:** How long the search engine took to retrieve your results.

✦ **Related Searches:** Other topics that contain your query or other searches Google thinks might be relevant.

✦ **Images:** Picture files that match your query. This comes from Google's Images vertical engine. Clicking the link would take you to the vertical search results; in this case, a page containing only images of roses.

✦ **News Results:** Any news results pertaining to your query or containing a keyword. These come from the vertical news engine. Clicking the link would take you to the news page.

✦ **Sponsored Links:** The paid ads. Note how some of them relate to a specific geographic location near you. This is thanks to the *local* vertical search engine.

✦ **Organic Results:** The listing results from a general search of Google's index, with algorithms applied to determine relevance.

✦ **Pagination:** Links to the additional pages of results.

✦ **Disambiguation:** (not pictured) The "Did you mean . . . ?" suggestions that usually displays after a misspelled search query or search queries that turned up very few results. It's Google trying to guess what you actually wanted. Because [roses] was spelled correctly, no disambiguation appears in Figure 3-1. You can test this feature for yourself by searching for [rozes] in Google.

Understanding the Golden Triangle

Knowing what is on the results page is important, but so is understanding how people read it. As it turns out, there is actually a predictable pattern in the way in which people read a results page. In 2005, Enquiro Research conducted a study to track people's eye movements while reading a typical search engine results page. They discovered a pattern that they called the *Golden Triangle*. The Golden Triangle identifies on a visual heat map how people's eyes scan a results page and how long they look at a particular result before moving on.

In Figure 3-2, you can see there is a common tendency for your eye to start in the upper left-hand corner and move down the page, and then out to the right when a title catches your attention. This eye-tracking pattern forms a triangle. You look the most at the top three or four positions on the upper left, a little bit at the ones in the middle, and with the last few results on the page, you tend not to look at all. So when you apply the Golden Triangle to figure out where you want your Web page to appear on the results page, the spot you aspire to is among the first two or three.

Enquiro White Papers

It should be noted that the full eye-tracking reports examine the results in much greater detail, focusing on intent, first and second looks, "scent," and the different reactions to three engines. If you're interested in delving deeper into this topic, the original 2005 report and a follow up 2006 report can be purchased from www.enquiroresearch.com.

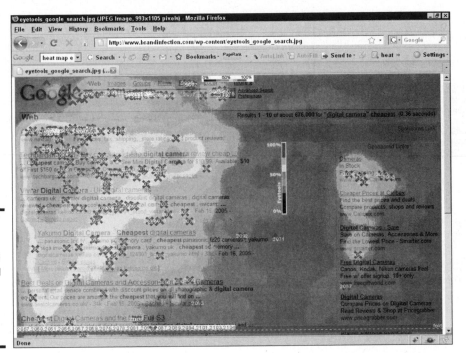

Figure 3-2: Enquiro dubbed this eyetracking study's results the Golden Triangle.

It's important to note that the size of the browser window matters. Although most screen resolutions are 800 x 600 or higher (with a growing percentage viewing 1024 px wide or larger), many users have their window minimized; in that circumstance, the Golden Triangle shrinks. Very few people scroll down to look at the results below the fold; that is, out of the visible browser window. The same is true of every results page, the Enquiro study found. So if your site ranks at the top of the second results page, it may actually be looked at more than the listings at the bottom of page one.

Discovering Blended Search

The search engines have historically indexed pages based upon the text content. Now the search engines are displaying other types of content integrated (blended) automatically onto the SERP. The intent of this blending is to satisfy the searcher and to engage them by making the results more relevant, essentially making the user happier with the search results.

User search behavior was similar across all search results pages until the advent of *blended search* results. Blending search results are something that the search engines have been doing recently with their searches. A *blended search* gives you results that the engine thinks would be useful to you, by including results from their *search verticals*, specialized engines that search only one type of content, like images, videos, news, local results, or blog posts.

Your focus here is to recognize blended search and understand that a blended search is the search engine's way of trying to give you the most relevant results possible by giving you results drawn from multiple sources. Note the differences between the general search in Figure 3-1 and the blended search in Figure 3-3. The images at the top are brought in from Google Image Search as a result of blended search. It requires no effort on the part of the user to receive blended search results. Any query that the search engine algorithms consider to be a candidate for a blended result will have such results. Try this yourself with a query for a popular musician or movie and see what happens. Searching for a person or event in the news recently is another good way to see blended search in action.

The results for the blended search include news items, images, and local results and many other types of engagement objects. These might be results that aren't exactly what you are looking for, but Google thinks they might be useful, so they include them. Notice how the inclusion of an image seems to break up the page. This is important because it changes the eye-tracking patterns in the Golden Triangle.

Results of the blended search on the Golden Triangle

With a traditional results page, the Golden Triangle theory says that you want to be in a top spot for maximum exposure, based on how people's eyes scan the search results page. In 2007, Enquiro released another study (this time as a free white paper) focusing on the impact of the search engines' integration of other verticals into their main results. They concluded that blended search results change how the eye tracks the page. Figure 3-4 shows what happens when test subjects were shown a results page with a blended result included.

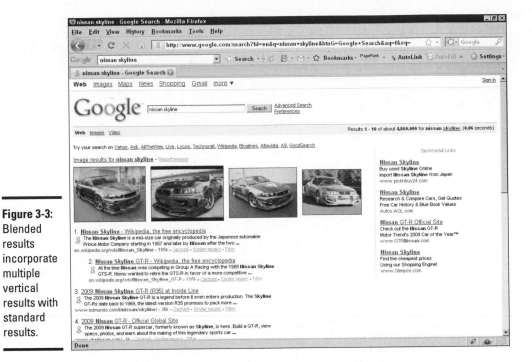

Figure 3-3: Blended results incorporate multiple vertical results with standard results.

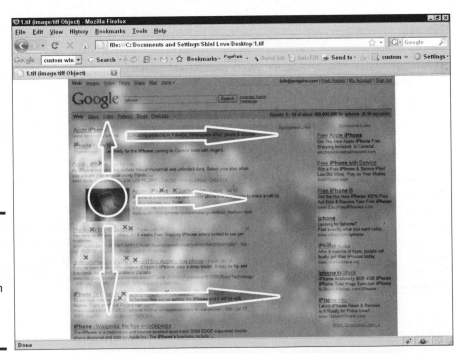

Figure 3-4: The Golden Triangle becomes distorted on a blended results page.

Instead of eye tracking forming a triangle as users' eyes move down and out from the upper-left corner, they briefly glance at the left-hand corner, and then look down to check out the image and very briefly look at the text beside it, before looking lower to check out the listing that is immediately underneath the image.

Humans are drawn to images because they include color and stand out against a text-filled page. Pictures are different, so people are automatically drawn to them. The inclusion of an image high in the results also leads us to mentally cut the page in half. This means that a link that achieves a much-coveted third or fourth spot on the results page may get ignored completely. That's right: Almost no one looks at the link above the image. Instead, nearly everyone looks at the link below the image.

However, inclusion of an image with the link doesn't automatically mean the image gets a thorough scanning. We can determine quickly whether an image is relevant and move on just as fast if we deem the image irrelevant. Note in Figure 3-5, where the image is not relevant to the search, how fast the eye scans and moves on.

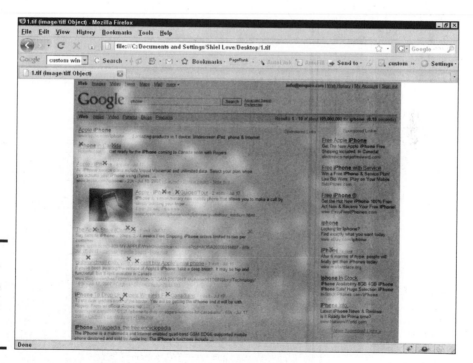

Figure 3-5:
Not quite what we're looking for, so we're moving on.

Understanding the effect of Blended Search

You can see why blended search impacts search engine optimization in a big way. The Golden Triangle research shows how adding an image into the search results, especially one that pops up high on the page, leads searchers' eyes to jump to it, making the top spots on the page not as important as they used to be. This is subject to change in the future as people become more used to the idea of blended results, but, for right now, we're still drawn to the image first. Which means that, in a blended results page with an image, instead of being the number one or number two result, you might actually be happy in the number four spot, under the image.

Understanding how changes to the search results page can affect traffic and click-throughs is important. This information comes in handy when you're fine-tuning your optimization campaign. Armed with the knowledge that your industry is often in the news, you can guide your site to sit in those coveted hot spots on the search page and gain more traffic.

Chapter 4: Getting Your Site in the Right Results

In This Chapter

✓ Seeking traffic as your real goal

✓ Avoiding spam

✓ Understanding how behavioral searching impacts your ranking

✓ Introducing intent-driven search

✓ Using vertical search engines to your advantage

✓ Getting into local search results

✓ Signing up for paid ads in the various search engines

I f the Internet were a mall, Google would be the biggest department store and the Yahoo!, Microsoft, and Ask department stores would be the smaller stores in between. But a mall is more than just its department stores: You can also shop in dozens of specialty stores, food venues, merchant carts, and so on. In this chapter, you meet the specialty stores of searching, the vertical engines, and find out how to make sure your product (your Web site) displays on those stores' shelves.

In this chapter, you discover how to put your products in front of your customers by changing your focus to traffic, not rankings; avoiding spam tactics that could hurt your Web site; and understanding the way that behavioral and intent-based search changes what your audience sees on the search results page. You also find out about how to get into the local search results and how to get started with a pay per click campaign in the main engines.

Seeking Traffic, Not Ranking

First, a couple of reminders are in order. Your search-engine-optimization efforts, if done well, can earn your site a higher ranking in search results pages. However, do not confuse the means with the end. Keep in mind your real goal — getting lots and lots of people to visit your Web site. What you really want to do is drive more Web traffic your way, and ranking represents just one means for achieving that end. In this chapter, you discover another reason to set your sights on traffic rather than ranking — technological advances (namely behavioral targeting and personalization) are causing ranking to become less important.

Avoiding Spam

In the search engine world, cheating is known as spam. *Spam* involves deliberately building Web pages that try to trick a search engine into offering inappropriate, redundant, or poor-quality search results. It's not only unethical, but can also get your Web site removed from an index entirely, so you definitely want to avoid it.

Here's a basic spam illustration: Site A is well written, content-rich, and exceptionally relevant for the search query [sailboat rigging.] Site B is not as well written, not as content-rich, and is considered not as relevant. Site B implements a few spam tactics to trick the engine into believing they're more relevant, and suddenly Site B outranks Site A for searches on [sailboat rigging]. What's the result? It lowers the users' satisfaction with the relevancy of their search results in that search engine, hurts the user experience because they didn't find what they needed, and slaps the face of those working at the search engine company who are responsible for making sure that users actually see relevant content and are happy.

Is it any wonder that the search engines enforce spam rules? It's one thing to want to improve the quality, presentation, and general use of keyword phrases on your Web page, and an entirely different thing to go about tricking the engines into higher rankings without providing the real goods. (Because unintentional spam can still get your site in trouble, you might refer to Book I, Chapter 6 for some specific spam techniques to avoid.)

A note about spam: Spam is largely based on perception. When you get e-mail that you do not want, you consider it spam even though you might have opted to receive emails from that company. However, if you're planning a trip and get e-mail about your travel destination, you don't think that e-mail is spam, even if it was unsolicited. Your interest makes the e-mail not spam. Search engines do the same thing by targeting ads to your interest. This leads to more clicks and higher user satisfaction surrounding advertising.

Understanding Behavioral Search Impact on Ranking

Search engines use a technique called *behavioral search* to customize a results page based on the user's previous search behavior. Behavioral targeting basically tracks the searches you've run and adjusts new search results to include listings the search engine assumes will interest you based on your recent and past searches. It doesn't replace all of the results you'd normally get with a regular search, but it may throw in a few extra ones it thinks would be useful to you.

Have you ever noticed that sometimes your search results differ from another person's search results — even when you both type the same query into the same search engine? This is a scenario that is becoming more and more common. Before you think this means that search engine optimization is completely futile and throw your hands up in exasperation, read on. Here is what's really going on.

Search engines can individually customize search results based on the user's:

✦ Recent search behavior

✦ Location

✦ Web history

✦ Demographic information

✦ Community

The major search engines use more than just keyword ranking to determine the order of results. Remember, they're trying to deliver the most relevant listings possible for every search. As a result, they've recently started taking this down to the individual-user level. With behavioral search and personalization, results revolve around users, not a single boiler plate algorithm.

Behavioral targeting particularly affects the *paid results* you see (that is, ads or sponsored links that site owners have paid the search engine to display on results pages, based on keywords). For instance, if you run a search for [coffee mugs] followed by a search for [java], the search engine throws a few extra paid results for coffee-related products at the top or sides of the page. (Note that this kind of advanced targeting costs advertisers a pretty penny; the coffee sites might get charged double when a user clicks their behavioral-targeting-enhanced listing, compared to their standard pay-per-click rate. For more details on how pay per click works, see Book X, Chapter 2.)

The *organic results* (non-paid listings that display on results pages) also may show slightly different listings or listings in an altered order. Even if you're not logged in, the data from your search history may influence your search engine results, compared to the search results you would see if you were a new searcher for [java]. Your previous search for [coffee mugs] influenced the search engine to assume you meant [java] as in coffee, rather than the computer language.

Personalizing results by location

Thanks to some fairly simple (and occasionally inaccurate) technology, search engines can tell where you are! Your computer's IP address identifies your approximate city location to a search engine, which can then personalize your search results to include local listings for your search terms. This technique, often called *geotargeting*, comes into play the most when you search for items that involve brick-and-mortar businesses or services that need to be provided locally (for example, the search terms "furniture reupholstery" or "house painters" would bring up some local businesses mixed in with the other results).

Personalizing results by Web history

Google, for one, tries to further understand searchers' intentions by looking at their personal *Web history*, or the complete records of their previous Google searches and the Web sites they've visited or bookmarked. How far back they go is unclear. It's important to note that Google can only track your Web history while you're signed in to your Google account. Because the extra services like free e-mail and customizable home pages are truly wonderful, many people have these accounts and may not realize their surfing behavior is being recorded. Google does give you ways to block this, however.

Personalizing results by demographics

Search engines often know demographic information about you such as your gender, age, home address, or city, as well as your interests. You may provide this information to them when you first sign up for an account. Yahoo!, for example, has a Tell Us About Yourself section on their form where you can optionally enter your gender and birth date. They don't get it without your consent. However, lack of direct input doesn't mean they're not going to try to infer information about you based on what you have told them. Your income could be assumed from your location or your gender based on your search history. They also learn about you by tracking what you do within their site. For instance, if you do a search on their map and, for map-searching convenience later, mark your home address as your starting location, the search engine reasonably assumes that that's where you live.

Opting out of personalized results

All of these personalization techniques enable search engines to target your search results more specifically to your individual needs. If the result gives you more relevant listings, it may not be a bad thing. (At least, that's the position the search engines take.)

You might want to opt out of personalized results because of privacy concerns. However, when you're evaluating keywords and doing SEO research, you definitely don't want the results you see to change based on your personal information. You want to see the results that show to most people, most of the time.

Here's how you can opt out of personalization in Google:

1. **To turn off personalized search for a particular query, just add &pws=0 to the end of your search results page URL.**

For example, after running a search for [coffee mugs] on Google, type **&pws=0** at the end of the URL in the navigation bar. These few extra characters appended to the end of your search string stop Google from personalizing your results.

2. **Opt out of session-based personalization.**

Recently, Google began making it more obvious when your search results are customized by displaying the message Customized Based on Recent Search Activity near the upper-right corner of the window (see Figure 4-1). If you click the adjacent More Details link, you see a page explaining why your results were customized, and offering you a way to see your results without these changes. Unfortunately, clicking this link for every search is something of a pain, but it is another option.

3. **Google's Web History feature only tracks you while you're signed in to your Google account, so if you sign out, it's turned off — until you sign on again.**

Google does offer a Yes/No switch to turn it off altogether and ways to delete history records or pause tracking temporarily, but all of these options are a little buried. To find them, sign in to your Google account, and then click the Help link for the options under the heading, The Personalized Google Experience. (Note that turning off Web History does not prevent Google from applying behavioral search targeting to your searches based on session behavior, so you may still need steps 1 and 2.)

Figure 4-1:
A Google search results page showing customized results.

Using Verticals to Rank

Getting into a vertical of a general search engine (like Google, Yahoo!, and Live Search) is fairly simple and requires little extra work. Ranking is another story. Ranking in a vertical is a lot like ranking in a general search engine. In order to optimize images, video, shopping, news, blogs, and RSS feeds, you must tailor your listing so that certain attributes are even more specific. In the next few sections, we highlight the most important attributes for ranking in each vertical.

Video

With the advances in streaming technology and faster Internet connection speeds, video is becoming more and more popular as time goes on. Like increasing the rank of your Web site, you can use similar techniques to make sure your video has a chance of achieving a high page rank.

Getting search-engine ranking for your video is as simple as this:

+ **Place keywords in the *metadata* of a video.** Meta data is descriptive text, containing mostly keywords, that can be placed in the HTML of the video file. You want this text to both describe the video and give the spiders something to look at.

+ **Place keywords in your video's filename.** Remember to keep your keywords for both the metadata description and the filename specific and relevant.

+ **Use YouTube (www.youtube.com) to host your video.** YouTube was acquired by Google a couple of years ago, so any video on YouTube gets spidered and indexed a lot faster than it would on other video hosting sites.

+ **Link from your video to your Web site.** This could help drive up your site's traffic and ranking. Of course, you especially benefit from this strategy if the video you post becomes popular (but don't ask what makes a video popular, because not even Hollywood can predict accurately what people will like).

+ **Include text about the video in the page area surrounding the video link, if possible.** Keep in mind that video, along with images, can be spidered. Spiders can read and index the Meta data and the text surrounding the video, as long as the text is descriptive of the video, full of keywords, and relevant to a user's search. In Figure 4-2, note the description box and the list of keywords, which are all hyperlinked. Remember, Google loves this.

Keep in mind that because YouTube.com is a separate site, the video is not considered "your" content. You want to host the video on your own site as well so that you get credit for it as part of your content. Always link back to your site in the description of the video and in the video file itself.

Figure 4-2:
Your video
on YouTube.

Images

You can apply many of the tips we stated in the previous "Video" section to images, as well. Images and video can be identified by topic as long as the text surrounding them relates to the image or video. Spiders are also looking at the filename, so instead of naming your image file 00038.jpg, call it red-porsche.jpg or something equally descriptive. Definitely include Alt attribute text for every image on your Web site. *Alt attributes* are used to describe an image for users who are using screen readers or when an image does not display. In some browsers, this text becomes user-visible when they move their mouse over the image. Spiders also read and index this text. With so many eyes looking at it, it's worth the effort to write something meaningful. For example, the HTML of the image of the red Porsche could look like this:

```
<img src="redporsche.jpg" ALT="Red 2005 Porsche with leather
    interior">
```

A short, simple, descriptive phrase is all you need for the Alt attribute. Stuffing it with keywords, however, is considered evil and might get your site dropped (see Book I, Chapter 6 for more info on that point). Keep it simple, keep it short, and keep it to the point. Consider the size of the image as a guideline: Smaller images probably only need a couple words to explain what they are. Larger images might require several words. Don't go overboard. If you have paragraphs of information about the image, consider putting that on the Web page as content.

News

Getting into a news vertical is a bit tricky. You might have a company Web site with a news site that you frequently update with articles and recent events, yet it won't rank in a news vertical. Why? Google considers a site a news site if it is updated multiple times a week by multiple authors. Your company News page, for example, would not be considered for inclusion in Google News because even though it might be updated several times a week, it's all written by the same person (or in this case, company). Compare this to a site like MarketWatch.com, which is updated multiple times a day by many different authors.

The easiest way to make your company news available for news searches is to send out a press release of your article. You can choose from a variety of different news wire services (PRNewswire, PRWebDirect, MarketWire, and so on); the fees vary depending on the length of your article, the geographic region you want to cover, and other factors. After you submit your press release, it's available for any news agency to pick up and publish, increasing your company exposure and potentially your site traffic.

You can monitor who picks up your news using either the optional tools provided by your news wire service (for a fee), or by creating a free Google Alert. You can sign up for a Google Alert at www.google.com/alerts and enter your company name, keywords, or other descriptor for your search terms. Google then automatically e-mails you whenever an article relevant to your keywords hits the Web!

Shopping

Shopping verticals usually get their information by using an RSS feed. *RSS* is short for Really Simple Syndication, and it is a method for distributing frequently updated content. Basically, people who receive an RSS feed see a page that displays all of a Web page's recent updates or uploads in a standardized format. An RSS document (which is called a *feed*) contains either a summary of content from an associated Web site or the full text that the spiders come and look over. We go over it a little more in depth later in this chapter, but what you need to know about it here is that shopping verticals use RSS feeds to check for new products. Google's shopping vertical, Google Product Search, uses spiders along with RSS feeds to check for new content, and they're the only shopping vertical out there that's truly free to vendors. Yahoo! Shopping provides an e-commerce template to small business vendors without a Web site, letting them build their own Yahoo! Shopping site that is entered into their shopping search engine for a fee based upon their expected sales, (the higher the sales you expect, the higher the fee). Users can log onto http://smallbusiness.yahoo.com/merchant/ to sign up or take the tour for more information.

Blogs and RSS

Blogs (short for "Web logs") have been increasing in popularity for the past couple of years and are starting to have their own vertical search engines. The same is true for RSS feeds. The thing is, in order for a blog site to rank in a vertical search engine, it needs its own RSS feed. Bloggers using software such as WordPress, Moveable Type, or Blogger have these feeds automatically created for their sites.

Other ranking features beyond having an RSS feed vary between search engines; blogs usually rank based on their own merit (content and update frequency are key), and based on however the algorithm is set up for that particular search engine. Google has a beta version of a blog vertical called Google Blog Search (`blogsearch.google.com`). Figure 4-3 shows a typical Google Blog Search result page.

Figure 4-3:
A Google
Blog search.

Showing Up in Local Search Results

You now know that local search engines provide another playing field for your Web site to attract potential customers. Better yet, they give you a much smaller field, where your business has an excellent chance of being a star player. In this section, you discover the how-to and follow step-by-step instructions (which are accurate at the time of this writing) for getting your site to show up in local-oriented searches. Note that there is no charge for submitting a basic local listing, so think of this as free advertising! You can submit your listing to all three of the big search engines.

Getting your site into the local engines has another benefit. The traffic for local terms in a broad-base engine (such as Google) far outweighs any sort of search volume in a local-only search engine. Search engines like Google, Yahoo!, and Microsoft Live Search are the first stop for a consumer in search of a solution. However, listing your business in the local search engines also ensures that your site shows up for general searches that include *geo-targeting* (search queries that contain a city, ZIP code, or other geographic term). For example, if you have a florist's shop in the Bronx, your shop's Web site would come up when someone searches for [Bronx florist].

Getting into Google Local

Much like their main search index, Google Local is the most popular local vertical out there. Submitting your site to Google Local enables you to show up for local queries, appear on Google Maps for searches there, and of course, appear for relevant general queries via blended search when Google detects that a local result is appropriate. Here is a step-by-step guide to getting your site listed in Google Local:

1. **Check Google Local (local.google.com) to see if your business is already listed. Search for your company name or type of business, followed by a space and your city or ZIP code.**

2. **If your listing isn't there yet, go to https://www.google.com/local/add/login.**

3. **Sign in to your Google account.**

   If you have ever signed up for a Gmail or iGoogle account, you can enter that e-mail address and password. If you don't have an account yet, choose Create a New Google Account and sign up for free.

4. **Submit your free business listing by following the online instructions.**

   You can specify your hours of operation, payment options you accept, and descriptive text. Click Add Another Category and choose up to five categories for your business — these help people find your business when searching, so be sure to choose well.

5. **Select a verification method, either by**

   • Phone (immediate), or

   • Postal mail (within two weeks)

Enrich your business listing for free and get maximum exposure: After your business is listed in Google Local, you can add coupons to entice local customers. Google also lets you upload up to ten photos and five videos at no extra charge.

Getting into Yahoo! Local

Yahoo! (www.yahoo.com) is an extremely popular home page for many people on the Web and, as a result, their local product receives a fair amount of traffic. Like Google, Yahoo! also integrates their local results into map search and incorporates them in blended search results. Follow these simple steps to increase your site's exposure for relevant local searches:

1. **Check Yahoo! Local (local.yahoo.com) to see if your business is already listed. Enter your company name or type of business, your city, or ZIP code, and click the Search button.**

2. **Scan the results to see if your business is already listed. If not, go to http://listings.local.yahoo.com.**

3. **Click Sign In near the top of the page and sign in to your Yahoo! account.**

   (You would have a Yahoo! account if you've ever created a free e-mail or My Yahoo! account.) If you are a new user, click Sign Up instead and create an account.

4. **Create your listing using the online form.**

   You can specify hours of operation, payment methods, and so on. Be sure to pick the two best categories for your business.

5. **Verify the listing and submit it.**

Yahoo! offers a basic listing for free, but if you want to add coupons, photos, a logo, and so on, you have to upgrade to an "enhanced" listing with a small monthly fee. Note that Yahoo! has no official verification system in place, so to protect your business from being added incorrectly by someone else, you might want to jump on this.

Getting into MSN Local (local.msn.com)

Microsoft's local product is the new kid on the block, but this scrappy underdog is worth the effort it takes to sign up. Follow this step-by-step list to get into the local results and capture a new market:

1. **Go to https://llc.local.live.com/ListingCenter.aspx and click Add Listing.**

2. **Enter your business information in their first form to check if your listing already exists.**

3. **If your listing is not found, you need to sign in to your Windows Live ID account. (Sign up if you don't have one.)**

4. **Complete the online forms per their instructions and submit your listing.**

5. **Choose the most appropriate categories.**

6. **Wait two or three weeks for verification via postal mail.**

Making the Most of Paid Search Results

We briefly went over paid search results in Book I, Chapter 2 for Google, Yahoo!, and Microsoft Live Search. If you're wondering what the difference between them is, think of it like buying a commercial on television. Running a commercial during the biggest sporting event of the year is going to be much more expensive than running it at 3:00 A.M. on a local station. The same is true for buying an ad on Google versus buying an ad on one of the less-trafficked search engines. It will be cheaper on the smaller engines, sure, but the odds of someone seeing it are going to be about as low as the price. Price also depends on the popularity of the keyword being bid on. Your best bet for the widest reach when you're getting started with PPC ads is to advertise on one of the three larger engines. Keep in mind that for the most visibility possible, you should probably advertise on as many as you can. In this section, we break PPC ads down for you in terms of how to buy on each of the engines, how much you'll be paying, and who is going to see your ad.

Google AdWords

Google AdWords (`adwords.google.com`) is Google's paid search program. It lets you create your own ads, choose your keyword phrases, set your maximum bid price, and specify a budget. If you're having trouble creating ads, Google has a program to help you create and target your ads. It then matches your ads to the right audience within its network, and you pay only when your ad is clicked. How much you pay varies greatly depending on the keyword because competition drives the bid price. For instance, a keyword like *mesothelioma*, the cancer caused by asbestos, runs about $56 *per click*. Lawyers love this one because a case could arguably net them hundreds of thousands of dollars, so it's worth getting the one case per hundred clicks, and multiple competitors drive the price up through bidding wars.

Signing up for Google AdWords

You can activate an AdWords account for $5, choosing a maximum *cost-per-click* (how much you pay when the ad is clicked) ranging from one cent on up; there's really no limit. Google provides a calculator for determining your daily budget, along with information on how to control your costs by setting limits. Google also has stringent editorial guidelines designed to ensure ad effectiveness and to discourage spam. Payment can be made by credit card, debit card, or direct debit, as well as via bank transfer.

Placement options

With Google AdWords, you have three placement options available to you. The most common is for your ads to appear on Google search engine results page based on a keyword trigger. The second option allows your site to show up in the search results pages of Google's distribution partners like AOL and Ask.com. The third option is site-targeted campaigns in which you can have your ads show up on sites in Google's content network (via Google's AdSense publisher platform). Site-targeted campaigns are based on a cost-per-thousand-impressions (CPM — the M stands for mille and is a holdover from the old printing press days) model with $0.25 as the minimum per 1,000 impressions.

Google has also recently introduced limited demographic targeting, allowing advertisers to select gender, age group, annual household income, ethnicity, and children/no children in the household (which raises the price, but also increases the potential effectiveness of your ad).

Most people want to advertise on Google because their ad has a chance of appearing across a wide range of networks, like America Online, HowStuffWorks, Ask (U.S. and U.K.), T-Online (Europe), News Interactive (Australia), Tencent (China), and thousands of others worldwide. Notice in Figure 4-4 how Google tries to target the ads based on the content of the Web page where the ads appear.

The major benefits of Google AdWords PPC advertising are

+ **An established brand:** Google gets the most searches (61.5 percent in June 2008).

+ **Strong distribution network.**

+ **Both pay-per-click and pay-per-impression cost models.**

+ **Site targeting** with both text and image ads.

+ **Costs automatically reduced** to the lowest price required to maintain position.

+ **Immediate listings** mean your ads go live in about 15 minutes.

+ **No minimum monthly spending or monthly fees.**

✦ **Daily budget visibility.**

✦ **Multiple ads** can be created to test the effectiveness of keywords.

✦ **Keyword suggestion tool.**

✦ **Conversion tracking tool** that helps identify best performing keywords, define your target market, and set an ad budget. You can easily import your search campaign, pay on a cost-per-click (CPC) basis, and access millions of unique users.

Figure 4-4:
A screen-shot of Google ads.

Yahoo!

Yahoo! Search Marketing (`searchmarketing.yahoo.com`) was formerly Overture, and before that GoTo — the original pay-per-click engine. It differs from Google because its human editorial process means that it takes longer for ads to go live. It used to be that your rank was based solely on your bid, but Yahoo! is making changes so that their model is more like Google's.

Signing up for Yahoo! Search Marketing

Yahoo! Search Marketing offers two sign-up options:

✦ **Fast Track:** Provides assistance with campaign setup, keyword selection, ad copy, budget advice, and strategy for a fee of $199. You get a proposal that shows estimated clicks and cost. Ads go online within three business days of your approval.

✦ **Self Service:** Processed online as advertisers create their own bidding strategy with ads subject to review. E-mail notification informs you when the ad goes live, usually within three business days. A full-service option is available if desired, where a Yahoo! Search Marketing specialist provides a proposal showing keywords and projected costs within ten business days, subject to client approval before going live.

Besides the time it takes for campaigns to go live, there are also differences in payment policy. Yahoo! requires advance deposits to cover *click-throughs* (every time a user clicks a paid result ad) and has monthly minimums. If you fall short, you are charged for the difference. If your account runs out of funds, Yahoo! stops the campaign and requires a minimum deposit of three days' worth of clicks based on recent campaign activity to reactivate the campaign.

Placement options

Yahoo!'s exact algorithm for ranking paid ads is a secret, but it's basically

```
Bid Price x Quality Score = Ad Rank
```

Quality score is based on the ad's CTR (click-through rate), the relevance of the ad to the keyword, and the quality of the landing page the ad is sending the user to. Yahoo! Search Marketing offers *geo-targeting*, which identifies users' locations by their IP addresses and gives them local results. You benefit most from geo-targeting if you are a local business. (Note that sometimes the user's IP address happens to originate in a completely different city than where they actually are, so geo-targeting is still not a perfect solution.) Yahoo! Search Marketing also offers ad testing, campaign budgeting, and campaign scheduling.

Like Google, YSM offers several placement options — in their own search listings, on their partner sites (which includes AltaVista, Excite, Go2Net, InfoSpace, and all the Yahoo! properties), and on their content network (through Yahoo! Publisher Network), which includes Cool Savings, CNN, Consumer Review Network, Knight Ridder, and many more. Figure 4-5 shows a typical Yahoo! pay per click ad.

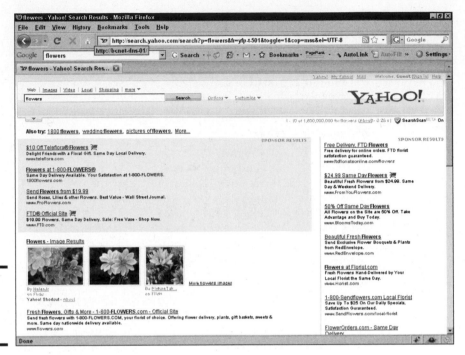

Figure 4-5:
A screen-
shot of a
Yahoo! ad.

Here are some of the benefits of Yahoo! Search Marketing:

✦ **Return on investments (ROI):** Yahoo has one of the highest return on investments (ROI) of any of the search engines.

✦ **Geotargeting** for local businesses.

✦ **Costs less** than Google.

✦ **Business-oriented:** Much more business-oriented than Google.

✦ **Campaign budgeting and scheduling.**

✦ **Large distribution network.**

✦ **Choice of either Fast Track or Self Service** when building your advertising campaigns, with Yahoo! helping you to create the most effective advertising campaign for a fee.

Microsoft Live Search

Microsoft's paid search program is called adCenter (`adcenter.microsoft.com`). AdCenter is the newest of the pay per click options and one of the most advanced. One thing they offer is a keyword research and optimization tool, based in Excel, which enables you to manage keyword lists, keep precise metrics, and more.

Microsoft adCenter

Signing up for Microsoft adCenter costs $5. After that, you only pay when someone clicks your ad, with cost-per-click bids starting as low as $0.05/click. You can import your existing search campaign using Microsoft adCenter and quickly build or expand keyword lists with adCenter's Add-in (beta) for Excel 2007.

Placement options

Microsoft adCenter allows you to target your ads based on user demographics, such as gender, marital status, age, and so forth. You have to pay more to restrict your advertising in this way; the price per click increases or decreases depending on whether someone you picked for your target demographic is clicking your ad. On top of that, adCenter allows you to run your ads on specific days of the week or certain times of day. If you have an ad that targets teenagers, for example, you can choose to have your ad run after 3:00 P.M. on weekdays and all day on weekends in order to achieve higher visibility.

Like Yahoo! and Google, adCenter allows search ads in Live Search results and display ads on Microsoft adCenter Publisher. Opportunities for display ads include RSS feeds to their shopping site, banners, and e-mail. They target smaller business owners with this one, and the cost is $3,000 to $15,000 per month.

Microsoft is the latest engine to have done studies proving that audiences exposed to both search and display ads together deliver a greater positive brand lift (that is, user recall and positive associations with the brand) than either type of campaign can yield on its own.

Figure 4-6 shows a typical search ad (left) and a typical display ad (right).

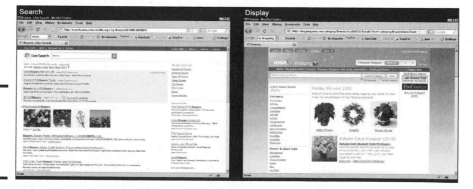

Figure 4-6:
An MSN
search ad
next to a
display ad.

These are some of the benefits of Microsoft Live Search adCenter:

+ **Demographic Targeting:** Allows you to target specific demographics
+ **Cost by Segmentation:** Adjusts cost per click to target demographic
+ **Search and Display:** A useful tool for small businesses
+ **Tools:** Keyword search and optimization tool
+ **Reach:** Your ads appear on Microsoft's content network, which currently covers about 43 million users
+ **Conversion Rates:** adCenter typically returns better ROI than other engines
+ **Costs Less:** Bids are usually lower than either Google or Yahoo!

Chapter 5: Knowing What Drives Search Results

In This Chapter

✔ Searching like a power user

✔ Using advanced operators to supercharge your search engine optimization

✔ Finding specific file types in the vertical search engines

✔ Understanding the difference between high traffic and high conversion

✔ Capturing more conversions using the Long Tail approach

*I*n this chapter, you discover how to use the search engines like a pro through the use of advanced operators, targeting vertical engines. You also find out the difference between high traffic and high conversion terms, plus why it's imperative to capture the so called *Long Tail* of search. Becoming an expert searcher gives you an edge for doing market research, keyword analysis, and much more. The expert-searcher skill set definitely complements your role as a search engine optimizer, so we're devoting a whole chapter to it. At the end of this chapter, you get to apply your newfound skills to enhancing your Web site with keywords targeted for your audience.

A typical search returns many results (commonly in the millions) and may include lots of irrelevant listings. Because search engines find what you tell them to search for, an overly large result set can be chalked up to a too-broad *search query* (the terms typed into the search box). You probably already know some simple techniques for narrowing a search, such as adding more specific terms (such as [bass fishing vacations] instead of just [bass fishing]), or including quotation marks around words that must be an exact phrase. For instance, searching for ["bass fishing vacations"] in quotation marks reduces the result set to just a few hundred listings, compared to more than 600,000 without the quotes. You may even know to click the Advanced Search link to access additional search fields that let you specify what to exclude as well as include. We offer more tips along this line in this chapter.

Using Advanced Search Operators

Search engines have come up with additional tools called *advanced search operators* to give power users even more control when searching. Advanced search operators are special terms that you can insert in your search query to find specific types of information that a general search can't provide. Several of these operators provide useful tools for SEO experts as well as others who want very specific information, or who want to restrict their search to very specific sources. These operators have a particular meaning to each of the different search engines, but not all engines accept the same operators.

Type the advanced search operators at the beginning of your search query, followed by a particular *domain name* (the base URL of a Web site, such as bruceclay.com). This type of query modifies the search to dig deeper into the engine's *algorithms* (the mathematical formulas the search engine uses to weigh various factors and establish a Web site's relevance to a search). The returned page provides entirely different results than the average search.

For example, say you type this query into a Google search box (substituting your own Web site domain name): [link:www.yourdomain.com]. The Google results page would include a list of some of the Web pages that actually link to your Web site. In this particular case, the advanced operator used is [link:] followed by the site's domain name. (Note that you cannot put a space between the operator and the domain name.)

You have numerous operators at your fingertips that can provide significant and useful information. Another very helpful operator is the [site:] operator. If you type [site:] into the search box before the domain name, the search engine results tell you how many pages are within that particular domain and its sub-domains. Those results can also provide information on pages that have been indexed more than once, which in turn provides information regarding duplicate content. It also provides information about pages that are being dropped out of the search engines. You can see how powerful this can be for SEO!

You can also put additional search terms in your query. For example, this search would list all the pages on the given Web site: [site:bruceclay.com]. If you were looking for something specific on the site, however, you could add more search terms to the end. For instance, to find pages on the Web site that contain the word *training* you would type this: [site:bruceclay.com training].

Table 5-1 below shows several advanced operators for the three big engines and describes their use. It should be noted that Yahoo redirects most advanced operators to their advanced search console, Site Explorer, located at http://siteexplorer.search.yahoo.com/.

Table 5-1   **Advanced Search Operators for Power Searching
on Google, Yahoo!, and Microsoft Live Search**

Google	*Yahoo!*	*Microsoft Live Search*	*Result*
cache:			Shows the version of the Web page from the search engine's cache
link:	**link:**	**link:** or **linkdomain:**	Finds all external Web sites that link to the Web page (Note: In Yahoo! you must type in **http://**) (Note: in Microsoft Live Search, there must be a space between the colon and the domain name.)
	linkdomain:		Finds sites that link to any page within the specified domain
related:			Finds Web pages that are similar to the specified Web page
info:			Presents some information that Google has about a Web page
define:	**define:**	**define:** or **definition:**	Provides a definition of a keyword. There has to be a space between the colon and the query in order for this operator to work in Yahoo! and Microsoft Live Search.
stocks:	**stocks:**	**stock:**	Shows stock information for ticker symbols (Note: Type ticker symbols separated by a space; don't type Web sites or company names). There has to be a space between the colon and the query in order for this operator to work in Yahoo! and Microsoft Live Search.
site:	**site:** or **domain:** or **hostname:**	**site:**	Finds pages only within a particular domain and all its sub-domains
allintitle:			Finds pages with all query words as part of the indexed Title tag
intitle:	**intitle:** or **title:** or **T:**	**Intitle:**	Finds pages with a specific keyword as part of the indexed Title tag. There needs to be a space between the colon and the query to work in Microsoft Live Search

(continued)

Table 5-1 *(continued)*

Google	Yahoo!	Microsoft Live Search	Result
allinurl:			Finds a specific URL in the search engine's index (Note: You must type in http://)
inurl:	inurl:	inurl:	Finds pages with a specific keyword as part of their indexed URLs
		inbody:	Finds pages with a specific keyword in their body text

Combining operators for turbo-powered searching

Whether you are an SEO expert or just now gleaning the basics of the search engine optimization industry, you may often find that you need to combine some of the commands to pinpoint the information you need.

For example, you find yourself wanting to determine how many pages on a site have a particular keyword phrase in their Title tag (one of the HTML tags contained in the HTML code that's located at the top of a Web page). Because Title tags are weighted quite heavily in most search engines' algorithms, this information would be very useful in your search engine optimization work. Fortunately, it is possible to combine multiple search operators to find information just like this.

To find out how many pages on a site have a particular keyword phrase, you could type the following query in either Google or Yahoo!: [site:www.sample domain.com intitle:keyword phrase]

Your query is basically asking, "Within the site, how many pages have this keyword phrase in their Title tags?"

However, keep in mind that many combinations of basic and advanced search operators do *not* work. For example, you cannot combine a [site:] command in Google with an [allintitle:] search, as we have below: [site:www.sample domain.com allintitle:keyword phrase]. This query doesn't always work.

A few types of search operators can never be used in combination with another operator. For your reference, we have included them below:

✦ Every Google [allin] operator

✦ Operators that request special information (for example, define:, stocks:, and so on)

✦ Search operators that are specific to a page (cache:, related:, url:, and so on)

Discovering which combinations work and which ones don't is a matter of trial and error.

Searching for images

When doing search engine optimization, you find that it's useful to know how to find specific types of files quickly. The vertical search engines and other file-type-specific sites (such as YouTube for videos) can make your life easier looking for image files, video files, news articles, blog posts, or maps. And if you can find the specific file, you can be sure it has been indexed by the search engine.

To search for image files, you can click the Images link located near the search box on all of the major search engines and then type in your search terms. Doing this restricts your search results to show *only* image files (file types such as JPEG and GIF, which include photos, diagrams, drawings, stars, lines. . . basically any static graphic on a Web page).

Besides the entertainment value of seeing tons of pictures on any subject, image searches also give you an easy way to make sure that the images on your Web site have been indexed by the search engine. For example, if you have a photo of a ten-gallon jar of peanut butter on your Web site, you can search for it by clicking Images and then typing descriptive text about your image, like [peanut butter jar]. If your webmaster gave the image an ALT attribute (text that displays in place of an image if it cannot display for some reason — for more details, see Book IV, Chapter 1) like "Ten-gallon peanut butter jar," you can use the ALT attribute as your search query. If the search engine spidered your Web site and found the image, it also should have indexed the ALT attribute. To really target your search, you can first tell the search engine to look *only* within your Web site: [site:www.yourdomain.com "Ten-gallon peanut butter jar"]. Using quotation marks (" ") around the query tells the search engine to return only pages with that exact text on them.

Searching for videos

Videos are being used more and more inside Web sites. Sites like YouTube store millions of videos that can be watched by anyone, anywhere, on nearly any subject. You can search within these sites for videos, but you can also do a broader video search using a vertical search engine.

From the Google, Yahoo!, or Microsoft Live Search page, click the Videos link near the search box and then type in your search terms. Your results only include video files that have been indexed by that search engine and that match your search terms.

Searching for news

Similar to running an image or video vertical search, you can click a News link on the major search engines near the search box to find news articles. The search engines consider a "news" site to be a site that has multiple authors and frequent postings. Additionally, Google requires that news sites have at least four numbers that aren't a date in their URLs. (So your company's News page that shows your own press releases probably wouldn't qualify.)

In Google, the News vertical search engine only keeps articles published within the last 30 days. If you want to search for any news older than that, you can use Google's news archive search. Google's news archive indexes full-text content dating back to about 1800. (Google partnered with organizations such as *The Wall Street Journal*, *The New York Times*, *Time*, the *Guardian,* and *The Washington Post*, and massive data aggregators including Factiva, LexisNexis, and HighBeam Research, to obtain their information.) You can click News Archive Search on the Google News search page, or go to `http://news.google.com/archivesearch` to search Google's news archives.

Searching through blogs

Blogs, which is short for *Web logs*, are rising in importance in online marketing. Though still new, these social marketing communities allow individuals to publish articles, comments, images, videos, and more as part of a running conversation online. A mention of your company with a link to your Web site on a well-read blog can potentially bring hundreds or thousands of people to your site. Because you generally have no warning when something like this might occur, such a sudden spike in traffic, though welcome, might overwhelm your server's capacity.

On the flipside, you might be reviewing your server logs and find that your site had nine times the normal traffic at 11:22 this morning, and you'd like to know why. The cause may have been someone's blog post, and you want to know what it said.

If there's a blog (or two or twenty) for your industry, it's a good idea to subscribe to it to keep your ear to the ground. You'll get to know more than just information; you'll also get to know the people in your industry. Think of it as passive networking and market research; plus it will help you figure out who the authoritative voices are in your industry. If every blog links to Blog A, it's a good bet that Blog A is someone you should be paying attention to. Blogs are also a great way to find out what people think about your industry.

You can search through blogs using Google's tool (which is still in beta testing as we write this). Go to `blogsearch.google.com` and search as you would through any vertical. Your results contain links to blog sites only, and you can even isolate posts that were only published in the last hour, last 12 hours, last day, or within a range of dates.

Finding news through a regular search

You sometimes see news items through the regular search page (not Google News). One way is to enter a search query that reads like a headline of a recent event. For instance, if you enter [man invents self-washing car] and this world-shattering news has just broken, your results will very likely consist mostly of newspaper article links. Also, search engines blend news stories into a regular search results page if a recent story is considered highly relevant to your search. In a blended search, Google usually places the news item in the first or fourth position on the search results page.

You may also find other blog searches helpful: Yahoo's is `www.ysearch blog.com`, Microsoft has one at `blogs.msdn.com/livesearch`, and there are plenty of others (to find them, do a search for [blog search]).

Searching with maps

We probably don't need to say much about map searches because anyone who has ever needed directions has probably already used them. Online mapping is a fast-moving industry where the technology continues to advance at lightning speed. Companies spend a lot of money and time to improve their interactive maps because visual map tools attract visitors in droves. What's good for you, though, is that maps are more than a tool for driving directions; they're also a great way to perform a local search.

Click the Maps link at Google, Yahoo!, or Microsoft Live Search, and you see a large map image topped by a simple search field. This is a friendly, visual interface for finding a local dry cleaner, or orthodontist, or pet groomer. The search field is very flexible; you can enter a type of businesses, a specific company name, an address, or just a city. When your business shows up in a local search, not only can a user see your information on the left, but also your location pinpointed on a map. (Note: If your business does not show up, we highly recommend you submit it to the three major search engines' local search indexes. For instructions, see Book I, Chapter 4.)

Distinguishing between High Traffic and High Conversion Search

You want to attract lots of people to your Web site. But it's not just about quantity — you want quality traffic. You want to attract visitors who come and stay a while, and find what they're looking for on your site. What you really need are customers. In the world of search engine marketing, site visitors who become customers are called *conversions*. They came, they looked, they bought. They were converted.

When you design for search engine optimization, it's important to keep in mind that you want high conversion rates, not just high traffic. You need to consider the Long Tail phenomenon (coined by Chris Anderson in an October 2004 *Wired* magazine article, and frequently discussed in SEO circles ever since).

The *Long Tail* is a statistical concept that says that items that are in comparatively low demand can nonetheless add up to quite large volumes. For example, a large bookstore sells dozens of books from the bestseller lists every day. These popular titles make up only about 20 percent of the store's inventory, yet their sales amount to more than half of the bookstore's total revenue. The slower, incremental sales of the remaining 80 percent of the store's inventory typically generate about 20% or more of the store's revenue. Individually, no one book sells a large number of copies, but added together, the revenue is substantial.

You can apply the Long Tail concept when you're choosing keywords for your Web site. The graph in Figure 5-1 represents different keywords (across the horizontal axis) and the quantity of searches, or traffic, that each keyword generates (up the vertical axis). The keywords that have high potential traffic appear at the left end of the graph, followed by keywords that are less frequently searched. Notice how the potential traffic drops off in a *Long Tail* as you move to the right.

Figure 5-1: Long Tail traffic is incremental traffic that added together brings greater return than head terms.

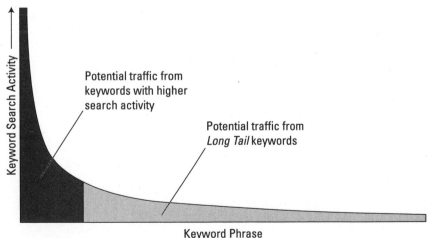

Potential traffic from keywords with higher search activity

Potential traffic from *Long Tail* keywords

Keyword Search Activity

Keyword Phrase

Don't ignore the long-tail traffic. In our bookstore example, this would be the equivalent of emptying all of the shelves except for the bestsellers' table — and cutting revenue substantially.

Think about focusing your keywords for your target audience. You want to use some specialized phrases in your keywords to attract long-tail traffic. A specialized keyword phrase might be three, four, five, or more words in length. A person coming to your Web site after searching for [compact rechargeable cordless widgets] would be more likely to purchase the item on your site than a person who had just searched for [widgets]. You might not have very many searches for that phrase, but the few who did search for it saw your listing (because it moved way up in the search engine results) and became conversions.

For more in-depth information on keyword selection, see Book II, Chapter 2.

Book I
Chapter 5

Knowing What
Drives Search
Results

Chapter 6: Spam Issues: When Search Engines Get Fooled

In This Chapter

✔ Finding out about the different types of search engine spam

✔ Understanding the consequences of using spam

✔ Being wary of guaranteed results and other false promises

In this chapter, you find out about techniques used to fool or trick the search engines into delivering a higher listing on the results page, which we call *spam*. We go over some of the more popular methods that have been used, and then we delve into the guidelines search engines use to define what they consider spam, as well as our Search Engine Optimization (SEO) code of ethics.

Understanding What Spam Is

When you normally think of Spam, the first thing that comes to mind is either the canned meat product or the junk e-mail that's clogging up your inbox. (Or the Monty Python skit . . . "Spam, spam, spam, spam" . . . ahem.) When we here in SEO-land talk about spam, however, we mean something a little different than meat by-products, unwanted e-mails, or British comedy troupes. Search engine *Spam* (also sometimes known as *spamdexing*) is any tactic or Web page that is used to deceive the search engine into a false understanding of what the whole Web site is about or its importance. It can be external or internal; it may violate the search engines policies directly, or it may be a little bit sneakier about its misdirection. How spam is defined depends on the *intent* and *extent*. What is the intent of the tactic being used, and to what extent is it being used?

If you stuff all of your *metadata* (text added into the HTML of a page describing it for the search engine) full of *keywords* (words or phrases relating to your site content that search engines use to determine whether it's relevant) with the sole intent of tricking the search engine so that you will receive a higher page rank on the results page, that's spam. Also, if you do that all over your Web site, with your `Alt` attribute text (text used to describe an image for the search engine to read), your links, and keywords all over the site, trying to trick the search engine *spider* (the little programs that search engines use to read and rank Web sites) into giving you the highest rank possible, it's a little harder to claim to the search engine that it was simply an accident and it was done out of ignorance.

Most technologies that are used in the creation, rendering, and design of Web sites can be used to trick the search engines. When this happens, or is even so much as *perceived* to happen, it's considered spam. Search engine companies do not like spam. Spam damages the reputation of the search engine. They're working their hardest to bring you the most relevant results possible, and spam-filled pages are not what they want to give you. A user might not use the search engine again if they get spammy results, for starters. So if someone's caught spamming, their site could be penalized or removed entirely from the search engine's *index,* (the list of Web sites that the search engine pulls from to recreate its results pages).

You can report spam if you run across it by contacting the search engines:

✦ **Google:** spamreport@google.com

✦ **Yahoo!:** http://help.yahoo.com/l/us/yahoo/search/spam_abuse.html

✦ **Microsoft Live Search:** http://feedback.search.msn.com

✦ **Ask:** information@ask.com

Discovering the Types of Spam

In this section, we talk a little about what types of spam there are in SEO-land, and what *not* to do, in order to keep your site from getting penalized or even pulled out of the engines by accident.

Spam is any attempt to deceive the search engines into ranking a page when it does not deserve to be ranked. Note that in this section we describe spam that is known to be detected and punished by the search engines.

Do not attempt any of the discussed methods as they will result in your site being branded as a spammer. This chapter is not meant to cover every type of spam out there on the Web: just to give you the knowledge you need to recognize when a tactic might be venturing down the wrong path. Spammers use other advanced techniques that may also be detectable by the search engines so avoid any attempt to deceive the search engines.

Hidden text/links

One of the more obvious ways to spam a Web site is inserting hidden text and links in the *content* of the Web page (content of a Web site being anything that the user can see). All text has to be visible to the user on the Web site. Hidden content can be defined as text that appears within the rendered HTML code that is not visible on the page to the user without requiring user-interaction in order to see it. Hidden text can simply be a long list of keywords, and the hidden links increase the Web site's popularity. Examples of using hidden text and links are

✦ **White text/links on a white background:** Putting white text and links on a white background renders it invisible to the user unless the text is highlighted by right-clicking on the mouse. Spammers can then insert keywords or hyperlinks that the spiders read and count as relevant.

✦ **Text, links, or content that is hidden by covering with a layer so it is not visible:** This is a trick that people use with CSS. They hide spider-able content under the page that can't be seen with the naked eye or by highlighting the page.

✦ **Positioning content off the page's view with CSS:** Another programming trick spammers use.

✦ **Links that are not clickable by the user:** Creating a link that only has a single one by one pixel as its anchor or using the period on a sentence or no anchor at all. There's nothing for a user to click on but the engine can still follow the link.

Using invisible or hidden text is a surefire way to get your site *banned* so it no longer shows up in the engines. The reasoning behind this is that you would want all of your content visible to the user, and any hidden text is being used for nefarious purposes.

Figure 6-1 shows what we mean by hidden text on a background. Usually, you'll find this as white text on a white background, but it could be any color so long as it's not visible to a user (black on black, gray on gray, and so on.) This is spam, and will get your site banned.

Doorway pages

A *doorway page* is a Web page submitted to search engine spiders that has been designed to satisfy the specific algorithms for various search engines, but is not intended to be viewed by visitors. Basically they do not earn the rankings but instead deceive the search engines into rankings by design and keyword stuffing tricks that you'd never want to put on a page for a user to see. Doorway pages are there to spam the search engine *index* (the database of information from which search engines draw their primary results) by cramming it full of relevant keywords and phrases so that it appears high on the results page for a particular keyword, but when the user clicks on it, they are automatically redirected to another site or page within the same site that doesn't rank on its own.

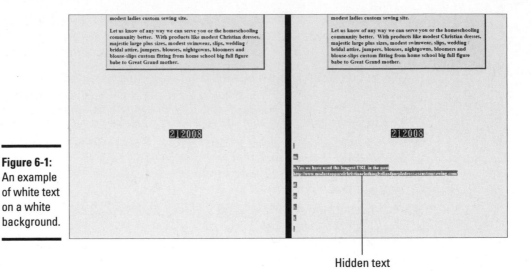

Figure 6-1:
An example
of white text
on a white
background.

Hidden text

Doorway pages are only there for the purpose of being indexed and there is no intention to have anyone use it. Sometimes more sophisticated spammers build a doorway page with viewable, relevant content in order to avoid being caught by the search engine, but most of the time, a doorway page is made to be viewed only by a spider. Doorway pages are often used in tandem with *deceptive misdirection*, which we discuss a couple of sections later.

Deceptive redirection

Has this ever happened to you? You do a search for a cartoon you used to love as a kid, and you click on one of the links on the results page. But instead of the page you were expecting, you get an entirely different Web site, with some very questionable content. What just happened here? Behold the headache that is *deceptive redirection. Deceptive redirection* is a type of coded command that redirects the user to a different location than what was expected via the link that was clicked upon.

Spammers create shadow page/domains that have content that ranks for a particular *search query* (the words or phrase you type into the search box), yet when you attempt to access the content on the domain you are then redirected to an often shady site that is commonly for porn, gambling, or drugs, that has nothing to do with your original query.

The most common perpetrators of deceptive redirects are also a spam method: doorway pages. Most doorway pages redirect through a `Meta refresh command` (a method of instructing a Web browser to automatically refresh the current Web page after a given time interval). Search engines are now issuing penalties for using meta refresh commands, other sites will trick you into clicking a link or using JavaScript (another computer programming language) to redirect you. Google now considers any Web site that uses a meta refresh or any other sneaky redirect (such as through JavaScript) to be spam.

Not all redirects are evil. The intent of the redirect has to be determined before a spam determination can be made. If the page that is redirected to is nothing like the page expected, then it is probably spam. If you get exactly what you expect after a redirect, then it probably isn't spam. We discuss a lot more about redirects in Book VII, Chapter 3.

Cloaking

Another nefarious form of spam is a method called cloaking. *Cloaking* is a technique in which the content presented to the search engine spider is different than that presented to the users' browser, meaning that the spiders see one page, while you see something entirely different. Spammers can do this by delivering content based on the *IP addresses* (information used to tell where your computer or server is located) or the *User-Agent HTTP header* (information describing whether you're a person or a search engine robot) of the user requesting the page. When a user is identified as a search engine spider, a server-side script delivers a different version of the Web page, one that contains content different than the visible page. The purpose of cloaking is to deceive search engines so they display the page when it would not otherwise be displayed.

Like redirects, cloaking is a matter of intent rather than always being evil. There are many appropriate uses for this technique. News sites use cloaking to allow search engines to spider their content while users are presented with a registration page. Site selling alcohol require users to verify their age before allowing them to view the rest of the content, while search engines pass unchallenged.

Unrelated keywords

Unrelated keywords are a form of spam that involves using a keyword that is not related to the image, video, or other content that it is supposed to be describing in the hopes of driving up traffic. Examples include putting unrelated keywords into the `Alt` attribute text of an image, placing them in the metadata of a video, or in the `Meta` tags of a page, and any time an unrelated keyword is used. Not only is it useless, but it also gets your site pulled if you try it.

Keyword stuffing

Keyword stuffing occurs when people overuse keywords on a page in the hopes of making the page seem more relevant for a term through a higher keyword frequency or density. Keyword stuffing can happen in the metadata,

`Alt` attribute text, and within the content of the page itself. Basically, going to your `Alt` attribute text and typing **porsche porsche porsche porsche** over and over again is not going to increase your ranking, and the page will likely be yanked due to spam.

There's also a much sneakier method of using keyword stuffing, using hidden text in the page, or hiding large groups of repeated keywords on the page (usually at the bottom far below the view of the average visitor) or using HTML commands that cause blocks of text to be hidden from user sight.

Link farms

You might envision a "link farm" as a pastoral retreat where docile links graze in rolling green pastures, but alas, you would be wrong. A *link farm* is any group of Web sites that *hyperlink* (a link to another part of the Web site) to all the other sites in the group. Remember how Google loves links and hyperlinks and uses them in their algorithm to figure out a Web site's popularity? Most link farms are created through automated programs and services. Search engines have combated link farms by identifying specific attributes that link farms use and filtering them from the index and search results, including removing entire domains to keep them from influencing the results page.

Not all link exchange programs are considered spam, however. Link exchange programs that allow individual Web sites to *selectively* exchange links with other relevant Web sites are not considered spam. The difference between these and link farms is the fact that the Web site is selecting relevant links to its content, rather than just getting as many links as it can get to itself.

Avoiding Being Evil: Ethical Search Marketing

We didn't spend this chapter describing spam just so that unscrupulous users could run out and use it. Sure, the spam might bump their page rank for a little while, but they will be caught, and their site will be pulled from the index. So why use it?

For too long, many SEO practitioners were involved in an arms race of sorts, inventing technology and techniques in order to achieve the best rankings and get the most clients. Unfortunately, some developed more and more devious technology to trick the search engines and beat the competition. Thus we have two types of techniques used in SEO:

✦ **White hat:** This is all SEO techniques that fall into the ethical realm. White hat techniques involve using relevant keywords, `Alt` attribute text, simple and clear metadata, and so on. White hat techniques clearly comply with the published intent of the various search engine quality guidelines.

✦ **Black hat:** These are the SEO techniques we've spent describing in this chapter (among others that we haven't covered.) Black hat techniques are sneaky, devious, and attempt to game the engines to promote content not relevant to the user. These techniques are deceptive and generally break (or at least stretch) the search guidelines, commonly leading to spam penalties that are painful at best and devastating at worst.

REMEMBER

With the search engines implementing aggressive anti-spam programs, the news is out: If you want to get rankings, you have to play well within the rules. And those rules are absolutely "No deception or tricks allowed." Simply put, honest relevancy wins at the end of the day. All other approaches fade away.

Generally, the search engines all adhere to a code of conduct. Little things do vary from search engine to search engine, but the general principle is the same:

✦ Keywords should be relevant, applicable, and clearly associated with page body content.

✦ Keywords should be used as allowed and accepted by the search engines (placement, color, and so on).

✦ Keywords should not be utilized too many times on a page (frequency, density, distribution, and so on). The use should be natural for the subject.

✦ Redirection technology (if used) should facilitate and improve the user experience. But understand that this is almost always considered a trick and is frequently a cause for removal from an index.

✦ Redirection technology (if used) should always display a page where the body content contains the appropriate keywords (no bait and switch).

You *can* get back into a search engine's good graces after getting caught spamming and yanked out of the index. It involves going through your page and cleaning it up, removing all of the spam issues that caused it to get yanked in the first place, and re-submitting your page for placement into the index. Don't expect an immediate resubmission, though. You have to wait in line with everyone else.

Realizing That There Are No Promises or Guarantees

Say that you know that you won't use spam in order to increase your page ranking in the search engines. You understand that it's unethical and is more trouble than it's worth. But at the same time, you need to increase your page rank. The simple solution is to hire an SEO organization to do the optimizing for you. But beware: Although you might not use spam, there's a chance than an unscrupulous SEO will.

A code of ethics applies to people in the search engine optimization industry. Beware of those who promise or guarantee results to their clients, or allege a special relationship with a search engine or advertise the ability to get priority consideration when they submit. People who do so are usually lying. Remember, there is no way to pay your way into the top of the search results page. Yahoo! does have a program called Search Submit Pro where, for a fee, you can submit your page and be guaranteed that you'll be spidered frequently, but they do not guarantee rankings, and they are the only large engine with this sort of program (see Book I, Chapter 2 for more details). Also avoid those that promise link popularity schemes, or to submit your site to thousands of search engines. These do not increase your ranking, and even if they do, it's not in a way that would be considered positive and the benefits, if any, are usually short-lived.

Unfortunately, you are responsible for the actions of any company you hire. If an SEO creates a Web page for you using black hat tactics, you are responsible and your site could be pulled entirely from the search engine's index. If you're not sure that what your SEO is doing, ask for clarification. And remember, like in all things, *caveat emptor*. Buyer beware.

Following the SEO Code of Ethics

The discussion of any SEO Code of Ethics is like a discussion on politics or religion: There are more than two sides, all sides are strongly opinionated, and seldom do they choose the same path to the same end. Most Search Engine Optimization (SEO) practitioners understand these ethics, but not all practitioners practice safe-SEO. Too many SEO practitioners claim a bias towards surfers, or the search engines, or their clients (all are appropriate in the correct balance), and it is common for the SEO pros to use the "Whatever it takes" excuse to bend some of the ethical rules to fit their needs. This does not pass judgment; it simply states the obvious.

Although the industry as a whole has not adopted an official code of ethics, the authors of this book have drafted a specific code that we pledge to adhere to with respect to our clients. We have paraphrased this code here but you can read the original at http://www.bruceclay.com/web_ethics.htm

✦ Do not intentionally do harm to a client. Be honest with the client and do not willfully use technologies and methods that are known to cause a Web site's removal from a search engine index.

✦ Do not intentionally violate any specifically published and enforced rules of search engines or directories. This also means keeping track of when policies change and checking with the search engine if you're unsure of whether the method or technology is acceptable.

✦ Protect the user visiting the site. The content must not mislead, no "bait and switch" tactics (where the content does not match the search phrase) are used, and the content is not offensive to the targeted visitors.

✦ Do not use the continued violation of copyright, trademark, service-mark, or laws related to spamming as they may exist at the state, federal, or international level.

✦ All pages presented to the search engine must match the visible content of the page.

✦ Don't steal other people's work and present it as your own.

✦ Don't present false qualifications or deliberately lie about your skills. Also, don't make guarantees or claim special relationships with the search engine.

✦ Treat all clients equally and don't play favorites.

✦ Don't make false promises or guarantees. There is no such thing as a guaranteed method of reaching the top of the results page.

✦ Always offer ways for your clients to settle internal and external disputes. There will be competition among your clients. Make sure there's a way to mediate conflict if it ever comes up.

✦ Protect the confidentiality and anonymity of your clients with regard to privileged information and supplying testimonials.

✦ Work to the best of your ability to honestly increase and retain the rankings of your client sites.

In a nutshell? Don't be evil. Spammers never win and winners never spam. What works in the short term won't work forever, and living in fear of getting caught is no way to run a business.

Book II
Keyword Strategy

The 5th Wave   By Rich Tennant

"Maybe your keyword search, 'legal secretary,love,fame,fortune,' needs to be refined."

Contents at a Glance

Chapter 1: Employing Keyword Research Techniques and Tools....87
Discovering Your Site Theme 88
Doing Your Industry and Competitor Research 92
Researching Client Niche Keywords 93
Checking Out Seasonal Keyword Trends 93
Evaluating Keyword Research 95

Chapter 2: Selecting Keywords 97
Selecting the Proper Keyword Phrases 97
Reinforcing versus Diluting Your Theme 99
Picking Keywords Based on Subject Categories 104

Chapter 3: Exploiting Pay Per Click Lessons Learned............109
Analyzing Your Pay Per Click Campaigns for Clues About Your Site ...110
Reducing Costs by Overlapping Pay Per Click
    with Natural Keyword Rankings...114

Chapter 4: Assigning Keywords to Pages 117
Understanding What a Search Engine Sees as Keywords 117
Planning Subject Theme Categories..118
Choosing Landing Pages for Subject Categories 121
Organizing Your Primary and Secondary Subjects 121
Understanding Siloing "Under the Hood"...122
Consolidating Themes to Help Search Engines See Your Relevance....124

Chapter 5: Adding and Maintaining Keywords...................129
Understanding Keyword Densities, Frequency, and Prominence.........130
Adjusting Keywords 133
Updating Keywords...134
Using Tools to Aid Keyword Placement 134

Chapter 1: Employing Keyword Research Techniques and Tools

In This Chapter

✔ Discovering your site theme

✔ Brainstorming for keywords

✔ Creating a keyword-based outline

✔ Choosing related keywords

✔ Researching keywords by niche

✔ Evaluating keywords

*I*n this chapter, we talk about picking and choosing your keywords. This is an extremely important step. You might say the mantra of search engines should be "keywords, keywords, keywords." Search engine *spiders* (the bots that go through your page gathering Web page data) are looking for keywords that match or closely relate to the search query. A *keyword* is a specific word or phrase a search engine looks for in its index (the list of Web sites it looks at during a search), based on what the user typed as the search query. For example, *cars* is a keyword.

It seems simple enough: just figure out a couple of great keywords and go! Unfortunately, there's more to picking keywords than that. Say you've got a Web site that specializes in selling custom-made classic automobiles. But the site isn't receiving the *traffic* (number of visitors) it should. Here's a tip: Think about what kind of keywords you used in your Web site. You might be using general words like [automobiles] and [vehicles], but how many people actually type in a search query of [classic automobiles]? Nine times out of ten people are going to be looking for [classic cars]. Little distinctions like this can make a big difference in the traffic you're receiving.

In this chapter, we talk about how to pick good, solid, relevant keywords. You discover that one of the first things you must do is to identify the theme of your Web site. Secondly, you sit down and brainstorm all the keywords you think fit your theme. And we're not talking five or ten keywords here: We're talking dozens or hundreds or thousands. Then we talk about creating a good outline for those keywords and researching your market to find out what the competition is doing and what your potential customers are searching for. We also discuss culling unproductive keywords so you can focus on the most relevant ones.

Remember, relevancy = higher ranking = more traffic for you.

Discovering Your Site Theme

The first thing you need to figure out is your Web site's theme. The *theme* is the main thing that your site is about. It's the central concept of whatever your site is doing on the Web. Again, it seems simple enough, but it's very important to know *exactly* what it is that you're about. If you are a Web site that specializes in selling customized classic cars, you need to figure exactly what that means, narrowing down the kinds of cars you consider to be classic, the types of customization you do, and so forth. Also consider where it is that you'll be going with this Web site. Think about whether you only want to handle classic cars, or if you might also want to broaden your scope and include newer models. Be thinking about whether there's a broad enough market out there for customized classic cars, decide whether you might include both domestic and foreign cars, newer cars, and so on.

You also need to think about your service area. Are you a local-only business, or could you take things to a national or international level? Try to break it down in very specific terms.

Write down the things that you feel your Web site is about, and all of the things that you are *not* about. So, if you're creating a site about customized classic cars, you would write things like

✦ We work on only classic cars built from 1950–1970

✦ The cars we work on are American-made; no foreign vehicles

✦ Customization means we do paint, chrome, and upholstery

✦ We do engine work or can install an entirely new engine if necessary

✦ We do not install "banging" stereos; that's the guy down the road

✦ We are a local business, but are willing to accept clients from out-of-town and out-of-state.

Brainstorming for keywords

After your theme is clear in your mind and you've clarified what your business is really about, you have a good starting point for your keyword brainstorming sessions.

Brainstorming is an appropriate first step for choosing good keywords. At this point, there are no bad keywords; you just want to compile a big list of possibilities. Here are some possible viewpoints to consider and questions you can ask yourself:

✦ **Natural language:** What would I search for to try to find my product?

✦ **Other perspectives:** What would someone else call what I have to sell?

✦ **Customer mindset:** How do "normal" people talk about the products or services I offer?

✦ **Industry jargon:** What do the "experts" call my products or services?

Write down whatever you think would be the major keywords you will be using. Ask your friends, ask your relatives, ask your associates, ask your employees and coworkers. It's a matter of throwing things at the wall to see what sticks and what doesn't. Figure 1-1 shows a simple mind map. Tools like this can help you come up with new topics and concepts that might relate to your site.

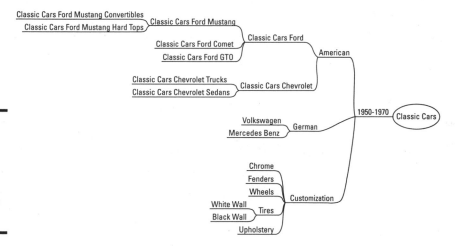

Figure 1-1:
Brain-
storming
your
keywords
with a map
outline.

Building a subject outline

After you have a large list of keywords that you might want to use, your next step is to create an outline using those keywords. Start with the broadest ones at the top level and break the list into categories and subcategories, getting more specific as you go deeper.

A keyword outline for our customized classic cars Web site could look something like this list. Notice how the keywords build on each other as you delve deeper into the subject:

Classic cars

Classic cars 1950–1970

Classic Cars American

Classic Cars Ford

> Classic Cars Ford Mustang

>> Classic Cars Ford Mustang Convertibles

>> Classic Cars Ford Mustang hard tops

> Classic Cars Ford Comet

Classic Cars Chevrolet

> Classic Cars Chevrolet trucks

> Classic Cars Chevrolet sedans

Classic cars German

Classic cars Volkswagen

Classic cars Mercedes Benz

Classic cars customization

> Classic cars customization paint

> Classic cars customization chrome

> Classic cars customization fenders

> Classic cars customization wheels

> Classic cars customization tires

>> Classic cars customization tires white wall

>> Classic cars customization tires black wall

> Classic cars customization upholstery

You can see how the breakdown goes from very broad terms to more specific terms. These all represent things that people might search for when they are looking up classic cars, or customization, or both, and can all be used as keywords. This is a very small, simple outline. You can go into even more breakdowns and come up with even more specific keywords as appropriate for your site.

Remember to list as many keywords that relate to your theme as you can. The broader base you have to work with, the better chances you have of identifying good, solid, relevant keywords.

Choosing theme-related keywords

Now, take your nice, long list of hundreds of potential keywords and go through and match them to your theme. Figure out whether you will be doing custom work for a Ford Anglia as opposed to Ford Mustangs, and whether you want to include Dodge at all. Also start thinking about keyword phrases, like [Ford Mustang convertible] or [1960s Ford Mustang hardtops]. Qualifiers such as *convertible* or *1960s* thrown in at the beginning and end of a main keyword turn it into a keyword phrase, and they help you figure out how narrow you want the search to be. This is especially important if you have a local business because you want to rank for the local search query, such as [Poughkeepsie classic car customization]. When you feel like you have some good usable keywords, drag out your thesaurus and look up synonyms for those words. Anything that relates to your keyword or has the same meaning is another good keyword.

Don't forget to use the search engines to discover synonyms. As shown in Figure 1-2, the tilde character (~) before any word in a query triggers a synonym search in Google. In the query [~classic cars], *classic* is the word that we're looking for synonyms for. In the search engine results pages (SERPs), words like *antique* and *muscle* are bolded in addition to the searched words *classic* and *cars*.

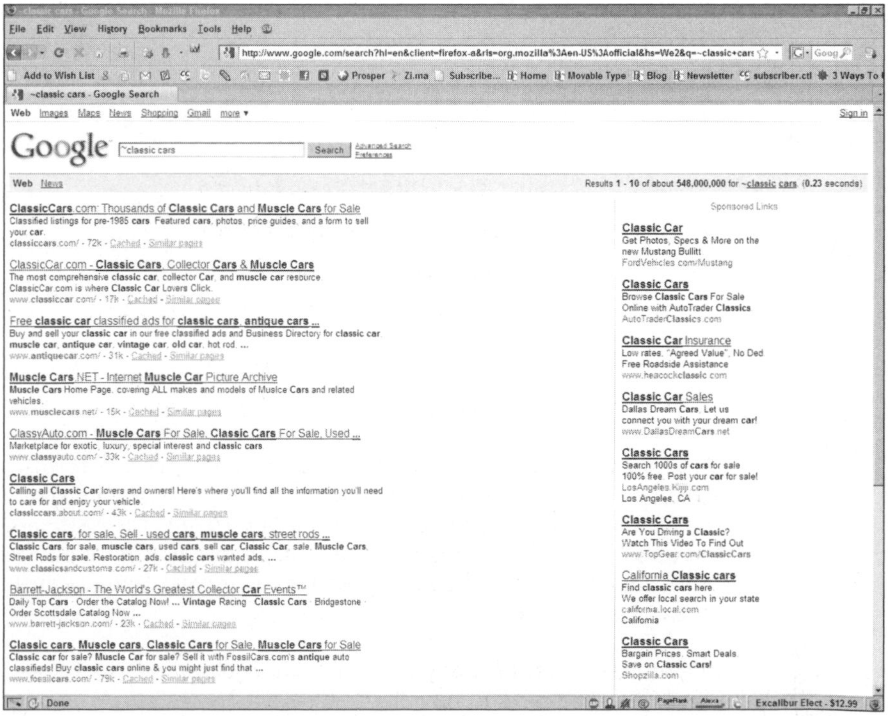

Book II
Chapter 1

Employing Keyword Research Techniques and Tools

Figure 1-2: Using a tilde before a word in a query triggers a synonym search in Google for [~classic cars]. Notice the bold terms in the titles and descriptions.

Doing Your Industry and Competitor Research

Now it's time to check out the competition. With any business, it's an important step in feeling out the market. With industry research, you need to know what keyword your competitors are using in their content and what kind of traffic they're getting. One of the easiest ways is to look them up on the search engines. Use the keywords you came up with during your brainstorming session and plug them into the query window. Google bolds your search terms in the search results, so pay attention to those words and the text surrounding them. Google also provides you with disambiguation options when appropriate, as in a "Did you mean ___?" phrase. In Figure 1-3, the search for [classic car customization] returns 115,000 results. The top ten results returned are worth mining for keyword ideas.

Figure 1-3: A Google search result for [classic car customization].

Check out the highest listings and make note of the keywords they use on their pages. The guys who have the highest rank are your competition for those keywords, and to have such a high listing on the search engine, they're obviously doing something right. For a really in-depth look at how to do research on your competition, check out Book III.

After you've identified who your competitors are, it's time to do some research. Look at any print materials they've put out, along with what's on their Web site. Pay attention to how they market themselves, and what words they use to describe themselves. This is important especially if you're looking to draw industry traffic to yourself or obtain links from other industry sites. Look at their site's navigation, check out their metadata, and read their content and press.

Researching Client Niche Keywords

After you know what keywords your competition is using, it's time to start thinking about what your targeted visitors are using to search for your product or services. The language the industry uses and the language the customer uses are often two entirely different things. For example, people in the auto industry use the words *auto* or *vehicle*, but the guy on the street is not going to refer to his Ford as his *auto:* He's going to call it his *car.* The same goes for search queries. Most people are not looking for [classic automobiles]; they're going to be looking for [classic cars].

You can find out what the man on the street is saying by actually going to the man on the street. Check out Internet forums, interest groups, and newsgroups that relate to your business and make note of what people are writing in their posts. What words do they use when referring to your type of business or the product that you sell? Those can be used as keywords. Talk to your clients. Communication is key to figuring out what they're looking for.

Also, pay attention when people call your business and ask questions. Those are the kinds of questions that people are asking the search engine. One person's slightly questionable phrasing can be another person's usable keyword.

Checking Out Seasonal Keyword Trends

Some keywords retain their popularity and relevance throughout the year, like [Ford Mustang] or [California]. Others see rises and spikes throughout the year due to seasonal trends. Holidays are a good example. More people buy Christmas tree ornaments in December than in July, and the majority of costume sales happen before Halloween. The same is true of the actual seasons themselves because people look for things at certain times of the year. More people look for bathing suits in the months before summer and for snowboards in the winter (see Figure 1-4).

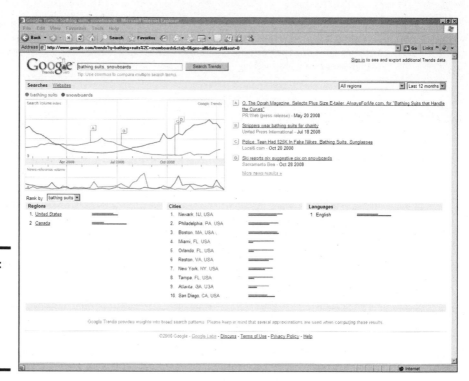

Figure 1-4:
Google
zeitgeist
showing
seasonal
keyword
trends.

You can use tools provided by the search engines to see keyword spikes and trends. End of the year reports such as Yahoo!'s Top Trends report, `http://buzzlog.buzz.yahoo.com/toptrends2007/`, and Google Zeitgeist, `www.google.com/intl/en/press/zeitgeist2007/`, along with Google Trends, `www.google.com/trends`, which measures how often a keyword is used during a given day, providing the most popular examples and measuring when the spikes happen.

You may find it important to note spikes and trends in your keywords: While certain things immediately come to mind during a given holiday (for example, flowers and chocolate for Valentine's Day), other keywords and keyword phrases that are much more loosely connected might spike during that time period as well. Around February 14th, you might notice a rise in searches for engagement rings, vacation listings for second honeymoons, and wedding-related searches. Restaurant searches and hotel listings also probably spike, along with clothing, shoes, and jewelry. As you saw when you did keyword brainstorming, one broad high-traffic term can be broken down into smaller traffic, specific terms. These more specific terms are every bit as relevant as the broad term, and they generally have less competition. Remember the Long Tail when considering possible keywords.

Seasonal keywords are important to keep track of because you can use them to tailor your site to draw in that seasonal traffic. Many stores receive the bulk of their revenue from seasonal purchases, so it's a good thing to keep in mind when building your Web site.

Evaluating Keyword Research

After you've done your research and your brainstorming, you hopefully have acquired a good long list of keywords that can be used. Now it's time to figure out which ones you'll actually be using.

In figuring out how often your keywords are searched for, you can use a variety of tools for keyword evaluation. Using some of these tools, you can monitor how often a certain keyword is searched, what the click-through rates are, and whether it would be a good, usable keyword to keep. Some tools you have to pay for, but there are free ones out there. A couple of examples:

✦ **Google AdWords:** Google has its own keyword tracker, shown in Figure 1-5. You used to have to be a member of Google AdWords to access the keyword tracking tool, but now it's a free service located at `https://adwords.google.com/select/KeywordToolExternal`. (Yahoo and Microsoft both have keyword tools as well.)

✦ **Search Engine Optimization/KSP:** Bruce Clay, Inc. provides a free keyword tool at `www.bruceclay.com/web_rank.htm#seoksp`. Simply type your keywords into the Keyword Activity search box. You'll get keyword counts, plus demographic information.

The following services are paid services, so you have to cough up a little bit of cash for them. They actually do research and check out your competition for you, so they might be something you want to invest in. That doesn't mean you get out of doing the brainstorming and researching yourself; they just make it easier.

✦ **SEOToolSet:** In addition to the free tools offered by Bruce Clay, Inc, you can also subscribe to a full suite of fully integrated SEO tools. Far more robust than the free versions, the SEOToolSet is available for $39.95 a month.

✦ **Wordtracker:** A keyword tracking service that you have to pay for, but they do offer free trials. Theirs is an annual subscription of $369 US a year (`www.wordtracker.com/`).

✦ **Keyword Discovery:** Made by Trellian, this is another paid keyword tracking tool. You can subscribe for $49.95 a month at (`www.keyword discovery.com/`).

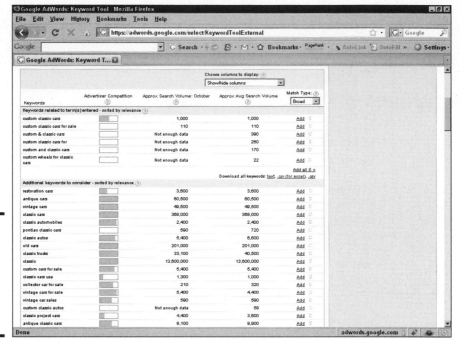

Figure 1-5:
The Google AdWords free keyword tracking services.

You need to cull the least relevant keywords off the list right away. If your business is customizing only American cars as opposed to foreign ones, you can do away with words like [foreign], [Anglia], and [Volkswagen]. Don't worry: You've still got a pretty big list to choose from. You're just narrowing the focus a bit. When you're clipping out keywords, remember that keywords that are supportive of a strong branding exercise, that result in sales more often than other keywords, or that have very high profit margins should all be retained.

Using the tools and brainstorming methods we describe in this chapter, you can come up with a pretty sizable list of keywords. Also using the keyword tracking tools, you can also get rid of a bunch of irrelevant, low-traffic keywords right away and pick a good list to focus on. Remember, you're not looking for five or ten keywords: You're looking for hundreds of good keywords, depending on the size of your site.

Although it might seem like a good idea to concentrate on the broadest, most general keywords out there, it's actually not. What you want are keywords that give you conversion. A keyword that brings 60 visitors to your site, 10 of whom make a purchase, is much more desirable than a generic keyword that brings in thousands of visitors who only come in, blink, and then hit Back on their browser. Statisticians attribute this to the fact that people use generic keywords when gathering information, and more specific keywords when they're ready to open their wallets. We explain this phenomenon more in the next chapter of this minibook.

Chapter 2: Selecting Keywords

In This Chapter

✓ Selecting proper keyword phrases

✓ Reinforcing versus diluting your site theme

✓ Selecting subject categories

✓ High traffic keywords

✓ High conversion keywords

*I*n this chapter, we take that nice long list of keywords you put together in the previous chapter and actually go through and select the best of the bunch. (If you haven't yet put together such a list, what are you waiting for? Go back and do it now!) In this chapter, you discover what makes a good keyword phrase, especially in terms of a *search query* (the words you type into the search engine window). You also discover the deal with subject categories and how they help you when choosing your keywords. Also, we talk about high traffic keywords and high conversion keywords, and what the difference between the two is.

Selecting the Proper Keyword Phrases

When you're doing a search, you must have the proper phrase to use as a search query. Just like a *keyword* is a single word used as a search query, a *keyword phrase* is two or more words typed as a search query. For example, [Poughkeepsie classic car customization] is a good example of a keyword phrase.

Search engine users find what they are looking for by searching for specific keywords or keyword phrases and choosing the most relevant result. You want your site to have as many opportunities to be included in those search results as possible. In other words, you should try to use every keyword phrase that you think someone might search for in order to find your site.

Usually when people do a search, they type in a keyword phrase instead of just a single keyword. Fifty-eight percent of search queries are three words or longer. So having keyword phrases on your site increases your chance of appearing higher on the page rank (because more keywords match the search query). The *click-through rate* (how many people click your listing to go to your site) also increases, due to more words matching the search query. Your *conversion rate* (how many visitors actually purchase something, sign up, or take whatever action is appropriate on your site) also increases because you're more likely to have what the user is looking for.

Search engine users are becoming more savvy as time goes on, and they have learned that a single keyword is probably going to be too broad of a search to return the results they're looking for. A good example is what happens when you do a search for [security]. You might be in need of a security guard service, but doing a quick search on Google with the keyword [security] gives you results as varied as the Wikipedia article on security, the Department of Homeland Security, the Social Security Administration, and many listings for computer security software. Using the keyword phrase [security guard service Poughkeepsie], on the other hand, turns up map results listing local businesses, two local business sites for hiring security guards, and a couple of news articles about security services in Poughkeepsie.

You can see why it's a good idea to have proper keyword phrases, and not just single keywords, on your Web pages. Your keyword phrase [Poughkeepsie classic car customization] could be used as a heading for your paragraphs, placed in the `Heading` tags (HTML tags used for paragraph headings) or as the title of your Web page (using the `Title` tag in the HTML code).

It is best to use simple, everyday language that searchers are likely to type in. As a general rule, we recommend including multiple uses of each keyword phrase, enough to be prominent on the page without forcing your keywords into your content. You want it to mention each keyword a couple of times while making sure that it still sounds natural. Additionally, you should avoid using only general phrases; be sure to include detailed descriptive words as well. If your keywords are too general, they are likely to be up against too much competition from others targeting the same keywords. However, if your keywords are too specific, fewer people search for those terms, resulting in fewer potential visitors. It's a balancing act, and the rules aren't hard and fast. You need to find the right mix for your site by finding the keywords that bring traffic that actually converts — in other words, you want to put out the bait that brings in the right catch.

When putting keywords in the content of your site, make sure the words surrounding them are also good, searchable keywords. For example

+ Classic car customization in Poughkeepsie
+ Reupholstery for classic Mustangs
+ Chrome, wheels, and paint for classic automobiles
+ New York State classic cars

These can all be used as headings for paragraphs or as links to their own pages. Remember, search engines also look for keywords in *hypertext links* (where clicking a word or phrase takes you to another page within the Web site) within the page, and using a search phrase within the hyperlink leads to a higher search rank for that phrase.

You should also still include *stop words* (very common words such as *the*, *a*, *to*, *if*, *who*, and so forth, which serve to connect ideas but don't add much in the way of meaning to your content) in your search phrases. Google had removed stop words from its indexes for several years, but they now use them to perform much more precise searches. Plus, you don't want your Web site text to sound like machine language — "Come shop Classic Cars customization all your needs Poughkeepsie." Instead, you want your Web site to sound like English: Your true readers are real people, after all. You also don't want to give the search engines the impression that you're *keyword stuffing*; they're expecting natural-sounding text, which means full sentences.

Reinforcing versus Diluting Your Theme

Hopefully, you've already done your brainstorming and have a list of thousands of keywords you can use for your Web site. Unfortunately, you probably can't use *all* of those keywords, not unless you have a site that has hundreds or thousands of pages anyway. And even if you do, it's best to reduce the list somewhat: There is such a thing as too many keywords. What you want are keywords that are going to enhance your site theme and not dilute it.

Imagine that your Web site is a jar full of black marbles. That's a very focused theme with very focused keywords, so your site ranks high for searches for [black marbles]. Because you never talk about anything but black marbles, it's inherently obvious to search engines and visitors that your site is an expert on black marbles. Imagine that the jar of black marbles in Figure 2-1 is your site.

Perhaps you also sell white marbles on your site. If you just add the marbles in, with no order or emphasis, it becomes harder to say that your site is focused on black marbles. You are starting to dilute your focus. The search engine still ranks it pretty high for [black marbles] because this theme is still very obvious. You might even rank for [white and black marbles], but your rank for [black marbles] might drop because your focus is now not explicitly clear. Figure 2-2 shows how a mixed-up jar of marbles doesn't seem to be about either black or white marbles in particular, although it's still clearly about marbles.

Similarly, if you were to add gray marbles to the mix, you would further dilute the "theme" of the jar. The search engines might still rank you for [marbles], but your rankings for [black marbles], [white marbles], [gray marbles] would be much lower or be gone entirely. You aren't about just black marbles anymore. The more colors that you add — blue, green, red, pink, tiger's eye, clear, silver — the more diluted your theme of black marbles becomes. Figure 2-3 shows how adding more colors makes black marbles less of an obvious focus.

Figure 2-1:
Your site
is clearly
about black
marbles.

Figure 2-2:
A jar of
mixed black
and white
marbles.

By picking a clear site theme (in this case, black marbles) and removing
all of the other unnecessary marbles, you bump up your Web site's search
ranking because the search engine can clearly deduce that you are all
about black marbles. (Note: You *can* rank well for lots of different themes

successfully using a technique called *siloing*. For more on how to silo your Web site, refer to Book II, Chapter 4. Detailed instructions on siloing can be found in Book IV.)

Figure 2-3:
White, black, and gray marbles mixed together.

Keeping in mind that you want a clearly defined theme, take your nice, long list of keywords and choose the ones that represent your site's theme the best. Say your site theme is Classic Car Customization. Keywords that you would definitely need to use would be *classic*, *car*, and *customization*. But don't forget the industry standard words. When experts are looking to link to other resources, they use industry jargon to do their searches. This is why it's important to research both your industry and the people on the street, so you can attract both kinds of traffic. It's a good idea to include *auto*, *automobile*, and *vehicle* into your keywords because those are industry terms, even though users are more likely to search for [cars] than [automobiles].

Focusing only on keywords that are very broad, high traffic terms can lead to you not achieving a high ranking in the search engines and not getting good conversions from what traffic you do get. People tend to look for broad search terms only when they're first doing information gathering, and use much more specialized terms or phrases when they're getting ready to make a purchase. Broad search terms are good to have to bring people in, but make sure you also have much more specific keywords that go along with them as well.

Make sure that the specific keywords match your site theme and don't dilute it. For example, going back to the classic car customization business in Poughkeepsie, tossing in keywords like *Anglia, Ferrari, Italian,* and so forth could actually do more harm than good because the business doesn't deal with foreign cars. There's a difference between drawing traffic for traffic's sake and having people actually stay and visit your site. Unless your Web site makes money simply by the number of visitors (like sites that make their money from selling ads based on page views), you want to attract people who won't immediately hit the Back button on their browser.

Here are some things to remember when you're picking keywords:

✦ **Clarity:** Are they clear and concise?

✦ **Relevance:** Are they what you're actually offering on your Web site? (False advertising is *never* a good idea.)

✦ **Categorized:** Can they be grouped into understandable keyword phrases?

✦ **Audience appropriate:** Are they a good mix of both industry standards and what your clients use in their searches?

✦ **Targeted:** Are they specific to your product? Three, four, even five word phrases are best.

Start weeding out what won't work for you using the above criteria and taking into account the traffic and return on investment the keyword brings. This can be a pretty time-consuming process, but there are steps to take during the brainstorming process to make this as painless as possible.

Picking Keywords Based on Subject Categories

Having a clear site theme, plus many relevant keywords, is a good start. But now you're going to have to break it down into smaller categories in order to best organize your Web site and all those keywords you picked out. In Chapter 1 of Book II, we told you to make an outline of your list of keywords, grouping them into categories and subcategories.

The high-level terms represent broad keywords, and then they're broken into longer, much more specific keywords as you go down the outline. Using this detailed outline, you can arrange your subject categories for your Web site. You want to have distinct subject categories because it helps you when *siloing* (or theming) your Web site. Having a Web site that has grouped or related keywords and links allows a search engine to return a faster result, which in turn equals a higher page ranking.

High traffic keywords

The next step you want to take with your keywords list is to determine which ones generate a high amount of traffic and which ones have a high conversion rate. High traffic keywords are the keywords that bring the most people to your site.

With a high traffic keyword, the goal is not only to bring people to your Web site, but also to keep them there. If your word brings in a lot of traffic, but there's also a high *bounce rate* (people who stay at the landing page only briefly, and then hit Back on the browser), you have a problem. A high bounce rate indicates one or more of the following issues:

✦ The keyword is not relevant for your Web page.

✦ The text on the Web page is not relevant enough to the keyword.

✦ The content or layout of the Web page doesn't hold a user's interest.

✦ The page loads too slowly and users lose patience and abandon the page before it fully renders.

In any case, you want to look closely at the page with the particular keyword in mind and make appropriate improvements. Keywords that have a high bounce rate do not yield many conversions, and therefore do not generate any revenue (unless you have a Web site where you make money based on page views alone). If anything, high bounce rate keywords can cost you money by requiring a lot of site hardware and *bandwidth* (the speed data moves to and from your Web site) to support all the extraneous traffic.

What we recommend to help you analyze your keywords is to use a spreadsheet program like Microsoft Excel. Excel comes along with most Microsoft Office packages, so if you have Microsoft Word, chances are you already have Excel. Microsoft Excel allows you to arrange and compare data in rows and columns, similar to a paper ledger or accounts book. We're going to talk about Microsoft Excel, but there are other spreadsheet programs out there like Google Docs and PlanMaker.

We suggest you copy your entire keyword list and paste it into column A of an Excel spreadsheet, so you end up with a simple list of keywords, one per row. Depending on how big your list is, you may want to create a new tab for each subject category, separating their keywords into more manageable spreadsheets. Setting up a keywords spreadsheet comes in handy when you're keeping track of what keywords are working and which ones aren't. (Not an Excel whiz? Check out *Excel 2007 For Dummies*, by Greg Harvey, and published by Wiley.)

Now you can use the remaining columns (B, C, and so on) to store data about each keyword. The first piece of data you need to find is an estimate of how many times people search for the keyword each day.

You can use free tools like Bruce Clay, Inc.'s Search Engine Optimization/KSP tool to measure daily search activity for specific keyword phrases on the Internet across the major search engines. It's not just guesswork; you can see actual counts!

The following tools are available online for checking search activity by keyword (and many other search engine optimization-related tasks). We list them in no particular order, with the prices accurate as of this writing:

✦ Bruce Clay, Inc. offers a free keyword activity tool on its Web site. Use the Search Engine Optimization/KSP tool (`www.bruceclay.com/web_rank.htm#seoksp`) to find search activity counts, category information, and demographic data. The full toolset is also available for $39.95 per month and features more robust versions of the free tools.

✦ Wordtracker (`www.wordtracker.com`) is a paid tool that measures keyword traffic. Wordtracker offers both annual plans and monthly plans. The annual plan runs about $329 a year, and the monthly play costs $59 per month. They also offer a free trial version.

✦ Keyword Discovery (`www.keyworddiscovery.com`) offers a subscription service that runs about $49.95 a month.

Keep in mind that the figures are only estimates and should be taken as general guidelines. However, they give you a general indication of activity levels. For instance, if the keyword research tools say that keyword A supposedly has 20,000 searches a day and keyword B only 200, you can look at the numbers proportionally and trust that while the actual counts may vary, relatively speaking, keyword A is searched 100 times more frequently than keyword B.

On your spreadsheet, make column B *Searches* or *Activity*. Using one of the tools we mention above, enter your keywords and fill in the daily search activity count in column B for each keyword (shown in Figure 2-4). You may find it tedious to try out each keyword and copy the resulting activity number into your spreadsheet, but this data will be extremely useful for you in evaluating your keywords and improving your search engine optimization. You need benchmarks and figures, not just guesses, to make sure you're optimizing your site for the right keywords.

	A	B	C
1	Query	Searches	Volume
3	pga	5244	11.08230719
4	pga.com	2583	6.610499028
5	freegolfinfo	64	4.147764096
6	golf tips	1884	3.046014258
7	golf	176386	1.62022035
8	pga tour	4142	1.360985094
9	michigan football	5105	0.777705768
10	golf swing	1596	0.777705768
11	pga golf	1406	0.712896954
12	pga championship	504	0.583279326
13	mgoblue	311	0.583279326
14	putting tips	133	0.518470512
15	golf shank	22	0.453661698
16	michigan wolverines	2587	0.453661698
17	golf lessons	463	0.453661698
18	us open	6077	0.388852884
19	online golf tips	8	0.388852884
20	university of michigan	4948	0.32404407
21	golf schools	1657	0.32404407
22	how to play golf	394	0.32404407
23	free video golf lessons	5	0.32404407
25	stratton	976	0.259235256
26	swing plane	15	0.259235256

Figure 2-4:
A keyword spreadsheet lets you compare data for each keyword.

High conversion keywords

You want to understand what keywords are going to result in buyers versus just window shoppers. It's nice to get a lot of traffic, but it's better to get conversions, and it's best to have both *ROI* (return on investment) and high traffic. A high conversion keyword means you have a keyword that brings you a lot of sales, sign-ups, entrants, or whatever action your site considers a conversion. A high conversion keyword could be a high traffic keyword as well, but not necessarily so.

A low traffic keyword may be okay if it is also a high conversion keyword. For example, if you have a keyword that brings only ten visitors a year, but one of those visitors becomes a sale that equals half a million dollars, that's a good keyword. You wouldn't want to remove that keyword from your site for a minute! Sometimes these types of keywords are called *elephant words* — big words that are so laborious to type and so obscure in usage that only a very serious searcher would think of entering it in a query. One elephant word is *mesothelioma*, which is the type of cancer that results from asbestos poisoning. Law firms love *mesothelioma* as a keyword, because even though it doesn't bring them a huge amount of traffic, people searching for the term usually mean business, and even one legal case can generate a huge amount of revenue. On the other hand, if you optimize for a keyword that brings you a million visitors and only one conversion that isn't worth much money, it's time to consider dropping that keyword phrase unless that term is a branding term for you and you want to keep it for the name recognition.

Choosing keywords and optimizing for them requires a certain amount of guesswork, science, finesse, and practice. There are few hard and fast rules — for each item, you must weigh the pros and cons and make lots of decisions. Over time, you develop a feel for search engine optimization and it becomes easier. However, it's extremely important to both track and test your keywords as you go along with your Web site. This process is ongoing, so be patient and let yourself go through the learning curve. And remember that the kinds of tools and analytics you've begun to use in this chapter are an SEO's best friend.

Chapter 3: Exploiting Pay Per Click Lessons Learned

In This Chapter

✔ **Analyzing pay per click campaigns**

✔ **Testing keywords through pay per click ads**

✔ **Building your brand with pay per click ads**

✔ **Eliminating low click-through keywords**

✔ **Overlapping paid ads with organic ranking to reduce costs**

*B*uying pay per click ads can be a useful part of your overall search engine optimization strategy. *Pay per click* (which are paid ads, showing up under "sponsored links" on a search results page, that site owners have negotiated with the search engine to display when certain keywords are searched) can complement the work you're doing to move your listing up in the *organic results* (the normal search results). And because it's relatively fast to set up pay per click ads, they can be an easy way to jumpstart your Web site's performance in search results.

To buy a pay per click ad, you go to the chosen search engine's paid search Web site (listed in Book I, Chapter 4 under "Paid Search Results") and bid on a particular keyword phrase that you would like your ad to display for. From then on, the search engine tracks how many times people click your ad, and bills you monthly for the total clicks. Generally, the highest bidders are awarded the top positions on the search results (though with Google, some relevance factors do affect the order). For more information on buying pay per click ads, you could pick up a copy of *Pay Per Click Search Engine Marketing for Dummies* by Peter Kent (published by Wiley). In this chapter, you'll learn why these ads are useful to your search engine optimization efforts and how to use them to build your brand and reduce your cost of conversion.

Analyzing Your Pay Per Click Campaigns for Clues About Your Site

You can use pay per click (PPC) ads to provide clues that help you optimize your Web site for organic results, such as:

✦ What keywords produce traffic (lots of visitors) to your site

✦ What keywords don't produce traffic to your site

✦ What keywords bring the right kind of visitors to your site (i.e., ones that convert to customers)

✦ Some real traffic volume numbers from that search engine for a particular keyword

What's nice about using PPC for this kind of research is that you can test ads scientifically. (Note: It's difficult to set up scientific tests of keywords in the natural search rankings because the search engine's methods are largely a secret, and their algorithms are constantly in flux.) With PPC, you can control which ads display for which keywords, and set up comparison tests. For example, you could test:

✦ Two different versions of an ad to see which wording draws more people

✦ An ad placed on two different keywords to find out which keyword is more effective

The various statistics and analytical tools offered by Google AdWords, Yahoo! Search Marketing, and Microsoft adCenter are a nice benefit to purchasing paid ads through these search engines. The data you collect through them helps you refine your Web site's theme(s) and keywords. In turn, this knowledge helps you to improve your site's ranking in organic search results as well as paid results by targeting better keywords for your pages.

Keep in mind that pay per click campaigns require constant monitoring and revision. Bid prices can fluctuate, and you have to make adjustments based on the performance of your ads. Over time, you must change your listings, removing the under-performers and adding new ones. You want to identify keywords that are costing far more than the profits they generate and discontinue them, while keeping track of these lessons learned to apply them to your natural search engine optimization as well. For these reasons, it is important to use the search engines' analytics tools mentioned previously to measure the effectiveness of your ads and to harvest data that helps you optimize your campaign.

Be aware that pay per click data does not necessarily represent how the same keywords would behave in natural search results; it only provides clues. However, it's a start in the right direction. Organic search engine op timization can take months of trial and error to produce results. By comparison, a pay per click campaign benefits you immediately with listings placed on the first page of search results, an increase in traffic, and some useful data. These benefits can help start your SEO efforts off quickly and give you some good indications of what might be the best keywords for your site.

Brand building

You want your company name to be seen and recognized in your industry without becoming generic — that's branding. When you think Nike, you think of a lifestyle, not merely a pair of running shoes. When your company is branded, it becomes a search keyword all by itself. Successful branding associates you with your particular industry so tightly that you're nearly synonymous. The key word here is *nearly*, of course. You don't want to have your brand name become so watered down that you lose control of how people use it. For instance, when you sneeze, do you reach for a tissue or a Kleenex? When you need a paper copied, do you photocopy it or Xerox it? A recent brand struggling with this problem is Google. They've been fighting to remind people that you're not "googling your blind date," you're "performing a search on your blind date using Google." Walking that line is probably a long way down the road for most businesses, however.

**Book II
Chapter 3**

**Exploiting Pay
Per Click Lessons
Learned**

You can build awareness of your brand instantly by purchasing pay per click ads. Every time your company name shows up visibly in search results for a particular search query, it helps to build your brand. If your business is selling classic custom cars, you can make your name appear on search results for [classic custom cars] simply by bidding for that keyword phrase with the search engines. Although it might take months of search engine optimization work to bring your listing up to the first page in the natural search results, pay per click gives you a way to increase your branding right away.

 We usually recommend that clients buy ads for their own company names. You'd be amazed how many companies do not show up in natural search results even for searches on their own name. This is brand nonexistence, at least on the Web. If you want to generate brand awareness, taking out PPC ads on your branded terms is a quick fix that should be on your to-do list. And if your company already does rank well in the natural search results for your branded terms, including a PPC ad as well, only strengthens your branding. According to studies done by Microsoft, companies with the top organic spot and the top paid listing receive a greater brand lift than those appearing in either location alone.

When you're building your brand name, make sure your brand goes first in the `Title` tags on your Web site. For example, a page on our company site could have a `Title` tag that looks like this:

```
<title>Bruce Clay Inc. - Search Engine Optimization
   Services</title>.
```

When you put your brand name first, it shows up first in your search results listing (as well as at the top of the browser window when someone is on your Web site). This exposure helps to give your brand a sense of authority. Be aware, however, that this does sacrifice some relevancy in the mind of the user when searching on non-branded terms.

Identifying keywords with low click-through rates

Pay per click ads let you easily test different keywords for your ads. Ads should be written with good marketing copy that is highly relevant to the keyword phrase you're bidding on. After you've accomplished that, you can find out which keywords yield the most *click-throughs* (people clicking the link) and *conversions* (people who not only visit your site, but also buy what you offer). You can conversely weed out those keywords that have low click-through and low conversion rates.

After all, just being listed on a search results page is of little value if people don't click through to your site. With pay per click ads, you can find out which search terms work best at generating the kind of traffic you need. Broad search terms such as *cars* are probably not a good place to put your ad money. First of all, these types of broad terms are heavily searched, which makes the bidding for them more competitive. The per-click cost for a broad term would be very high (measured by price per click times traffic) and might not be worth it. Also, although *cars* is searched frequently, the click-through rate is very low. Even if someone does click your listing and visit your site, broad search queries tend to have low conversion rates because the people usually are just seeking general information and not ready to take action such as making a purchase.

As a best practice, bid on everything that has a positive ROI and test, test, test — always test . . . never stop.

What you want are keywords that specifically draw people to your site and result in conversions. Here are a few facts you can keep in mind:

✦ Approximately 58 percent of search queries contain at least three words.

✦ Short, one- or two-word search queries tend to be used for information gathering; those searches usually don't convert well into customers.

✦ When users refine their search by using longer queries, they tend to be more seriously looking for a product or service.

✦ In general, users are getting more sophisticated and using more refined searches (that is, typing in longer search queries).

When choosing good keywords for your site, keep in mind the Long Tail effect we covered in Book I, Chapter 5. The *Long Tail* is a statistical concept that says that items that are in comparatively low demand can nonetheless add up to quite large volumes. The idea is that longer, more specific keyword phrases may not get a lot of traffic, but when people do search for them, the likelihood of click-through and conversion is quite high. Take our classic custom cars Web site example. A long-tail keyword phrase such as *1965 Ford Mustang GT* might make an excellent keyword phrase for a pay per click ad linked right to the Ford Mustang page on the Web site. Although the phrase might not get searched very often, someone typing in this search query would probably be a serious shopper — or at the very least, will find exactly what he's looking for on your Web page.

You want to purchase long-tail keyword phrases for pay per click ads for several reasons:

+ They are relatively cheap to buy because fewer sites bid on them.

+ The *bounce rate* (percentage of people who click a listing but then bounce right back to the search results by clicking the Back button) tends to be low because your Web page closely relates to the search query.

+ Fewer searches mean fewer clicks, so your costs remain low.

+ The pay per click ads let you test different keyword phrases and find out what people search for that leads them to your site.

+ You can apply what you learn with your pay per click ads directly to optimize your Web site for effective keywords, which can help you to rank in organic search results. Your ranking may go up fairly easily for these long-tail keywords because they're less competitive.

+ Long-tail traffic adds up, and that makes it attractive.

If you have ads that people aren't clicking on, the keyword might not be the problem. A low click-through rate could be due to a number of factors:

+ Your ad copy may not be written well.

+ Your ad may not be relevant to the search term.

+ The audience your ad is targeting is not the same as the people who are searching for that term.

Because there are several variables, it may be difficult to pinpoint exactly why a given ad has a low click-through rate. You can actually learn more from ads with high click-through rates than you can from those that underperform. If you've found a winning combination of ad copy and relevant keyword terms and it's bringing the right kind of traffic to your Web site, you've found marketing gold. By all means, apply the same types of keywords to your Web site to improve your organic search engine optimization, as well.

Reducing Costs by Overlapping Pay Per Click with Natural Keyword Rankings

Pairing your search engine optimization work with a pay per click campaign often yields the best results. Don't just do one or the other. If you have the budget, doing both organic SEO and pay per click together is the best strategy.

Research supports the use of PPC ads in addition to organic search results ranking for your targeted keywords. If your company name appears in two places on the results page, you get higher impact and brand awareness — and more clicks on both the ad and the listing than you would if only one displayed. Studies have shown that when your company listing appears in the organic results *and* in a paid ad on the first results page, people get the impression that your company is an expert. As a result, they click your organic listing far more often than they would if no pay per click ad displayed. See Figure 3-1 for an example of a search ad paired with an organic ranking.

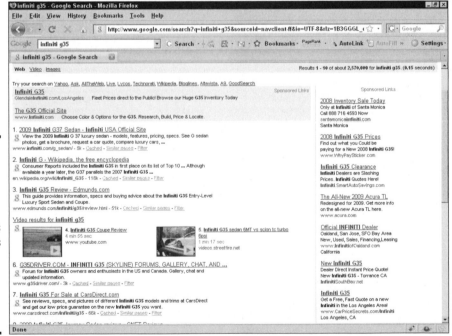

Figure 3-1: Displaying a paid ad as well as an organic listing raises a company's perceived expertise, branding, and click-throughs.

You benefit when your pay per click ads work in conjunction with a high page ranking in the organic results. It's interesting to note that when both display, although click patterns depend upon the keyword, some studies have shown that clicks go up for both the listing and the ad. Nevertheless, most people click the organic listing rather than the paid ad. Either way, you're still generating more traffic to your site by having both an ad and a good ranking.

In addition to perceived expertise and more click-throughs, your company earns better brand recognition by displaying in two places on the search results page. And on a practical level, your site also controls more real estate on the page — leaving less room for competitors.

Chapter 4: Assigning Keywords to Pages

In This Chapter

✔ Knowing what search engines see as keywords

✔ Planning your site's themes

✔ Creating landing pages that attract and hold visitors

✔ Organizing your site into subject categories

✔ Consolidating themes for maximum ranking value

*I*f you've read Chapters 1 through 3 of this minibook, you've already done a lot of the prep work for assigning keywords to pages. In this chapter, you use all of that research and prep work as we explain how you can assign keywords in a way that helps make your Web site most accessible to search engines. You want to make it as easy as possible for the search engines to find out what your site is about because the more relevant your site is to a user's search query, the higher your site is likely to show up in the search results.

Understanding What a Search Engine Sees as Keywords

In this section, we take a step back first and talk about what search engines really see as keywords. When someone enters a search query, the search engine looks for those words in its index. Here are some general things the search engine looks for:

✦ Web pages that contain the exact phrase.

✦ Web pages that have all the words of the phrase in close proximity to each other.

✦ Web pages that contain all the words, although not close together.

✦ Web pages that contain other forms of the words (such as *customize* instead of *customization*). This is called *stemming*.

✦ Web pages that have links pointing to them from other pages, in which the link text contains the exact phrase or all of the words in a different sequence.

✦ External Web pages that link to this site from a page that is considered to be about the same keyword.

✦ Web pages that contain the words in special formatting (bold, italics, larger font size, bullets, or with heading tags).

The preceding items are some of the clues a search engine would use to determine your site's keywords. They are not listed in order of priority, nor do they represent an exhaustive list because the search engines keep their methods a secret. All mystery aside, the search engine's main goal is to give users the *most relevant* results. If a search engine cannot clearly connect a user's query to keywords on your Web page, it won't return your site in the search results.

You should also put each page's keywords into its `Meta` keywords *tag* (part of the HTML coding for your Web page). Opinions are divided within the SEO industry on this point, however. Around 2005, the search engines said they would no longer weigh the keywords tag heavily, if at all, because so many Webmasters had abused it by cramming it full of words that didn't pertain to their site. Although this obviously lessened the overall importance of the keywords tag, it has been our experience that a keywords tag containing appropriate phrases that are also used in the page content definitely helps your Web page to rank highly. In addition, Google recently recommended that sites use the keywords tag to list common misspellings of their company name or products. This confirms that Google does indeed consider the keywords tag in some searches.

Planning Subject Theme Categories

Search engines rank individual pages but they do look for overall site-wide themes in determining how relevant your Web page is to a search query. As a general rule, the home page should use more broad range terms, and the supporting pages should use more specific and targeted terms that help support the home page. By using this method, you enable the search engines to understand and index your site's contents because this is the organization they're expecting. And better indexing means better inclusion on search results.

Here's a general guideline about keywords, topics, and themes: A Web page's first paragraph should introduce its keywords. If a keyword is repeated in every paragraph, it's a topic. If the Web site has multiple (we recommend six or more) interconnected pages related to the topic, we consider that a theme. Search engines consider a site with multiple pages of unique, informative content on a theme to be highly relevant.

You need to choose a main theme for your Web site. What is your whole Web site about? For instance, our classic custom cars Web site might have a main site theme of *custom cars* or of *classic cars*. Which one makes the most sense depends on two things: which theme most accurately fits the business and vision of the Web site, and which theme is searched for the most. To find out which phrase gets the most number of searches, you need to use a keyword research tool such as those covered in Book II, Chapter 2. Here, we suffice to say that the phrase [classic cars] receives about four times the number of searches that [custom cars] does, so we use *classic cars* as our main site theme.

The preceding example points out an important principle: You should not plan your site theme and structure based solely on what makes sense to you. Instead, do research to find out how people search and lay out your Web site accordingly. This is essential to your design.

Book II Chapter 4

Assigning Keywords to Pages

Assuming that you want your site to rank in searches for its major theme, you want to

+ Make sure your site theme is included in your home page's title tag and Meta tags (HTML code located at the top of a Web page — we show you how this is done in Book IV).

+ Use your site theme in your page content, so that the search engines interpret the theme as keywords for your Web page. Making your theme part of the keywords helps a Web page come up in searches for those keywords. (You learn more about keyword strategy in Chapter 5 of this minibook.)

After you've got your main site theme, you need to organize the site content. If you already have a Web site, try to view it with fresh eyes because the current organizational structure might not be the most conducive to good search engine ranking. In our experience, many Web sites are disjointed arrays of unrelated information with no central theme. Yours may not be that bad, but as you read through the recommendations in this chapter, you may find that you're light on content, have too much of the wrong type of content, or need to do some major reorganization. As Figure 4-1 shows, you need to figure out how best to divide your site into subject categories.

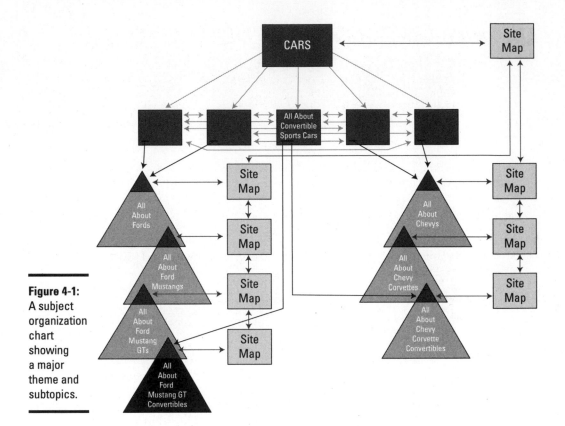

Figure 4-1:
A subject
organization
chart
showing
a major
theme and
subtopics.

Look at all of the content, products, services, and so on, that your Web site offers. Is all of the stuff on your site well-organized into categories and sub-categories? Do those breakdowns match the way people search for what you offer? Depending on the size of your Web site and the diversity of its subject matter, you could have a single site-wide theme, or a structure with hundreds of subject theme categories and subcategories. Some keyword research is in order here as well to make sure you're dividing up the infor-mation according to how people search. For instance, the classic cars Web site could separate its content either by body type (sedans, coupes, convert-ibles, vans, and so on), by make (Chevrolet, Ford, Oldsmobile, and so on), by year of manufacture (1950, 1951, 1952, and so on), or by some other method. It turns out that people don't usually search for cars by body type, such as [sedan cars], or by year [1959 Oldsmobiles]. Instead, most people looking for cars search by make and model, like [Oldsmobile Ninety-Eight]. For maxi-mum ranking in search engines, therefore, this Web site ought to organize its contents by make, and then by model. Of course, based on how people search in your industry, your subcategories will vary.

Choosing Landing Pages for Subject Categories

You should organize your Web site into categories not just because it's neater that way, but also so that your site can rank well for any of its subject themes. Rather than having all inbound links point to your home page only, you should create an array of highly targeted pages representing all of your categories. For each subject category in your Web site, you want to choose a landing page.

A *landing page* acts as the primary information page for a subject category. It's the page where all *hypertext links* (text that can be clicked to take the user to another Web page) related to that subject should point. Your Web site's landing pages present the all-important first impression to site visitors. You want to make sure your landing pages not only put your best foot forward, but also interest visitors enough to entice them to go further, and hopefully convert to customers. They have to look good to users *and* search engines.

The primary subjects for our classic cars Web site are the different makes of cars, and each one needs a landing page. The Ford landing page needs to contain some general information about Ford cars; a separate Oldsmobile landing page should contain some information about Olds cars; and so on. Your landing pages need to have enough content so that people reaching them from a search engine feel satisfied that they've come to the right place. You want the content to engage visitors enough so that they want to stay. You also need your landing pages to link to other pages on your site that offer more detailed information within the subject category and lead to opportunities to buy, sign up, or take whatever action your site considers a conversion.

Organizing Your Primary and Secondary Subjects

Search engines look for depth of content. Your landing pages should each have at least three or four pages of supporting information that they link to. These sub-pages need to be within the same theme as the landing page that they support. Having several sub-pages linked from each landing page that all talk about the same subject theme reinforces your theme and boosts your landing page's perceived expertise on the subject.

Now that you've decided on primary subjects for your Web site, each with its own landing page, you need to decide whether further stratification is needed. Do you have natural sub-categories under your primary subject categories? If so, you probably want to create landing pages for this second tier, as well. For our classic cars Web site, the secondary subjects under each car manufacturer would be the different models of cars, and we'd create a landing page for each model. So the Ford landing page could link to individual landing pages for Ford Mustang, Ford Falcon, Ford Thunderbird, and so on.

The concept of organizing a Web site's content into distinct subject categories, each with its own landing page and supporting pages, is called *siloing.* Refer back to the diagram in Figure 4-1 to see how our classic cars Web site could be arranged into silos.

Here are a few recommendations for building landing pages:

- ✦ Keep each landing page's content focused on its particular subject category.

- ✦ Make the content engaging — consider including video, audio, images, or dynamic elements along with highly relevant text (not in place of it!).

- ✦ Customize the keywords on each landing page to reflect that page's subject theme.

- ✦ Be sure to include the keywords in the page content as well as in the `Meta` tags.

- ✦ Include links to secondary pages in the same category.

- ✦ Don't include links to secondary pages under different subject categories.

A note about links: Hypertext links that lead to each landing page should contain your page's keywords. You want the linked text that the user clicks (the *anchor text*) to be meaningful. Google keeps track of links to determine the relevancy of each of your Web pages. The link Ford Mustang Information and Pricing gains you a lot more points than Click Here because your page is not really about Click Here — it's about Ford Mustangs. You definitely want to use good, keyword-rich anchor text for links going to landing pages in your Web site. You don't have as much control over the links that other Web sites use to link to your pages, but as much as possible, try to have those links also show descriptive anchor text.

Understanding Siloing "Under the Hood"

Now that you understand the importance of grouping content on your site, you might be wondering how to accomplish it. If you have a gigantic Web site with thousands of pages that need to be reorganized, don't panic. You can do your siloing in two ways. Either can be successful, but you get the most bang from your buck by doing both.

✦ **Physical silos:** Ideally, the physical structure of your site — the directories or folders — should reflect your silo organization. This is the simplest, cleanest way to do it, and keeps everything nicely organized as your Web site grows. With this organization, you want the top level folders to be your primary subject categories, the next-level folders to contain the secondary subject categories, and so forth. So a directory structure for our classic cars site might look something like Figure 4-2:

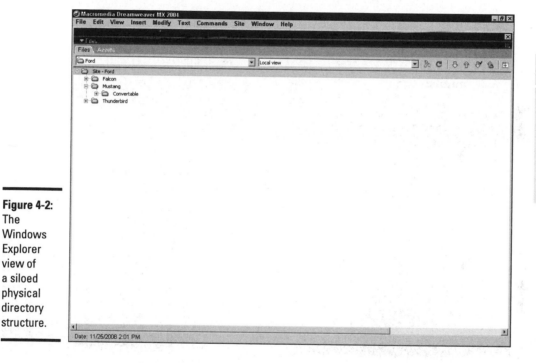

Book II
Chapter 4

Assigning Keywords to Pages

Figure 4-2:
The Windows Explorer view of a siloed physical directory structure.

Arranging the physical directories to match your siloing scheme is fine if you have the luxury of starting a site from scratch, or if your site is small enough to move things around without too much pain and effort. However, if you have a very large site or a very stubborn *Content Management System (CMS)* (software that helps you create, edit, and manage a Web site), you need a more flexible solution.

✦ **Virtual silos:** Web sites that cannot adjust their directory structures can accomplish siloing by creating *virtual silos*. Instead of moving related Web pages into new directories, virtual silos connect related pages using links. You still need to have a landing page per subject, and links on each landing page identify the sublevel pages within that subject silo. So no matter how the directories are set up for our classic cars Web site, the Ford landing page would have links to Ford Falcon, Ford Mustang, and Ford Thunderbird pages. Because search engine spiders follow the links as they move through a Web site, this virtual silo organization does not confuse the spiders, no matter how your underlying files and folders are set up.

✦ **Doing both:** Incorporating virtual and physical silos can be very powerful for a site that has pages that should exist in more than one silo or category. For a complete view of siloing and architecture, refer to Book IV.

Consolidating Themes to Help Search Engines See Your Relevance

In order to rank well in search results for a particular keyword phrase, your Web site must provide related information that is organized in clear language that search engines understand. When your textual information has been stripped away from its design and layout, does it measure up to be the most relevant aggregate information compared to that of other sites? If so, you have a high likelihood of achieving high rankings and attracting site visitors who are researching and shopping for products and services.

As we mentioned in Chapter 2 of this book, we often explain the importance of creating subject silos by using the analogy that most Web sites are like a jar of marbles. A search engine can only decipher meaning when the subjects are clear and distinct. Take a look at the picture of the jar of marbles in Figure 4-3.

In this jar are black marbles, white marbles, and gray marbles all mixed together with no apparent order or emphasis. It would be reasonable to assume that search engines would only classify the subject as *marbles*.

If you separated out each group of marbles into its own jar (or Web site), they would be classified as a jar of black marbles, a jar of white marbles, and a jar of gray marbles (Figure 4-4).

Figure 4-3:
A typical
Web site is
a jumbled
mixture of
items, like
this jar of
marbles.

Figure 4-4:
Each jar
(or site)
is clearly
about one
color of
marbles:
black, white,
and gray.
There is no
opportunity
for
confusion.

However, if you wanted to combine all three marble colors into a single jar, you could create distinct silos within the site that would allow the subject themes to be *black marbles*, *white marbles*, *gray marbles*, and finally the generic term *marbles*. (See Figure 4-5.) Most Web sites never clarify the main subjects they want their site to become relevant for. Instead, they try to be all things to all people.

Your goal, if you want your site to rank for more than a single generic term, is to selectively decide what your site is and is not about. Rankings are often damaged in three major ways:

✦ By having too little content for a subject on your Web site

✦ By including irrelevant content that dilutes and blurs your theme

✦ By choosing keywords that are not well matched to your theme

Do you have your themes poorly defined, spread out in pieces over a number of different pages? Or are you mixing dissimilar items together on a page, so that no central theme emerges (similar to the first jar of marbles in Figure 4-3)? Both of these cases may be preventing the search engines from seeing your Web pages as relevant to your keywords. If your Web site is not currently ranking well for a keyword phrase, consider both possible causes. You may have too little content for a theme, in which case you need to increase the number of pages that contain keyword-rich content on that sub-ject. Conversely, if you have irrelevant or disorganized content, you might need to consolidate your subject themes by separating and concentrating them into silos, like the marbles in Figure 4-5.

Figure 4-5:
A Web site
can contain
multiple
subjects
if they are
clearly
organized
into silos.

Chapter 5: Adding and Maintaining Keywords

In This Chapter

- ✔ Figuring out keyword densities
- ✔ Adjusting keywords
- ✔ Updating keywords
- ✔ Using tools to aid keyword placement

*I*f you've been doing what we suggest as you read the past four chapters, you've brainstormed, you've done your research, you've categorized your keywords, and created *landing pages* (the Web page the user comes to when clicking a link) for your subject categories. So now what? Now you actually get to add keywords.

There is an art to placing keywords on your Web site. You can't simply type *car, car, car, car, car, car* again and again. For one thing, that's considered spam and will get your site pulled from the search engine index. (For our purposes, *spam* is any type of deceptive Web technique meant to trick a search engine into offering inappropriate, redundant, or poor-quality search results. For more details, see Book I, Chapter 6.) For another thing, a user who sees "car, car, car, car …" would immediately hit Back on the browser window. Remember, you want to *keep* people so that they will stick around and be converted from a visitor to a customer (or however your Web site defines converted). To do that, you have to create searchable, readable content for your Web site.

But what do you do with those keywords we made you gather? In this chapter, we talk about how to distribute them on your pages, and how to determine the number of times you need to use them. We also discuss how to maintain your keywords. Unfortunately, the Internet is ever-changing and so is the market. In order to maintain your relevancy, you're also going to have to adjust and update your keywords regularly. But not to worry: There are tools out there that help you measure your keywords' performance and analyze your competition's keywords, and we show you how to use them.

Understanding Keyword Densities, Frequency, and Prominence

Keyword density is a term we use in SEO-land. It's the measurement of the number of times a keyword or keyword phrase appears on a Web page, compared to the total number of words on the page. To determine density, you take the number of words on the page (say, 1,000 for a long page) and the number of times that the word appears on that page (maybe 23 times). Divide 23 by 1,000 to get a density of about 2.3 percent. Keyword density is one of the factors a search engine spider looks at when determining whether a Web page is relevant to that search. Frequency is another factor that SEOs look at: It's simply how many times a word appears on the page; in this case, 23 times. The combination of frequency and density is the prominence — higher density and more instances lead to greater prominence of the term.

These factors collectively are why it's important to have searchable text on your Web page, and especially on each landing page. That doesn't mean you have to write a novel on your landing pages. Search engine spiders generally put more weight on the first 200 words on a Web site, including words in your navigation, headings, and so on. It's important to make sure that your keywords appear throughout the page but especially right up front so that search engines and your visitor know what you're all about from the get go. You can elaborate further from there on, of course.

With keywords, the spiders are looking at these three things:

✦ **Frequency:** How often a keyword is used on a Web page. Any word (or phrase) is considered a keyword if it's used at least twice in the page. (Note that search engines do not include stop words such as *and*, *the*, *a*, and so forth as keywords, although they may be part of keyword phrases.)

✦ **Density:** Keyword density is like frequency, but it measures what percentage of the total page content the keyword appears. You're going to want to have each keyword comprise no more than five percent of the total page content.

✦ **Distribution:** This measures whether the keyword is evenly distributed throughout the page and the site. There is some debate over whether placing keywords higher on the page gives a boost to your rankings. In general, it's better to sprinkle the keywords evenly through the page in a normal writing fashion. Natural-sounding text is easier to read, and scores better with search engines.

You can visualize keyword distribution if you imagine all the content of a Web page arranged horizontally in a box, so that the beginning of the page is at the far left and the last words on the page are at the right edge.

Figure 5-1 shows the distribution of a keyword on a given page. The chart shows that the keyword phrase *peanut butter* occurs once near the beginning of the page, a couple of times near the middle of the page, and not at all near the end. Although a more even distribution would be better, search engines could tell from this distribution that the word *peanut butter* is an important keyword for this Web page.

1 Word Phrases

Keyword	Meta Title	Meta Desc	Meta Keywords	Heads	ALT Tags	First Words	Body Words	All Words
Count	5	13	29	25	3	200	299	432
butter	20 % (1)	15.4 % (2)	24.1 % (7)	12 % (3)	33.3 % (1)	3 % (6)	3.3 % (10)	5.6 % (24)
peanut	20 % (1)	15.4 % (2)	17.2 % (5)	8 % (2)	33.3 % (1)	2.5 % (5)	2.7 % (8)	4.4 % (19)
soy	-	-	13.3 % (4)	8 % (2)	-	1 % (2)	1.3 % (3)	3 % (9)
organic	-	-	6.7 % (2)	4 % (1)	-	1 % (2)	0.9 % (2)	1.7 % (5)
recipes	-	-	6.7 % (2)	-	-	1 % (2)	1.3 % (3)	1.7 % (5)
about	-	7.7 % (1)	-	-	-	1.5 % (3)	1.3 % (3)	1.3 % (4)
nuts	-	-	3.3 % (1)	-	-	1 % (2)	0.9 % (2)	1.3 % (4)
milk	-	-	-	-	-	2 % (4)	1.8 % (4)	1.3 % (4)
store	-	-	-	-	-	2 % (4)	1.8 % (4)	1.3 % (4)
all	20 % (1)	7.7 % (1)	-	-	-	0.5 % (1)	0.9 % (2)	1.3 % (4)
roasted	-	-	3.3 % (1)	4 % (1)	-	1 % (2)	0.9 % (2)	1.3 % (4)
information	-	-	-	-	-	1 % (2)	1.3 % (3)	1 % (3)
how	-	-	3.3 % (1)	-	-	0.5 % (1)	0.9 % (2)	1 % (3)
syrup	-	-	-	-	-	1.5 % (3)	1.3 % (3)	1 % (3)
low	-	-	-	-	-	1 % (2)	1.3 % (3)	1 % (3)
history	-	7.7 % (1)	-	-	-	0.5 % (1)	0.9 % (2)	1 % (3)
facts	-	-	-	-	-	1 % (2)	1.3 % (3)	1 % (3)
buy	-	7.7 % (1)	3.3 % (1)	-	-	0.5 % (1)	0.4 % (1)	1 % (3)
fun	-	-	-	-	-	1 % (2)	1.3 % (3)	1 % (3)
just	-	-	-	-	-	1 % (2)	0.9 % (2)	0.7 % (2)
perfect	-	-	-	-	-	1 % (2)	0.9 % (2)	0.7 % (2)
great	-	-	-	4 % (1)	-	0.5 % (1)	0.4 % (1)	0.7 % (2)
use	-	-	-	-	-	1 % (2)	0.9 % (2)	0.7 % (2)
look	-	-	-	-	-	1 % (2)	0.9 % (2)	0.7 % (2)
contact	-	-	-	-	-	0.5 % (1)	0.9 % (2)	0.7 % (2)
peanutbutterville	20 % (1)	-	-	-	-	-	0.4 % (1)	0.7 % (2)
near	-	-	-	-	-	1 % (2)	0.9 % (2)	0.7 % (2)
malt	-	-	-	-	-	1 % (2)	0.9 % (2)	0.7 % (2)

Figure 5-1:
A linear distribution chart for a keyword across a Web page.

Book II Chapter 5

Adding and Maintaining Keywords

In order to have proper keyword distribution, you can't clutter up your page with keywords or just dump them on the page. When writing your text, form sentences that use those keywords. Remember what we said about keyword phrases as well. Search engine users are getting more sophisticated these days and entering search queries that contain three to four words instead of just two or three. If you're a good writer, you're going to have to tame some of those habits you learned while writing papers. Good writers are encouraged to use synonyms and rephrase things to keep from being too repetitive. This makes a document easier to read, surely, but it won't help with your site rankings. Because your search engine ranking is going to be measured using a math equation, it's better to think of your site in terms of supplying the equation with numbers.

For instance, if you want to rank high for a query like [classic cars], you're going to have to keep using the words *classic cars* in your page instead of using *these* and *them* and so forth. Use discretion when doing this; otherwise, your page could become unpleasant to read. A good example of how to properly spread keywords is this book. Notice how many times we say a particular word, like *keyword*, and how we distribute it through the text. We don't say "Choose your keywords during your keyword research for keyword optimization purposes using keyword tools." That level of repetition is unnatural-sounding. Instead, we mention keywords every now and then, when it's appropriate. On the other hand, we don't just say *keyword* once and then spend the rest of our time trying to find flowery ways to refer to keywords. Your competition is a good way to get an idea of what looks natural to search engines. For more on how to analyze your competition's pages, read Book III, Chapter 1.

Remember that search engines count every instance of a word on a Web page (except if it's showing in a graphic — computers can't "read" images). This includes all words in the article text plus that in headings, navigation elements, links, and HTML tags. Here's an example, and remember this is just a recommended guideline, of how you might evenly distribute a main keyword throughout a page that had 750 words divided into five paragraphs:

✦ Once in the `Title` tag

✦ Once or twice in the description `Meta` tag (in the HTML code)

✦ Once or twice in the keywords `Meta` tag (in the HTML code)

✦ Once in the first sentence of on-page (user visible) text

✦ Twice in the first 200 words (including the first sentence)

✦ Once each in paragraphs two, three, and four

✦ Once or twice in the last paragraph

On the flip side, there is such a thing as using too many keywords — that's how you venture into the realm of spam through keyword stuffing. (Refer back to spam definitions in Book I, Chapter 6.) Remember our sample sentence about keywords from a few paragraphs ago? That's a stuffed sentence. There's no guaranteed magic number for keyword frequency or density, but it's a good rule of thumb to keep your keyword below five percent of the total number of words on the page. The better way to do it is to make it sound natural as compared to your competition. Use a keyword too often, and you could trip an alarm on a keyword stuffing filter. Keywords repeated too often also work against user retention and could bring down the conversion rate. For a commercial Web site, you want to keep customers around so they'll make purchases, and you risk driving them away with too much repetition. For an informational or reference Web site, the goal is to have as many visitors as possible stick around and read the information available. Badly written text does not make someone want to stay on your Web site. Figure 5-2 shows a made-up example of a Web page with keyword stuffing.

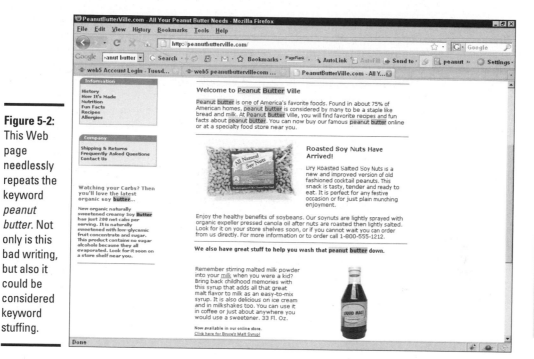

Figure 5-2: This Web page needlessly repeats the keyword *peanut butter*. Not only is this bad writing, but also it could be considered keyword stuffing.

There is a question of whether the Big Three search engines (Yahoo!, Microsoft Live Search, and Google) measure keyword densities differently. As with all areas of SEO, there's some argument over this issue. Generally, however, there's agreement that Google is less tolerant of heavy keyword usage than Yahoo! or Microsoft. And because all search engines continuously try to refine and improve their spam filters, you don't want to get too close to the line of what might be unacceptable.

Want to make sure a search engine doesn't miss your keywords? You can draw more attention to keywords by applying special formatting, such as strong `strong` or emphasis `em`, changing the font size, or using `Heading` tags. Putting them in the page titles (in the HTML `Title` tags) and the description and keywords `Meta` tags (also in the HTML code) is also recommended.

Adjusting Keywords

After you optimize your Web site for your selected keywords, be aware that your job is not done. Search engine optimization involves continual monitoring, testing, and tracking. You need to keep track of how your keywords are performing as you go along. If a keyword is not drawing in as much traffic as you think it should be, or it's drawing in the wrong kind of traffic (visitors who don't convert), it's time to go in and change it. (This is why you do a bunch of research into your competition, and to look up synonyms while you're at it.)

If a keyword is not working out, sitting around and hoping it eventually will is not going to increase your rank. SEO is not an exact science; it requires tweaking, fixing, and adjusting things. If one keyword is not working for you, perhaps its synonym might. If you find that you're getting traffic but no conversions, that's a sign that you need to look deeper into whether this is a useful keyword or if you're just wasting time trying to fight that battle.

It's more than okay to go in and adjust your keywords as needed. Do some testing between different keywords and compare the results to find your best performers. If a word's not working for you, stop using it! There are words out there that *will* bring your targeted audience, and all you need to do is make the proper adjustments to find them.

Updating Keywords

The thing about keyword maintenance is that it's not an exact science. There is no one guaranteed keyword out there that will always bring you a ton of traffic today and into the future. For one thing, no one knows what the Internet will look like two years from now, let alone five or ten. Vernacular changes very rapidly. In 2000, Google was a small upstart search engine; today, Google so dominates the industry that it's become a word in the dictionary and is often used as a verb. You can't stay still in the online world. Things that are common sense to us today might not stay that way.

For example, in the late nineties, you used a cellular telephone. Nowadays, it's a cell phone. If you're abroad, you don't use a cell phone, you use a mobile. A term that made sense as a keyword five years ago might not make sense today. The moral of the story is that you can't do your keyword research once and then say you're done. You have to keep researching as you go along, especially if you're making plans for the long term.

Using Tools to Aid Keyword Placement

Like tools for measuring how often a keyword is searched (which we covered in Book II, Chapter 4), there are also tools out there that aid you in researching keyword densities of a certain page. You want to use these tools to check out the competition. Not only do you need to know what keywords your competitors are using, but also in what frequency and density.

There's a couple of ways you can go about this. You can count the keywords by hand and probably drive yourself nuts. Or you can use a helpful tool called Pagè Analyzer. *Page Analyzer* measures as a percentage how much your keyword is used compared to the total number of words on your Web page. Our Page Analyzer measures frequency and prominence and graphs the density. Figure 5-3 shows a screenshot of the free Page Analyzer from the SEOToolset.

Tag Information

Tag	Count	Stop Words	Used Words	Length	Description
Title	7	2	5	52	PeanutButterVille.com - All Your Peanut Butter Needs Error: Title is too short (5 words). The title should be between 6 and 12 words Error: Title is out of sequence. The title should be before the Meta Description and Meta Keywords tags.
Description	19	6	13	101	At Peanut Butter Ville learn about the history of peanut butter and buy all of your nut butters here. Error: Description out of sequence. The Meta Description should appear between the Title and Meta Keywords tags. Warning: Description is missing a word that appears in the Title.
Keywords	32	3	29	209	peanuts, roasted nuts, soy, soy products, soy butter, soy nut butter, peanut butter, buy organic peanut butter, organic foods, peanut butter and jelly, recipes, peanut butter recipes, how to make peanut butter Error: Keywords out of sequence. The Meta Keywords should appear below the Title and Meta Description tags. Warning: Keywords is missing a word that appears in the Title or Meta Description
Headings	25	-	25	-	<h2>Watching your Carbs? Then you'll love latest organic soy butter... <h1>Welcome to Peanut Butter Ville <h1>Roasted Soy Nuts have Arrived! <h2>We also have great stuff to help you wash that peanut butter down. Error: Heading tags are out of sequence. Heading tags should appear in hierarchical order (H1, H2, H3, ...)
Link Text	35	5	30	199	AREAMAP Allergies Allergies Contact Us Contact Us Frequently Asked Questions Fun Facts Fun Facts History History How It's Made How It's Made Nutrition Nutrition

Figure 5-3:
The elements of Page Analyzer.

Using a page analyzer allows you to keep track of your competition in order to see what the search engines prefer and why. We also advise you to keep track of the results by using an Excel spreadsheet (see Book II, Chapter 2 for more details on that). This is something you should do periodically in order to keep track of the progress of your competition.

You can find many page analyzers out there, but the one we're going to discuss is available for free at www.seotoolset.com/tools/free_tools.html. As of this writing, it was the fourth tool down. To use it, simply type in your Web site's URL into the query window and click the Check Keyword Densities button. After a minute, you see a results page like the one in Figure 5-4 for our training site, www.peanutbutterville.com.

As you look down the report, the items in red indicate that your keyword density may be too low to rank across all engines. The items in blue indicate that your keyword density may be too high to rank across all engines.

The first thing you're going to see after you've placed your Web page into the Page Analyzer is your Google PageRank (the algorithm Google uses to measure and assign importance and weight to the links in your page and the links to you). Peanutbutterville.com has a PageRank of zero because of a lack of inbound links.

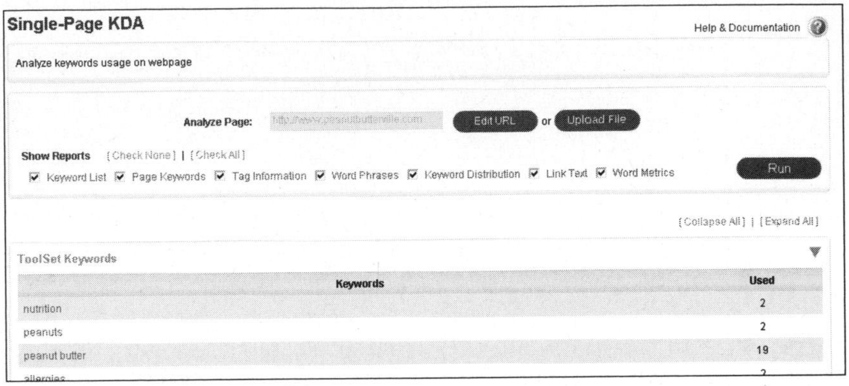

Figure 5-4:
The Web
site www.
peanut
butter
ville.
com in
the Page
Analyzer.

In Figure 5-5, you can see that you're next given a list of common words on your site. These are the keywords the Page Analyzer found on your Web page. A Page Analyzer (and a search engine) considers a word a keyword if it is used more than twice, including keyword phrases. In a full version of the toolset, you can actually enter in the keywords from your list and the Page Analyzer measures them and provides you their stats.

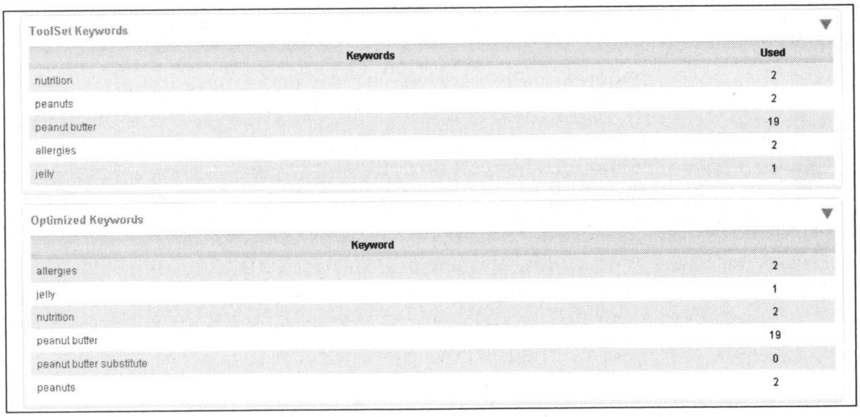

Figure 5-5:
Word lists
in the Page
Analyzer.

In Figure 5-6, under the headings "Title Tag," "Meta Description Tag" and "Meta Keywords Tag," you can see all of the text the Page Analyzer found in your Title tag and Meta tags for this page. Title tags are what you name your Web pages in the HTML coding of the site. It's very important to place a keyword or keywords in your page titles. The Meta description and keywords tags are other items in the HTML code at the top of each page. These are not visible to the user, but search engine spiders read them and measure them as part of your keyword density.

Tag Information					▼
Tag	**Count**	**Stop Words**	**Used Words**	**Length**	**Description**
Title	7	2	5	52	PeanutButterVille.com - All Your Peanut Butter Needs
					Error: Title is too short (5 words). The title should be between 6 and 12 words.
					Error: Title is out of sequence. The title should be before the Meta Description and Meta Keywords tags.
Description	19	6	13	101	At Peanut Butter Ville learn about the history of peanut butter and buy all of your nut butters here.
					Error: Description out of sequence. The Meta Description should appear between the Title and Meta Keywords tags.
					Warning: Description is missing a word that appears in the Title.
Keywords	32	3	29	209	peanuts, roasted nuts, soy, soy products, soy butter, soy nut butter, peanut butter, buy organic peanut butter, organic foods, peanut butter and jelly, recipes, peanut butter recipes, how to make peanut butter
					Error: Keywords out of sequence. The Meta Keywords should appear below the Title and Meta Description tags.
					Warning: keywords is missing a word that appears in the Title or Meta Description
Headings	25	-	25	- -	<h2>Watching your Carbs? Then you'll love latest organic soy butter... <h1>Welcome to Peanut Butter Ville <h1>Roasted Soy Nuts have Arrived! <h2>We also have great stuff to help you wash that peanut butter down.
					Error: Heading tags are out of sequence. Heading tags should appear in hierarchical order (H1, H2, H3, ...)
Link Text	35	5	30	199	AREAMAP Allergies Allergies Contact Us Contact Us Frequently Asked Questions Fun Facts Fun Facts History History How It's Made How It's Made Nutrition Nutrition Recipes Recipes

Figure 5-6: Measuring keywords in the Title and Meta tags, using the Page Analyzer tool.

The Page Analyzer can let you know if a title is too long or too short, whether too many keywords are used or not enough, and whether you're in danger of a spam violation. Figure 5-7 shows the stats page. This lists every word or phrase that's used at least twice on your Web page. The columns also indicate where your keywords appear in your page, and how many times the keyword is used in that particular section. For instance, in Figure 5-7, the word *butter* is used once in the Title tag and ten times in the body text of the page. It also tells you what percentage out of the total amount of words the keyword accounts for.

The Page Analyzer also tells you by one, two, three, and four-word phrases how your keywords are spread across your page. Figure 5-8 shows the Page Analyzer report for your keyword multi-word phrases. Densities on multi-word phrases are usually significantly lower than single words. Although a density of four or five percent might make sense for a single word, your multi-word phrases should be quite a bit lower than that (depending on your industry — more on that in Book III).

Keyword		Meta Title	Meta Desc	Meta Keywords	Heads	ALT Tags	First Words	Body Words	All Words
Word Phrases									
1 Word Phrases									
	Count	5	13	29	25	3	200	299	432
butter		20 % (1)	15.4 % (2)	24.1 % (7)	12 % (3)	33.3 % (1)	3 % (6)	3.3 % (10)	5.6 % (24)
peanut		20 % (1)	15.4 % (2)	17.2 % (5)	8 % (2)	33.3 % (1)	2.5 % (5)	2.7 % (8)	4.4 % (19)
soy		-	-	13.3 % (4)	8 % (2)	-	1 % (2)	1.3 % (3)	3 % (9)
organic		-	-	6.7 % (2)	4 % (1)	-	1 % (2)	0.9 % (2)	1.7 % (5)
recipes		-	-	6.7 % (2)	-	-	1 % (2)	1.3 % (3)	1.7 % (5)
about		-	7.7 % (1)	-	-	-	1.5 % (3)	1.3 % (3)	1.3 % (4)
nuts		-	-	3.3 % (1)	-	-	1 % (2)	0.9 % (2)	1.3 % (4)
milk		-	-	-	-	-	2 % (4)	1.8 % (4)	1.3 % (4)
store		-	-	-	-	-	2 % (4)	1.8 % (4)	1.3 % (4)
all		20 % (1)	7.7 % (1)	-	-	-	0.5 % (1)	0.9 % (2)	1.3 % (4)
roasted		-	-	3.3 % (1)	4 % (1)	-	1 % (2)	0.9 % (2)	1.3 % (4)
information		-	-	-	-	-	1 % (2)	1.3 % (3)	1 % (3)
how		-	-	3.3 % (1)	-	-	0.5 % (1)	0.9 % (2)	1 % (3)
syrup		-	-	-	-	-	1.5 % (3)	1.3 % (3)	1 % (3)
low		-	-	-	-	-	1 % (2)	1.3 % (3)	1 % (3)
history		-	7.7 % (1)	-	-	-	0.5 % (1)	0.9 % (2)	1 % (3)
facts		-	-	-	-	-	1 % (2)	1.3 % (3)	1 % (3)
buy		-	7.7 % (1)	3.3 % (1)	-	-	0.5 % (1)	0.4 % (1)	1 % (3)
fun		-	-	-	-	-	1 % (2)	1.3 % (3)	1 % (3)
just		-	-	-	-	-	1 % (2)	0.9 % (2)	0.7 % (2)
perfect		-	-	-	-	-	1 % (2)	0.9 % (2)	0.7 % (2)
great		-	-	-	4 % (1)	-	0.5 % (1)	0.4 % (1)	0.7 % (2)
use		-	-	-	-	-	1 % (2)	0.9 % (2)	0.7 % (2)
look		-	-	-	-	-	1 % (2)	0.9 % (2)	0.7 % (2)
contact		-	-	-	-	-	0.5 % (1)	0.9 % (2)	0.7 % (2)
peanutbuttersite		20 % (1)						0.4 % (1)	0.7 % (2)

Figure 5-7:
A Page
Analyzer
shows
statistics
for every
keyword.

There are no guarantees when it comes to SEO. The tools we've described in this chapter are just that, tools — they can only help you do a task more easily, not tell you what to do. Search engine optimization is not only about keywords, either. If you only adjust your keywords, you only upgrade your page to an okay page instead of an excellent page. Competitor research (Book III), site design (Book IV), content (Book V), linking (Book VI), site environment (Book VII), and analysis are all vital components to succeeding.

The more practice you have with researching, updating, and maintaining keywords, the less you need tools like the Page Analyzer. When you have more experience, you can look at a page and see if the keyword density needs tweaking, but it takes practice and patience to get to that point!

Maintaining keywords is only one part of search engine optimization. The gold standard of a Web site is to achieve algorithmic immunity. *Algorithmic immunity* means that your page is the least imperfect it can be, across the board. So if the search engines' algorithms were to change (as they do frequently), like, say, lessening the importance of links and stressing the importance of on-page factors again, your Web site won't be affected because it's optimized across the board. Keywords are important, certainly, but there are also many other factors to consider before your page is the least imperfect it can be.

2 Word Phrases

Keyword	Meta Title	Meta Desc	Meta Keywords	Heads	ALT Tags	First Words	Body Words	All Words
Count	5	13	30	25	3	201	227	303
peanut butter	40 % (1)	30.8 % (2)	33.3 % (5)	16 % (2)	66.7 % (1)	5 % (5)	4.4 % (5)	10.6 % (16)
butter ville	-	15.4 % (1)	-	8 % (1)	66.7 % (1)	1 % (1)	0.9 % (1)	2.6 % (4)
soy butter	-	-	6.7 % (1)	8 % (1)	-	1 % (1)	1.8 % (2)	2.6 % (4)
fun facts	-	-	-	-	-	2 % (2)	2.6 % (3)	2 % (3)
soy nuts	-	-	-	8 % (1)	-	1 % (1)	0.9 % (1)	1.3 % (2)
recipes allergies	-	-	-	-	-	1 % (1)	1.8 % (2)	1.3 % (2)
history how	-	-	-	-	-	1 % (1)	1.8 % (2)	1.3 % (2)
facts recipes	-	-	-	-	-	1 % (1)	1.8 % (2)	1.3 % (2)
naturally sweetened	-	-	-	-	-	2 % (2)	1.8 % (2)	1.3 % (2)
butter buy	-	15.4 % (1)	6.7 % (1)	-	-	-	-	1 3 % (7)
how its	-	-	-	-	-	1 % (1)	1.8 % (2)	1.3 % (2)
more information	-	-	-	-	-	1 % (1)	1.8 % (2)	1.3 % (2)
low carb	-	-	-	-	-	1 % (1)	1.8 % (2)	1.3 % (2)
nutrition fun	-	-	-	-	-	1 % (1)	1.8 % (2)	1.3 % (2)
its nutrition	-	-	-	-	-	1 % (1)	1.8 % (2)	1.3 % (2)

3 Word Phrases

Keyword	Meta Title	Meta Desc	Meta Keywords	Heads	ALT Tags	First Words	Body Words	All Words
Count	5	13	29	25	3	200	299	374
peanut butter ville	-	23.1 % (1)	-	12 % (1)	100 % (1)	1.5 % (1)	1 % (1)	3.2 % (4)
nutrition fun facts	-	-	-	-	-	1.5 % (1)	2 % (2)	1.6 % (2)
peanut butter buy	-	23.1 % (1)	10.3 % (1)	-	-	-	-	1.6 % (2)
all rights reserved	-	-	-	-	-	-	2 % (2)	1.6 % (2)
history its nutrition	-	-	-	-	-	1.5 % (1)	2 % (2)	1.6 % (2)
fun facts recipes	-	-	-	-	-	1.5 % (1)	2 % (2)	1.6 % (2)
facts recipes allergies	-	-	-	-	-	1.5 % (1)	2 % (2)	1.6 % (2)
its nutrition fun	-	-	-	-	-	1.5 % (1)	2 % (2)	1.6 % (2)

4 Word Phrases

Figure 5-8: The Page Analyzer stats for keyword phrases.

Using the SEOToolSet for a broader view

Similar to the Page Analyzer is a *multi-page analyzer*, which measures the keyword density of multiple Web pages, so you can check out what your competition does and compare them with your own Web site. Reading a multiple page analyzer is a lot like a single page analyzer, so we're not going to break that one down separately for you. Unfortunately, multiple page analyzers are generally only available as a paid option, but they are dead useful. We cover how to mimic the multi-page analyzer in Book III, Chapter 2.

Book III
Competitive Positioning

The 5th Wave   By Rich Tennant

"Our customer survey indicates 30% of our customers think our service is inconsistent, 40% would like a change in procedures, and 50% think it would be real cute if we all wore matching colored vests."

Contents at a Glance

Chapter 1: Identifying Your Competitors 143

Getting to Know the Competition..143
Figuring Out the Real Competition..145
Knowing Thyself: Recognizing Your Business Advantages..................147
Looking at Conversion as a Competitive Measure.............................148
Recognizing the Difference Between Traffic and Conversion................149
Determining True Competitors by Their Measures..............................151
Sweating the Small Stuff...152

Chapter 2: Competitive Research Techniques and Tools.........153

Realizing That High Rankings Are Achievable.................................153
Getting All the Facts on Your Competitors....................................154
Calculating the Requirements for Rankings....................................155
Penetrating the Veil of Search Engine Secrecy...............................171
Diving into SERP Research...172
Doing More SERP Research, Yahoo! and Microsoft Style......................174
Increasing your Web Savvy with the SEMToolBar...............................175

Chapter 3: Applying Collected Data 179

Sizing Up Your Page Construction..180
Learning from Your Competitors' Links...187
Taking Cues from Your Competitors' Content Structure.......................190

Chapter 1: Identifying Your Competitors

In This Chapter

✔ Getting to know your competition

✔ Figuring out the real competition

✔ Knowing your strengths and weaknesses

✔ Looking at conversion in a competitive market

✔ Discovering the difference between conversion and traffic

Like any business, you need to know what you're up against. Knowing who your competition is and figuring out how to beat them are the hallmarks of good business planning. Online businesses are like any business in that regard, but online and traditional businesses have some slight differences in how you build a competitive strategy, especially when it comes to search engine optimization.

In this chapter, we discuss how to figure out who your competition is and how to make their strengths and weaknesses work for you. You figure out how to research who your competitors are for the coveted top search engine rankings. Also, your competition in the brick-and-mortar world might not be the same as your competitors online. Finally, it's one thing to know your competition; it's another to put that information to use. Not to worry: We've got you covered in this chapter.

Getting to Know the Competition

With any business, you want to feel out the market. Who are you competing with, and how are they doing? This is important because it gives you an idea of how to run your own business. If somebody's succeeding in your space, they're doing something right. You also need to know what other people are doing wrong so you can capitalize on that and avoid their mistakes.

Say your business is customizing classic cars. You restore, repaint, and rev up any old model American car. To figure out your competition, sit down and think about the kind of competitors you think would be in your market. Who is your competition? Other classic car customization places. Other people who do paint and body work. Other businesses that offer simple customization services. Write them all down, even ones you think would only be loosely connected. Figure 1-1 is a brainstorming graph of your business and what you do that links your competition to you.

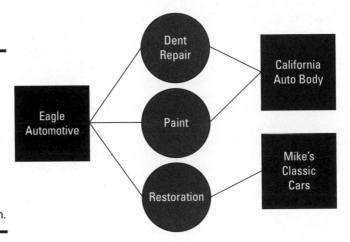

Figure 1-1:
A bubble graph is a good organizational technique for assessing your competition.

Taking this list, now go and research all of these other companies, while asking yourself some questions about these areas of their business:

+ **Tactics:** How do they advertise?

+ **Similarities:** What services do they offer that are similar to yours?

+ **Differences:** What services do they offer that are different?

+ **Success rate:** Do they get more or less business than you?

+ **Opportunities:** What are some of the things they are doing that you could be doing, too?

This approach is a good way to start market research. You also need to remember to continue doing this, as businesses, and especially Internet businesses, are subject to changing their tactics and offerings. Every market differs, but you probably want to do a review of your competitors four to six times a year.

The other important thing to keep in mind about doing research for your competition in the search engines is just how much their results can differ in *a day.* And because different search engines use different algorithms, the page Google ranks number one — say, [classic car customization] — could be in an entirely different position over on Yahoo! and yet another for Microsoft Live Search. You have no guarantee that all three engines even have the same page indexed.

Another problem is that sometimes a spider has not crawled a page in the index for more than two weeks (or longer). Although two weeks is not a long time to us, in those two weeks, that Web site could have been taken offline, been completely redone to reflect changes in the business, or had screwy code attached to attain a higher rank for the site. Search engines are not infallible, so it's best to continue to research the competition often to maintain the most up-to-date information possible.

Also, the playing field changes between the brick-and-mortar world and the online business world, so make a list and check it multiple times. Just because you have a cross-town rival for your business doesn't mean that he's online, or that you won't have other competitors to worry about. In the real world, you see competitors coming. Online, they appear from nowhere. You have to be vigilant.

Figuring Out the Real Competition

Part of knowing who you're competing against is knowing who is actually drawing the customers you want, and who is just limping along, especially when it comes to search engine optimization. Who you think your competition *should* be and who *actually* pops up on those search results pages are sometimes two completely different things.

Doing a quick search on Google for your business's *keywords* (the words people use when doing a search) might turn up those that you think of as your competition, as well as others that are completely out of the blue. Book II teaches you how to pull together a keyword list that gives you a good starting point for finding your competition. Take a typical search, like in Figure 1-2, which shows the SERP (search engine results page) for [classic car customization].

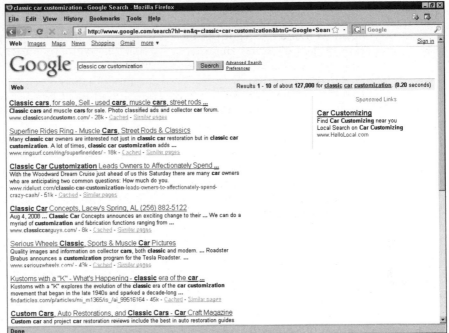

Figure 1-2:
A Google
search
result for
[classic car
customiz-
ation].

The search page yields a mixture of listings for Web sites related to the search term:

+ Classic car sales

+ Customization businesses

+ Auto parts dealers

+ Stereo dealers

+ Articles on classic car customization

+ Auto club memberships for car restorers

Note the different types of businesses. Are they what you'd thought they'd be? These sites represent the true competition in the search engine world for [classic car customization] because they're ranking high for those keywords. Try out other, more specialized keywords as well, and make note of who's ranking for them. Are they actual businesses like our example? Or are they something that's only tangentially related to classic car customization?

Another good idea is to do a search for your actual business name to see if your brand is ranking. If you don't occupy the number one position for your business name, find who does and what they're doing to rank higher. Because if they've got the spot you want, with *your name*, they're obviously doing something right.

For example, going back to your car customization business, your biggest competitor in your hometown is Bob's Customized Classics. Bob is everywhere you look. He's got print ads, he's got billboards, and he's got a *really* annoying commercial. He markets himself very well. But when you go online and do an online search for your keywords [classic car customization], Bob is nowhere to be found. In fact, you find out Bob doesn't even have a Web site! What you see ranking number one for your most important keyword phrase is Motormouth Mabel's Classic Car Boutique down in Boca Raton.

Mabel's Web site is gorgeous. It's SEO-friendly, full of spiderable content, no Flash, and plenty of links. Mabel, not Bob, is your real competition when it comes to the Internet. Because when people do a search in the search engines, they're going to go to her instead of Bob. So although Bob is your competition in the brick-and-mortar world of your hometown, Mabel's the one you need to be studying if you want to get anywhere with your online presence.

Your other competitors might not even be related to classic car customization, but because they rank high for your keywords, you should study them to understand their online methodology. After you know their tactics, you can figure out how to beat them. If you're doing searches for a keyword and none of the competitors are even in the same ballpark in terms of your business, you might have a keyword that isn't appropriate to your business, and you should reconsider optimizing for it.

Knowing Thyself: Recognizing Your Business Advantages

Part of being able to market yourself is actually understanding yourself and your niche. This might seem like common sense, but the truth is a lot of businesses out there can't decide exactly who they are and what they're selling. Knowing what your strengths and weaknesses are gives you a huge advantage because you can work on reducing your weaknesses while emphasizing your strengths.

The first part of knowing yourself is figuring out what you do best. In this example, you customize classic cars, certainly. But maybe what you do *best* is repair work. You can take a rusted-out hunk of a Comet and have it up and running within weeks, with a shiny new paint job to boot. So one of the strengths you would play to on your Web site is restoration. Emphasize that on your Web site. Have a section devoted entirely to car restoration, with subsections linking to that.

Think about what makes you different than Bob or Mabel. Bob does restoration as well, but he doesn't have an Internet presence like you do. That's a point for you and gives you an advantage over Bob. Mabel has a gorgeous, SEO-friendly Web site, but she doesn't have much on there about actual car restoration, so there's an advantage point for you to build on.

The lighter side of competitive research

Doing competitive research can also be a good way to think up new tools, tricks, or toys to add to your Web site to attract users. You may discover that your competitors are writing confusing "How-To" articles that would be much clearer as instructional videos. Or they may have an article listing the latest baby names, which could easily be turned into a fun tool — take the initiative and create it. Users love interactive content. Be continuously looking for creative ways to make your site more interesting and more useful to your visitors.

Knowing what your weaknesses are is also very important. Mabel's got a great Web site. Your Web site is not as good (yet). She's also a national business, while you still are fairly local. Those might be points you want to build on in order to make yourself equal with your competition. Streamline your Web site and filter out or downplay your weaknesses. If necessary, completely take your site down and rebuild it from scratch.

Be aware of what makes you different. If you offer a service that many other people are offering, what makes you stick out from the rest of the pack? Do you offer other services that the competition doesn't? Are you quicker or more efficient? Make sure to keep a note of this when researching the competition. What are they doing, and how do you do it better? Or how will you do it better? Make yourself valuable to the customer.

Compare your Web site to your competition's: You have to make yourself equal before you can set yourself apart. Make sure you match what your competition offers in your own way and then provide content that explains why you're unique, more trustworthy, and better overall: in other words, make it obvious that you're the first choice to fit the visitor's needs. *You* know that you are made of awesome; now you just have to convince everyone else.

Looking at Conversion as a Competitive Measure

When you go through your competitors' sites, you're essentially looking for anything they have that gives them an advantage — any special content that appeals only to a certain sector or that is attracting links. Obviously, you're not using their site as a blueprint to copy, but there's something about venturing off your own Web site and seeing things from a visitor's eye that can alert you to holes you would have missed otherwise.

If you are bringing your business online, you're going to want a return on your investment. If you are a shopping site, you want sales. If you are an information site, you want people to hang out and read your content. If you're advertising a newsletter, you want people to sign up for it. These are examples of *conversions* (the actions that a Web site wants visitors to take). Getting conversions, not just visitors, is your goal if you have a Web site.

Your keywords are an important part of this. A good, relevant keyword that you rank well for brings people to your site, and if your bottom line depends on the number of page views you're getting (how many people are viewing your Web site), you're pretty much set. However, if your keywords aren't providing you with conversions, they could be actually doing you more harm than good. Keywords that aren't generating conversions won't pay for the time, labor, or the bandwidth they take up.

Here is a conversion checklist to help you decide whether your keywords are effective:

✦ Is your keyword bringing in traffic?

✦ Is that traffic bringing you conversions?

✦ Are you able to sustain yourself based on those conversions? For example, say you have a keyword that brings only one or two conversions a year, but those conversions are worth two million dollars each. That keyword is a keeper.

✦ Is this a great keyword for branding or for an emerging product area? The only reason to keep a keyword that isn't earning you money is if that keyword has value as a brand or future investment.

Conversions also depend on your competition. You want to do better than the other guy. It's a simple fact of marketing. But you want higher conversions versus high traffic. A Web site that pulls in twelve hundred visitors a month but only has three conversions is less of a threat than a Web site that has maybe ten visitors a month, but six conversions.

Recognizing the Difference Between Traffic and Conversion

While you're looking at your competitors, make sure that you're also looking at which keywords are making sales versus drawing lots of window shoppers. Take note of how specialized they are. People search for broader terms when they're still doing their research and more specialized terms when they're getting ready to make a purchase. Your competitor who is ranked high for a general keyword might not be raking in the sales like the competitor dominating all the niche terms. Sometimes it takes users a lot of time and research to decide, so conversions may be slow to happen on broad terms.

Mabel's Classic Car Boutique might have a fantastic, high-ranking Web site, but if she has very few conversions, she's not really someone you should be looking at when trying to set the bar for yourself in the competitive market. High traffic does not always equal a high conversion rate.

Although a Web site may be high-ranking and well-designed for prime search engine optimization, it's pretty much moot if the site does not provide what the user is looking for. If your site's revenue depends entirely on traffic, you want a lot of traffic. But even in that scenario, you also want that traffic to stay around and visit the other pages within your site. Web pages with a lot of traffic and a high bounce back rate (which means they didn't check out more than one page on the site, or look at the main site for longer than a few seconds) aren't Web pages with a high conversion rate.

On the flip side, you might have a Web site that provides a newsletter, and the only way to get conversions is to convince people to sign up for your newsletter. A lot of traffic is good, yes, but it only matters if the people who are coming to your site do what you want them to do. If no one signs up for your newsletter, you get no conversions.

Along the same lines, if you have a keyword that draws in a lot of traffic, but doesn't provide you with very many conversions, the keyword could be more trouble than it's worth. It's using up bandwidth and server space to handle all of the traffic, not to mention all the time and effort you spent doing your SEO, but not providing you with any income.

A good example of the difference between a lot of traffic and actual conversions is a company we know that needed some optimizing. This company did well for itself in the mail-order business, but not so well online. Their Web site was not at all search-engine-friendly. After determining that changing the site's technology was not an option, they created a research or content site, as a sister site to the original, that was designed to draw in traffic and then send people to the actual, not-optimized Web site where they could make purchases. For a while, this worked well, with increased traffic and sales, until the company decided to pull down the sister site because they felt it was drawing traffic away from their original site! Never mind that the sister site was designed to bring in traffic in order to create conversions for their original site.

The lesson here is that the company shot themselves in the foot by confusing traffic with conversions. The sister site increased their sales by drawing in the window shoppers and funneling the true customers to the original Web site. Keep this in mind while checking your *server logs* (records that measure the amount of traffic your site receives), and don't freak out if you're not getting insanely huge numbers. If you're making a lot of sales, it really doesn't matter.

Determining True Competitors by Their Measures

Knowing your competition is very important. In terms of competition, you have three basic types: the local brick-and-mortar business, the online powerhouse, and the large corporate brand name. These are all different markets and need to be treated differently in terms of competing with them. What you need to do after doing the research on your competition is to figure out who you're really competing against. Look at all the information you've gathered. Is Bob, your local business competitor, your main competition, or is it Mabel's online Web site? Or are you competing against the big kids on the block, like Ford and Chevy? It all depends on who you are and what you're trying to sell. Bob is not your competition online because he doesn't even have a Web site! Mabel pops up first in the search engine results, but she doesn't do quite what you do. And as for the large corporations, it's probably not even worth trying to compete with them for their broad terms.

Consider another example. Say that your brother owns his own car customization business, but he restores only Volkswagen vans. He doesn't want to rank for the term [Volkswagen] because his is a specialized business and Volkswagen is too broad a term. Most people searching for [Volkswagen] alone would probably not be looking to restore a Volkswagen van. If he were to focus solely on the keyword [Volkswagen], it would do him more harm than good because the term is too broad and is already a brand name. What he would want to do is rank for the keyword phrase [Volkswagen van restoration] or [Volkswagen bus restoration].

REMEMBER

Brands are something to watch out for. Most people doing a search for [Nike], for example, are not actually looking for running shoes. They're looking for the brand itself. Trying to rank for the keyword Nike is probably not in your best interest because Nike markets a brand more than it does a singular product. If you were trying to sell running shoes while also trying to rank for the keyword [Nike], it's probably not going to work very well. You are much better off concentrating on your niche market than trying to tackle the big brands.

So assume that you've crossed out the big corporations and the smaller businesses that aren't really relevant to what you're doing. You've got a list of Web pages that are your true competition. They're the ones that customize classic cars just like you do, and rank high on the search engine results page. So how are they doing it?

There are tools out there to help with determining how your competition is doing. Comscore, Compete, and Hitwise are three such Web sites that offer tools designed for online marketers, giving them statistics and a competitive advantage. Comscore (www.comscore.com), Compete (www.compete.com), and Hitwise (www.hitwise.com) provide tools that measure or gauge Internet traffic to Web sites. They collect Internet usage data from panels, toolbars, and ISP log panels. Essentially, they can measure who's coming in to your Web site and from where. They also can gauge your competition. They can tell you how much your competition is bidding for a certain keyword, how much they spent on that keyword, and more. They can also track your brand name. They're a statistical tool that online advertisers and site owners use to rank sites in various categories on estimated traffic.

Unfortunately, all of these services charge a fee for their services, although Compete does offer a limited free service called MyCompete. They actually cost a pretty penny: ComScore does not publish their pricing, Compete starts at $199 a month for an individual plan, and Hitwise starts at $695 per report, so if you think it's worth the investment, look into them. They're useful tools for measuring the traffic to your site and where that traffic came from, along with the traffic on your competitor's Web sites.

Sweating the Small Stuff

Take advantage of what you can control. Every little piece counts, whether it's market research, knowing what kind of traffic your competition is getting, what keywords they're using, or something else. *Do* sweat the small stuff: It really counts in search engine optimization.

But don't get discouraged because of all the competition out there: Many companies out there don't know *anything* about search engine optimization. Most major companies don't even bother with it. Your competition probably doesn't know as much as you know at this point, and you can use that to your advantage.

Chapter 2: Competitive Research Techniques and Tools

In This Chapter

✓ **Finding out how to equal your high-ranking competitors**

✓ **Calculating what your site needs to gain high ranking**

✓ **Running a Page Analyzer**

✓ **Using Excel to help analyze your competition**

✓ **Discovering other tools for analyzing your competitors**

✓ **Diving into SERP research**

✓ **Using the SEMToolBar for competitor research and more**

*I*f you read the previous chapter and followed our suggestions, you spent some time finding out who your real competitors are on the Web, and you might have discovered that they are quite different from your real-world, brick-and-mortar competitors. You also found out that for each of your main keyword phrases, you probably have a different set of competitors. If you're starting to feel overwhelmed that you'll never be able to compete in such a busy, complicated marketplace, take heart! In this chapter, we show you how to get "under the hood" of your competitors' sites and find out *why* they rank so well.

Realizing That High Rankings Are Achievable

No matter what type of market your business competes in — whether broad-based or niche, large or small, national or local, corporate or home-based — you can achieve high rankings for your Internet pages by applying a little diligence and proper search engine optimization (SEO) techniques.

Your site may not be coming up at the top of search engine results for a specific keyword (yet), but someone else's is. The Web sites that do rank well for your keywords are there for a reason: The search engines find them the most relevant. So in the online world, those pages are your competitors, and you need to find out what you must do to compete with them. What is the barrier to entry into their league? You need a model for what to change, and analyzing the pages that do rank well can start to fill in that model.

The top-ranking Web pages are not doing things perfectly. That would require that they know and understand every single one of Google's more than 200 ranking signals and are targeting them perfectly, which is highly improbable. However, they're working successfully with the search engines for the keyword *you* want. The Web pages listed may not be perfect, but if they rank at the top, they are the *least* imperfect of all the possible sites indexed for that keyword. They represent a model that you can emulate so that you can join their ranks. To do that, you need to examine them closely.

Getting All the Facts on Your Competitors

Identifying your competition on the Web can be as easy as typing your main keywords into Google and seeing which pages rank above your own. (Note: If you know that your audience uses another search engine heavily, run your search there as well. But with a market share at more than 60 percent and climbing, we think Google offers the most efficient research tool.)

You want to know which Web pages make it to the first search engine results page. After you weed out the Wikipedia articles and other non-competitive results, what are the top four or five Web pages listed? Write down their Web addresses (such as www.wiley.com) and keep them handy. Or, if you did more in-depth competition gathering in the last chapter, bring those results along. We're going to take you on a research trip to find out what makes those sites rank so well for your keywords.

You need to know as much as you can about the Web pages that rank well for your keywords. The types of things you need to know about your competitors' Web sites can be divided into three categories:

✦ On-page elements (such as content and `Title` tags and metadata)

✦ Links (incoming links to the page from other Web pages, which are called *backlinks*, as well as outbound links to other pages)

✦ Site architecture

One basic strategy of SEO is this: Make yourself equal before you set yourself apart. But you want to analyze the sites that rank well because *they are the least imperfect*. You can work to make your site equal to them in all of the ranking factors you know about first. When your page can play on a level field with the least imperfect sites, you'll see your own rankings moving up. After that, you can play with different factors and try to become *better* than your competition and outrank them. That's when the fun of SEO really starts! But we're getting ahead of ourselves.

Calculating the Requirements for Rankings

As you look at your keyword competitors, you need to figure out what it takes to play in their league. What is the bare minimum of effort required in order to rank in the top ten results for this keyword? In some cases, you might decide the effort required is not worth it. However, figuring out what kind of effort *is* required takes research. You can look at each of their Web pages and see them as a human does, to get an overall impression. But search engines are your true audience (for SEO, anyway), and they are deaf, dumb, and blind. They can't experience the images, videos, music, tricks, games, bells, and whistles that may be on a site. They can only read what's there, count everything that can be boiled down to numbers, and analyze it. To understand what makes a site rank in a search engine, you need research tools that help you think like a search engine.

Table 2-1 outlines the different research tools and procedures we cover in this chapter for doing competitor research. Although SEO tools abound, you can generally categorize them into four basic types of information-gathering: on-page factors, Web server factors, relevancy, and site architecture. For each category of information gathering, we've picked out one or two tools and procedures to show you.

Table 2-1   Information-Gathering Tools for Competitor Research

Tool or Method	Type of Info the Tool Gathers
Page Analyzer	On-page SEO elements and content
Site Checker	Web server problems or health
Google [link:domain.com] query	Expert relevancy and popularity (How many links a site has)
Yahoo! Site Explorer	Expert relevancy and popularity
View Page Source	Content, HTML (How clean the code is)
Google [site:domain.com] query	Site architecture (How many pages are indexed)
Microsoft Excel	Not an information-gathering tool, but a handy tool for tracking all the data for analysis and comparison

Of the three types of information you want to know about your competitors' Web pages — their on-page elements, links, and architecture — a good place to start is the on-page elements. You want to find out what keywords your competitors use and how they're using them, look at their content, and analyze their other on-page factors.

Behind every Web page's pretty face is a plain skeleton of black-and-white HTML called *source code*. You can see a Web page's source code easily by choosing Source or Page Source from your browser's View menu. If you understand HTML, you can look under the hood of a competitor's Web page. However, you don't have to understand HTML for this book, or even to do search engine optimization. We're going to show you a tool that can read and digest a page's source code for you, and then spit out some statistics that you'll find very useful.

We do recommend that you know at least *some* HTML or learn it in the future: Your search engine optimization campaign will be a great deal easier for you to manage if you can make the changes to your site on your own. You can check out *HTML 4 For Dummies,* 5th Edition by Ed Tittel and Mary Burmeister, published by Wiley, if you need a primer on HTML.

Cleaning up the on-page elements of your Web site alone may give you a lot of bang for your SEO buck. Because they're on your own Web site, you have a lot of control, and changes such as modifying your Meta tags should take little effort. Often sites see major leaps in their search engine ranking just by fixing what's out of whack in their Web pages.

You may be tempted, in the early stages of your research, to conclude that a competitor's site doesn't deserve its high rankings. But don't. As you continue to collect data, you will discover why they rank well. Gathering accurate data and plenty of it can mean the difference between drawing brash conclusions and forming an effective strategy.

Grasping the tools for competitive research: The Page Analyzer

The Page Analyzer tool tells you what a Web page's keywords are (by identifying every word and phrase that's used at least twice) and computes their density. *Keyword density* is a percentage indicating the number of times the keyword occurs compared to the total number of words in the page. We also cover the Page Analyzer in Book II, Chapter 5, as it applies to analyzing your own Web site. When you run a competitor's page through the Page Analyzer, it lets you analyze the on-page factors that help the Web page rank well in search engines. Subscribers to the SEOToolSet can simply run the Multi-Page Analyzer, but for those just using the free version of the Page Analyzer, we've included a step-by-step process to building a comparison tool for yourself.

Because you're going to run the Page Analyzer report for several of your competitors' sites and work with some figures, it's time to grab a pencil and paper. Better yet, open a spreadsheet program such as Microsoft Excel, which is an SEO's best friend. Excel comes with most Microsoft Office packages, so if you have Word, chances are you already have it. Microsoft Excel allows you to arrange and compare data in rows and columns, similar to a paper ledger or accounts book. (We're going to talk about Microsoft Excel, but you might have another spreadsheet program such as Google Docs and PlanMaker, and those are fine, too.)

Here's how to set up your spreadsheet:

1. **In Excel, open a new spreadsheet and call it** Competitors.

2. **Type a heading for column A that says** URL **or something that makes sense to you.**

In this first column, you're going to list your competitors' Web pages, one per row.

3. **Under column A's heading, type the URL (the Web page address, such as** www.bruceclay.com**) for each competing Web page (the pages that are ranking well in search results).**

You can just copy and paste the URLs individually from the search results page if that's easier than typing them in.

Now you're ready to run the Page Analyzer report for each competitor. You can use the free version of this tool available through our Web site. Here's how to run the Page Analyzer:

1. **Go to** www.seotoolset.com/tools/free_tools.html.

2. **In the Page Analyzer section (the fourth tool down), enter a competitor's URL (such as** www.competitor.com**) in the URL to Check text box.**

3. **Click the Check Keyword Densities button and wait while the report is prepared.**

While you run this report for one of your own competitors, we're going to use a Page Analyzer report we ran on a competitor for our classic custom cars Web site. The whole Page Analyzer report contains a lot of useful information (including ideas for keywords you might want to use on your own site), but what we're trying to gather now are some basic counts of the competitor's on-page content. So we want you to zero in on a row of data that's about halfway down the report shown in Figure 2-1, which shows a quick summary of some important page content counts.

Next, you're going to record these summary counts in your spreadsheet. We suggest you create some more column headings in your spreadsheet, one for each of the following eight bold items (which we also explain here):

✦ Meta Title: This count shows how many words are in the page's *Title* tag (which is part of the HTML code that gets read by the search engines).

✦ Meta Description: Shows how many words are in the Description Meta tag (also part of the page's HTML code).

✦ **Meta Keywords:** Shows how many words are in the Keywords Meta tag (ditto).

✦ **Heads:** The number of headings in the text (using HTML Heading tags).

✦ **Alt Codes:** The number of Alt attributes (descriptive text placed in the HTML for an image file) assigned to images on the page.

✦ **Hyperlinks:** The number of links on the page.

✦ **All Body Words:** The number of words in the page text that's readable by humans.

✦ **All Words:** The total number of words in the page content, including on-screen text plus HTML tags, navigation, and other.

Now that you have the first several columns labeled, start typing in the counts from the report for this competitor. So far, your Excel spreadsheet should look similar to Figure 2-2, which shows data from the first competitor filled in.

The summary row

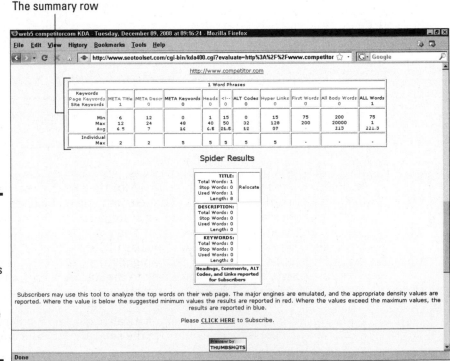

Figure 2-1:
The summary row of a competitor's on-page elements from a Page Analyzer report.

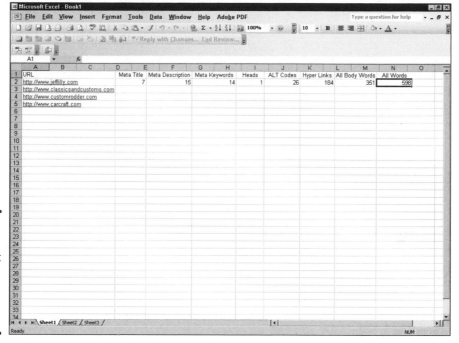

Figure 2-2:
Using a spreadsheet makes gathering competitor data easier.

Book III
Chapter 2

Competitive
Research Techniques
and Tools

Next, run the Page Analyzer report for each of your other competitors' URLs. You're just gathering data at this point, so let yourself get into the rhythm of running the report, filling in the data, and then doing it all over again. After you've run the Page Analyzer for all of your competitors, you should have a spreadsheet that looks something like Figure 2-3.

After you've gathered some raw numbers, what can you do with them? You're trying to find out what's "normal" for the sites that are ranking well for your keyword. So far you've gathered data on eight different factors that are part of the search engines' ranking systems. Now it's just simple math to calculate an average for each factor. You can do it the old-fashioned way, but Excel makes this super-easy if you use the AutoSum feature in the toolbar. As Figure 2-4 shows, just click to highlight a cell below the column you want to average, click the triangle next to the AutoSum tool, and then select Average from the small menu that appears.

When you select Average, Excel automatically selects the column of numbers above, so press Enter to approve the selection. Your average appears in the highlighted field.

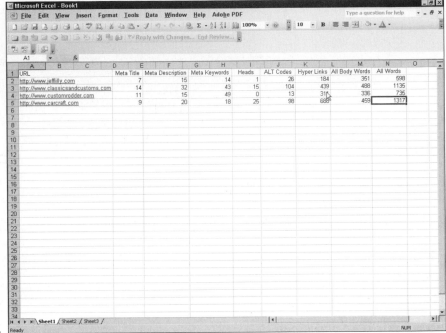

Figure 2-3:
The
spreadsheet
showing
data
gathered
by running
the Page
Analyzer.

You can create an average for each of the remaining columns in literally one step. (You can see why we like Excel!) In Figure 2-4, if you look at the black-outlined cell next to the word Averages, notice the slightly enlarged black square in the lower right-hand corner. Click and drag that little square to the right, all the way across all the columns that have data, and then let go. Averages should now display for each column because you just copied the AutoSum Average function across all the columns where you have data.

Figure 2-5 shows what your finished spreadsheet might look like, with the Page Analyzer data from all of your top competitors and an average for each of the eight ranking factors.

You can next run a Page Analyzer on your own Web site and compare these averages to your own figures to see how far you're off from your target. For now, just keep this spreadsheet handy and know that you've taken some good strides down the SEO path of information gathering. In the next chapter, we go into depth, showing you how to use the data you gathered here, and begin to plan the changes to your Web site to raise your search engine rankings.

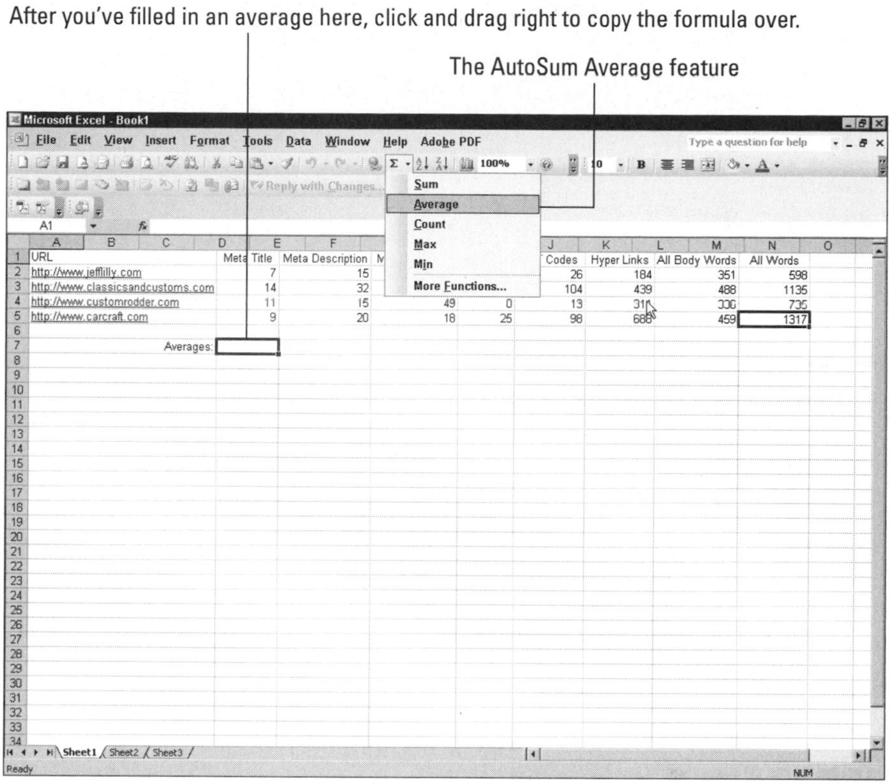

After you've filled in an average here, click and drag right to copy the formula over.

The AutoSum Average feature

Figure 2-4:
Excel's tools let you compute averages effortlessly.

The Multi-Page Analyzer makes short work of analyzing all your competitors' Web pages at once. Unfortunately, we don't know of any free versions of this tool, but you can subscribe to a number of different SEO tool vendors online who provide this and many other worthwhile tools for a fee, including the SEOToolSet. Fees for these vary based on the product, but the SEOToolSet is $39.95 per month.

Discovering more tools for competitive research

Beyond the Page Analyzer, there are some other tricks that you can use to size up your competition. Some of this may seem a little technical, but we introduce each tool and trick as we come to it. We even explain what you need to look for. Don't worry: We won't turn you loose with a bunch of techie reports and expect you to figure out how to read them. In each case, there are specific items you need to look for (and you can pretty much ignore the rest).

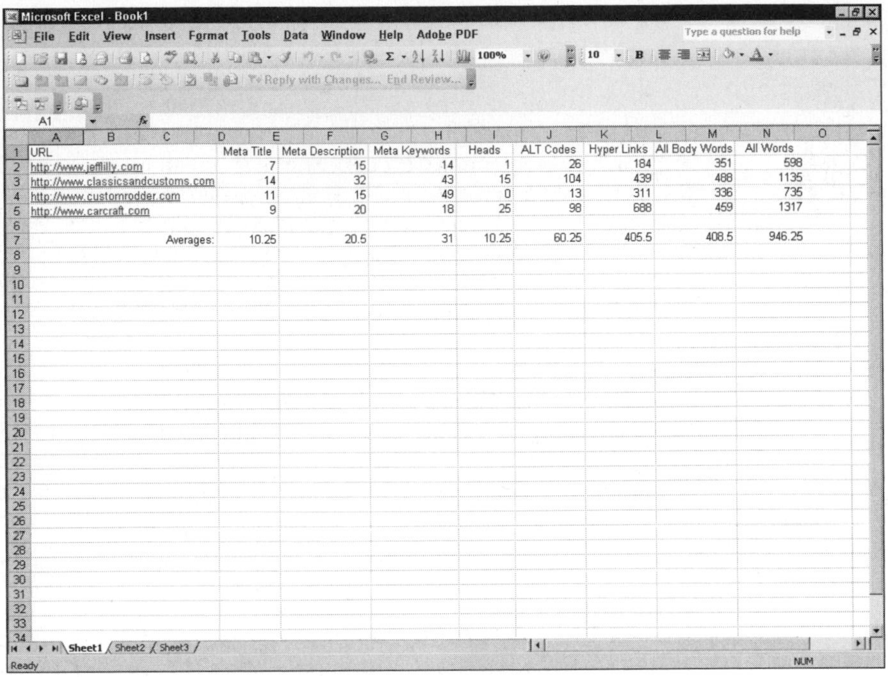

URL	Meta Title	Meta Description	Meta Keywords	Heads	ALT Codes	Hyper Links	All Body Words	All Words
http://www.jefflilly.com	7	15	14	1	26	184	351	598
http://www.classicsandcustoms.com	14	32	43	15	104	439	488	1135
http://www.customrodder.com	11	15	49	0	13	311	336	735
http://www.carcraft.com	9	20	18	25	98	688	459	1317
Averages:	10.25	20.5	31	10.25	60.25	405.5	408.5	946.25

Figure 2-5: Averaging the data from competitors' Web pages lets you quickly compare your own Web site and see where you're behind.

Mining the source code

Have you ever looked at the underside of a car? Even if it's a shiny new luxury model fresh off the dealer's lot, the underbelly just isn't very pretty. Yet the car's real value is hidden there, in its inner workings. And to a trained mechanic's eye, it can be downright beautiful.

You're going to look at the underside of your competitors' Web sites, their source code, and identify some important elements. Remember that we're just gathering facts at this point. You want to get a feel for how this Web page is put together and notice any oddities. You may find that the page seems to be breaking all the best-practice rules, but ranking well anyway somehow — in a case like that, they're obviously doing something else very right (such as having tons of backlinks pointing to the page). On the other hand, you might discover that this is a very SEO-savvy competitor that could be hard to beat.

To look at the source code, do the following:

1. **View a competitor's Web page (the particular page that ranks well in searches for your keyword, which may or may not be their home page) in your browser.**

2. **From the View menu, choose Source or Page Source (depending on the browser).**

As you look at the source code, keep in mind that the more extra stuff it contains, the more diluted the real content becomes. For good search engine ranking, a Web page needs content that's as clean as possible. Too much HTML, script, and coding can slow down page loading time, bog down the search engine spiders, and, most importantly, dilute your keyword content and reduce your ranking. Webmasters may not agree with this principle, but from an SEO perspective, a Web page should be a lean, mean, content-rich machine. Want to see if your competitor is doing things right? Look for these types of best practices:

✦ Use an external *CSS* (Cascading Style Sheet) file to control formatting of text and images. Using style sheets eliminates font tags that clutter up the text. Using a CSS that's in an external file gets rid of a whole block of HTML code that could otherwise clog the top section of your Web page and slow everything down (search engines especially).

✦ JavaScript code should also be off the page in an external JS file (for the same clutter-busting reasons).

✦ Get to the meat in the first hundred lines. The actual text content (the part users read in the Body section) shouldn't be too far down in the page code. We recommend limiting the code above the first line of user-viewable text overall.

You want to get a feel for how this Web page is put together. Pay attention to issues such as

✦ **Doctype:** Does it show a Doctype at the top? If so, does the Doctype validate with W3C standards? (Note: We explain this in Book IV, Chapter 3 in our recommendations for your own Web site.)

✦ **Title, description, keywords:** Look closely at the Head section (between the opening and closing `Head` tags). Does it contain the `Title`, `Meta` Description, and `Meta` Keywords tags? If you ran the Page Analyzer for this page earlier in the chapter, you already know these answers, but now notice how the tags are arranged. The best practice for SEO puts them in this order: Title, Description, Keywords. Does the competitor's page do that?

✦ **Other `Meta` tags:** Also notice any additional `Meta` tags ("revisit after" is a popular and perfectly useless one) in the Head section. Webmasters can make up all sorts of creative `Meta` tags, sometimes with good reasons that may outweigh the cost of expanding the page code. However, if you see that a competitor's page has a hundred different `Meta` tags, you can be pretty sure they don't know much about SEO.

✦ **Heading tags:** Search engines look for heading tags such as H1, H2, H3, and so forth to confirm what the page is about. It's logical to assume that a site will make its most important concepts look like headings, so these heading tags help search engines determine the page's keywords. See whether and how your competitor uses these tags. (We explain the best practices for heading tags in Book IV, Chapter 1, where we cover good SEO site design.)

✦ **Font tags, JavaScript, CSS:** As we mentioned in the previous set of bullets, if these things show up in the code, the page is weighted down and not very SEO-friendly. Outranking it might end up being easier than you thought.

Seeing why server setup makes a difference

Even after you've checked out the source code for your competitor's pages, you're still in information-gathering mode, sizing up everything you can about your biggest competitors for your chosen keywords. The next step isn't really an on-page element; it's more the foundation of the site. We're looking beyond the page now at the actual process that displays the page, which is on the server level. In this step, you find out how a competitor's server looks to a search engine by running a Site Checker utility.

Generally, an SEO-friendly site should be free of server problems such as improper *redirects* (a command that detours you from one page to another that the search engine either can't follow or is confused by) and other obstacles that can stop a search spider in its tracks. When you run the Site Checker utility, it attempts to crawl the site the same way a search engine spider does and then spits out a report. In the case of our tool (available as part of the SEOToolSet for free on www.seotoolset.com), the report lists any indexing obstacles it encounters, such as improper redirects, robot disallows, cloaking, virtual IPs, block lists, and more. Even if a page's content is perfect, a bad server can keep it from reaching its full potential in the search engine rankings.

You can use any Site Checker tool you have access to, but we're going to recommend ours because we know it works, returns all the information we just mentioned, and it's free. Here's how you can run the free Site Checker:

1. **Go to www.seotoolset.com/tools/free_tools.html.**

2. **Under the heading Site Checker, enter the URL of the site you want to check in the Web Page text box, and then click the Site Checker button.**

The SEOToolSet Site Checker tool reads the robots text (.txt) file on a Web site, which contains instructions for the search spiders when they come to index the site. Because you don't want the first thing a search engine finds to be a File Not Found error, you definitely want to have a robots text file on your own Web site. Even an empty file is preferable to having *no* file at all. Search engines always check for one, and if no file exists, your server returns a File Not Found error. (More on robots text files in Book VII, Chapter 1.)

When we ran the Site Checker report for our classic cars site's top competitor, it looked like Figure 2-6.

In the report shown in Figure 2-6, you can see that they have a Sitemap. xml file which serves to direct incoming bots. The more important item to notice, however, is the number 200 that displays in the Header Info section. This is the site's server status code, and 200 means their server is A-okay and is able to properly return the page requested.

The chart in Table 2-2 explains the most common server status codes. These server statuses are standardized by the World Wide Web Consortium (W3C), so they mean the same thing to everyone. The official definitions can be found on their site at `www.w3.org/Protocols/rfc2616/rfc2616-sec10.html` if you want to research further. We go into server code standards in greater depth in Book IV. Here, we boil down the technical language into understandable English to show you what each server status code really means to you.

Figure 2-6: The first page of the Site Checker report for a competitor's Web page.

Table 2-2   Server Status Codes and What They Mean

Code	Description	Definition	What it Means (If It's on a Competitor's Page)
200	OK	The Web page appears as expected.	The server and Web page have the welcome mat out for the search engine spiders (and users too). This is not-so-good news for you, but it isn't surprising either because this site ranks well.
301	Moved Permanently	The Web page has been redirected permanently to another Web page URL.	When a search engine spider sees this status code, it simply moves to the appropriate other page.
302	Found (Moved Temporarily)	The Web page has been moved temporarily to a different URL.	This status should raise a red flag. Although there are supposedly legitimate uses for a 302 Redirect code, they can cause serious problems with search engines and could even indicate something malicious is going on. Spammers frequently use 302 Redirects.
400	Bad Request	The server could not understand the request because of bad syntax.	This could be caused by a typo in the URL. Whatever the cause, it means the search engine spider is blocked from reaching the content pages.
401	Unauthorized	The request requires user authentication.	The server requires a login in order to enter the page requested.
403	Forbidden	The server understood the request, but refuses to fulfill it.	Indicates a technical problem that would cause a roadblock for a search engine spider. (This is all the better for you, although it may only be temporary).

Code	Description	Definition	What it Means (If It's on a Competitor's Page)
404	Not Found	The Web page is not available.	You've seen this error code; it's the Page Can Not Be Displayed page that displays when a Web site is down or nonexistent. Chances are that the Web page is down for maintenance or having some sort of problem.
500 and higher			The 500–505 status codes indicate that something's wrong with the server.

The other thing you want to glean from the Site Checker report is whether the page is cloaked. The Cloak Check runs through the site identifying itself as five different services — Internet Explorer, Mozilla Firefox, Googlebot, Slurp, and MSNbot — to ensure that they all match (Figure 2-7).

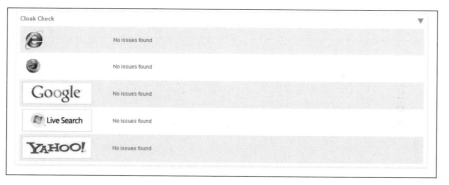

Figure 2-7: Cloak Check information from the Site Checker report.

Book III
Chapter 2

Competitive
Research Techniques
and Tools

To manually detect whether a competitor's site uses *cloaking* (showing one version of a page's content to users, but a different version to the spiders), you need to compare the spiderable version to the version that you are viewing as a user. So do a search that you know includes that Web page in the results set, and click the Cached link under that URL when it appears. This shows you the Web page *as it looked to the search engine* the last time it was spidered. Keeping in mind that the current page may have been changed a little in the meantime, compare the two versions. If you see entirely different content, you're probably looking at cloaking.

Tracking down competitor links

So far, we've been showing you how to examine your competitors' on-page elements and their server issues. It's time to look at another major category that determines search engine relevance: backlinks.

Backlinks are the hypertext links that a user clicks to jump from one Web page to another. You can have backlinks on your own site, such as when you include navigation links to your main landing pages in the footer throughout your site, or they can be links on third-party Web sites.

Why do search engines care so much about backlinks? Well, it boils down to the search engines' eternal quest to find the most relevant sites for their users. They reason that if another Web page thinks your Web page is worthy of a link, it must have value. Every backlink to a Web page acts as a vote of confidence in that page.

The search engines literally count these "votes." It's similar in some ways to an election, but with one major exception: not every backlink has an equal vote. For one thing, the anchor text of the link itself makes a big difference. *Anchor text* refers to the actual words that can be clicked, and backlinks must contain your keywords in their anchor text to tell the search engine what your site is about. If the link is simply Click Here or the URL, the search engine won't actually count it as a vote. (We cover the other factors that make inbound and outbound links count towards your search engine ranking in Book IV, Chapter 4.)

In the search engines' eyes, the number of backlinks to a Web page increases its *expertness* factor (and yes, that is a word, because we say so). Lots of backlinks indicate the page's popularity and make it appear more trustworthy as a relevant source of information on a subject. This alone can cause a page to rank much higher in search engine results when the links come from related sites and use meaningful, keyword-rich anchor text.

You can find out how many backlinks your competitors have using tools that the search engines themselves provide:

✦ **Using Google:** In the regular search box, type the query [**"domain. com" -site:*domain.com***], substituting the competing page's URL for `domain.com`. This returns all pages that mention your site, usually as a link (and if it isn't, you can ask them to make it a link!) You can also use [link:domain.com] but the numbers are less accurate.

✦ **Using Yahoo!:** Go to `http://siteexplorer.search.yahoo.com` and enter the competing URL in the Explore URL box.

You may want to run these tests for both the `www.domain.com` and `domain.com` (the second time, without the `www.` in front). Sites may have these URLs as separate Web pages. Searching with the non-www version produces results from www and non-www, plus any other sub-domains the site may be using.

You may notice that there's a huge disparity between the counts that Google and Yahoo! return. (For example, when running our classic custom cars competitors through both tools, Google link: command returned 175 links versus Yahoo! returning 12,102 links. Like we said, the disparity is *huge*.) That's normal. Google's `link:` operator shows you only a sample set of the link data, not an exhaustive list (no matter what they say). Yahoo!'s results, on the other hand, show you everything — they include not only every hypertext link that they are aware of, but also image links, every time the URL is used in text somewhere (even if it's not linked), and even redirects. So you either get too little or too much, but that's okay for SEO purposes.

You can look at the numbers to get an idea, proportionately, of how many inbound links each Web page has that's outranking yours. The numbers aren't really accurate in themselves, but they give you a gauge for comparison. For instance, if you're trying to optimize your classic custom cars Web page for the same keyword as a page that has 12,000 backlinks to it, and your page only has 50, you know it's going to be an uphill battle. In fact, you might decide that optimizing that page for that keyword isn't where you want to spend your energy . . . but we cover making those kinds of decisions in the next chapter.

You want to track your competitors' backlink counts; this is very useful raw data. We suggest adding more columns to your competitor-data spreadsheet and record both the Google and Yahoo! numbers there so you can compare them to your own.

The link results display in pretty much random order. If you want to work with them, you can export the Yahoo! link results using the Export Results to: TSV link. This dumps all the link data into a TSV (tab-separated value) file that you can import into an Excel spreadsheet (each value in its own cell), and then re-sort as desired.

Sizing up your opponent

If you walk onto a battlefield, you want to know how big your opponent is. Are you facing a small band of soldiers, or an entire army with battalions of troops and air support? This brings us to the discussion of the Web site as a whole, and what you can learn about it.

So far we've focused a lot on the individual Web pages that rank well against yours. But each individual page is also part of a Web site containing many pages of potentially highly relevant supporting content. If it's an army, you need to know.

To find out how big a Web site is, you can use a simple Google search with the `site:` operator in front of the domain, as follows:

1. **At Google.com, enter [`site:domain.com`] in the search box (leaving out the square brackets, and using the competitor's domain) and then click Search.**

2. **When the results page comes up, scroll to the bottom and click the highest page number that shows up (usually 10).**

   Doing this causes the total number of pages to recalculate at the top of the page.

3. **Notice the total number of pages shown at the top of the page (in Results 91 - 100 of about ###).**

   The "of about ###" number represents the approximate number of indexed pages in the site. (Google never tells anyone everything they know.)

4. **Now navigate to the very last page of the results by changing the "start=" value in the URL to 999 and press enter.**

   The count shown there represents the filtered results. Google doesn't actually show you as many pages as it claimed to find at first. A very large disparity between the two counts most likely indicates that there are lots of pages with duplicate content in this Web site.

For performance reasons, Google doesn't display all of the indexed pages, but omits the ones that seem most like duplicates. If you truly want to see all of the indexed listings for a site, you can navigate to the very last results page of your [site:] query and click the option to Repeat the Search with the Omitted Results Included. (Even then, Google only shows up to a maximum of 1,000 listings.) Pull out your competitor-data spreadsheet again and record the total number of indexed pages (filtered and total) for each site in new columns.

If you want to check the number of indexed pages in Yahoo! and Microsoft Live Search, we recommend you try the free Search Engine Saturation tool available from Marketleap (`www.marketleap.com`).

Comparing your content

You've been pulling in lots of data, but data does not equal analysis. Now it's time to run research tools on your own Web page and find out how you compare to your competition.

Run a Page Analyzer report for your Web page, and compare your on-page elements to the figures you collected in your competitor-data spreadsheet (earlier in this chapter). Next, check your own backlink counts using Google and Yahoo! (see the previous section for details on how to do this). Record all the numbers with today's date so that you have a benchmark measurement of the "before" picture before you start doing your SEO.

After you have metrics for the well-ranked pages and your own page, you can tell at a glance how far off your page is from its competitors. The factors in your spreadsheet are all known to be important to search engine ranking, but they aren't the *only* factors, not by a long shot. Google has more than 200 factors in its algorithm, and they change constantly. However, having a few that you can measure and act on gives you a starting place for your search engine optimization project.

Penetrating the Veil of Search Engine Secrecy

The search engines tell you a lot, but not the whole story. Search engines claim that the secrecy surrounding their algorithms is necessary because of malicious spammers, who would alter their sites deceptively for the sole purpose of higher rankings. It's in the search engines' best interests to keep their methods a secret; after all, if they published a list of dos and don'ts and just what their limits and boundaries are, then the spammers would know the limits of the search engines' spam catching techniques. Also, secrecy leaves the search engines free to modify things any time they need to. Google changes their algorithm frequently. For instance, in just six months in 2007, Google's algorithm changed 450 times. No one knows what changed, how big the changes were, or when exactly they occurred. Instead of giving out the algorithm, search engines merely provide guidelines as to their preferences. This is why we say that SEO is an art, not just a science: Too many unknown factors are out of your control, so a lot of finesse and intuition is involved.

Book III
Chapter 2

Competitive Research Techniques and Tools

Other factors can complicate rankings as well. Here's a brief list of factors that have nothing to do with changes on the Web sites themselves that can cause search engine rankings to fluctuate:

✦ The search engine changed its algorithm and now weighs factors differently.

✦ The search engine may be testing something new (a temporary change).

✦ The index being queried is coming from a different data center. (Google, for instance, has more than 100 data centers in different locations, which may have different versions of the index.)

✦ The search engine had a technical problem and restored data temporarily from cache or a backup version.

✦ Data may not be up-to-date (depending on when the search engine last crawled the Web sites).

If it seems like playing on the search engine field is too unpredictable, remember that at least you're in good company. Your competitors can't control the game any more than you can. You don't know what the search engine is looking for exactly, and you don't know all the parts of the algorithm; however, you do know some of the ranking factors. So *do* sweat the small stuff when it comes to SEO — work on everything you can. The exciting thing is that your competitors may know less than you do, or may be completely ignorant when it comes to optimizing their sites.

Within the broad field of marketing, Internet marketing represents a narrow specialty. In that narrow field is the narrower field of search marketing and within that is search engine optimization. As Figure 2-8 shows, SEO is an extremely specialized field. All marketers don't know Internet marketing, all Internet marketers do not know search marketing, and all search marketers don't know SEO. Search engine optimization is really the technical end of Internet marketing, and it takes a somewhat technical mind to grasp it.

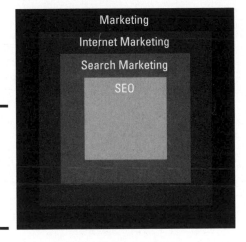

Figure 2-8: SEO is a specialty within a specialty within a specialty.

Diving into SERP Research

You can use the search engines to help you analyze your competitors in many ways. You're going to switch roles now and pretend for a moment that the high-ranking site is yours. This helps you better understand the site that is a model for what yours can become.

Start with a competitor's site that's ranking high for your keyword in the search engine results pages (SERPs). You want to find out *why* this Web page ranks so well. It may be due to one of the following.

✦ **Backlinks:** Find out how many backlinks the Web page has. Run a search at Google for [`"www.domain.com/page.htm" =site:domain.com`], substituting the competitor's Web page URL. The number of results is an indicator of the site's popularity with other Web pages. If it's high, and especially if the links come from related, industry sites with good PageRank themselves, backlinks alone could be why the page tops the list.

✦ **Different URL:** Run a search for your keyword on Google to see the results page. Notice the URL that displays for the competitor's listing. Keeping that in mind, click the link to go to the active page. In the address bar, compare the URL showing to the one you remembered. Are they the same? Are they different? If they're different, how different? Although an automatic redirect from `http://domain.com` to `http://www.domain.com` (or vice versa) is normal, other types of swaps may indicate that something fishy is going on. Do the cache check in the next bullet to find out whether the page the search engine sees is entirely different than the one live visitors are shown.

✦ **Cached version:** If you've looked at the Web page and can't figure out why it would rank well, the search engine may have a different version of the page in its cache (its saved archive version of the page). Whenever the search engine indexes a Web site, it stores the data in its cache. Note that some Web sites are not cached, such as the first time a site is crawled or if the spider is being told not to cache the page (using the `Meta` robots `noarchive` instruction), or if there is an error in the search engine's database.

To see the cached version of a page:

1. Run a search on Google for your keyword.

2. Locate the competitor's listing in the results. Click Cached in the last line of the listing.

3. View the cached version of the Web page. At the top of the page, you can read the date and time it was last spidered. You can also easily view how your keywords distribute throughout the page in high-lighted colors.

A good way to look at Web pages the way a search engine spider sees them is to use the text-only Lynx browser. Google actually recommends (in their Webmaster Guidelines at `www.google.com/support/webmasters/bin/answer.py?answer=35769`) that you use a text browser such as Lynx to examine your site, which helps you see your site exactly how a search engine sees it without the benefit of video, images, audio, or any other Engagement Object. You can install the Lynx browser for free, so if you're interested, go for it. If you don't want to install an entirely new browser, we recommend installing the SEMToolBar (`www.bruceclay.com/web_rank.htm#semtoolbar`), which has a View Text mode that accomplishes the same thing without requiring you to leave your IE or Firefox browser.

Doing More SERP Research, Yahoo! and Microsoft Style

There is a difference between SERP research with Google and SERP research with Yahoo! and Microsoft Live Search. For one thing, you might find the rankings quite different; the competitor you've been analyzing may not even show up in the top-ranking Web pages for these other search engines. Because Google has the lion's share of traffic, many sites focus their optimization efforts there exclusively. Whether you want to examine your competitor's pages as seen through Yahoo! or Microsoft's eyes depends on how much your target audience tends to use those search engines. Do you get enough potential traffic to warrant SEO efforts on multiple fronts? That's up to you, but here's how you can do it.

To check backlinks:

✦ Using Yahoo!, go to `http://siteexplorer.search.yahoo.com` to check how many backlinks a Web page has. Enter the URL for the competing Web page in the Explore URL text box. At the top of the Results page, the number of Inlinks represents Yahoo!'s backlink count.

✦ Microsoft hasn't actually built a tool to check backlinks in their search engine. We suggest using a third-party free tool called the Link Popularity Check, available at `www.marketleap.com`. This gives you figures for Google, MSN (Microsoft Live Search), and Yahoo!, so you can pull out the MSN ones.

To check for URL differences:

Follow the same procedure that we discuss in the "Different URL" bullet of the previous section "Diving into SERP Research," but this time, run your searches in Yahoo! (`www.yahoo.com`) and in Microsoft Live Search (`www.msn.com`).

To check the cached pages:

✦ In the Yahoo! search results, click Cached beneath the competitor's listing to view the cached version of the page. You can see your search terms highlighted on the cached page, but Yahoo! doesn't reveal the date and time it last crawled the site.

✦ For Microsoft Live Search, click Cached Page below the competitor's listing. The cached version of the page displays, showing the date the site was last indexed at the top (but with no highlighting on your keywords.).

Increasing your Web Savvy with the SEMToolBar

As you're running searches for your keywords to scan the competition, it's helpful to have special intelligence about the results. There are many free *browser plug-ins* (software applications that enhance a Web browser's existing features) available online that you can install to display extra information about each Web page at a glance. These plug-ins make your competitor and keyword research quicker and easier, necessitating less switching back and forth between tools. Our SEMToolBar (available free at `www.bruceclay.com/web_rank.htm#semtoolbar`) is one such plug-in. The toolbar has some incredibly useful features that can help you with competitor research and optimizing your Web site. It also supports 20 different languages and has features that help if you're trying to optimize a site for another geographical market, whether inside the U.S. or abroad.

You can install the toolbar for Internet Explorer or Mozilla Firefox browsers. After it's installed, it shows up at the top of the browser window with your other toolbars. The SEMToolBar gives you a big advantage for doing competitive research, finding keywords, identifying your target demographic so you can cater your landing pages to them, looking for sites to request links from, or just checking out someone's Web site.

Here's how it changes search engine results pages (SERPs) so you can see more data on the fly:

✦ **Keyword statistics:** A box with important keyword data displays at the top of the SERP. The various results include approximately how many times the keyword is searched each day, the categories it's considered to be part of, statistics related to paid search advertising for that keyword, the demographics (age and gender) of people who search for that keyword, and the keyword's search volume over the past 12 months, shown as a line graph.

✦ **Search result info:** SERPs look a little different because the toolbar numbers the results so that it's easier to see ranking and also adds an extra line below each result. The extra line shows you when each domain was registered, how many backlinks the page has, its PageRank, and other facts that the average Web user doesn't know. You can even highlight certain domains/pages so they stand out in search results, allowing you to easily spot your results every time you search. These features work in Google, Yahoo!, and Microsoft Live Search. (You can see a toolbar-enhanced SERP in Figure 2-9. Clicking on the + box to the left of the annotation gives you additional data.)

Enhanced SERP with the SEO toolbar

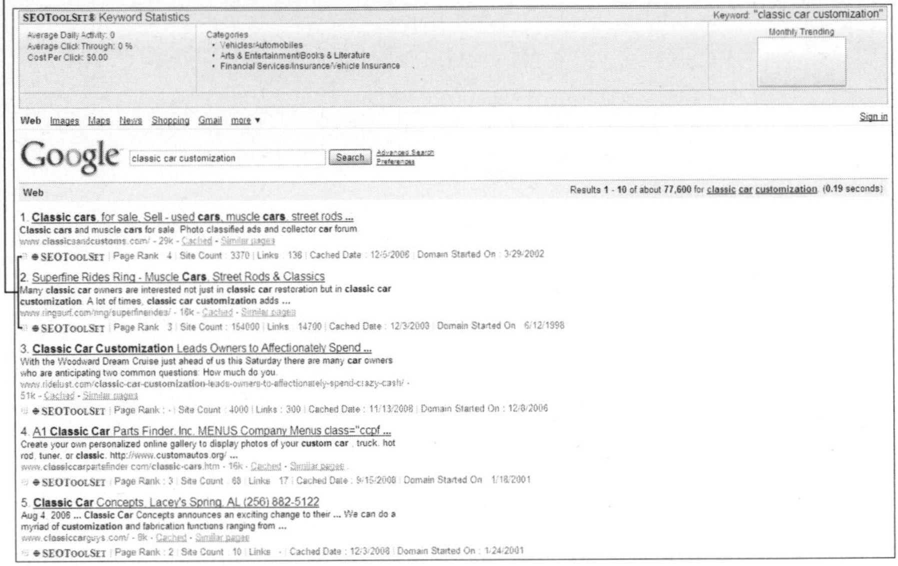

Figure 2-9:
The toolbar enhances SERPs with keyword statistics and facts about each Web page.

The toolbar also helps you when you're browsing the Internet. You can look at the toolbar to see things about the current Web page, like its backlink count, PageRank, date the domain started, and other facts that help you determine how viable the Web page is. When you're looking for good sites to request links from, for instance, the toolbar can really come in handy to give you the scoop on a potential candidate.

You can conveniently run searches from the toolbar directly and specify the search engine, keywords, and *proxy location* (where you want the search to run from). For instance, imagine you're working on an Australian version of your Web site and you want to see how you're ranking there. You could run a search as if you were in Sydney, even though you're really in California. This feature is called *proxy search*, and it lets you run a search as if you were physically at a computer in another place.

Being able to run a search as if you're in another place gives you a huge advantage when optimizing a site for local search somewhere else. Search engines increasingly personalize the results to each individual searcher and localize the results geographically, when it's appropriate. So proxy search gives you a way to get around these obstacles and run searches from another place (without having to buy a plane ticket and go there).

The SEMToolBar is free, but it is powered by the SEOToolSet, which is a subscription-based service (available at $39.95 a month). If you are a subscriber to the SEOToolSet, the toolbar gets even more robust, with tie-ins to the full tool set. For instance, the extra line beneath search results also shows how much a particular page known to the SEOToolSet has gone up or down in rankings for a particular keyword. However, you don't need to subscribe in order for the toolbar to be extremely useful to your optimization efforts. The SEMToolBar has other features geared to helping you do SEO beyond what we've covered here. We invite you to download it and try it out for yourself.

Chapter 3: Applying Collected Data

In This Chapter

✔ Applying best practices to your page construction

✔ Identifying what's natural for your competitors

✔ Sizing up what engagement objects you need

✔ Building your link equity with a little help from your competitors

✔ Examining how your competitors organize their content

✔ Applying your analysis to help with content siloing

Your real competitors online are the sites that show up at the top of the results whenever someone searches for your *keywords* (words or phrases people enter as a search query), not necessarily the big name brand in your industry. So if you want your classic car customization business to rank well in the search engines, for example, you can run searches for your main keywords to see who your competition is.

If you just finished the exercises in Chapters 1 and 2 of this minibook, you should have a spreadsheet full of data on your top competitors. Looking at the Web pages that the search engines find most relevant for your keywords is a crucial step in your search engine optimization (SEO). Looking at them, you can find out what's "natural" for your competition. For example, you could find that all of the top-ranked Web pages have more than 1,000 words of text. You can be pretty sure that if you're going to rank well for that keyword, you're going to have to beef up your page's content to match the competition.

Search engines include many different page factors in their *algorithms* (in this context, formulas for determining a Web page's relevance to a keyword), which they use to decide the order Web pages are listed in a search engine results page (SERP). For each ranking factor, it's impossible to know exactly what the search engine considers to be a "perfect" score. But you can look at the top ranking sites for clues because they're most consistently ranked for top keyword categories. Of the more than 200 different ranking signals in Google's algorithm, some are known, but many remain a mystery. For all of the known ranking factors, the sites that rank well are the ones that are the "least imperfect" in the search engine's eyes. So it's a good idea to try to make yourself equal to them before you try to set yourself apart.

In this chapter, you take the data you've gathered on your top competitors and apply it to your own Web site. In other words, you're going to figure out how to make yourself equal and then better than your competition. We talk about the best practices for some of these page elements, which help you make good decisions on how far to go in making yourself equivalent. You also look beyond page elements to other data about your competitors, including their *backlinks* (incoming links to a Web page), their content structure, and what kinds of images, videos, and other types of objects they have on their site to engage users. All of this helps you understand what you need to do to make your site compete in the search engines.

Sizing Up Your Page Construction

It's time to look at your own Web site and see how it's measuring up. Examine your main *landing pages*, which are the pages best suited for searchers looking for your main keywords. You generally need a minimum of one landing page with at least five secondary or supporting pages/articles dedicated to each of your main keywords so that users searching for them click your link and arrive at a page that delivers just what they're looking for. You should also have secondary keywords on those pages, but the point is to have focused content that has the main keyword distributed throughout. (For more information, check out Book II, Chapter 3.)

Landing page construction

The way your landing pages are put together matters to search engines and helps them determine the relevance of each page. The engines count everything that can be quantified, like the total number of words, how many times your keywords are repeated on the page (prominence), and so forth. It pays to make your page construction line up with what the search engines consider to be optimal for each of these elements as much as possible.

In the previous chapter, we explained how to do research on your top competitors using the *Page Analyzer* report (which compiles statistics about a Web page such as its *keyword density*, a percentage indicating the number of times the keyword occurs compared to the total number of words in the page). We recommended that you put your data in a spreadsheet like the one in Figure 3-1, which pulls together stats from four different competitor's Web pages.

Notice that there are eight columns of data for each competitor, and the numbers they contain are straight off of the Page Analyzer report. Also notice the Averages row at the bottom, which is simply the mean of each column. It's a pretty simple way to figure out what's considered normal (or "natural") for the top-ranking competitors for your keyword, in the search engines' eyes. These eight categories represent on-page elements that you can compare to your own Web page.

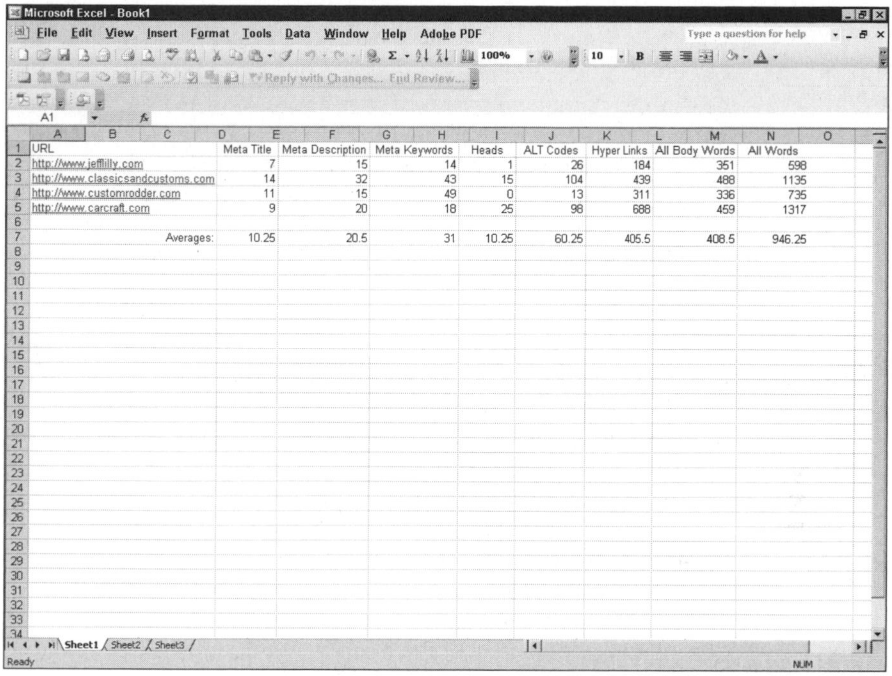

URL	Meta Title	Meta Description	Meta Keywords	Heads	ALT Codes	Hyper Links	All Body Words	All Words
http://www.jefflilly.com	7	15	14	1	26	184	351	598
http://www.classicsandcustoms.com	14	32	43	15	104	439	488	1135
http://www.customrodder.com	11	15	49	0	13	311	336	735
http://www.carcraft.com	9	20	18	25	98	688	459	1317
Averages:	10.25	20.5	31	10.25	60.25	405.5	408.5	946.25

Figure 3-1:
Spreadsheet showing competitor data from a Page Analyzer report.

After you've studied your competitors, it's time to run your own Web pages through the Page Analyzer to get your starting figures for comparison. Here's how to run the Page Analyzer:

1. **Go to www.seotoolset.com/tools/free_tools.html.**

2. **In the Page Analyzer (the fourth tool down), enter your page's URL (such as www.*yourdomain.com*/pageinprogress.html).**

3. **Click the Check Keyword Densities button and wait until the report displays.**

Keep in mind that for each item, the best practices just give you a starting point for your analysis. As we mentioned, the top sites are imperfect, so there is room to vary your analysis because your goal is first becoming equal to and then better than your competition. Your market may require certain page elements to be much shorter or longer than the guidelines recommend. Remember that your page construction should make you competitive for your keywords and make judgment calls backed up by real-world results. SEO requires ongoing monitoring and tweaking because the nature of rankings is transitory. Search engine rankings fluctuate, and you have to make tweaks to adapt. Your target number for each element can be changed over time as you get more of a feel for what the search engines consider most relevant.

After you have your data in hand, you can dig into your analysis. In this list, we cover what we consider to be the SEO best practice for each item and how it lines up with the competitors' natural usage based on the averages in Figure 3-1. Knowing those two things, you can decide what to do on your own page (these numbers are examples only; your industry will be different):

✦ **Title:** The `Title` tag is a line of HTML you put in the Head, or top, section of a Web page's HTML code.

    Best practice: 6 to 12 words in length

    Competitors' average: 10.25

    Recommendation: Because the search engines are rewarding these sites with top rankings *and* their natural average falls within best practices, you should make your `Title` tag 10 words in length.

    • **Meta description:** The `Meta` description is another HTML tag that goes in the Head section of a Web page.

    Best practice: 12 to 24 words in length

    Competitors' average: 20.5

    Recommendation: The top-ranking sites seem to be following best practices here, so go ahead and match them by putting 20 or 21 words in your `Meta` description tag.

✦ **Meta keywords:** The `Meta` keywords tag also goes in the Head section and gives you a place to list all your keywords for the page.

    Best practice: 24 to 48 words in length

    Competitors' average: 31

    Recommendation: They've done it again, falling within best practice guidelines. You should make your `Meta` keywords tag about 31 words long.

✦ **Headings:** This refers to the number of Heading tags on the page (which are `h#` formatting tags applied to headings and subheadings).

    Best practice: There's no minimum/maximum guideline for Heading tags; however, you should have a single `H1` tag at the top of the page for your main headline because search engines look for this. Use `H2`, `H3`, and so on through the page for subheadings that help break up the text in natural places.

    Competitors' average: 10.25. However, notice that the competitors don't agree on this: Their Heading counts are 1, 15, 0, and 25.

    Recommendation: Where you have one or two competitors that are completely out of range of the rest, you shouldn't try to match the average. Follow the bulk of the sites or best practices instead.

✦ **Alt codes:** `Alt` attributes are alternate text attached to images that briefly describe the image to search engines (and users). In the Page Analyzer, the `Alt` codes figure represents the total number of words included in `Alt` attributes on the page.

> **Best practice:** For every image, you should include an `Alt` attribute (incorporating keywords, if appropriate). The length of the `Alt` attribute depends on the size of the image, but should not exceed 12 words per image for the largest images. (See Book V, Chapter 2 for the mathematical rule of thumb for this.)

> **Competitors' average:** 60.25

> **Recommendation:** There's a wide disparity between the four sites (26, 104, 13, 98). You should probably follow the best practices rather than the average here.

✦ **Hyperlinks:** This figure represents the total number of words included in link *anchor text* (the text a user can click to follow a link) on the page.

> **Best practice:** There's only a vague guideline for this: The number can vary widely. You do want some links on the page, but don't be overly link-happy, or the search engines could suspect your page of *spam* (deceptively trying to manipulate the search engines). The anchor text for each link should contain meaningful text. Beyond that, best practice says to have between 12 and 172 words in anchor text. (See, that's a big spread.)

> **Competitors' average:** 405.5

> **Recommendation:** Whew! The average here is way above the best practice limit of 172, and most of the sites match it. This may be a case where what's natural for your market trumps best practices. At least if you start with a high number, you're in the ballpark of your competitors, and you can experiment with lowering it later after you're ranking high.

✦ **All Body words:** This refers to the number of words in the Body section, which is the part between the beginning and ending `Body` tags, or the main page content that users see. The count excludes *stop words* (little words like *a*, *an*, *but* and others that the search engines disregard).

> **Best practice:** You should fall within the range of your competitors, but a landing page needs at least 400 to 500 words of readable content as a general rule to establish its relevance to a keyword.

> **Competitors' average:** 408.5

> **Recommendation:** All the competitors' pages have a similar count and it falls within best practices, so this average is probably a sweet spot you'll want to match or slightly exceed.

✦ **All words:** This is the total number of words in the page minus stop words, so it includes the Body section as well as other sections that may or may not be visible to users.

> **Best practice:** There's no minimum or maximum guideline here, so match your competitors as long as they're in keeping with other SEO best practices (such as keeping the HTML code uncluttered, and so on.).

> **Competitors' average:** 946.25

> **Recommendation:** Aim to have sufficient text in the Body section, and to keep your HTML clean. This number usually takes care of itself.

Want more info on page construction? See Book V, Chapter 3 for additional recommendations on building effective, SEO-friendly page elements.

Content

To make sure your landing pages have enough focused content to be considered relevant for their main keywords, you can look at two things: the search engine's *cache* (stored version of a page) and a Page Analyzer report.

Google's cached text-only version of a Web page is the best way to see how much content the search engines have actually *indexed* (included in their database of Web pages, from which they pull search results).

To view Google's cached text version of a page:

1. **Run a Google search to bring up the Web page.**

Try putting an excerpt in quotation marks to find an exact match.

2. **Click the Cached link in the result for your Web page, which is next to the URL (Web address).**

3. **In the gray box at the top of the page, click Text-Only Version.**

This text-only view is what Google sees, and your keywords are highlighted. This view is useful because

✦ You can find out how much text Google indexed.

✦ You can see visually how many times you used each keyword.

✦ You can tell how evenly you distributed the keyword through the page.

If you find that the page has very little textual content that can actually be read by the search engines, your design might be relying too much on non-text elements like images or Flash. (*Adobe Flash* is a multimedia software program used for building animated and interactive elements for the Web.) Although these elements may be good for your users, they're not very readable to a search engine. In general, landing pages need a *lot* of text-based content so search engines can figure out what they're all about.

The Page Analyzer report further breaks down how keywords are used on a Web page. It identifies all of the single and multi-word keyword phrases. It also tells you whether the keywords are used in all the right places (for instance, any word used in the `Title` tag is expected to also be in the `Meta` description tag, the `Meta` keywords tag, and throughout the page).

For more help using the Page Analyzer to optimize your landing pages, see Book V, Chapter 3.

Engagement objects

Before leaving the subject of page construction, there's a hot topic you need to know about: *engagement objects*™. These are non-text elements such as images, videos, audio, or interactive elements on a Web page that help engage users. Not only do they make your page more interesting to a user, but they are also now becoming increasingly important as a search engine ranking factor.

With the rise of *blended search* (also known as *Universal Search* in Google), search engine results pages (SERPs) are now able to show a combination of different types of files to a searcher. So a search for [1969 Ford Mustang] can return photos, videos, and so on, in addition to Web site links, all on the same SERP (as shown in Figure 3-2 below).

The search engines (particularly Google) want to provide the most relevant and engaging results to their users, so having engagement objects on your Web site can actually make you rank higher in search results than your competitors.

**Book III
Chapter 3**

Applying Collected
Data

Figure 3-2:
Blended
search
results
combine
many
different
types of
listings.

Take a look at your top competitors' Web pages as a user would and notice their engagement objects. Keep your own Web site in mind so you can make a list of things you might need to add. Besides getting an overall feel for how these sites engage their users, look to see how extensively they incorporate engagement objects such as

✦ **Images:** Notice the number of photos, illustrations, diagrams, charts, and so on. Also pay attention to size. Larger images with good `Alt` attribute text and good surrounding text can get indexed and actually returned as a search result itself, so notice whether the competitor has anything like this.

✦ **Video:** Video is extremely important these days for getting noticed on the Web. The best method is to embed the video right into your landing page and also upload it or a portion of it to a video-sharing site like YouTube. Include a keyword-rich description and a link back to your site, and you'll probably get traffic as a result. Consider this: YouTube's internal search function now gets more total searches than Yahoo!. Depending on how you look at it, that means YouTube is the second most visited search engine in its own right. Obviously, YouTube's site search isn't a true search engine, but you better believe that the traffic is true traffic. If your competitors haven't been savvy enough to upload videos to YouTube and embed videos on their sites yet, here's a good way to one-up them. Being where people can find you is critical.

✦ **Audio:** Look for embedded audio files within the site, which is another type of element that's good for user engagement. Audio files are expected on music-industry sites, but other sites might benefit from a creative use of audio, as well. Google can now parse soundtracks and generate a text of the words that can be subsequently indexed. This clearly shows that audio is a valid content form.

✦ **Flash:** Flash files (SWF) can also help a site rank, especially if there's lots of explanatory text and if it's something that attracts people's interest enough to link to it. (Note that a site built completely in Flash, however, can't be very competitive in searches because it lacks sufficient text content.) Check out your competitors' use of Flash. If they all have some Flash elements that help engage users, you're probably going to need to build some, too.

There are many other types of engagement objects, and lots more to say about the best ways to include them on your Web pages. Please see Book X, Chapter 2 to get more information.

Learning from Your Competitors' Links

What else can you learn from your competitors? You can find out who's linking to them.

Besides your page construction, another big factor in your search engine ranking is your *link equity*, which is the value of all the backlinks coming to your Web pages. The search engines consider every link to your Web page to be a "vote" for that page. The more votes your page has, the more "expert" your page appears to be. Based on the links pointing to your site, the search engines either increase or decrease how relevant your site is for particular keyword searches. The quality of your backlinks also matters; one testimonial-grade link from an authoritative Web site in your field is an important endorsement and can be worth more than thousands of links from unrelated and inconsequential sites in terms of your link equity.

You want to have a natural variety of backlinks to your landing pages, from sites with a range of different link equity values themselves. However, it's good to keep in mind what the gold standard is so that you can recognize a nugget when you see one and go after it. The most ideal backlinks come from a Web page that is

✦ Well-established (that is, an older site that's become trusted)

✦ An authority within your industry, with lots of backlinks coming to it from related sites, as well as some links out to other authority Web sites;

✦ Focused on the same subject as your Web page, even using some of the same keywords;

✦ Using meaningful anchor text that contains your keywords in the link to your page.

You may have some of these "ideal" candidates in mind already: sites that are well-respected and established authorities in your field. It's very likely, however, that you don't have nearly enough backlink candidates in mind yet. That's where looking at your top-ranking competitors comes in handy.

You can look at your competitors' links primarily to find good backlink candidates for your own site. The top-ranking competitors for your keywords probably have vetted worthwhile links that you could benefit from, too. After all, your competitor deals with the same type of information and customer that you do. If that third-party site finds it useful to link visitors to the competitor's site, they might find your site equally useful for their visitors to know about.

You can see a list of all the indexed backlinks a competitor has by running a search engine query:

✦ **In Google:** In the regular search box, type the query [`link:domain.com`], substituting the competing page's URL for `domain.com`.

✦ **In Yahoo!:** Go to `http://siteexplorer.search.yahoo.com` and enter the competing URL.

The results come out in pretty much random order. You can go page by page and read through them, copying the ones that look promising as a possible backlink candidate into another document for follow-up. Be picky here: You don't want any spammy links, and some may simply not be worth the time to pursue. If there are hundreds of link results, we suggest you export them from Yahoo! by clicking the Export Results to: TSV (Tab Separated Values) link. Then you can export the data into a spreadsheet program like Microsoft Excel and re-sort it as desired.

Suppose your competition has about 50 backlinks. How many do you really need to be competitive? In most cases, reasonably close is sufficient. Focus on developing links in a natural fashion — buying links en mass or devoting huge amounts of time to obtaining reciprocal links is not a good way to gain links as the search engines have ways to detect these links and they have very little, if any, SEO value.

If you have the SEMToolBar installed, scanning the link results looking for good candidates gets much easier. (The *SEMToolBar* is free software that can be downloaded into your Internet Explorer or Mozilla Firefox browser from www.bruceclay.com/web_rank.htm#semtoolbar.) For one thing, the results are numbered. More importantly, you'll be able to see extra information about each backlink, including its approximate *PageRank*. So at a glance you can tell which Web pages are the heavyweights with the search engines. However, be sure you're choosing sites that are relevant to yours; otherwise, the sites won't help your link equity very much. (See Chapter 2 of Book III for more information on the SEMToolBar.)

After you've decided which Web sites you'd like backlinks from, you can begin your link-building campaign. Spend a little time looking at the candidate's Web page. You want to know what it's about so that you can make sure your own Web page has something of value to those users. Another thing you might find is something amiss on the third-party site, like a broken link or missing image, which you can offer to them when you contact them with a request.

Never pay for a link to build your link equity. You can pay for advertising, if you want to attract more visitors or promote your site, but not to increase your link equity. Buying links that look deceptively like regular links can get you in trouble with the search engines, especially Google. According to Matt Cutts, who's currently the head of Google's Webspam team, link buying is being addressed by improvements to the search engine's algorithm. When they detect a paid link, they typically give it no value. Selling links is even more of a gamble: If it's a big problem, Google may drop your PageRank to let you know that they know about the purchased link, and you'll wind up nowhere in the search engine results. Webmasters have the right to put anything on their site, but Google also reserves the right to take action so that the best results are delivered to their users.

You can read about link-building strategies in depth and see a sample link solicitation letter that you can send to a Webmaster in hopes of getting a link in Book VI, Chapter 4.

**Book III
Chapter 3**

Applying Collected Data

Taking Cues from Your Competitors' Content Structure

You may have a lot of great content on your Web site, but if it's jumbled and disorganized, the search engines might not figure out what searches it relates to. This is why you should consider *content siloing*, which is a way of organizing your Web site into subject themes by linking related pages together. Content siloing lets you funnel link equity to your landing pages, which reinforces to the search engines how relevant those pages are for their keywords. Linking is so important that it can override the actual content of the page. Siloing is comprised of two parts. One is internal linking and another relates to page and site architecture. Consider a good site map: one that, in a very detailed schematic, outlines the entire structure of a document. Siloing means that all the links on the Web site follow that outline exactly without any straying from topic to topic. Literally, the anchor text links do more to inform Google than the content in those pages. (Siloing is a big subject, with its own chapter devoted to it. See Book VI, Chapter 3 for the full scoop.)

Looking at the top-ranking competitors' Web sites, you can get some clues as to how they've organized their content. This can benefit you in two basic ways:

✦ You can tell how well organized the competitor's content is. If they aren't using siloing, that could be an advantage point for you.

✦ You can get ideas for beefing up your own content or for different ways you might organize your site.

Go to a competing Web page from a search results link. What can you learn from this landing page about how it fits into the entire site, and whether it uses siloing?

First, looking at the navigation structure may give clues. This navigation example shows a fairly clear directory structure — it looks to be organized first by car make (Ford), and then by model (Mustang). This site may have its content siloed:

```
www.autocustomizing.com/ford/mustang/customize-your-mustang.htm
```

Now look at this URL, which contains codes and *parameters* (auto-generated URL characters that carry information to the receiving page about the user) that make it impossible to read:

```
www.pallatinacars.com/svcse/php?t=37481&_cthew=13%3A2
```

Obviously, sometimes the URL structure is informative, and sometimes not. Because the URL is another piece of communication the search engines use to try to understand what a page is about, you want your pages to have meaningful keywords in your URLs. Although there is very little weight placed on keywords in the URL, don't miss that opportunity. Human visitors appreciate the clarity even if the search engines don't. And if the sites you're competing against have gobbledygook in their URLs (like the second one we mentioned), you'll have another advantage.

Second, you can tell if a site is well-organized into silos by looking at its internal links. We're not talking about the main navigation menu so much, but about the related hyperlinks on the competitor's landing page. See if there are links to pages full of supporting information on the same topic. Then as you click to view those supporting pages, look to see whether they contain links back to the landing page, but none to other pages outside of that topic. If so, that site is probably siloed.

If they don't have a siloed linking strategy, you might see

✦ No links to related pages on the landing page, or

✦ The same set of links on every page you look at, or

✦ A haphazard assortment of links to various areas of the Web site, with no clear subject focus

Here are some questions you should answer about your competitors:

✦ Does the competitor's site organize the main content categories in a clear, readable hierarchical and empirical structure with clear indexable (spiderable) navigation?

✦ Does the competitor's site have quality content on each major category section?

✦ How well does the site link to related articles and site guides?

If the competitor *isn't* siloing, and the vast majority of sites are not, that could give you an advantage as you create a theme for your site contents and implement linking within silos.

Detecting rel="nofollow" links

For the purposes of siloing, you only need to look at the links that are "followed" by the search engines. Links that have a rel="nofollow" attribute attached to them in the HTML code don't count for passing link equity. (By the way, the presence of a rel="nofollow" attribute on a Web site may itself provide a clue that there's an SEO expert on staff, and the site may be siloed.)

To see "nofollow" links more easily, you can install a free plug-in for the Mozilla Firefox browser called Search Status (currently in version 1.27). If you install this plug-in, links with a "nofollow" attribute automatically show

up highlighted in pink on any Web page. Here's how you can get and use Search Status:

1. In your Mozilla Firefox browser, go to www.quirk.biz/searchstatus/.

2. Click the big Download Search Status button, and then scroll down a bit and click the Firefox icon. Complete the installation procedure as directed.

3. After it's installed, you see some new icons in the lower-right corner of your browser window. Right-click on the Quirk icon to open the context menu for options and select Highlight Nofollow Links.

After you've figured out whether the competitor's site is organized into silos, take a look around and see what tips you can take from them. First of all, you might discover they've covered something that you missed, like an article about how to preserve the original upholstery of a classic car so that it lasts for decades. Your site visitors probably want to know that, too, so make a note to write a new article to fill that hole.

A well-siloed Web site might also give you good ideas for organizing content. For instance, your silos might be set up by type of service (body work, reupholstering, complete restoration, and so on), whereas on a competitor's site, you see siloing by car make and model. The test of a good silo structure is how much traffic you're bringing in by being relevant to important keywords. If your structure is bringing in visitors and giving you enough *conversions* (sales, sign-ups, orders, or whatever action you want people to take on your site), you shouldn't tear it down.

You might still learn something from another site's silo structure, however, that you could apply as a horizontal silo within your current structure. A *horizontal silo* involves linking across silos very deliberately to create a secondary silo structure that can rank for other types of search queries. So if your silo structure is by services, you could consider linking together your page titled Reupholstering a Ford Mustang to your pages for Restoring a Ford Mustang and Ford Mustang Body Work, and so on. That would create a set of horizontal silos that might help you rank higher for searches that include [Ford Mustang] as a keyword.

For more help with siloing and overlaying a horizontal silo, check out Book VI, Chapter 3.

Book IV
SEO Web Design

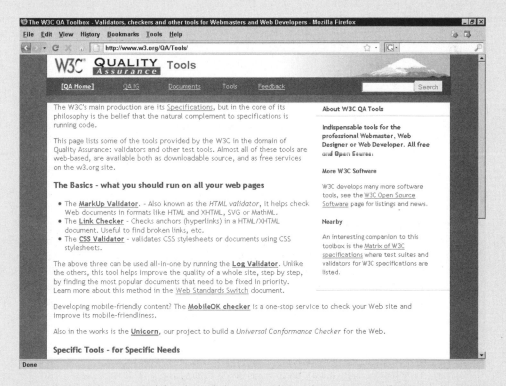

Online validator tools like these help you make sure your site is W3C-compliant.

Contents at a Glance

Chapter 1: The Basics of SEO Web Design **195**

Deciding on the Type of Content for Your Site.. 196
Choosing Keywords 197
Using Keywords in the Heading Tags 201
Keeping the Code Clean.. 203
Organizing Your Assets 205
Naming Your Files 206
Keeping Design Simple... 208
Making a Site Dynamic 211
Develop a Design Procedure 212

Chapter 2: Building an SEO-Friendly Site **215**

Preplanning and Organizing your Site 215
Designing Spider-Friendly Code... 216
Creating a Theme and Style 218
Writing Rich Text Content.. 219
Planning Your Navigation Elements... 220
Implementing a Site Search 224
Incorporating Engagement Objects into Your Site.................................. 226
Allowing for Expansion 230
Developing an Update Procedure.. 231
Balancing Usability and Conversion 232

Chapter 3: Making Your Page Search Engine-Compatible. **241**

Optimizing HTML Constructs for Search Engines.................................. 242
Using Clean Code.. 256
Making Your Site WC3–Compliant... 257
Designing with sIFR 261
Externalizing the Code 268
Choosing the Right Navigation 269
Making Use of HTML Content Stacking.. 271

Chapter 4: Perfecting Navigation and Linking Techniques **275**

Formulating a Category Structure.. 276
Selecting Landing Pages 281
Absolute versus relative linking 283
Dealing with Less-Than-Ideal Types of Navigation................................ 284
Naming Links.. 288

Chapter 1: The Basics of SEO Web Design

In This Chapter

✔ Deciding on your site content

✔ Choosing keywords

✔ Using H# tags for headings

✔ Cleaning up your page code

✔ Organizing your assets

✔ Naming files

✔ Making your site dynamic

✔ Developing a design procedure

In this chapter, you discover the basics of site design with search engine optimization in mind. Building a Web site is like baking a cake in a lot of ways, and one of the first things you have to do is gather together your ingredients.

In this chapter, we first guide you to deciding on the content and the types of keywords that you want. Then we discuss *H# or heading tags* (HTML code applied to headings) and page headings, and the importance of using clean code for your site. You find out how to organize and name all of the assets on your page, including images, videos, and podcasts. After you have everything organized, you discover how to actually construct your site.

We finish off the chapter by discussing keeping your page simple and neat, creating dynamic content for your site that is still seen as relevant by the search engines, and developing a design procedure so that everyone on the team is on the same page.

We talk a lot about HTML in the upcoming pages; however, we don't attempt to teach you HTML in this book. We strongly recommend that you learn at least the basics of HTML before you attempt SEO. Even if you aren't going to be the one doing the optimization on your Web site, it's a good idea to learn the basics. If you want to be good at search engine optimization (SEO), you need to understand both the marketing end *and* the technical end. If you know the basics of HTML, you can communicate with your IT guys in their own language, which prevents them from claiming something can't be done if it actually can. It also allows you to be able to catch mistakes others might miss, helps you research your competition's Web sites, and is just generally good to know.

Deciding on the Type of Content for Your Site

We have stated this time and time again throughout this book, and we'll continue to do so because it's important: You must know what your business is about. It colors how you choose your keywords and how you arrange your site. You need to know if you have a research or an e-commerce site, or if it's both. How can you tell? Here are a few ways:

✦ **Research:** A research site's keywords should lean towards how-to types of phrases. As in, [How do you fix a lawnmower?] or [How do you say where is the consulate, I lost my password? in Spanish?]. Or even more specific keywords like [Mustang] or [John Wilkes Booth]. These are keywords that people use when they do research. If you have a site that provides information, such as recipes, lists of dead historians, or classic auto club newsletters, you want your keywords to be research-based. Research Web sites typically use words like [research], [reviews], [how to], [information], and so on.

✦ **E-commerce:** If you have an e-commerce site, your site is designed to sell things. Your keywords are geared more towards users who want to make purchases. That could include the keyword [free] because who wouldn't want free stuff? Also, you'd include much more specific keywords like [Ford Mustang Convertible with leather interior] because people search for broader terms when doing research and more specific terms when they're ready to make a purchase. E-commerce sites have calls to actions in their content, using terms like [buy now], [purchase], [shopping cart], and so on.

✦ **Research *and* e-commerce:** Some sites provide both information and purchasing opportunities. You can have a site that provides tons of information and recipes for the best barbecuing techniques, and have things like grills and barbecue sauces available on your Web site for purchase.

Knowing what kind of a business you have (and what kind of Web site you want to build/redesign) helps you to pick out your keywords. Separate them into information-type keywords and transaction-type keywords. This means thinking about whether the keyword would draw someone doing research to your site, or someone ready to buy something.

You have to do research and *continue* to do it. SEO is not like doing research for a tenth-grade English essay, where you do it once and then never have to do it again. The market changes constantly and you have to be able to keep up with it. See Book II, Chapter 1 for more information on keyword research.

Choosing Keywords

After you've decided what kind of site you're building and separated your lists of keywords for that site, you have to choose what keywords will go where. You need to know what keywords to assign to each page in order to

+ Focus the page content

+ Make it faster for the viewer to understand the content

+ Make it easier for a search engine *spider* (or *robot*, referring to the search engine programs that come read your site and index its contents) to determine what each page is about.

Running a ranking monitor to discover what's already working

If you have an existing Web site, you have to first establish a *benchmark;* that is, that you should find out what's currently working before you begin rearranging things. You need to find out which of your Web pages already rank well in the search engines, and for which keywords. For instance, if you have a page on your site that's already ranking in the top five listings for one of your keywords, you should just designate that as the main page for that keyword and leave it alone. Check on which keywords are working for you and which aren't and don't fix something that's not broken. Conversely, if you have a page that is consistently not ranking for any keywords, it's time to fix that page.

To help you evaluate your keywords, you can take advantage of a useful tool called a ranking monitor. This tool is extremely helpful for keyword research and keeping track of how your pages are ranking, both now and further on down the road as the market grows and changes.

**Book IV
Chapter 1**

**The Basics of SEO
Web Design**

A *ranking monitor* tells you where your pages rank in the search engines for each keyword, or if they rank at all. At the time of this writing, we don't know of any ranking monitor available for free; however, subscribing to a paid monitor is worth the cost. At the risk of sounding self-promotional, the monitor available with our subscription SEOToolSet at `www.seotoolset.com/` works and is fully integrated with many useful tools. The full suite of tools is available for $39.95 a month, but you can search online for others. No matter which you choose, you need to be looking for a ranking monitor that

✦ Checks multiple search engines (domestic and international)

✦ Includes historical data, so you can see trends over time

✦ Is "polite" to the search engines by automatically spacing queries over time, or allows you to customize the crawl rates to use time delays

✦ Supports proxy (remote location) queries

✦ Offers multiple languages

✦ Is schedulable

✦ Runs from a server and not from your desktop

✦ Integrates with other tools to allow for analysis

Figure 1-1 shows a typical ranking report from the SEOToolSet. For every one of the site's keywords (which are pre-entered), the report shows if any page on the site ranks for that keyword, what number rank it has in each of the search engines, and the search activity (roughly the number of search queries per day). Clicking on the keyword reveals which URLs specifically are ranked.

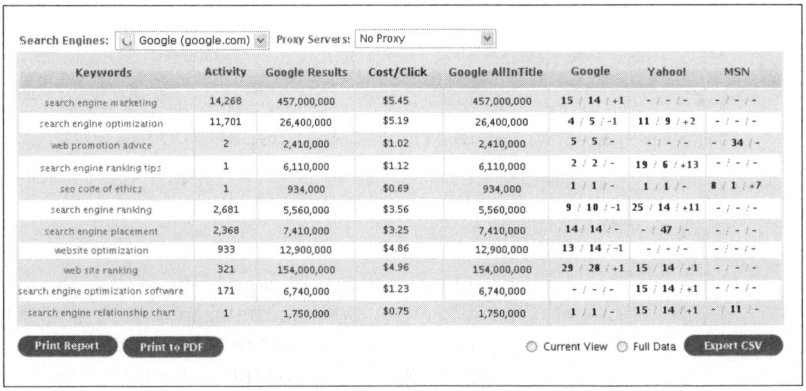

Figure 1-1:
Ranking reports identify which pages rank well for your keywords.

Keywords	Activity	Google Results	Cost/Click	Google AllInTitle	Google	Yahoo!	MSN
search engine marketing	14,268	457,000,000	$5.45	457,000,000	15 / 14 / +1	- / - / -	- / - / -
search engine optimization	11,701	26,400,000	$5.19	26,400,000	4 / 5 / -1	11 / 9 / +2	- / - / -
web promotion advice	2	2,410,000	$1.02	2,410,000	5 / 5 / -	- / - / -	- / 34 / -
search engine ranking tips	1	6,110,000	$1.12	6,110,000	2 / 2 / -	19 / 6 / +13	- / - / -
seo code of ethics	1	934,000	$0.69	934,000	1 / 1 / -	1 / 1 / -	8 / 1 / +7
search engine ranking	2,681	5,560,000	$3.56	5,560,000	9 / 10 / -1	25 / 14 / +11	- / - / -
search engine placement	2,368	7,410,000	$3.25	7,410,000	14 / 14 / -	- / 47 / -	- / - / -
website optimization	933	12,900,000	$4.86	12,900,000	13 / 14 / -1	- / - / -	- / - / -
web site ranking	321	154,000,000	$4.96	154,000,000	29 / 28 / +1	15 / 14 / +1	- / - / -
search engine optimization software	171	6,740,000	$1.23	6,740,000	- / - / -	15 / 14 / +1	- / - / -
search engine relationship chart	1	1,750,000	$0.75	1,750,000	1 / 1 / -	15 / 14 / +1	- / 11 / -

Figure 1-2 is a chart showing your page rankings over time, giving you a history of how your site ranked overall over time and a handy bar graph to go along with it. It's important that you be able to track your rankings over time so that you know whether your search engine optimization efforts are working. Keep good records of all your changes so that you'll be able to relate it back to the rise and fall in your graph.

Figure 1-2:
This
screenshot
from the
SEOToolSet
shows
overall
keyword
ranking
over time.

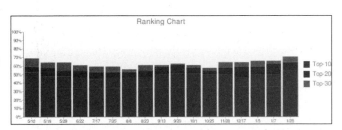

It's important to choose a ranking monitor that won't constantly hammer the search engines. (By hammer, we mean it won't constantly query the search engines. You don't want them to spider your site at full speed if it impacts your ability to do business by overloading your servers. We think it's just polite to return the same courtesy to the search engines.) We *recommend* you choose an online ranking monitor instead of a desktop one to be sure you don't get your personal IP banned: You don't want to limit your ability to do your own Google searches. If your monitor hits the engines with too many searches too fast, the search engine may identify your monitor as a machine and require you to prove you're a human user every time you try to run the application.

Choose a ranking monitor that either auto-spaces its queries or lets you request delays between searches because scraping at the search engines constantly gets you into trouble and will produce inconsistent data. The SEOToolSet ranking monitor waits several seconds between each query, just to be polite.

You should rerun a ranking monitor at regular intervals, storing up a history of biweekly or monthly ranking reports that you can compare to each other. There's no real benefit to running monitors more often as search engines change algorithms regularly, and less frequent monitors give better history and don't take up so much data. (Not to mention that you need to wait to see if your SEO edits on your Web pages were picked up by the engines in the first place.)

**Book IV
Chapter 1**

**The Basics of SEO
Web Design**

Having an archive of dated reports allows you to see your progress over time because each one is like a snapshot of your current SEO work. Especially as you begin implementing search engine optimization throughout your Web site, you want to run a ranking monitor regularly. You will definitely appreciate the trending reports in the long run.

Matching Meta tags and keywords to page content

After you've run the ranking monitor, you can identify the pages that rank well for particular keywords. Consider those ranking keywords as being assigned to those pages. Remove other unrelated keywords so that your page stays focused very clearly on its main keyword. You want to follow some SEO best practices for how you assign keywords to a page. We go into depth on this throughout this book, but here's a brief list to start with.

When assigning keywords to your Web pages, select one to five main related keywords (or keyword phrases) for each individual page. Allow two or three supporting keywords (or keyword phrases) per page. Supporting keywords may be suitable for developing pages around, as well, increasing your depth of content.

Make sure all keywords on the page relate to one another: Too many unrelated (but well-ranking) keywords can dilute the theme and bring your rankings down. If the page is about painting a classic Mustang, make sure the keywords all relate to painting a classic Mustang. Your page content should also include synonyms and clarifying words that a user would be looking for. Slang terms are excellent clarifying words because they mimic the way people actually speak: [stang] or [pony car] for Mustang wouldn't be considered secondary keywords, but they're important to proving your expertise to your visitors.

If you already have a Web site and need to tweak it for ranking, take a look at the page you have and think about where you can enhance it. Going back to the classic car customization example: If you have a page on your site that's mostly about tires but it also has a paragraph about rims and a line or two about wheel axels, that page is a little disjointed. Because the page is primarily about tires, make it *all* about tires and create a separate page for rims and another page for axels. Then pick two or three really good supporting keywords for your tires page.

After you choose your main and supporting keywords for each page, you are going to arrange them strategically. You should put keywords in

✦ The page's Title tag.

✦ The Meta description and Meta keywords tags (metadata appears in the Head section of the HTML code and defines the page content).

✦ In the headings on the page, especially in your H1 tag.

✦ In the page content.

Search engines look at the `Title`, `Meta` description, and `Meta` keywords tags not only to understand what your page is about, but also to grab text to display in your search results listing. Search engines pull the descriptive text that displays on their results pages from any of several different sources depending on the search query and the engine itself: from the `Meta` description tag, from the page content, occasionally from the Open Directory Project (DMOZ), and Yahoo! often uses the description from a site's listing in the Yahoo! Directory.

See Book VI, Chapter 3 for more help creating `Title` and `Meta` tags.

Using Keywords in the Heading Tags

When you're structuring the HTML coding for a Web page, it can look a little like an outline, with main headings and subheadings. An important place to have keywords is in those headings, placed within `Heading` tags.

Heading tags are part of the HTML coding for a Web page. Headings are defined with `H1` to `H6` tags. The `H1` tag defines the most important heading on the page (usually the largest or boldest, too), whereas `H6` indicates the lowest-level heading. You want to avoid thinking of headings as simply formatting for your pages: Headings carry a lot of weight with the search engines because they're for categorization, not cosmetics. You can control what each heading looks like consistently through your site using a CSS style sheet that specifies the font, size, color, and other attributes for each `Heading` tag. Here's an example of what various heading tags can look like:

```
<H1>This is a heading</H1>
<H2>This is subheading A</H2>
<H2>This is subheading B</H2>
<H3>This is a lower subheading</H3>
```

Search engines pay special attention to the words in your headings because they expect headings to include clues to the page's main topics. You definitely want to include the page's keywords inside `Heading` tags.

`Heading` tags also provide your pages with an outline, with the heading defining the paragraph that follows. They outline how your page is structured and organize the information. The `H1` tag indicates your most important topic, and the other `H#` tags create subtopics.

You should follow several SEO best practices for applying `Heading` tags. First, you want to have only one `H1` tag per page because it's basically the subject of your page. Think of your `H1` tag like the headline of a newspaper article: It wouldn't make sense to have more than one. You can have multiple lesser tags if the page covers several subsections. In feature articles in newsletters, you occasionally see sub-headlines that are styled differently than the headline: Those would be the equivalent of an `H2`.

Say that you have a page that describes how you can customize classic Mustang convertibles. Your very first heading for your page should be something like this:

```
<H1>Customizing Classic Mustangs</H1>
```

Your second paragraph is about customizing the paint job for the convertible. So it should have a heading that reads:

```
<H2>Customizing Paint for Mustangs</H2>
```

When you view the code of your page (which you should most definitely do even if you have someone else create it for you), it should look something like this:

```
<H1> Customizing Classic Mustangs s</H1>
<p>200 words of content about Customizing Classic Mustangs
    using the keywords.</p>

<H2> Customizing Paint for Mustangs </H2>
<p>200 words of content about Customizing Paint for Mustangs
    using the keywords</p>

<H2> Customizing Upholstery for Mustangs </H2>
<p>200 words of content about Customizing Upholstery for
    Mustangs using the keywords.</p>
```

When assigning Heading tags, keep them in sequence in the HTML, which is how the search engines can most easily read them. Heading tags should follow the outline structure you used in school for an outline or a technical paper. If you wanted to add an `H3` tag, it would have to follow an `H2` in the code. Similarly, if you had an `H4` tag, it could only follow an `H3` tag and not an `H2`.

Heading structure is a relatively simple concept, but you would be surprised at how many Web sites use the same type of heading for every paragraph, or just use their `Headings` tags to stuff keywords into the HTML code. In reality, many sites do not even use `Heading` tags, so it should a quick win to place appropriate headings on your site. Absolutely avoid any headings that look like this:

```
<H1>Mustang Mustang Mustang Ford Mustang</H1>
```

This tag is unacceptable to search engines (to say nothing of your visitors), and is considered spam. See Book I, Chapter 6 for more on what may be considered spam.

The words in each `Heading` tag should be unique and targeted to the page they're on. *Unique* and *targeted* means that your `Heading` tag's content shouldn't be duplicated anywhere across the site. If the heading on your tires page is "Classic Mustang tires," "Classic Mustang tires" shouldn't be the `H1` on any other page in your site.

Search engines look for uniqueness on your page. For example, if you have an `H1` heading of `Ford Mustang Convertible` at the top of two different pages, the search engine might read one of the pages as redundant and not count it. Having unique `Heading` tags allows the search engine to assign more weight to a heading, and headings are one of the most important things on the page besides the `Title` tag (which is discussed in Book IV, Chapter 3).

If you want to have any of the elements on your Web site (`Title` tags, `Heading` tags, `Alt` attributes, and so on) help your pages rank in a search engine, they all need to be unique. It may take a little more time to go through and think up unique, relevant, keyword-rich tags for everything, but it's worth the effort. The little things count when it comes to SEO.

Keeping the Code Clean

Another part of building a search engine-friendly Web site is keeping your code clean and simple. When we talk about code, we're talking about languages like HTML, XHTML, AJAX, JavaScript, and the like. Coding supplies the building blocks of your Web site. If we were talking about building a house, the code would basically define the walls, floors, insulation, light fixtures, kitchen sink, and everything right down to the color of the paint in the bathroom.

We assume that you already know a little bit about HTML, CSS and JavaScript code and what it looks like. In this chapter, we assume that you're at the planning stage of your SEO campaign, gathering your assets and starting to visualize a big-picture plan for your Web site. In the next chapters, we cover how to apply what you've visualized to make an SEO-friendly site. But first, there are a few more concepts to grasp.

You want to streamline your site's code so that it's an easy read for the search engine spiders. Keeping the code as clean as possible, as it relates to SEO, means some specific things:

**Book IV
Chapter 1**

**The Basics of SEO
Web Design**

✦ Get to each page's content as soon as possible in the HTML view. You want your keywords to start showing up early in the search engine spider's crawl.

✦ Code using as little on-the-page *markup* (formatting and other types of on-the-fly HTML codes, such as `Font` tags, which could be controlled in a CSS style sheet instead) as possible. If you have useless tags in your code, get rid of them.

These are great goals, but how can you achieve them? These best practices can slash the code clutter right out of your Web pages:

✦ Use an external *CSS* (Cascading Style Sheets) file to define the look of your Web site, rather than relying on inline formatting.

✦ Move any JavaScript code into an external .JS file when possible. Include simple calls to the JavaScript file from your pages, which keeps the on-page code short and sweet.

You may also have extraneous tags lying around in the HTML. Code gunk buildup can happen if you've cut and pasted content from another source (like an old Web page of yours, or from Microsoft Word or other programs that add a ton of unnecessary HTML code to your text). Or you may have been working on a particular page for so long that it's acquired excess tags like barnacles on a ship's hull. Go through and remove all of the extraneous tags and code from your pages including extra carriage returns. Simplifying your code streamlines the site and makes it easier to read for the search engine spiders. If they read too much redundancy or if your page code appears too complex, they're less likely to assign a lot of weight or relevancy to your page. Just as two drops of dye in a small glass of water has a lot more impact than two drops of dye in a barrel of water, effectively, the messy code could be "diluting" the strength of your keywords.

A couple of programs are available to clean up your code if you've got a bunch of gunk hanging out in the HTML. The cheapest is your friendly neighborhood text editor, Notepad. If you're used to reading HTML, just opening it up and looking at the raw code can help you tidy up pages one at a time. If you're using a UNIX/LINUX server, save your work in UNIX format.

For those who aren't able to read HTML like it's English, there are other tools out there that can help. Adobe Dreamweaver (a Web design and programming application) allows you to create Web pages in a WYSIWYG view ("What you see is what you get," or the way the page looks to visitors). It can actually write the HTML code for you as you type text and move things around. This helpful program can also help you clean up cluttered code. It contains an option to review an .HTM file for unnecessary code and offers to clean it up for you, as you can see in Figure 1-3.

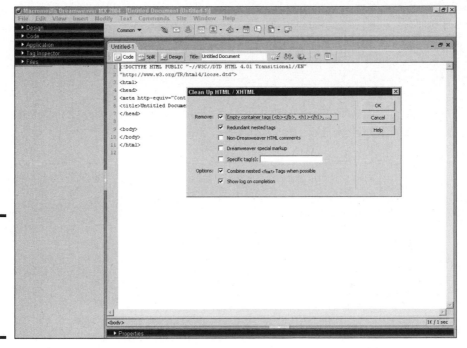

Figure 1-3:
You can
use Adobe
Dream
weaver to
help clean
your code.

Dreamweaver can correct bad coding syntax and remove code that doesn't need to be there. It even can help you convert all of your Font tags to CSS and reorganize the HTML in a format that the search engine spiders will be more easily able to follow, which streamlines your code for you.

Organizing Your Assets

Making a Web site is kind of like baking a cake. You have to have all of your ingredients together and the recipe before you get started; otherwise, you could be in the middle of mixing only to find out that you have no eggs. It's why we have you go through all of these steps first in order to make sure you have everything ready before you begin.

If you're just starting a Web site, it's important to organize your assets. What's going to go on your Web site? Sift through everything that you have. Remember, users love dynamic content, so in addition to that must-have readable, well-written text, include images and video to enhance user interest and engagement.

Go through all of your print materials, if you have any, and choose images that you can use on your Web site. Do you have a commercial? How about an interview that you did for radio or television? Gather all of these things together and go through them. If something is useless, chuck it because clutter will always be clutter. But if you find an image or a video you think will work with your site, use it!

Besides text, you might want to consider putting the following types of engagement objects on your Web site:

✦ **Files:** First things first, organize your files into proper categories. And by files we mean everything. Your pages, your data, your images, videos, and podcasts, if your have any. Main subjects go first, and then go down the line into subcategories.

✦ **Images:** If you have print materials, you probably have images. Use those images to enhance your Web site (and make *sure* you have the copyrights to use those images). Adding images can also help your page rank because of the ability to use keywords in the Alt attribute text (the HTML coding of the image), plus the ability to rank in image-centric *vertical search engines* (search engines that look for a specific type of file or location).

✦ **Videos:** If you have any commercials or videos lying around, consider uploading them and using them on your site. Especially upload it to YouTube, which allows you to add to your outside links. Search engines can't see a video, but videos can still enhance your rank by containing keywords in the text surrounding the video (such as if you put the video in a table cell with keyword-rich text above or below it), and by appearing in their own vertical results.

✦ **Podcasts:** If you have a radio show, it's not that hard to stream it online and create podcasts that are downloadable.

If you have any of these engagement objects, gather them together and keep them organized. Engagement objects don't stop there, consider also blogs, news, books, maps — anything that could catch the eye and engage a user with your site that isn't just a standard text-based Web page. You'll thank yourself later when you're actually building your Web site and have lots of content choices handy.

Naming Your Files

After you've gathered your assets together and separated the wheat from the chaff, you need to name them as you're uploading them. How you name your files is important because a search engine looks at the filename as an indication of what's in the file, so this is another good place to have keywords.

Instead of naming your image of a red Ford Mustang like this:

*0035001.jpg

Rename the file as you're uploading it to describe it, something like:

*ford-mustang-1967.jpg

Not only is the file now easier for you to identify when building your pages down the line, but it also now contains three keywords that search engines can read and add to their algorithms for ranking.

Use filenames that make sense to both the search engine and the user. You might understand the gibberish you just used as a filename, but someone else who doesn't know you or your sense of humor might not. Also, use full words instead of abbreviations. Searchers generally don't use abbreviations in their search queries unless they're very common.

The same advice is true for naming video and podcast files. Make sure that the filename is descriptive and simple: It helps you and the search engine in the long run.

When naming your files with phrases, don't leave spaces between words. Nor should you use an underscore (_) to separate words. Search engines interpret the underscore as its own character, so it's like naming your file *fordxmustang*, which misses an opportunity to use your keywords when a search engine spiders it. It's possible that search engines can figure it out, but better to name your files properly than take the chance of a misread.

Instead, if you have to use spaces (remember, search engines can parse words from Web pages filenames without any help), use periods or hyphens. They won't be read as a separate character. That way, you can have files that look like this:

ford.mustang.1967.good.condition.jpg

or

ford-mustang-1967-good-condition.jpg

Even without spaces, periods, or hyphens in your filenames, a search engine can actually parse out up to 500 words that are *concatenated* (run together without spaces). You might want to use a hyphen in places where there could be confusion in the parsing, either for a search engine or for a user. In those cases, you might want to throw in a dash or some periods in order to make it legible. For example, the distinction between mensexchange.jpg and mens-exchange.jpg is an important one, after all.

Eyetracking studies done by Enquiro research have found that users are not likely to click on a long URL in the results page. They tend to click the result below the hideously long URL instead. So when you're naming the pages and files in your Web site, keep the length down to a reasonable level.

As descriptive as it is, you wouldn't want something like this as your base domain name:

`www.reallycoolclassiccustomcarsatareasonableprice.com`

Also follow a standard of using either all lowercase or all uppercase in naming files. Apache servers are case-sensitive: Lower- or uppercase makes a difference to them. The pages /FordMustang.html and /fordmustang.html are not considered the same to a case-sensitive server. Also, do not use more than two hyphens in a page URL, and avoid having more than one hyphen in the domain name. Filenames (like our ford-mustang-1967-good-condition.jpg example) are mostly exempt from this rule (we've found examples with 14 hyphens in the filename), but we still recommend economy in your naming conventions.

Keeping Design Simple

When it comes to designing your site, the old adage *KISS* is good advice: "Keep It Simple, Sweetie." Make your Web site as straightforward and easy to navigate as possible. Make sure the links and instructions are clear and not horribly complicated. Also, be aware of how much Flash you are using. Adobe Flash is a multimedia program that allows you to place animation on your Web site. There are many major companies out there with big shiny Web sites that contain lots of complicated and cool-looking Flash. But here's a secret about those sites: a search engine can't read them.

A search engine is basically deaf, dumb, and blind. It cannot see what the viewer sees; it can only read the code. It can't read a page like a person reads it (yet). The search engines are trying to emulate what a person will see and react to, but technology isn't there yet, and they have to make do with reading the code.

Web sites built entirely in Flash generally don't have searchable content. A search engine, being blind, deaf, and dumb, can't see the Flash animations that describe all the cool things the Web site has to offer because all they can see is the Flash plug-in in the HTML code. See Figure 1-4, for example. It's got some well-designed Flash, but a search spider can't see any of it, so it can't read any of the keywords or follow any of the links on the site. The capabilities of the search engines and of this technology are evolving rapidly. We may one day see Flash become as spiderable as text, but that day hasn't arrived yet.

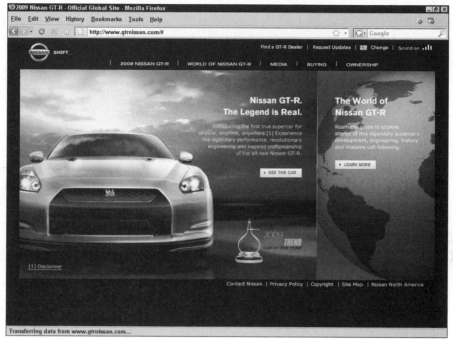

Figure 1-4:
Although a human can read this, a search engine robot can't.

That's not to say that your Web site can't contain Flash, but make sure there's readable content that goes along with it. A few Flash movies on the page is a good thing for user experience, provided they are relevant and are accompanied by a reasonable amount of companion text. Also, make sure that the Flash is not too complicated for the page, or for the user. Some sites create mini applications using Flash and include them on their Web sites. If that's your site, don't miss an opportunity to pull good text content out of the application to include on your pages, as well. For instance, if your Flash contains instructions on how to use it within the Flash itself, grab that text and make it part of the text on the page. Also, if you use Flash, place a description of the Flash content in the actual text of the page. That makes it easier for the user to understand, and a search engine spider can read it and use it in your ranking. It's a win/win situation.

Also, many Web sites include a Flash animation as the *splash* page (sort of like a site's welcome mat), and users have to sit and wait for it to load and play before going on to the actual site. In general, these pages are usually skipped. Most people want to go to the content right away instead of having to sit through a minute of pretty, but useless, animation. If your site has one, you should probably remove the Flash intro.

Here's another hint for your Web site. Some people out there think it's a cool idea to include some music that plays when a user visits their Web site. We can tell you right now that many people do not enjoy this. There is nothing more annoying than visiting a site and being unable to find the music player to turn off the background music. The only people who enjoy having music playing on the page are the ones who put it there in the first place and the ones who pay to have it there. We would recommend that unless you have a site that actually sells music, don't include background music on your site. And if you really must, make sure it defaults to off.

Keeping the content on your page simple and easy to navigate not only helps you get better rankings, but it also means that your user has a much better experience and will return to your site again. Follow this general rule: If it looks cool but is a pain in the rear to use, users won't use it. Figure 1-5 is a great example of a simple, easy-to-use Web site.

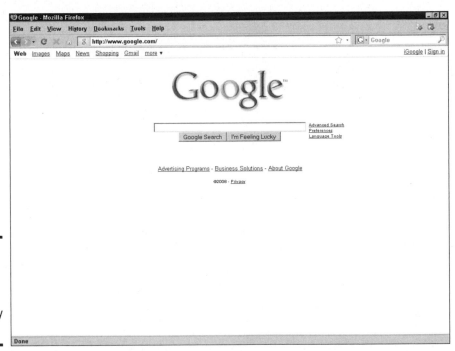

Figure 1-5:
Google is committed to clean, user-friendly design.

Google's home page is clean, simple, doesn't have any extraneous clutter, and is pretty self-explanatory when it comes to what the page does. The less you have to explain to your users, the better. Of course, Google doesn't have to worry about ranking for anything, but that doesn't mean their simple and clean design ethic can't work for you, too. Ask yourself if you are putting only what you need onto a page and avoid the tendency to cram in just one more thing.

Making a Site Dynamic

A *dynamic* Web site is a site that is built using a template and a *CMS* (content management system) that gives you control of how to define your Web page that pulls information from a database. This means that the pages don't exist until someone asks for them. If you have 10,000 products, you're not going to build 10,000 individual pages by hand. Instead, you use a content management system to build it dynamically on the fly. A CMS actually generates the page that a search engine spiders by taking the information in your database and plugging it into a template Web page, so the CMS is responsible for creating all of the tags, content, and code that search engines see.

The most important thing you need in order to have a dynamic site, and we really *cannot* stress this enough, is to have an SEO-friendly CMS. Any CMS that supports SEO completely allows you to access and edit these tags as well as to set rules for generating tags that are SEO friendly. That means that you can focus on the content on your Web site. That content is what builds the page that the user sees. You need to be able to make changes to the H# tags and control the metadata on each page separately. *Every* element must be customizable.

If you cannot customize your current CMS, get a new one. End of story. If you can't write a `Title` tag individually, you're out of luck when it comes to SEO. If you can't control your `H1` tag, you're out of luck. Chuck your inflexible CMS and get one that allows you to control page tags and content; otherwise, you can't do *any* of the SEO we've been talking about. PixelSilk from Smart Solutions is a low-cost CMS that was designed from the ground up to be SEO-friendly. For simple Web sites, you could use a blogging software like the highly customizable WordPress, which is a free and open source.

Keep this list in mind when searching for a good CMS. They must be able to

✦ Customize HTML templates

✦ Produce unique `Title` tags

✦ Produce unique `Meta` description/keywords tags

✦ Produce unique `Heading` tags (H#)

✦ Categorize content by groups

Develop a Design Procedure

Developing a design procedure for your Web site is also important. Keeping a procedure the same through all parts of the design process helps you if something goes wrong. If your design procedure is a set procedure, it's easier to pinpoint where the goof-up happened and fix it.

When developing a design procedure, create a style guide for your Web site conventions and best practices. If you use a template style guide, all images are named the same way, like with periods for spaces, and they are all saved under the same file. All videos are named in a standard way and go in their own folder, and so on. This prevents confusion down the line.

If you have a design team, make sure they're all on board with the style guide and that any newbies you bring in are trained to follow it. Also make sure it's a procedure that everyone can follow. Sure, it may all make sense in your head, but it needs to make sense to everyone else, too. (Besides, don't be too sure that what makes sense to you now will make sense to you in six months.) Document every last bit of your procedure, and if you have the resources, hire a technical writer to take it all down and rework it so that it's understandable for everyone else.

Here's a handy checklist for things you should be keeping in mind when you're coming up with the standard design procedure for your Web site:

✦ Know what your site is about

✦ Know your page themes

✦ Know the major categories/silos

✦ Know the subcategories

✦ Know your keywords and how you research and choose them

✦ Know whether or not your site is e-commerce, research-oriented, or both

✦ Know how you arrange your files

✦ Have a set standard for naming files

✦ Have a set standard for naming `Title` tags

✦ Keep track of all of your titles and headings in order to avoid redundancy

✦ Know the color scheme, fonts used, and the visual standard

Having a set standard in place before you start also helps to keep the process as quick as possible and results in the least amount of headaches for everyone involved. It also makes doing your SEO much easier because you don't have to waste time redefining your goal with every single page edit.

Chapter 2: Building an SEO-Friendly Site

In This Chapter

✔ Designing your Web site to be SEO-friendly

✔ Creating a style that attracts your targeted audience

✔ Planning your site navigation

✔ Implementing a search within your Web site

✔ Incorporating interactive media to enhance your search engine rankings

✔ Creating pages that convert

*I*n this chapter, you find out how to design Web sites with search engine marketing in mind. For many sites, search engine ranking is viewed as a part of the launch, but not as a part of the design. If you are fortunate enough to be newly building your Web site, you can construct it with search engine friendliness from the ground up. It's more likely, however, that your site already resides on the Web. Search engine optimization (SEO) is a new phase of your site's development, but it's better late than never. This chapter contains many rules of thumb that can help you design — or retrofit — a site to be SEO friendly.

Preplanning and Organizing your Site

As we covered in the last chapter, you should start your SEO planning by inventorying your assets. What do you have that can possibly enhance your Web site? List all of your potential assets, not just those that are already online. Be creative and very open-minded at this point. Take stock of all of the following:

✦ Written materials you or your company has produced — brochures, catalogs, articles, user manuals, tutorials, online help, customer correspondence, and so on.

✦ Videos of interviews, television spots, commercials, award acceptances, speeches, company events, or other.

✦ Audio recordings of radio interviews, original music, or other.

✦ Photos of products, people, events, buildings, properties, or other.

✦ Images that go along with your products and services, such as logos, statistical charts, diagrams, illustrations, and so on.

The items you gather may become site assets, but for now they're just ingredients waiting to be used. Looking to the materials your business produces outside your current Web site, you can probably find a lot of original content that, with a small amount of reformatting or updating, could enrich your online site.

To help you decide which elements to put on what pages, you need a combination of research and planning. The research half involves keyword research (covered in Book II) and competitor research (covered in Book III) — activities that give you lots of guidelines for your SEO work. The types of guidelines you may come up with through research include

✦ Your site's main purpose (research, e-commerce, or a mix of both)

✦ Your site's main keywords

✦ How much content you need to be competitive

✦ What kinds of content you need

✦ Which existing pages already rank well (so you don't want to change them)

✦ How your site should be organized to best compete in your Internet market

Armed with this research, you are ready to enter the planning stage. Based on the guidelines you developed, you can determine what areas of your Web site need work. Or if you're building your site from scratch, you can lay out a big-picture site plan like a storyboard or a flow chart. Put your ideas for each page on paper. This organized approach lets you pair up items from your inventory of available content with your site's needs and move through the planning stage.

Designing Spider-Friendly Code

Whether you're writing your own HTML or hiring a Webmaster to do it for you, you want to keep your site's underlying code spider-friendly. Basically, you need to streamline your site's code so that the search engine spiders have an easy time crawling your pages and figuring out what the pages are about. You do this by keeping the code as clean as possible. We covered this in the last chapter, but just as a reminder, for search engine optimization (SEO), here are some coding best practices:

✦ Use an external Cascading Style Sheet (CSS) file to define the look of your Web site.

✦ Use an external .JS file to hold any JavaScript code you plan to use.

✦ Use as little inline *markup* (formatting and other types of on-the-fly HTML codes, such as Font tags to define the font style, and so on) as possible.

Creating a CSS file gives you a source from which to control the look of your entire Web site. In your CSS file, you can define, for instance, that all H1 headings should be Arial, size 3, bold, navy blue, and centered. Next week, if you change your mind and decide to make your headings purple instead, you can simply edit the definitions for your H1 style in your CSS file and viola — every H1 heading throughout your entire site is now purple. That's a lot more efficient than going page by page through your site, manually updating every instance of an H1 tag, and it eliminates the risk that you'll miss one.

Not only is an external CSS efficient, but it also provides a few other big advantages. Having a CSS file allows you to remove inline formatting such as font tags from your page content and instead insert a CSS tag identifying what style to apply. The result is much less HTML code cluttering your pages and significantly less page complexity. Less code means smaller file sizes. Smaller file sizes mean your pages load faster for your site visitors, and the search engine spiders have less junk to wade through as they read your text. It's a win/win/win for all involved!

If your site incorporates JavaScript, you want to externalize it as well, for similar reasons. Move the JavaScript off your individual Web pages and into a separate .JS file. Then your pages can include a single line of code that *calls* (that is, instructs the browser and spiders that the information in the file should be used in reference to the content on the page) to the JavaScript file, rather than tons of code on the page. Because JavaScript code can get really long and cumbersome, this decision alone may cut the size of a Web page in half. Less code makes for spider-friendly pages with uncluttered text and clear themes.

One online business implemented just these two best practices on their Web site, creating external files for their JavaScript and using CSS, and they reduced 20,000 lines of code to just 1,500. The keyword-rich content rose to the top of the page, and along with it their site's rankings across their keyword terms in the search results.

Creating a Theme and Style

When it comes to design styles, people tend to have certain expectations about what's appropriate. Elegant restaurants don't seat people at tables with plastic chairs and red, yellow, and blue toy blocks for decoration. Neither do preschools decorate their rooms with Persian rugs and neutral colors. A typical business designs for their intended audience, so assessing who makes up their target audience is one of the first things they have to do. Online businesses should be no different, but many Web sites overlook this step in their zeal to just "attract visitors, lots of visitors!"

Knowing what *kind* of visitor you want to attract influences lots of style decisions. It helps you make these types of design decisions:

✦ A color palette for the site

✦ The kinds of photos and graphics to include

✦ An appropriate reading level for your audience, including the complexity of the words and sentence structures

✦ The best tone to use when writing

✦ Font and layout choices that appeal to your target audience

✦ The complexity (or simplicity) of information to include

✦ The number of fun or interactive elements your site needs

✦ How "flashy" your site needs to be to attract and hold your audience

If you know the type of visitor you want, you can design your Web site to attract and hold those people's interest once they arrive. When we say *design*, we don't just mean the cosmetic look and feel, but also the site's voice and themes. Your site's main theme should be a focused idea of what your site is all about, using terms and keywords that match how your audience searches. For instance, if you have a business that customizes people's classic cars, your main site theme is classic car customization. We cover assigning keywords and themes more in Book II, Chapter 4, but basically, after you've determined your main site theme, you can organize your content into categories and subcategories (that is, subtopics under the main site theme) and choose a specific primary keyword for each one. Every category-plus-keyword pair should have its own landing page within your Web site, so that people searching for those keywords can click your listing and arrive at a page that's specifically relevant to their search query. (A *landing page* is the particular Web page a user comes to when clicking a link.)

So far, we've talked about theme in reference to the keywords and information your Web site provides. The site's theme is what the whole site is about; each page's theme is a subtopic and has content and keywords focused on that subtopic. Frequently, the word *theme* also applies to the design theme, or the look and feel of a Web site. Keep in mind that the design theme a Web designer creates must integrate with the site's main content theme and be right for the target audience. They're all interrelated.

A design theme for a Web site needs to support the site's main theme. For example, if you have a Web site that offers dog kennel franchises, the design theme needs to include dog-related graphics in the same way the text talks about dogs. Similarly, the overall look needs to appeal to your target audience, just as the text should be tailored to dog-loving entrepreneurial adults. If you do market research to further narrow your target audience, you can make the site even better. Look at your current customers to determine what type of person tends to convert from a window-shopper to a customer. For instance, if it's usually women who become dog kennel franchisees, you can modify your site theme to appeal more to women. If it's usually married couples who go into the dog kennel business, by all means, include text references to this as well as images of happy couples watching over lots of tail-wagging pooches.

Writing Rich Text Content

People do read, especially online. "Content is king" is a frequently stated maxim of Internet marketing experts because it's true. To have a successful Web site, you need lots and lots of content on your pages. How much content do you need? The answer depends somewhat on what is normal for your industry. When you research the sites that rank well for your keywords, some of the things you want to find out are how many indexed pages they have, as well as the quantity, quality, and structure of the keyword content on the high-ranking pages competing with yours. (Note that Book III explains how to do competitive research in detail.) When you know what level of content is currently succeeding in the search results pages for your keywords as an average, you get an idea of how many pages and words you need in order to play in their league.

We recommend that you have a minimum of 450 words of text content per page. That's a general rule, based on all of our experience helping companies do SEO. If that sounds like a lot to write per page, think about it this way: The page that you're reading right now has about 450 words on it. Fewer than 450 words makes it hard to convince the engines that you're a subject-matter expert. In fact, depending on the industry and keyword, 450 might still be too few. The SEO industry averages around 1,000 words per page and this is true of other industries as well. Still, 450 is a good initial target number.

Writing that much text for every page might sound like a daunting task, but keep in mind how it can help you:

+ **Expertise goes up:** Search engines look for a site's expertise about a subject, and having a greater amount of relevant text signals that your Web page is a subject-matter expert.

+ **Trust factor goes up:** Users coming to your landing pages stay longer and trust it as more of an expert source if there's more content for them to read that matches their query.

+ **Keyword relevancy goes up:** Long pages give you more opportunities to use your keywords without overusing them and creating spam.

+ **Depth of content:** Multiple pages built around the same theme allow you to capitalize on niche and Long-Tail keywords that support your main keywords.

The second main principle you should know about text content is this: In addition to needing lots of text on your site, you also want that text to be focused. Search engines (and users, for that matter) come to a Web page seeking something specific. You want the content of each page to be focused on its keyword theme. This makes the page relevant to the user's search query.

Making each page's content relevant and focused helps the page rise in the search engine rankings. This concept ties into *siloing*, which is the process of organizing your site themes and content into categories and subcategories, each with its own main keyword. (You can read a full explanation of siloing in Book IV, Chapter 4.) For example, in your dog kennel franchise Web site, you might have a page focused on how much expected revenue a franchise can generate. In your more than 450 words of content, you wouldn't want to include a discussion of different dog food brands or grooming techniques. Including non-focused content like that would only dilute the content of your page. Instead, you want to have lots of information about kennel rates, expected monthly revenues, and revenue-related content.

For lots more in-depth recommendations, tips and guidelines on writing good content, see Book V.

Planning Your Navigation Elements

Navigation elements make up the roads and highways of your Web site. They're the transportation system that can help people move smoothly from place to place, following clear signposts through well-marked paths. On the other hand, a Web site's navigation can make people frustrated and hopelessly lost, causing them to press the first Back button and get out of town.

If you create a good navigation plan right from the start, it's easy for site visitors and search engine spiders alike to move around your site. In fact, if your site doesn't have a good navigation system, it's unlikely that the search engines can thoroughly index your site. Sites with a clear directory structure, siloed content, and easy-to-follow navigation are at an advantage over sites without these foundational elements.

For maximum readability to the search engines, you want to make your navigation elements text links. That said, there are ways to help the search engines read non-text navigation elements (such as Flash or image mapping), which we get into in Book IV, Chapter 3. Nevertheless, you're going to get the cleanest, best read from simple text link navigation.

Figure 2-1 shows a sketch of a typical Web page's navigation plan: It has three basic areas for navigation links: top, bottom, and side (either right or left, with left being more common). We explain what the differences are at an initial design level, so you can evaluate what you're currently doing for site navigation if your site is already in public use. If your site is still in the design phase, you can start planning how you'll build your navigation. (Note that we go into depth on navigation in Chapter 4 of Book IV.)

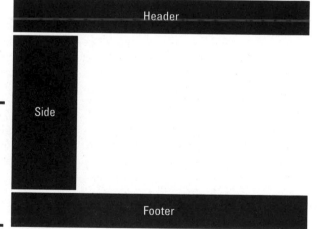

Figure 2-1: The three basic areas for navigation links on a Web page.

Don't be tempted to use frames to create your navigation, unless you don't want the spiders following those links. When you put content inside a frame, spiders see it as its own separate page, so it can't be indexed as part of the current page's content. Frames split up a page and remove all the association of your navigation to your content for the search engines.

Top navigation

Top navigation simply refers to the links at the top of the page. Usually these are the "pretty" ones, the ones you want people to notice and use to get to the main sections of your site. Also called "global" navigation, top links often display site-wide, showing up conveniently on every page. Links commonly found in your top navigation include

✦ **Home page:** A link to the home page is required for good site navigation (though it shouldn't be labeled *Home* — more on that in a second).

✦ **About Us:** You want to provide easy access to information on who owns/ operates the Web site. This gives credibility to your site both in a site visitor's eyes and to a search engine. An About Us link usually goes at the far right end of your top navigation.

✦ **Contact Us:** A link to a contact information page also gives you credibility, not to mention customer service points! Some sites don't have room for this in the top navigation, so alternatively you can include the contact info on your About Us page.

✦ **Category/theme-specific links:** Include other links that give quick access to your main site categories.

Although these are common elements in the top navigation, they're not necessarily items that *you* want to have dominate your top navigation — it depends on your business strategy. For example, the About Us page and Contact Us page don't necessarily do anything to enhance your overall site theme.

Good labels are critical. Because your global navigation appears throughout your site, the *anchor text* of every link (which is the text label of the link, or what people click) carries a lot of weight. *Internal links* (links on your own site going to other pages within your site) still count with the search engines and contribute to your link equity.

Because anchor text must be relevant to count toward your link equity, you want to make sure that your navigation elements contain meaningful keywords so that you can profit from all those links. (*Link equity* refers to assigning expertise and authority to a Web page based on the number of links leading to it. We cover this in more detail in Book VI, but it's an important ranking factor with all the search engines.)

Why shouldn't your Home page be simply called Home? We know of a window blinds company that radically improved their search engine ranking simply by changing their global navigation link from Home to Window Blinds. Within days, their Web page jumped from the third to the first page of the search results for the keyword [window blinds] after this one simple change.

Footer navigation

Footer navigation refers to the navigational links at the bottom of a Web page. Because search engines crawl all the way through a page, you can take advantage of another prime chance to show your keywords and increase your site's navigation and usability. Sites that have top navigation elements in Flash or images should use this chance to restate all those links in search-engine friendly text at the bottom of the page. Footer navigation usually appears in a less conspicuous font, not trying to attract attention and simply offering a service to anyone who goes looking for more links to global topics. The footer is not the place for a link to every single page on your site, nor is it the place for links to pages outside of your site: Those honors belong to your site map and resource page, respectively. The footer should include links to the pages linked in your top navigation as well as any additional user friendly pages that weren't important enough to be in your main navigation, such as your privacy policy, your Contact Us page, and industry affiliations like the Better Business Bureau.

Your footer navigation generally should include

✦ **Top navigation links (again):** You want to repeat all the links that are in your top, global navigation if your top navigation is in Flash or JavaScript and therefore not spiderable. Consider using anchor text that is more descriptive.

✦ **Contact Us:** You definitely want a link here to your contact information (especially if you left it out of your top navigation). This is good business practice so that people can contact you, but it also makes tons of sense for SEO. Local businesses that let spiders freely crawl all over their physical business address could wind up in local search results, too.

✦ **Physical address:** Include your physical address and local telephone number in your footer, especially if you're targeting local business. Both search engines and visitors use street addresses as a way to verify that you're a real business and not merely a scammer.

✦ **Legal stuff:** We recommend you include a privacy policy, copyright, and terms of use (if appropriate). These can be separate links in your footer even if they all go to the same legal-content page. You definitely want a privacy policy and copyright for your site — search engines look for these links because they help confirm that you are a "real" company with accountability. Your trust factor increases, both with the public and the search engines, and because they can simply be inconspicuously placed at the bottom of each page, there's no reason not to do it.

✦ **Site map:** Include a link to your HTML site map to help the search engines and your users find their way to every bit of your content.

✦ **Link magnets:** If you have any piece of content that you're particularly known for, or that people often come looking for on your site, providing a link there on every page of your site will satisfy users and ensure that search engines consider it a significant page.

Side navigation

Side navigation elements typically include category-specific links. Side navigation is context-sensitive: The links vary from page to page. This helps with siloing because you can reinforce the landing page's theme by including links to supporting pages. You can put these links in a table cell along the side of your page.

Implementing a Site Search

Many sites offer a Search box right on their Web pages that lets users search for information within the Web site (see the example in Figure 2-2).

Search box

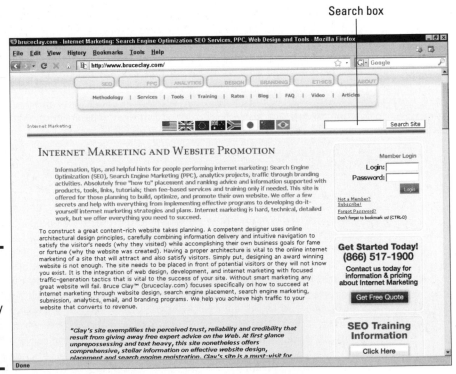

Figure 2-2: A site search offers a way to search within the site.

Site searches are essential if your Web site has tons of pages, such as for a magazine with years of archived issues, a large store with thousands of products, or other extensive amounts of content. Smaller sites might also want a site search, but this decision should be made carefully. If you're thinking of adding a site search, consider the benefits and the potential drawbacks and be sure to implement a site search that's effectively customized for your site.

The two major benefits of implementing a site search are

✦ **Improving usability:** Ideally, a site search should improve usability and user retention. If your site search helps people find what they're looking for after coming to your site, it's doing good. For example, a site search is essential for a shopping site such as Target's site (www.target.com), which tries to keep users within the store after they arrive. Say a user comes to the Target site after running a Google search for [snow shovels]. If the user next wants to find [tire chains], Target's handy search function offers a quick way to find more products, add them to the same cart, and check out one time. The user gets better convenience, and the Web site keeps a customer and increases its revenue.

✦ **Providing direct user feedback:** A site search provides you with a cache of valuable information. Your visitors leave a trail that tells you what they want in their own words. It's perfect as a feedback tool — users come to you and type in exactly what they're looking for. By tracking all of these searches and the user experience following each one, you can identify weaknesses in your site processes, keywords you may have overlooked, pages of content you need to add, and also what's working successfully or not working at all.

The main drawback of a site search occurs when it does not improve usability. Many site searches fail to provide what the user is looking for and become a side door where many visitors exit. You don't want to confuse and lose your site visitors by giving them a technical tool that doesn't perform as expected. So examine your Web site carefully in order to determine whether the risk is worth it. If you have clear navigation and well-organized content, you might be better off letting users find their way around rather than giving them a shortcut to nowhere.

If you do decide to implement a site search, be sure to do it right. You want your site search to control the selection and presentation of results to make sure you've maximized the opportunity to give users what they need. When done well, an effective site search can prevent site abandonment and eliminate the multitude of brief, one-time visitors. It can guide users along the conversion path, getting them hooked along the way and encouraging them to explore. To make sure, watch your site analytics closely after you deploy a site search to see whether it's routing people well or causing them to take the nearest exit.

To be effective, your site search must be paired with good navigation and a well-siloed site. This combination is key to giving the user a good experience and to developing the relationship between your brand and the customer. Here are some tips for maximizing your site search on an e-commerce site:

✦ List all major product categories and subcategories on your home page for easy navigation. If you have more than 99 categories, consider multiple pages so you stay within Google's Quality guidelines of less than 100 links per page.

✦ Put a free form site search box on every page with content that can lead to further searches. Like Google search, this is a box where anything can be typed and get a potential answer.

✦ Implement guided search queries, where a user selects from a rigid predetermined list to help narrow their search.

 • Provide site search for items by brand, price, color, sale, and so on.

 • Provide site search for featured products in every category.

 • Include every brand in every category in your site search database.

 • Include bestsellers in every category.

In some cases, your site may require separate search capabilities, or you may have to choose which kinds of search to offer. The same underlying principles apply to non-e-commerce sites. Allow the site search to find your information in a variety of ways, broken down by lots of different categories, subcategories, and cross-categories. You want to give users many ways to get results, and avoid search failure.

There are many free or inexpensive site search kits you can use to incorporate a vertical search into your Web site. Google offers a site search option at http://www.google.com/sitesearch/ that's easy to get started with and fairly inexpensive. Another way to go is to buy a behavioral search engine that tracks user actions and customizes the results per individual. Collarity (www.collarity.com) is an example of this type of search engine. Paired with the free Google Analytics tool, any site search offers a good way to track user queries. Check out Book VIII for more on analytics in general, Book VIII, Chapter 3 covers Google Analytics in more detail.

Incorporating Engagement Objects into Your Site

It's a good practice to include *engagement objects* on your Web site. By *engagement objects*, we mean any type of interactive media object that gets users excited and offers them a way to connect to the content. This section specifically covers video and audio files. Including these types of rich media makes your Web site appear technically advanced to both users and search engines and engages your visitors.

Incorporating engagement objects into your Web site can also improve your search engine rankings. The reason is because of a concept called *blended search*, which is the mixing of different types of content in the search results. For instance, if you search on Google for [classic Ford Mustang], Google may include more than just Web page links in your results. You might see photographs of restored Ford Mustangs at the top of your results page. Also mingled into the listings you might find a video link to a recent classic car show featuring Ford Mustangs. You might find a news article about a classic Ford Mustang that was the getaway car in a recent heist. Or you might find listings of classic car shops and other local businesses in your city that specialize in Ford Mustangs. Mixed in with these you would also see the top-ranked Web pages for the keyword phrase that you entered. Now that there's blended search, the search engines show whatever types of files they determine to be the most relevant results. (As a side note, Google calls their blended search product Universal Search, and many in the search engine marketing community use that name to refer to all engines' blended search offerings.)

The concept of blending different types of files within a single search results set has raised the value of putting media on your Web site. Some ranking factors have to do with what interactive media you have on your site. You want your site to get in on this action! You may find that just by adding some engagement objects to your Web site, your rank increases, especially if your competitors aren't currently using any on their sites. At the very least, you have an opportunity to satisfy the visitors better than your competition.

Embedding interactive files the SEO-friendly way

Some sites offer video or audio files by displaying them in a separate pop-up window with no text. This has some value for visitors, but because search engines can't do much to understand the contents of a video or audio file, and because the pop-up window doesn't provide the spiders with any context that would help them understand the media's contents, the site has missed a valuable opportunity to enhance its keyword relevance with this great content.

A better way to handle video and audio files is to embed them right into your Web pages. Let the video play from right on the Web page that also includes descriptive text about the video. Give users a hyperlink to let them hear an audio clip of a Ford Mustang engine on your Ford Mustang landing page, and let the anchor text and the sentences in the code surrounding the image help to support your page's keyword relevance. Some files, like MP3 that contain clean narrative, can be indexed by the searches, but this isn't perfect. The key to including video and audio files effectively is to place them in proximity from a code view to on-topic text that the search engines can read.

Video

You can include videos on your Web pages if they're relevant to your topic. Basically, anything that can be shown in a short video that is relevant to your Web page could be used: Just make sure it's ethical and within acceptable standards for your industry. If you can, you should always be hosting your videos on your site. You can upload them to YouTube as well, but it's your content and you should have it on your site. The possibilities are endless, but here are some examples of videos you might include, just to give you some ideas:

✦ **Product demo:** Include a small video demonstrating your product or service's features and benefits. You can do this in a straightforward way or comically. For example, the Blendtec blender company uses video extremely effectively by showing videos of its product pulverizing things you'd never think to put in a blender (a shoe, an iPhone, and so on). The engaging videos alone have attracted thousands of interested buyers to the site (www.willitblend.com/), and have become a viral Internet phenomenon in their own right.

✦ **Speech:** If you or someone notable from your company speaks in public, you could capture a digital video of an appropriate speech. Just a snippet might be enough.

✦ **Tour:** A video can be a tremendously effective tour guide. Show off your company building, impressive equipment, state-of-the-art facilities, or beautiful location — just pick something that can be well shown through a short video.

✦ **Interview:** You could interview one of your own personnel to give site visitors a "face-to-face" greeting, introduce one of your executives, or just give a video update of something newsworthy for your business. Alternatively, you could do a brief customer interview and post a live testimonial about your product or service.

Compression rates on the Internet mean that to keep file sizes down, you often have to sacrifice video quality for speed. Put your money into making sure that the audio is crisp and clean. When it comes to quality, studies have shown that as long as the audio is decent, users will watch a video even if the picture quality is lacking. For more tips on the technical aspects of uploading videos to your site, see Book V, Chapter 2.

Audio

We confess that Web sites that greet their visitors with audio blaring really annoy us! From a usability perspective, making every person who comes to your site scramble to find their volume control buttons and do damage control with whomever may have heard their computer erupting in sound is a bad idea. You definitely want to avoid that. With that disclaimer made, we want to explain the *appropriate* use of sound files. Because in the world of SEO, embedding an audio file or offering a podcast carries weight with the search engines — not to mention users.

Consider what types of audio files you might offer in your site. Some ideas include

✦ **Sounds:** If your site has anything to do with nature, consider offering nature sounds (waterfall, mockingbird calls, hyenas whooping, and so on). You could demonstrate how quiet your product is by recording its noise compared to, say, a roomful of football fans after a touchdown play. Or, you could use on-topic recordings of bells ringing, trains whistling, tires screeching . . . this list is going downhill fast, but you get the idea.

✦ **Music:** We suggest that you include music on your site only if your site is about music. (Background music for the sake of ambiance alone can be annoying, but as long as you default it to off and offer a volume control, it could be effective.) If you're a recording artist, by all means, include lots of links to your music and make sure to include keyword-rich song titles in the anchor text.

✦ **Speaking:** You could include a recording of a presentation, speech, sermon, training, poetry reading, or other public speaking event that's relevant to your page topic and keywords. This makes for excellent SEO-friendly content.

✦ **Interviews:** A Q&A session with one of your own staff or a notable person in your industry could be recorded and offered on your Web site. If you hire a new executive, consider interviewing her talk-show–style as an introduction that you can post on your Web site.

✦ **Podcasts:** To make your site even more advanced, host a podcast that site visitors can subscribe to. With a *podcast*, users can download digital audio recordings of a radio show or other type of regular program and listen to it on an iPod or other device. These are great for lessons, weekly recaps, radio shows, or even mixes of your favorite music with some commentary sprinkled in.

**Book IV
Chapter 2**

Building an SEO-Friendly Site

From an SEO perspective, there's a right way and a wrong way to add video and audio files to your Web site. You can read our specific recommendations for keeping your audio and video files SEO-compliant and user-friendly in Book V, Chapter 2.

Allowing for Expansion

When you're building your Web site, remember to allow for future expansion. A Web site is never "finished" any more than a business can ever set itself in stone. To be successful, especially in online marketing, you must stay flexible and allow room for growth — including on your Web site.

Database engineers have to think about future growth when they create a new database structure. They do not want to be in a position where the entire database needs to be torn apart and rebuilt simply because it cannot accommodate adding another layer of storage. Similarly, you don't want to box yourself in when it comes to your site design. To some extent, you can foresee future needs and plan ahead logically. Think about

✦ **New products or services:** Try to predict what types of add-on product lines or services may come down the pike and need to be added to your site.

✦ **Expanded content:** You've read how important it is to have lots of content supporting your keywords, so try to identify where you have content holes that need to be filled with new pages of supporting information.

✦ **Enhanced features:** If you'd like to someday enrich your site by starting a blog or other interactive community feature, envision how this might fit into your site.

Despite your best efforts, however, you probably cannot predict all the changes coming in the future. For this reason, you want to keep your Web site design, navigation, structure, and even name somewhat open. For example, a business called George's Ford-Only Customization Shop has prevented itself right away from ever being able to expand to Chevrolets. Similarly, you wouldn't want your Web site's domain name to be restrictively specific. Today, your business might be all about repairing truck fenders, but if you choose the domain name www.truckfenderwork.com, you'd be stuck having to create a new URL if you want to expand your business to work on all-body work or on cars as well as trucks.

Because constant growth is the rule, you want to make your Web site structure modular. We cover the concept of *siloing* in Chapter 4, which involves breaking your Web site content into categories based on keywords. A proper silo structure allows you to add new silos without breaking your site's current linking architecture or navigation system. You can simply snap on another silo adjacent to the existing ones at the same structural level.

Developing an Update Procedure

You may be a one-man shop now or the only person in your company's Web development department, like the Lone Ranger working to save the day. Or you might be part of a large team developing a voluminous Web site. Whatever your situation is today, the fact is that it will change. People may leave the company, you could be transferred, and new people could be hired. To survive the personnel changes that inevitably happen, your Web site must have a documented update procedure.

In the previous chapter, we covered creating a design procedure that functions as a style guide for your Web site. Here, we want to help you expand that document to cover an update procedure, as well. You've done the research to know what your site needs in terms of SEO. If you don't write down guidelines related to search engine optimization and include them in a style guide that new Webmasters, IT staff, marketing directors, and others can refer to, all of your SEO progress could be lost. After all, without an education in SEO best practices, and without knowing how to do site analysis and competitive research (as you find out how to do in this book), people can make Web site decisions that drop them right out of the search engine rankings. We've seen it happen.

Write down your update procedures, including your SEO dos and don'ts, to lay out the blueprint for others to follow. Make them as exhaustive as possible. To get you started, some items to cover in your style guide and site update procedure would be

+ **File naming:** Specify how you name new pages, images, videos, audio files, and so on. You probably have developed syntax for these things, so you want to write down those standards. (We cover good file naming in Book IV, Chapter 1.)

+ **Directory structure:** How you name and structure your file folders should also be documented so that when someone creates a new silo or wants to add a new picture, they know how to do it.

✦ **Redirects:** Document what your procedure is for redirecting traffic away from a no-longer-needed page. Because there are several types of HTML redirect codes and only a 301 redirect is good practice for SEO, instructions could help prevent a costly mistake. (For more information on redirects, see Book VII, Chapter 3.)

✦ **Linking:** You want to be sure to cover your procedure for adding new links. Explain why anchor text must contain relevant keywords (never just Click Here) and give guidelines for linking within silos, not between them, as a general rule. You may want to cover linking very thoroughly because it's so important to SEO — you can find lots more information on good linking strategies in Chapter 4, as well as the rest of Book VI.

✦ **New pages:** Your procedure for adding a new page to your site should ask some critical questions, such as: What goal does this page meet? Does it fit into the silo? What are its main keywords? Whoever sets up the new page should be able to write down answers to these questions. In addition, because there are a number of things that must be carefully reviewed before a new page goes live, a checklist is helpful. Your new-page checklist should contain all the steps needed to make sure that the page is SEO-friendly and ready for the public. We suggest you start with the sample checklist we included in Book I, Chapter 1, and adapt it for your site.

Balancing Usability and Conversion

This chapter is all about building an SEO-friendly site. However, we aren't recommending that you design a Web site just for the search engines. Your SEO goal must be *balanced* with the need to create a user-friendly site. Unless you balance SEO-friendliness (to help people find your site) with user-friendliness (to make people want to stay there), you won't be able to achieve your true objective, which is conversion.

Conversion refers to whatever action you want your site visitors to take. That may be buying something, joining a group, signing up for a newsletter, registering for a seminar, filling out a survey, or just visiting more pages. Whatever your definition is for conversion, your real goal involves more than just generating traffic to your site's front door. When those people arrive, you want them to do something.

Usability and SEO working together

Usability refers to the way a person uses, or experiences, your Web site. Every few months, a familiar discussion resurfaces in the SEO community's forums, blogs, and newsgroups: When you are designing a Web site, who should you be targeting, the search engines or the humans? Which should take precedence in your site design, and how do you serve both? Luckily, balancing these complementary needs is not as complicated as it seems. Search engine optimization and usability can work hand in hand. In fact, many of the things that are good for search engines benefit human visitors as well.

Some marketers are adamant that usability take priority over SEO, arguing that an unusable Web site can be at the top of the search engine results pages and still never make money. The reverse is pointed out as well — search engine optimization has to come first because the most perfectly usable site in the world still has to have visitors who use it before it is worth anything.

The confusion arises because people commonly mistake what the goal of each approach really is and makes the assumption that the two are incompatible. In many people's minds, SEO advocates a complicated set of rules to follow, games to play, pages to write, links to attract, and hoops to jump through. Usability has also grown to complex proportions, incorporating the use of personas, *conversion funnels* (the path that a visitor takes to get to a conversion, most commonly a purchase) and psychology degrees in human factors. But if you strip away all of the ways in which both are done, their goals are remarkably similar. Search engine optimization is the process of designing a Web strategy that gives search engine spiders the best picture of the Web site possible. Usability is the process of designing a Web strategy that gives visitors the most satisfactory experience possible.

Although some techniques very clearly support either usability or search engine optimization — users simply don't care if your page is *W3C-compliant* (following HTML standards set by the W3C) as long as it loads properly in the browser, for example — the two objectives aren't often going to come into conflict. As long as you recognize that the ultimate goal is to maximize the potential of your Web site, the conflict remains minimal.

You need to focus first on the things that SEO and usability have in common and then put the rest into balance. SEO is about more than simply ranking well in the search engines. The key is to rank well in the search engines for the keywords that are *most* relevant. If your site is the most expert and best for your human visitors, your SEO campaign should be working to demonstrate that to the search engines. Table 2-1 lists a few examples of how improving the usability of your site often benefits your SEO campaign, as well.

Book IV
Chapter 2

Building an SEO-Friendly Site

Table 2-1	Usability Improvements Often Go Hand-In-Hand with SEO
Usability Improvement	*SEO Benefit*
Do research to find out where your target users are looking for you	Combines with keyword research
Develop each landing page so that it's well suited to help particular users based on their search query	Optimizes pages around specific keywords
Build a larger network of links coming from external Web pages so that more people can find your site	Increases the perception to the search engines that your site is an expert and raises your link equity
Discern where your target audience "lives" online when they aren't on your site	Identifies where you need to be getting links because chances are, those sites are relevant
Make your site navigation clear and easy to travel for users	Also allows search engine spiders to get around your site more easily
Write clean copy that states exactly what you offer visitors	Helps search engines determine what each page is about
Use clarifying words so that your terms make sense in context	Helps search engines understand what queries are relevant to your pages
Put your site on a fast, stable server to provide good site performance to users	Speeds the search engine spiders along their way
Create user-friendly error screens that explain the problem and give users links to other options when a page can't be displayed	Optimizes the 404 Page Can Not Be Displayed error page and redirected pages so that search engines can move through them easily to functioning pages on your site

So when you consider your visitors' needs in order to boost your site's usability, the nice part is that you also usually support your SEO efforts. But what if there are conflicts? If the best way to serve your visitors seems to go against SEO best practices, there probably is a way to compensate.

We've found that there is nearly always a technical solution for achieving SEO, no matter what the site owner is trying to accomplish. Here are two scenarios where the site's usability objectives needed a technical solution for SEO:

✦ **Basic example:** A Web designer wants to use a single image as the entire home page of a site. Knowing that search engines need to find content in order for that page to rank, you as the SEO consultant can use HTML to put content into the page, remove any words from the graphic and reset them as text, and use a .CSS file to position the elements and give style to the page.

✦ **A more complicated example:** To provide the kind of content its users need, a site uses query strings to dynamically build the page from a database rather than the page being static. To help optimize that site for search engines, a technical solution could involve renaming directories so that the URL of each page contains meaningful keywords and a link structure is implemented to assure crawlability; as a result, the search engine spiders can see what the site is about based on its well-labeled physical directory structure.

So between usability and SEO, which is more important to your Web site's success? The answer is that they're both equally necessary and, thankfully, can work hand in hand. Build your site for *all* of your visitors, human and spider alike. Instead of taking the approach that one or the other is sufficient, realize that by doing them in tandem, your Web site can be stronger, easier to navigate, more accessible to your target audience, and can generate more conversions.

Go for conversions as your main target. As you monitor your site traffic and conversions, you may notice a strange phenomenon: Sometimes being number three or four or five on the search results page is better than number one. Sure, you get far more traffic in position one, but consider a typical scenario. Say a woman wants to buy a pair of designer shoes. She searches for the designer name and [shoes] and then begins clicking through the results. At the first Web site, she looks around and finds a pair she likes, but she doesn't purchase them because she isn't sure she's found the best style or the best price. She clicks the second, third, and fourth sites to continue her shopping and price comparisons. At the fourth site, she's done with price comparisons and has discovered that every site sells the shoes for the same price. She's now ready to buy, and clicks Add to Cart on site number four: Because she's already on the site, it's the most convenient place for her to make her purchase. So site number four wins the conversion. You have two choices: Be site number four, or be one of the first three sites that didn't secure the conversion and figure out why not. In this case, ranking number one might not get you the sale unless your site was a lean, mean, converting machine.

Creating pages that sell/convert

Most people come to a Web page and decide whether to stay there within the first three seconds. That means that you have only three seconds to convince someone that your page offers what they're looking for. For each of your landing pages, ask yourself questions such as

✦ **Curb appeal:** Is the site able to satisfy the intent of the query and is it appropriate to the visitor?

✦ **Impressions:** At first glance, what does my page seem to be about?

✦ **Focus:** Is it clear that this page is about the keyword?

✦ **Ease of use:** How easy is it to achieve the desired task?

✦ **More details:** Can a visitor easily access more detailed information if desired?

✦ **Conversion:** Can a visitor easily navigate to where a conversion can take place?

You also want to consider your goal for each page and see if you're achieving it. This differs from deciding what the keyword is for each page. For instance, you may have a landing page on your classic car customization Web site centered on the keyword [Chevrolet Camaros]; your text may be all about restoring classic Chevy Camaros; your images might depict classic Chevy Camaros; and so far, that's all good. But your goal for this page is a different issue. Your goal may be to get the user to click through to more pages on your Web site. Your goal may be to have the user download a coupon for a free tire rotation. Your goal may be to entice the user to set an appointment, make a phone call, order a service, make a purchase, or something else. In short, the page's goal can be measured in terms of what you want visitors to do while on this page.

To help determine each page's goal, ask yourself three questions about every page on your Web site that requires action (such as landing pages):

✦ **What:** What action is required?

✦ **Who:** Who must take that action?

✦ **How:** What information does the visitor need in order to know how to take the required action?

After you have each page's goal firmly in mind, usability really comes into play. Think of yourself as a professional usability expert for your Web site. You want to design your pages in a way that helps your site visitors successfully reach the goal. Don't just assume that you know what's best. Someone who knows the site and industry has a completely different opinion than a prospective user of the site. All the different needs and viewpoints of your potential audience should be explored. This is why if you have the budget for it, a professional usability expert can be worth her weight in gold.

For example, professional usability experts can help brick-and-mortar stores decide how to lay out their shelves for highest potential revenue. They can advise a bookstore owner that people tend to turn to the right when entering a store more often than they turn to the left, and the bookstore can apply this information by positioning a bestseller table to the right of the entry. Groccry stores are a great example of user psychology in action as well: You have to pass right through all the really tempting packaged goods, like doughnuts and chips, to get to the staple items, like milk and eggs, that are usually on your shopping list.

On your Web site, you want each of your landing pages to meet a particular goal. Often you want the landing page to work as a funnel, collecting visitors and sending them through to some other page on your site. For instance, an Add to Cart link near the product information is a fairly standard way to turn a window shopper into a customer, and if your site then displays a clear Proceed to Checkout or similar link, you can funnel the person to a page where they can make a purchase. If your site isn't about e-commerce, you still want to have clear signposts that lead visitors from each landing page to a conversion page. (Note: We cover more about conversion funnels in Book VIII, Chapter 2.)

Engineering a Web site for human interaction does not always follow common sense. There's a whole usability science about how to design Web pages for maximum return, and that's outside the scope of this book. If you want to research it, we recommend starting with the Web site UsabilityEffect (`www.usabilityeffect.com/`). The site owner, Kim Krause Berg, began in the field of SEO and then moved to a career in usability consulting, so she understands both sides. You can discover a lot from the articles and other resources on her site.

Keep in mind that all usability theories remain just that — theories — until proven through user testing. You might add a button that says Free Tire Rotation Coupon on your Web site's home page, but until you analyze how many times people click the button to download the coupon, you don't really know if it's an effective conversion device. You would also want to know whether adding the coupon link draws more traffic to your site, or alters your search engine ranking. To go a step further with your user testing, you might also try a few different versions of the button, varying its look or placement, and gather comparison data. However you approach it, you're going to want to prove your usability theories with some real-world testing.

Creating a strong call to action

Do your Web pages have a clear "call to action," enticing people to do whatever action the Web page requires? If not, this could explain a less-than-satisfactory conversion rate.

You need an effective call to action on any page where you want the user to do something. This goes back to knowing what your goal is for each page, whether it's to click through to another page, add an item to a shopping cart, or some other action. Because Web sites typically lose a percentage of people at every step along the way to conversion (known as *conversion dropoff*), you want their journey to be as direct and clear as possible.

The most effective calls to action make use of an imperative verb (like *Add* or *Sign Up* or *Create*) and a compelling benefit. Some of the very best calls to action are actually graphics or buttons that catch the visitor's eye but don't dilute your content with needless commercial language that could bias the search engines. If your site is research-oriented, you might want to obscure the words *Buy Now* by placing them into an image so that the search engines don't think that you're a retail site. This example could be from a business-to-business site. It's very motivating for an engineer seeking this type of solution:

```
Attend our Web cast "Process Excellence for Supply Chain
Management" and learn how to reduce costs with our
process-driven approach to align business practices within
your organization.
```

Your call to action must tell visitors exactly what you want them to do. If you want them to buy your product, you could scatter multiple calls to action in strategic places within your copy, telling them how to do it (such as `Click here to buy Brand X now`). If you want them to contact you by phone, list your phone number and provide instructions ("Call us Monday–Friday from 8–5 PST at 1-866-517-1900"). Repeat the number in bold text throughout your copy and again at the end. But be wary of spamming the page. Repeating your call to action only works if you don't annoy the visitor.

You should use meaningful words in the anchor text of any call to action in order to reinforce why the user would want to do it. The anchor text can clarify why a user would click by incorporating keywords. For example, if you have links in your copy to sign up for your newsletter, include a brief description in every link like "Car Restoration Newsletter" rather than just "Sign up for our newsletter." Descriptive anchor text on your calls to action adds value for users and also helps build link equity for your site with the search engines.

You want to make sure that you're not inadvertently thwarting anyone from getting to the point of conversion with confusing messages, broken links, or other weaknesses in your site. This is where micro-management is appropriate — gather lots of site analytics from your IT department and closely examine how effective your conversion path is every step of the way. You need this to help you identify problems, and then test and improve, test and improve again, and then again — it's an ongoing process.

A strong call to action is critical, but it's just one factor that helps you achieve conversions. In the end, your conversion rate reflects your ability to persuade visitors to complete their intended actions from A to Z. It is a measure of your effectiveness and of customer satisfaction overall.

Book IV
Chapter 2

Building an SEO-Friendly Site

Chapter 3: Making Your Page Search Engine-Compatible

In This Chapter

✔ **Conquering HTML constructs**

✔ **Using clean code**

✔ **Designing with sIFR**

✔ **Externalizing code**

✔ **Validating HTML with W3C**

✔ **Choosing the right navigation**

✔ **Implementing the table trick**

✔ **Positioning with Div tags**

*I*n this chapter, you get down to the nitty-gritty stuff that makes your page stand on its own. In addition to worrying about links or content, you have to get the nuts and bolts right. Your SEO strategy is only as strong as its weakest link, so make sure that every part of the chain is forged as tough as you can make it. Attention to the small stuff pays off big-time in the long run.

Success with *on-page optimization,* the changing of the underlying code of a Web page for SEO reasons, isn't something that you can just guess at or just hope that you luck into. You need to understand every element of a Web page and use it to the fullest potential. Knowing how spiders are going to see and react to your page is absolutely critical to your optimization efforts. For example, mistakes with JavaScript can lead to a *spider trap,* where a spider gets caught in an endless loop and is forced to abandon the page because it has no other alternative. In this chapter, we cover the things that make your page search engine–friendly and what the biggest pitfalls are. Getting these elements right is essential if you're going to obtain and retain traffic and rankings in the long term.

In this chapter, we show you how to create clean, attractive HTML pages that properly render in the browser and give search engines a clear path to index the page and understand its value to their users. You discover how to write every part of your page, from your HTML code to your JavaScript and CSS, in a way that supports your ranking goals.

Optimizing HTML Constructs for Search Engines

At first, the Web was made up in great part by research papers posted by academics. They were formatted in a specific way and most of them were heavily text-based. These days, the Internet contains document types of every shape and size. Images, videos, Flash pages — you name it, someone's built it — and they all serve their purposes in the construction of a successful Web site. (You can find more about optimizing media content in the "Choosing the Right Navigation" section in this chapter and still more on video optimization in Book V, Chapter 2.) Nevertheless, when you get down to the basic structure for a Web page, you're still looking at HTML.

HTML pages are the building blocks of your Web site, so it's worth it to take the time to construct them well. Unlike humans, search engines evaluate pages based on the code. Because search engines cannot understand images or similar content forms, that content is invisible to them, leaving them to only see the content in the text of an HTML page. You want to write your code so that it will be very easy for spiders to understand. You don't want to bury the content down in the code. This is intuitively obvious to Web designers and seasoned search engine optimizers, but many people don't take the time to put it into practice. In this section, we break down, define, and explain how best you can optimize each of the so–called *on-page* elements of a successful Web page.

The Head section

The task of optimizing every HTML page begins in the head section. The Head section is where search engines are first introduced to your page and where they first discover what the page is all about. This section makes that infamous first impression that you only get one shot at. But the job of the Head section isn't only to impress the search engine. Search engines like to share the wealth when it comes to information, so parts of your Head section get starring roles on the search engine results page. Time to get those parts camera-ready!

The four important tags in the Head section are the `Title`, `Meta` description, `Meta` keywords, and `Meta` robots tags. Metadata, is quite simply, data about data. It is descriptive of the rest of the page. Each of these help to define for the search engine what's coming up in the page and how it relates to other pages: the first three by defining the content, and the last by defining how the search engine should handle the information and links on the page. You can find out more about how these first three tags can affect your site's search engine rankings in the next few sections. For more on the `Meta` robots tag, jump to Book VII.

Optimizing Title tags for ranking and branding

The undisputed headliner of the head section is the `Title` tag. Although the various search engines out there don't tell us how important any one element is in their algorithms, most industry experts agree that the `Title` tag is one of the most critical. Because the `Title` tag not only shows up in your browser window but also in the search engine results, it's easy to infer that this tag naturally has some impact in the search engine's ranking algorithms. The following code (and Figure 3-1) show you how a `Title` tag appears in HTML.

```
<title>Good Titles Use Keywords like Ford Mustang 1967
    specs</title>
```

Figure 3-1:
The `Title` tag in Google search results.

Title tags in Google search results

Getting this tag right has many benefits — increased ranking, branding, and click-throughs. Getting it wrong severely hinders your page's chances at ranking in the search engine — duplicate `Title` tags are considered spam and are filtered, poorly written ones won't garner click-throughs, and your branding purposes won't be served. Leaving out the keywords hurts your chances to rank for those words.

The `Title` tag, although short, tells the search engine what your page is about. The maximum number of characters allotted for the `Title` tag is 62 to 70, depending upon search engine. You have just a few words to inform, entice, and reinforce your brand to search engines and their users. In order to get your message through, you need to be specific with keywords. Entice searchers with calls to action and use "research" words like *how to* and *information*. Figure 3-1 displays a `Title` tag as seen in Google's search engine results pages.

So what to do about this short, yet critically important piece of content? In order to maximize the effectiveness of your `Title` tag, you need to make some solid decisions first:

✦ **Focus:** Your page must have a single explicit subject. Put keywords related to that focus in the `Title`.

✦ **Silo:** Your page must support the theme of the page above it and be supported by the pages that link below it. Theme level keywords should appear in the `Title`.

✦ **Branding:** Some pages are critical to support branding; others are not. If branding is an issue, include branded keywords in the `Title`.

After you've decided on your focus, theme, and brand emphasis, you're ready to start writing your tag. Even though the actual length of your `Title` tag varies depending on your industry standard, you can follow some basic guidelines to get started. The two most important terms to remember are *unique* and *keyword-rich*. You need to make sure that you're writing unique, keyword-rich titles for your pages. The title of your page should belong only to that page, and not be used anywhere else on your site. If you're following your focus, theme, and branding guidelines, you should already be using words in a combination that won't be repeated somewhere else. Your title should not be sensational or contain keywords that you don't expect to rank for. Be sure that you have only one `Title` tag per page. Duplicate `Title` tags are a severe issue that could lead to filtering of your pages by the search engines, denying them the ability to rank for key terms.

Your title should be fairly short. Google cuts your title off after 70 characters, so you need to get your message right up front. Although Google indexes the whole tag, you want users to see your relevance immediately.

Put the keywords up front, and make them enticing for people to click through. If branding is an issue, put your company name at the end unless that is the main thrust of your SEO strategy. For example, Nike doesn't put running shoes at the front of their title: They put Nike first because their brand is their most important keyword. Notice that in Figure 3-1, the words *search engine optimization* are bolded wherever they appear. Google bolds search query words that appear in the title, which may lead to higher click-throughs. Eye-tracking studies have shown that people are naturally drawn to bold-faced type.

Be aware that there *is* a difference between being keyword-rich and being spammy. Spam by excessive repetition of keywords only hurts, not helps, your `Title` tag. Always strive to play within acceptable boundaries when it comes to SEO. The margin of safety changes all the time and without any warning at all.

Writing a Meta description

Working your way through the tags in a typical Head section, the next stop is the `Meta` description tag. Search engines use the `Meta` description tag in their results, so this is an important tag to get right. Write your `Meta` description like a sentence, describing what visitors can expect to find on the page after they click through from the search engine. If you fail to provide a `Meta` description, search engines often select text off the page that may or may not be a good representation of your page's real value. In Google, this extraction is called an *autosnippet*, and it contains the words found in the query whenever possible. It is in your best interest to craft a unique, targeted `Meta` description tag for every page. The following code displays a sample `Meta` description tag as it would appear in the raw HTML of a Web page:

```
<meta name="description" content="Your description tag should
    use keywords, describe the theme and purpose of the page
    and be fairly short. It is structured as a sentence.">
```

The `Meta` description should be about twice as long as your `Title` tag. Like the title, words used in the search query that are also found in the description are bolded, giving your listing another opportunity to catch the eye of the searcher. Google displays up to 160 characters for the description, sometimes extracted from the page content. If the `Meta` description is used for search engine results, you must put your best information right up front. No one but the spider sees it if you don't. Figure 3-2 shows a `Meta` description tag appearing in Google's search results.

**Book IV
Chapter 3**

**Making Your Page
Search Engine-
Compatible**

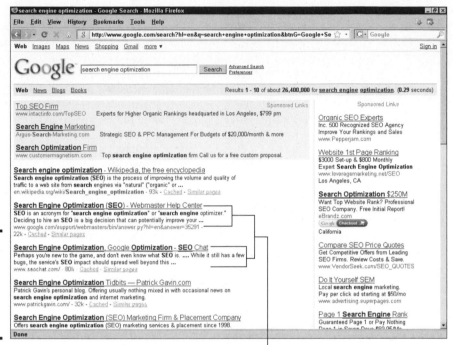

Meta description in Google search results

Figure 3-2:
A Meta description in Google search results.

Your description should answer the question "What is this page about?". Try not to repeat any word more than twice; any more than that may look unnatural to users and to the engines. Ask yourself what your target audience would be looking for when searching for you and write your metadata to address that person. Notice in Figure 3-2 that descriptions are in sentence form and give you a very clear idea about the content on the linked page.

Like your Title tag, your Meta description tag must be unique; that is, it has to be unlike any other on your site and targeted to the content of the page it's on, or you run the risk of *duplicate content* (that is, content that appears elsewhere on your site or the Web) penalties. Duplicate content is commonly filtered out of the search results by the engines because it's not in their users' best interests to show the same or similar pages more than once. Even if everything else on your page is unique and useful, a duplicate tag in the head section can spell disaster for your rankings. The metadata must match your content, using the same words. Think of your metadata as the advertisement and the content as your product. Don't be guilty of false advertising!

Writing a useful Meta keywords tag

In the past, it used to be simple (well, okay, easier) to get ranked in the search engines. Use your keywords in the page's metadata (including `Title` and `Meta` description as well as the keywords tag) and throughout the displayed body of the page, and within days or even hours, you could be on the top of any search engine you liked: Infoseek, AltaVista, Excite, or Yahoo!. But times have changed, and search engines have developed algorithms that are much more sophisticated, containing many more variables. The `Meta` keywords tag, which is basically a place to list all the relevant keywords for your page, is very easy to abuse because it's not a user-visible tag and invites *keyword stuffing* — putting every word, not just relevant ones, into the content of the tag. As a result, the `Meta` keywords tag suffered a serious devaluation. To be frank, you are never, ever going to rank on the basis of your `Meta` keywords tag for any competitive term.

So why still use it? Although some engines claim that they don't even bother to index the `Meta` keywords tag, they still usually read and store it. Although the `Meta` keywords tag is not a major factor in rankings, it's still better to sweat the small stuff and do everything right from the get-go. It only takes a few minutes to do it right and you won't be penalized for having them (unless you spam by keyword stuffing). You can never go wrong by using a `Meta` keywords tag, and you only hurt yourself if you don't use this valid piece of HTML data. The following code shows you how to format a `Meta` keywords tag in HTML:

```
<meta name="keywords" content="First Keyword Phrase, Second
    Keyword Phrase, Repeated Keyword, Keyword">
```

Optimizing a `Meta` keywords tag is simple. Essentially, the only thing this tag requires is that you list all the keywords and keyword phrases that are important to your page. A general rule is that if a keyword was important enough to be included in your title and `Meta` description, it's important enough to include in your keywords tag. As a best practice, order your keyword phrases from longest to shortest (four-word phrases, and then three-word phrases, and then two-word phrases, and so on). This keeps you organized and gives the search engines the most targeted and usually the most valuable words right up front.

WARNING!

Don't go overboard. Remember, excessive repetition could be considered spam. Try not to repeat any single keyword more than twice. If you stick to a keywords tag approximately twice the length of your `Meta` description tag, you're playing on safe ground.

Body section

Other than the page title which appears at the very top of your browser window above the menu, all of the user-visible content is located in a page's body section. As your site aims to satisfy the needs of users and search engines alike, dedicating ample time to producing high-quality body content is critical to creating a search-engine friendly site that serves the needs of your users.

After a search engine spider reads the summary-style information provided in a page's head section, it should find that the content within the body section also supports the established keywords. The vast majority of text content, links, and images are located in the body section. Having a significant amount of keyword-rich text content in the body section is absolutely necessary to achieving a Web page optimized for search engines.

Headings

Within the body section, the heading acts like the headline of a newspaper, identifying the topic of sections or paragraphs of a Web page. As such, it plays an important role for search engines looking to classify the subject matter of the page. Because of this, search engines give heading text significant weight in their ranking algorithms; thus, it's very important that you optimize headings in line with your ranking goals.

As with a table of contents or outline, the heading is usually made up of short phrases, generally not complete sentences. Within the page, there are often sub-sections with their own sub-heading tag designations. Hence an H1 tag may be followed by H2 tags. Figure 3-3 displays an H1 heading tag used in content.

When you're writing an H1 tag, you must include the most important keywords of that section of your Web page, which are likely to be the keywords also used in the Title and Meta tags. When seen together with the other keyword-optimized page elements discussed throughout this section, all of your page's significant text work together to support the spiders' recognition of your keywords as your site's area of expertise. For this reason, we recommend that you always use at least one H# tag on every page of your site. Thanks to CSS and special CSS/Flash customization methods like scalable Inman Flash Replacement (sIFR), you can use H# tags throughout a page without ruining the design. You don't need to use an image where you can place search engine and spider-friendly text instead.

Heading tag on page

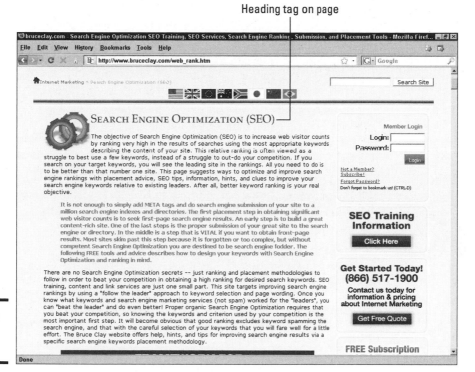

Figure 3-3:
A heading
on a page.

You can use multiple headings as needed, but they should always be used in hierarchical order. An H1 tag is given more weight than an H2 tag. It's rare that there would be more than one H1 on a page because pages generally only have one major subject. (There are exceptions to this rule; we have multiple H1 tags on our homepage at BruceClay.com because we have a very long page that is defining multiple top level topics.) All other subjects naturally fall below that top level listing. Following an H1 tag, the next heading on the page can be represented by the H2 tag. In other words, heading tags should not be used out of order. The H1 tag should be followed by the H2 tag, which can be followed by the H3 tag, if needed.

Don't use excessive headings: Too many can actually dilute the theme of your page. Think of this structure as a table of contents and you can't go wrong.

Each heading throughout the page should be unique. Because the purpose of the heading is to summarize the unique content of the page or section, each heading should naturally be unique as well. However, the content within a heading tag should be similar to the content in the `Title` because both share the task of summarizing the page content and including significant page keywords.

Try to keep headings from being too long. Because they are serving as a headline for the page, headings must be concise and to the point. Notice that the heading in Figure 3-3 acts as more of a title describing the subject of the page. A heading should usually be only a few targeted words and never more than a single sentence. Including an entire paragraph in a heading tag would likely be considered spam by the search engines. Here are a few points to remember about headings:

✦ Use heading tags as a headline for your page.

✦ Use heading tags in hierarchical order, following an H1 with an H2, and then H3, and so on.

✦ Keep headings short and unique.

✦ Don't use headings for styling text. Use CSS instead.

Content

Search marketers often say that content is king. Regardless of its relationship to royalty, tests show that content weighs heavily in search engine rankings. Although search engines are rapidly developing the capabilities to index other types of media, in most cases, you're dealing with a search engine spider that is deaf, dumb, and blind. Spiders cannot see images, watch videos, listen to podcasts, fill out forms, or use any other advanced features of your Web site although they can detect that those engagement objects are present and are expanding their ability to index that content. For this reason, it's imperative that you have enough sentence-structured text content on your page for a search engine to adequately determine what your page is about. The amount of content necessary to be competitive varies by industry, but the trend is that the amount of content has steadily increased over time for all industries. Discover how much content is right for your industry by doing competitive research (as described in Book II, Chapter 1).

If you're just starting out and haven't done competitive research, plan for a minimum of 450 or more words of good, relevant, useful text content on your important pages. Your content should always be unique to the page it's on and should naturally incorporate the keywords found in your title, description, and headings. The reason for this is simple: The first three tags define what the page is about; therefore, it is only logical that those words are repeated again in the text content on your site. Don't fall into the trap of discussing something without ever naming what it is or relying on the images on the page to provide context. Remember that the search engines aren't able to look at the picture and understand what you're talking about. If your page is about Ford Mustangs, you need more than a picture of the car to let the search engines know that. Say what you mean.

Use synonyms and related words in order to reinforce your keywords. When discussing shoes, you should also be using words that help define what sort of shoes. Are the related words *heel*, *leather*, *instep*, *size,* and *designer*? Or are they *horse*, *anvil*, *iron,* and *mare*? You can see that many very different mental pictures are painted by placing the keyword *shoes* in context.

There's practically no maximum number of words you can put on a page: A search engine just keeps reading. (Your visitors might not, though! If you don't have anything interesting to say, stop talking.) You should have all the words discuss the same subject matter for SEO, but long pages are not frowned upon by search engines. There used to be upper limits on how large of a page that the search engines would index, but those have gone out the window.

While the search engines might be happy to read your 50,000 word opus, you need to keep in mind user fatigue. If you find yourself discussing several topics on a very long page, you might consider breaking it up into two or more pages. This adds depth to your site by expanding the number of pages you have on a keyword phrase and also allows you to manage the site's themes.

When it comes to formatting the text on your page, remember, people tend to scan text on the Internet. Keep paragraphs short and direct. Give the facts as concisely as possible. Customers don't want to spend a long time reading if the Web page isn't going to satisfy their requirements. Tell your customers who you are, what your product is, and why they should choose you over your competitors. Use lists, **bold**, and *italicized* text to direct your visitors' eyes to important words and concepts.

If you are writing content for your own Web site, your first response might be to feel frustrated. What on earth are you going to write about? Everyone knows everything that you could possibly tell them and you're not a writer anyway. But that's just the thing: They *don't* know everything, and you *are* an expert on the topic even if you're not the world's best writer.

For most people, the hardest part of adding content to their Web sites is the writing of the content in the first place, but it doesn't have to be. There are lots of themes for you to write on and many topics available for you to write about. For e-commerce sites, this might include a well-written product description, user reviews, tips and tricks, or the inclusion of some frequently asked questions.

Remembering that most people on the Web are there to do research. You should address the concerns that your visitors may have and give them a reason to buy whatever you are selling (literally or figuratively). Search engines look for research words, like *how to* and *tips* as markers that indicate that page will satisfy a user doing research.

Suppose for example that you're in the business of selling cowboy boots. You are an expert in your area. Brainstorm everything you can think of that relates to cowboy boots, even if it's only somewhat related. After you have all your ideas down, pick a few of the best. For example, you probably want to focus a section of your site on the keywords [buy cowboy boots]. Everyone, you think, knows about how to buy boots. It's just a matter of finding the right fit and style. You don't need to explain it to your site's visitors. But it's one of your keywords, so you sit down and write all the obvious information.

Of course, you know how to check the fit of your boots and which styles work best for which people. It's obvious to *you* that your jeans should be tucked inside your boots if you're working outside and that you should take certain steps to care for your boots.

But most people *don't* know these things. That's why they're coming to your site in the first place. Your expertise is a valuable resource for the development of content. Explaining something that is obvious to you is probably the best way to introduce new customers to your products. If a visitor who is an expert comes into your site, having correct and informative content reinforces to them that your site is worthwhile.

Write your first draft with the page's keywords in mind. Use your keywords as a guide for the content. Tape them to the side of your monitor or put them at the very top of the document so they're on your mind as you write. Don't worry about keyword densities or forcing the words in. If it doesn't sound natural to use the keyword, don't use it. The first draft is just to get the information out.

Take a look at the tone of your piece:

✦ **Match your audience:** Are you writing to the right audience? Baby boomers and teenagers have very different ways of expressing themselves, not to mention widely different cultural touchstones, and writing the same way to each of them is probably not going to work. You have to speak their language.

✦ **Engage the reader:** Your content should get the user involved and offer them ways to connect to the material.

✦ **Solve a problem:** Does your content solve a problem or help the customer make a decision? Fighting fear, doubt, and uncertainty increase your conversions as visitors learn to trust you.

✦ **Educate:** If you're in a highly technical area where your customer isn't likely to know enough to ask intelligent questions, have you educated them enough to feel comfortable in making their decision?

Revise your draft with these ideas in mind. Knowing your audience means putting in the kinds of words that they will be looking for: the same kinds of words that help them understand what the best choice of products is for them.

 After your next draft, ask someone else to read it over for you. The best person for this task is someone who fits the profile of a site visitor. Have them read it aloud to see if it is easily readable and answers their questions in an easy to understand way. If not, revise the content to meet their understanding. You might even find that you're going to need another page of content in order to answer their questions.

After you have a final draft, incorporate your final product into the destination page, and use a page rating tool to determine the validity and strength of the document. Tweak it if necessary. Keep in mind how the content supports the Web site theme as a whole. This ties into the linking strategies discussed in all of Book VI.)

The final thing to remember about writing for search engines is that there is no magical formula for writing the perfect copy. You're going to have to put in hard work and attention to detail to meet the needs of both the search engines and your human visitors. Start writing and go from there.

Links

Links within the body section provide *anchor text*, which is the text that the user clicks on in order to follow the link to a new page (see the following code). When they are measuring the relevance of the Web page, search engine spiders consider the anchor text of links pointing that page. The keyword used within the anchor text of the hyperlink is not added to the *keyword frequency* of your Web site (how many times a keyword is used and how far apart in the text), but it does add to the relevance of the target page Web page in the search engine.

```
<a href="http://www.mydomain.com/bikerboots.html">Motorcycle
    Boots</a>
```

Links have a lot of power when it comes to a Web site appearing high in the search engine results page. How many links a particular page or site has is part of the algorithms search engines use, simply because it's saying that your page or site has meaning and carries a certain amount of expertise. It's like being the most popular kid in school because everyone says you have all of the answers.

With anchor text, you're basically describing to the search engine what the page you're linking to is about. So if you provided a link with the words `the world's greatest page` as the anchor text, the engine reads that and adds it to the relevance of the page. So if all of the hyperlinks to that page within your Web site say the same thing, that it's the world's greatest page, the engine's going to pick up on that like a giant blinking neon arrow and say that your page is the world's greatest page when someone enters that search query.

Two types of links can be used in the body section: relative links and absolute links. An *absolute link* is a link that contains the whole file path, so when it appears in code, it begins with `http://`, as shown here:

```
<a href="http://www.classiccarcustomization.com/fords/
    mustangs/tireoptions.html">
```

That's the whole file directory in the link itself. A *relative* link references a file located in a physical directory relative to the current page or the root of all directories, so it can simply start with the page name and leave off the `http://` and domain. If you're on the page `www.classiccar customization.com/mustangs/paintoptions.html`, you could use `<a href-"tireoptions.html">` to reach `http://www.classiccar customization.com/mustangs/tireoptions.html`.

You can use two periods before the filename to indicate that the page is located one directory up (closer to the root) from the directory the page is located in. For example, the HTML on the same page — `<a href="../tire options.html">` — indicates that the link goes to a page located at `www. classiccarcustomization.com/tireoptions.html`.

Relative links are a bit of a shortcut, and on the whole we recommend that you don't use them, especially if you're building your site from the ground up. When you use a relative link, it works only in relation to the page that the link is contained on. So `tireoptions.html` is only going to work if there's a `mustangs/tireoptions.html` for it to link to.

If the directories were to get switched around or taken out for whatever reason, the relative link would no longer work: Where it linked to no longer exists. So if the page with the link on it (in this case, `paintoptions.html`) was moved to the /mustangconvertible directory, the relative link of <a

`href="tireoptions">` would not work anymore because there's no `tire options.html` page located in the /mustangconvertible directory. A link to `/tireoptions.html` and an absolute link would still work. Without the leading slash (/), the link only goes to the current directory.

An absolute link is easier to maintain than a relative one because it is very clear what you're linking to and why, and there will be no confusion if the location of a page changes. Although fixing one or two broken links isn't a big deal, if every link on your site is relative, you'll have a huge repair project every time you decide to reorganize your page. And forget about reusing snippets of code from page to page. Relative links, unlike absolute links, rarely still take you to the page you intended if you happen to reuse the code on another page.

Bottom line: The absolute link `<a href="http://www.classiccar customization.com/mustangs/tireoptions.html">` always gets you to the Tire Options page. A relative link like `<a href="tireoptions. html">` gets you there only if you're starting from the same directory. In the long run, absolute links are less of a hassle.

Images

Images in the body of your site are also pretty important. Not only do they add to the overall aesthetic of your Web site and provide a visual of the product if you're trying to sell something, they also add weight and relevance to your ranking. Images aid users and they provide search engines with additional clues about the page. Images can also appear in *vertical search engines* (search engines that look for a specific file type only).

Images should contain keywords in their filenames (when they're named properly; see Book 4, Chapter 1 for more info). A search engine can read the filename and add it to the overall relevancy of the page. Also, although search engines cannot see images, they can read `Alt` attribute text. *Alt attribute text* is the HTML code that describes the image. The `Alt` attribute is designed to be an alternative text description for an image. The `Alt` attribute displays before the image is loaded (if it's loaded at all) in the major browsers, and instead of the image in text-based browsers such as Lynx. `Alt` is a required element for images in order to help vision-impaired people and can only be used for image tags because its specific purpose is to describe images. Stuffing many keywords into the `Alt` attribute text is considered spam and can get you pulled from a search engine's index (list of Web sites they crawl during a search). Instead, `Alt` attribute text should be a short descriptive phrase that clearly describes the content of the image. In the sample code, "1967 Ford Mustang with dented rear fender" is the `Alt` text for the image named ford.dented.fender.jpg.

```
<img src="ford.dented.fender.jpg" alt="1967 Ford Mustang with
   dented rear fender">
```

Make your images relevant to the overall content of the page. You can't have a picture of a duck on a page about classic cars, for instance — not unless the duck is driving a classic car. Another way a search engine can "see" an image is by the descriptive text around the image, so the image had better be relevant to the text describing it. As we mentioned previously, the image name, if it contains keywords, also helps to identify the image to the search engines. The identification of the image related to the keywords of the page it's on allows the image to contribute to the page as content. This helps your relevancy.

Using Clean Code

When designing or building your Web site, it's important to keep the code as clean as possible. If you have useless tags in your code, get rid of them, and code in as little markup as possible. That means no extraneous tags lying around in the HTML. You want to streamline your site's code so it's an easy read for the search engine spiders. If you can define something in 200 tags instead of 400, cut out all of the tags you do not need.

Code gunk buildup can happen if you've cut and pasted code from another source (like an outdated Web page of yours) or if you've been working on a particular page for so long that it's acquired excess tags. Go through and remove all of the extraneous tags and code from your page. Simplifying your code streamlines the site and makes it easier to read for the search engine spiders. If spiders read too much redundant stuff, they're less likely to assign a lot of weight or relevancy to your page, and are likely to throw out one of the pages.

With clean code, the goal is to have a high amount of content with the least amount of markup. This means there's more content going on than HTML coding. Figure 3-4 shows two different pages' HTML code side by side. On the left is a messily coded image of a table, and on the right is the clean version of the same table. Note the difference between the messy code and the clean code: The clean code has a higher content to code ratio. The less code a search engine has to read, the faster it can spider your page, and the sooner it gets to the content of your Web site, the better. The first 200 words of a page carry the most weight, so it's important to get the spider to the actual content as soon as you can.

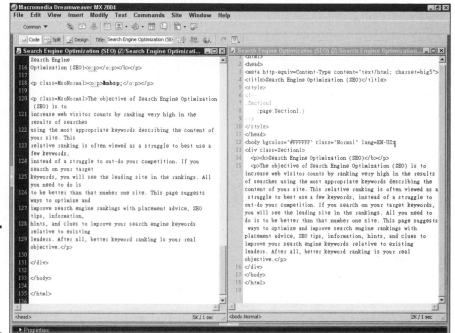

Figure 3-4:
Note how the clean code has more content in it.

Making Your Site WC3–Compliant

One of the ways to get your code nice and clean is to validate it. *Validating* code means making your Web site WC3 compliant. The *World Wide Web Consortium* (W3C) is an international consortium where member organizations, a full-time staff, and the public work together to develop Web standards. Their mission statement is "to lead the World Wide Web to its full potential by developing protocols and guidelines that ensure long-term growth for the Web."

W3C goes about achieving this by creating Web standards and guidelines. It's basically like health code guidelines for a restaurant. A Web site needs to meet certain standards in order to be as least imperfect as possible. Since 1994, W3C has published more than 110 such standards, called W3C Recommendations.

A compliant page is known to be spiderable and the links crawlable, so although the search engines do not require W3C compliance, it's not a bad idea. If you have complex or just plain ugly Web page code, or you're having issues getting your pages crawled and indexed, validating your code to W3C standards might help.

On the front page of the W3C's Web site (www.w3.org) is a sidebar called W3 A to Z, which contains all sorts of links. Bookmark this page: These links are a great reference to help you understand the standards that the Web is built on.

Here's something about search engines: The harder they have to work to read your site, the less often and less thoroughly the search engines index your site. Because more content tends to mean more authority, you are less likely to receive top ranking. In fact, if a search engine has to work too long at reading your page, it might just abandon it all together.

So it's a good idea to follow the W3C standards, simply because they make for a faster, more efficient page that is set up the way a search engine expects to find things. It's like having your house swept clean and in order when the spiders come to visit: It makes them like what they see. (Internet spiders, that is. It doesn't work that way for the arachnid variety.) If your site doesn't comply with the W3C standards, the search engines might not crawl all of your pages on your site. Because you can't rank pages the search engines don't know about, that's a big problem.

To comply with W3C, every page should declare a *doc type* (document type) and validate itself. To declare your doc type, include a line at the very top of your of HTML code, which declares the document as an HTML document and identifies the type of HTML you are following. Because HTML has changed since the early days, some versions are different than others. Declaring a doc type is telling the search engine what it's going to be reading. It's important to comply with your declared doc type. If you don't, you confuse the search engine spider, and it takes longer to crawl your pages.

To validate your page, go to www.w3.org/QA/Tools/#validators on the W3C Web site and use the free tools on that page, as seen in Figure 3-5.

These are tools that you can use to basically "proofread" your site in order to make sure they comply with the W3C standards.

The first tool on the site is the MarkUp Validation Service, shown in Figure 3-6. Also known as the HTML validator, it helps check Web documents in formats like HTML, XHTML, SVG, or MathML. Plugging your site's URL into the box allows the tool to check your Web site to see if the code matches the declared doc type.

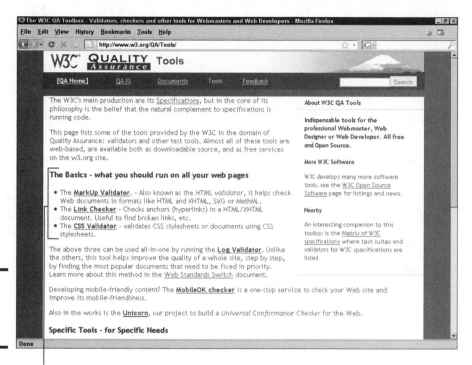

Figure 3-5:
The W3C
validator
tools.

The W3C validator tools

The second tool is the Link Checker (see Figure 3-7). It checks anchors (hyperlinks) in a HTML/XHTML document. It's useful for finding broken links, redirected pages, server errors, and so on. There are some options for your search, like ignoring redirects and the ability to check the links on the pages linked to from the original page, as you can see in the figure below, and you can also save the options you set in a cookie, to make it quick to run it again in the future. If you don't select summary only, you can watch it go through each link on the page. Most of the time, you just need to run the tools without making any adjustments so don't stress about the options. Many other link checkers are also available out there. This tool is great for checking one page (if you were putting up a single new page with a lot of links, for example), but for spidering a whole site, we prefer Xenu's Link Sleuth, which is a great (and free!) link-checking tool that makes sure all of your links work. It's available at `http://home.snafu.de/tilman/ xenulink.html`.

The third tool on W3C's site is the CSS Validation Service, which validates CSS stylesheets or documents using CSS stylesheets. As shown in Figure 3-8, it works a lot like the Markup Validation Service. Just put in the URL of the site you wish to have validated.

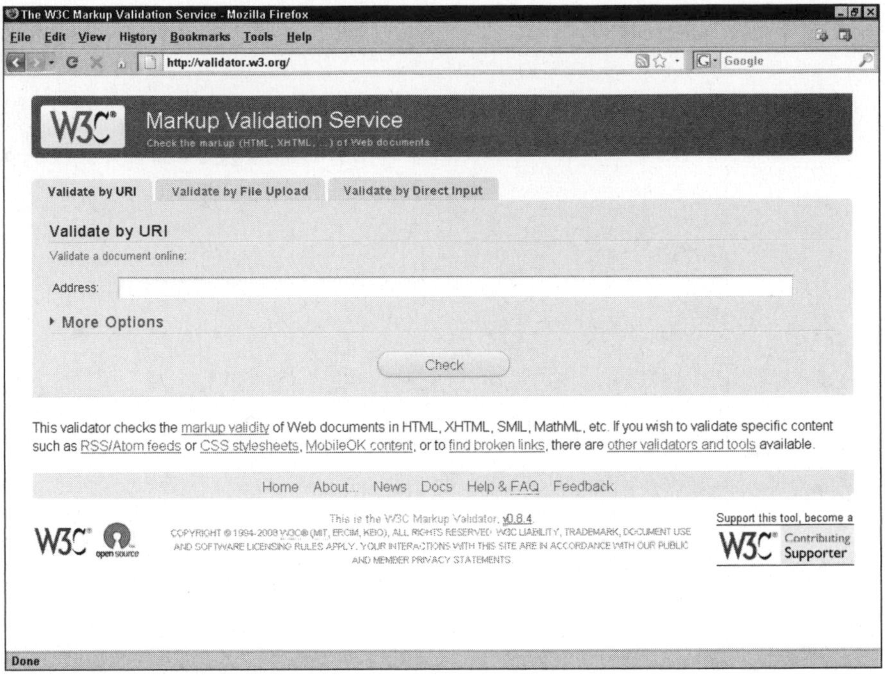

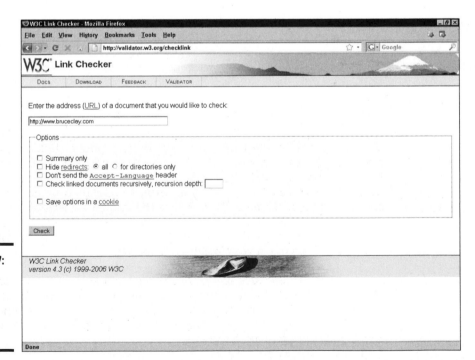

Figure 3-6:
A Web site
URL in the
markup
validator.

Figure 3-7:
The Link
Checker
validator
from the
W3C.

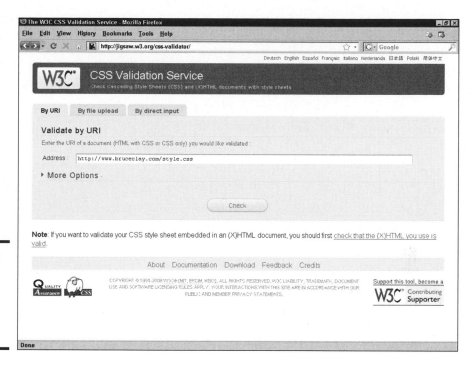

Figure 3-8:
The CSS
Validation
Service
from the
W3C.

Validating your CSS ensures that your site looks picture perfect whenever a standards-compliant browser (like Firefox) or spider (like Google) comes by and checks it out.

Designing with sIFR

Typically, HTML pages allow the use of standard browser fonts (Arial, Verdana, Times New Roman, and so on) only, or you must use a graphic in place of the text as an alternative in order to keep the type of typography you want. The downside of using graphics in place of text is that you lose accessibility and the image is not as strongly weighted as equivalent text content would be. Some audiences, like the visually impaired and colorblind, and all search engines, cannot read graphics, and therefore, they can't see what text is showing within your images. Using images also uses more bandwidth and slows down your Web page's load time.

Scalable Inman Flash Replacement (sIFR), developed by Mike Davidson and others, is a powerful technology that enables you to use just about any font you want on Web pages without sacrificing search-engine friendliness or accessibility. You or your Webmaster must have some knowledge of HTML and CSS in order to make this work.

You can download the official sIFR 2.0.2 release (full) from Mike Davidson. This is a free tool and is available at www.mikeindustries.com/blog/files/sifr/2.0/sIFR2.0.2.zip.

In this section, we walk you through how to use sIFR, so you need the following things to get started:

✦ sIFR 2.0.2 release from Mike Davidson

✦ sIFR tutorial files (available for free download at www.bruceclay.com/sIFR_tutorial_bruceclay.zip)

✦ Adobe Flash MX or newer

✦ A HTML/CSS editor (HTML Kit, BBedit, and so on) or a text editor (Notepad, TextEdit, and so on)

After you've gathered these together, you're ready to begin your sIFR tutorial. To use your choice of font with sIFR, you need to first generate a Flash file that contains the font data.

1. **In Abobe Flash MX, open the file named font.fla, which is contained in the tutorial download.**

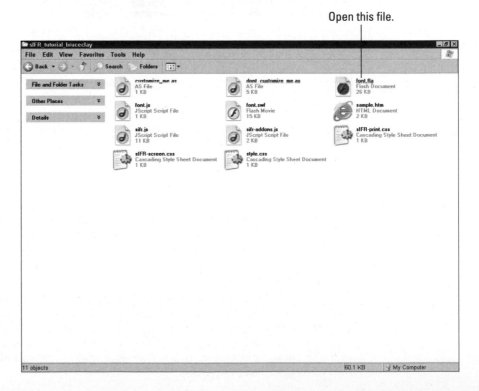

Open this file.

2. **Double-click on the movie clip called holder from the library palette.**

The holder movie clip

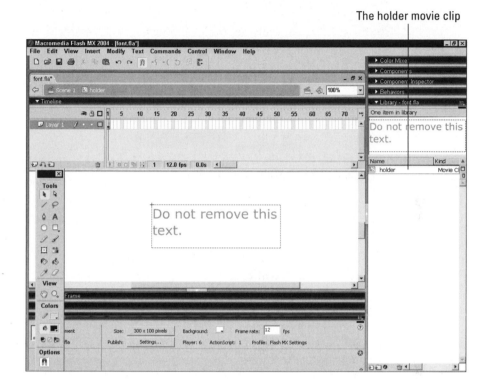

Inside the holder movie clip is a text field called txtF.

3. **Set the font of text field txtF to another font you like and then go back to Scene 1. Save (File⇨Save) and publish (File⇨Publish) the Shockwave (font.swf) file.**

4. **Next, from the downloaded .zip file, open the file style.css in your HTML/CSS or text editor.**

   As shown in the following figure, you have set font definitions for H1 and P tags, which apply to the sIFR fonts. You may change them or add more definitions as needed.

5. **Next, open font.js.**

   Here is where you specify which Shockwave (.swf) file sIFR should use — the file that contains the font data. Also, this is where you set the text color, text background color, padding, and alignment for the sIFR fonts. In this case, you are using the font file font.swf, which you just generated, and have declared two sets for H1 and P tags corresponding to the definitions declared in style.css.

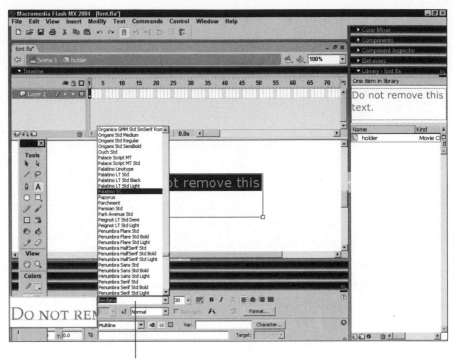

Select a new font

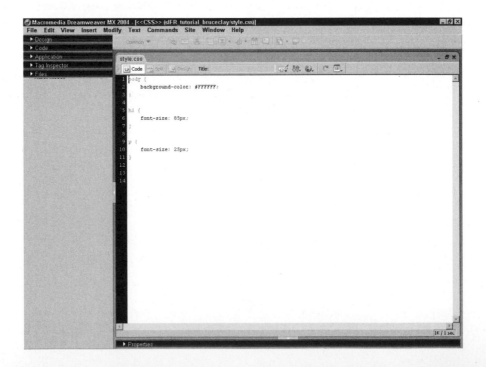

6. **Next, create a new HTML document similar to the one shown in the following figure. In the head section, link to the three CSS files (style. css, sIFR-screen.css, and sIFR-print.css) and the two JavaScript files (sIFR.js and sIFR-addons.js).**

   These files are *required* for sIFR to work.

7. **Now you can start inserting your page contents, applying the CSS definitions you set up in style.css. Insert an open/close `<p>` tag containing some page content text.**

8. **Finally, right before the closing `Body` tag, you should link to the font.js JavaScript file.**

Link to these files.

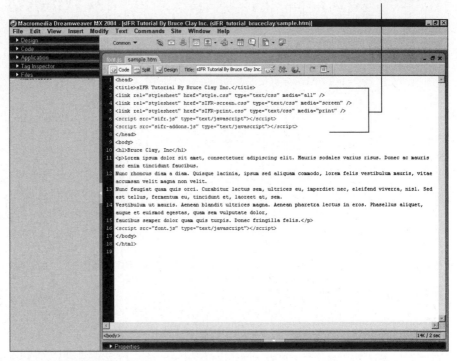

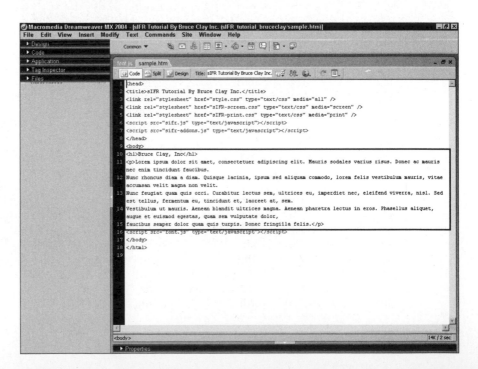

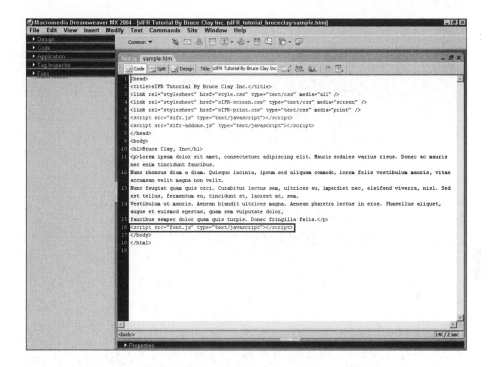

9. Preview your HTML document in a Web browser.

The result should look something like the following image. If you've done it correctly, you now have fonts that are readable by both the user and the search engine.

Using sIFR allows you to use whatever font your heart desires, without it dragging down your page load time or making it invisible to a search engine spider. For the sIFR fonts to be seen, the user must have Flash and JavaScript turned on in their browser; otherwise, the text reverts to a standard substitute. Most users will have no trouble viewing the content in sIFR. It's handy, and best of all, it's free.

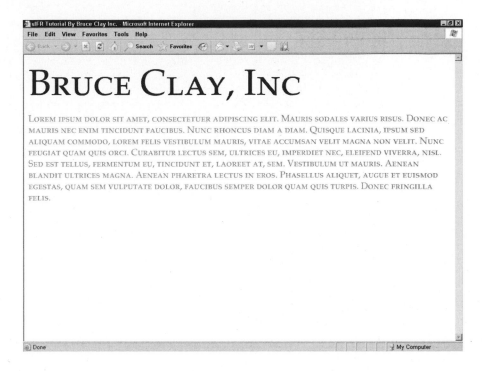

Externalizing the Code

When you're working with CSS and JavaScript, it's important to externalize the code. Externalizing the code is basically putting all your definitions in a file, putting that file on your site, and using a single line of code within your actual pages to tell the browser (and engines) where to find it. Because the code represents the building blocks of your Web site, there's going to be a lot of it. Just the JavaScript for your analytics alone can take up dozens of lines of code, maybe even hundreds. Externalizing your code is streamlining your process.

Not only does it reduce the size of your page to externalize CSS and JavaScript, giving your browser less to load, but if you want to go in and change all of your headings to blue, all you need to do is go to the glossary page where all the terms are defined, change that particular code to `blue`, and the change appears throughout your Web site. You don't have to go through every single page and do it by hand. The advantage for SEO is that externalizing your code makes the page code much cleaner, thus making the content to code ratio much higher overall.

Choosing the Right Navigation

You can allow a user to navigate your site in several different ways. There's text-based navigation, which means all of the *navigation info* (links, information about those links, any cool little widgets you have, and so on) is listed in the text. There's image-based, which means you click an image linked to another page or a section of an image map (the image is on a layer that allows for attaching links and other goodies) and navigate via that. Then there's navigation using scripts such as JavaScript or technology such as Flash to build your navigation. For search engine optimization, we recommend that you use text-based navigation. You can, if you really want to, use any of the other ways to build a navigation system for your site, but they all have significant drawbacks when it comes to search engine optimization.

Image maps

Using an image map for your site navigation doesn't help with SEO because you don't have any anchor text to take advantage of. Your anchor text is important because it tells the search engine what that page you are linking to is about. When a page is linked to the anchor text `classic cars`, search engines tend to think "Hmm, this must be about classic cars." The more links you have with that anchor text pointing into that page from other pages, the more it's like a giant blinking neon sign telling the search engine that this page is about classic cars. The search engine then assigns more weight to the link and increases the perceived relevance of the linked page.

Because an image map does not contain any readable text, any text that is contained within the image is not going to be seen by a search engine spider. A spider is deaf, dumb, and blind and can only understand the code on the page, not what a human user sees. Any text within the navigation is not counted toward your overall page rank. The only text it's going to read is the `Alt` attribute text. And because you have one image for the navigation, that's only going to be one `Alt` attribute tag. Some designers break up a big image into several smaller images so that they can use multiple `Alt` attribute tags, but `Alt` attribute tags still do not carry as much weight as hyperlinked text, especially because it's very easy to deceive a search engine with spam in the `Alt` attribute tags.

You also must consider the possibility that users do not have images turned on in their browser, usually because they're still on a dial-up connection and they want pages to load sometime this century. (They are still out there.)

Flash

Another type of navigation system is Flash. There have been some advances when it comes to Flash: Newer versions of the program have made non-animated Flash file text readable by a search engine, but this is only for the latest versions, and search engines still won't be able to read any of the links or anchor text.

Also, some search engines see Flash files as files separate from the page they're attached to, and do not count the Flash content towards that over-all Web page. Flash can also be annoying because it can break, slow down load time, or start playing unwanted music or videos. Many people choose to turn Flash off on their browsers in order to avoid Flash-based advertise-ments, and they wind up stranded on your page if your navigation is Flash-based because they won't even be able to see it.

JavaScript

If Flash is not very usable, JavaScript is even less so. JavaScript is a program similar to Flash, but very little of it is readable at all by search engines, often the spiders can't follow any of the links contained therein, and it's a bad idea to use a navigation system that's pure JavaScript, like AJAX. JavaScript is hard to spider and hard for some visitors with dated technology to use. Users browsing with JavaScript turned off find your site completely unusable if it relies solely on JavaScript navigation.

Text-based navigation

Text-based navigation is the navigation you should rely on when designing your page. Search engines can read the content of your text and can use the anchor text in the links to assign weight and relevance to those pages. Text is also clean, simple, and easy-to-use, and you don't run the risk of users being unable to see it in their browsers because all browsers can read text.

Not only is text easy to both read and use, but it's also highly controllable and customizable. You can add Flash elements and JavaScript to the text using CSS and still have it be understandable to a search engine.

A word about using frames

Frames have fallen by the wayside as site design has advanced in the past several years, but a few sites out there still choose to use them. Our advice is to not be one of them. Search engines read a frame as a completely sepa-rate page, so if your navigation is in a different frame than your page con-tent, they're being read as two separate pages. Splitting up the relationship between your content is a bad idea. Just don't do it.

If you decide to use images, Flash, or JavaScript for your navigation, at least use a text-based footer on the page that offers alternative text links to your pages and to your site map, so that search engines can follow that and can do a read-through of your site.

Making Use of HTML Content Stacking

Content stacking is writing the HTML in such a way that the page content is delivered to the spiders before any scripts or navigation elements. A search engine puts the most weight on the first 200 words of a Web page, and then less weight on the remaining words that are left. If the first 200 words on your Web page are all HTML code setting up your navigation and you don't start with your actual content until about word 580, you might end up with a low rank. That doesn't mean you have to chuck your navigation system and start afresh; we here in SEO-land can suggest a couple of tricks to ensure that the spider reads the content of your page first. One is called the *table trick* and the other is `div`tag positioning.

Implementing the table trick

Your Web page is developed in tables, and by the time the search engines encounter your "main content," it is too far down the page for the spider to consider it important. Generally, the text at the top of the page is the more important text, and sometimes site design pushes the main body content hundreds of lines from the top of the page's source code.

A normal Web page usually has a header, a navigation bar that is usually on the left side of the page, and the main content on the right. The search engines usually look at many page attributes, for example, title, description, and at least the first 200 words of your content. The engines spider your whole page, but if your navigation bar lists many products, the search engine may not encounter your main body within the first 200 words.

Most of the search engines read a table a certain way. They find the opening `Table` tag and look for the first `"table row"` `<tr>`. They begin to read each `"data set"` `<td>"data"</td>` inside the "table row" from left to right until they find the closing `</tr>` tag. They try to keep going until they find the closing `Table` tag. They continue until they have crawled the entire page. Your main body content is usually where you would have most of your keyword phrases and the relevant body text that you want the search engine to index. Knowing that the spider tries to figure out your theme within the first 200 words of your site, you want it to see the relevant text as soon as possible. The best way to do this is using CSS positioning, but if you've got to stick with tables, we SEO types rely on something we call the *table trick*.

A search engine normally reads a page in this order: first, the top navigation; second, left navigation; third, page content; and fourth, footer. That puts two cells of content before your page's nice keyword rich content. The table trick pushes your left-side navigation bar down below your body content and pulls up your body content so that it usually is within the first 200 words. The trick is to insert a blank cell after the first cell. The order is now as follows: first, top navigation; second, the blank cell; third, the page content, fourth, your left navigation; and fifth, the footer. You can see how the table trick works in the before (left) and after (right) examples shown in Figure 3-9.

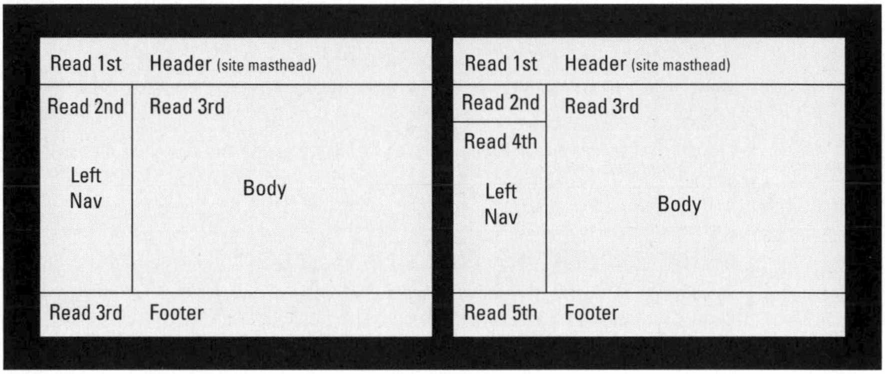

Figure 3-9:
The output for the table trick results in five cells where there were once four.

Read 1st	Header (site masthead)		Read 1st	Header (site masthead)	
Read 2nd	Read 3rd		Read 2nd	Read 3rd	
			Read 4th		
Left Nav	Body		Left Nav	Body	
Read 3rd	Footer		Read 5th	Footer	

Div tag positioning

Unfortunately, using a table trick can cause the left navigation to appear slightly lower on the page than it did before the table trick was implemented. The gap between the global site header and the left navigation becomes just a bit larger. This problem is generally not even noticeable. However, the height of the empty data cell changes depending on the length of the main page content. The left navigation may appear to jump up and down ever so slightly when you go from a longer page to a shorter page, or vice versa.

There is an alternative solution that does not create the same style problems as a table trick. It involves using CSS positioning to reorder the content in the code. The easiest implementation involves putting the left navigation content within one Div tag and all of the main body content within another Div tag. Then, using CSS, you would float the left navigation Div tag to the left and the body content Div tag to the right.

Using an inline style, the parsed HTML would be as follows at its most basic level:

```
<Html>
<Head>Head Section</Head>
<body>
  Global Header Content
  <div style="float: right;">Body Content</div>
  <div style="float: left;">Left Navigation  Content</div>
  Global Footer Content
</body>
</Html>
```

By using the Float property in CSS, the page renders the same no matter how you order the Div tags. Obviously, the whole reason for restructuring the code is to get the body content higher up in the source code. Thus, you would opt to put the content Div before the left navigation Div tag.

You can take this recommendation one step further. You can also place the header (or top navigation) of the site and reposition it in the code using CSS. Unfortunately, it is not possible to use the float attribute that we used above to reposition the site header. There is no float:top or float:bottom in Cascading Style Sheets. However, CSS allows you to place Div or Table tags in absolute positions on the page. By using absolute positioning, the page's main content can be read before anything else on the page.

If you use absolute positioning for your Div tags, be sure to avoid using negative numbers as a position because this puts the content outside of the user viewable frame. Spammers have been known to use CSS positioning to place keyword-stuffed content outside of the viewable browser window (for example, style=position:absolute; top:-1000px, which places the content 1,000 pixels above the top of the page). Because of past abuse, search engines routinely look for this type of spam.

Chapter 4: Perfecting Navigation and Linking Techniques

In This Chapter

✔ **Formulating a category structure**

✔ **Building landing pages for silos**

✔ **Absolute versus relative linking**

✔ **Types of navigation**

✔ **Naming links**

In this chapter, we talk about how to physically structure your site in the most efficient way possible with siloing. *Siloing* is the process of categorizing your Web pages into subject themes in order to group related content. In this way, you present clear and straightforward subject relevancy that increases your site's perceived expertise to the search engines.

Search engines award keyword rankings to the site that proves that it is least "imperfect" for the relevancy of a subject or theme. That means that the more clearly on-topic a site is for a user's search query, the more relevant it is, and the more likely it is to appear near the top of search results. Search engines try to dissect a site into distinct subjects that add up to an overall theme that represents a straightforward subject relevancy. If a search engine can clearly understand what you're talking about, they're going to consider you more of an expert on the subject and award you a higher rank than the other guy who's diluted his theme and cluttered his page with junk that's not relevant to his site. More often than not, a Web site is a disjointed array of unrelated information with no central theme and suffers in search engines for keyword rankings. If you visit a Web site and you wind up not being exactly sure whether it's about electric shavers or rubber pants, odds are a search engine isn't going to know either. Siloing a Web site helps to clarify your Web site's subject relevance.

In this chapter, we discuss how to physically arrange a site for siloing. We go much more in depth on siloing in Book VI, but this chapter gets you started. The first thing we talk about is formulating a linking structure and landing pages: what they are and why they're important. Next we revisit absolute versus relative linking. Finally, we discuss the types of navigation to use when building a silo, and finish off with the naming of links.

Formulating a Category Structure

Formulating a category structure is basically grouping your site content to put all of your categories together into related directories. In Book IV, Chapters 1 and 2, we talk about picking major categories and smaller subcategories to go with them. If you've already done this, formulating a category structure shouldn't be so bad.

First you need to figure out which page is the most important, and then have all of your other pages point to it. What page do you think represents you best? What page do you want your visitors to first see when they visit your Web site? This is the first step in figuring out your linking structure because you need to decide your categories and what you want to link to where. This is important to keep from diluting your theme.

Going back to the jar of marbles analogy we discussed in previous chapters: If you have black, gray, and white marbles all bunched together in a jar, it's hard to figure out what the "subject" of the jar is. Is it a jar of black marbles with some white and gray mixed in, or a jar of white marbles with black and gray marbles mixed in, or a jar of gray marbles, or something else? Search engines function much the same way when they index a page or a site. Search engines can only decipher the meaning of a page when the subjects are clear and distinct. Take a look at the picture of the jar of marbles in Figure 4-1. How would search engines classify it?

In the jar, you can see black marbles, gray marbles, and white marbles all mixed together with seemingly no order or emphasis. It would be reasonable to assume that search engines would classify the subject as a jar of marbles.

If we then separate out each group of colored marbles into separate jars (or Web sites) as in Figure 4-2, they would be classified as a jar of black marbles, a jar of white marbles, and a jar of gray marbles.

However, if you wanted to put all three marbles (categories) into a single jar (Web site) as in Figure 4-3, you would create distinct silos or categories within the site that would allow the subject themes to be black marbles, white marbles, gray marbles, and finally the generic term *marbles*. Most Web sites never clarify the main subjects they want their site to become relevant for. Instead, they try to be all things to all people.

Categorizing your Web site makes it easier for a search engine to read and understand the page's content, and it also helps the user navigate the page.

Figure 4-1:
A mixed
jar of
marbles —
how would
a search
engine
classify it?

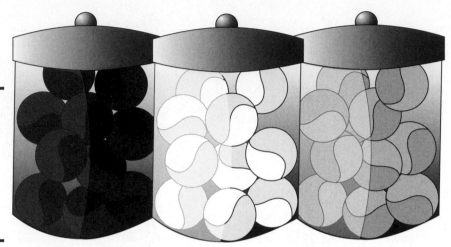

After you have your categories and subcategories picked out, now it's time to upload them and set up your site's directories for easy navigation and siloing. When building a directory structure, it's important to not go too deep. The *directory structure* refers to where your files physically exist within the folders on the site. For example, take a look at the following URL of a Web page. The full address identifies the directory where the page physically resides:

```
http://www.customclassics.com/ford/mustangs/index.html
```

The URL lets you know where the page is. Notice that there are only two subdirectories under the main domain. Having too many levels of subdirectories does the following things:

✦ The farther the file is from the root directory, the less important it seems to the search engines.

✦ Long directory paths make long URLs, and studies have proven that users avoid clicking long URLs on a search results page.

✦ Long URLs are more apt to cause typos. This could cause broken links within your Web site (if Webmasters use absolute linking); also, users could make mistakes typing in your URL.

Therefore, don't get category-happy. Making your directory structure ten directories deep is bad; having five deep is bad too. Having three levels of directories is not as bad, but it's not great either. We recommend going no more than two directories deep.

**Book IV
Chapter 4**

**Perfecting
Navigation and
Linking Techniques**

Figure 4-3:
This jar
has three
distinct
themes, or
silos.

For example, your classic car Web site only has one main category (the car's make) and two subcategories (model and year). If you have enough content to support multiple sublevels (a minimum of five pages for each category), you could set up the directory structure with two levels. The top level folders would be labeled with the make; the subfolders would be named by the model. Each page within the subfolder could represent a particular year. So the directory structure would look something like this:

```
http://www.customclassics.com/ford/delrio/1957.html
http://www.customclassics.com/ford/fairlane/1958.html
http://www.customclassics.com/ford/mustang/1965.html
```

Note how shallow the directory structure is.

The grouping of content on the site is very significant. One of the ways to think about it is to think of a Web site as compared to a book: The table of contents describes the overall subject in the introduction and then breaks down into different chapters that support that major subject. The different chapters are the different top level folders, whereas each chapter is made up of HTML pages that may be compared to the individual files within that folder.

The folder or directory is the physical organization of the files (pages) in that root directory. Because a spider cannot physically read the files on the server or in a database (it takes a content management system to format pages), you can use several strategies for dynamically organizing data, making even the most ornery Content Management Systems (CMS) flexible for implementing directory structures. There are two separate ways to understand how a directory structure looks visually — by the URL structure and by folder view:

```
http://www.classiccars.org/index.shtml
http://www.classiccars.org/Ford/index.shtml
http://www.classiccars.org/Business_Partnerships/Support_
    Other_Businesses.shtml
http://www.classiccars.org/Business_Partnerships/Value-Added_
    Partnerships.shtml
http://www.classiccars.org/Chevy/index.shtml
http://www.classiccars.org/Chevy/Comet.shtml
```

Notice how none of the URLs are longer than one main category and two subjects long. Knowing how to group related subject files on your Web site provides greater primary and supporting subject relevancy while also lending a strategy for identifying which sections of your site require greater amounts of content.

Three major subjects define what impact link structure has on implementing silos on your site:

✦ Internal site linking is how the pages are linked within the span of your site, whether it be linking between major silos or cross-linking related subject pages.

✦ Outbound, or external, linking represents the offsite links to other sites that are subject-relevant and provide resources to users that your site can't offer.

✦ Finally, backlinks are the format by which other Web sites link to the pages on your Web site. You should understand the difference between links from sites that support your theme and links from sites that have no subject matter relevance. The first are good, but the second kind may dilute your subject relevancy.

Having sites with unrelated subject matter link to your site causes the relevancy to be diluted. The purpose of inbound links is to reinforce subject relevance. This is a major issue for sites that purchase links because the links often originate from a completely irrelevant site.

Selecting Landing Pages

When you're ready to choose your subject categories, go through and pick what you think would be the most important pages, the ones you want the users to see in the search results and ultimately land on. These are the aptly named *landing pages*. A landing page can be any or all of three things. One, it can be the first page a user lands on when clicking the link to your site during their search query. Two, it's the page a user lands on after clicking a paid ad. Or three, it's the page at the top level of a silo.

When choosing a page on your site to be a landing page, keep in mind that it should be a big topic with lots of pages there to support it. If you have less than five pages of support for this page, it's probably not a landing page. See Figure 4-4 for an example of a landing page with its supporting pages.

Figuring out your landing page depends on what keywords you chose for the page. You want it to be a gateway page to the rest of your site. It should contain the broad keywords you need to draw in the query, and then funnel the user to the other pages with the more specific information they need.

**Book IV
Chapter 4**

**Perfecting
Navigation and
Linking Techniques**

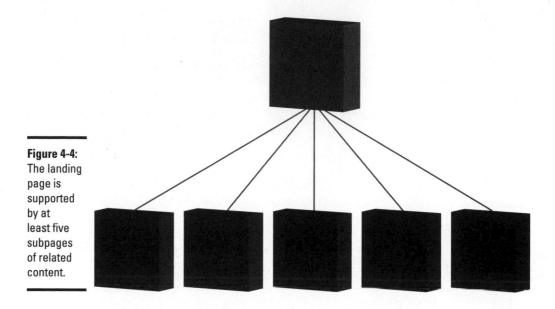

Figure 4-4:
The landing page is supported by at least five subpages of related content.

You should be thinking about these questions: Does the landing page content answer the search query? Does it contain enough information on that page or on its subpages that provide information for a search query? If a user doesn't find what they're looking for on your Web site, they're not going to stick around and explore the rest of your site. Remember, you want people to explore your site, and having a well-crafted silo not only helps your search engine rankings, but it also enhances the user experience.

One thing to keep in mind is that every page on your Web site has the potential to be a landing page. One of your subpages could be drawing all of the traffic because it contains more relevant information than the actual landing page. This is not a bad thing; it just means one page ended up being a better landing page than the one you thought of. So it's important to optimize every page just in case. Make sure it reads naturally and is not too forced or obvious. A search engine robot can't read a Web page, but a human user knows when things on a page seem stilted or forced. When linking your pages, you can link as much as you like within a silo, but if you have to change the subject, always try to link to the landing page of the other subject, not to any subpage. If you must link to a non-theme–related, non-landing page, you need to use a `rel="nofollow"` parameter on the link.

It's also important to link only to landing pages in the silo. A normal silo looks like Figure 4-5, where the subpages link either to other subpages in the same silo or the landing page. Notice that they don't link across to other subpages. A good comparison of siloing is to think of it like a pyramid, where the top tier is supported by the level below it, and so on, throughout the pyramid.

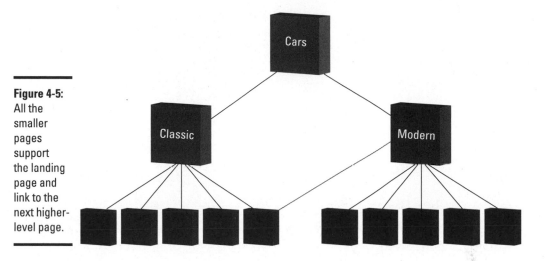

Figure 4-5:
All the smaller pages support the landing page and link to the next higher-level page.

Absolute versus relative linking

In a Web page's HTML code, there are two ways you can include a link: relative links and absolute links. An absolute link is a link that contains the whole URL of the file you're linking to. When it appears in code, it looks the same as when it appears in the browser's address bar:

```
<a href="http://www.classiccars.com/fords/mustangs/
    tireoptions.html">Anchor Text</a>
```

That's the whole file directory in the link itself. A relative link looks like only part of a full path URL:

```
<a href="tireoptions.html"> Anchor Text</a>
<a href="../tireoptions.html"> Anchor Text</a>
```

When designing your Web site, we recommend that you don't use relative links, especially if you're building your site from the ground up, so you won't have the added headache of having to go and clean them up later. When you use a relative link, it only works in relation to the next directory up. For example, a link from mustangs/paintoptions.html to `<a href="tireoptions.html">` is only going to work if there's a mustangs/tireoptions.html for it to link to.

If the pages that were linking out were to get moved somewhere else, the relative link would no longer work because where it linked to would no longer be valid. So if the page was moved from the /mustangs directory to the /mustangconvertible directory, the relative link of `<a href="tireoptions,html">` would break because there is no `tire options.html` page in the /mustangconvertible directory.

An absolute link is easier to maintain in situations like this because it's very clear what you're linking to. There's no confusion if the pages move because absolute links outbound from it still work.

Use the full qualified URL (that is, the link target that begins `http://domain.com`) every time you create a link. Not only is it easier for the engines to understand, but there are also fewer mistakes in the coding of the Web site, and any mistakes can easily be caught and corrected.

Dealing with Less-Than-Ideal Types of Navigation

In Book IV, Chapter 3, we describe the various types of navigation used in building Web sites and recommend what is best to use and what is best to avoid. For SEO, it's important to use text-based navigation because it's clean, simple, and can be seen by both the search engine and the user.

Unfortunately, you can't always use text as your navigation system. Sometimes you have a boss who wants the bells and whistles, and you can't convince them that text links work best. Sometimes your CMS (content management system) won't allow you to use only text. And sometimes competing in your industry demands those bells and whistles, and users won't trust your site without them. For example, a movie site would require Flash animation and navigation in order to show movie trailers; a user would think something was terribly wrong with a movie site that's entirely text-based.

Fear not, for there is a way around these problems in your navigation. You can work around the problems with using images, JavaScript, and Flash for your navigation in order to still rank in the search engines. There is a technical way of working around every problem. It may require a little more work, but if the bells and whistles are something you *have* to have, these tips help, especially in terms of keeping your silos neat and clean.

Images

To quickly recap the previous chapter, using images for your site navigation is not advisable. Because an image map does not contain any readable text, any text that is contained within the image is not going to be seen by a search engine spider. A spider can only understand the code on the page, not what a human user sees. So any text within the navigation is not counted towards your overall page rank. The only text it is going to read is the `Alt` attribute text. If you have only one image for the navigation, that's only going to be one `Alt` attribute tag. `Alt` attribute tags do not hold a lot of weight with a search engine because they are easily stuffed with keywords and are spammable.

When you're building a silo, however, using image-based navigation can be useful. If you need to remove keywords that otherwise dilute your page's target, you can place them in an image, rendering them unseen by a search engine, but still visible to a user.

For example, say you have a page you want to rank in the search engines for research-type search queries. To make this happen, you need to remove any call-to-action keywords such as *purchase* or *buy now* from your Web page. Having those keywords on your page enters it into ranking against e-commerce sites, and you run the risk of diluting your page theme and losing the rankings you really want, which are the ones for a research site.

The simple solution is to place all of the call-to-action keywords within an image, which renders them invisible to a search engine but still visible to the user. It's important to keep keywords that do not pertain to your particular silo (remember, they run along a common theme, like a certain model of car or colors of paint) invisible to a search engine.

JavaScript

The problem with JavaScript when used in site navigation is that it can confuse the search engine with too much or too little information, especially if the JavaScript navigation is the primary way of getting into a silo. Using JavaScript in the form of a drop-down menu as your site navigation might look pretty and keep navigation convenient, but the search engine reads all of this information in each page and attributes it to every single page, as Figure 4-6 shows. Every page on the site would have the unrelated link to the Contact and About pages, which don't need a global link.

If your drop-down menu links to other unrelated pages, the search engine is going to read all of the unrelated keywords and include them when weighing relevancy. For example, your page is about black marbles, but the JavaScript navigation also links to all of your pages on white marbles, blue marbles, green marbles, and pink marbles. When every page on the site links to every other page on the site, it dilutes the page content and weakens the silo.

The solution is to pull the navigation off the page into its own separate JavaScript file. That way, the navigation isn't read as part of the page but as its own separate page, and doesn't dilute your landing pages and silos.

**Book IV
Chapter 4**

**Perfecting
Navigation and
Linking Techniques**

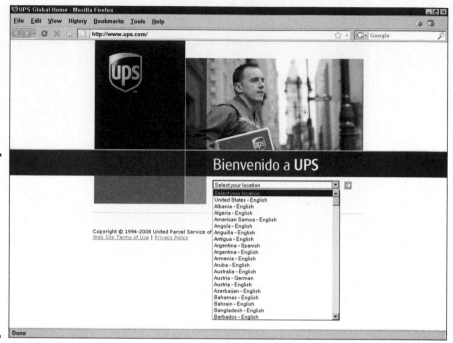

Figure 4-6:
The search engine reads all of the information in a drop-down menu and attributes it to that page.

Flash

Flash content is generally not advisable when doing search engine optimization, simply because a search engine can't read it. There have been some advances with the latest version of Flash that make the text created in Flash readable by spiders, but because it's so easily spammable, it does not carry as much weight as plain text would. Some companies' Web sites require the usage of Flash in order to compete, or to look reliable. The Bruce Clay, Inc. Web site, for example, uses Flash navigation for the top of the page as in Figure 4-7.

However, putting your navigation in Flash also can be a problem for people who have Flash turned off in their browsers in order to avoid Flash-based ads or to keep their browsers from crashing because of a slow-loading modem. In those cases, when they arrive at your Web site, they're not going to be able to see anything or navigate your site.

Flash navigation

Figure 4-7:
The main navigation for www. bruce clay. com is in Flash.

The easy way to fix this problem is to have a text-based version of the information at the bottom of the page in the footer that the search engines can read and use it in their rankings. People who have Flash turned off can also see the text links on the page, as in Figure 4-8.

Text-based navigation

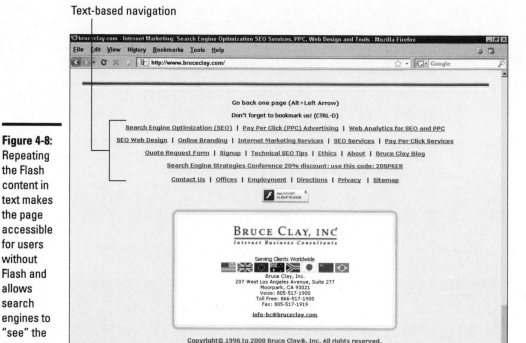

Naming Links

The naming of links, or writing the *anchor text* (the words that make up the actual link someone clicks) is one of the most important aspects of siloing. Providing anchor text for a link tells the search engine what the page that's being linked to is about. If the page content talks about tires, and the anchor text says it's about tires, and any other links to that page all contain the word tires, that's a giant neon arrow to the search engine that that particular page is about tires.

The headings of the page should also match the anchor text that's linking from outside the page. It's positive reinforcement for the search engines. If the sign that says *Pancakes* is pointing to a building that advertises pancakes in the window, it's a pretty safe assumption that the business sells pancakes. That goes double if there are multiple signs pointing to the building saying *Pancakes*.

Another way of working with anchor text is to vary the actual anchor text. In the case of the signs, it would be something like "Let's go eat at the pancake place," "This place makes great pancakes," and "Let's go here for pancakes." You can expand this as well and say the page is about all types of pancakes, so you'd want to link back using synonyms for pancakes like *flapjacks*, *hot-cakes*, and other types of pancakes. Using synonyms creates good varying anchor text, assuming there were no pages about those on your site. They all mean the same thing, but the different wording allows for the anchor text to match a greater variety of search queries.

Slight variations in your anchor text wording also sound more natural. That's the way people talk. It's important to keep your link names as natural-sounding as possible. Not only is it uncomfortable for users to read things that seem stilted or forced, but also the search engines expect to find text that sounds natural, and may suspect spam otherwise.

Book V
Creating Content

Embedding a video in Flash lets you closely associate text with the video.

Contents at a Glance

Chapter 1: Selecting a Style for Your Audience 293

Knowing Your Demographic 294
Creating a Dynamic Tone 299
Choosing a Content Style. 301
Using Personas to Define Your Audience. 301

Chapter 2: Establishing Content Depth and Page Length 307

Building Enough Content to Rank Well. 308
Developing Ideas for Content. 309
Using Various Types of Content 312
Optimizing Images 313
Mixing in Video 315
Making the Text Readable 318
Allowing User Input 322
Creating User Engagement 323
Writing a Call to Action. 325

Chapter 3: Adding Keyword-Specific Content 327

Creating Your Keyword List. 327
Developing Content Using Your Keywords 329
Optimizing the Content. 334
Finding Tools for Keyword Integration 338

Chapter 4: Dealing with Duplicate Content. .341

Sources of Duplicate Content and How to Resolve Them. 342
Intentional Spam. 351

Chapter 5: Adapting and Crediting Your Content 355

Optimizing for Local Searches 356
Factoring in Intellectual Property Considerations 359

Chapter 1: Selecting a Style for Your Audience

In This Chapter

↙ **Knowing your target audience**

↙ **Looking at your current customers to understand their demographics**

↙ **Interviewing and researching to analyze your target audience**

↙ **Choosing the right tone to engage your audience**

↙ **Using personas to define your audience**

↙ **Understanding the benefits and drawbacks of using personas**

The slogan "Content is king!" has been stated and restated in every blog, forum, conference, and seminar that has anything to do with search engine optimization (SEO) or Internet marketing. Content includes all the stuff inside your Web site: everything from the words you read, to the pictures and videos you view, to the audio you listen to. In this chapter, we teach you all about the most important content element for SEO — the words on the page. The text content draws people to your site, starting with the brief title that shows up on a search results page. Content holds a visitor's interest long enough to read your page and, hopefully, move on to do more. Content is what gives your Web site credibility with both your visitors and other sites so that they want to endorse you with a link or purchase. Content tells the search engines what you're all about. Content proves (or disproves) that you know what you're talking about.

And content takes hours and hours and laborious days to create. If you feel overwhelmed by the need to write tons of new content, we understand. The prospect of writing page after page of content can make many people want to crawl under the nearest desk, but the truth is, your Web site really cannot do without it. Good content and plenty of it is needed if you want to rank well with the search engines and attract users who convert into customers (however you define that conversion). For this reason, these chapters on content creation may be the most valuable pages in this book.

Good, relevant content is your single most SEO potent tool. It allows you to do the following:

✦ Differentiate your site from the masses.

✦ Attract expert links to your site.

✦ Develop a loyal site following and brand.

✦ Launch your site higher in the search engine rankings.

In this chapter, you think through how to create the best content for your site's purposes and target audience. You first need to understand who your site needs to appeal to, so we begin by discussing what demographic information you need to know about your target audience and how you can find it out. Next, you learn how to choose a dynamic tone and style that can effectively communicate with your audience and yield conversions. Last, you find out how to create a *persona* (a profile that represents your target audience based on calculated averages of their buying processes and demographics) so that you can design appropriate content that satisfies a specific, highly targeted group.

Knowing Your Demographic

Before you communicate anything, asking "Who is my audience?" is a great first step. You might be an expert in your field, but unless you can explain what you know in a way that your target audience understands, you can't communicate your expertise. With your Web site, your job is not only to communicate, but also to persuade because you want *conversions* (visitors who make a purchase, sign up for a newsletter, or whatever action your Web site requires). Understanding who your audience is becomes even more essential in order to better target your conversions.

Many new Web marketers make the mistake of thinking they don't have a target audience: They see the Internet as a vast crowd of people and just want them to come to their site. But attracting visitors to your site who convert requires *specific* targeted marketing. The Internet population includes many types of people, and the more precisely you can figure out who your target visitors are, the more effective you can be at attracting and holding their interest and making conversions.

Finding out customer goals

Beyond knowing *who* your target audience is, you also want to find out *what* they need. You know what your Web site offers. Now turn your chair around and look at your site from the other direction. Why would a person come to your site? What goal would they be trying to meet?

You want to be sure to meet your visitors' needs first before trying to motivate them to do anything else. Imagine you've spent two hours working and sweating in the hot sun to fix a broken sprinkler in your yard. You finally get it under control and walk toward the house for a cold drink. You have only one thing on your mind: your thirst. If another family member meets you at the door to show you something, how attentive will you be? You're probably not going to give them much attention until your need for cold refreshment is satisfied.

Similarly, your Web site visitors come to your site with a need in mind, and your first priority should be to meet that need. It may be to get information. It may be to research a product to buy. It may be to find a better price, free shipping, or some other special deal on a product they've already decided to buy. When you figure out what your site visitor's goals are, you can make sure your Web pages deliver.

Meet your visitor's goal in the easiest, quickest way possible. If your site sells choir robes, you want to help your visitor pick out the right styles, fabrics, sizes, and quantities as smoothly as possible. You can present lots of textual information to help them make the best choices, but you don't want to distract them with cute videos of choir performances, mix in song lyric downloads, or clutter up your shopping cart page with Flash animations. Their goal is to purchase choir robes. Your goal is to help them do it as directly and pleasantly as possible. Do this by leaving clues in your copy for your visitors. Tell them how to accomplish their goal. Remember that the trigger words for shopping and research differ: *buy*, *free*, and *sale* appeal to different visitors than do *how-to*, *step-by-step instructions*, and *more information*.

The more you know about your target audience — who they are and what their goals are — the more effective your Web site can be.

Looking at current customer data

The best way to begin researching your target audience is to look at your existing customers. (We call them "customers" for ease of writing, but depending on your business model, you might call them subscribers, members, clients, or another term.) What do you know about the people already on your customer list? You probably won't succeed in gathering all of this information, but here are a few types of demographics to look for. These facts are helpful in profiling your target audience:

✦ **Gender:** Are most of your customers male, female, or are they evenly split?

✦ **Age:** Maybe your customers fall into a single age group, for example, tweens, teenagers, college students, young adults, 30-somethings, and so on.

✦ **Location:** Do you know where your customers live? They may be concentrated within a given geographic area, in which case being included in local search engines and utilizing local ads might be part of your strategy.

✦ **Marital status:** Do you know whether your customers tend to be single, married, or divorced? You can cater differently to married couples and singles with your site design and style.

✦ **Education:** What level of education do your customers have? This ties into the age category, too, but if your audience is made up of adults, knowing whether they never attended college or hold master's degrees definitely impacts how you can communicate with them. (Note: Book V, Chapter 4 explains writing for different grade levels.)

✦ **Occupation:** Do you know what field your customers are in specifically? If your Web site offers an industry-specific product, it's obviously an important factor for your target audience. But even if you offer products to the general public, knowing customer occupations can help you with target marketing. If you know, for instance, that a lot of nurses like your product, one place you might want to develop links to your site (or run ads, and so on) could be on sites that are popular with nurses.

✦ **Beliefs:** What do you know about their religious, political, or philosophical beliefs? For instance, if your site collects signatures for various petitions, knowing how your typical petition signer leans politically helps you target the right audience for your site.

✦ **Lifestyle/situational:** What do you know about their lifestyles? You may find a trend among your customers to be single parents or married couples with children; apartment renters or homeowners; city dwellers, suburbanites, or farmers; boat owners or horse owners or other. Whatever extra information like this you can gather gives you useful clues about your target audience.

✦ **Much more:** Customize this list with other types of pertinent information for your Web site marketing. You probably won't be able to get all the information you want, but having a wish list is a good start. Income level, ethnicity, and hobbies are all excellent things to know about your customers. Much of this information is easily obtained just by asking for it. The registration process on many sites often asks for these facts. If your registration process includes the ability to do so, turn it on and see what you learn.

Researching to find out more

In addition to examining the customer data you have, you can look at industry statistics. Find out what data is available out there. Do some homework online and track down information sources. If there's a trade association for your industry, see if they can provide statistics, member rosters, and other types of information. You might find news articles, court cases, studies, or who knows what else, but see what's out there that gives you more information about your typical customer.

Interviewing customers

Next, consider interviewing past and current members of your target audience to find out more about them. A typical method is to ask users to complete a form on your Web site. It might be a sign-up form at the beginning of your conversion process, or a feedback form you pop up on the screen at the end of a process. Or you might prefer to interview the old-fashioned way and directly contact people by mail, phone, or e-mail. A survey can work great, although you may need to offer some incentive to the user for filling it out (a discount, a coupon, or some other prize).

You can e-mail people a link to complete a survey online. Sites like www.questionpro.com make setting up an online survey very easy to do; you just need to plan the questions you want to ask (see Figure 1-1). The costs can be nominal, depending on what services you use.

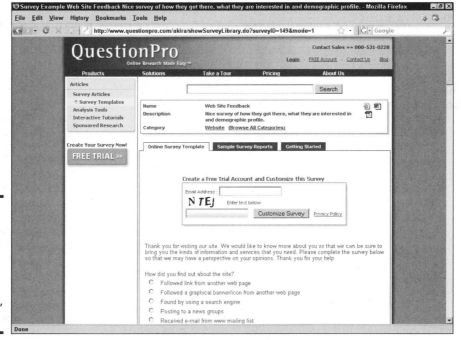

Figure 1-1:
Online surveys are easy to set up and can be inexpensive, too.

When interviewing people, try to gather some personal demographic information (such as the items in the previous bulleted list) as well as some feedback about their experience on your Web site. It's a golden opportunity for valuable feedback from past customers. Here are some good things to learn during your interview:

✦ How the person found your Web site

✦ What their impression was of the site

✦ Whether they had any difficulty getting around your site, or whether they found it easy to use

✦ Whether they were pleased with the service or response they received (if applicable)

✦ What type of product or service were they looking for

Include these two questions in your survey to get a technical picture of your customers' awareness:

✦ How often do they go online and how long do they spend there?

✦ Which of your competitors' sites do they visit?

You can also use your surveys in conjunction with the data your analytics tool gathers to discover information about their browsing habits that will help you understand your customers' online habits. You can easily get this data with a simple server-side script that captures header data:

✦ The type of computer they use

✦ The *ISP* (Internet service provider) they use to access the Internet

✦ The speed or type of Internet connection they use (broadband, cable modem, dial-up, and so on)

✦ What Internet browser they prefer

The answers to these questions give you an idea of how tech-savvy your customer base is. For instance, the Microsoft Internet Explorer (IE) browser dominates with roughly 75 percent of total market share currently (because Windows comes with IE preinstalled). However, the Mozilla Firefox browser tends to be heavily used by people in Web technology fields (such as SEO). So if you find your users prefer Firefox, that might be a clue that they're more technical than the average user, which can influence how you set up your Web site and write your content. On the other hand, if your users get to the Internet through their AOL interface and stay there throughout their Web session, you know you're probably dealing with a less technical user base.

If you have any professional associations in your industry (the SEO community has SEMPO, for example), check with them to see if they've done any
demographic research, which is likely more cost-effective than conducting
your own research. This is a particularly good idea for a new site that might
not yet have a large user base to interview.

Using server logs and analytics

Your Web site's server logs contain valuable data about your visitor counts
and their behavior. It's also a good idea to have *analytics* embedded in your
Web pages, which are program routines a Web site can use to track user
behavior on the site. Talk to your IT department or Webmaster and see what
they can tell you about your Web traffic and the user behavior on each page.

If you would like more analytics operating on your Web site or want to know
all the choices out there, we cover Web analytics in detail in Book VIII. We
also recommend you check out the following resources:

✦ **The Web Analytics Association (`www.webanalyticsassociation.
org`):** The trade association for Web analytics professionals is a good
source for information.

✦ **Google Analytics (`www.google.com/analytics/`):** Free analytics help
and resources from Google.

✦ **Omniture (`www.omniture.com`):** One of the top vendors for analytics
programs.

In addition, some tools can look at your recent Web site traffic and tell you
where visitors came from and what search terms they used to find your Web
site. These are extremely valuable for SEO. Knowing where your users come
from can give you clues to their goals. For instance, if your site sells shoes
and you find a lot of visitors coming from youth soccer sites, they're likely
looking for children's soccer shoes and cleats. This information can help you
style your site to help those visitors find exactly what they need.

Creating a Dynamic Tone

The writing for your Web site should

✦ Engage your target audience with an appropriate style and tone. For
example, this book uses a conversational tone that wouldn't be appropriate in a scholarly journal. A site targeting teens might rely more heavily on modern slang than a site targeting baby boomers.

✦ Lead visitors to the goal you have for each Web page.

✦ Meet the visitor's need with relevant content as directly and quickly as
possible.

You want to write engaging text that's appropriate for your target audience and meets your site goals. As a general rule, effective Web site copy should be dynamic in the sense of being (as the Encarta dictionary defines it) "vigorous and purposeful, full of energy, enthusiasm and a sense of purpose." As we discuss earlier in the chapter, each of your Web pages should have a goal that matches the perceived visitor's goal, which may be to gather information, clarify a question, sign up for something, make a purchase, or something else. The text on each page should engage readers and lead them to fulfill the goal.

The tone of a written piece can make or break it. *Tone* refers to the writer's attitude toward the subject matter and toward the reader. Tone creates an emotional response in readers. The wrong tone can turn off an audience within the first sentence or two.

When people talk about the way a piece "comes across," they're talking about its tone. In speaking, people call it the "tone of voice," and it affects communication powerfully. Dogs, for example, can tell a lot by the sound of their master's voice: They might come running or hide their tails based solely on their master's tone. In written communication, an author's tone comes through in more subtle ways. Word choice, sentence length, punctuation, grammar, sentence structure — all of these and more convey the tone.

Your writing tone should support your site goal and be appropriate for your target audience. For example, if you're a heavy metal band promoter, you wouldn't want to greet your visitors with rainbows and ponies, and a jaunty message like, "You've arrived! Mr. Ponypants wants you to have a super fun day!" The bouncy, enthusiastic tone is all wrong for the target audience and would probably have visitors heading straight for their Back button. There's nothing wrong with heavy metal or ponies, but typically fans of each aren't found in the same company. Instead, you'd want the tone to come across as rebellious and rowdy, meeting your target audience in the same spirit they're showing. Only then would you be able to achieve your site's conversion goal, which is to engage people and interest them in becoming clients.

Look at your current Web site and ask yourself how you feel when you read it, but don't just stop there. Read it out loud to yourself or someone else to see if it flows nicely to the ear. This is usually an enlightening experience. Ask someone you know to read it with fresh eyes to give you this feedback. Ask them to tell you what attitude comes through the writing. How does it make them feel: happy, lighthearted, positive, hopeful, enlightened, or wanting more? Or does it make them feel uncomfortable, belittled, creepy, angry, annoyed, or frustrated?

Think about what response you would want your target audience to have when they read your Web site. The emotional response your tone evokes in your readers can make them want to stay or run away, so choose it carefully.

Choosing a Content Style

After you know who your target audience is, you can adjust your Web site to be appropriate for them. We talk in Book IV, Chapter 2 about tailoring your Web site design to your target audience. Now in Book V, we focus on tailoring the content style to your target audience.

Listen to your customers. The words they use to talk about your industry and your products and services could be very different from how you describe the same things. Jargon that may be commonplace in your offices won't necessarily be familiar to your potential clients. You want to incorporate their words into your Web site. Not only does this ensure that people understand what they're reading on your site, but it also adds keywords that people search for when they to try to find you.

You also must listen to the *way* in which your customers talk: not just the words they're using, but how they're using them. If your target audience is children, you don't want your Web site to read like a dry academic text, or you'll just bore them. If your target audience is medical researchers, your Web site can be written in a more academic style with longer words and sentences. You want to make visitors feel that they've come to the right place. You can do this when you support relevant content with a style and tone that feel natural and appropriate. So use a style that reaches your target audience and feels natural for the content.

Using Personas to Define Your Audience

To help you evaluate your Web site from your target customer's perspective, you can create a fictional Web persona based on all the customer data you accumulated. A *persona* is like a role, and it includes how a person acts, talks, thinks, believes, and so on. The customer Web persona you create is a profile that represents your target audience based on calculated averages of your customer's buying processes, goals, and demographics. Companies use personas as user archetypes to help guide their decisions concerning product launches, new features, customer interaction, and site design. It's easier to evaluate things from a particular Jane Doe's or John Doe's perspective than just imagining a vague customer group. By understanding the goals and patterns of your audience, your company can create archetypes to help create services to satisfy a specific, highly targeted group.

Your goal is to create a persona that encompasses the most complete picture of your target audience. In fact, you may want to create several personas, depending on your Web site's various goals and how varied your customers are. Linda the mother of two has different motivations for being on your site than Debbie the high-powered sales exec or Fred the college student. Creating more than one persona allows you to produce the maximum amount of appeal to your real-life customers. Creating effective personas helps you

✦ Understand (and keep in mind) your target audience's goals and beliefs.

✦ Develop the most effective voice for your company's Web site.

✦ Determine what products/features are and are not accepted by your audience.

✦ Get to know your audience on a more personal level.

✦ Build a shared vocabulary between you and your audience to avoid confusion.

✦ Enable your company to make informed decisions.

Creating personas

Creating personas helps you identify your customers' buying decision processes to allow you to maximize your conversion rate. Acquiring and analyzing the type of data listed earlier in this chapter can help you develop a more complete picture of who your audience really is, how they spend their time, and what they value as being important. After looking at this information, you can start to see patterns emerge. These patterns are the basis for the personas you create.

In looking for patterns, notice the similarities and differences between your customers through your research. Keep in mind that personas represent your audience's behavior patterns, not job descriptions, locations, or occupations. Although it's important to be aware of this information, these details should not be the basis of your archetypes. A properly defined persona gives you a well-rounded picture of your customers' attitudes, skills, and goals; it's not just a résumé that only offers a surface view.

After you have your data, group the information in a way that makes the most complete picture of a person. This includes assembling key traits (such as behavior patterns, and similar buying processes) to try and form a cohesive "person." You should be able to use the collected information to form a small group of "people" that you feel represent your audience. Each persona (like your real audience) should be different, wanting and looking for different things.

When you are creating your personas, *do not* model them after someone you know. This would alter how you work with them. A persona should be a purely fictional character that you feel best represents some segment of your audience. Keeping it fictional forces you to concentrate on your audience and address their needs.

After you have your persona, don't keep her (or him) to yourself. Share it with the other members of your company to get their insights. They may have valuable opinions that help you narrow down or fill out the personality of your customer. Use this time to fill in any blanks. Name your persona to differentiate her from the others: Don't just call her *Jane Doe*. Choose a name that you can believe in, not one that's just a stand-in.

Using personas

You now have your persona: You've named her, you know where she comes from, and you know what she's looking for. But you're not done. It is now time to put your persona into action. Use your persona to role-play:

✦ **Case studies:** Imagine your persona coming to your Web site for various purposes. Walk through the processes the persona would use.

✦ **User testing:** Using your persona, try out a feature of your Web site. You can also use your persona when running different keyword searches, starting at a search engine, and find out how quickly relevant information can be found on your site.

✦ **New feature evaluation:** Try out any new pages or features of your Web site from your various personas' points of view and see how easy they are to use.

✦ **Product decisions:** Coming from each of your personas' perspectives, think through how useful a new product would be. You may be able to identify whether the product meets a typical user's need as is, or needs some value-add-on to have better marketability.

✦ **Design decisions:** See your Web site design through a persona's eyes to determine whether the colors, placement, layout, bells and whistles, and other design elements make it easier or harder for visitors to achieve their goals.

✦ **Customer service:** Use your personas to find out how easy it is to get help when using your Web site. Remember, your Web persona doesn't know that you have an exhaustive Help system linked from the site map, or that clicking a tiny link somewhere in the footer launches a live chat window. The persona only knows what it can easily see during its process, so this is a valuable way to find weaknesses in your Web site.

Here is an example of a persona and how you can put it to use:

Jane is a competitive personality. Social status is very important to her and she appreciates it in others. She tends to be impulsive and doesn't mind the impersonality of doing things online as long as she is able to get what she needs quickly and efficiently. She is looking for verifiable results and quantifiable bottom lines. Social interaction is not important to her. She is willing to pay more to get a little extra. She is unmarried and does not see marriage in her near future.

Jane is very Internet-savvy and uses the Internet for 10 or more hours per day. She has multiple e-mail accounts from various service providers and does all of her shopping and banking online. Jane works for an Internet company and has just purchased a modest condo in the suburbs outside a large metropolitan city.

By analyzing the profile of Jane, you can better target her needs. Based on this, you can see that her primary concern is for quick, expert information. Jane is an impulsive buyer; the key to acquiring her conversion is to give her information in a quick, easy-to-read format while touching on her desire for prestige. You can guess that when she first visits your site, her eye quickly scans the content for keywords. If you lose her interest for a moment, she's gone.

The profile also gives you an idea of Jane's experience level with your product. This can help you decide how to target her. Here are two example scenarios:

Scenario A: Jane at a technology-related Web site: If you are a technology company, you know that Jane has a certain experience level with your breed of product. You can assume that Jane likely understands the basic workings of your merchandise without you having to break things down step-by-step. Based on her Internet savvy, you know she likely has little or no problem navigating through your site, but if she doesn't find what she's looking for immediately, she will likely take off and visit one of your competitor sites. At this stage in her life, brand loyalty comes second to quick service.

Scenario B: Jane at a non-technical Web site: If your product is home- and garden-related, you know that Jane needs a lot of detailed information to better understand how your product or service could benefit her. You need to make sure your information is presented upfront so that Jane doesn't wander away from your site. You know that Jane just purchased her first home. It's likely she is looking for easy ways to spruce it up. How can you gear your marketing campaign to address this? Perhaps there's a way to market your product as a "timesaver" so that she can focus on other things. Is Jane likely to have a pet? Maybe your product can do a better job of keeping her pet safe. By understanding Jane, it allows you to target her more efficiently.

Using Jane's persona helps you identify the language that most likely appeals to her and satisfies her motivations and needs. When you're testing out new features or campaign plans, make sure to keep Jane in mind. Ask yourself these types of questions for each of your personas:

✦ **Benefits:** Does this feature offer a clear benefit to this persona?

✦ **Level of explanation:** What, if anything, do I need to provide this persona with to help her understand this benefit?

✦ **Wording:** What kind of language should I use? Does this persona understand industry jargon, or do I need to define terms in the page content for her?

✦ **Style:** How can my writing style fit this persona, and give her what she's looking for most naturally and directly?

✦ **Tone:** What tone would seem most natural to this persona? Would a tone that's friendly, professional, enthusiastic, subdued, energetic, calm, or other best suit her goals and influence her to stay on the site and move toward my Web page's goal?

✦ **Clarity:** Does this persona realize the problem this feature is supposed to address? How much do I need to spell out?

Benefits of using personas

Personas provide many benefits. First, by speaking with your customers directly while gathering the data to create your personas, you have taken the first important steps to creating brand loyalty. Taking time to ask them about their needs and their interests shows them that you are interested in who they are, not just that you are out to make a sale. You want to learn about them, their goals, and what is important to them so that you can make your product better for *them*. Customers are likely to remember such a move and are more likely to do business with you in the future. By investing in them, you have made it easier for them to invest in you.

Secondly, your personas can alert you to problems you might not have known about. For example, while doing your research, you may discover that your customer base is larger and wider than you imagined. Knowing this shows you that there are two or more very different audiences that you must address. This could lead to creating a whole new product or set of instructions to fit more advanced users, while still catering to your more inexperienced ones. It could also lead to adding more pages to your Web site, or incorporating more appropriate text on each page.

Drawbacks of using personas

Many companies resist the idea of personas because they don't understand how they work. They may design personas that are too vague to be efficient in helping with the direction of their company. If not done correctly, personas may cause companies to pigeonhole their audience, negating the basic purpose of creating personas.

Another drawback of using strict personas is that no matter how much research you do or how deeply you analyze it, you can never know 100 percent for sure that your customers feel exactly the way that your fictional personas do. If you tailor your campaigns too closely to a persona, you risk alienating some of your other customers. This is why it's important to create multiple personas: You have a better chance at targeting the largest number of users.

At the end of the day, despite your best efforts at analyzing your customers' personalities, all you are left with is a best guess about what they're looking for and who they really are. Using Web personas allows your guess to be an educated one and provides your company with an invaluable tool to help keep users' interests in mind.

Chapter 2: Establishing Content Depth and Page Length

In This Chapter

✔ **Writing for maximum readability**

✔ **Varying content to increase user interest and search-engine ranking**

✔ **Formatting your text for optimum readability**

✔ **Enabling user-generated content**

✔ **Writing an effective call to action**

Search engines find out what your Web pages are about by reading them. They read everything they can find on your site — the text on your pages, the text in your HTML code, the names of your files and directories, and the *anchor text* in all your links (which is the text someone clicks in order to follow the link). They also read the anchor text of any inbound links to your site from other people's Web sites to find out what they've written about you. Using all of this textual information along with a few other factors like links and engagement objects, search engines determine what your site is about, what search terms your Web pages are relevant for, and how much of an authority you are on your topics — and then rank you accordingly.

Because of this focus on written words, a successfully optimized Web site must have a lot of content. A home page with a single graphic and no textual content can't rank well with the search engines, no matter how cool it looks. On the other hand, a page with a lot of words but no cohesive theme also won't rank well, and for the same reason: The search engines can't figure out what the page is about. The right balance is to have enough content *and* to have it focused on a theme. Then the search engines can index your site and know exactly what it's about.

In this chapter, you find out how to develop content ideas, how to integrate various types of content for a blended approach, and all about the rules for optimizing images and video. You also discover the importance of formatting text so that it's readable and how you can allow user input to build a stronger site. Finally, you find out how to create user engagement by writing effective calls to action.

Building Enough Content to Rank Well

How much content do you need in terms of words per page and pages per subject? Before we tell you our SEO best practices, we want to stress that the answer greatly depends on what is normal for your industry and keywords. When you research your competitors' sites that rank well for your keywords, some of the things you want to find out are how many indexed pages they have and how many words are on the pages that outrank yours. (Note that Book III explains how to do competitive research in detail.) Analyzing these figures among your competitors gives you an indication of what level of content is currently succeeding in the search engines for your keywords. This helps you know how many pages and words you need to play in their league.

Now for the best practices. We recommend that you have a *minimum of 450 words of text content per page.* That's a general rule, based on our experience across multiple niches. Again, this is a guideline. If all of the top-ranking pages for your keywords have more than 1,000 words each, you may want to consider 1,100 words on your page in order to compete. (Remember that there are many factors in the algorithm and amount of content is only one of them.) But if your research hasn't indicated that you need an unusually high number of words for your industry, 450 words gives the search engines enough content to work with and gives users a satisfying amount of information, as well. It's a little less than one page of typed copy using a 12-point font and single line spacing. In fact, the page that you're reading right now has more than 450 words on it, so you can get an idea of what that amount of content looks like. Also, the number of words you need on a page has been steadily increasing over the years. When we first started recommending adding content back in 1997, we set our minimum at merely 75 words. Today, the number of words on top-ranked pages in some competitive markets is actually closer to 1,000 words on a page. This variance is why analyzing your competitors is so crucial.

As a general rule, you need at least five pages to support each theme. You should have *at least five supporting pages for each theme landing page* on your Web site. (A *landing page* is your primary page of information on a particular topic or subtopic, so it's the page where you want users to land when they search for those keywords and click your listing.) Keep in mind that the required minimum number of pages varies depending on what your competitors have. The search engines want to return the most relevant results to a user's search query, and they want their users to be satisfied. It makes sense that the search engines would rank most highly the sites that seem to be the experts, or authorities, in the subject the user is interested in.

For instance, if you're trying to rank for the *keyword phrase* [Ford Mustang], you're going up against sites that have dozens of related pages about Ford Mustangs including facts, forums, customer reviews, multimedia, and so on.

(A *keyword phrase* is a search query containing two or more words that your Web page content relates to.) That kind of competitive environment would require you to have a lot more than five pages of content on Ford Mustangs in order to be considered as much of an authority as the other sites are. You'd need to really beef up your site to make it into the top 10–20 search results.

If you've already worked on categorizing your Web site into subject themes, as we explain in Book II, Chapter 4 and elsewhere, you should have a good idea of what "holes" you need to fill in your Web site. As you go through this chapter, keep in mind your list of landing-page topics and what you need in terms of new content either on those pages or on supporting pages. Figure 2-1 shows a sample Web site in the construction stage. As you can see, it looks like Topic A needs more pages.

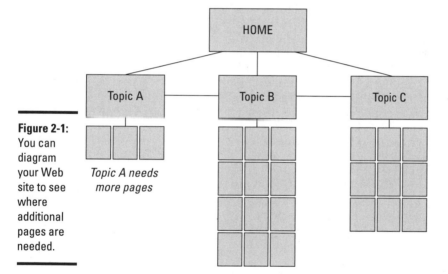

Figure 2-1: You can diagram your Web site to see where additional pages are needed.

Topic A needs more pages

Developing Ideas for Content

You may feel overwhelmed at the thought of writing pages and pages of content for your Web site that have at least 450 words each, but take heart. There are lots of ways to get ideas for content, and even some shortcuts for creating it.

In this section, we help get you started with four ways to find content ideas:

✦ **Brainstorming**: You want to tap into your own creative juices first. Get input from your employees and coworkers, too.

✦ **Looking at competitors:** Don't copy them, but you can definitely get ideas from them.

✦ **Utilizing your offline materials:** Repurpose what you've already written.

✦ **Listening to customers:** Find out what they want to know.

Brainstorming to get ideas

The best source of original content for your Web site may be yourself. You and the other people in your Web-site business are authorities in one thing: your own business. You know the most about your Web site's goals, products, services, clientele, methods, expertise, history, personnel, and so forth. You might discover that a lot of that information would be interesting and useful for your site visitors. For example, you could ask the founder to write a three-paragraph history of how the company got started (or have someone interview him and write it up). Or you might write about your operations or your facilities like a tour guide, complete with pictures. When you write about your company, industry, and products, it's easy and natural to include lots of keywords, which benefits your SEO efforts. You probably have a wealth of interesting information about your company and its products and services that could be turned into Web site content.

Brainstorm other kinds of content ideas, too — at this stage, accept any idea that could be useful and engaging to your target audience. Make a list of all possible articles, stories, topics, tidbits, quotes, and so on. Don't stop at just what you're able to create. Consider things that you could write as well as subjects you could find someone else to create. You're just idea-gathering now, so be as creative as you can.

Looking at competitors for content ideas

One of the best ways to fill content holes on your Web site is to do some competitive research to see what others in your industry are writing about. You want to see what they're doing right, where they're missing the mark, and what you could add to your site that they haven't even thought of yet.

Travel your competitors' Web sites like a user and discover what they have to offer. In particular, look at the landing page that is competing with your own for the same keyword. Notice its content as well as the various supporting pages linked from it. (Note: You also can do some serious analysis of these pages using the procedures we describe in Book III, Chapter 2, but right now you're just trying to get some ideas for new content.)

When you go through your competitors' sites, you're essentially looking for anything they have that gives them an advantage — any special content that appeals only to a certain sector or that is attracting links. You are not using their site as a blueprint to copy, but venturing off your own Web site and seeing things from a visitor's eye that can alert you to holes you would have missed otherwise. You can get ideas for original content that can be just as good as, or better than, your competitor's.

What you're looking for depends on your content needs. If you're looking to beef up the number of pages on your site, look at what your competitors offer and how they're marketing themselves, and then find ways to differentiate yourself. You want to make yourself equal to the competition before you can set yourself apart. Make sure you match what they offer in your own way and then provide content that explains why you're unique, more trustworthy, and overall just better-suited to fit the visitor's needs.

One thing you can notice is how they structure their information compared to how your site does it. For instance, if the two Web sites sell competing products, compare how they're each presented. Your page might offer a description in paragraph form only, whereas your competitor includes a complete bulleted list of features with links to view a schematic diagram, product dimensions, installation instructions, and consumer reviews. In that situation, you know you have some writing to do in order to boost your content about that product.

You also could get ideas for how to present similar information better. For example, say your product is cowboy boots. A brief mention on a competitor's site about the importance of breaking in your boots before the beginning of rodeo season could spark the idea to write a whole article about this on your site. Or your competitor's site might have a chart showing boot sizes compared to normal shoe sizes. That's useful information that could help the consumer make a purchase decision, so you want to add this feature to your Web site — but do it better. You might add a third column with the corresponding sock sizes. Or make it a neat, interactive tool rather than a static chart. Or enhance it with illustrations of different sized feet . . . you get the idea. Develop a page debating the eternal question: to tuck your jeans into your boots or not to tuck? Have customers respond and send in pictures with their explanations.

By looking at competitors, you can identify holes in your own site as well as ideas to set your site apart. You want to be continuously looking for creative ways to make yourself more interesting and more useful to your visitors. As much content as there is on the Web, a lot of it can be improved. It can be written to be clearer, updated to be more interesting, or tweaked to allow users to interact with it in a fresh way. Be on the lookout for these types of opportunities to make your site stand out.

Utilizing your offline materials

One shortcut to creating Web site content is to pull from what you already have. Review everything your business has ever written to see if it can be repurposed for your Web site. Brochures, flyers, catalogs, articles, manuals, tutorials, online help resources, and even customer correspondence may contain volumes of helpful content. Do you have a user manual or instructions to go with one of your products? Consider replicating it online in

HTML. The same goes for marketing materials, text on packaging, or other printed collateral. The writing may need to be updated, but starting with content makes your job much easier than starting from a blank page.

Frequently asked questions (FAQs) can be a popular Web site feature, and they're very useful in helping user find the information they need. If your company maintains a support staff for customer assistance, they may already have an FAQ list started that includes the right answers. If you work for a company, ask around to find out what your various departments already have documented that could be polished a bit and used on the Web.

Listening to customers

You want your Web site to serve your customers and target prospects, so try to address what they'd like to know. Talk to your customers. Ask some questions. Also talk to your support people to find out what customers ask about frequently. You may find great ideas for articles to add to the Web site (and help out your support department as a bonus). If you have a site search, you can mine those queries as well. What is of interest to one customer might be valuable to more, particularly if variations on the same keyword phrase keep popping up.

You might also check blog sites for your industry, your area, or your target demographic (whichever of those apply) to see what people are talking about related to your keywords. You can use Google's blog search (`http://blogsearch.google.com`) and type in your keyword phrases, your company name, or other pertinent search terms. You can get some excellent ideas for Web site content by listening to what's being talked about. Just make sure that the ideas relate closely to your Web business so you don't dilute your themes with unrelated content.

Using Various Types of Content

Search engines may be deaf, dumb, and blind, but users aren't, and search engines understand that. So far in this chapter, we've focused on writing text that gives the search engines lots of content to rank you with. Now we want to turn to the other side of the equation: creating content to engage your users.

Pictures, movie clips, sounds — all these things help hold a visitor's interest on your Web site. Including other types of content besides text is a good idea for many reasons. The advent of blended search made these files important for search engine rankings, as well. (*Blended search* is the search engines' method of combining different types of listings in a search results page, such as Web pages, news articles, pictures, videos, blog posts, and so on.) Google and the other search engines consider these engagement objects among the factors that help a Web page rank well. If two pages are otherwise equal, it makes sense that the search engine would prefer to send its users to a page that has pictures, videos, or other types of content to make the experience more engaging.

Optimizing Images

When you include pictures, video, or other non-text elements in your Web site, you need to describe them in the surrounding text. This is the key to optimizing your multimedia elements so that search engines know what they're about because the search engine spiders can't watch a video or see a picture. You must explain the image or video or any other non-text element using words.

For images (including JPEG, GIF, and other types of picture files), you have several places where you can put descriptive text that the search engines can read. You can refer to what the image is about in the following locations:

✦ **Text surrounding the element:** Include descriptive text either above, below, or next to the picture, video, or other non-text element. A caption or a lead-in sentence that explains what the image shows works well. This gives search engine spiders text they can read and index, but it also helps communicate your intended meaning to users.

✦ **Filename:** The file names of your image, video, and other types of multimedia files contain actual words.

✦ **Alt attribute:** You can also put brief descriptive text into the `Alt` attribute attached to any image. For example, `alt="1968 Ford Mustang California Special Gas Cap"`.

Naming images

Because both people and search engines are going to read your file names, make sure to use good, descriptive words in your image, video, and other types of multimedia files. Here is another opportunity to provide readable content (with keywords, if appropriate) to the spiders. Instead of naming your image A1234.jpg, call that photo of a skier falling on his face skier-face-plant.jpg so the search engines know what it is, too.

To separate words, don't use a space or an underscore (underscores are seen as an alpha character, rather than as punctuation). Instead, use a hyphen or a period to separate words in your filenames. But try not to over-use them either — just because you can have many dashes in a URL doesn't mean that you should.

Alt attributes and the law

You want to help all types of visitors access your Web site, including people with disabilities. It turns out that there's an easy thing you can do to make your site easier to use for people with vision impairments, and that is to use `Alt` attributes on your images. Not only does that improve your site for visitors, but it's also now the law.

The Americans with Disabilities Act (ADA) states that persons with disabilities may not be denied equal access to goods and services. In 2006, a court ruled that this applied to Web sites as well as physical retail establishments. The case, which was between the National Federation of the Blind and Target.com (www.

target.com), resulted in a ruling that Web sites must accommodate vision-impaired users by putting `Alt` attributes on every image. Vision-impaired people navigate the Web using screen-reading software. The software vocalizes the text and describes the graphics by reading their `Alt` attributes. If an `Alt` attribute is missing, the screen reader actually says the image's URL out loud! This doesn't help anyone, and is definitely user-unfriendly!

Put `Alt` attributes on your images to communicate what the image is about and include your keywords. It's a win-win for you, the search engines, and your users.

Also, keep file names brief. Remember that long filenames cause URLs to get longer, too (such as if one of your images gets returned in an image search). Because people generally avoid clicking long URLs, keep your names to a reasonable length. Six words in a filename would generally be too much. Keep it simple: a picture of a Ford mustang with a dented fender shouldn't be called fordmustang-with-a-dented-fender.jpg, just call it dented-ford-mustang or mustang-dented-fender.jpg. You'll have on-page text and `Alt` attributes to explain to the engines what the content of the image is.

Size matters

We've already said that you want to write descriptive text around images and in their `Alt` attributes. But how much text you use depends on the size of your image. For example, if you have a 50 x 70 pixel photo of a writer's face next to an article, it's enough to just put the person's name in the caption. You could include a longer description of her credentials in the byline copy, but you wouldn't need an entire paragraph of text captioning a small image like this. On the other hand, larger pictures should have longer text descriptions. If the image is important enough to take up a lot of screen space, it's important enough to tell the search engines about. Explain the picture with at least a sentence of text.

If pictures help engage your users, big pictures can satisfy them even more. If you are offering very large images, you might want to put them on a separate page so that only users who really want to see the full-size view have to wait for them to display. However, you don't want the search engines to miss the fact that that picture is part of your page's content, and not some separate, unrelated page. To keep it related, you can show a thumbnail or small version of the image on your original page, with text description, Alt attributes, and the works. Then if a user clicks to view the full-size image in a separate window, consider including a text description there, too — but definitely give it an Alt attribute and filename that describes what's in the image.

When writing Alt attributes for images, make the length proportionate to the image's size on-screen. Create a brief Alt attribute for a small image, and longer ones for large images. As a general guideline, we believe the Alt content should not exceed 12 words.

Mixing in Video

Video enriches your Web site with rich media content that search engines are increasingly looking for. For quick reference, here's a summary of the best practices for mixing in video, which we explain shortly:

✦ **Placement:** Embed the video on the page it relates to, rather than in a separate window.

✦ **Descriptive text:** Include an explanation of the video in the surrounding text.

✦ **Saving:** Save the video file inside the current silo directory, rather than in a central video directory. (Note: You can find out more about silos in Book VI.)

✦ **Play:** Don't start playing a video automatically. Let users start it themselves.

✦ **Size:** Choose a viewing size that fits your audience. The standard video sizes are 320 x 240 pixels (small) and 640 x 480 pixels (larger).

✦ **Quality:** Render your video in a file size that fits your audience. Tech savvy audiences generally have faster connections and can handle larger file sizes. Likewise, urban areas are more likely to have broadband access than rural areas. A media-centric audience will put up with longer download times to get better quality than an audience that just wants an answer right now. Find the balance between good quality and fast download speed.

✦ **Length:** Shorter videos obviously are easier to download and more convenient to watch. Although the content largely determines the length, short is better than long on the Web. Plan to make videos around two or three minutes long. Five minutes is an extremely long time on the Web and it's rare for very long videos (anything more than ten minutes) to do well.

✦ **Posting:** In addition to posting your video on your site, to help your video get noticed, post it to a video-sharing site like YouTube (www. youtube.com) or Metacafe (www.metacafe.com) and link it back to your Web site.

Placing videos where they count most

To include a video on your Web site, the SEO best practice is to embed it within the current page. Don't show it in a pop-up window where it's isolated from the text describing it because you want the spiders to see the video as part of the current page. Many sites move videos into separate windows with no title or text, but this is a lost opportunity from an SEO perspective. Unless you describe the video in words the spiders can read, more than likely it won't be ranked with your content because the search engine cannot tell what it's about.

If you're worried that your page may load too slowly if you embed the video, here's one possible solution. The video can be collapsed when the Web page initially loads, displaying only a link to it. Then if the user clicks the link to watch the video, it can expand and play within the page. This technique uses an expandable `Div` tag that works like a toggle switch, expanding or collapsing the video at the user's choice. You may find that this improves the usability of your page because the user stays in control.

Saving videos, and a word about formats

Where you save the video file matters, too. If your video shows the inside of a Ford Mustang and plays from your Ford Mustang page, save the file inside a directory in your Ford Mustang silo rather than, say, in a root/video directory that's all about cars. That way, the search engines know for certain that it's a video about Ford Mustangs.

Several different video formats are available (Flash, QuickTime, Windows Media, and so on). Currently the Flash format (SWF) seems to be the most popular and offers some advantages over the others. The first is usability — the Flash format may be the easiest for your visitors to use simply because so many browsers have the Flash Player plug-in installed. The second advantage relates more specifically to SEO. Using the most recent version of Adobe Flash, you can show static text right alongside the video that you created within Flash. Figure 2-2 shows a Flash design within a Web page that plays a video and has text above and beside it.

Because the major search engines can read stationary text within newer versions of Flash, adding text to the video file is a perfect way to get it indexed by the search engines. However, you should recall that because of the potential for spam, search engines may not give that Flash content the same weight that on-page text has.

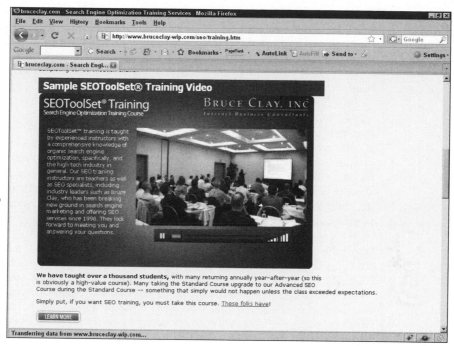

Figure 2-2:
Embedding
a video in
Flash lets
you closely
associate
text with the
video.

If you use another video format, the search engines can still pick it up. Your
descriptive text needs to be in the page text near your embedded video link.
You can also include text in the `Title` attribute of the video file (in the HTML
code, it would look like `Title="Your text here"`). Search engines may or
may not look at the `Title` attributes, and it's definitely not necessary.

Sizing videos appropriately for your audience

When you're deciding how big to make your video, consider your audience
first. If they tend to have the latest technology and fast Internet connections,
you can feel free to upload large-display, good quality videos without too
much concern for their big file size. But if your audience is varied, or not
technically savvy, you may want to stick with smaller files that can easily
stream over lower Internet connection speeds. There are two standard sizes
for video play on the Web: 320 pixels wide by 240 pixels high (small), and
640 pixels wide by 480 pixels high (twice as big).

Choosing the "best" video quality

Quality in this sense refers to the resolution of the video image (how clear it
looks compared to the original) and how clean the audio sounds. The higher
the quality, the bigger the file. You might be tempted to put a full-size, full-
quality video on your site because it looks and sounds great on your desktop,

but after it's online, it may be too large for anyone to download. Weigh what's best for your audience. Studies have been done on video quality, and if you have to pick between decent picture quality and decent audio quality, go with audio quality. Most people are willing to put up with reduced picture quality as long as they can hear the audio clearly, but not the other way around. That said, you can probably keep the audio quality at 128 kbps (kilobytes per second) maximum and meet the dual objectives of good audio quality and good download speed.

Choosing the right video length

Shorter videos are easier to watch than longer ones, download faster, and don't get "stuck" in the middle as often. People also prefer to watch a video that they know will take only a few minutes of their time, versus long ones. They may be reluctant to start a video that requires a lot of time to watch. A software company began creating Flash tutorials that were 15 to 20 minutes long for users to view online (modeling them after the step-by-step approach that had always worked in live trainings). The tutorials seemed like a big success until someone examined the server logs. Of all the people who started watching the tutorials, only 3 percent watched them all the way through, with 90 percent exiting within the first two minutes. Needless to say, their next tutorials were two minutes or under in length.

Posting your videos to increase traffic

Videos can attract users to your site who wouldn't otherwise find it. One strategy is to upload your videos to a video-sharing site like YouTube (www.youtube.com) or Metacafe (www.metacafe.com) and link the videos back to your site. When people see them, they might be enticed to visit your site and explore your other content. This is a good practice, but the real advantage of including video on your site comes from getting higher rankings in the search engines.

Making the Text Readable

Your text content needs to be plentiful and focused for the search engines, but it also needs to be readable for your users. Here are some tips for improving your text's readability:

+ **Use a spelling checker:** When your writing includes spelling errors and typos, what does that say about your company? It may communicate that you are unprofessional, that you have no quality control, or that you simply don't care — none of which are good impressions to give your site visitors. Spelling checkers don't catch everything, but they can point out things that aren't even words. Then have someone proofread to catch any remaining problems.

✦ **Break your writing into smaller chunks:** When we recommend a minimum of 450 words per page, we aren't suggesting you put it all into one gargantuan paragraph. It's difficult to read large blocks of text on a screen. Short paragraphs of three to five lines are easier to track with your eyes. It's also easier to hold your readers' interest and keep them moving to the next thought when you separate a piece into short sections. You can use bullets, a Q&A (question and answer) format, lists, subheadings, and other techniques to make your text more digestible.

✦ **Use bullets:** Bullet points make for easy reading. They visually parse the text into small, digestible bits. Readers can see at a glance how many there are, what they relate to, and how long it's going to take to read through the list. You don't have to stick to the standard black dot style, either, but keep in mind that some kind of bullet created in text (rather than using a graphic bullet) also signals to search engines that these are bullet points, which helps them decipher what your content is about. For a good sample of how this works, look at a news story on CNN (www.cnn.com), which summarizes the main points of the article in bullet points above the full text, making the article easy to skim while offering more information to an interested reader.

✦ **Choose the best reading level for your audience:** One of the metrics you should look for when you're analyzing your competitor's pages is the average reading level. Known as the Flesch-Kincaid readability score, it measures the corresponding U.S. grade level of written text. So for instance, a Flesch-Kincaid score of 8.0 would indicate an eighth-grade reading level; a score of 16.2 would mean it's appropriate for people with four years of college education. The free version of the Page Analyzer in the SEOToolSet returns this number, as will Microsoft Word. To turn on the advanced page statistics in Word, go to Tools, Options, Spelling & Grammar, and then select the Show Readability Statistics check box. (See Figure 2-3.) Run a spell check on your document. After the check is complete, a box pops up with information related to the general ease of readability of your document.

To come up with a number, the Page Analyzer and Word analyze the average number of syllables per word and words per sentence. For the Flesch-Kincaid score, a lower number is more difficult to read; higher is easier. The Flesch grade level corresponds roughly to the American school system. A grade of 9.6 would be about the reading level of a high school freshman midway through the year. If you find your pages scoring way too high or too low for what's natural in your market, you should adjust your word length and sentence structure.

✦ **Name your nouns:** Don't write about "the thing"; call it by name every time. Don't overuse pronouns like "it," "them," "that," or "those;" instead, spell out what you're talking about. When you clarify what you're writing about each time, you prevent reader confusion *and* give the search engines more uses of your keywords.

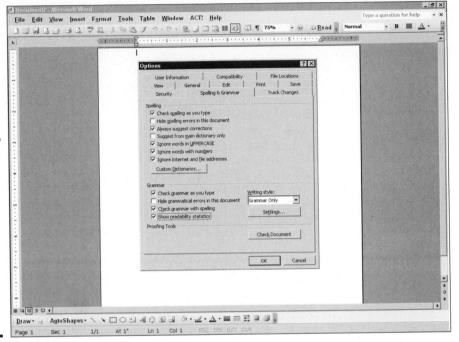

Figure 2-3:
Turning on readability statistics in Word gives you the Flesch grade level and Flesch-Kincaid score of the document.

✦ **Be careful with acronyms:** Jargon alphabet soup — those three-letter acronyms that separate "us" from "them" and identify who's in the know from outsiders who haven't got a clue what everyone is talking about — doesn't belong on your Web site without being clearly defined. Not only do you risk ostracizing site visitors who don't know your acronyms, but also you risk keeping search engine spiders in the dark. Instead, use the good journalistic practice of writing out the phrase the first time it occurs on every page, followed by the acronym in parentheses. You might also consider spelling out your phrase in every usage if it improves your keyword density. If you must use acronyms exclusively, you can use the Acronym HTML tag — this helps users by allowing them to mouse over the word to get the full definition. There's no SEO value in the tag because search engines ignore the tag as it can be spammed.

```
Example: <acronym title="Search Engine
    Optimization">SEO</acronym>
```

✦ **Allow white space and margins:** Empty space around text makes it easier to read, so don't think of white space as wasted screen real estate. Use margins and spacing to avoid a cluttered look. Edge-to-edge text looks like too much to read, so people won't try. Also consider indenting paragraphs by wrapping the left or right edge of your text nicely alongside a graphic. This can add visual appeal as well as reduce the width of your paragraph and increase readability.

✦ **Select readable fonts:** You can specify typefaces that are *serif fonts* (fonts that include little strokes at the ends of characters, such as the feet on a capital A) or *sans-serif fonts* (fonts without serifs, such as Arial, Verdana, and others) for your body text. Although users may have their own opinions on this, sans-serif fonts are considered the king of Web text because serifs often make small letters less readable on a computer monitor. And to keep from cluttering your HTML with inline font tags, be sure to specify what typefaces to use on headings, captions, body text, and so on, using an external CSS (Cascading Style Sheet). (For more on that, see Book IV, Chapter 1.)

It's important to note that even if you specify what typeface you want to use, the font cannot show up if users do not have that typeface installed on their computers. For this reason, specify multiple fonts or end your font command with a generic command, such as `serif`. This way, if a user's browser can't find the exact font you wanted, it can at least substitute a similar font. (Note: You can use sIFR as a way to get around this and incorporate special fonts if you really want to — see Book IV, Chapter 4.)

✦ **Choose backgrounds and colors for readability:** The most readable text is black type on a white background. You can vary from that, but do so carefully. For your main body copy, do use dark fonts against a light background for maximum contrast and readability. Using *reverse copy* (light text against a dark background) should never be applied to an entire Web site. Not only is it harder to read, but also you risk letting your users print out blank pages when they choose File➪Print (white text tends to not show up on white paper).

Also be careful of having too little contrast between your background and type colors. You've probably watched presentations where the slides were illegible because they had peach text on a beige background, or some similar combination. It's the same principle on your Web site. Make the words stand out. In addition to usability, adequate contrast between text and background is an extremely important point for search engines: Text that is too similar in color to the background could be considered hidden text and marked as spam.

✦ **Plan for printing:** People may want to print out your Web pages, so be sure to create a print style sheet that defines how all of your site fonts should translate for printing, and how to lay out the content on an 8 1/2" x 11" piece of paper. You should also specify the images to print, removing unnecessary ones in order to save your users time, ink, and paper. Neglecting to create a print style sheet can cause printing nightmares, and people can waste tree-loads of paper in the process.

Allowing User Input

Letting users contribute content directly to your Web site meets at least two goals simultaneously: It adds more content to your site and stimulates higher user engagement. Although you might feel nervous about letting other people write text that appears on your Web site, the advantages make it definitely worth considering. And you can still hold the reins to make sure your site contains accurate and constructive information. The primary SEO motivation for allowing User Generated Content (UGC) is to add unique content to pages that would otherwise contain only duplicate content.

One of the best applications of user-generated content is reviews. Letting users write their own reviews of your products and services is a fantastic way to get content on your site. Users write about your products in their own words, which become natural language search terms. This might help you capture *Long Tail queries* (search queries for long, specific phrases that indicate a serious, conversion-ready searcher) if you make sure those pages can be crawled by the search engines.

It's great for business, too. Facilitating online user reviews of your products or services can help you sell them. Consumers also trust user-generated content more than traditional sales copy. After reading reviews, people are often more likely to purchase because they have more faith in what they will receive. Educated consumers also make better customers, with less potential for returned merchandise.

Web site owners often fear that people will write bad things about their product or service and negatively impact their brand. However, statistics show that the majority of user reviews are positive. For instance, the online-reviews Web site Yelp (www.yelp.com) says that 85 percent of reviews are positive. Similarly, the site Bazaarvoice (www.bazaarvoice.com) claims that 80 percent of all reviewers award four or five stars.

That being said, you can always expect a few people who write defaming, nonsensical, or offensive comments that don't belong on your Web site. To take care of unwanted reviews, you should

✦ Monitor your user-generated content, either automatically using a service, or manually, so that you can remove the offending entries.

✦ Consider tracking the IP addresses of reviewers, so that you can identify someone who leaves a truly malicious comment.

✦ Consider requiring an account logon for anyone who submits a review. The drawback is that your security gate may dissuade people from participating, but it would give you assurance that you're dealing with customers only.

✦ Allow users to comment on other people's reviews (with a link such as "Was this helpful?"). Then the reviews can become self-regulating to a certain extent.

Negative feedback can often help a business, so don't shun it entirely. Negative reviews help people understand the product's limitations and further builds trust. ("It didn't work for them, but their situation is different than mine.") Online reviews can also alert you to cases where your products or services truly did fall short, so that you can address the problems. When a disgruntled user has a legitimate issue that you read about in the user-generated content, you can immediately contact the person to resolve it. After the person's issue is resolved, she might be so happy that you end up getting another, completely positive review of your customer service.

Another interesting thing to note about negative review is that they can actually help build trust. Many people say that they don't trust a product that doesn't have anything but positive reviews. Negative reviews actually validate the user's sense that nobody's perfect.

Besides reviews, you might consider adding these other types of user-generated content to your Web site:

✦ **User forums:** These discussions can become free-for-alls, but they also allow significant user interaction and provide you with excellent feedback from your user group. You can decide whether to participate with "official" responses or not.

✦ **Comments:** News sites do this all the time. After an article, they put a Comments link and let people respond. The number of comments can even make the article appear more popular, relevant, or interesting.

✦ **Blogs:** If you want to post opinion-style content in the form of blog articles, or just let your site visitors do it, a *blog* (literally, Web log) may be right for you. You probably need to blog on a regular basis (weekly or other) in order to keep conversations going.

Creating User Engagement

A lot of what you learned in high school English class can help with your Web site writing and make it more engaging to read:

✦ **Choose strong verbs that convey action.** Avoid overusing the "forms of be" verbs (*is, are, was, were,* and so on) because they stick a sentence together with all the excitement of white glue. Instead, generate interest with active verbs like *drive, soar, infuse, create,* and so on.

Also avoid using the passive voice, which dulls down your writing and makes it sound like a dry treatise or a political science textbook. English teachers suggest asking, "Who kicked whom?" in order to find out what a passive-voice sentence really means. Here's a passive sentence that lacks excitement: "Up to 20 pairs of skis can be stored in the MegaRack ski hauler." You can rewrite it by identifying a subject ("you") and making it active: "You can pack skis for a 20-person ski party into this trunktop MegaRack ski hauler."

✦ **Show, don't tell.** Your Web site needs to persuade people, interest them, and draw them in with good content. For this reason, you should write as if they're there, not just reading about an event after the fact. Newspaper reporting tells what happened: "On Friday night, Racer Rick won the Indy 100 driving a bumper car." But to engage your readers, you want to show them what you're talking about. Describe the scene when the race began; what Racer Rick looked like; how his bumper car looked compared to all the formula ones on the track; what people said before, during, and after the race; the blow-by-blow of the race action; and the spectacular finish. Don't just tell people about your product or service; make them feel it.

✦ **Use sensory words.** Your text needs to make readers feel, taste, touch, hear, and see what you're talking about — experience it themselves — rather than just read a report about it. You achieve this using sensory words and good descriptors. For instance, "The XJ-7 ski pole improves your downhill speed" tells the facts. But "Wrap your fingers around the XJ-7's form-fitted grips and hold on tight as you zip around curves, adjusting your descent with light touches of your diamond-tipped poles to the snow-packed ground racing beneath you," makes your readers experience it. Not to mention that you can integrate your keywords more easily into a descriptive paragraph.

✦ **Be specific and give details.** As we stated earlier in this chapter, your writing needs to call things by name. Don't be vague — it leads to ambiguity and confusion for your readers. Because *you* know exactly what you mean, you generalize or put together phrases that don't make sense to someone unfamiliar with your business. To help you improve your text, you might ask someone who's a complete novice to review your copy and point out anything that's unclear.

✦ Also, try not to use pronouns like *it* and *that*, or generic words like *stuff* or *thing*, when you can use words packed with meaning instead. As a bonus, restating the proper name of the thing you're talking about helps the search engine understand better that your page is about that thing, whether it be ski poles, cowboy boots, or search engine optimization.

Keep in mind that your Web site is never "done." Good writing, if you remember your high school or college composition courses, involves continuous revision. When you think you are finished and that the writing is good enough, you should put the pages away for a few days, do something else, and then come back and look at them again. More than likely you can find a few more things that can be made better. And as always, try to have fresh eyes look at what you've written. Someone who has not seen it before can usually see things that you could not see because of your familiarity with the subject.

Writing a Call to Action

You know the goal you have for your Web page visitors — to make a purchase, sign up for your newsletter, subscribe to your RSS feed, sign a petition, become a member, or something else. *Calls to action* are the words that clearly give users that opportunity. "Buy your XJ-7 poles now," and "Try out the new XJ-7 ski poles," and "See the XJ-7's new colors," all represent calls to action that can be linked to a page where the user can purchase the XJ-7.

For search engine optimization, you should include descriptive words in your calls to action. Notice that every previous example mentions the name of the product (XJ-7) and something meaningful about it. If your call to action says only "Buy now," or "Add to cart," you're missing an opportunity to clearly specify (to the search engines) that this is the page where the XJ-7 can be purchased. Your Web site design may have a standard interface that includes generic options under every product listing, but you could consider also including a more specific text link under the product description. Or for another example, if you have links in your copy to sign up for your newsletter, include a brief description in every link like "Car Restoration Newsletter" rather than just "Sign up for our newsletter."

To be most effective, a call to action should use an imperative verb (like *See* or *Try* or *Buy*) and a compelling benefit. The following example could be from a business-to-business site. A call to action like this would be very motivating for an engineer seeking this type of solution:

```
Attend our Webcast "Process Excellence for Supply Chain
    Management" and learn how to reduce costs with our
    process-driven approach to aligning business processes
    within the supply chain.
```

Your call to action should tell visitors exactly what you want them to do:

✦ If you want them to buy your product, you could scatter multiple calls to action in strategic places within your copy, telling them how to do it (such as "Click here to buy Brand X now").

✦ If you want them to contact you by phone, state your phone number and instructions ("Call us Monday–Friday from 8–5 EST at 1-800-999-9999"). You could repeat the number in bold text throughout your copy and again at the end.

Be wary of spamming the page. Repeating your call to action only works if you don't annoy the visitor. From an SEO perspective, it's possible to configure a page for a user, for a search engine, and for your conversion objective.

An effective call to action entices the user to click. It motivates the user to move further into the conversion process. Often, you won't be able to know conclusively what phrasing works best until you've tried them. So if you're debating between three different calls to action, you could set up a test alternating between versions, tracking how many people clicked on each as well as the eventual conversion rate (how many of those clicks resulted in an actual sale). Then you would know which call to action is most effective for your current audience and Web site.

Chapter 3: Adding Keyword-Specific Content

In This Chapter

✔ Creating your keyword list

✔ Developing content using your keywords

✔ Including synonyms to widen your appeal

✔ Optimizing your content for search engine rankings

✔ Analyzing the reading level of your text using Flesch-Kincaid

✔ Finding the best tools for keyword integration

You may have a Web site already up and running, or you might be in the planning stages of a brand new site. Either way, you should be ready to identify where you have content holes that need to be filled. In this chapter, you hone your skills at creating content that can rank well with the search engines.

First, ask yourself: What is your Web site about? The answers to this question give you a foundation for all your content planning and writing. Some sites try to be everything to everybody, but those sites don't rank well in searches. When a site's content is unfocused and too general, search engines can't figure out what the site is about. The site doesn't demonstrate expertise in any one thing, so the search engines don't know what search queries the site is relevant for. The result? The site doesn't rank well in search results.

You must clearly know your site's main subject *themes*, or the primary categories of information in your site, as a first step to planning and writing effective content. In a nutshell, you need to identify your themes, categorize them into pages, and then create focused content on those subjects. This is what we cover in this chapter. (For more on how to theme a Web site, see Book II, Chapter 1.)

Creating Your Keyword List

After you know your Web site's main subject themes, you can begin building a keyword list. A *keyword* is any word typed as a search query. Search engines try to give users what they're looking for by searching for those keywords among their indexes of Web sites, and then displaying the most relevant results. You want your Web site to be considered the most relevant for the keywords that match what your site is about. You need to choose your keywords so that you can proactively create focused content that can be considered most relevant.

Your first step in building a keyword list should be to brainstorm. At the brainstorming stage, write down every keyword word or phrase that comes to mind for your themes. You can filter them later; for now, you just want to amass the longest list you can of one-word, two-word, three-word, and longer potential keywords that relate to your Web site. (Note that the multi-word phrases are important to plan for because people tend to search for more specific queries when they're ready to make a decision, but shorter queries when they're just doing research.) To get more input, ask other people what they would call the information, products, or services you offer. Ask people involved in your business or industry, but also ask your neighbor, your niece, or others who are unfamiliar with your industry. You're trying to find all the ways someone might try to find what you have to offer.

After you've brainstormed, the next step is to organize your long list of potential keywords into subject categories, broken down from the broadest to the most specific. If your Web site is about customized classic cars, an outline might look something like this:

```
Classic Cars
Classic Cars 1950s
Classic Cars 1960s
Classic Cars 1970s
Classic Cars American
Classic Cars Ford
Classic Cars Ford Mustang
Classic Cars Ford Mustang Convertibles
Classic Cars Ford Mustang Hard Tops
Classic Cars Ford Comet
Classic Cars Ford GTO
Classic Cars Chevrolet
Classic Cars Chevrolet Sedans
Classic Cars Chevrolet Trucks
Classic Cars Customization
Classic Cars Customization Paint
Classic Cars Customization Upholstery
Classic Cars Customization Upholstery Leather
Classic Cars Customization Upholstery Vinyl
```

These are all terms people might search for when they are looking up classic cars, or customization, or both, and all of them can be used as keywords on your Web site. You can go into even more breakdowns and come up with specific keywords into the hundreds or thousands, as appropriate for your site.

After you have your initial keyword list, you need to evaluate the keywords and identify which ones are your main subjects. Then organize the more specific subtopic keywords beneath them. You want to structure your Web site to assign each of your main keywords to a specific *landing page* (the page you want users to come to because it's the best source of information for that topic on your site). For instance, you'd want to build a landing page for the keyword phrase [Classic Cars Ford Mustang] that has focused content on Ford Mustangs, and that links to subpages of supporting information about Ford Mustangs. Doing this makes it easier for search engines to know that the page is relevant to searches for [Ford Mustangs] or [classic Ford Mustangs] or [classic Mustang cars], and so on. We recommend that you include a minimum of five subpages supporting each of your landing pages in order to present depth of content to the search engines. Organizing your site into categories like this is called *siloing* (theming), and it's covered at length in Book VI, Chapter 1.

Weed out keywords that don't support your subject themes: Unrelated words that show up too frequently on a page dilute the page's subject relevance. For instance, if your Ford Mustangs page lists all the possible tire and wheel options and mentions "tires" too many times, the search engines might think it's a page about Ford Mustang tires, and lower its ranking for the keyword [Ford Mustang].

For more help selecting good keywords, see Book II, Chapter 2.

Developing Content Using Your Keywords

After you have your categories and subcategories mapped out, look at your Web site content and choose (or plan) a landing page devoted to each one. For every landing page, you also want to assign a primary keyword or keyword phrase. In other words, your site needs to have a focused page on each of your important keywords.

Your goal is to have the search engines recognize what each one of your landing pages is most relevant for, so that it can show up in search results for its keywords. And the better you can focus your content on those targeted keywords, the higher your URL is likely to be in the list.

Your Web site's landing pages present the all-important first impression to site visitors. You want to make sure your landing pages not only put your best foot forward, but also interest visitors enough to entice them to go further, and hopefully convert. The pages have to look good to users *and* search engines.

As a general guideline, the pages at the top of each silo (your landing or index pages) should have at least 450 words of text content, and be supported by at least five subpages (each with at least 450 words) within the same theme. Writing that much content may sound overwhelming, but you can tackle it as you would any big project. Develop a strategy for adding at least 450 words to each page. Setting a schedule and producing *X* number of pages every week eventually builds up a site that can serve as a subject matter expert in the areas that are important to your business. Focus not on gimmick pages, *link bait* (short-lived attention-getters) Top 10 lists or other flash-in-the-pan strategies, but on developing content that will satisfy researchers and convert them to buyers. (For more on link bait, see Book VI, Chapter 1.)

Your landing pages need to have enough content so that people reaching them from a search engine feel satisfied that they've come to the right place. You want the content to engage visitors enough so that they want to stay. You also need your landing pages to link to other pages that offer more detailed information within the subject category and lead to opportunities to buy, sign up, or take whatever action your site considers a conversion.

Beginning to write

When writing your Web content, it's best to use simple, everyday language that searchers are likely to type in. As a general rule, we recommend including a keyword or keyword phrase enough to be prominent so that someone who read the page would be able to pick out what the most important word was. Don't force your keywords into your content. Let it sound natural.

Additionally, you should avoid using only general phrases; be sure to include detailed descriptive words as well. If your keywords are too general, they are likely to be up against too much competition from others targeting the same keywords. However, fewer people search for very specific terms, resulting in fewer potential visitors. It's a balancing act, and the rules aren't hard and fast. You need to find the right mix for your site by finding the keywords that bring traffic that actually converts: In other words, you want to put out the bait that brings in the right catch. Also keep in mind that the broader keywords go on the upper landing pages and more specific keywords on the subpages, and that you might need to focus on several more specific variations of a keyword phrase in order to rank for the broader term.

When you start to write a new page, stay focused on the page's theme. Write as much as you can about that subject theme, even if the information seems totally obvious to you. What seems obvious to you probably would be new information to someone unfamiliar with your subject. After all, that's why someone would come to your site: to read what a subject expert has to say. Begin by stating the obvious; it establishes your credibility when your visitors find information they already know to be true on your pages and they'll be more likely to trust your site to give them further information.

As you write your first draft, don't worry so much about keyword placement. Do include your keywords, but let the language flow naturally around the topic. Later you can analyze what you've written and refine things like keyword density and distribution (but more on that under "Optimizing the Content," later in this chapter).

To test whether your writing comes across as natural, try reading it out loud. Text that sounds like conversational language engages readers.

Keeping it relevant

Make sure that you don't dilute the subject theme by including irrelevant information. Some pruning might be necessary if you're working on an existing page rather than starting one from scratch. If the page is all about Chevrolet Camaros, keep the discussion focused on that car model, without a lengthy discussion of how it compared to the competing Pontiac Firebird back in the 1970s. Too many mentions of another type of car can dilute your Camaro theme and confuse the search engines, thereby reducing your subject relevance to [Chevrolet Camaros].

Including clarifying words

You want to include secondary words that help clarify what your keywords are about. For example, if you have the keyword [apple] for one of your pages, the search engines are going to look at all of the text near the word *apple* to figure out whether your page is about the fruit or the computer. If this was your Web page, you could use words like *software*, *computer*, or other related terms to clarify that you mean Apple as in computer.

You want to put your clarifying words close to your keywords in the text. The closer the proximity, the stronger the correlation.

Another reason to include clarifying words is to match more search queries, especially Long-Tail queries. *Long-tail queries* are longer, targeted search phrases that aren't frequently used, but generally have a high conversion rate because searchers entering these queries know exactly what they're looking for. Search engine users are becoming savvier as time goes on, and they know that a single keyword is probably going to be too broad. A good example is what happens when you do a search for [security]. You might be in need of a security guard service, but doing a quick search on Google with the keyword [security] gives you the Wikipedia article on security, the Department of Homeland Security, the Social Security Administration, and many listings for computer security software. Using a Long-Tail search query like [security guard service Poughkeepsie], on the other hand, turns up map results listing local businesses, two local business sites for hiring security guards, and a couple of news articles about security services in Poughkeepsie.

You can see why it's a good idea to include supplemental words and phrases on your Web pages. Search engines can match queries to words that can be found in close proximity to each other on your page, even if they never appear as a phrase. So for instance, if your Web page has the heading "Oldsmobile Ninety-Eights Make the Coolest Convertibles," and the body copy contains all of these words in close proximity as well, your page would be found relevant to the search query [Oldsmobile Ninety-Eight convertible], even though you never used the exact phrase.

Including synonyms to widen your appeal

Synonyms of your keywords also need to show up on your Web pages, in your HTML tags, and in the anchor text of links to your pages. People don't use the same words to describe things, so it appears more natural to search engines to find backlinks to your pages using a variety of different terms that all mean roughly the same thing.

Including keyword synonyms also helps you match more search queries. People search for things in their own words, not yours. For instance, if you have a page on your classic cars site all about Oldsmobile Ninety-Eights, you should make sure your keywords include both [Ninety-Eight] spelled out and the numeric [98], because people could search either way. In another example, a Web page that sells ski boots would optimize that page for the keyword phrase [ski boots]. But they'd also want their listing to display when people search for [ski footwear], [snow boots], or [winter apparel]. Unless they have synonyms like these within the page, the search engine won't find it relevant and won't include it in the search results.

Also, don't forget nicknames! If your main subjects have common nicknames, these are important to include — possibly as keywords, but at least in your body content. For instance, on your classic cars site, your Chevrolet Camaro page should include the word [Chevy], your Ford Mustang page should include the nickname [Stang], and so forth.

Of course, your hunt for good synonyms could begin in a thesaurus. Even better, find out what words Google thinks are synonymous with your keywords. Do this:

1. **For a Google search, enter a tilde (~) character in front of a keyword, such as [~Mustang].**

2. **View the results page, and notice that synonyms appear in boldface type.**

   Google formats the word *Mustang* in bold, and also any words Google considers closely related or synonymous with *Mustang*. So you can see ideas for additional words you should probably use in your page. You can run a synonym search for keyword phrases, as well — put tildes in front of every word, such as [~Ford ~Mustang ~trim], or just in front of selected words, like [Ford Mustang ~trim]. Doing this search bolds some additional words of interest: trimming, Ford, and so on.

Dealing with stop words

Stop words are words that the search engines typically ignore because they are so common. They don't contribute to any meaningful content but they are absolutely essential in your writing. Words like *a, the, at, to, will, this, and,* and *with* are all stop words that make your text sound more natural. Here's what Google says about stop words:

"Google ignores stop words when they're placed in searches alongside less common words. For example, a search for [The Sound and the Fury] will only return results for the terms "Sound" and "Fury." However, a search that only includes stop words — [The Who], for example — will be processed as is."

Although the search engines typically do not count stop words, writing without them would turn your pages to gibberish. Ranking well for your keyword is worthless if your potential customers don't like your site well enough to buy your product or service. Remember the rule is always to write for your customers first and the search engines second.

As a final note about stop words, you *can* include them in your keyword phrases. For example, a search for [holiday on ice], which is the name of a touring ice show, does bring back slightly different results than a search for [holiday ice]. It looks like the algorithm is intelligent enough to recognize phrases that contain stop words, rather than discard them completely.

Freshness of the content

As a general rule, the more often your site has fresh changing content, the more often the search engines want to index it. News sites, for example, have to be crawled constantly because of how frequently they post new stories. On a lesser scale, if you have a blog on your Web site that has new activity every day, the spiders generally crawl your site more often than a site that updates once a month.

If your site content gets indexed in news searches or blog searches, you definitely need fresh content to stay near the top of those engines. Without frequent posts, your articles fade into the oblivion of the search results' back pages.

Your ranking in normal search results does not change based on how frequently you're spidered. Where you might suffer as a result of infrequent search engine indexing, however, is if you've made SEO-related changes to your site. You might have an entire board of directors waiting to see the results of your latest SEO edit, and weeks could go by until the spider revisits your page.

Periodically, you should review your site content to make sure it stays fresh. See if anything has changed, and either update or add to the text that's there. This is pretty much common sense, but it has the added benefit of providing fresh content to keep the spiders coming back to your site.

Dynamically adding content to a page

You may use a content management system (CMS) that takes your content and automatically builds your Web pages from it. If so, you'll want to make sure it's dynamically adding content properly, taking into consideration everything you know about SEO and good content writing. For instance, the text should sound natural, use your keywords in the appropriate amount and distribution, and make sense. Also, make sure that the `Title` and `Meta` tags in the page's `Heading` section are being created properly emphasizing appropriate keywords, with every page unique.

You don't want to ever lose control of your Web site by using a poor-quality CMS that is not configurable. Because search engines decide whether your pages are relevant for search queries based on having keyword-rich focused content, and unique headings and tags, you can't afford to let an inflexible CMS limit how much you can customize each page.

Another thing to avoid is auto-generated text. Generally, machine-written content sounds unnatural and won't do a good job representing you either to users or to the search engines. (For more discussion of content management systems, see Book VII, Chapter 5.)

Optimizing the Content

When you have pages of content to work with, you can refine them for search engine optimization (SEO). If you haven't already set up the text content in an HTML document, do so now because part of what you need to optimize is the HTML code behind the page.

Looking at your page in the HTML code view, your first step is to do what we call "getting the red out." (In Page Analyzer, things that need to be corrected are displayed in red text, so it's easy to figure out where to start.) You want to fix the blatant SEO issues, the ones that are the most obvious and often the easiest to fix. Here's what to look for:

✦ **Title tag:** The Title tag should appear first in your HTML code's Head section. It should be unique and contain your page's main keyword (with no word repeated). Normally the Title tag should be between six and twelve words in length (brief).

✦ **Description Meta tag:** The Meta description tag should appear second in your HTML Head section. It needs to contain all of the keywords used in the Title tag, and should be written like a sentence because this is often what search engines display within a result listing. Any word should not appear more than twice. The length guideline is 12 to 24 words.

✦ **Meta keywords tag:** The Meta keywords tag should appear third in your HTML head section and should contain all of the words used in the Title and Description tags. It can be written as a list separated by commas, starting with the long phrases and ending with single words. No single word should be used more than four times, and the total length should not exceed 48 words.

✦ **Heading tags:** Heading tags (H#) set apart your on-page titles and sub-headings, and search engines analyze them to determine your page's main ideas, so make them meaningful. You want to use an H1 for the first and most important heading on the page only. Second-level headings should be given H2, third-level headings H3, and so forth; also, they should never be placed out of order. Just think back to school term papers, outlines . . . When the search engines were built, their main purpose was to index educational, technical, and professional papers, and very little else. The code hasn't changed much since the engines were built: They still rely on the same basic principle they started with.

A good heading length is from one to five words, but how many headings you should have on a page depends on the content of the page. Only use an H# tag when it defines a sub-change in the content structure, much like a table of contents outlines the structure of a book. You will almost never have multiple H1 tags (how many pages have more than one main topic, after all?), but could have multiple H2, H3, and so on, if the content supports it.

For example:

```
<h1>Ford Reviews</h1>
    Content about Ford Reviews (200 words)
    <h2>Mustang Reviews</h2>
    Content about Mustang Reviews (200+ words)
    <h2>Ford F-150 Reviews</h2>
    Content about Ford F-150 reviews 200+ words again.
```

In the preceding example, the H1 and H2 tags are used properly. Think about it as a school or technical paper. It has to follow an outline format completely. You can have an H3 heading, but only if it's below an H2 tag.

If you had a section for the engine specs of the Ford Mustang, for example, that could be considered an H3.

The usage of H4 and H5 tags would have to be, again, related sub-content to the H3 tag, and so on.

Remember that the spider reads the page from a code view, not the way the page is laid out for visual presentation. They do not yet have the capability of modern browser emulation.

Digging deeper by running Page Analyzer

After you've gotten the red out, you can work on optimizing the body content you wrote. We suggest you run the page through Page Analyzer:

1. **Go to www.seotoolset.com/tools/free_tools.html.**

2. **In Page Analyzer, enter the page's URL (such as www.*yourdomain*.com/pageinprogress.html).**

3. **Click the Analyze Page button and wait until the report displays.**

The Page Analyzer report compiles lots of useful information for you to analyze your page content and plan improvements, as we explain in a moment. We suggest you look at the following six areas to diagnose issues and improve your page: the Heading section, frequently used words, reading level, keyword density, keyword frequency, and keyword distribution.

✦ **Head section problems:** You can see at a glance if you overlooked any of the "getting the red out" steps we discussed previously because the report shows exceptions in bright red text. For instance, if you used a word in your Meta description tag but forgot to include it in the Meta keywords tag as well, under the heading "Meta Keywords Tag," you would see this message:

```
META Keywords is MISSING a word that is in either the
    TITLE or META Description.
```

✦ **Frequently used words:** Figure 3-1 shows a table from the report that lists two-word phrases that are used at least twice in the page.

Looking across the rows, you can also see what section of the page each phrase appears in, whether it's in the Title, Description, Keywords, headings, image Alt codes, or something else. Because search engines look for repeated words to ascertain what your page is all about, look carefully at these tables. The most frequently used words appear at the top: These should be your keywords. You also want to make sure you don't have frequently repeated words that might distract the search engines from understanding your main page theme. You can see how this report can save you hours of manual work counting instances and trying to make sure your keywords, synonyms, clarifying words, and so on are adequately used.

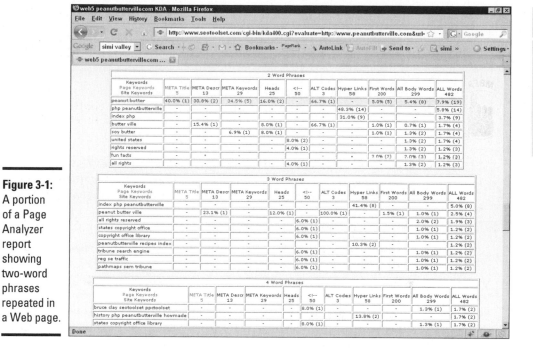

Figure 3-1:
A portion
of a Page
Analyzer
report
showing
two-word
phrases
repeated in
a Web page.

✦ **Reading level:** Above the word tables, the report shows you details about your text's reading level. Because you want your site to be appropriate for your target audience, this is important. The row (not shown in the figure) labeled "Kincaid Grade Level" identifies the U.S. school grade level that your writing matches. If it says 16.0, that means your text is appropriate for someone with four years of college education. The Kincaid score is based on the average number of syllables per word and words per sentence. If you find your pages scoring way too high or too low for your target audience's education level, you should adjust your word length and sentence structure. For instance, a Web site directed at tweens needs to have a low Kincaid score (around 5.0 to 8.0), but that reading level would not be appropriate for a site targeting doctoral candidates.

You can also check your documents Flesch-Kincaid score and Flesch grade level in Microsoft Word. Check out Chapter 2 in this minibook for instructions on how to turn on your readability statistics in Word.

✦ **Keyword density:** You also want to check the *keyword density* of your main keywords in the page, which is how much of the total text that keyword represents. The report shows the density as a percentage in the ALL Words column for every keyword (see the far right column of Figure 3-1). Keyword density is one of the factors a search engine spider looks at when determining whether a Web page is relevant to that search. The ideal density for your important keywords depends on what's considered normal for the high-ranking sites for that keyword. If all of your top-ranking competitors have a 7 percent keyword density for the phrase [classic cars], 7 percent should be your starting target. Go below that and you risk being left out of the search engine rankings for that phrase. Go above that, and you could be considered spam.

You can find out the typical keyword density for your competition by running Page Analyzer on their Web pages and calculating the average you receive. You may also subscribe to tools that produce this data in one step, such as the Multi-Page Analyzer from the SEOToolSet, which can be found at www.seotoolset.com. (For more help doing competitive research, see Book III. Detailed instructions on how to approximate the results of the Multi-Page Analyzer are available in Book III, Chapter 2.)

✦ **Keyword frequency:** Because the use of keywords is so crucial to your search engine optimization, also examine your *keyword frequency* (the number of times the keyword appears on the page). This number shows in parentheses in the All Words column of the Page Analyzer report. And as with keyword density, you need to size up your competitors to find out what number to shoot for.

✦ **Keyword distribution:** One last measurement that affects your search engine ranking for a particular keyword is the *distribution*, or placement throughout the page. Your site might use the keyword phrase [classic cars] the right number of times (frequency) and in the right proportion to the total amount of text (density), but it also needs to distribute the phrase *regularly* throughout the page. If it's only used in the top quarter of the page, the search engines assume that your page as a whole is not as relevant to classic cars as it would be if the phrase appears throughout the copy evenly.

Finding Tools for Keyword Integration

In this section, we recap tools we've mentioned elsewhere to give you a handy list for your reference. These tools can help you analyze your Web page content to make sure you've set up your keywords effectively. They are shortcuts that show you some key factors that the search engines look for to determine relevance. Remember, in almost every case, the search engines themselves are going to be your best asset in terms of analyzing your market.

✦ **Page Analyzer (www.seotoolset.com/tools/free_tools.html):** The Page Analyzer is your primary keyword analysis tool. It lists all keywords on the page (words used at least twice, minus "stop" words like the, and, but, and so on). It shows you each keyword's density and frequency. It also identifies problems in your Title tag and Meta tags and analyzes the reading level of your text.

✦ **Copyscape (www.copyscape.com):** This free tool lets you check for duplicates of your Web page copy elsewhere on the Web. You want to make sure you have original content on your site because duplications can cause your page to be filtered out of the search engine's index. (We cover avoiding duplicate content in the next chapter.)

✦ **Keyword Activity (www.seotoolset.com/tools/free_tools. html):** Part of analyzing keywords is finding out how often people search for them. This free tool lets you check search activity by keyword (and do many other search engine optimization-related tasks). You can also do keyword research using the free Search Engine Optimization/ KSP, available at **www.bruceclay.com/web_rank.htm#seoksp.** Alternative recommended tools that give you robust reporting (for a fee) include

• **Wordtracker (www.wordtracker.com)** is a for-pay tool that measures keyword traffic. Wordtracker offers both annual plans and monthly plans. The annual subscription runs about $329, and the monthly plan costs $59 per month. They also offer a free trial version.

• **Keyword Discovery (www.keyworddiscovery.com)** offers a subscription service that runs about $49.95 a month.

✦ **Keyword distribution using a browser:** Mozilla Firefox (www.mozilla. com/en-US/firefox/) and (www.google.com/chrome).

Available as a free download, Mozilla's Firefox browser is one of the most powerful SEO tools out there, with multiple add-ons that allow power users to slice and dice almost any aspect of a Web site. Right out of the box, Firefox lets you do a rough keyword distribution search on a page. Ctrl+F brings up a search box: Just type in your keyword, and then select Highlight All to see where the words fall on your page.

Also available as a free download, Google's new Chrome browser (still in beta as of this writing) has some nifty features. One of its best features is the ability to see how a word or phrase is distributed throughout a page visually. With any Web page open, simply press Ctrl+F to activate a drop-down search box. Then type in the word or phrase you want to find. Figure 3-2 shows how every instance is automatically highlighted in yellow, and colored bands appear in the vertical scroll bar representing each time the selected word or phrase is used in the page content. Seeing a keyword's distribution at a glance like this can help you distribute it evenly throughout your page.

✦ **Synonym search (www.google.com):** Search using a tilde (~) character in front of one or more of your words, and Google displays those search terms *and their synonyms, commonly associated and related words* in bold on the results page. This can be an excellent way to discover additional words you can optimize for on your Web page.

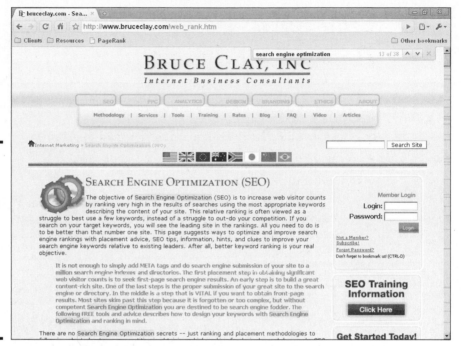

Figure 3-2:
Google
Chrome
lets you see
a word's
linear
distribution
using
colored
banding in
the scroll
bar.

Competitive analysis tools

It's a competitive world, and ranking well has everything to do with what your keyword competitors are doing. The optimal keyword density, frequency, and distribution are determined by analyzing the top-ranked sites. The search engines are clearly accepting the keyword density, frequency, and distribution of the top sites, so being better than these competitors is often simply a matter of careful page editing:

✦ **Page Analyzer:** You can run Page Analyzer on the top-ranked Web pages to analyze their keywords and page content, as well as using it on your own Web site.

✦ **Multi-Page Analyzer (www.seotoolset.com):** This is a paid tool, available through our SEOToolSet, which looks at multiple competitors' Web pages and analyzes them in one fell swoop for you. There are many similar products available online, so check your existing SEO tools subscription to see if you already have access to a similar report. You can do the comparisons by hand (see Book III, Chapter 2 for instructions), but a tool like this one saves you time.

Chapter 4: Dealing with Duplicate Content

In This Chapter

✔ Understanding duplicate content so you can avoid it

✔ Recognizing how content can become duplicated

✔ Resolving duplicate content issues

✔ Understanding how a federal copyright can protect your Web site

✔ Handling your content being stolen

In this chapter, you find out how to avoid having duplicate content on your own Web site and why that's important. We also explain how your content can become duplicated (copied) on other Web sites and the variety of causes for it, ranging from accidental to downright malicious. Because you want to protect your original Web site content and prevent duplication as much as possible, we list all of the various sources of duplicate content and give you some recommendations for how to deal with each type of situation.

There aren't many hard and fast rules in search engine optimization (SEO), so when we get to state one, we like to do it with gusto:

You *must* avoid duplicate content at all times.

Duplicate content refers to text that is repeated on more than one Web page either on your site or on other sites. When a search engine's indexing process (the software that crawls the Web, reading and indexing Web site content into a searchable database) detects that a page on your Web site is a copy of another page on your site or anywhere else on the Internet, the spider tries to make a determination of which page is the original, true version, and it may or may not be accurate. Although there is no penalty for duplicate content, the filtering of duplicate content could hurt your ranking in other ways. The perceived original page can be included in search results, but the other page won't make the cut. It's not that the copycat page is penalized in the search engine's *index* (the searchable database of Web site content). The search engines filter it out of search results pages because they don't want to give users redundant listings, and other Web sites link indiscriminately to whichever form of the duplicate content they like best, which dilutes your link equity. Therefore, having duplicate content can be a bad thing for your search engine rankings.

Sources of Duplicate Content and How to Resolve Them

Content can become duplicated either intentionally or by accident. There's a saying that "Imitation is the sincerest form of flattery." Well, you can do without this kind of flattery when it comes to your Web site. Whatever the copycat's motivation is, you don't want people copying your original content if you can help it.

There are two basic types of duplicate content:

✦ **Outside-your-domain duplicate content.** This type happens when two different Web sites have the same text (like we've been talking about so far).

✦ **Within-your-domain duplicate content.** This second type refers to Web sites that create duplicate content within their own *domain* (the root of the site's unique URL, such as `www.domain.com`).

Sites can end up having within-your-domain duplicate content due to their own faulty internal linking procedures, and often Webmasters don't even realize they have a problem. (We explain some of these in the next few sections.) If two or more pages within your own site duplicate each other, you inadvertently diminish the ability for one or the other being included in search results. In some cases, an unknowing Webmaster causes half or more of a site's pages to be completely ignored by the search engines because of duplicate content issues.

You can end up with duplicate content within your own site for a variety of reasons, such as having multiple URLs all containing the same content; printer-friendly pages; pages that get built on the fly with session IDs in the URL; using or providing syndicated content; problems caused by using localization, minor content variations, or an unfriendly content management system; and archives.

Multiple URLs with the same content

Even with sites under your own control, you may have duplicate content resulting from any of the following sources:

✦ Similar pages in the same Web site (`www.yourdomain.com`)

✦ Similar pages in different domains that you own (`www.yourdomain.com` and `www.yourotherdomain.com`)

✦ Similar pages in your www. prefixed site and the non-www version (`www.yourdomain.com` and `yourdomain.com`)

When search engines find two pages with nearly the same content, they may include both pages in their index. However, they only take one of these pages into consideration for search results. The search engines do this because they want to show users a variety of listings — not several that are the same. To make the entire body of your Web site count, you want to ensure that each of your Web pages is unique.

But here's the rub: the search engines may consider two pages the same even if only *part* of the page is duplicated. Just the headings, the first paragraph, the `Title` tag, or any other portion being the same can trigger "duplicate" status. For instance, if you use the same `Title` tag on multiple pages, the search engines might see them as duplicate pages just because they share that single, but important, line of HTML code.

To avoid issues with duplicate content, you always need to write *unique* headings, tags, and content for each page in your Web site.

Finding out how many duplicates the search engine thinks you have

A good place to start looking at duplicate content is to find out how many of your Web pages are currently indexed, versus how many the search engines consider to be duplicates. Here's how:

1. **At Google, type [site:*domain*.com] in the search box (leaving out the square brackets and using your domain), and then click Search.**

2. **When the results page comes up, scroll to the bottom and click the highest page number that shows (usually 10).**

   Doing this can cause the total number of pages to recalculate at the top of the page.

3. **Notice the total number of pages shown in "Results 1 - 10 of about ###" at the top of the page.**

   The "of about ###" number represents the approximate total number of indexed pages in the site.

4. **Now navigate to the very last page of the results.**

   The count shown there represents the filtered results. The difference between these two numbers most likely represents the number of duplicates.

For performance reasons, Google doesn't display all of the indexed pages and omits the ones that seem most like duplicates. If you truly want to see *all* of the indexed listings for a site, you can navigate to the very last results page of your [site:] query and click the option to Repeat the Search with the Omitted Results Included. (Even then, Google only shows up to a maximum of 1,000 listings.)

To discover the number of indexed pages in Yahoo! and Microsoft Live Search, we recommend you try the free Search Engine Saturation tool available from Acxiom Digital at `www.marketleap.com`.

Avoiding duplicate content on your own site

When it comes to cleaning up duplicate pages on your own Web site, which you have control over, after all, don't spend time wondering, "How similar can they be?" Just make the content different. Stick with the best practice of having unique, original content throughout your site. Stay away from the edges of what might be all right with the search engines and play within the safe harbor.

To keep your site in the safe harbor, here are some ways you can avoid or remove duplicate content from within your own Web site:

✦ **Title, Description, Keywords tags:** Make sure that every page has a unique `Title` tag, `Meta` description tag, and `Meta` keywords `Meta` tag in the HTML code.

✦ **Heading tags:** Make sure the heading tags (labeled `H#`) within the body copy differ from other pages' headings. Keeping in mind that your headings should all use meaningful, non-generic words makes this a bit easier.

✦ **Repeated text, such as a slogan:** If you have to show a repeated sentence or paragraph throughout your site, such as a company slogan, you should consider putting the slogan into an image on most pages. Pick the one Web page that you think should rank for that repeated content and leave it as text on that page so that the search engines can spider it. If anyone tries to search for that content, the search engines can find that unique content on the page you selected.

For example, if your classic car customization Web site has the slogan, "We restore the rumble to your classic car," you probably want to display that throughout your site. But you should prevent the search engines from seeing the repetition. Leave it as HTML text on just one page, like your home page or the About Us page. Then everywhere else, just create a nifty graphic that lets users see the slogan, but not search engines.

✦ **Site map:** Be sure that your *site map* (a page containing links to the pages in your site, like a table of contents) includes links to your preferred page's URL, in cases where you have similar versions. The site map helps the search engines understand which page is your *canonical* (best or original) version. Matt Cutts, head of Google's Web Spam team, defines canonicalization as "the process of picking the best URL when there are several choices." The canonical URL is the one that is chosen at the end of the process, with all others being considered duplicates (*non-canonical.*)

✦ **Consolidate similar pages:** If you have whole pages that contain similar or identical text, decide which one you want to be the canonical page for that content. Then combine pages and edit the content as needed.

If you do need to consolidate pages to a single, canonical page, a few precautions are in order (see the upcoming numbered step list for details). You don't want to accidentally wipe out any link equity you may have accumulated. *Link equity* refers to the perceived-expertise value of all the inbound links pointing to your Web page. You also don't want to cause people's links and bookmarks suddenly to break if they try to open your old page.

When consolidating two pages to make one your main, canonical version, take these precautions:

1. **Check for inbound links.**

   Do a [link:*domain.com/yourpage*.html] search in Google or use the back-link checker in Yahoo Site Explorer to find out who's already linked to your page. If one version has 15 links and the other version has 4,000, you know which one to keep: the one that 4,000 people access.

2. **Update your internal links.**

   Make sure that your site map and all other pages in your site no longer link to the page you decided to remove.

3. **Set up a 301 redirect.**

   When you take down the removed page's content, put in its place a *301 redirect*, which is a type of HTML command that automatically reroutes any incoming link to the URL with the content that you want to retain. (Note: For help on this, see Book VII, Chapter 4.)

Avoiding duplications between your different domains

Most Web sites today operate both the domain that begins with www. and the domain without this prefix (such as `www.yourdomain.com` *and* `your domain.com`). You do not want to duplicate your site content between these two domains. Instead, set up a 301 redirect from one root domain to the other and keep only one set of your Web documents in production. (Note: It doesn't matter whether you redirect the www or the non-www version, although it may be more common to make the `www.` version the main site.) Users coming to either URL can get to the same content.

If you own multiple domains with the same content, you can solve the problem of duplicate content with the same technique. Decide which domain you want to rank well for your keywords and redirect the other domains to that one. Or if you truly need separate sites with duplicate content, know that you're going to pay a price when the search engines pick one page version that they decide is the authoritative one and ignore your others. (You can learn technical solutions to get around some of these issues, as well. See Book VII for more details.)

Printer-friendly pages

A common practice that inadvertently creates duplicate content within a Web site involves printer-friendly pages. *Printer-friendly pages* are separate pages designed for printing, without the heavy images and advertisements that eat up a lot of printer ink. Recipe sites are notorious for these, but many sites offer both an HTML version and a text-only version of each page so that their users can easily print them. The printer-friendly page has its own URL, so it's actually a twin of the HTML page.

You don't need to have separate text-only pages for printing. The best way to allow easy printing, keep your users happy, *and* follow SEO best practices is to use *CSS* (Cascading Style Sheets, an efficient way to control the look of your site by defining styles in one place). A print style sheet within your CSS can reformat your HTML pages on-the-fly so that they can be easily printed. Inside your CSS file, you can specify how a page should automatically change when a user chooses to print it. Your CSS can control print formatting such as page width, margins, font substitutions, and which images to print and which to omit. Creating a print style sheet within your CSS file is a much more elegant solution than duplicating your pages with printer-friendly versions.

If you do not want to use CSS for printable pages, you have to find ways to avoid several problems if you have twin versions of each content page, one for viewing and one for printing:

✦ **Link equity gets reduced.** This problem is common to all forms of duplicate content. People are going to link to both versions, so the link equity value for your content is effectively split between the two pages. Because link equity helps search engines determine how much authority a Web page has for a relevant search query, a diminished link equity value means your page won't rank as well in search results.

✦ **If you decide to consolidate the pages down the line, inbound links could break.** Because people are going to link to both versions, when you're ready to do away with printer-friendly pages, existing links may break. (Note: You want to create 301 redirects for those pages, which would fix the links, but would cost you some initial work and ongoing vigilance to keep those codes in place forever.)

✦ **Double the maintenance is a hassle.** If you have printer-friendly duplicate pages on your site, you already know that anytime you want to make a change to one, you have to remember to make the same change on the other. (We thought we'd mention that this is a pain, in case you didn't know already.)

✦ **Search engines pick just one page.** Having two versions of a page on your site forces the search engines to pick the one *they* think is the original and filter out the other one from their search results. And because the text-only version is probably much easier to spider than your beautiful HTML version, they may choose the printer-friendly page particularly if your printer friendly page has received more backlinks than your HTML version. So basically, you lose control over which version greets first-time visitors coming from a search results page.

If you currently have printer-friendly versions of your pages as separate URLs, we suggest you convert to a print style sheet in an external CSS file. You won't need the Printer Friendly Version hyperlinks on your pages anymore (unless you want to leave them for usability, maybe changing the wording) because whenever a user prints a page using File⇨Print or Ctrl+P, your CSS automatically takes charge and delivers a printable version.

When getting rid of printer-friendly pages you no longer need, be careful. Check for inbound links, update any internal links you may have to those pages, and set up a 301 redirect on the removed page. You want to make sure not to hurt your link equity or cause your users any problems when you remove a page.

If you decide you still want to keep your printer-friendly text versions, circumvent the duplicate content problem by putting a `noindex` command in the HTML code to prevent search engines from crawling these pages. You'd probably lose some links, but at least the search engines wouldn't confuse these pages with your main content.

Dynamic pages with session IDs

Many Web sites track the user's *session* — the current time period the user is active on the Web site since logging on. Sometimes these sites add a session ID code to each page's URL as the user travels the site. This is a really bad way to handle passing a session ID from page to page because it creates what looks like duplicate content. Even though the page itself has not changed, the varying parameters showing at the end of each URL causes search engines to think they are separate pages.

In fact, you don't want to put any type of variables directly into your URL strings except for ones that actually correspond with changed page content. You need unique content for every URL. If your site passes session IDs through the URL string, here are two ways to fix it:

✦ **Stop appending session IDs.** Ideally, you should correct your Content Management System (CMS) or server application so that it no longer creates URLs with session IDs. Use *cookies* (small bits of code that the server assigns to a user's browser that tracks the user from page to page) instead to serve pages.

✦ **Show spiders friendly URLs.** This is a more advanced solution, but you could consider using "user agent sniffing" to detect search engine spiders. If the page detects it's a search engine spider, it could deliver parameter-free URLs to them. This sniffing is invisible to the spider and, with a 301 on the old URL pointing to the rewritten URL, the spiders have a URL that they can index.

It's very important to deliver *exactly* the same content to a search engine as to a user; delivering different content would be considered spam.

Content syndication

Content syndication simply means sending out your Web site content to others. The big upside of syndicating your content is having more people read your stuff, which in turn can lead to increased traffic coming back to your Web site. The potential downside of syndication is duplicating your content. In essence, you are trading potential search engine ranking for direct links and the traffic that your feed brings in.

An RSS feed is a typical example of content syndication. *RSS* is a method of distributing links to new content in your Web site, and the recipients are people who've subscribed to your RSS feed. Even though your RSS feed sends out lots of copies of the same text, you can avoid a duplicate content problem by only sending out a snippet of your article, not the whole thing. (You can read more details on RSS in Book VI, Chapter 2.)

Then there is the problem of press releases. Press releases are posted on wire services for the express purpose of being picked up and duplicated on as many sites as possible. If your company puts out press releases, don't stop. Even though they do become duplicate content that may not bring any unique ranking to your Web site, they may generate traffic and backlinks. You distribute a press release for other reasons than search engine ranking, like branding, public relations, investor relations, and so on. These are legitimate goals, too.

You might also use more traditional ways of syndicating your content, where you create the content and receive a fee from other sites who want to use it. For example, newspaper artists draw their cartoons and then use a syndicate to make them available to any news organization that cares to run them, in exchange for a fee. However, if you syndicate your Web site content, you are very likely to run into duplicate content problems. If an expert-level Web site takes your content, chances are *they'll* become the canonical source for that information. For instance, if a big city news organization decides to fill one of its columns with your articles, chances are that the search engines will determine that the news site takes precedence over yours (because it's the 800-pound gorilla), and they would outrank you for that content if someone searched for it. If the sites are equal in every other way, however, the search engines look through their indexes to determine the original, or earliest, source of the content, and filter out the copies that came later as duplicates.

Localization

Many Web sites repurpose the same content for various locations. For example, a large real estate company with brokerage offices through the state may offer the same template to all of their brokers, customized only with a different city name and local property listings. Or a national cosmetics company gives local representatives their "own" sites, but all of them have the same standard template and content.

For local searching, a site like one of these may do all right. For instance, if you search [real estate listings Poughkeepsie], you will probably find brokerage sites that are located in Poughkeepsie, including the ones built with the same template and duplicated content. However, if the Poughkeepsie broker himself would like to rank for a broader search query like [New York properties,] he's probably out of luck. His Web site won't have enough unique content about that keyword phrase to rank in the search results. Doing a quick find and replace with a keyword to create "new" targeted pages (like changing Poughkeepsie to Albany) is not enough to create unique content and is in fact considered spam by the search engines. You must have unique content on unique pages in order to survive and thrive in the search engines.

You can use a template to create many Web sites, but here's how to do it without creating duplicate content. You need to do more than just a Find and Replace for a few terms. Customize the content for each location, including the headings, Title tags, Meta tags, body content, and so on. Unless you're located in a highly competitive demographic market area such as Chicago or New York City, your template-based site may be sufficient if you're only after local search business.

If you want to rank for non-local search queries, you absolutely need to customize your site content and make it unique. Depending on what kind of traffic you hope to attract through the search engines, you probably need to make changes to your content focused on improving both the quality and quantity.

Mirrors

On the Web, a *mirror* refers to a full copy of a Web page or site. The mirrored version is an exact replica of the original page. Yes, this is blatantly duplicate content, but there are a couple of legitimate reasons to mirror a Web page.

One reason to mirror a Web page is user convenience, such as when multiple Web sites offer copies of a download file so that users can access it at each location. Another legitimate reason is to display a backup version of a page that's temporarily down. For example, a site called Slashdot (www.slashdot.org) posts reviews of tech-related articles with a link to view the full article on the original site. In its heyday, Slashdot was so popular that whenever they posted a new review, many thousands of people would try to follow the article link at once, instantly crashing more than one unsuspecting site server under this sudden flood of traffic (this was called "the Slashdot effect"). To solve the problem, Slashdot began setting up a mirrored version of each new article on its own server, redirecting its users to the mirrored version only if the original site was unavailable. The mirror page's content is counted toward the original URL because it is a temporary redirect.

Mirroring should never be done deceptively. Hackers and pornography sites are notorious for mirroring sites, having content in 20, 30, 40, or more locations because of how frequently their sites are discovered and taken down. You want to ensure that search engines consider you a legitimate company with original content. Unless you have a need to put up a temporary page such as the ones mentioned above, try to avoid using mirrors on the Web.

CMS duplication

Many sites use a *content management system* (CMS), which is a software program that helps create and maintain Web pages. Some CMSs, however, have a problem: They generate duplicate content. It's just the way they're programmed. Or is it?

Your CMS should allow you to customize all parts of your Web pages, from the body text to the `Title` tags to the anchor text of links. If your CMS currently doesn't allow this, talk to your IT department and ask them to revise the settings. If that doesn't work, we recommend scrapping your inflexible system and starting over with a CMS that allows you to make these changes. Seriously, it's that important.

According to a September 2008 Google Webmaster Blog post, most site owners who ask about duplicate content are worried about issues like having multiple URLs on the same domain point to the same content. This is a situation that many CMSs create naturally. The example given in the blog post was

```
www.example.com/skates.asp?color=black&brand=riedell
```

and

```
www.example.com/skates.asp?brand=riedell&color=black
```

Both of these URLs bring up the same Web page, but they're different URLs because the CMS put the parameters for color and brand in a different order.

If that example looks like your site, you should realize that this can be prevented. Your CMS needs to facilitate ordering logic that controls the sequence of parameters in URLs. Where the page content remains unique, there should be no change to the URL.

Similarly, if your Web site lets users navigate to a page from various categories, be sure that there's only one copy of each file, not multiple copies. For instance, an e-commerce site selling ladies shoes might have separate navigation choices for dress, casual, sandals, pumps, open-toe, closed-toe, and so forth. One shoe could fall into many different categories, but no matter how the user navigates to find it, that unique shoe should have only one page at only one URL address.

Archives

After your Web site has been up for a while, you eventually need to trim some older content to keep the current information uncluttered. If the older pages are still useful, you can put them into an *archive* (storage area where older content is out of the way, but still accessible). Just be careful that your archive doesn't create duplicate content problems with current information on your site. (Without correction, duplicate content issues are almost always the case with blogging software and with news content.)

Keep one best practice in mind when you set up an archive: Do *not* change the archived page's URL. It's best to let pages stay in their original locations when you set up an archive, so that the URL stays golden through time. If you must change a URL, remember to do a 301 redirect to the new name.

Active blog sites tend to need archiving sooner than other content pages because they fill up with text and comments so quickly. Blog software programs generally include prior posts at the bottom of new posts and create copies of blog posts for appropriate categories or time periods, so duplicate content is sort of built-in. They also automatically move older posts into archive directories. If your blog is updated regularly and actively commented on, you don't really have to worry about this because the search engines are used to seeing this behavior. However, if you don't publish a lot of new content to your blog, the search engines filter out pages that seem to duplicate each other.

Intentional Spam

Now we want to address the more serious issue of people taking your content on purpose. If you've got loads of useful and engaging information, there is a good chance that someday it will wind up being intentionally copied and republished on someone else's site. This kind of duplicate content happens frequently, and it can damage your site's reputation and authority with the search engines.

There is no excuse for taking someone else's page intact, adding a different façade, making a few top-of-page cosmetic changes, and then uploading it to another site. Sometimes it even still contains the original displayed text and links! Unfortunately, there is no fool-proof defense against someone taking your content from the Web.

To deter others from copying your content, we recommend that you display a copyright notice on your Web site and register for a federal copyright. These two proactive steps can help you defend your Web site against intentional spam. It's a good idea for you to register for a federal copyright of your Web site as software. This is a low-cost and important step in your anti-theft effort. Even though all content carries copyright naturally, you want to actually file for a copyright registration because only a federal copyright has enough teeth in it to help you fight violations of your copyrights legally, if it ever comes down to that. (See Chapter 5 of this minibook for instructions on how to go about filing for a federal copyright.)

With a federal copyright on file, you have legal recourse if things get ugly. You also carry a lot more weight when you tell people your work is copyrighted with the U.S. government and then ask them to remove it from their site. The federal copyright can be enforced throughout the U.S. and internationally, so it has some real teeth in it.

In the next few sections, we list different types of intentional spam, with tips for what you can do to protect your Web site.

Scrapers

Scrapers are people who send a robot to your Web site to copy (or "scrape") the entire site and then republish it as their own. Sometimes they don't even bother to replace your company name throughout the content. Scraping a site is a copyright violation, but it's also more than that: It is theft, and, if the content is protected by a federal copyright, the thief can be sued in federal court.

If your Web site has been scraped, you need to decide what your objective is. Will you be satisfied simply to get the content pulled down? Or do you feel that the other party's actions are so serious and malicious that you want to sue for damages? You need to decide how much money and effort you're willing to spend, and what outcome you're really after.

If your site is scraped, your first step can be a simple e-mail requesting that the site stop using your content. Often this is enough to get it removed. You can also report them to the search engines or the *ISP* (Internet Service Provider) that hosts their site domain. If you notify them that the site has been scraped and provide some proof, they may shut the site down.

Because scraping is a crime, you may choose to file a police report for theft. You should have printouts and other evidence that the text is yours and that it has been stolen to back you up. You can even hire a lawyer and serve them a cease and desist order, demanding that they take down the offending Web pages or face legal action. As a last resort, you can file a lawsuit and fight it out in court.

Clueless newbies

Clueless newbies are what we call people who take someone else's Web site content but don't realize they've done anything wrong. They may be under the mistaken impression that everything on the Internet is fair game and free for the taking. They may not realize that intellectual property laws apply to the Internet just as they do everywhere else.

If your content has been stolen by a clueless newbie, we suggest you e-mail them. Tell them that it's copyrighted material and kindly ask them to take it down. If you're feeling generous, as an alternative, you might suggest that they only include an excerpt or summary of your content, link to your site instead, and put a `Meta` robots `"noindex"` tag on their page so that the search engine spiders won't crawl it. The newbie site owner may comply, and you have taught him or her a lesson in Internet etiquette. But even if they don't comply, the duplicated page is probably a low risk to you. A new site generally doesn't have much authority in the search engine's eyes, so their site may not hurt your rankings. They have no right to your content for their own commercial use, however, so you don't have to let them use it.

Stolen content

When you work hard to create unique, engaging content for your own Web site, it can be frustrating for you or even damaging to your search engine rankings when that content gets stolen and duplicated on some other site.

We suggest that you regularly check to see if your Web site content has been copied and used somewhere else. To check this, use the free service at Copyscape (`www.copyscape.com/`). Figure 4-1 shows how straightforward Copyscape is to use; you just type in your site's URL. If the site has been scraped, you see the offending URL in the results.

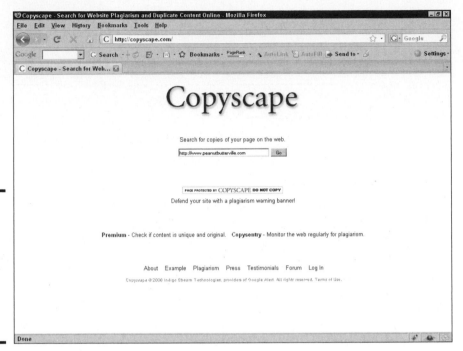

Figure 4-1:
Copyscape
lets you
find copies
of your
Web site
anywhere
on the
Internet.

When your content is stolen, you may see it appearing everywhere. Like playing the Whack-A-Mole arcade game, you might succeed in getting one site to remove your stolen content, only to find it popping up on another.

If you're in the Whack-A-Mole situation and lots of other sites now have your content, hopefully you have a federal copyright and can follow some of the recommendations we give earlier in this chapter. If you don't have a federal copyright, you may have only one recourse: changing your content. It's unfair, it's a pain, but if you don't have a registered copyright, you can't do much to stop people from stealing your stuff. Being unique on the Web is more important to your search engine rankings than playing whack-a-mole trying to stop thieves from taking your content, so rewrite your own text to be different than theirs. Enforce your copyright when you find people ripping you off, but don't think that it will solve your problem.

Chapter 5: Adapting and Crediting Your Content

In This Chapter

✔ Optimizing your content for local search

✔ Creating region-specific content

✔ Maximizing local visibility

✔ Understanding intellectual property ownership

✔ Knowing what to do when your content is stolen

✔ Filing for a federal copyright

✔ Incorporating content from other Web sites

✔ Giving credit to original authors

*I*f you've applied the ideas laid out in the previous chapters of this book, you are well on your way to a successful Web site. Your Web site hopefully contains lots of engaging content that your users love, with pages focused on your *keywords* (specific words or phrases entered in a search query) so that search engines can clearly establish your site's subject relevance.

In this chapter, you find out how to ensure that your site turns up in *local searches*, which are search queries intended to find businesses based on a specific location. You can do things to make sure that your business comes up when someone looks for "car customization in Poughkeepsie," for example, and we're going to tell you about them.

In the previous chapter, we covered the evils of duplicate content in many of its forms (site scraping, duplicate pages within the same domain, printer-friendly pages, dynamic pages with session IDs in the URLs, content syndication, localization, mirrors, archives, spam, and stolen content). Now we want to provide the remedy. Here, you discover what to do if your content is stolen by some other Web site. By the time you finish reading this chapter, you'll be well-armed to deal with this inevitable problem.

We also explain how you can incorporate content from other sites, if you should ever want to do that. After an entire chapter on how to avoid creating duplicate content, we figured it's time to balance the subject with information on how to use content from another site the *right* way: Sometimes, as with news sites, you'll need to do it.

Optimizing for Local Searches

The search engines logically interpret some types of search queries as local, or location-based, searches. For example, you might search for any of the following:

✦ [dog groomers]

✦ [dry cleaners]

✦ [chimney sweep services]

The search engines know that these search queries most likely mean you are looking for someone in your local area who can provide a service. If you live in Poughkeepsie, New York, it's unlikely that you'd be looking for a dry cleaner in Miami. It's also unlikely that you're interested in dry cleaning techniques, or the history of dry cleaning, or any other research-type information. Because the search engines want to satisfy you with relevant results (they want you to keep coming back to them), they're going to assume your intent is to find a local business and give you a list of dry cleaners in and around Poughkeepsie.

The search engines know where you're located. They have two ways of figuring this out: First, while doing a search at some point, you might have specified a city. Second, your computer's *IP address* (the numeric "Internet Protocol" code assigned to your computer) identifies your approximate location.

You can do local searches in three ways:

✦ **Logical local searches:** Sometimes search queries just logically bring up local businesses or services (like [dry cleaners], and so on).

✦ **Geographic search terms:** Search queries can include a city or ZIP code, such as [dry cleaners Miami], [dog groomers in Sacramento CA] or [chimney sweep services 90210].

✦ **Map searches:** People can search directly on a physical map (using a map interface) to find local businesses in a selected area.

Keep in mind that your own home location may not be the only city where you'd like your Web site to rank in local search results. For instance, if you do classic car customization nationwide, and you know that Detroit, Michigan has a huge concentration of classic car buffs, you could make sure your content is optimized to rank for a Detroit local search with your *keywords* (search terms relevant to your Web site). We explain how to optimize for local searches in the next sections, but consider that there may be several "local" areas that you want to optimize for, not just your own physical location.

Creating region-specific content

You need to let search engines know *where* you do business, so that your Web pages get returned in local searches. You need to adapt your content for localized searches. You shouldn't just copy pages and use a Find and Replace command to substitute different city names on each. That approach creates duplicate content (a bad thing because it damages your site's ability to rank well in search results for having unique and relevant information). It also doesn't satisfy your users or the search engines that you really do business in those locations.

To optimize your content for local searches:

✦ **Show your physical address.** If you have a brick-and-mortar location, be sure to include the address and local telephone number prominently somewhere on your Web site, preferably on the home page. Make sure that the page containing this information is linked from your site map, so that search engines can easily find it. (A *site map* is a page containing links to the pages in your site, like a table of contents.) Showing your address and contact information to users also makes them feel more comfortable doing business with you because you're not just a virtual company being operated from some post office box.

✦ **Mention your location.** In your Web site text, mention the name(s) of the city or cities where you do business. It depends on your site structure and goals, but consider devoting specific pages to locations and then talking about what you do in that location throughout the text. So you might have one page about your classic car services in Poughkeepsie, another about Yonkers, and so on.

✦ **Talk about things related to the location.** Don't just give the city name. Also mention geographic terms related to it, as you would naturally in conversation. For instance, if you're establishing that you do business in Los Angeles on a given page, you could also include "Hollywood" or "sunny Southern California" in the text.

Maximizing local visibility

If you run a local search in Google, the first thing that displays are local business listings pinpointed on a handy map, as shown in Figure 5-1.

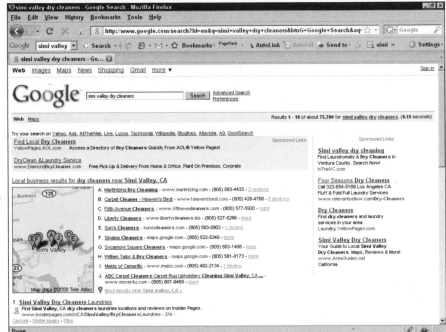

Figure 5-1: Business listings display at the top of a local search results page.

To be included in these local listings, the business owners of these sites at some point completed a business listing form with Google. If you haven't done this yet, take a little time now and register your business with the local directories for all the major search engines (Google, Yahoo!, and Microsoft Live Search). For detailed instructions, see the "Showing Up in Local Search Results," section in Book I, Chapter 4.

In addition to getting your business into the search engines' local directories, you don't want to miss being included in other online local directories. Do some research to find out what's out there for your specific industry and region. For example, in our local area, there's a weekly publication called *The Kitty Letter* that lists available rental properties. Smart real estate agents here make sure to include their rental listings in this local directory.

For your classic car customization Web site, that's a national business, so you could research and become a member of various local clubs or directories for classic car enthusiasts. Try to find out what kinds of publications or Web sites serve specific market areas and have your business listed in them.

To find these types of sites, simply enter search queries into the search engines that include specific locations, such as [classic car directory New York], [classic car clubs Detroit], and so on.

Your goal is to be visible not just for the big keyword searches. You also want to be found by the people who are looking for you in their own home-towns. Your site accomplishes this when you make it visible on a local level.

Factoring in Intellectual Property Considerations

Not everyone realizes that Web sites are the intellectual property of their owners. Your Web site content is your intellectual property, just as much as a book is the intellectual property of its author and publisher. And as intel-lectual property, your Web site is governed by copyright laws that protect it, especially if you've obtained a federal copyright (we get to that shortly).

Nevertheless, Web site content is often stolen and republished. If you've cre-ated lots of great content for your site, we almost guarantee that sometime, somewhere, you'll see your content pop up on someone else's site. It's inevi-table.

This book is not intended to replace legal advice. You should seek a copy-right lawyer in order to get the full picture regarding your legal rights and options.

What to do when your content is stolen

How can you respond when your Web site content is copied and posted on some other Web site? There are a number of things you can do if your con-tent or entire site is stolen:

✦ **E-mail a request:** A good first step can be a simple e-mail request to the site's Webmaster or contact person. Ask nicely for them to stop using your content. Often, this is enough to get it removed.

✦ **Report it to the search engines:** You can file a report of copyright infringement with the search engines to have the offending Web pages removed from their index. This procedure is allowed under the Digital Millennium Copyright Act. For instructions, see `www.google.com/dmca.html`.

✦ **Report it to their ISP:** You can also find out which *Internet Service Provider* (ISP) is hosting their site and contact the ISP. If you notify them that the site has been scraped and provide some proof, they may shut the site down. (You can use the WHOIS Lookup at `www.whois.net` to identify information about a site's registered owners, including the domain servers that host the site, which is the same as the ISP.)

✦ **File a police report:** Because theft is a crime, you can file a report with your local police or sheriff's department. You should have undisputed evidence that the text is yours and that it has been stolen. Print the offending page as displayed, and then print the HTML code for that page so that you have it. Call a friend to have them witness the theft, as well. See if their site contains a references or clients page. If so, write down the names and URL of these sites so that you can notify them of the theft a little later. You might also run a search to discover the list of sites that link to the offending pages ([link:offendingdomain.com]), and later send them all e-mails informing them of inadvertently supporting a scraped site and inviting them to link to the "source" of the content instead.

✦ **Send a cease and desist order:** You can have a lawyer draft a cease and desist order, demanding that they take down the offending Web pages or face legal action. The downsides with this approach are that it's costly and it gives the other party advance warning if you plan to file a lawsuit later. So before you do this, be sure to put together all the evidence recommended in the last paragraph.

✦ **File a lawsuit:** In serious cases where your business has been materially damaged, you can hire a lawyer and sue the other party. But make sure you have lots of evidence. Follow the recommended ideas for evidence gathering under the previous "File a police report" bullet.

The preceding list is not meant to be a step-by-step procedure. You can pick and choose from these suggestions based on your situation. But remember that you have options in case someone does steal your content.

Filing for copyright

To protect your Web site content, we recommend that you do two things:

✦ Display a copyright notice on your Web site.

✦ Register for a federal copyright.

These are two proactive, low-cost steps that can help you defend your Web site against theft. When you've registered for a federal copyright of your Web site as software, you have legal recourse if things get ugly. Only a federal copyright has enough teeth in it to help you fight violations of your copyrights legally. Your words also carry a lot more weight when you tell people your work is copyrighted with the U.S. government when you are asking them to remove your content from their site. The federal copyright can be enforced throughout the U.S. and internationally, so it has some real teeth in it.

The U.S. Library of Congress manages the U.S. Copyright Office. The U.S. Copyright Office considers Internet pages to be software programs. To have a copyright simply requires that the work contain a valid copyright notice as follows: © year author name (such as © 2009 John Wiley & Sons, Inc.).

Registering a copyright is not mandatory, but this is a time-proven effective step. After you register your site, the copyright stays in effect. Unless you completely replace your site with a new one, as "software," your future Web site updates continue to be protected by your initial registration.

To register, you should refer to the filing procedures required by the U.S. Copyright Office. Registering a copyright is not mandatory, but it is a reasonable step. You can handle the registration online — see their Web site at www.copyright.gov/.

On an international level, the U.S. government became a member of the Berne Convention in 1989 and fully supports the Universal Copyright Convention. Under this Convention, any work of an author who is a national of a Convention country automatically receives protection in *all* countries that are also members, provided the work makes use of a proper copyright symbol (©). The degree of protection may vary, but some minimal protection is defined and guaranteed in that agreement. Jurisdiction for prosecuting violations lies exclusively with the federal government.

Using content from other sites

Now, what if you want to use *other* people's content on your site? Perhaps you've seen a chart or image online that is relevant, useful, and perfect for your site users; or maybe you read an article in a magazine that says exactly what you want to tell your users. You also realize that reusing something that's already written is undoubtedly the fastest way to add bulk to your site. So you believe your site simply *must* have these things. Can you — should you — use them?

Be careful! You don't want to have duplicate content on your site, because that won't help and could even harm your site rankings. You also don't want to be deceptive and make it look as if it's your original creation. Deceiving your users or the search engines usually backfires (your pages could be filtered out of search results, you could damage your reputation with customers, and so on).

But say that you've found something you know would add tremendous value for your users. Here are some best practices for the times you need to use external content on your Web site:

✦ **Read the site.** Often sites will have a copyright or legal page that details their use permissions. Starting with the legal page gives you guidelines on what you'll be able to reasonably expect to be allowed to use.

✦ **Get permission.** If you want to republish something you saw on some-one else's site, ask for permission. It won't work with every Web site owner, but it's still a good idea. When you make your request, be sure to say you'll give a link back to their site and give them credit.

✦ **Do not use the whole thing.** Whether it's a full article, a full poem, a full page, or other, do not republish someone else's content in its entirety (unless you have an agreement with the owner).

✦ **Excerpt or summarize it.** You can write a brief summary or review in your own words, rather than displaying the original text (give a link instead). Don't use more than an excerpt if you're posting the original words. For instance, if it's a magazine article you wanted, you could write a review, rebuttal, or summary, and give a link to read the article on the original site. The most you should copy directly is a short excerpt in a quote.

✦ **Set it apart with quotation marks or as a block quote.** The idea is to make it clear to users that the excerpted text is quoted, not original to you. You can also make that clear to search engines by indenting the text with a `Blockquote` HTML tag.

Some people claim "fair use" when reusing other people's content. The doctrine of fair use says that under some circumstances, it's not a copyright violation to quote another's work. This is a confusing part of copyright law, and the line between fair use and infringement is very fuzzy. One clear guideline is that you can't use the borrowed content for profit in any way. If you have an ad or sell things anywhere on your site, it's considered a "for profit" Web site. Basically, no business qualifies for fair use. In the area of copyright infringement, as in so many others, it's best to keep your Web site in the safe harbor and follow the best practices listed here.

Crediting original authors

When you do use someone else's content, give credit where credit is due. Attribute the work to its author or to the originating Web site. In addition to setting it apart with quotation marks or as a block quote, include a line that says something like: "Used by permission of . . ." or "Courtesy of . . ." or "Provided by . . ." and identify the name of the author. If you weren't able to get permission, you still can mention where the information comes from. You may also want to include the cite attribute in a quote or blockquote tag. The cite attribute is used in the Quote `Q` and `Blockquote` tags to reference the source for material that originally appeared elsewhere.

The Q tag is used for short, inline quotes, such as

```
<P>According to a World Research Foundation article, <I><Q
   CITE="http://www.wrf.org/news/news0017.htm">In nine
   double-blind studies comparing placebos to aspirin,
   placebos proved to be 54 percent as effective as the
   actual analgesic</Q></I></P>
```

Note that you may want to include the quoted text in italics — as in the preceding example — or in quotes, since most browsers do not render the Q tag correctly by placing it in quotes or italicizing it.

The Blockquote tag is used for longer quotes, usually where an entire paragraph or more is referenced. For example:

```
<BLOCKQUOTE CITE="http://www.wrf.org/news/news0017.htm ">
   <P>I don't believe that the use of placebos is immoral
   or unethical. In reality, it seems that the medical
   profession's lack of understanding and utilization of the
   mechanism of the placebo in the healing process is tragic,
   shortsighted and cowardly. Cowardly in the aspect that
   it has been far easier for doctors to simply say that
   the placebo response is worthless, and nothing more than
   someone's wishful thinking or trickery of the mind. The
   bottom line is the response; for whatever reason, placebos
   seem to work... patients get better.</P>
<P>An interesting statistic has shown that virtually all
   newly introduced surgical techniques show a decrease in
   success over time. Is this also a placebo response?</P></
   BLOCKQUOTE>
```

Some browsers indent blockquote text on both the left and right side, but you should not count on this formatting to occur. Also note that Blockquote may contain block-level elements such as P (paragraphs) and Table (tables), but they may not be contained within inline elements (such as A, B, I, U, or Strong tags.

Also, be sure to link to the source. Give your users a link back to view the original article in context. This keeps your "borrowing" above board, boosts your credibility, and improves the users' experience. Plus, by treating the originating author respectfully, you may just build a business relationship that yields long-term benefits.

Book VI
Linking

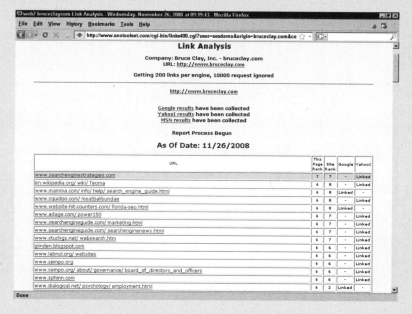

*A Link Analysis Report showing Web pages
that link back to a particular page.*

Contents at a Glance

Chapter 1: Employing Linking Strategies 367

Theming Your Site by Subject..367
Implementing Clear Subject Themes 375
Siloing...377
Doing Physical Siloing..378
Doing Virtual Siloing..380
Building Links...385

Chapter 2: Obtaining Links 389

Researching Links..389
Soliciting Links...393
Making Use of Link Magnets and Link Bait..............................397
How Not to Obtain Links 399
Evaluating Paid Links 400
Working with RSS Feeds and Syndication 401

Chapter 3: Structuring Internal Links 405

Subject Theming Structure...405
Optimizing Link Equity 407
Creating and Maintaining Silos 408
Building a Silo: An Illustrated Guide......................................410
Maintaining Your Silos...414
Including Traditional Site Maps..415
Using an XML Site Map 418

Chapter 4: Vetting External Links 421

Identifying Inbound Links..421
Avoiding Poor Quality Links 422
Identifying Quality Links...426
Finding Other Ways of Gaining Link Equity 429
Making the Most of Outbound Links......................................430
Handling Advertising Links 431
Dealing with Search Engine Spam 432

Chapter 5: Connecting with Social Networks 435

Making Use of Blogs 435
Discovering Social News Sites 437
Promoting Media on Social Networking Sites 438
Social Media Optimization...440
Community Building...442
Incorporating Web 2.0 Functioning Tools................................445

Chapter 1: Employing Linking Strategies

In This Chapter

✔ Theming your site by subject

✔ Implementing siloing

✔ Tackling link building

In Book IV, Chapter 4, we briefly discuss *siloing*, which is a way of arranging your Web site according to themes that allows for prime search engine optimization. In this chapter, we go into the meat and bones of siloing.

Siloing your site is one of the most important things you can do for search engine optimization. It organizes your Web site so that a search engine (and a user) can get a good clear picture of who you are and what you're about. A non-siloed site versus a siloed one is like the difference between having a bookshelf with books and DVDs and CDs and knickknacks all crammed into the same shelves versus a bookshelf with books on one shelf, CDs on another, DVDs on a third, and knickknacks on the fourth. It's easier to figure out where things are on the organized bookshelf versus the messy bookshelf.

In this chapter, we discuss how to build categories and themes for yourself and how to incorporate those into your silos. We also discuss how to build those silos yourself and how to use link building.

Theming Your Site by Subject

You can do many things to your Web site to provide evidence of subject relevance. One of these things is understanding what it means to theme a Web site. Theming is grouping Web site content in a manner that matches the way people search. One site can have many themes. Each theme can have sub-themes. In our classic car customization site, the main theme is customizing classic cars; a sub-theme is restoration of classic Mustangs.

In order to rank for your keywords within Google, Yahoo!, and Microsoft Live Search, your Web site has to provide information that is organized in clear language that the search engines can understand. When your information has had all of its design and layout stripped away, is it still the most relevant information when compared to other sites? If so, you have a pretty good chance of achieving high rankings and in turn attracting users looking for those products and services. In order to do so, you have to be thinking about the following things:

✦ The subject themes your Web site is currently ranking for in the search engines.

✦ The subject themes your Web site can *legitimately* rank for. (False advertising is *always* a bad idea.)

✦ How to go about properly implementing those subject themes.

As you may have seen throughout this book, we often explain the importance of creating silos for your subject themes by using the analogy that most Web sites are like a jar of marbles. Search engines can only decipher the meaning of a Web site when the subjects are clear and distinct. Take a look at the picture of the jar of marbles below in Figure 1-1 and think about how search engines would classify the theme(s) of the jar.

In the jar, you can see black marbles, gray marbles, and white marbles all mixed together with seemingly no order or emphasis. You can reasonably assume that search engines would classify the only theme as "marbles."

If you then separate out each group of colored marbles into separate jars (or sites) as in Figure 1-2, they would be classified as a jar of black marbles, a jar of white marbles, and a jar of gray marbles. Now your site could rank for the narrow terms [black marbles,], [white marbles,] and [gray marbles,] but you would be lucky to rank for the generic term [marbles].

If you wanted to keep all three types of marbles together in a single jar (or Web site) and go after the very important generic term, you would go about creating distinct silos or categories within the jar (or site) that would allow the subject themes to be black marbles, white marbles, gray marbles, and finally the generic term [marbles,] as in Figure 1-3.

Most Web sites never clarify the main subjects they want their site to be relevant for. Instead, they try to be all things to all people and wind up with a jumbled mess.

Figure 1-1:
Our jar
of mixed
black, white,
and gray
marbles.

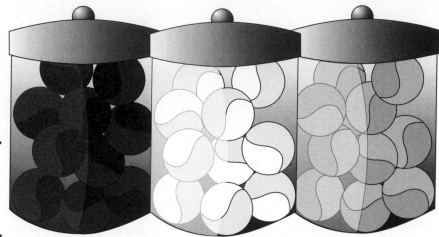

Figure 1-2:
Now your
marbles are
easier to tell
apart.

The goal for your site, if you want to rank for more than a single generic term, is to *selectively* decide what your site is and is not about. Rankings often are damaged in two major ways: by including irrelevant content, or by having too little content for a subject on a Web site.

So what subject themes are you currently ranking for?

The best places to start to identify what themes are your most relevant are your keyword research and the data from your Web site. You can start by examining the data from the following sources:

✦ **Web analytics.** (These are program routines embedded in your Web pages that are designed to track user behavior.)

✦ **Pay-per-click (PPC) programs.** (See Book X, Chapter 1 for more details on pay per click.) You can use PPC traffic to estimate whether a keyword is worth targeting in your SEO campaign.

✦ **Tracked keyword phrases.** All of the phrases you are tracking in your monitors are valuable sources of information when you apply competitive research tactics (see Book III, Chapter 2 for mining themes.)

Each of these sources of information can provide the history of who visits the Web site and why. They won't tell you why the site isn't ranked for desired keywords directly, but they help you understand what keyword phrases your site currently ranks for organically and which visitors find your site relevant.

Figure 1-3:
Arranging
the marbles
by theme
allows you
to keep
them in the
same jar
and still be
able to tell
them apart.

Web analytics evaluation

You have several ways to obtain the data or logs for the search engine spider history and the footprints of visitors to your site. First off, you may go right to the source and download the actual log files from your server using FTP. If your server comes with a free log file analyzer, you can use that, or you can use a program like Web Trends (`www.webtrends.com/`) or dozens of other desktop applications that help decipher Internet traffic data. Many businesses also use on-demand services that use cookies and JavaScript to pull live data on the patterns of search engines and visitors. These businesses do so through an online service like the exceptionally powerful Omniture (`www.omniture.com/en/`), ClickTracks (`www.clicktracks.com/`), or Google Analytics (`www.google.com/analytics/`), which is a free service. However you access the data history, you are looking for the search terms that brought users to your site. Book VIII focuses on Web analytics and guides you through many of your options.

PPC programs

You can also find clues to the words that your current site is relevant for by evaluating the words that you bid on with pay per click programs offered by all major search engines. Often, companies bid on words that they would *like* to be relevant for within the organic search arena, but that for one reason or another they have not yet achieved ranking success.

Tracked keyword phrases

The last and most accessible method of discovering your Web site's most important subject themes is to find out which keyword phrases are currently the best ranked. What phrases are pulling people to your Web site? Running a keyword monitor, checking your Web analytics program reports and server logs, and using tools like the one found at the SeoDigger Web site (`www.seodigger.com`) are all ways to discover which queries are already bringing you traffic. Obviously these aren't the only terms that you'll want to focus on in your SEO campaign, but they are important to optimize for so that you don't lose the traffic they're already bringing you. Pair them with your new keyword list when you do your organization.

After you identify your keywords and implement them in your campaign, you want to continue to track them, paying close attention to which keywords are bringing traffic and, of that traffic, what percentage of visitors are converting.

Keyword research

After creating a starter list of 10–100 keyword terms that appear to be most relevant to your company's product or services, it's time to begin keyword research. During the process of keyword research, the first goal is to grow that keyword list as large as possible. Cover as many relevant subjects that can be remotely connected to the Web site's subject themes as you can. Use Trellian's Keyword Discovery tool (`www.keyworddiscovery.com`) or Wordtracker (`www.wordtracker.com`) to identify keywords and synonyms that are related to the site's subject matter. Another excellent tool is the Google Keyword Tool from Google AdWords (`https://adwords.google.com/select/KeywordToolExternal`). Refer to Book II for the nitty-gritty on keyword research techniques.

After you answer the question of where the site currently ranks, you know two major factors: what you are ranked for and not ranked for in the search engines. The next challenge is to understand what subjects your site is legitimately relevant to and why you are ranked as you are currently.

Book VI
Chapter 1

Employing Linking
Strategies

Many site owners get incensed that they are not better ranked for terms they feel they are relevant for. These owners feel that engines misjudge the value of their site. A poor mechanic always blames his tools. There *are* rare exceptions where the tools are at fault, but 99 percent of the time, the problem is that the site is not focused enough on its dominant topics. Owners try to cram in too many things at once, and the search engine has a hard time figuring out what the site actually is supposed to be about. Your task is to figure out what your site is about after stripping away all the visual hoo-has and getting down to the actual content.

Page Analyzer

A great place to begin is to run Page Analyzer within the SEOToolSet. (Non-toolset subscribers can use the tool on SEOToolSet.com on the Free SEO Tools page — `www.seotoolset.com/tools/free_tools.html`.) Page Analyzer reveals the density, distribution, and frequency of keyword phrases used throughout the page (for more information on this subject, please see Book III, Chapter 2). By running the main pages of your site through this tool, you can begin to identify if the major themes are used throughout the titles, `Meta` tags, headings, `Alt` attributes, and body content. If your terms are absent, make a note that the keyword densities seem low. Evaluate how often a phrase is repeated in each major category element and take note of the commonly repeated phrases and infrequently repeated phrases. Are all the terms concentrated only near the top of the pages? If so, make a note that the distribution of the keywords could stand to be more spread out. Don't bunch them all together.

Multiple Page Analyzer

SEOToolSet subscribers can use Multi-Page Analyzer to further help their siloing efforts. After evaluating, if the pages throughout your site contain keyword rich densities, compare your pages to that of the top 10 competitors for your major keyword terms. Using Multi-Page Analyzer, you are given a report that summarizes why the competitors' sites ranked highly and recommends how to adjust your own pages to have keyword densities similar to those of the top ranked sites.

Using search engine operators for discovery

The last test is to evaluate each major engine by using the following search index operators in Table 1-1. Take a moment to discover all the ways you can extract Google's index data and then highlight two separate functions: the [site:domain.com] command and the [link:www.domain.com] command. In Google, the two most relevant measurements of rankings are how many pages a site has about a subject, and how many inbound links reference the site. Please note how the link: command requires the fully-qualified URL. The purpose of using these commands is to better understand the scope or size of competitive Web sites. Use these tools to research why the competition ranks, and create a graph that documents the contrast between your site and the competition. (For more on researching your competition, see Book III, Chapter 2.)

Table 1-1	Advanced Search Operators for Power Searching on Google, Yahoo!, and Microsoft Live Search		
Google	*Yahoo!*	*Microsoft Live Search*	*Result*
cache:			Shows the version of the Web page from the search engine's cache.
link:	**link:**	**link:** or **linkdomain:**	Finds all external Web sites that link to the Web page. (Note: In Yahoo! you must type in **http://**.) (Note: in Microsoft Live Search, there must be a space between the colon and the domain name.)
	linkdomain:		Finds sites that link to any page within the specified domain.
related:			Finds Web pages that are similar to the specified Web page.
info:			Presents some information that Google has about a Web page.
define:	**define:**	**define:** or **definition:**	Provides a definition of a keyword. There has to be a space between the colon and the query in order for this operator to work in Yahoo! and Microsoft Live Search.

Google	Yahoo!	Microsoft Live Search	Result
stocks:	stocks:	stock:	Shows stock information for ticker symbols. (Note: Type ticker symbols separated by a space; don't type Web sites or company names.) There has to be a space between the colon and the query in order for this operator to work in Yahoo! and Microsoft Live Search.
site:	site: or domain: or hostname:	site:	Finds pages only within a particular domain and all its sub-domains.
allintitle:			Finds pages with all query words as part of the indexed Title tag.
intitle:	intitle: or title: or T:	Intitle:	Finds pages with a specific keyword as part of the indexed Title tag. There needs to be a space between the colon and the query to work in Microsoft Live Search.
allinurl:			Finds a specific URL in the search engine's index (Note: You must type in http://.)
inurl:	inurl:	inurl:	Finds pages with a specific keyword as part of their indexed URLs.
		inbody:	Finds pages with a specific keyword in their body text.

Implementing Clear Subject Themes

After you know what you are ranked for, what you're considered to be relevant for, and hopefully have performed some analysis on the data you gathered so you can determine why your competition ranks the way they do, you're still not done. For each keyword phrase you've identified, you need to make a decision: Is it worth the work to write dozens of pages of content to rank for a subject you don't *already* rank for? To make this decision, consider whether your site is really about that theme, and whether adding more content about the subject could make your site become *less* relevant for more important terms. You do not want to dilute your site. You need to sit down and figure out whether you're willing to make the commitment to establish a theme and do the work required.

There are many ways to establish a clear theme: Begin by visualizing the primary and secondary categories that you would prefer for your site. If you don't have a clear idea of what the primary theme of your Web site is, search engines and users are going to be confused as well. You can start figuring out your primary theme by creating a simple outline. Think of this chart like a business's organization chart, except for themes. Define the major theme or primary subject that you want to become relevant for and create an organization chart or linear outline to cement your ideas in place. Often, it's not until you actually put pen to paper that major subject complications or contradictions surface. Look at Figure 1-4 and note how one main topic is supported by several smaller subtopics.

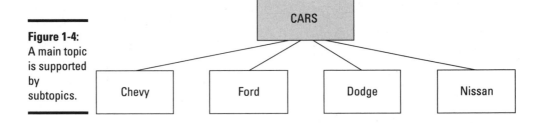

Figure 1-4:
A main topic is supported by subtopics.

Or you can use a simple bulleted list, like this:

✦ Major theme
  • Subtopic 1
  • Subtopic 2
  • Subtopic 3
  • Subtopic 4

Creating an organization flow chart is a third way to lay out your subject themes visually. The Organization Chart is an easily accessible tool that can be found within Microsoft Visio, or you can use another organization chart creation software program. Using one of these visual representations of your themes and subtopics (outline, bulleted list, or organization chart) provides the opportunity to visually explain to others involved in the Web site what the focus of the Web site should be and what subjects actually serve to distract the search engines from the main subjects.

After completing this exercise, ask yourself what keyword phrases users actually type into the search engines when looking for this information. This helps in organizing your broad phrases for the large, traffic-heavy pages for your site, and the smaller, more specialized phrases that go on your sub-pages.

Siloing

After you have your main themes and subtopics laid out on paper, you can match up your Web site content. You may have a good *landing page* (a page that users come to from clicking a search result or an outbound link from another site) for each main topic; if not, that's going to be at the top of your list. Next, you want to make sure you have enough subtopic content, or sub-pages, to support each main topic. You also want to make sure that every page's content is focused on its particular theme. In other words, it's time to start arranging your Web site into silos.

One way to visualize a silo is to think of a pyramid structure. Look at Figure 1-5 and notice the top tier. That's a landing page, which has the big broad terms you want to be ranking for. The pages underneath it are the supporting pages, which are the smaller subcategories you came up with to support the main term.

**Book VI
Chapter 1**

Employing Linking
Strategies

Figure 1-5:
A silo looks a lot like a pyramid, in that the main topic is supported by the smaller subtopics.

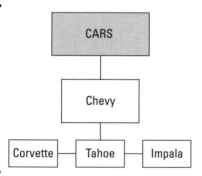

The top page receives the most support (and hopefully the most traffic) because it's the most relevant and focused page about its particular subject. Your site proves that it's the most important by the way it's structured, with supporting pages under the top page, and by the way you have your links set up. The way you set up your site should tell the search engines exactly what each page is about and which is the most important page for each keyword theme.

There are two ways of doing siloing. One way is *physical (or directory-based) siloing*, which involves building the directory structure to reflect your site themes and constructing your links to follow the structure of your directory, where subpages in a directory are also subpages in for a particular theme. The other way is through *virtual siloing,* which establishes what your main subject themes are based entirely on links without the reinforcement of your directory structure.

Doing Physical Siloing

One way you can do your siloing is to link in the same pattern as your directory structure. (The *directory structure* refers to the folders where your Web site files physically reside and how they are arranged.) When you upload files to your site, you place them in a directory. A siloed directory structure has a top-level folder for each main topic, subfolders within each main-topic folder for its related subtopics, and individual pages inside (as shown in Figure 1-6). Linking then naturally follows this structure, effectively reinforcing your directories through links.

Figure 1-6:
A siloed file directory structure.

When building a directory structure, be sure not to go too deep. For example, take a look at the URL of the page. The full address is the directory of where the page is. Observe:

```
http://www.customclassics.com/ford/mustang/index.html
```

The URL lets you know where the page is. Notice how the page named "index.html" is saved within the folder named "mustang," which is a subfolder of the main directory "ford." This page is only two levels deep in the site structure, which is good.

Too many levels of subdirectories can have the following negative effects:

✦ The more clicks it takes to get from the home page to the target page, the less important it is deemed by the search engines.

✦ Long directory paths make long URLs, and studies have proven that users avoid clicking long URLs on a search results page.

✦ Long URLs are more prone to typos. This can discourage deep linking or even cause broken links to your Web pages from other sites. Also, users can make mistakes typing in your URL.

So don't get category-happy. Making your directory structure ten directories deep is bad, having five levels is bad, and even having three levels of subdirectories is still not great. Although there's no hard and fast rule, you should try to remain quite shallow: One or two level deep is usually sufficient. The closer the page is to the root of the directory, the more important your page looks to the search engine.

For example, your classic car Web site only has one main directory level (the car's make) and two directory levels of subcategories (model and year). The directory could look something like this:

```
http://www.customclassics.com/ford/delrio/index.html
http://www.customclassics.com/ford/delrio/1957.html
http://www.customclassics.com/ford/delrio/1956.html
http://www.customclassics.com/ford/fairlane/index.html
http://www.customclassics.com/ford/fairlane/1958.html
http://www.customclassics.com/ford/fairlane/1959.html
http://www.customclassics.com/ford/mustang/index.html
http://www.customclassics.com/ford/mustang/1965.html
http://www.customclassics.com/ford/mustang/1966.html
```

Note how shallow the directory structure is: No page is more than three directory levels away from the root.

The other thing to keep in mind when working with physical siloing is the difference between absolute and relative linking. A *fully qualified link* provides the entire URL within the link, and a *relative link* is only linked to a file within the current directory. A fully qualified link looks like this:

```
<a href="http://www.classiccars.com/ford/mustang/tireoptions.
    html">
```

A root-relative link looks like this:

```
<a href="/ford/mustang/tireoptions.html">
```

And a directory-relative link looks like this:

```
<a href="tireoptions.html">
```

When you use a relative link, it's only going to work in relation to the current directory (or the next directory up, if you use slash characters relative to the root of the site). So a link to `tireoptions.html` works only if there's a file called `tireoptions.html` for it to link to in the same directory as the file you are linking from.

With fully qualified linking, there is no confusion about where the file is located and what it is about. A fully qualified link has the added bonus of being very clear for the search engine to follow. Fully qualified links allow the search engine spider to have the full address when it follows a link and ensures that the pages being linked to can be found and indexed when the spider returns in the future. Using relative links, or links that are not fully qualified (with the `http://www` URL), can send the spider to a wrong place. Fully qualified links make links easier to maintain and ensure that the search engine spider can always follow them.

Whenever you move files, links need to be updated. Absolute links break absolutely if you rearrange folders, whereas if you picked up an entire sub-directory and moved it somewhere else, relative links actually still work. The disadvantage of relative linking is not being able to see at a glance the complete path where a file exists, which may make it tougher to maintain.

Doing Virtual Siloing

You may have your Web site directories currently set up in a non-siloed structure, with thousands of files and hundreds of folders already in place. Or, you may need to maintain a directory structure that does not reflect your site theme for some other reason. Never fear: As with most difficulties, there is a technical solution that can still enable you to silo your site and achieve better search engine optimization.

You can make the theme of your Web pages clear to the search engines even if you do not follow your directory structure so long as you connect your pages on the same theme through internal linking. This is called *virtual siloing*.

If you want to think about it in the simplest terms possible, the Internet is a series of Web pages connected by hyperlinks. A Web site is a part of the great Internet soup, being both a member of the whole vast network and an individual group of pages unique unto itself. What search engines attempt to do is collect information from individual sites into content groups: "This site means this, and that other site means that, and so forth." They try to determine every site's content and give it a category. Search engines award the Web sites that have the most complete subject relevance with high rankings for those keywords.

The difference between physical siloing and virtual siloing is that in physical siloing, it's about how you set up your directory structure and links. Virtual siloing is about setting up your links regardless of your directory structure. It's achieved through the *anchor text,* the text that is hyperlinked that describes the actual link; the *backlinks*, the links going to your site from external sites; the *external links*, the links going out of your site; and *internal linking*, which are the links within your site.

Anchor text

The anchor text for a link tells the search engine what the page that's being linked to is about. Clicking a link that says "tires" should take you to a page about tires. Because if the page is about tires, and the anchor text says it's about tires, and any other links to that page all contain the word tires (or synonyms of tires), that creates a giant blinking neon arrow to tell the search engine that that particular page is about tires. Anchor text is the hyperlinked text that explains what the link is and what the page it is linking to is about. It sometimes helps to think of anchor text as your ability to vote for what keyword phrase the target page should rank for.

Book VI Chapter 1

Employing Linking Strategies

Backlinks

Inbound linking (also called backlinks) is perhaps the most well known and often discussed of the link structure elements in search engine optimization. These backlinks are the links that point into your site from an outside Web site. You might be saying to yourself, "Hold up, I can't control what people say about me." That is true, to an extent. However, having a page on your Web site instructing visitors how you prefer to be linked to or even offering an appropriate code snippet helps both you and the people you want to link to you. Supporters and people interested in spreading the word about you are likely to add mention of your site to their personal or even company Web site. Your Web site can suggest to these people what the most appropriate way to link back to your site might be. Many videos or links provide several different ways of linking back to themselves, or embedding themselves on a Web site. You can similarly offer links back to items on your site: All you have to do is provide the appropriate code.

So what are some of the ways a search engine measures the value of a backlink?

Keyword-rich anchor text

The link's anchor text should contain appropriate relevant keywords (such as cars, Corvette, Impala, Chevy Cavalier, and so on). The link text must also match the target page subject in order to be considered relevant.

Relevant Web sites link to relevant categories

A relevant Web site linked to the most relevant category on your Web site offers the highest value. A link from a Web site that has little or no relevance doesn't help your site with expertise or authority. It won't hurt your site, however, in most cases. Irrelevant links harm a Web site only if the links turn out to be purchased in mass quantities as part of a link farm and you reciprocate the link. (*Link farms* are networks of Web sites built for the express purpose of driving up link popularity.) In most cases, the worst thing that happens is that the links are filtered and no value is passed to the target page or site.

Natural link acquisition

It's important to have other high-ranked Web sites pointing links to your site; however, if the only Web sites that link to your site are PageRank 5 or higher, it may seem artificial or suspicious to search engines. It's more common to see a variety of new and more established sites linking to your site, acquired naturally over time rather than instantaneously. It doesn't harm your rankings to have good links and there's no reason not to solicit links from relevant experts in your industry, but a natural link distribution is something to keep in mind.

Ethical site relationships

Choosing to seek links from other ethical Web sites has a lasting effect on your Web site's rankings. On the other hand, choosing sites that deliberately try to boost link popularity through *link farms* or other schemes to fool the search engines may lead to a drop in rankings or more drastic search engine penalties such as being removed from the index itself. When you're engaged in link building efforts, give serious thought to the types of people that you're asking to link to you.

Purchased links

On the whole, we recommend that you don't buy links. The only time we do recommend buying links is for the purpose of advertising in order to increase your site traffic — not to increase your link popularity. Buying links for commerce purposes (traffic) is acceptable but buying for link equity is deceptive SEO and is spam. We cover more on buying links in the section "Link buying," later in the chapter.

External links

Links from your Web site to other Web sites are called *external links*. Often, the drive to build backlinks dominates site owners' link structure projects, whereas external linking remains ignored and misunderstood. Some companies are mistakenly concerned that they could lose traffic and customer sales if they link their site to other relevant sites' information, products, or services. After all, why should you link to your competition? Well, failing to link out harms your search engine rankings. The effort devoted to attracting backlinks is only effective when balanced with appropriate external linking to relevant expert sites. External links count towards your search engine rank because it's natural that an expert site would be connected with other related sites in its industry (or subject "community," as the search engines call it). Being a competent reference source is important for SEO.

External link anchor text

The anchor text that points away to another site must be evaluated with the same scrutiny given to backlinks. Evaluating the competition is critical to understanding why a site has high keyword rankings. The phrases used in link anchor text should reflect the same type of keywords that the site is trying to rank for.

In order to pass on subject relevance, you don't need to link to direct competitors; rather, you can choose compatible or related Web sites. Often, subject experts are education-related sites, as well as other compatible services that *complement* your services, rather than confusing or confiscating your users.

Do *not* sell links for SEO. Obviously, many sites use advertising to support themselves: We're not talking about that. We're talking about the guy who offers you a $1,000 a month for an undisclosed paid link on your home page. Google has made it very clear that they do not like links that are bought for the purposes of trying to game their algorithm. If you're going to sell link advertisements on your site, make sure they're clearly labeled as such. Link selling, no matter how tempting, can be met with search engine penalties and possibly a complete Web site ban that removes the Web site from the search engine.

Internal linking structure

The last part of virtual siloing is building subject relevance using the navigation and on-page elements of your Web site. This means arranging the main subjects in the most straightforward way possible in order to build subject relevance and organizing your navigation menus to categorize the content of your site. Remember the pyramid that we talked about at the beginning of the chapter? The broader terms are supported by the lesser terms, and the lesser terms are supported by the even lesser terms, and so forth.

Every silo needs to be assigned a main landing page focused on that silo's primary subject theme. The landing page should have at least five pages of support for it, and so on. Linking should stay within the silos or point to other important landing pages. Look at Figure 1-7, which shows a graph of a silo with one big broad page and five smaller subcategory pages, each with their own attached supporting pages.

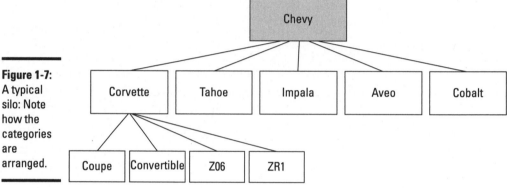

Figure 1-7:
A typical silo: Note how the categories are arranged.

When you're building your silo, the smaller pages should not link cross-category. Your page on Ford tires should not link to a page about Chevy tires, for instance. Instead, have both pages link to a separate landing page about tires. Too much cross-linking between unrelated subjects dilutes the silo and confuses the search engine.

You can also use a couple of tricks with cross-linking in order to keep the links streamlined, but they should be used sparingly. If you must cross-link theme supporting pages (not landing pages), we suggest that you add the `rel="nofollow"` attribute to a link to keep the search engine from following the link. This allows unrelated pages to link to each other without confusing the subject relevance.

The `nofollow` attribute is not a substitute for having a good linking strategy, and every page on your site must be linked to from at least two perfectly normal, followable links on perfectly normal, indexable pages.

Excessive navigation or cross linking

When it is impossible to remove menus or other links that contradict subject relevance categories, instead use technology to block the search engine spiders from indexing those specific elements and maintain quality subject relevance:

✦ **JavaScript:** Great for drop-down menus, forms, and other elements that you don't want the spider to follow. You can use JavaScript to prevent the search engine from indexing a menu if, for example, your whole site's navigation menu shows at the top of every page (which could confuse the spiders).

✦ **Iframes:** If you have repetitive elements, add an iframe to isolate the object to one location and eliminate interlink subject confusion.

✦ **Flash:** Effectively remove a menu or content links from the search engines' view by placing your content or menu within a Flash object, which spiders can't follow. This technology is developing rapidly and may be spiderable in the near future, but for now, proceed with caution.

✦ **AJAX (Asynchronous JavaScript and XML):** AJAX applets are gorgeous Web 2.0 applications that can be used to create engagement, but that can't be indexed in search engines, providing the perfect haven for content, menus, and other widgets for the user's eyes only.

Striking a balance between these three elements of link structure (inbound, outbound, and internal site linking) serves to create maximum subject relevancy.

Building Links

Link building goes back to what we were talking about earlier in this chapter about inbound links. It's about getting external sites to link to you. We go over this more in depth in Chapter 2 of this minibook, but here are a few different ways you can solicit links to your site:

✦ Link magnets

✦ Link baiting

✦ Link requests

✦ Link buying

Link magnets

When we say *link magnets*, we mean elements on your site that you build in such a way that people naturally want to link to them. Much like a magnet attracts iron filings, these site content elements simply attract links. People happen upon your site, find the link magnet, and decide that it's relevant and worthy of a link, so they stick a link to your content on their site. This happens because someone finds your page both useful and interesting, and it's a process that happens over time. But it means that the link is generally going to be from someone who is actually interested in your industry, not just in your gimmick. Remember, search engines judge you based on your expertise, and good quality links from relevant sites add to that.

The Search Engine Relationship Chart available at Bruce Clay's site (`www.bruceclay.com/serc`) is a good example of a link magnet. People in the search engine optimization industry find it relevant to their sites and useful for reference, so they link to it. We continue to keep the chart updated, so it always reflects the current state of the ever-changing search engine land-scape. For this reason, the chart maintains its relevance over time, as opposed to something brief and flashy that has no long-term value.

Link bait

Link bait is an accelerated version of a link magnet. *Link bait* is anything that is deliberately provocative in order to get someone to link to you. Examples would be a cartoon that someone did of your boss, or a video depicting wacky hi-jinks in your office that was linked to a few well-read blogs.

Link bait, unlike link magnets, is usually more broadly appealing in scope and probably isn't targeting your core market. Like any other non-relevant link, a link generated from link bait is often not one that would be considered a high quality link in general. But it does have the bonus of bringing a lot of traffic to your site, and hopefully a few of those visitors may poke around your site and decide to give you a permanent link.

An excellent example of link bait is any kind of viral marketing. Blendtec, a blender company, gets tons of links and traffic off of their videos on their Will It Blend? site, where they put all manner of strange and surprising things into their blenders (like rakes, marbles, and iPhones) and post the videos on the Internet. Most sites linking to Will It Blend? are not directly related to blenders, commercial or retail, and certainly can't be considered blender "experts" by the search engines, so those links count for less.

Link requests

Link requests are just what they sound like: e-mailing or contacting someone and asking for them to link to your site. If you find a site related to your subject themes that you would like a backlink from, you can contact them, providing them with information on what your site is, why you think it would be good to link to your site, and the anchor text with which you'd like to be linked to. It's basically like going door to door with your Web site and having to recite your pitch over and over again. Out of a neighborhood of 100 houses (or a hundred e-mails sent), you might get one or two takers. But is it worth the time and the effort for those two links? Link requests do work, but there's not a lot of return for the time you put in. It's not something we recommend.

Link buying

By ad link buying, we don't mean going out and selling or buying links to your own site for SEO link building purposes. There are two loose groupings of link buying: buying advertising for traffic purposes but not for SEO, which is acceptable; and buying a link for SEO purposes that is not a qualified testimonial, which is considered deceptive and if detected could result in a spam penalty.

Acceptable link buying is paying for a link on someone's advertising site. You *must* do it strictly for advertising and traffic purposes only, and not for link popularity. Google doesn't like to consider paid links and does not assign weight to a paid link. Paid links may pass some value until detected, but after they're detected, you lose all SEO value and could incur a penalty. If you do have a paid link on someone else's site, ask them to place a `rel="nofollow"` attribute on it. This attribute alerts the search engines that link equity should not be passed via that link. This is also important because if Google discovers a sold link on the site, it might stop passing link equity to all of the links on the site.

If you decide the traffic and advertising is worth the effort, it's perfectly acceptable to pay a site to have them run your banner or text link ad. Be aware, however, that part of the whole "paid links" issue is that you have to pay for it.

A word about reciprocal links: *Reciprocal links* are when two sites link to each other: site A to site B *and* site B to site A. This exchange of links is essentially a barter and generally does not contribute much, if anything, to link equity, but they are not harmful. Links between authority sites are natural and expected, whereas links between non-expert sites are of limited value. As a bartered link exchange, reciprocal links are essentially purchased; you are simply "paying" by giving a link in return. Building a link campaign based on reciprocal linking is largely a waste of time, but don't hesitate to link to a site that links to you if that site would be useful to your users.

Chapter 2: Obtaining Links

In This Chapter

✔ Researching links

✔ Soliciting links

✔ How not to obtain links

✔ Evaluating paid links

✔ Working with feeds and syndication

✔ Creating a press release

*I*n the previous chapter, we talk a little bit about getting people to link to you, and how it affects your overall ranking within the search engines. Having links from good reputable Web sites lends to your site's overall credibility and is used in the search engine's *algorithm* (formula that measures a Web page's overall relevancy to the search query) to determine whether you can be considered an "expert" in your field. Remember, the search engines want to give their users the best results possible, because if they give the user what they want, users come back and continue to use the search engine.

In this chapter, you find out how to research and solicit links for your site. You also find out how *not* to obtain links, and how to properly evaluate paid links. The last thing we cover is how to work with RSS feeds and syndication.

Researching Links

You can acquire new *backlinks*, or inbound links to your site, in a number of ways. Examples include writing articles, creating new widgets for your site, and so on. Each technique can produce results, but the amount of time and effort that goes into them can be costly. So it makes sense to consider attracting high-quality links to your site with good content — especially if you have limited time, effort, and money to pursue new links. You can read more about what makes good content in Book V.

The benefit of good content is that it can attract quality links on its own (and those links are likely to stay there), as well as help you build your business reputation. The idea is to attract long-term expert testimonial links to your site. It makes you seem more authentic and trustworthy to the users and search engines alike. Although developing good content also takes time and effort, the added benefit of building your reputation as an authority in your industry has lasting value and allows you to compete more successfully on the Internet.

If you've already got that exciting and interesting content all ready to go (lucky you), and you want to be more proactive about obtaining links, you can go about it in several ways. First, you need to think about what kind of sites you want to link to you. Brainstorm about places that might link to you, and vice versa. Think about your competition and who's linking to them and especially why. Take note of whether your competition uses paid advertising (such as banner ads) or hosts banner ads on their own site in exchange for another site hosting there.

After you have a working list of possible sites, you have a long list of points to consider when you start thinking about soliciting links from different Web sites. If you're going to spend money, the cost of advertisements has to be justified based on the potential increase in traffic and brand awareness, not the potential ranking benefit. Any ranking boost you receive is only an additional side benefit; do not get too attached to that boost, eventually the paid link will be detected and discounted. Pages that are visited often on your site are better targets for purchased links or advertisements.

The quality and reputation of the site that links to you is crucial. Though Google states that there is almost nothing another site can do to harm yours, *almost nothing* is not the same as *absolutely nothing*. Links from unethical sites, such as sites involved in spam or unethical search engine results page (SERP) manipulation, can seriously damage your reputation and rankings if they show up in large quantities, and you could even wind up pulled from the *index* (the database of Web sites that search engines maintain for all queries). Never solicit links from any site that you suspect may be engaged in spam or unethical practices.

A brief explanation of PageRank

PageRank is a term that is unique to Google. Google considers a hyperlink to a page to be a vote of confidence for that page. Every site on the Web has a certain PageRank, or PR, based on these votes and how much PageRank inbound the linking pages have. PageRank is distributed within a site based on links: those coming from third-party sites and from the site's internal linking. Usually, the home page of every site has the most PageRank because it has the most direct links from other sites and because it is commonly linked to from every page internally. The terms *link popularity* or *link equity* are often used synonymously with PageRank. They refer to the same concept, but are more generic and can thus be used when discussing any search engine.

Try to pursue links from sites that are strongly related to the industry or overall themes of your Web site. But while you're doing that, bear in mind that a link from a newer site can have just as much value (or more) if the site has a lot of link popularity or authority within the search engines. Also consider that a newer site could potentially drive much more traffic than an older site with stale content, an old design, and little or no maintenance. It's a matter of trial and error.

Try to obtain links from sites with varying PageRank values. (Note: the Google Toolbar PageRank scale ranks pages from 0 to 10, with www.google.com being a 10.) A natural distribution of links to any given page includes a majority of links from PR3 or lower pages. Generally, there should be fewer links from PR4 pages, even fewer from PR5, and so on. With that said, do not avoid getting a link from a higher PR page if you are obtaining it in an ethical way.

Your links should be formatted so they can be counted toward your link equity. They should not include a rel="nofollow" attribute or otherwise block the spiders from following and indexing links. Don't create links using JavaScript, AJAX (Asynchronous JavaScript and XML), or Flash (with rare exceptions) as they will not be spiderable. Each link should also directly connect to the designated page in the target site. Links acquired should point to different landing pages within the site, as well as the home page. They should be based on topic relevance of the anchor text and the page they are being referred from.

Make sure linking sites are not part of a *link farm* (sites that exist only as thousands of links for the sole purpose of fooling the search engines) or another search engine spam network.

Reciprocal links (an "I'll link to your site if you link to mine" swap) should be avoided as a general solicitation practice. However, this doesn't mean that you should *never* have reciprocal links. Remember, the search engines want to do what's best for your users. If your user would find value in a site that links to you, by all means, link back.

Ads or other bartered links should only be obtained from relevant sites. Linking to a spam network puts you in danger of getting pulled from the search engine index, so be very careful and review all sites accordingly.

Develop a list of the preferred anchor text you would like to see on each URL from which you are seeking inbound links. Your anchor text describes to the search engine the subject of the page linked to. It's like a sign that you point to yourself. Ideally, all links should use the preferred anchor text you provide to the site. If any "tailoring" occurs, be sure main keywords are present (that is, not removed). Realistically, you do not control the site linking to you, so in the end, it's up to the linking site to use whatever anchor text they feel is best. Suggested link text is just that: a suggestion.

Links should remain on the original URL from the date placed and should not move around. The goal is to achieve link stability and longevity. Check back occasionally on solicited links to find out if they're still there.

Use social media sites (social networking sites like Facebook, communication sites like Twitter, social news sites like Digg, social bookmarking sites like Delicious, and so on) to generate interest in your site. The goal is to get others to see the post and then post about the article elsewhere. However, be aware that links from non-related blog pages, social media sites, wikis, or forums only help your link popularity in a limited fashion (see the section "Making Use of Link Magnets and Link Bait" later in this chapter for more details).

Linking pages should ideally have unique content, and not content used on other domains. The `Title` and `Meta` tags on linking pages should also be unique.

In some cases, an inbound link from a high quality education (`.edu`, but not student accounts) site should be considered. Inbound links from an `.edu` site can hold increased value when the link is relevant (for example, the `.edu` links to your page discussing research in which that educational institution is involved). These links can also pass link equity even if those pages are not relevant to the pages they're linking to simply by virtue of their own authority.

Although obtaining links from directories is a good way to build the link popularity of a new Web site, your long-term link building strategy cannot consist solely of directory links. The vast majority of your links should be from non-directory based sites.

Sites with a top-level country domain (for example, `.co.uk` for the United Kingdom, `.co.nz` for New Zealand, and so on) should try to obtain links from other sites that have the same *top-level domain* (TLD) designation and are hosted in the country associated with that top-level domain. Links from other top level domains are fine as well, but you absolutely need links from other sites in the same TLD as your domain. The more links that you can obtain from sites hosted in that country, the more likely it is that your site ranks well in search engines specific to your country.

Linking sites should reside on different IP address ranges than your site. Additionally, there should not be a large number of links from the same C-block of IP addresses. (The C block is the third set of numbers in an IP address. In the sample IP address, 255.168.219.32, 219 is the C-block.) If all of your links are from the same C-block, it looks unnatural and spammy. Excessive linking between sites on the same IP ranges might be seen by search engines as a link farm community.

Links should be obtained gradually over time, not in the span of a few days or weeks. This allows your link growth to appear more natural and reduces the risk of search engines flagging your Web site for forced or artificial increases. This guideline is far more important in regards to advertisements, as they can be obtained at a much faster rate.

Soliciting Links

After you've figured out which sites you want to obtain links from, you can go about the process of actually soliciting them. But how do you do that? Do you go politely from site to site, knocking on their doors like a vacuum cleaner salesman? For maximum benefit to your SEO efforts, you want to obtain non-purchased links from respected Web sites that are related to your subject themes. The search engines reason that if your site is expert, other people in your industry naturally want to link to you, without having to be paid to do it.

Requesting unpaid backlinks

One approach to obtaining a natural backlink from a related site involves contacting the Webmaster or site owner directly and making a request. Link solicitation can be a very laborious process, but the benefit of choosing the right "linking fit" can be enormously beneficial to both you and the other site. If you can communicate this to them, your chances of actually obtaining your specific link request is much better.

First, you need to determine which sites are the best candidates for your link solicitation. You may know of some off the top of your head; if so, great. A tried-and-true method for obtaining relevant links, though, is to discover what sites link to the Web pages that already rank for your keywords. Chances are that if the Web site has linked to your competitor, it might be a good candidate to link to you.

To discover what sites link to your competitors, follow these steps:

1. **Identify your competition: Run a search on Google.com (or Yahoo.com or Ask.com) for your search terms, the keyword you're trying to rank higher for.**

2. **Go through the results one at a time, opening the pages if you have to in order to understand what kind of site they are.**

   If the page is a direct competitor or is not likely to link to your site, move on to the next URL in the results. (If the page is not a direct competitor, search for information on how to contact the site's Webmaster. These sites could be good backlink candidates, too.)

3. **Make a list of the Web pages (URLs) that rank well for your keywords.**

    These are your competitors.

4. **After you've identified your competition, find out who links to them by running your competitors' URLs through the Link Analysis Report that's available as a free tool on our SEOToolSet Web site (`www.seo toolset.com/tools/free_tools.html`) or through another comparable tool.**

    The paid version of the SEOToolSet has a competitive link analysis tool that compares six sites and their linking schemas that is also useful for this.

Look over the report, which shows external pages with backlinks to your competitor. Figure 2-1 shows a Link Analysis Report from the SEOToolset (version 4.0) that found sites that link to the sample page. You can see that each URL is hyperlinked, so you can click to follow the URLs and look at the pages as needed.

Here's what you should look for as you review the various URLs shown on the report:

✦ **Newness:** If the page already links to your Web page, examine the anchor text and see if it would be better to change it or even point to a more relevant page on your site. If it's already a good link, ignore it. You want to find *new* candidates for backlinks.

✦ **Relevancy:** Make sure the content on the Web page relates to your page content. You don't want to solicit irrelevant links that won't pass any link equity. Also, the page should not have dozens of links to non-related sites.

✦ **Appropriateness:** We get into this more in Chapter 4 of this minibook, but you don't want to solicit links from bad neighborhoods. If the page is nothing more than a list of 100 random links with no content or theme, or full of paid ads, or looks spammy, or smells fishy . . . you don't want any part of it.

When you've determined good Web pages to solicit backlinks from, make a list of their URLs, including whatever information you can find on their site for how to contact their Webmaster.

When you have a list of Web pages you'd like links from, you're almost ready to contact them. We say "almost" because there's a little more preparation you can do so that your correspondence is customized for them and doesn't come across like junk mail. What follows is a recommended scenario that you can use for soliciting a link. After you read through this, we explain what we mean by "preparation":

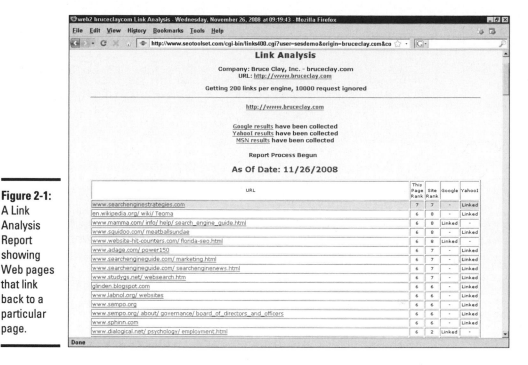

Figure 2-1:
A Link
Analysis
Report
showing
Web pages
that link
back to a
particular
page.

Write an e-mail that's customized. Do not start with "Dear Webmaster" if you want to stand out from the rest of their inbox fodder. Do not use generic boilerplate text (although you can start with something generic and then modify it).

In your e-mail, explain that you've looked at their page (giving the URL) and feel that it relates well to the subject matter of your Web page (give the URL of your page as well). You can call this subject or theme by name to further personalize your message. If a particular section of the page seems most related, specify it: That proves that you actually read their page, and it may give you a better-placed link near relevant surrounding text.

If you've identified any technical problem with their site, such as a broken link, typographical error, missing graphic, server error, or other, you can offer this information to them. For example, you could say, "By the way, when I was on your page yesterday, I noticed a broken link about halfway down to the Squiggly Slalom Ski Shop. Thought you could use that information — we Webmasters have to stick together." Tools are available to help you locate broken links or other problems with another person's Web page. We suggest running the Link Checker tool, which is available for free on the W3C (World Wide Web Consortium) site at `www.w3.org/QA/ Tools/#validators`.

Praise the sites that they link to already and say that you noticed there's an existing link to another site that offers similar services/information/products, or whatever, to yours, so you wondered . . .

Then, if you have a link magnet of some sort that you think is relevant to their site, suggest that they consider visiting your cool chart, table, interactive tool, or other widget to see if they believe it would add value for their site visitors. You don't have to ask for the link; if they like it, they'll make that decision on their own.

Close the e-mail with your name and contact information so that the Webmaster knows you're a real person, not just a computer.

The link-request e-mail you construct based on the preceding steps contains some specific information that you gather before sending the request. This preparation may take a little time, but a valuable link may be worth five or ten minutes. After all, you're trying to start a business relationship that could have value in itself. In the best-case scenario, they give you a backlink that lasts for a long time to come and may end up passing you quality traffic to your site that goes beyond better rankings.

Writing a customized link request can show the other site's Webmaster that you know what you are talking about, illustrate your expertness, and demonstrate your commitment to success for both parties. In this case, putting yourself in their shoes might also prove helpful. You don't want to scare them by coming on too strong. Consider how you would react to the same type of request and adjust your approach accordingly. In some cases, it might be appropriate to pick up the phone and call them, or even visit their offices in person. (Visit them in person *after* you've made phone or e-mail contact, please: We don't want to encourage cyber-stalking!) It all depends.

Soliciting a paid link

Obtaining a free link is not always possible. On those situations, you may want to come up with a plan to approach Web sites about direct advertising on their site. In that case, you have to determine a price point that is not only acceptable to you, but to the other site as well. In some instances, a partnership may be developed that benefits both parties without any fees actually being exchanged. But however the paid link is secured, you want to be sure that you get a link from the most relevant page with the best anchor text possible.

Remember that obtaining a paid link does not necessarily give you a direct SEO benefit. The search engines do not pass link equity through links that have been identified as paid, so you only want to buy links if traffic or advertising, not rankings, are what you're really after. In fact, if Google detects paid links on a Web page, it may stop passing PageRank through any of the links on that page, whether they're really paid or natural.

Here's how to solicit a paid link from another site:

1. **Determine if there are advertising possibilities on the Web site.**

2. **If there are no listed advertisement packages, you may want to contact the Web site owner or Webmaster to propose privately paying for an advertisement on their Web site.**

3. **Try to obtain text links with optimal anchor text located on the most relevant pages for your subject theme.**

   If the paid link you solicit is formatted as an image or banner, this may increase your *click-through rate* (thc number of visitors who click your link) and traffic. Ideally, any links that you obtain (paid or not) should have surrounding text related to your subject and not be one among dozens of non-related links. Again, this isn't done for the SEO benefit. Image links/banner links are less likely to pass the same weight as good anchor text. In fact, most large sites that sell banner ads run them through redirects or advertising networks that more than likely use iframes (embedded frames that display a separate page in the frame) and pass no link equity at all. Paid advertisements are strictly for advertising, not for link building.

Making Use of Link Magnets and Link Bait

Another way of attracting links is to set yourself up as a link magnet or put out some link bait and wait for the links to come to you. We introduce these concepts in the previous chapter, but we elaborate on them here. *Link magnets* are typically creative Web applications, tools, how-to guides, reference materials, or any information that is unique and valuable to users. *Link bait* is content created for the purpose of attracting attention and links. The difference between the two is that a link magnet is for the purpose of attracting relevant links, whereas link bait is mostly good for short-term traffic. Rarely, link bait can translate into long-term links, but that's only if you have good content to go along with the video or blog or other tantalizing things you've just released.

Generating information, applications, tools, or ideas that people talk about is a surefire way to generate links: This is the benefit of a link magnet. Developing an idea for a link magnet takes some dedicated brainstorming and creative thought, as well as a good understanding of your target audience and what they might find useful or even humorous. For example, research that generates data or insights into the differences between competing services might be highly valued by a technology audience.

Creative insight that grabs everyone's attention and generates discussion is what you're after. When you come up with an idea, actual construction of the link magnet may also require hard work, although some link magnets can be developed with little effort.

Articles

Adding an article section to your site or posting articles on a blog can be a valuable source of links. Not only are articles a good way of adding keyword-rich content to your site, but they can also be a good way of attracting links. Other sites frequently link to articles that provide useful advice or information in order to share it with others.

There is a difference between articles that you write to provide information about your products or company and articles that can be deemed link-worthy. The latter tends to be non-commercial, informative, and entertaining, whereas the former tends to be more marketing-oriented, like a page describing your product or service that is not designed to garner links and draw traffic, but is merely to give more information to people already interested in you.

The key to writing articles that generate links is to make sure the article is something that viewers want to read and share with others. Think of it as an article you would read in a magazine, not just something written strictly for SEO value.

Many different types of content can be used as link bait:

✦ **Top 10 lists:** These have nearly become cliché online, but can still be effective if they are new and fresh.

✦ **How-to guides:** Explain how to do something in a clear and easy way. Visuals, like images or videos, can be helpful.

✦ **Articles about hot button issues:** Debate a controversial industry-related topic.

✦ **Resources:** Offer new research, information, tools, charts, and graphs.

✦ **Humorous and off-beat material:** Include funny stories and topics.

✦ **Games:** They can be developed for fun that may or may not be related to your industry.

Videos

Using engagement objects such as images and other rich media can be an integral part of link building. Blended search (searching for different types of content, such as text, videos, photos, and so on) is becoming a bigger part of search engine algorithms as they mix various types of files into search results. Some people online are looking for more than just static Web pages. You can utilize video, Flash animations and videos, and podcasts to reach this audience. Not only does this help your overall Internet marketing campaign and raise brand awareness, but it can also help generate quality links.

Videos can be used as link magnets and link bait and can be a great way of increasing awareness of your Web site. The key to a good video link magnet is to make your video unique and link-worthy. The video should incorporate branding and advertising strategies, but above all, it should be entertaining.

Videos from YouTube (www.youtube.com) currently rank high in Google video results. Although videos on YouTube can increase exposure for your company, they do not necessarily build link popularity for your Web site. However, YouTube can be used to raise awareness for the video link magnets that are hosted on your site. You can do so by posting shortened video clips on YouTube that link back to additional or higher quality videos posted on your Web site.

The best way to build link popularity with a video link magnet is to embed the video into a Web page on your site. This way, anyone linking to the video is directly linking to your site, which is of course the primary reason for creating a link magnet. However, showing up on a search results page as a blended result might be a secondary goal as well. You can increase the likelihood of meeting that goal by adding links from your site to the videos you have put on YouTube.

One famous example of a video link magnet is the "Will It Blend?" series of videos done by Blendtec, a company that manufactures blenders. Blenders may seem like a boring product for a video, but Blendtec makes their videos entertaining by obliterating all sorts of items in their blenders and styling the demos like a 1960s game show. Blendtec posts their videos on YouTube, but they also integrate them into their Web site.

After you have created a video link magnet, you need to promote it. Issuing a press release is one way to do this. (See the section, "Creating a press release" later in this chapter for more on how.) You can also bring awareness to your video through social news sites like Digg (www.digg.com) and Reddit (www.reddit.com), as well as social bookmarking sites like Delicious (www.delicious.com), StumbleUpon (www.stumbleupon.com), and Furl (www.furl.net). Twitter (www.twitter.com) is a great way to build a community and put out information as well.

How Not to Obtain Links

As with many things in life, there is a right way to go about obtaining links, and there is a wrong way. We've put together a handy list of what *not* to do when trying to get links to your site.

✦ **Do not spam.** This means no sending of mass e-mails like, "Dear Webmaster, can you please link to me? Here is the anchor text I want to use. XOXO. Me." If you are soliciting links from a Web site, make sure to customize *each* and every e-mail you send.

+ **Avoid incestuous linking.** If you build a vast network that only links back in on itself, or only back to itself, it's considered incestuous linking. This is a huge no-no for Google, and there are actual penalties involved that could result: Your site could be removed from the index or subjected to heavy ranking penalties instead of just having your links disregarded as part of the PageRank.

+ **Do not buy links for ranking.** You can buy links in terms of traffic and for advertising, but buying a link for ranking is a definite no-no for Google, which disregards the weight of paid links and possibly any and all links on that page.

+ **Do not use run of site links.** Run of site links happen when a site has links to your site on every single one of its pages. These kinds of links are heavily discounted and are usually immediately flagged as paid links at best and spam at worst.

+ **Do not use link farms.** There's more about link farms in Book I, Chapter 6. Link farms are spam, and you incur penalties for using them. You could get your site yanked from the index; if this happens, you need to clean it up and grovel to the search engines to get back in.

+ **Do not solicit links from irrelevant sites.** It does not matter if the site is very, very popular: It won't help you if your content is in no way related to their content: like, say, your dog grooming business soliciting a link from a gossip site like Gawker (www.gawker.com).

+ **Do not set up several different sites all with the purpose of linking to yourself.** This is spam. Spamming is bad.

In general, think about how you would want people to try to obtain links from you. Treat others as you want to be treated. Also, always avoid sneaky, underhanded, or devious techniques. You will be caught and will have to do it the right way anyway. It saves you the time and effort of cleaning up your page and the hassle of begging Google to consider resubmitting your site into the index.

Evaluating Paid Links

When soliciting paid links, remember to do it *only* for the traffic or the advertising. Soliciting a paid link in order to increase your ranking is definitely not recommended. Google hates that. A lot. But if you've decided to try and solicit some paid links for the advertising traffic, you need to properly evaluate the Web sites you are looking at in order to make sure you get a quality link and don't get ripped off.

First, check out the site and see how much traffic they are getting. Also take a good hard look and determine whether they're using spam techniques. If you think that they're a good legitimate site, send them a solicitation letter. Suggest a trial run for your ad — you could pay them for a month's worth of advertising, so you can check and see if your traffic goes up.

There are other methods of gauging/estimating traffic to a site before you purchase advertising. Most sites that are serious about selling ads have demographical and traffic data available. Sites like Hitwise (www.hitwise.com), comScore (www.comscore.com), Compete (www.compete.com), and even Alexa (www.alexa.com) can give you some idea of what they can do for you.

One thing to monitor is the quality of the traffic your advertisement is bringing you. Is it bringing you conversions or just a lot of traffic? It might not be worth the money you spend on the ad if the traffic does not bring you any conversions. Instead, you can wind up just paying for the ad and the extra fees when your server gets hammered by all the new traffic.

Working with RSS Feeds and Syndication

Another way of going about obtaining links is working through RSS feeds and syndication. *RSS* is a method of offering a convenient way to distribute content on your Web site that you'd like others to use. In other words, it's a mechanism to "syndicate" your content.

No one agrees for sure on what *RSS* stands for. RSS was introduced by Netscape in 1999 and then later abandoned in 2001. They said it stood for *Rich Site Summary.* Another version of RSS pioneered by UserLand Software supposedly stands for *Really Simple Syndication*. In yet another version, RSS stands for *RDF Site Summary*. The reason for so many different names is because there's some rivalry over who invented RSS. But the purpose is all the same: It's a program that publishes new information updates from Web sites.

One way of thinking about RSS is to compare it to the funny pages in the newspaper. The artists draw their cartoons and then, through their syndicates, the cartoon is made available to any newspaper that cares to run it, in exchange for a fee. Syndication of Web content via RSS can be an easy way to draw attention to your material, bringing you some traffic and perhaps a little net fame, depending on how good your information is.

So how does RSS syndication work? When you publish a new Web page about a particular topic, you want others interested in that topic to know about it. You can do so by listing the page as an item in your RSS file. You can have the page appear in front of those who read information using RSS readers or *news aggregators*, which are software programs that allow users to subscribe to and read RSS feeds. RSS also allows people to easily add links to your content within their own Web pages. Bloggers are a huge core audience that loves RSS feeds, and bloggers are the gossip columnists of the Internet. Telephone, telegraph, or tell a blogger, and the information gets out there.

There are several RSS or news aggregators out there that you can use. We mention a couple here, but this isn't even the tip of the iceberg. A little searching around will turn up the feed reader that's just right for you:

✦ **NewsIsFree (www.newsisfree.com/):** A free service. With it, you can create customized pages for different topics, and then have headlines from various resources automatically filled into those pages.

✦ **Feedreader (www.feedreader.com/):** A small, free software-based tool. Just enter the URL of a feed, and the headlines are brought back and made viewable within the application.

✦ **Radio UserLand (http://radio.userland.com/):** Another long-standing news aggregator. This one starts out with a free 30-day trial, and then you pay an annual fee of $39.95. Enter the URL of a news feed, and it's added to your personal list.

✦ **Google Reader (www.google.com/reader/):** An easy-to-use feed reader that also enables you to share, comment on, and trend items. It's integrated with your Google account. As with most things Google, it's completely free.

Creating a press release

Internet press releases are an effective and economical solution for distributing information to the public. After a press release is sent out through a third-party company, the information it contains is usually archived on that company's Web site. Most of the companies that offer this service allow you to write your own content, including links to your site. This ensures that you not only acquire an inbound link, but also that it's from a page with relevant content and optimized anchor text.

Press releases should be written once every couple months (minimum), discussing new services that are being offered, the latest deals available, and what is happening on your site in general. You can generate press releases for significant announcements or events worthy of a press release. It's possible to do all your press release writing yourself, or you can hire a writing service to generate your release for you. It all depends on how confident you are in your ability to write for journalists.

A good company to distribute press releases is PRWeb. Their Web site is located at www.prweb.com. For more information on how to write an effective press release, visit www.prweb.com/pressreleasetips.php. PRWeb is priced from $80 to $360 per press release, depending on the package and reach that you choose for your distribution.

You should create a handful of links in each press release you send out, using different anchor text that links to various landing pages on your site. The links ideally go to the home page and high-priority landing pages for your most profitable and most searched services. When linking to pages, be sure to use one of the page's top keywords as the anchor text rather than, or in addition to, the URL.

Here are some other tips for writing an article or press release:

✦ **Avoid sounding like an ad.** No one likes to read a press release that offers nothing more than a commercial. Gather quotes from relevant parties to support your assertions and work them into your text.

✦ **Avoid promoting your company or product too much in articles.** If your article seems too much like a sales pitch, people are less likely to read or link to it.

✦ **Offer something new.** Provide something new in your article. Avoid repeating the same information that may be online elsewhere.

✦ **Use keywords in the title.** The article should have a catchy headline that encourages people to want to read, but that also includes the keyword phrase you are targeting. Others will likely link to the article with the title, so including the main keyword phrases helps incorporate keyword-rich anchor text into the links.

✦ **Avoid keyword stuffing.** Use a natural writing style that appeals to your audience and avoid overusing or "stuffing" keywords.

✦ **Be truthful.** Don't use articles or link bait to lie to your visitors, as they will never return to your site if you can't deliver something you promise.

✦ **Tackle controversy.** Don't be afraid to tackle a controversial subject. Articles that cause people to think or want to debate the topic can make them more apt to want to post a link about it elsewhere.

✦ **Always opt to use the exact phrase you are trying to optimize in your articles.** If your keyword is *SEO training*, it should appear right up front, not just in the title, but in the first sentence and throughout your text. Just like optimizing a Web page, you need to remember what you want people to consider the point of your article.

Book VI
Chapter 2

Obtaining Links

A press release can also be used to help promote and bring awareness to your link magnet. For example, if you have created a chart or checklist as a link magnet, write an article that shows how helpful your chart, widget, illustration, or checklist can be and send out a press release announcing its launch and covering the main advantages.

Spreading the word

After you have written an article, you need to let people know about it. Of course, you should link to your article on your Web site, but you also need to spread the word to other Web sites, and social media is a great way to do this. One way you can do this is through a Share link on your articles that includes links to submit your content to social news sites like Digg, Reddit, Delicious, and StumbleUpon. These sites allow users to submit articles they find interesting, and then the rest of the community votes and comments on them. You can also promote your article on other social networking sites like Facebook (www.facebook.com) and MySpace (www.myspace.com), on your blog, or on industry-related forums.

The purpose of attracting links to your content from social media sites is not just to get the link popularity from the links. After all, the benefit of these types of links is short-lived because news changes constantly. The real reward is that social media sites help generate traffic and awareness. Your goal is to spread the word about your article and get people to read it and want to share it with others by linking to it and discussing it. Hopefully, permanent and valuable links are built as a result.

Chapter 3: Structuring Internal Links

In This Chapter

✔ **Theming your Web site by subject**

✔ **Optimizing link equity**

✔ **Creating and maintaining silos**

✔ **Understanding site maps**

✔ **Figuring out XML site maps**

Siloing is a way of arranging your Web site according to themes that allows for prime search engine optimization. We discuss siloing a bit in the previous chapters, but, in this chapter, we go into how to actually build and structure your site in order to have the best silos possible.

First, we review the subject theming of your site, and then we discuss link equity. From there, we cover actually creating and maintaining your silos. This means we walk you through the setup, construction, and maintenance work necessary for good silos.

Another thing you read about in this chapter is a site map. There are two different kinds: the traditional site map and the XML site map. A traditional *site map* is a Web page that is designed to guide users to all the pages on your site. It's a little like an index page in the back of a text book where every page is listed and linked to, usually grouped by subject theme. An *XML site map* is a document designed specifically to be readable by a search engine. You can tell a search engine all about your site using this kind of document. Despite their confusingly similar names, the two types of documents aren't interchangeable and they both have their uses. In this chapter, we show you how to use both to your advantage.

Subject Theming Structure

We talk about subject theming, which is picking out your themes in order to better arrange your silos, in Chapter 1 of this minibook. Now you need to actually implement your themes into a silo structure. Look at Figure 3-1, which is a silo pyramid.

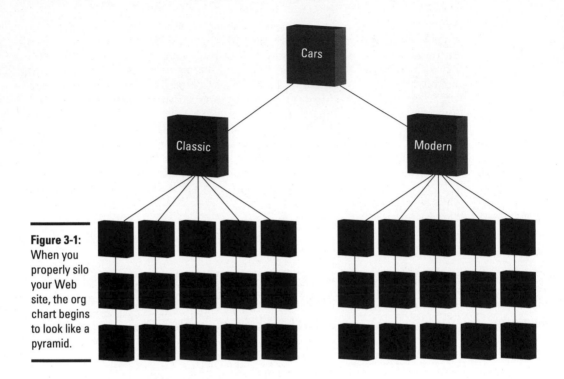

Figure 3-1:
When you properly silo your Web site, the org chart begins to look like a pyramid.

The example we're using is a classic car Web site. The very top of the page represents one of the broadest themes, which are the makes of cars, and this silo is for Ford.

You can accomplish siloing by setting up either directory-based silos, where the linking structure follows the physical setup of the site (physical siloing), or non-directory based silos, where the linking structure alone defines the theme (virtual siloing). These types of silos both create themes through linking, but they do so in different ways. Virtual silos create content and subject relationships through cross-linking alone to create theme, whereas physical siloing creates relationships by utilizing directory structure and links to group like content. They can both be used in the same site, depending on organizational structure.

In a physical silo, relationships between pages are created by grouping pages with like content in a single directory and linking those pages together. The names of the pages help to focus the subject matter of the directory. The theme of the directory is tied into the directory structure itself.

Directory structures require at least five pages of textual content that support whatever topic the directory is addressing. Directory silos must be very structured and highly organized.

In a virtual silo, the theme is created through linking. The names of each page are not important because the pages in the relationship are not necessarily in the same silo. The silo is defined by what pages are linked together. Thus, you are creating a theme based solely on links rather than hanging the linking framework on the directory structure. You have the landing page, or the main page, at the top of the silo, and, underneath, you have pages that support the main landing page's theme.

The difference between a primary and a sub-silo is like the difference between a main theme and a secondary theme. A primary silo should be on the main subject you're wishing to attract to your site. The sub-silos branch off from the primary silo, covering their own smaller subthemes. These sub-silos should both clarify and support the primary silo.

Optimizing Link Equity

Part of the *search engine algorithm* (how search engines rank your site) is measuring your *link equity* to see whether you're an expert on your subject. In broad terms, more links equals greater expertise, especially when the links are from expert sites that are relevant to your site. The more outside Web sites link to you, the bigger your "expert" status. (Note: We go over link solicitation much more in depth in the previous chapter.)

Say you're a member of the Better Business Bureau (BBB). Being a member of the BBB is a good practice for a business. It's a trust issue for your visitors who feel better knowing that you're a member. Naturally, you want to tell people this affiliation, so you place a link to the BBB on your Web site. Unfortunately, if you're like a lot of Webmasters out there, you were so proud of joining the BBB that you stuck a badge and link to their site on every page of your entire site. In doing this, you just gave a huge amount of link equity to a site that is not your own.

Link equity is something Google measures when reading your site to determine whether a site is an "expert" in that field. If many people are linking to you from relevant quality sites, obviously you must know something, or so the logic goes. Obviously you can create spammy links to fool the engines, but that won't last long. Valid links from other sites, on the other hand, contribute to your being recognized as an expert.

It's not a bad idea to link out to other sites. You *want* to link to other sites. It gives you an air of respectability when you point to others and say, "This person is also an expert in the field, and you should check them out." It makes you look like you know what you are talking about. There is also the added bonus of the person you have linked to turning around and linking back to you, thus proclaiming you to be an expert as well.

On the other hand, you have to be picky about who you link to and where you place those links on your site. (Check out Chapter 2 of this minibook for details on dangers to avoid with outbound linking.)

Creating and Maintaining Silos

If you're like most businesses, you probably already have a Web site, and you can't exactly chuck the whole thing out the window and start over from scratch. But there is a way to streamline and tweak your site to build better silos. It's a fairly easy process:

1. **Identify your main themes — these will be your main silos.**

2. **Identify the smaller subthemes, which are your subpages or support pages for your silos.**

3. **Identify the keywords for each page.**

   We go over choosing keywords more in depth in Book II. You should choose the broader keywords for the main themes and the more specialized keywords for the subpages.

4. **After you have your pages organized, you can start linking them together.**

There are three basic types of pages within your silos:

✦ **Landing pages** are the pages that you want to direct your users to. These are the main subjects that are supported by the smaller subpages.

✦ **Subpages** are the supporting information for your main subjects or landing pages. All landing pages need at least five subpages of information to support them, as a general rule. As it happens, these sub-pages may evolve into landing pages themselves if they have enough supporting material of their own.

✦ **Article pages** are classified as subpages. These are pages that contain articles, history, or any sort of information about your theme. These pages usually contain lots of text and are a good place to have concise keywords.

To correctly implement a directory silo, you would group like content into separate directories. Take Ford and Chevy, for example. You would create a directory for each theme, one for Ford and one for Chevrolet. Within these directories, you would have subsequent content-rich pages to support the overall theme of the directories. If you have two models of Ford you want to use, Mustang and Explorer, these would fall underneath the Ford page. You'd need further information about Mustang and Explorer, and all of the information regarding each model type would fall underneath its respective directory.

So, what if you want to link between the Ford directory and the Chevy direc-tory? You have a page underneath the Ford directory that discusses a model of Chevy that is very similar to a model of Ford, and you want to do a link between these two pages. Rather than linking from that model of Ford to the similar model of Chevy that complements it, you would only link from the model of Ford page to the Chevy landing page. Although you could link to the specific Chevy model page, you would need to add a `rel="nofollow"` attribute to that link because the model page is not a landing page for the silo. The reason for this is that if you have multiple links linking models of Ford and Chevy with Ford, you are diluting your theme, which makes it difficult for your keywords to stand out and tell the search engines what your pages are about. If you have two distinct categories, or silos, Ford and Chevrolet, it's much easier for your keywords to stand out and, conse-quently, be ranked by the search engines.

In your classic car Web site, you have your site split into two main catego-ries, Ford and Chevy. The Ford page would be one of your main landing pages, and the Chevy page would be another. Say also that you have addi-tional pages that discuss the specific years of cars, but they are located in different silos. These pages all link separately to your main landing page and they link horizontally to each other, thus helping to build the theme of that silo. See Figure 3-2 as an example of horizontal and vertical siloing.

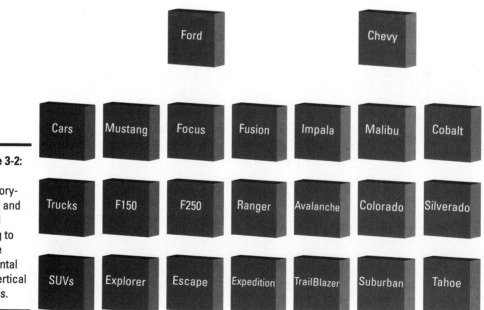

Figure 3-2:
Use directory-based and virtual siloing to create horizontal and vertical themes.

You must decide what you want to be ranked for: Do you want to be ranked for Ford as a general keyword, or for specific types of Fords? Siloing too tightly would mean that you would not be supporting your general term with your specific terms. In this respect, cross-linking within a silo would be okay. It all depends on which keywords you want to be ranked for. You definitely should target the more specific keywords that are relevant to your site, but you may also want to try to rank for more general keywords, which tend to be more competitive and harder to optimize your site for. To rank for general terms, you need to have some general content pages at the top of your site that link down into your category silos (picture an extra row above your pyramid of silos), but that don't receive links back up from the more interior pages.

Cross-linking between subjects dilutes your theme. The point of linking is to group similar subjects in order to tell the search engine what this section is about. You want a giant neon arrow pointing to your subjects on your site, and keeping them free of other unnecessary links and keywords helps to do that.

Say that you want to discuss Chevy as well as Ford. The Chevy page would have its own silo design. The landing page would be the Chevy page, and, as in the Ford silo, any pages that discuss varieties of Chevy would be the subsequent pages that would all link to the Chevy landing page, but not to each other.

In your Ford page, which discusses a particular year of Ford, you might also want to discuss a Chevy model manufactured in the same year. Rather than directly linking from the 1962 Ford page to the 1962 Chevy page, you would link from the 1962 Ford page to the Chevy landing page. The reason for this is that if you have multiple links linking different Ford years and Chevy with Ford, you dilute your theme, which makes it difficult for your keywords to stand out and tell the search engines what your pages are about. Again, it is possible to link from one page to the other directly if you use a `rel="nofollow"` attribute to block the passage of link equity.

Still confused? Not to worry. Siloing is a tricky process, so we've put together a handy illustrated guide in order to walk you through it.

Building a Silo: An Illustrated Guide

Start each silo with an index page. This is the main landing page, which is the big enchilada for your silo. This is where all the big broad keywords go within the silo's theme, and where you introduce yourself to the world as an expert on this subject. In your directory, you would call this the `index.html` page. So, the URL would read `www.classiccarcustomization.com/index.htm`, as seen in Figure 3-3.

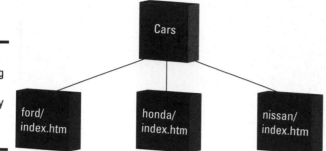

Figure 3-3:
The landing page of a silo, usually `index.htm`.

Branching off from the silo's landing page you would have several subpages that support the theme. If your silo theme is Ford, you would have subpages about the history of Ford, the different types of Ford models, pictures of Fords, some videos, and maybe some articles. Each of these subjects would get their own separate pages and would be named in the Ford directory as follows:

```
www.classiccarcustomization.com/Ford/index.html
www.classiccarcustomization.com/Ford/articles.html
www.classiccarcustomization.com/Ford/models.html
www.classiccarcustomization.com/Ford/pictures.html
www.classiccarcustomization.com/Ford/video.html
www.classiccarcustomization.com/Ford/history.html
```

Each of these subpages would link back up to the index page, but not to each other. When siloing, the rule of thumb is to link *up*. See Figure 3-4.

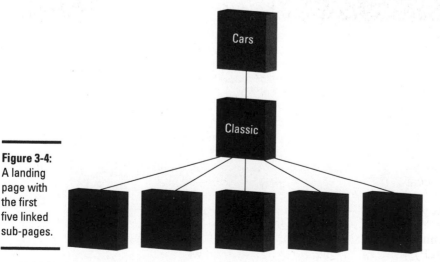

Figure 3-4:
A landing page with the first five linked sub-pages.

Any one of these subpages can become its own landing page as well. If you intend to make a subpage a landing page — for example if you want to rank for the keyword phrase [Ford history] — make sure that it has its own subpages to go along with it. You need at least five subpages of support for your landing pages. Doing this creates a smaller silo below the Ford silo, with just one overlapping page in common.

Next, build a sub-silo for the Ford Mustang content that you have. Mustang falls under Ford, so you would want a page devoted to the keyword [Ford Mustang] in the Ford silo, with a link from the Mustang page going to the Ford page, as in Figure 3-5.

That Mustang page simultaneously functions as a subpage within the Ford silo above it and as the landing page for the Mustang silo. In addition to this index page, the Mustang silo needs at least five subpages linking to the index page (they could be its own history, articles, years, pictures, and video subpages). The directory structure would look something like this:

```
www.classiccarcustomization.com/Ford/mustang/index.html
www.classiccarcustomization.com/Ford/mustang/history.html
www.classiccarcustomization.com/Ford/mustang/articles.html
www.classiccarcustomization.com/Ford/mustang/years.html
www.classiccarcustomization.com/Ford/mustang/pictures.html
www.classiccarcustomization.com/Ford/mustang/videos.html
```

The silo now resembles Figure 3-6, which goes down another level to show the Mustang silo.

Figure 3-5: The Mustang landing page is connected to the Ford landing page in this silo.

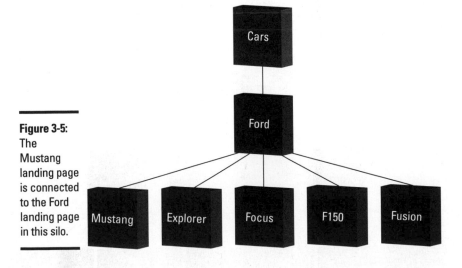

Now, if you want to have a link from one of the smaller Ford subpages to the Chevy subpages, you would not link directly between them. Instead, you would link the Ford subpage to the Chevy landing page, as in Figure 3-7. Remember, this method of linking is to avoid dilution of the silo themes.

But if you really want to have links between the subpages (usually to enhance the user experience), you can. All you need to do is use a non-spiderable method to link: Create the links in JavaScript, or in AJAX, or in an iFrame, or add a `rel=nofollow tag` to the link in order to keep the search engine spiders from following the link, as in Figure 3-8. This way, your silo still reads like you don't have any links between the subpages, but the user can follow the link with no problem.

Figure 3-6:
The sub-silo increases the relevance of the site for both Ford Mustang and the more general term *Ford*.

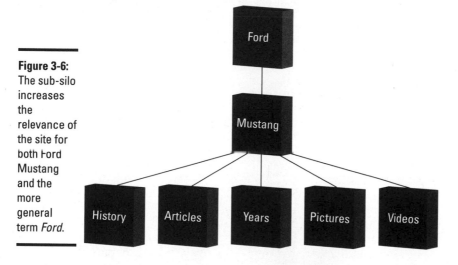

Figure 3-7:
The subpages link to the landing pages.

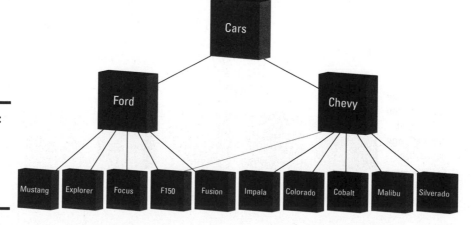

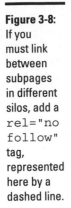

Figure 3-8:
If you must link between subpages in different silos, add a `rel="no follow"` tag, represented here by a dashed line.

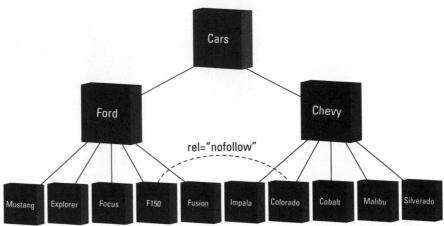

Maintaining Your Silos

Whenever you make content changes to an existing site, you run a risk of losing ground in the search engine rankings for a while. If your changes are well-planned and SEO-smart, your long-term gains are worth the risk. However, you need to know how to maintain your site with care.

It's pretty common for people to ask, "How can we modify our site to better focus our silos without losing our existing rankings?" Well, think of your site as a work that's constantly in progress. In order not to alienate visitors and keep your traffic consistent, consider expanding or growing your site one or two silos at a time and then carefully analyzing how each change you made affects your rankings. Also, don't change the site in one giant update and just hope everything is re-indexed properly. Hundreds of different configurations of silos may end up being a better fit; all it takes is constant tweaking in order to figure out what is working best for your site.

It is our experience that you can update an entire site all at once without any loss of ranking but it's not something that we would recommend doing without our help or the help of an SEO professional. It's very easy to make a mistake. We doubt that any improvement to a site will result in a loss of rankings but as these modifications are extensive and often involve other changes with less certain benefit, we strongly suggest that you exercise caution in your updates.

Part of the maintenance aspect of your site is watching your silos to see if they're a strong silo or a weak silo in the search engine rankings. One example of a weak silo is a silo without enough content in it. If you're not ranking for your theme, your silo probably needs more content, more links, or more pages added to it to strengthen it.

A critical part of maintaining any site is cutting back or pruning parts of the site that are diluting your theme. It is simply getting rid of clutter on your site. Keywords or pages that do not fit your silos and no longer belong on the site should be removed in most cases. Silo pruning also helps if you are doing a targeted promotion, like offering a coupon. You don't want that to index because it's going to dilute your site, so you use a piece of code (an iFrame, pop-up window, JavaScript link) to prune it out of the silo and insert the noindex command in `Meta` robots tag of the head section of the page. It's linked so the users can find it if you want them to, but the link and the content aren't indexed. Your users can see it, but not the search engines. Make it a routine part of site maintenance to remove links that decrease subject relevance.

TIP

If you prune a page that has backlinks, you should 301 redirect that URL to another page on your site so that you don't break those links and lose that link equity.

Including Traditional Site Maps

Traditional site maps are static HTML files that outline the first and second level structure of a Web site. The original purpose of a site map was to enable users to easily find items on the Web site. Over time, they also became useful as a shortcut method to help search engines find and index all the parts of a site. Today, we recommend that you have an XML site map, which effectively provides an easy-to-read link dump for the spiders to index. Although certain Web browsers can display an XML site map for users to read as well, you should offer both kinds of site maps (HTML and XML) if you want to be sure to cover both the search engines and your users. However you implement them, site maps play an important role in your siloed Web design.

A site map displays the inner framework and organization of your site's content to the search engines. Your site map reflects the way visitors intuitively work through your site. Years ago, site maps existed only as a boring series of links in list form. Today, they are thought of as an extension of your site. You should use your site map as a tool to lead your visitor and the search engines to more content. Create details for each section and subsection through descriptive text placed under the site map link. This helps your visitors understand and navigate through your site and also gives you more food for the search engines. You can even go crazy and add Flash to your site map! Of course, if you do include a Flash site map for your visitor, you must include a text-based site map as well because site maps must also aid users who aren't using advanced technology like Flash or JavaScript.

A good site map does the following:

+ Shows a quick, easy-to-follow overview of your site.
+ Provides a pathway for the search engine robots to follow.
+ Provides text links to every page of your site.
+ Quickly shows visitors how to get where they need to go.
+ Utilizes important keyword phrases.

When it comes right down to it, the purpose of a site map is to spell out the central content themes and to offer a cohesive representation of where to find information on your site. At its best, a site map is your table of contents; at its worst, it's just an index.

Now what do site maps have to do with content siloing? A well-planned site map can help improve the organization of a site and focus its theme, which may in turn influence rankings. The reality is that few sites make any real effort when creating an outline of the content on their site. They add content arbitrarily, either as brochure marketing or a sales tool, or because they are told they need it to qualify for keyword ranking. Instead, the site map should be the *first* document created in a Web site construction project, laying out all the structure and content to follow.

We can already hear dissenting minds arguing that you can engineer a site to qualify for high keyword relevance without tailoring the entire site by subject relevance. The reality, though, is that most organizations forget what their focus is, and the site often devolves into a mish-mash of competing subjects or is forced to remain stagnant, without any clear plan on how to expand content. Adding a well-designed site outline in the form of a traditional site map encourages organization without restricting creativity. A good site outline shows where the site is trying to go by offering a clear purpose. Since when is offering clarity a bad marketing or sales tool? Get everyone in your company on the same page with a well-conceived and well-rendered site map.

Site maps are very important for two main reasons. First, your site map provides food for the search engine spiders that crawl your site. The site map gives the spider links to all the major pages of your site, allowing every page included on your site map to be indexed by the spider. This is a very good thing! Having all of your major pages included in the search engine database makes your site more likely to come up in the search engine results when a user performs a query. Your site map pushes the search engine toward the individual pages of your site instead of making them hunt around for links. A well-planned site map can ensure your Web site is fully indexed by search engines.

Site maps are also very valuable for your human visitors. They help them to understand your site structure and layout, while giving them quick access to your entire site. They're also helpful for lost users in need of a lifeline. Often, if a visitor finds himself lost or stuck inside your site, he looks for a way to find what he's looking for. Having a detailed site map shows him how to get back on track and find what he was looking for. Without it, your visitor may just close the browser or head back over to the search engines. Conversion lost.

Here are some site map dos and don'ts:

✦ Your site map should be linked from your home page. Linking it this way gives the search engines an easy way to find it and then follow it all the way through the site. If it's linked from other pages, the spider might find a dead end along the way and just quit.

✦ Small sites can place every page on their site map, but larger sites should not. You do not want the search engines to see a never-ending list of links and assume you are a link farm. (More than 99 links on a page looks suspicious to a search engine.)

✦ Most SEO experts believe you should have no more than 25 to 40 links on your site map. This also makes it easier to read for your human visitors. Remember, your site map is there to assist your visitors, not confuse them.

✦ The *anchor text* (words that can be clicked) of each link should contain a keyword whenever possible and should link to the appropriate page.

✦ When you create a site map, go back and make sure that all of your links are correct.

✦ All the pages shown on your site map should also contain a link back to the site map.

✦ If you have a very extensive Web site, you should create a separate site map for each silo. These would link up to the site map of the silos above and below them, which would further reinforce your silo organization to the search engines. You would also create one master site map at the top level of your site — this would be the one linked from your home page — which contained links to all of the other top-level site map pages. The master site map would not contain all pages in your Web site, but would lead search engines and users to the appropriate site map for their area of interest. In essence, you need to silo your site map just like the rest of your site.

Just as you can't leave your Web site to fend for itself, the same applies to your site map. When your site changes, make sure your site map is updated to reflect that. What good are directions to a place that's been torn down? Keeping your site map current helps make you a visitor and search engine favorite.

Using an XML Site Map

Your XML site map should be constructed according to the current Sitemap Protocol format (which is regulated by www.sitemaps.org). Sitemap Protocol allows you to tell search engines about the URLs on your Web sites that should be crawled. An *XML site map* is a document that uses the Sitemap Protocol and contains a list of the URLs for a site. The Protocol was written by the major search engines (Google, Yahoo!, and Live Search) to be highly scalable so that it can accommodate sites of any size. It also enables Webmasters to include additional information about each URL (when it was last updated, how often it changes, and how important it is in relation to other URLs in the site) so that search engines can more intelligently crawl the site. Note that even though its name is similar to the traditional HTML site map, an XML site map is a totally different kind of document, and the two are not interchangeable. You shouldn't rely on an XML site map alone for your site.

XML site maps define for the spider the importance and priority of the site, better enabling the search engine to index the entire site and to quickly re-index any site changes, site expansions, or site reductions. This XML format offers excellent site indexing and spider access. Additionally, many site-mapping tools can diagnose your XML site map, informing you of duplicate content, broken links, and areas that the spider can't access. Sitemaps.org has a tool that constructs an XML file for you: This is a great place to start.

Google adheres to Sitemap Protocol 0.9 as dictated by www.sitemaps. org. Site maps created for Google using Sitemap Protocol 0.9 are therefore compatible with other search engines that adopt the standards of www. sitemaps.org.

A normal version of the XML code looks something like this:

```
<?xml version="1.0" encoding="UTF-8"?>
 <urlset xmlns="http://www.sitemaps.org/schemas/sitemap/0.9">
 <url>
<loc>http://www.example.com/</loc>
<lastmod>2005-01-01</lastmod>
<changefreq>monthly</changefreq>
<priority>0.8</priority>
</url>
</urlset>
```

Table 3-1 shows both the required and optional tags in XML site maps.

Table 3-1		Site Map Tags in XML
Tag	*Required or Optional*	*Explanation*
<urlset>	Required	Encapsulates the file and references the current protocol standard.
<url>	Required	Parent tag for each URL entry. The remaining tags are children of this tag.
<loc>	Required	URL of the page. This URL must begin with the protocol (such as http) and end with a trailing slash, if your Web server requires it. This value must be less than 2048 characters.
<lastmod>	Optional	The date of last modification of the file. This date should be in W3C Datetime format. This format allows you to omit the time portion, if desired, and use the YYYY-MM-DD format.
<changefreq>	Optional	How frequently the page is likely to change. This value provides general information to search engines and may not correlate exactly to how often they crawl the page.
<priority>	Optional	The priority of this URL relative to other URLs on your site. Valid values range from 0.0 to 1.0. This value has no effect on your pages compared to pages on other sites and only lets the search engines know which of your pages you deem most important so that they can order the crawl of your pages in the way you prefer. The default priority of a page is 0.5. We recommend setting your landing pages at a higher priority and non-landing pages at a lower one.

The XML site map also must

✦ Begin with an opening `urlset` tag and end with a closing `urlset` tag.

✦ Include a `url` entry for each URL as a parent XML tag.

✦ Include a `loc` child entry for each `url` parent tag.

As we explain earlier in this chapter, content siloing can be strengthened by both traditional site maps and XML site maps. A lot of evidence supports the adoption of complete site transparency in search engine optimization. That means that all the elements of your site should consistently offer subject relevancy. You can always work on different projects and use different methods, but a clear and concise method of building and maintaining your site is the best way to go. You are helped by using traditional site maps and XML site maps, which ensure that everyone is on the same page. Not only will your IT and marketing departments agree, but even the site users will be able to tell what your site is trying to say.

Chapter 4: Vetting External Links

In This Chapter

✓ Identifying inbound links

✓ Avoiding poor links

✓ Identifying quality links

✓ Making the most of outbound linking

✓ Handling advertising links

✓ Dealing with link spam issues

*I*n this chapter, we discuss inbound links. *Inbound links* are the links coming into your site. If you are Bob's Classic Car Customization, and you get a link from Motormouth Mabel's Classic Car Boutique, that's an inbound link. In addition to rankings by content, part of how search engines rank pages is based on inbound links. Google's description of their *PageRank* system (a part of Google's link algorithm) for instance, notes that Google interprets a link from page A to page B as a vote of confidence, by page A, for page B. That means that they read an inbound link from another page as a testimonial link in your page, as if it means, "Hey, this guy knows what he's talking about!" Unfortunately, like a lot of things in life, there are good inbound links and bad inbound links.

In this chapter, we discuss the difference between the good and the bad links, how to avoid the bad links, and how to figure out the good ones. We talk about making the most of outbound linking. We also discuss handling all of your advertising links and dealing with link spam issues.

Identifying Inbound Links

So how do you know who's linking to you? Well, going back to Chapter 2 of this minibook, we had you solicit a bunch of links from other sites. Generally, those are the links you're going to know about. It might be a good idea to check and see if the links are still there. Sometimes, for whatever reason, a site stops linking to you. Perhaps it's because they found someone better, perhaps it's because their site folded, renamed the page, redesigned their site, who knows? (And trust us, it's not you, it's them . . .) Not all links come from solicitation. Sometimes a site stumbles upon you and decides you'll be excellent to link to, and they just give you a link. You can achieve this just by being awesome (or, more clearly, having good design, a lot of relevant information, and interesting and dynamic content that the other site thinks their users would be interested in).

One way to find out who is linking to you is to go to Google and type in [link:*yourdomain*.com]. This is the command for Google to search for your inbound links but you won't get a comprehensive list this way. Google only shows a sample of the links they know about. To get a better list, use Yahoo!, go to `http://siteexplorer.search.yahoo.com` and use the site exploration tool to track your inbound links.

If you are a smaller site, you need to be checking on your links constantly. If you have 50 incoming links, all of those are going to count towards your *link equity* (how much weight Google assigns your links). If you are a large, fairly well-known site, it's not going to matter much when one or two sites stop linking to you, *unless* they are major sites . . . you need to manage those relationships. But little guys need all the help they can get, and every little bit helps.

There is also the possibility that the page linking to you has a very new link, and the search engines are not aware of it yet. However, this is for *new* links. If a site gave you a link a while ago (before the last time the page was crawled by the engine — you can see the last crawled date by looking at the Google cache of the page), but it's not in the index, there's probably a reason why, and it's probably not a good one. We go over that a bit more in this next section.

Avoiding Poor Quality Links

Inbound linking is generally a good thing — it tells the search engines that you have a vote of confidence in your "expertness" level — but some inbound links out there only hurt you in the long run. There are several kinds you should be on the lookout for: from non-harmful reciprocal links to the riskier incestuous links, Web rings, link farms, and bad neighborhoods.

Google can detect when you have bad links. They can take away the link's *PageRank* (part of their link algorithm that measures the value of the link to you) as well as the link and domain equity/authority and won't pass on any link value to your page. Google won't count the bad incoming link, and if they suspect you're doing something sneaky and devious with it, they even penalize you for it. The penalty could be as simple as removing all of the link equity of your site, or they could punish you by reducing your rankings on the results page. They may even remove your page or entire site from their index. Ouch! We've stated this before, but dishonesty (like crime) never pays.

Reciprocal links

Reciprocal linking is the least worrisome of the bad inbound links. If a site links to you, and you give them a link back, that's a reciprocal link. Unfortunately, doing this does limit the value of the link in either direction. Google's usually but not always going to rate those links as having no value.

The reasoning is that it is impossible for Google to judge the intent of every reciprocal relationship. Google doesn't know if your intent is good or if you're trying to trick them. Reciprocal links are bartered exchanges, so they might be treated just like an ad from a search engine perspective.

If you have a reciprocal link, don't expect it to carry any value, especially if you have a small site. If you are linking out, link to a non-competitive relative expert. However, if you want to provide some reciprocal links that would be valuable to your visitors, by all means do so. Just be aware that they may not count towards your link equity.

Incestuous links

Incestuous links occur when people link to their own properties or among a group of friends' sites and then try to pass the links off as legitimate links from outside sources. If you have several sites, and they all link to each other, and you're trying to pretend that you don't own half of those sites, that's some incestuous linking going on.

There are large networks that do link between their properties, like the Gawker Media Network, which has links between all of its sites (www.gawker.com, www.jezebel.com, www.io9.com, www.lifehacker.com, www.gizmodo.com, among many others). This is not incestuous linking by definition. They're linking within their network, yes. But they are, first, a large company and, second, not trying to hide the fact that they own the sites in the networks. Generally, this happens for user experience or for branding purposes. Large companies know that linking within their own networks doesn't mean they gain any link equity from it. In most cases, these links are for commercial value and perhaps credibility, but not for link equity or Page Rank. And most importantly, they're not trying to hide the fact that they do it. It's a general rule of thumb: If someone is trying to hide something that they did, they're probably doing something wrong.

We call these types of links *incestuous links* because they are no good and should make you feel icky. Smaller sites caught using them are punished. When you are caught using incestuous links, not only do you run the risk of having those links devalued, but your site could also be marked as spam, and you may have *all* of your links devalued. And that's not even the worst that can happen.

When you get penalized for this type of spam, your site can vanish from the index altogether. We know of one site (that shall remain nameless) using incestuous links and ranking really, really well, with a ton of link equity. Then Google made some tweaks to its algorithm and discovered that this particular site was using incestuous links. So Google punished them. The site's rankings dropped down to the thousandth place on every one of its keywords, and they couldn't even rank for their own name. Trust us when we say dishonesty doesn't pay.

Link farms

We discussed link farms in Book I, Chapter 5 when we were talking about *search engine spam*. Spam includes any sneaky, devious, or underhanded technique used to trick search engines into giving Web sites higher rankings. *Link farms* are literally pages of hundreds (or even thousands) of links on many sites that all link together. This is slightly different than incestuous linking as you might not own the properties involved. In general, you should be very suspicious if someone asks for a link from your site and offers you a link from a totally different site in exchange. That's a classic warning sign for a link farm.

Link farms are sites that have many different links to multiple different sites, all for the express purpose of passing link equity and giving those sites a higher rating in the search engines. Sometimes you can't help it if a link farm links to you, however. If you discover that your site is part of one, politely ask for it to be removed as soon as possible. Being caught as part of a link farm could lead to all of your links losing their link equity or even harsher penalties.

Web rings

Web rings are not necessarily spam. *Web rings* are any collection of Web sites from around the Internet that join together through interlinking in a circular structure. When you join a Web ring, you are automatically part of a circle of related Web sites. You can tell a site belongs to a Web ring because they usually have a *widget* (an interactive piece of HTML coding) that looks like Figure 4-1.

It's pretty easy to identify whether you're in a Web ring, as the presence of the widget is something of a clue. We don't recommend joining a Web ring because all of those links do not give you any link equity. On top of that, it probably isn't worth the traffic you'll be receiving.

You want *natural* links. People link to you because they feel that your site is worthwhile. Web rings are not natural links. And although they have fallen out of favor in recent years, they do still exist. And quite honestly, they're not worth the trouble.

Bad neighborhoods

Say you have a site that wants to link to you. You take a quick look at the site and check to see whether it's in the search engine's index by entering it into Google. But this site does not show up anywhere in the search results. Do you want a link from this site? Chances are, probably not.

Sometimes a Web site is not part of the search engine's index. It could be that the Web site is too newly created. But it is more likely that the Web site is from a *bad neighborhood*. This is a Web site that got yanked from a search engine index, and probably for a good reason. Either they were spamming or using other sneaky methods to try and fool the search engines, and they got caught.

Being part of a bad neighborhood or accepting links from a site that has been banished from the index is about the same as if you had suddenly associated with the bad kids at your high school. Your site gets flagged, and you come under suspicion of using spam techniques yourself.

Normally when Google "flags" you, your site gets a serious search by a human instead of their normal algorithms. That means that anything you have hidden from the search engines in images or with any other kind of technology is visible. It is a little bit like being audited. If the person doing the inspection catches you doing something wrong, you are penalized. You will most likely be punished by getting kicked out of the search index. If you catch any unsavory linkage from sites in a bad neighborhood, drop them an e-mail and ask for your site to be removed. Also, this is why we insist that you keep all things on your site above-board and clean — Google doesn't inform you if you have been flagged. They might send you an e-mail if you have Google Webmaster Tools, but otherwise, if you're flagged and they discover anything wrong, you are simply punished.

You can't help it if someone chooses to link to your site. But it's a good idea to avoid actively attracting unsavory attention. Try to avoid poor links whenever you can, and focus on attracting quality links that will add to your PageRank and grant you link equity. If you do get an unsavory link, try to distance yourself from them as much as you can.

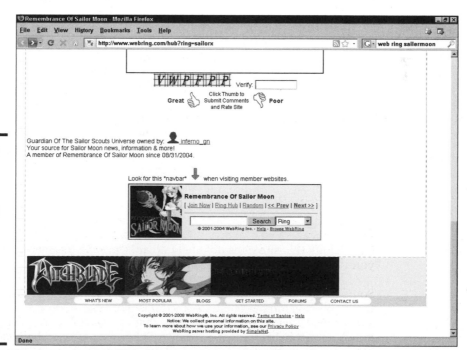

Figure 4-1: This is a Web ring for fans of a TV show; they were especially popular before search engines became ubiquitous.

Identifying Quality Links

So we've talked about the kind of links that you don't want to attract, but what about the ones that you do? *Quality links* are links that contribute to your perceived expertness and your overall link equity. These are the links that point to you and declare that you know what it is you're doing. Your classic car customization site would want the kind of links that shout, "These people are good at what they do, and we think you should check them out." Because those kinds of links establish you as an expert.

There are three different types of quality links that you want to attract:

✦ Complementary subject relevance links

✦ Expert relevance reinforcement links

✦ Quality testimonial links

Complementary subject relevance

Complementary subject relevance links come from a site that has similar content to yours. The site might not be exactly what you do, but its subjects and themes are close enough to be complementary. If you have a classic car customization site, and you receive a link from a Web site devoted to classic car enthusiasts, this is a complementary link. Your site discusses something that their site also discusses, and they have declared your site to be worth reading. This kind of link is worth more than a link from, say, Jill's House of Hamsters.

It doesn't matter if the link from the hamster site has great anchor text (the text that is the outgoing link). The search engine is going to read the surrounding text around the link on the hamster site, the overall content of the page, and the content of the site itself, and it's going to figure out that this is a site about hamsters, and hamsters don't really have anything to do with classic cars (unless, of course, instead of horsepower, your car runs on "hamster" power).

When the search engine notes that the site linking to yours doesn't have a whole lot of relevance to your subject, it's going to say that the link is not a quality link, and the link is not going to add anything to your overall link equity. It also doesn't matter if the page linking to your site has relevance. If the linking site has a page devoted to mesothelioma (the cancer caused by asbestos), but the rest of the site is about peanut butter, the mesothelioma page just looks crammed in there. It's going to dilute that site's theme, and it might raise a red flag with the search engines.

Figure 4-2 is a graph about the power of sites linking to you. The numbers are on a scale of 1 to 10, with 1 being the least relevant and 10 being the most, and the higher the number, the more your link equity goes up.

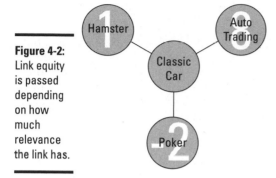

Figure 4-2:
Link equity
is passed
depending
on how
much
relevance
the link has.

The box in the middle is your classic car site. The circle with the 1, is Harry's House of Hamsters: It bears very little relevance to your site, so it carries very little weight. The box with the 8 is a link to a large, official auto-trading Web site. Because it is a large, official Web site with a lot of expertise on its own and it has relevance to your site, the worth of the link goes up. It's important to note that we're just using these numbers to represent varying weights given by relevance — we're not referring to PageRank at all here.

Then there's the -2 poker site that has linked to you. The poker site comes from a spammy, spammy industry, used to shady doings and basically being a headache for the search engines. Having a link from one of those sites not only gives you no link equity, but it might actually cause your site to get flagged for review if you have a lot of these kinds of shady backlinks. By associating with one of these sites, you make it easy for the search engines to assume that you are doing something shady, too. Though Google says that almost nothing someone else does can harm your site, that doesn't mean there's *absolutely* nothing at all. Don't sweat a few bad links coming to you, but do your best to only work on acquiring links from quality sites.

The links you need to be attracting are the kind that have relevance to your industry. Remember, link equity comes from how much of an "expert" in your subject you are, and the more people with similar content link to your site, the more of an expert you are.

Expert relevance reinforcement

It's natural to have experts link to other experts. If you are an expert in your field, you are naturally going to be linking to other experts in your field. It's like a Nobel prize-winning physicist name-dropping another Nobel laureate in economics, as opposed to a kid who won his school science fair.

Experts require validation from their peers. When scientists publish a science paper in a journal, they expect other scientists to go out and test the published theory on their own, in order to receive validation from these other scientists. The same is true for Web sites. If an expert Web site discusses you on their own site and then provides a link to you, claiming you as another expert, that just reinforces what you say on your own site.

To put it another way, if the biggest, baddest, classic car customization site on the whole Internet has a link and a section describing you and linking to your site, that is going to mean a lot more than your brother's very small classic car site giving you a link.

Quality testimonial links

We have discussed three kinds of linking sites in this chapter — the good, the bad, and the really ugly:

✦ The good kind of link is the "expert" industry site. A big name classic auto trader site linking to your classic car customization site, for instance.

✦ The bad kind of link is the site that really has no overall relevance to your subject (such as the hamster site linking to the classic car site).

✦ And then there's the ugly. The spammy, spammy poker site that offers nothing of value and only makes you look bad.

But there is one type of link that is considered the best of them all: the testimonial link.

A *testimonial link* is a link that appears in a paragraph in the context of a lot of relevant information and then points to you as another resource of information. Basically, it's like someone describing how to properly customize classic cars, and then providing a link to your site, as in the following example. Note that the text "classic car customization business" would serve as the anchor for a link back to www.classiccarcustomization.com.

```
There are many classic car customization businesses out
    there, but for the best, you have to check out Bob's
    Classic Car Customization, which has tons of resources
    for restoring and customizing every kind of classic Ford,
    Chevy, and 50s hotrod on the planet. Check out their
    gallery of restorations for some seriously cherry autos.
```

A testimonial link is worth a whole lot of link equity and is one of the best kinds of links you can receive (as long as it's not coming from any sites that practice the "worst practices for linking" we described previously).

Link equity is always an important thing to keep in mind when you're vetting external links. One good testimonial-grade link is worth a lot more than a hundred decent links or a thousand bad links. Link equity through a testimonial link is the highest grade of link equity possible. We're not quite sure why this is, other than Google says it is, so we're going with that.

Finding Other Ways of Gaining Link Equity

Another thing that carries a lot of link equity weight is a link from a *top-level domain* (the root of a Web site's URL) that ends in .edu or .gov. These are official domains that belong to colleges or the government. People only have access to these domains if they belong to either an educational establishment or they work for the government. No one else can have one. These are exclusive domains. So a link from an .edu site (from a university controlled page, not from a student-owned Web page) or a .gov site is harder to obtain and makes you look more like an expert. It's the difference between a link from Bob's House of Hamsters and Stanford University. The .edu or .gov link is considered more authoritative and thus passes a lot of link equity.

If you obtain an .edu or a .gov link, your site is presumably doing something worthwhile to earn it because .edu or .gov sites generally do not link out to just any old site.

Book VI
Chapter 4

Vetting External
Links

More about PageRank

Google scores a site's toolbar PageRank on a scale from 1 to 10, with 1 being worth the least and 10 being the highest. But there's a magnitude of difference between each level. It's kind of like the Richter scale in that a 5.0 level earthquake is 32 times greater than a 4.0, and a 6.0 is 1000 times greater than a 4.0.

It's worth noting that the PageRank that appears in the Google toolbar is for entertainment purposes only. That's right. That PageRank number in the corner? Meaningless — it is only an indication and is updated differently from the PageRank algorithm. On average, that number is many weeks out of date. Using that PageRank number as a basis for your actual PageRank is kind of like calling a psychic hotline — it might be accurate, but generally it's a shot in the dark.

The PageRank number in the toolbar changes every now and then, when Google updates it every so often. It *is* based off of a real number, but using it is like using a stethoscope to do an MRI. Real PageRank rank means something, but unfortunately there's no way to find out what your actual PageRank is. So the next time you overhear someone bragging about their PageRank number in the Google toolbar, just smile and nod: You know that the number should be purely for entertainment purposes.

Say you have an international site, like one that deals with customizing classic Volkswagen cars in Germany. You run your site from your office in the U.S., but your site is in Germany and hosted on a German server, with a URL such as www.classiccarcustomization.de. If you do have an international site, make sure you have at least one link from within your ccTLD. The acronym *ccTLD* stands for *country code top level domain*. For example, domains coming out of the United Kingdom end in .co.uk, domains from Japan end in .co.jp, and so on. So your German car site would need links from several .de sites (for Deutschland) because that is the local domain. Again, your goal is to look respectable and trustworthy. If you are trying to do business in another country, you look better if you have recommendations from that country than if all of your links are from American sites.

Making the Most of Outbound Links

Your outbound links are the links that you have going out of your site. It's important to actually have outbound links to resources and experts in your industry that help your visitors. It also shows the search engine that you recognize who the other experts in your industry are and helps them to define your site by association. Here's a quick list of things to keep in mind for your outbound links:

✦ **Link out to other experts.** Pick non-competitive sites that you feel are relevant to your own site and are experts in their subjects. Not only does it increase your standing in the search engines (experts linking to experts), but it also makes you appear more trustworthy to users.

✦ **Make sure the link is useful to your users.** Having a bunch of irrelevant links on your site damages your expertise in the eyes of the search engines. It also makes you look bad to your users. They're coming to your site for research, and if you can't give them any useful links to follow, they're probably not going to come back.

✦ **Relevancy is key.** Your links have to be relevant to your site, for you and the search engines.

✦ **Validate links.** Make sure your links are legitimate and won't get you in trouble with the search engines.

✦ **Be selective.** If you're associating with another Web site, make sure it's worth it — no bad neighborhoods, no irrelevant links.

Handling Advertising Links

We talk a little about buying advertising links on other sites in previous chapters. Buying links for anything other than advertising or traffic purposes is considered pointless in search engine–land and could even be harmful to your site. When you buy links, they do not do anything for your link equity.

When it comes to selling links or ads (because hey, you need the revenue), you can display them on your site in such a way so as not to get in trouble. You don't want the search engines to think that your site is a link farm, or that you're trying to fool them into treating paid ads as legitimate, equity-passing links. First, you have to state right off the bat that these are paid links. Call them ads, call them partner links, or call them sponsored links. Second, make sure that they have a `"rel=nofollow"` attribute included in the link tag, which alerts the engines that the link should not be considered a testimonial link and shouldn't pass link equity. Let the audience (and the search engines) know that these are paid links right away.

Using technology with advertising links

It's important to keep search engines from following advertising links on your site. You don't want the search engines to index them and pass link equity through them. The ads are there for the users, not for the engines.

One of the ways you can keep your page as clean as possible with the advertising links is by using technology to hide them. You can do this either with iframes (putting the links in an imbedded frame (iframe) on the page, which search engine spiders see as its own separate page) or using JavaScript. Remember that search engines do not crawl JavaScript, so they won't be able to see the ad. JavaScript has the added bonus of making the ad appear dynamic and attractive. You can also place the ad and the link in an image. Search engines can only read text, so they can't read or follow the ad in the linked image. You can also design your ad in Flash which the search engines cannot yet fully spider.

The last solution is simply to use a `rel="nofollow"` attribute on the link. A `rel="nofollow"` is an attribute that attaches itself to a piece of HTML code of the anchor tag (a) that tells the search engine not to follow the link. Users can still access the link, but the search engines won't follow it.

Example:

```
<a href="http://www.domain.
    com/page.html" rel="no
    follow">Link Text</a>
```

It's best to play on the safe side and be as transparent about your methods as possible. Do not do anything to confuse or deceive the search engines. The easiest way for a search engine to catch you doing something wrong is to look like you are doing something wrong.

It's important to note that you should always play by the search engines' rules and let them know that you do have advertising links on your site. Otherwise, you run the risk of the search engines devaluing all of the other links on the page.

Dealing with Search Engine Spam

As we discussed in Book I, Chapter 6, there are several different ways that someone can spam (deceive or trick) the search engine into giving their pages higher rankings or allowing them to rank for keywords that have nothing to do with their site. Search engine spammers also use links to practice their sneaky ways. Here are some of them:

✦ **Link farms.** A *link farm* is any Web site that links to a large, random assortment of different Web sites which all link back to each other. Most link farms are created through automated programs and services. Search engines have combated link farms by identifying specific attributes that link farms use and filtering them from the index and search results, including removing entire domains to keep them from influencing the results page.

✦ **White text/links on a white background.** Putting white text and links on a white background (or black text on a black background, and so on) renders the text invisible to a user unless it is selected with the mouse. Spammers can then insert text that is merely keywords or hyperlinks that the spiders read and mistakenly count as relevant.

✦ **Hidden text or links.** Spammers sometimes hide content by covering it with an image or other layered element so it is not visible. People also specify a negative page position so that the page technically stretches up higher or wider than the browser window. Or they hide spiderable content under the page content (layer) so that can't be seen with the naked eye.

The problem with link spam is that you cannot help who is linking to you. What you *can* do is disassociate yourself from them as quickly as possible.

You might drop a line to Google and report any link farms or any other unsavory links to their spam department (`www.google.com/webmasters/tools/spamreport`).

Google's site quality guidelines

The following is Google's policy when it comes to quality for the sites in their index. This was taken from the Google Webmaster Guidelines at `www.google.com/support/web masters/bin/answer.py?hl= en&answer=35769#3`. We include it here in its entirety as a handy guide. Be aware that Google does occasionally update their guidelines, and so you should monitor the Web site (or search for Google Webmaster Guidelines in Google) so that you're always playing within the rules.

These quality guidelines cover the most common forms of deceptive or manipulative behavior, but Google may respond negatively to other misleading practices not listed here (for example, tricking users by registering misspellings of well-known websites). It's not safe to assume that just because a specific deceptive technique isn't included on this page, Google approves of it. Webmasters who spend their energies upholding the spirit of the basic principles will provide a much better user experience and subsequently enjoy better ranking than those who spend their time looking for loopholes they can exploit.

If you believe that another site is abusing Google's quality guidelines, please report that site at `https://www.google. com/webmasters/tools/spam report`. Google prefers developing scalable and automated solutions to problems, so we attempt to minimize hand-to-hand spam fighting. The spam reports we receive are used to create scalable algorithms that recognize and block future spam attempts.

Quality guidelines — basic principles

Make pages primarily for users, not for search engines. Don't deceive your users or present different content to search engines than you display to users, which is commonly referred to as "cloaking."

Avoid tricks intended to improve search engine rankings. A good rule of thumb is whether you'd feel comfortable explaining what you've done to a website that competes with you. Another useful test is to ask, "Does this help my users? Would I do this if search engines didn't exist?"

Don't participate in link schemes designed to increase your site's ranking or Page Rank. In particular, avoid links to web spammers or "bad neighborhoods" on the web, as your own ranking may be affected adversely by those links.

Don't use unauthorized computer programs to submit pages, check rankings, etc. Such programs consume computing resources and violate our Terms of Service. Google does not recommend the use of products such as WebPosition Gold™ that send automatic or programmatic queries to Google.

Quality guidelines — specific guidelines

Avoid hidden text or hidden links.

Don't use cloaking or sneaky redirects.

Don't send automated queries to Google.

Don't load pages with irrelevant keywords.

(continued)

(continued)

Don't create multiple pages, subdomains, or domains with substantially duplicate content.

Don't create pages with malicious behavior, such as phishing or installing viruses, trojans, or other badware.

Avoid "doorway" pages created just for search engines, or other "cookie cutter" approaches such as affiliate programs with little or no original content.

If your site participates in an affiliate program, make sure that your site adds value. Provide unique and relevant content that gives users a reason to visit your site first.

If you determine that your site doesn't meet these guidelines, you can modify your site so that it does and then submit your site for reconsideration.

Chapter 5: Connecting with Social Networks

In This Chapter

✔ Link building with blogs

✔ Leveraging social news sites

✔ Defining media optimization

✔ Implementing social media optimization

✔ Building a community

✔ Using the tools in Web 2.0

In recent years, the world of *online social networking* (sites where people can meet and interact with one another) has exploded in popularity. You may have heard of sites like MySpace and Facebook, which allow users to create their own Web pages and connect with other users all over the globe. This kind of social networking has expanded to include news sites, entertainment media, and beyond.

Social networking is another way to find and attract links. The majority of links from *link bait* (media or articles specifically created to attract links) comes from social networking sites. Social networking is also a way to build your brand and a name for yourself. This is where true grassroots marketing begins, and if you're creative and smart enough, you can use social networks to your advantage.

In this chapter, we discuss what you need to do to take advantage: blogging, social news sites, media optimization, social media optimization, community building, and Web widgets.

Making Use of Blogs

Blog is short for Web log, and blogs are primarily an online conversation medium. Blogs can be anything from people's personal journals to talk about their day, their trip to the hair salon, and the rude guy who cut them off on the way to the grocery store, to media and corporate blogs describing new products and services. Blogs cover entertainment, politics, fashion, lifestyles, and technology. If you name it, probably somebody out there is blogging about it. Blogs should be updated daily, or at least a few times a week.

One way to use blogs is to set up a blog to your own Web site. A major benefit is increasing the amount of *content* (the text and media offered on your site) related to your subject matter because an actively-used blog site builds content rapidly. A blog also helps you by improving user engagement on your site and strengthening your customer service: Blogs provide a place for you to hear from your users and to interact with them. (For more information on setting up a blog, see Book X, Chapter 2.) In general, blogs take a lot of attention and time, get links very quickly, and lose them just as fast. Blogs, like all social media links, are high-maintenance and require consistent care.

Blogs can also benefit you when someone writes about your site or your company and links back to your Web site. The worth of a link from a blog depends, however. If an authoritative blog — such as Wonkette (`www.wonkette.com`) a political gossip blog, or Jalopnik (`www.jalopnik.com`), a car enthusiast blog — links to your Web site, that link could equal a whole lot of traffic for you, plus the prestige that comes along with it. On the other hand, most links from blogs are actually pretty worthless. You only see an increase in traffic within the first day or maybe just a few minutes; after that, the link cycles off the page, the blogger updates with new content, and your link is yesterday's news. Links from blogs are good for passing around link bait, but not a whole lot else.

Blogs also have the ability for users to comment on them. You can click a button at the end of the blog post and leave your thoughts, criticisms, or links of your own. Other users can reply to your comment, as can the author of the blog. Blog comments usually do not pass any link equity (the worth of a link as defined by the search engines). The `rel="nofollow"` attribute (an HTML code that tells search engines not to follow a link) was actually invented for blog comments. It was there to stop spammers from crashing blogs and cluttering up the comments page with useless, unrelated information. Most blog software programs apply a `rel="nofollow"` attribute to every link by default, so anything in the comments is not read by a search engine.

However, don't let the lack of link equity stop you from using the comments option and interacting with other readers on a blog. Like other forms of business networking, the comments section of a blog can be a great place to network with other people and find out what the guy on the street is saying about products or services in your industry. People interact with you in the comments section; they might decide to check out your site and wind up giving you a link from their Web site.

This type of link building by relationship building is a much slower process than the normal heavy traffic that you would receive if you were linked through the blog, but these kinds of links (and the traffic gained from them) based on a relationship formed through a blog stick around longer. Don't be afraid to interact in the comments section on a blog. Just be sure to practice good etiquette. Be who you are, not some fictitious persona. Also, don't go around trolling on other blogs. *Trolling* is the act of deliberately being rude and offensive just to make people angry on blogs and other Web forums, and most definitely gets you banned from the blog or site.

Discovering Social News Sites

Today, the Internet puts the news right at your fingertips, and there are hundreds of sources for news out there. You can go to a site like CNN (www.cnn.com) or any newspaper site and read articles at their source. But the Internet has turned news-reading into a social activity, too. A *social news site* is a site where news stories and articles from anywhere on the Web can be voted on by users, and the importance of a story or article is determined by the audience rather than by the editors of the site or source. Several social news sites are out there, but the big ones are Digg (www.digg.com/), StumbleUpon (www.stumbleupon.com/), and Reddit (www.reddit.com/).

When you read an article on a news site, a blog, or on an Internet-savvy company Web site, at the bottom of the article, you can usually find icons such as the ones shown in Figure 5-1.

Figure 5-1: Social news chiclets let readers submit or vote on an article.

These icons are called *chiclets*, which are Web icons that can be clicked to submit or "vote for" an article on a particular social news site. Each chiclet represents a different social news site. The Digg chiclet is a tiny icon of a figure holding a shovel (dig, get it?) When you find a story or article that you find interesting, you can click the Digg chiclet (or the chiclet for StumbleUpon, Reddit, or whatever). This takes you to Digg's Web site, where you can write a short description of the news item or article and then post it to the Digg network.

People on the social news network have the ability to click the link to the story and then vote "up" or "down" on the item. (On Digg, these are known as "digging up" or "burying.") The more positive votes an article receives, the closer it gets to the front page. With a social news network, users get to decide what stories are most important and entertaining.

With time, effort, and good luck, a site or article could make it to the first page. If it's your site or article, congratulations! But sorry about the server crash. Digg alone has five or six *million* hits from unique users a day. Digg has a huge community to draw from, as do StumbleUpon and Reddit, and the higher you appear on their news pages, the more traffic you get. Success with a social news site can be both a blessing and a curse: It has the possibility of generating more permanent links, but your server might not be able to handle the traffic.

An article's popularity varies from network to network because each network has its own unique appeal to different kinds of users. Digg's network tends to be generally young, male, liberal, and technology-savvy. Reddit's network is a little older, has a higher population of women, and is more mixed in its political views. The StumbleUpon network is geared more towards entertainment stories and less towards news, and its demographics are more mixed in terms of age and gender.

There are also smaller, more niche-oriented social news networks that focus on a particular demographic, like a particular gender, age group, or political affiliation.

Promoting Media on Social Networking Sites

Social media sites are another way to get links via relationship building. Posts that promote your engagement objects are good forms of link bait that can pay off with huge amounts of traffic and short term links. Taking advantage of the social media sites requires some advanced planning. After you've identified which site would be best for your subject, you still need to make some decisions about how, when, and what. If you plan to submit different forms of media to social networking sites, consider optimizing it for those sites first. The media in question includes videos, podcasts, and images.

If you have videos, put them on your Web site as well as on video-sharing sites like YouTube (www.youtube.com). People who view them on the other site read your description and hopefully will follow a link back to your site that you include in the description, as in Figure 5-2.

Figure 5-2:
Companies can upload their videos to YouTube with a link back to their site in the description.

Your media has to be engaging. Make it funny, creative, educational, and engaging or, if all else fails, controversial. You want to get people talking about it. Don't be afraid to make people angry, if it comes right down to it. One of the fastest ways to get links to a blog is to write something that is sure to make people angry, but turn the comments off. People go running back to their own blogs and newsfeeds to write what they think about you, with a link back to your site. This benefits you in terms of link equity. The thing about link equity is that Google doesn't care if a link is positive or derogatory. Google still passes link equity.

Another thing to keep in mind about your content is not to be stingy with it. Share it! A comparison has been made about media and the card game Canasta. In Canasta, a good strategy to win is to give away all of your best cards in the beginning so that you get them back at the end. Similarly, if you freely give away your media, people come to your Web site.

For example, you can put your images on the photo-sharing site Flickr (`www.flickr.com`) under the Creative Commons license, which allows you either to retain some rights over your image or to make it free for use in the public domain. (You can find out more about the Creative Commons license options at `http://creativecommons.org/`). You can make the images free for public use as long as they provide a link back to your site, which people generally more than happily provide. In any kind of photo-sharing network, you also have the option of tagging your photos with relevant keywords, as well as providing links to your site.

As with most links you want to attract, you want to attract media links naturally. You want links to come to you on their own because people find and enjoy the media you put out there and think your site is a relevant and entertaining place that they would recommend to other users to check out. You have to have a vested interest in creating quality content. Give the people out there something of value. An example is musician Jonathan Coulton, who makes all of his songs available for public use under the Creative Commons license on his Web site. He allows others to take his songs and use them for their videos and media projects. Using this, he is able to introduce his music to a much wider audience. Go to YouTube and check out how many people are using his music for their own projects and you'll get an idea.

If you have a classic car customization Web site, a good example of both utilizing video and giving things away would be to make a video about how to properly repair chipped paint on a classic car, or fix a dented fender. (Or, get a little silly and teach them to properly hang dice from a rearview mirror.) But you want to do so in a way that is clever and entertaining. For instance, you might dress up as ninjas while repairing the chipped paint. The easiest way to draw people to you is to be clever and entertaining. (This is why it's a good idea to watch those social news networks, so you can see what is funny versus something that is definitely *not* funny.)

You can also allow people to take your content that is under the Creative Commons license and post it on their own sites, as long as they give you a link back. People are usually more than glad to give you a link.

Social Media Optimization

Social media is any sort of online environment that allows social interaction, including blogs, social news sites like Digg (`www.digg.com`) and Reddit (`www.reddit.com`), social networking sites like MySpace (`www.myspace.com`) and Facebook (`www.facebook.com`), and others. Social media sites have become great for branding. Not only can they bring you inbound links, but they also provide great opportunities for reputation management because you can read and respond to what's being said about your brand.

Twitter (www.twitter.com) is a popular microblogging site that allows you to update your status via the Web or through text messaging (Micro-blogs are like blogs, but they only allow you to update a few words at time.) Google reads microblogs a lot because of how frequently they are updated. But even more than that, Twitter is a great way to control your branding because it allows you to go out and engage other users.

The important thing to remember is to snap up your brand name right away on each of the major social media sites. Go out and register your name and every variation that you can think of as fast as you can. You want to keep others from taking them and potentially using them to pretend to be you, damaging your online reputation (we go over this more later in this chapter). This has happened many times, and when someone does take your name before you can register it, there's not much you can do about it. So make sure you grab your own brand name.

What follows is a list of social networks at the time of writing that are good for search engine optimization (SEO). The Internet is an ever-changing entity, so it's safe to say that this list will change and expand, but these are good places to start. All of these sites allow followable links in your profile area for search engines:

- ✦ Digg: www.digg.com
- ✦ Flickr: www.flickr.com
- ✦ kirtsy: www.kirtsy.com
- ✦ LinkedIn: www.linkedin.com
- ✦ Current: www.current.com
- ✦ PostOnFire: postonfire.com
- ✦ BloggingZoom: bloggingzoom.com/
- ✦ coRank: www.corank.com
- ✦ Technorati: technorati.com
- ✦ MyBlogLog: www.mybloglog.com
- ✦ LinkaGoGo: www.linkagogo.com
- ✦ Bibsonomy: www.bibsonomy.org
- ✦ Mister Wong: www.mister-wong.com
- ✦ MyLinkVault: www.mylinkvault.com
- ✦ ClipClip: www.clipclip.org
- ✦ 9rules: www.9rules.com
- ✦ Associated Content: www.associatedcontent.com/

- Blogoria: www.blogoria.com/
- NowPublic: www.nowpublic.com/
- MemeStreams: www.memestreams.net/

The following is a list of current social bookmarking sites. These are sites where you can save articles or sites as a bookmark and share them with other people at the same time. None of these have a rel="nofollow" attached, so search engines read the links coming from them. Some are repeated from the previous list:

- BlinkList: blinklist.com
- Furl: furl.net
- Mister Wong: www.mister-wong.com
- Spurl: spurl.net
- Diigo: diigo.com
- Bibsonomy: www.bibsonomy.org
- RawSugar: www.rawsugar.com
- LinkaGoGo: www.linkagogo.com
- MySutff: mystuff.ask.com
- BuddyMarks: buddymarks.com/
- Connectedy: www.connectedy.com/
- MyLinkVault: www.mylinkvault.com/
- Jumptags.com: www.jumptags.com/
- OYAX: www.oyax.com/
- A1-Webmarks: www.a1-webmarks.com
- BookmarkTracker: www.bookmarktracker.com
- myVmarks: www.myvmarks.com
- Health Ranker: www.healthranker.com
- Yattle: www.yattle.com

Community Building

Community building is managing your reputation and brand building via the social networks. Social networks are not a traditional network, so traditional networking is not really going to work here. People on the Internet react differently. For one thing, traditional advertising, such as, "Our product is great, please buy it!" generally does not fly with the Internet audience. Many big companies do not do very well with Internet marketing, and that's because they're using the same types of traditional marketing messages that work in print and TV advertising. On the whole, Internet users are turned off by traditional marketing methods.

So what do you do in this situation? The solution is to give away control. That's right: There is only so much you can do for your brand, and, at a certain point, you must allow it to work for itself. When you're engaging others in a conversation on the Internet about your brand, you cannot control the conversation. You can only be a *participant* in it.

A Web site for a large car manufacturing company was able to find out about problems with its vehicles through its Internet *forums* (a message board where users can log on and post about topics on a related subject). If you are willing to use social networks and actually listen to what your users say, you can get some great feedback on your products and services, and on your competition as well. People are honest in forums (almost brutally so). Don't disregard the positive or negative feedback. This is good, usable information. You can see what you are doing right, and what your competition is doing right. On the flip side, you can also pinpoint where your weaker areas are, and where your competition is messing up.

Twitter (www.twitter.com) is also a great resource for this. You can pay attention to what people are saying about you, and you have the ability to search and listen in. With Twitter, you can *follow* people (that is, read all of their posts) and, in return, people follow you and read your posts. Figure 5-3 is an example of a Twitter page. Twitter consists of nothing but short posts (the maximum you can type in one post is 140 characters including spaces).

Companies can search for their names in your posts. A colleague *tweeted* (that's what Twitter calls posting) about Southwest Airlines when his flight was late, and, six minutes later, a Southwest Airlines representative was following him on Twitter.

Another example is a cable TV company that has used Twitter to help improve its reputation. The company does not have a great reputation when it comes to customer service. However, they assigned an employee to do nothing but manage a Twitter account for the company. His job is to sit on Twitter and catch tweets about problems with the company, respond, and then fix their problems. And he does. He offers technical solutions through Twitter, and then he calls and arranges for a service technician to come out to fix problems he cannot fix himself. This is an example of a company using social networks to the fullest. The company is using Twitter to fix problems and expand its reputation as a company that cares about its customers.

Figure 5-3:
When logged in, your Twitter home page has a profile box and timeline of updates from people you're following.

Another example is Zappos (www.zappos.com). Zappos is an online shoes retailer. Every employee is on Twitter, and they are encouraged to talk. This is community building for the company. Even the CEO has his own Twitter account. For Zappos, it's not just their product they're selling; they are selling customer satisfaction. They're selling themselves. With their products, they provide free overnight shipping. They don't advertise this, but when a user makes a purchase, Zappos e-mails them and informs them that they have free overnight shipping. Plus, they have a very easy return policy. Simply call them, and you are sent a box with a label, for no charge, and you are given a refund. The point of Zappos is not how much money a customer spends, but whether their customer is satisfied. This is a grassroots marketing campaign that works not only because their satisfied customers want to do business with them again, but also because they tell others about their experiences and bring in new customers to Zappos.

On the Internet, people are going to care more about a company that seems to be listening to them and engaging them. That is why it is important to always be genuine with your customers and with people on the social media sites. You have to be out there, talking to your customers. But be honest. People — on the Internet, and everywhere else — hate being lied to. If they find out you are not being genuine about yourself or your intentions, woe to you. As Shakespeare once (sort of) said, "Hell hath no fury like an Internet scorned."

Astro-turfing is a term used for a fake grassroots market campaign (a term based on AstroTurf, which is artificial grass). For example, it was discovered that several blogs praising Wal-Mart were fake. Supposedly these blogs were written by "real" customers, but they were actually written by Wal-Mart's public relations firm. This was uncovered because the bloggers sloppily provided links to their PR firm. Needless to say, that did not go over well with the Internet audience. Be warned: As soon as people find out they're being deceived, they turn on you.

Lonelygirl15 was a popular video blog series on YouTube, until it was discovered that the girl was an actress, and the blogs were scripted. Lonelygirl15's popularity dropped off sharply after that, and the video blog series is now defunct. If you are going to create something along these lines, be upfront right away that this is not real. Don't hide the fact that something is a marketing campaign. Users do not like feeling tricked.

You also have to be concerned about the problem of people taking your brand and then using it to harm you. On Twitter, there was a case where a company supposedly had two IT guys giving out advice on how to fix problems, both with account names that included the brand name. The trouble was that one of these IT guys was a fake and did not work for the company and was giving out particularly bad advice. Unfortunately, there wasn't much the company could do beyond letting people know that the person was not employed by their company. (This is also why it is important to keep track of your employees and what it is that they're supposed to be doing.)

If someone illegitimate does get a hold of your brand name, you can't do a whole lot other than distance yourself from him and make sure that your customers know that the guy that stole your name or who is pretending to be you is not affiliated with you in any way.

The Internet is still like the Wild West. There is no law out there to deter someone who registers your brand name, and no punishments for people who pretend to be you. The most you can do is register your Web site under a federal copyright and hope that gives you enough teeth to take out someone who steals your name. (See Book V, Chapter 5 for more on copyright infringement.)

Incorporating Web 2.0 Functioning Tools

What is Web 2.0? It's the current wave of technology aimed at bringing people together, enhancing creativity, and stimulating conversation. The next stage of the Web means going from static pages without any interaction to a living site that reacts to the users and gives visitors a way to affect the status of the page. Social networking sites, where you can upload your profile, talk to friends, and make new connections, are the most well known aspect of Web 2.0. When we talk about Web 2.0 functioning tools, we're actually talking about widgets. A *widget* is a piece of HTML code that can be imbedded in a page that a user can interact with. One social media professional likes to say that a widget is what's left of a page if you get rid of all the junk like the navigation, the template, and the footer and only leave the content. That's pretty accurate.

But there are other kinds of widgets as well. On many personal blogs are links to online quizzes. These quizzes can be about anything from personality, astrology, which TV show character you most resemble, or how long you can survive chained to a bunk bed with a velociraptor. For the most part, these quizzes are for entertainment purposes only. But all of these widgets feature a link for other users who see these quizzes and want to take them themselves, and will bring other users into that Web site. The results of the quiz come with a line of HTML code that you can use to post your results on your personal blog, or on your other social networking page (like Facebook or MySpace). The HTML coding presents an image with your results and link back to the site with the quiz.

A clever and entertaining widget can generate lots of traffic for your site and bring you plenty of links because all the widgets feature a link back to your site. These can be both fun and functional. For your classic car site, you could create a quiz that tells a person which classic car matches their personality most, along with an image and link back to your site.

It's very important to prominently display your link and not try to hide it. If you are hiding something, the search engines might think you are doing something wrong. The link must also be relevant to the widget and your Web site. Don't hide links to other sites in the widget; otherwise, the links from the widget are discounted. Also, beware of using widgets for spam. Don't use the widget for any sneaky, devious, or underhanded techniques. You will be caught and punished.

You can use other types of widgets for your site. Again, just make sure they're relevant. You might have a widget on your site that can tell your users what time it is in Tokyo, but if it's for your American classic car customization site, it wouldn't be relevant. What might be better is a quiz that determines whether your driving skills enable you to outrun a herd of rampaging wildebeests (because people respond to cleverness and creativity, and, when all else fails, wildebeests are always entertaining).

Another type of widget that might be worthwhile is a poll. Polls ask questions and publish counts of people's answers, like in Figure 5-4.

A poll is a way of engaging your audience and finding out what it is that they're actually thinking. Your audience also checks back to see how the poll is doing, and, if you leave a comments section with the poll, your audience can interact with one another and discuss the poll. Even if the poll doesn't actually mean anything, if you make it fun, it can help build community and bring you traffic. Another example of widgets includes a sports statistics ticker that constantly gives updates. It could include scores, who's won, who's on first, and so on. These are useful for sites that are related to sports in some way.

Stock market tickers are another excellent example of a widget. They give constant updates on how the stock market is doing that day — although these days, you might prefer to remain in the dark. These are useful for sites having to do with finances or brokerage firms. Pretty much anything you think of can be a widget. In most cases, if you have an idea for a widget, you need to build it yourself or hire a clever programmer to build it for you. Some companies do have widgets of their own that you can customize (like for a poll), but that's not always the case.

The primary results of widgets are traffic and engagement, and the secondary results are branding and linking. An effective and clever widget can be associated with your Web site and ultimately boost your brand.

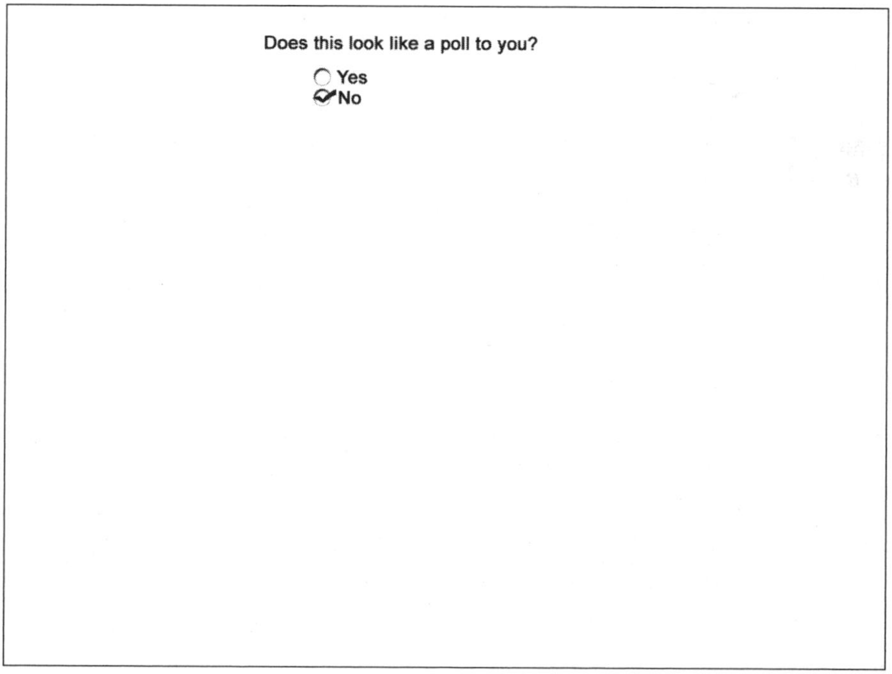

Does this look like a poll to you?

○ Yes
☑ No

Figure 5-4:
Even a very simple poll invites user engagement.

Book VII
Optimizing the Foundations

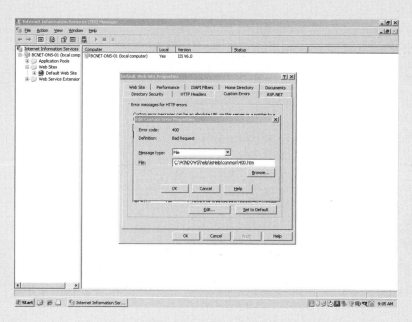

*Edit your IIS server properties to set up
a custom error page.*

Contents at a Glance

Chapter 1: Server Issues: Why Your Server Matters. 451

Meeting the Servers... 452
Making Sure Your Server Is Healthy, Happy, and Fast 453
Excluding Pages and Sites from the Search Engines............................. 458
Creating Custom 404 Pages 464
Fixing Dirty IPs and Other "Bad Neighborhood" Issues 468

Chapter 2: Domain Names: What Your URL Says About You 471

Selecting Your Domain Name.. 471
Registering Your Domain Name... 474
Covering All Your Bases 475
Pointing Multiple Domains to a Single Site Correctly 480
Choosing the Right Hosting Provider 481
Understanding Subdomains 484

Chapter 3: Using Redirects for SEO. 487

Discovering the Types of Redirects 487
Reconciling Your WWW and Non-WWW URLs 492

Chapter 4: Implementing 301 Redirects 495

Getting the Details on How 301 Redirects Work................................ 495
Implementing a 301 Redirect in Apache .htaccess Files..................... 496
Implementing a 301 Redirect on a Microsoft IIS Server...................... 499
Using Header Inserts as an Alternate Way to Redirect a Page 504

Chapter 5: Watching Your Backend: Content Management System Troubles 509

Avoiding SEO Problems Caused by Content Management Systems.....510
Choosing the Right Content Management System 515
Customizing Your CMS for SEO 517
Optimizing Your Yahoo! Store 519

Chapter 6: Solving SEO Roadblocks 523

Inviting Spiders to Your Site 524
Avoiding 302 Hijacks 528
Handling Secure Server Problems..530

Chapter 1: Server Issues: Why Your Server Matters

In This Chapter

✔ **Getting to know the servers**

✔ **Making sure your server is healthy and fast**

✔ **Excluding pages or sites from the search engines**

✔ **Passing instructions to search engines with a robots text file**

✔ **Using Meta robots tags**

✔ **Building a customized 404 error page**

✔ **Avoiding dirty IPs and bad neighborhoods**

Your *Web server* is the software application/service that runs your Web site. (The term *Web server* can be used to refer to both the hardware and the software that runs a Web site, but here we're talking about the software.) Anytime a user does something on your site, such as load a page or view an image, it's your Web server that receives the request and serves up what the user wants. Like a good waiter in a restaurant, your site's server should be as fast and efficient as possible so that your site visitors feel happy and well satisfied.

Server issues impact search engine ranking, from the type of server you use to how well it performs. Sites that frustrate users by being slow or unavailable are not the type of sites that any search engine wants to present in its results. A slow server, or a server that fails often, can cause a site to drop out of the search engine's *index* (the databases of Web site content that Google, Yahoo!, or Microsoft Live Search pulls from when delivering search results), or prevent a site from ever being indexed in the first place. A key and yet often overlooked point of failure for a Web site is the server environment where it resides.

If your site is up and running, you are either operating your own server equipment or using a hosting facility. Either way, you need to know what type of server you use. You also need to know something about the IP address that your site occupies. An *IP (Internet Protocol) address* is the numeric code that identifies the logical address where your site resides on the Web — as well as other server-level factors that can have a big impact on your success with your search engine optimization (SEO) efforts.

In this chapter, we discuss the importance of choosing the right server and keeping your server in optimal health. You also discover ways to identify server problems that can have a negative impact upon your search engine ranking so that you can address them.

Meeting the Servers

In the world of Web servers, two competitors hold more than 90 percent of the market share: Apache and Microsoft IIS. In this section, we give you some basic information on each server to introduce you to these two reigning heavyweights.

Using the Apache server

The most popular Web server on the market, the Apache HTTP Server is an *open-source software application* (a computer program whose source code is available for free to the public) maintained by the Apache Software Foundation. Currently in version 2.2.9, the Apache Web server supports approximately 50 percent of all sites on the World Wide Web. The fact that it's free may contribute to its popularity, but the Foundation people in charge say it also contributes to its strength because the entire Internet community can participate in identifying and fixing bugs and in improving the software.

For search engine optimization purposes, Apache is the best server available. Its configuration options make it the most flexible server, which is important because SEO requires constant monitoring and tweaking. Apache also gives you direct access to the server even if a third-party hosting provider runs your site. This is a crucial advantage over a straight Microsoft IIS server environment.

Using the Microsoft IIS server

The main competitor to the Apache server is Microsoft Internet Information Services (IIS). This *proprietary software* (meaning that it must be purchased from Microsoft) provides a platform for running a Web site. IIS is currently in version 7.0 and comes included with the Windows Server 2008 operating system for data centers.

Microsoft IIS is the next-best server available after Apache. The main disadvantage with IIS occurs if your site resides on a shared server operated by a third-party hosting provider. With an IIS server, only the administrator can access the server directly — so anytime you need to look at or make changes to your server files, you have to go through the hosting provider, which can cause delays and end up being a little frustrating. However, if you have a *dedicated server* (not shared with any other sites) that you can access directly, the IIS server can accommodate your SEO needs if you have administrator-level access rights.

You can overcome some of the administrator-rights requirements and get Apache-like, flexible functionality out of your IIS Web server. To do this, you need to install an ISAPI_Rewrite plug-in into IIS. *ISAPI* stands for Internet Server Application Program Interface, and ISAPI_Rewrite software can be obtained from several vendors. If you're using IIS 7.0, we suggest you download it directly from Microsoft. Another version that is excellent and that works well on IIS 5.0, 6.0, or 7.0 comes from Helicon Tech (www.isapi rewrite.com/). (For more information on ISAPI_Rewrite, see Chapter 4.)

Using other server options

A bunch of other little guys out there also offer Web servers. Sun Microsystems' Sun Java System is the most well known of the also-rans, but there's a plethora of others with intriguing names like AppWeb, Barracuda, Cherokee, Yaws, and IceWarp. Red Hat makes an *enterprise* (large-scale) edition of the Apache server that targets large clients with high-traffic demands. All of these have different limitations that you won't find with the Big Two (Apache and Microsoft IIS).

For your SEO efforts, you want to make sure that your site uses either an Apache or a Microsoft IIS server. We recommend these servers as only they provide the flexibility and performance you need.

Making Sure Your Server Is Healthy, Happy, and Fast

A slow server can spell disaster for your site. If the search engines keep trying to visit your site to no avail, eventually they may stop trying. They don't want to index a site that isn't going to load when users try to access it — search engines don't want to give their users unreliable, slow information. That kind of thing makes the search engine look bad.

If your Web site takes forever to load a new page, or links end in error messages, you also won't have happy site visitors. And you may lose their business for good.

To succeed with search engines and users, you need a fast, clean server. You should check your server's health regularly to ensure it's performing well. Here are three things you should look for:

+ **Malfunctions:** You need to make sure that your site remains free of server problems such as improper *redirects* (HTML commands that detour a request to a different page), script errors or malfunctions that could cause a page not to display.

+ **Fast processing speed:** Speed counts a lot with the search engines. Kind of like the postal service through rain, sleet, or snow, the search engine spiders have a lot of ground to cover as they roam the Internet. If your site bogs down their progress due to a slow server, they're less likely to crawl it completely and won't re-index it as often.

Servers, in the overall scheme of things, are pretty cheap. If you take the cost divided by the number of visitors per year, you are talking about pennies. You should therefore address speed issues head-on, buying servers any time performance is slow.

✦ **Clean and uncrowded IP:** Your IP address also matters and should be monitored because your site can be adversely affected if another site on your IP is caught *spamming* (intentionally trying to deceive or manipulate the search engines) or doing other dirty deeds.

Running a Check Server tool

One way to check the status of your server is to run a quick diagnostic utility called a *Check Server tool*. This is a utility that attempts to crawl your site the same way a search engine spider does. If the Check Server tool runs into any obstacles that could prevent the spider from indexing your site, it tells you about them on a report that the utility creates. Even if your content is perfect, a poorly functioning server can keep your site from reaching its full potential in the search engine rankings. It's a good idea to run this diagnostic tool on a regular basis.

You can use any Check Server tool you have access to. You can also use the free Check Server tool located on our Web site. To run our Check Server, do the following:

1. Go to `www.seotoolset.com/tools/free_tools.html`.

2. Under the heading Check Server, enter your Web site's domain (such as `www.yourdomain.com`).

3. Click the Check Server Header button and wait until the report displays.

A Check Server tool performs several different page requests and checks the returned status codes and the content. If they don't match up, by showing error codes or inconsistent page content, it may be that your server is showing the search engines an error, even though there's no real problem. Having this information lets you fix issues quickly, which is important because search engines often reduce Web site rankings due to Web server errors they encounter. At the very least, even if you encounter a common error that would not cause you to be dropped from the index, a "cleaner" site is likely to rank higher in the search engine results.

Right below the table on the first page of the report, you'll notice a number — in Figure 1-1, it's *200*. This represents the Web page's status as a search engine would see it. In this case, *200* means the page is normal.

Table 1-1 explains the most common server status codes. These server statuses are standardized by the *World Wide Web Consortium (W3C)*, an independent governance organization that oversees Internet standards, so they mean the same thing to everyone. We've boiled down the technical language into understandable English to show you what each server status code means about your Web page. The official definitions can be found on the W3C site at `www.w3.org/Protocols/rfc2616/rfc2616-sec10.html` in case you want to research further.

Server status code

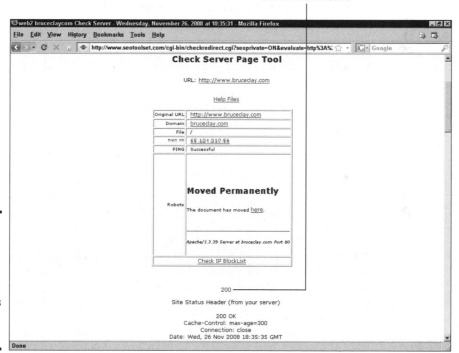

Figure 1-1:
The Check Server report identifies the server status code for a Web page.

Table 1-1   Server Status Codes and What They Indicate

Code	Description	Definition	What it Means
200	OK	The Web page appears as expected.	This is what you want to see. Your server and Web page have the welcome mat out for the search engine spiders (and users too).
301	Moved Permanently	The Web page has been redirected permanently to another Web page URL.	When a search engine spider sees this status code, it moves easily to the appropriate new page. A 301 Redirect status is *not* a problem for your search engine optimization.
302	Found (Moved Temporarily)	The Web page has been moved temporarily to a different URL.	This status should raise a red flag if it's on your Web server. Even though there are supposed to be legitimate uses for a 302 Redirect code, they can cause serious problems for your optimization efforts. Spammers frequently use 302 Redirects maliciously, so if you don't want a search engine mistaking your site for a spam site, avoid them.
400	Bad Request	The server could not understand the request because of bad syntax.	This could be caused by a typo in the URL. Whatever the cause, you don't want a search engine spider blocked from reaching your content pages, so investigate this if you see this status code on your site.
401	Unauthorized	The request requires user authentication.	Usually this means that you need to log in before you can view the page content. Not a good error for spiders to hit.
403	Forbidden	The server understood the request, but refuses to fulfill it.	If you find this status code on your Web site, find out why. If you want to block the spiders from entering, there ought to be a good reason.

Code	Description	Definition	What it Means
404	Not Found	The Web page is not available.	You've seen this error code; it's the Page Can Not Be Displayed page that displays when a Web site is down or nonexistent. You definitely do not want a spider following a link to your Web site only to be greeted by a 404 error! That's like visiting a house and finding the lights off and the doors locked. If your server check shows you have a 404 error for one of your landing pages, you definitely want to fix it ASAP.
500 and up	Miscellaneous Server Errors	The 500–505 status codes indicate that something's wrong with your server. Check it out.	

The other thing you can glean from the Check Server report is whether the page is cloaked. *Cloaking* (showing one version of a page's content to users, but a different version to the spiders) is a big no-no with the search engines, so if your page appears to be cloaked, you need to know about it. If the page uses cloaking, it says so right on the report.

Indulging the need for speed

You also want to monitor your site's *performance*, which is computer-speak for speed. The faster your server can deliver a page after it has been requested, the better. You want your human visitors to have a smooth, pleasant experience using your site because that leads to more *conversions* for you (which could be sales, sign-ups, subscriptions, votes, or whatever action that you want people to take on your site). More importantly for your search engine rankings, you want the search engine spiders to be able to move fast and freely through your site. The quicker they can get to your pages, the more pages they'll index and the more often they'll come back.

You can tell how long it takes a search engine spider to retrieve your Web pages. This information shows up as a call in your server log (a *server log* is a complete record of requests sent to the Web server and the server's actions in response). You should be able to check your server logs and establish a benchmark, and then regularly check it again for comparison. If checking your server logs sounds too complicated, try this easier way: Use the Web Page Analyzer free tool offered at `www.websiteoptimization.com/services/analyze/` instead. Either way, one factor that influences your search results ranking is your page response time, so this is a good thing to keep tabs on.

Many factors influence your Web site's performance. The user's Internet connection speed, location, and computer have a big impact on how fast they perceive your site to be, factors that are frustratingly out of your control. When a search engine spider comes to crawl your site, you can rest assured that on *their* end, things are humming. On *your* end, though, many things can affect site speed. These include server computing power (also known as *chip speed*) and setup, the amount of Internet bandwidth available compared to the amount of traffic, the efficiency of your HTML code and programming, contention with other sites sharing your IP, and whether you're the only site on your IP address, to name a few.

Excluding Pages and Sites from the Search Engines

Sometimes you need to block a spider from crawling a Web page or site. For instance, you may have a development version of your Web site where you work on changes and additions to test them before they become part of your live Web site. You don't want search engines to index this "in-progress" copy of your Web site because that would cause a duplicate-content conflict with your actual Web site. You also wouldn't want users to find your in-progress pages. So you need to block the search engines from seeing those pages.

Using a robots text file

The best way to exclude pages from the search engines' view is with a robots text (.txt) file. The *robots text* file's job is to give the search engines instructions on what *not* to spider within your Web site. This is a simple text file that you can create using a program like Notepad, and then save with the filename robots.txt. Place the file at the root of your Web site (such as `www.yourdomain.com/robots.txt`), which is where the spiders expect to find it. In fact, whenever the search engine spiders come to your site, the first thing they look for is your robots text file. This is why you should *always* have a robots text file on your site, even if it's blank. You don't want the spiders' first impression of your site to be a *404 error* (the error that comes up when a file cannot be located).

With a robots text file, you can selectively exclude particular pages, directories, or the entire site. You have to write the HTML code just so, or the spiders ignore it. The command syntax you need to use comes from the Robots Exclusion Protocol (REP), which is a standard protocol for all Web sites.

And it's very exact; only specific commands are allowed, and they must be written correctly with specific placement, uppercase/lowercase letters, punctuation, and spacing. This file is one place where you don't want your Webmaster getting creative.

A very simple robots text file could look like this:

```
User-agent: *
Disallow: /personal/
```

This robots text file tells all search engine robots that they're welcome to crawl anywhere on your Web site *except* for the directory named /personal/.

Before writing a command line (such as `Disallow: /personal/`), you first have to identify which robot(s) you're addressing. In this case, the line `User-agent: *` addresses all robots because it uses an asterisk, which is known as the *wild card* character because it represents any character. If you want to give different instructions to different search engines, as many sites do, write separate `User-agent` lines followed by their specific command lines. In each `User-agent:` line, you would replace the asterisk (*) character with the name of a specific robot:

> `User-agent: Googlebot` would get Google's attention.
>
> `User-agent: Slurp` would address Yahoo!.
>
> `User-agent: MSNBot` would address Microsoft Live Search.

Note that if your robots text file has `User-agent: *` instructions as well as another `User-agent:` line specifying a specific robot, the specific robot follows the commands you gave it individually *instead* of the more general instructions.

You can type just a few different commands into a robots.txt file:

✦ **Excluding the whole site:** To exclude the robot from the entire server, you use the command:

> ```
> Disallow: /
> ```

This command actually removes all of your site's Web pages from the search index, so be careful *not* to do this unless that is what you really want.

✦ **Excluding a directory:** (A word of caution — usually, you want to be much more selective than excluding a whole directory.) To exclude a directory (including all of its contents and subdirectories), put it inside slashes:

> ```
> Disallow: /personal/
> ```

✦ **Excluding a page:** You can write a command to exclude just a particular page. You only use a slash at the beginning and must include the file extension at the end. Here's an example:

```
Disallow: /private-file.htm
```

✦ **Directing the spiders to your site map:** In addition to Disallow:, another useful command for your SEO efforts specifies where the robot can find your *site map* — the page containing links throughout your site organization, like a table of contents:

```
Sitemap: http://www.yourdomain.com/sitemap.xml
```

We should point out that in addition to the previously listed commands, Google recognizes Allow as well. This is applicable to Google only and may confuse other engines, so we don't recommend using it.

We recommend that you always include at the end of your robots text file a Sitemap: command line. This ensures that the robots find your site map, which helps them navigate more fully through your site so that more of your site gets indexed.

A few notes about the robots text file syntax:

✦ The commands are case-sensitive, so you need a capital D in Disallow.

✦ There should always be a space following the colon after the command.

✦ To exclude an entire directory, put a forward slash *after* as well as *before* the directory name.

✦ If you are running on a UNIX machine, *everything* is case-sensitive.

✦ All files not specifically excluded are available for spidering and indexing.

Removing content from an index

If you discover that a search engine has indexed content from your Web site that you wanted to exclude, there is something you can do about it. The search engines offer ways to request that a particular URL be removed from their index. Here are links to get the instructions (or you can search for current info):

Google: `http://googlewebmaster` `central.blogspot.com/2007/04/` `requesting-removal-of-content-` `from-our.html`

Yahoo!: `http://help.yahoo.com/l/` `us/yahoo/search/siteexplorer/` `delete/`

Microsoft Live Search: `http://help.` `live.com/help.aspx?mkt=en-` `us&project=wl_webmasters`

To see a complete list of the commands, robot names, and instructions about writing robots text files, go to www.robotstxt.org.

Always be aware of your robots text tag. Mistakes here can absolutely destroy your site's rankings in the search engine. Here's a story that's unfortunately all too common about a business that learned about this the hard way. The company had a huge Web site and multiple development environments where they made changes and tested new pages before those pages went live. Of course, they had a robots text file set to Disallow: / all pages on the test site because they didn't want the search engines to index an in-progress copy of their Web site.

After a major revision, they moved the finished test site into place, replacing the old site files entirely — including the robots text file. Unfortunately, they neglected to take out the Disallow: / command. Soon the search engines stopped crawling their pages. Their site started to drop like a boulder in the rankings, and no one knew why. It took them three days to figure out that the cause was their robots text file! By simply changing one line of code in that file, they fixed the problem, but it was a costly lesson. Their estimated revenue loss topped $150,000 per day. The moral of the story: *Don't forget to update your robots.txt when you upload a new site!*

As a further safeguard, make it part of your weekly site maintenance to check your robots text file. It's such a powerful on/off switch for your site's SEO efforts that it merits a regular peek to make sure it's still "on" and functioning properly.

Using Meta Robots tags

Besides the robots text file, there is also another way you can prevent search engines from seeing something on your site. On an individual Web page, you can include a special tag in the HTML code to tell robots not to index that page, or not to follow the links on that page. You would place this tag after the other *Meta tags,* which are part of the HTML code located in the head section of a Web page.

Using Meta robots tags is less efficient than using a site-wide robots text file for two reasons. First, robots sometimes ignore Meta robots tags, and second, these tags slow down the robots reading your pages, which may decrease the number of pages they're willing to crawl. Also, this method can give your Webmaster headaches because the tags have to be maintained on the individual pages, rather than in a central file.

The Meta robots tag below tells the search engine robot not to index the page *and* not to follow any of the links on the page:

```
<META NAME="ROBOTS" CONTENT="NOINDEX, NOFOLLOW">
```

You could use this tag to tell the robot to read and index the page's content, but not to follow any of the links:

```
<META NAME="ROBOTS" CONTENT="INDEX, NOFOLLOW">
```

The next tag instructs the robot to ignore the page's content, but follow the links:

```
<META NAME="ROBOTS" CONTENT="NOINDEX, FOLLOW">
```

Being wise to different search engine robots

Not all search engines are created equal. We focus on Google, Yahoo!, and Microsoft Live Search because they account for nearly all search-generated traffic on the Web. Even among these three, however, you find a few slightly different options for your robots.txt file and `Meta` robots tags.

For example, you can use a different `Meta` robots tag per search engine to partially control where the two-line description that accompanies your page's link on a search engine results page (SERP) should come from. To see what we're talking about, look at Figure 1-2, which shows a typical SERP result with its two-line description highlighted.

Each link gets a description

Figure 1-2:
Search
engines
display
a brief
description
with each
link.

The search engines pull SERP descriptions from varying places, depending on which seems most relevant to the user's search query. They often pull information from a *directory* that they either manage or contract with, which is a hand-assembled set of Web site data arranged like a list. Different search engines work with different directories.

✦ **Google:** Google uses one of three sources for their search engine results descriptions: the *Open Directory Project* (ODP), which is a hand-assembled, human-edited directory of Web site data (go to www.dmoz.org if you want more information on this ambitious project); the Meta description tag on the Web page itself; or a snippet from the on-page content containing the searched-for keywords and some surrounding text (also referred to as an *auto-snippet*).

✦ **Yahoo!:** Yahoo! displays a description pulled from its own Yahoo! Directory, the Meta description tag, or the on-page content.

✦ **Microsoft Live Search:** Live Search pulls descriptions from either the Meta description tag or the on-page content. They don't currently use a directory.

You can prevent the search engines from using the directories, if you feel the manually edited description there is either out-of-date or inaccurate for some reason. For SEO purposes, it's always better to avoid showing someone else's description for your pages. If you like their wording, use it on your Web page, but we recommend that you exclude the directories. By using the proper Meta robots tag, you can force them to pull descriptions from your Meta description tag or your Web page.

The following tag instructs Google not to pull the description from the Open Directory Project:

```
<meta name="robots" content="noodp">
```

The following tag tells Yahoo! not to use the description contained in the Yahoo! Directory (YDIR for short):

```
<meta name="robots" content="noydir">
```

Within a Meta robots tag, you can include multiple commands by separating them with a comma and a space. To tell all robots not to pull descriptions from either directory, you could write the tag like this:

```
<meta name="robots" content="noodp, noydir">
```

Creating Custom 404 Pages

You've seen it probably a hundred times — *File 404: Page Can Not Be Displayed*. It's the error page that means, "Sorry, you're out of luck. The Web page you wanted is broken or missing, and you can't see it right now. So go away!" A user will probably do only one thing when presented with this 404 error page, and that's hit the Back button.

You can give your Web site visitors and search engines a much better experience when there's a problem displaying a page. You can present them with a customized 404 error page that's actually helpful and friendly rather than the standard browser-issued version.

This issue matters to your SEO efforts, too. If the spiders find a default 404 page on your site, you've thrown a roadblock in front of them that they have no way to get over. Search engines can't hit the Back button or use the other advanced features of your Web site. All they can do is follow links. If they come across a bad link and you don't give them anywhere else to go, they leave your site. This may result in entire sections of your site not being indexed. Creating a custom 404 page that includes links to other pages on your site helps prevent this from happening. You have to give the engines something to follow.

Designing a 404 error page

Here are tips for creating a user-friendly and SEO-friendly 404 error page for your Web site:

✦ **Design the page to look like your Wcb site.** Keep your users feellng like they're still on your site and everything's under control.

✦ **Apologize and tell them what happened (such as "Sorry, the page you requested is unavailable.").** Your message should match the tone of your site, but consider making it humorous to keep your readers engaged, such as, "The well-armed monkeys normally operating this Web page are engaged in full-scale warfare at the moment. To avoid the flying fur, try one of the escape routes suggested below."

✦ **Offer suggestions with links to other pages they might want to go to.** Include helpful descriptions in the links. ("Read about our car customization services. See picture of 'new' classic cars. Hear what our customers say about us.")

✦ **Include a link back to your home page, with meaningful keywords in the *anchor text* (visible link text that a user can click).** Don't call it Home.

✦ **Include a link to your site map.** This is especially important for search engine robots because they can follow that map to get around your entire site. Providing access to your site map becomes even more beneficial because the engines continually return to your site to see if those nonexistent pages have returned. If they have, the search engines re-index them. If they haven't, the robots still find your 404 page and all of your relevant links.

✦ **If you have a good programmer, customize the page contents based on where the user had a problem.** For instance, if the page was supposed to show Ford Mustang steering wheel options, the message and links could dynamically change to offer them a way to get to another Ford Mustang page in your site, rather than just showing them a generic error message.

✦ If you are running a sale, put images linked to your current ads on the page.

✦ Put a search box on your error page, front and center. Let users type in what they're looking for and go to that exact page on your site.

✦ Put a `Meta` robots tag on your custom 404 error page. Tell the search engines that they should follow the links on the page, but not index it:

```
<meta name="robots" content="noindex, follow">
```

✦ Do not redirect your 404 error page (for more on handling redirects properly, see Book VII, Chapters 3 and 4).

✦ Be sure your 404 error page passes a 404 error code, which stops search engines from indexing it. Many sites forget this step, and their error pages can show up in search results (see Figure 1-3).

Error pages can accidentally show up in search results

Figure 1-3:
It's embar-
rassing to
have your
error pages
rank with
the search
engines.

Customizing your 404 error page for your server

After you've created your 404 error page, you need to customize it for your server. The instructions vary depending on which server you use, so we've provided a list of options in the next few sections.

Apache

For an Apache server, you need to add some code into your .htaccess file that instructs the server to present a custom page (in this case, 404.php) instead of the standard error, in the event of a particular error occurring (in this case, ErrorDocument 404):

```
<IfModule mod_rewrite.c>
    RewriteEngine On
    ErrorDocument 404 /error-pages/404.php
</IfModule>
```

If you like, you can enhance the user-friendliness of your site even more by creating custom pages for other types of errors, as well. In the following code snippet, the server is being told to display five different custom pages that have been built for different kinds of errors that could occur on the site:

```
<IfModule mod_rewrite.c>
    RewriteEngine On
    ErrorDocument 404 /error-pages/404.php
ErrorDocument 403 /error-pages/403.php
ErrorDocument 401 /error-pages/401.php
ErrorDocument 500 /error-pages/500.php
ErrorDocument 501 /error-pages/501.php
</IfModule>
```

Microsoft IIS

It's also easy to configure a custom 404 error page in the Microsoft IIS server environment, if you have the administrator rights to access the server. (If you have to beg your ISP staff to do it, it may take longer, but it's still possible.) You simply make changes within the Properties dialog box to point various errors to their correct pages. To get ready, you need to have your site up on your IIS server (at least one page, anyway) and have already created a custom 404 error page. We call the page 404error.aspx in the following steps:

1. **Open the Internet Services Manager.**

   Typically, this is located in your Programs list under Administrative Tools.

2. **Click the plus sign (+) next to your server name to expand the list.**

3. **Locate the Default Web Server (or other, if you've renamed it), and then right-click it and choose Properties.**

4. **Open the Custom Errors tab.**

5. **Select the error 404 from the list, and then click the Edit button.**

6. **Browse and select your custom error page (400.htm is shown in Figure 1-4, but you should name yours 404error.aspx or similar).**

7. **Click OK to exit the dialog box.**

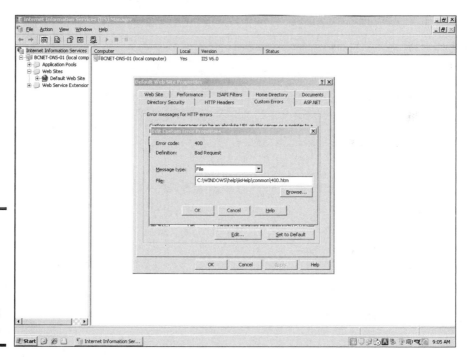

Figure 1-4:
You can edit your IIS server properties to set up a custom 404 error page.

Book VII Chapter 1

Server Issues: Why Your Server Matters

Monitoring your 404 error logs to spot problems

You can find out a lot by monitoring your *404 error logs* (the server record of every time a page could not be displayed on your site). The error log can alert you of problems with your Web pages so that you can fix them. You may also notice people linking to your site with an incorrect URL, in which case you could redirect (using a 301 redirect) those bad links to another page that is valid. Because 404 errors are a major reason why people abandon a site, tracking where your site gets 404 errors can help you capture and hold visitors, improving your traffic and your bottom line.

Fixing Dirty IPs and Other "Bad Neighborhood" Issues

It's a good idea to know the IP address of your site and monitor it to make sure it remains clean. It's like renting an apartment. Just because the neighborhood was quiet and peaceful when you first moved in, that doesn't mean it won't change over time and become an undesirable place to live.

IP addresses come in two flavors: virtual and dedicated. If you're using a *virtual IP address*, it means that there are multiple Web sites, as many as your server allows, using the same IP address you are. If you're using a *dedicated IP address*, you are the only site on that IP.

We recommend that you use a dedicated IP for your site. Even so, you still need to monitor it to make sure it stays clean because you can also be affected by bad behavior of other IPs within the same *C block*. (The second to the last set of digits in an IP address, such as the *179* in the IP address 208.215.179.146, identify the C block. It's similar to an area code for a telephone number, except that unlike your area code, you can change C blocks. You can move your site to a new IP address and C block if you have trouble with the one you're in. Call your hosting company and tell them you want to be moved.)

If you do share a virtual IP with other sites, which is often the case with small or brand new Web sites, it's like being in an apartment building. Similar to living in an apartment building, it's important that the IP isn't full of bad neighbors, even though that's pretty much out of your control. If the search engines find out you're next door to a spam site, for example, your site could be tainted by association. Google has indicated that it is difficult to be tainted by surrounding sites, but why take a chance? We recommend being in clean IP blocks whenever possible.

The other drawback of using a virtual IP is that occasionally, a search engine or a user navigates to your Web site by your IP address rather than your URL (usually only if your server is configured incorrectly). If you're on a virtual IP, they may not be able to find your site. Any of the various sites located on that IP could come up; it'd be the luck of the draw. And do not forget that shared IPs may mean that your server performance will slow down based on the traffic load of your neighbors.

To find out your Web site's IP address, look no further than our free Check Server tool, which we covered earlier in this chapter. The report identifies your DNS IP address. See Figure 1-1.

Diagnosing your IP address's health

After you have an IP address, you can find many tools on the Web that can evaluate whether it's clean. By "clean," we mean that the IP is not on any *IP blacklists*, which are lists of sites suspected of illegal acts such as child pornography, *e-mail spam* (sending unsolicited e-mail indiscriminately to tons of people), or *hacking* (attempting to break into computer networks and bypass their security). You may have never done anything unethical on your Web site, but your IP's history with previous sites (or other current sites, if you're on a shared IP) could still haunt you.

Being blacklisted is bad news. Most major e-mail services (Hotmail, Yahoo!, AOL, Gmail, and so on) block any e-mail coming from a blacklisted IP address, so being blacklisted seriously affects your ability to communicate with the outside world. For instance, it harms your ability to reply to sales inquiries, and thus can cost you money.

Being blacklisted also puts you in hot water with the search engines. Search engines refer to these IP blacklists for purposes of spidering, indexing, and ranking of Web sites. We don't know how much the IP blacklists influence the individual search engines, and Google indicates that it should not, except in severe cases, impact your rankings. However, the search engines do flag your site and watch it closely because they assume that a site involved in e-mail spam has a high likelihood of being involved in other types of spam. Simply put, you become guilty by association.

To find an IP checker tool, do a search on Google for ["ip blacklist" check]. We found several free options this way — one you might try is MX Lookup (www.mxtoolbox.com). Alternatively, we recommend the monitoring reports at DNSstuff (www.dnsstuff.com), which are available for a paid subscription only.

When you run an IP check, it shows you the status of your IP with many different blacklists. If you see any red flags, you need to take steps to *get off of that blacklist ASAP*:

1. **Contact your ISP (Internet Service Provider) and request a change to a clean IP.**

   Better yet, try to move to an entirely new C block. You want to get as far away as possible.

2. **As an alternative, ask your hosting provider to clean up the neighborhood and then petition the search engines to have the IP marked as clean. They can do that.**

3. **If your hosting provider won't cooperate, then cut your losses and change hosting providers.**

   However, this problem should never occur. There is no excuse for an ISP operating blacklisted IP ranges.

4. **Be sure to run an IP check on your new IP address when you get it.**

   You want to see for yourself that you're moving into a good neighborhood. If you can, try to check the target IP before you are moved to it.

The diagnostics available through Google Webmaster Tools (www.google. com/webmasters/tools/) are extremely helpful. After you sign up your Web site (which is free), Google verifies your site and then sends a spider to check it out. You receive a report that quickly tells you if they found anything wrong. Hearing in Google's own words that your site is A-OK is reason enough to celebrate, but you get the added bonus of lots of cool tools to try. (See Book VIII if you want more coverage of analytics and the Webmaster Tools.)

Chapter 2: Domain Names: What Your URL Says About You

In This Chapter

✔ Choosing your domain name

✔ Registering your domain name

✔ Understanding country codes and top-level domains

✔ Securing domains for common misspellings of your name

✔ Considering domains with alternate extensions

✔ Choosing the right hosting solution

✔ Knowing how search engines view subdomains

S hakespeare once said, "A rose by any other name would smell as sweet," implying that a name does not affect an object's essential makeup. That may be true, but a Web site is not a rose — your site's name is critical to its success. Your *domain name* (the root of your site's URL address, such as *yourdomain*.com) must be chosen strategically, based on your business goals. Pick a good domain name, and you've got a foundation for a successful online presence.

In this chapter, we explain some guidelines for selecting an appropriate domain name for your Web site. You discover the basics, like how to register for a domain name and how to pick a hosting service to get your site up and running. You also find out about securing variations of your domain name in order to protect your *brand* (company name) long-term.

Selecting Your Domain Name

Picking the right domain name for your Web site depends on your business strategy. You need to decide how you want people to find you on the Web. You have basically two ways to approach choosing a domain name — by brand or by *keywords* (search terms that people might enter to find what your site offers).

If you have a unique brand name and want people to be able to find your Web site by searching for your brand, you should secure your brand as your domain. Having a brand for your domain name makes sense if any of the following is true:

✦ Your brand is already established and recognized (Nike, Xerox, and so on).

✦ You have advertised or plan to advertise to promote your brand.

✦ Your brand is your own name (such as `bruceclay.com`) or very unique.

✦ You want your site to rank well in search results for your brand name.

As an alternative, you could choose a domain name containing keywords that identify what your business does. For instance, if your business is called Marty's Auto but your Web site is focused on your classic car customization business, you might get a lot more mileage out of `classiccarcustomization. com` as a domain name than out of `martysauto.com`. Search engines can parse the domain name to recognize the distinct words *classic car customization*, and your keyword-laden domain name would make your site more relevant to searches for those terms. Also, the business name *Marty's Auto* doesn't identify what services you really offer — it could be auto sales, auto repair, or other. Unless you plan to heavily advertise and build *Marty's Auto* into a brand, you'd be better off choosing a keyword-centered domain name.

You may run into problems getting your first choice of domain name because someone has already registered it. People often buy domain names that they don't intend to use, just so they can turn around and sell them later. Your desired domain may fall into that category, in which case you can try to contact the domain owner and negotiate to buy it from them. However, that isn't always possible, especially when the domain is legitimately operating as a thriving Web site. So in this case, you need to be creative and start thinking of alternative domain names that would work for you.

Here are a few points to keep in mind when trying to come up with a good domain name:

✦ **Length:** Shorter is better than longer in a domain name. There are three reasons why: The URL string for your files can be shorter, and people tend to avoid clicking long URL links on search results pages; a short URL is easier to remember than a long one; and there are fewer opportunities for typos when someone enters your URL in a browser window or sets it up as a link.

✦ **Multiple words:** Search engines have no trouble parsing words that are *concatenated* (run together without spaces). Most Web site domains for businesses with multiple-word brand names run the words together, such as `bankofamerica.com`, `bestwestern.com`, and so on. Concatenating domain names is the best practice. However, sometimes, you may need to separate words visually to make them easier for users to understand. When you must separate words, use a hyphen. The search engines interpret hyphens as word spaces; underscores (_) don't work well because they count as alphanumeric characters. Imagine you own a tailoring business called the Mens Exchange and that you're interested in branding exactly that name. But wait a second: The domain `mensexchange.com` could be parsed two ways. To make sure the site name isn't misunderstood, a hyphen is needed; `mens-exchange.com` prevents any misunderstandings.

We recommend you use no more than one hyphen (or two at the most) in a domain name — more than that can make your site look suspicious to the search engines, like *spam* (deliberately using deceptive methods to gain ranking for irrelevant keywords). Although none of the engines ban you for having a multi-hyphenated domain name, they may still think that your domain buy-cheap-pills-and-try-free-poker-here.com looks a little suspicious. What's more, your visitors do too.

✦ **Articles:** Part-of-speech articles like *a*, *an*, and *the* may help you create a unique domain if they make sense with your name. For instance, Hershey's has a Web site at `hersheys.com` that's consumer-targeted and all about chocolate. But for their investors, they have a separate domain at `thehersheycompany.com` that's full of company-related news and information. In most cases, you're not going to need the article, so don't even worry about it.

You also want to consider your future plans as much as possible. It might be hard to foresee how your business may change and expand, but try to avoid boxing yourself in. For example, Marty's Auto might decide to branch out and also do classic car brokering and resale, or possibly include current-model car customization, bicycle customization, or another type of expanded service. In those cases, the domain name `classiccarcustomization.com` may become too restrictive in the long run.

As a general rule, you want to choose a domain name that will last. This makes sense from a usability point of view because you want your customers to rely on your Web site, bookmark it, and come back often. It's also important from a search engine optimization (SEO) perspective. The search engines consider domain age as a factor when ranking sites. The longer your domain has been continuously registered and active on the Web, the higher your score is for the age factor. Granted, this is only one of more than 200 different ranking factors Google considers, but that doesn't make it insignificant. Because competition can be so tight on the Web, you want every advantage you can legitimately get.

Remember in the 2008 Summer Olympics when Michael Phelps won a swimming relay by 1/100th of a second? That was in a field of only eight swimmers. When you consider how many thousands of competitors you could face on the Web, you see why every little advantage can make such a big difference. In SEO, you need to sweat the small stuff. Having a domain that endures is a small thing that can pay off big with long-term customers and search engine rankings.

Registering Your Domain Name

To find out whether a domain has already been taken, start by just typing it into the Address bar of your Web browser and seeing what comes up. If you see an error message saying "Address Not Found" or something similar, you might think you're in luck and have located an available domain. But sometimes a domain may be taken even though no site displays, or it may look taken when in fact the domain holder would like to transfer it to someone else.

A more foolproof way to check for available domains is to go to a *domain name registrar* (a company accredited and authorized to register Internet domain names) and use their domain name search tool. A domain name search tells you whether the name is available and then quotes prices to register it to you if it is. Domain name registrars we recommend are

✦ Register.com (`www.register.com`)

✦ Moniker (`www.moniker.com`)

✦ Go Daddy (`www.godaddy.com`)

✦ Namecheap (`www.namecheap.com`)

✦ Whois.net (`http://whois.net`)

✦ Domain.com (`www.domain.com`)

✦ Network Solutions (`www.networksolutions.com`)

Also check with your Web site hosting company to see what they can do for you. Many provide all the same services as a domain name registrar.

If a domain is available, you can claim it on the registrar's Web site. The standard price to register a `.com` domain name is $9.95 a year or greater (international domains can cost much more), although you may be able to secure it for two or more years up front at a discount.

In the future, you'll need to renew your domain name registration. You don't *buy* a domain name; they're only licensed for a period of time. So when your current registration is near its expiration date, you need to re-register it, and then repeat this process throughout the life of your Web site.

If a domain name you really want is already taken according to a domain name search, look at the Web site. See if it looks like a real site doing business, or just a placeholder site, or better yet, just brings up an error. All of these could indicate that someone has registered the domain name but hasn't gotten around to creating a site yet — or that they don't intend to. Domains are often purchased on speculation and sold later. In these cases, you may be able to negotiate with the domain holder to obtain the domain. There's no telling what the initial price might be that the domain holder would require, but it may be worth it to you to negotiate a deal. Some sites, such as Moniker (`www.moniker.com`), also operate periodic auctions where domains are auctioned by their holders.

You can find out the name and contact information of the registered domain holder using the WHOIS Lookup tool on the home page at `http://whois.net`. Then try your best persuasive techniques and see what happens.

Covering All Your Bases

You may want to register other domains in addition to your main URL. Most companies try to cover all their bases — not just to attract more *traffic* (visitors) to their site, but to protect their brand and their future online business as well. Securing other domain names besides your primary domain can be an important proactive step for your Web site, but you want to do it strategically. This section covers why you might want to have more than one URL. We also help you understand the variety of choices beyond the .com domains, so you can make informed decisions.

Country-code TLDs

You may be wondering what to do about all the other types of domains besides `.com`. There are many domain name extensions other than the familiar `.com` extension, such as `.net`, `.org`, `.me`, and so forth. Known as *top-level domains*, or *TLDs*, they represent the topmost part of a domain name under which all domain names within that TLD are registered. So `.com` is a TLD, and all domain names that use the `.com` extension (`wiley.com`, `amazon.com`, and so on) fall within that TLD.

Who's in charge of the domain system, you ask? The Internet's domain name system is managed by the Internet Corporation for Assigned Names and Numbers, or *ICANN* for short. This not-for-profit international organization coordinates the Internet globally, creating technical naming and numbering standards to ensure that every Web site and computer on the Internet can be identified uniquely, which is a technical necessity. You can read more about ICANN on their site (`www.icann.org`).

There are two main types of TLDs within the Internet's domain name system: country-code TLDs and generic TLDs.

Country-code TLDs have a dot followed by two letters. Below are a few examples of country-code TLDs:

.au	Australia
.ca	Canada
.de	Germany

.eu	European Union
.fr	France
.il	Israel
.mx	Mexico
.us	United States

When a country-code TLD is established, the country can issue domain registrations for that TLD as they see fit, according to their own local policies, so the rules vary from country to country. We recommend that you obtain a domain *within the country's TLD* for anywhere you think you might do business. Secure your domain name if you can. You need to research the rules for establishing a domain in each country, however. Here are some specific examples:

✦ **.de:** If you want to do business through a German domain (.de for Deutschland), they require that you either live in Germany or have a physical business located there.

✦ **.ca:** Canada has less stringent requirements; if you have a relative who lives in Canada, you can obtain a .ca domain.

✦ **.us:** If you're located in the U.S., by all means pick up a .us domain name. The .us domains aren't very common yet because most companies use .com, but some notable examples are Delicious.com (a popular social bookmarking site), which started life at the much more complicated http://del.icio.us, and directory pages for each ZIP code that contain information about that locality (such as http://www.93065.us).

✦ **.co.uk:** Sometimes a country-code TLD looks more complicated than a simple two-letter code. The United Kingdom, for example, chooses to register domains with an additional second-level domain specified in their extensions. So a business Web site in England typically ends with .co.uk; an English non-profit group would have a site ending in .org.uk; and so forth.

✦ **.fm:** The Federated States of Micronesia has reserved the TLDs .com.fm, .net.fm, .org.fm, and others, but makes money by allowing anyone in the world to register a .fm domain. Although this is unconventional, .fm has become popular with sites related to FM radio and Internet radio (such as the social music site www.last.fm or the Internet marketing industry site, www.webmasterradio.fm).

✦ **.tv, .me:** Occasionally a country goes so far as to sell the rights to operate its TLD. This happened with the .tv country code (for Tuvalu) and the .me country code (for Montenegro).

Generic TLDs

Generic TLDs are usually three or more letters long. The most common are
.com, .net, and .org, but there are about 20 TLDs total at this time. Some
can be registered by anyone who's interested, but others require that you
meet certain eligibility requirements. Table 2-1 below shows the different
generic TLDs and details on who can obtain their domains. (Note: The "spon-
sor" of a generic TLD is responsible for administering the policies and ensuring that all domain registrants meet the eligibility requirements.)

Table 2-1   The Most Popular Generic Top-Level Domains (TLDs)

TLD	Purpose	Our Comments
.biz	Restricted to businesses. Sponsored by NeuStar, Inc. of Sterling, Virginia.	Theoretically restricted, .biz has a reputation for being home to less than sterling Web businesses and spammers.
.com	Generic use (unrestricted).	Originally intended for commercial sites, this is the most popular TLD (with more than 60% of all sites). People think of this extension by default, so we recommend that you have a .com domain. Some browsers even have a keyboard shortcut (Ctrl+Enter) for adding www. and .com around a domain name in a browser to make these URLs easier to type.
.edu	Reserved for post-secondary institutions accredited by an agency on the U.S. Department of Education's list of Nationally Recognized Accrediting Agencies (in other words, American colleges). Sponsored by EDUCAUSE in Boulder, Colorado.	
.gov	Reserved exclusively for the U.S. government. Sponsored by the General Services Administration of Fairfax, Virginia.	
.info	Generic use (unrestricted).	Originally intended for informative sites, this TLD has really taken hold with millions of registered, active domains.

(continued)

Table 2-1 *(continued)*

TLD	Purpose	Our Comments
.mil	Reserved exclusively for the U.S. military. Sponsored by the DoD Network Information Center of Columbus, Ohio.	
.net	Generic use (unrestricted).	Originally intended for networks, anyone can now register for a .net domain.
.org	Generic use (unrestricted).	Originally designed for organizations such as non-profits, this TLD can now be used for any type of site.

We didn't include the other generic TLDs in Table 2-1 — .aero, .arpa, .asia, .cat, .coop, .int, .jobs, .mobi, .museum, .name, .pro, .tel, and .travel — because they're rarely used, and we don't think most site owners need to consider them in their SEO or business strategies. But if you can, buy them! (For a complete list of TLDs with more details, see ICANN's official data at http://iana.org/domains/root/db/.) Of course, if you are running a museum, by all means grab up classiccars.museum. It'll be a conversation piece, if nothing else.

After you've chosen your domain name, we recommend that you register every variation you can. Pick up the .com, .net, .org, and so on — as many as are available. Remember, this is your future business reputation you're protecting. If you set up your Web site at www.classiccarcustomization. com but don't secure the other TLDs for that domain name, down the road, someone may build a competing site at www.classiccarcustomization. org. Potentially they could confuse your customers, take away some of your traffic, or even damage your reputation by using your brand name for different purposes. By locking up those other domains now, you could be safe, not sorry.

Vanity domains

A *vanity* domain is an easy-to-remember Web address used to market a specific product, person, or service. You would obtain a vanity domain with your users in mind, not search engines. Movies often register a vanity domain in addition to their primary location on the studio's Web site. For example, the 2008 movie *The Dark Knight* snatched up the vanity URL www.thedark knight.com to capture all the *direct type-in traffic* (users who type a URL directly into their browser's address bar) of people looking for the movie by name. However, www.thedarkknight.com redirected you automatically to http://thedarkknight.warnerbros.com/dvdsite/, a subdomain on the Warner Brothers studio site containing the movie's Web pages.

Obtain a vanity domain if you want to market your product or service with a simple Web site address. A long, complicated URL doesn't look good in ads and isn't easy for people to remember. You might also want to register relevant, really good vanity domains just to keep your competition from getting to them first.

Misspellings

Another good idea is to register domains that are commonly misspelled versions of your main domain name. Not only might this help you rank better for your misspelled brand name in the search engines, but also it helps you capture the *direct type-in traffic*, or the people who type a URL directly into the address bar of a Web browser. Figure 2-1 below shows a typed-in URL, which bypasses the search engines and takes the user straight to a Web site (assuming the URL is entered correctly).

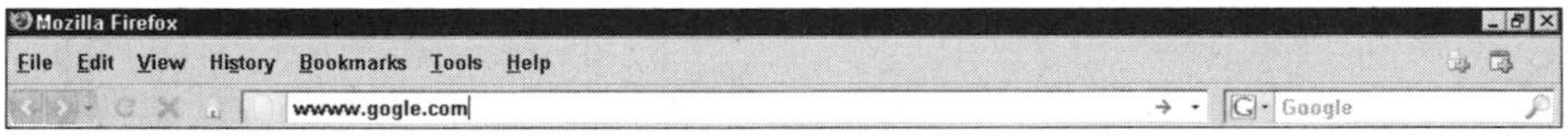

Figure 2-1:
Users
sometimes
type a URL
directly into
the address
bar to open
a Web site.

Google, for example, has covered their bases by securing close misspellings of their domain name. If you type `www.gogle.com` into your browser's address bar and press Enter, you instantly get redirected to `www.google.com`. This also works with `www.googlee.com` because Google has registered it, too.

To support your `www.classiccarcustomization.com` Web site, you also might want to pick up the misspelled versions (such as `www.classicar customization.com`), as well as the hyphenated versions `www.classic-car-customization.com` and `www.classiccar-customization.com`, and then redirect them all to your primary site. For ideas on the common misspellings of your brand name, look no further than your customer correspondence (such as letters and e-mails).

Consider all the ways people might try to find you and make all paths lead to your site. Secure all the different variations of your actual domain name that are available and make sense.

Pointing Multiple Domains to a Single Site Correctly

After you've registered a bunch of domains, you need to know what to do with them. Having multiple domains all point to a single Web site is usually bad for search engine optimization because the search engines think you're trying to index multiple Web sites all for the same content. They can tell that it's duplicate content (by matching long text strings, file sizes, and so on), and they usually only use one site and throw the others out of their search results.

You can correct this problem by using an *IP funnel*. This is a method for funneling many domains to a single *canonical site* (your primary, main Web site) correctly, so that search engines won't view your multiple sites as deceptive or misleading.

With an IP funnel, you don't have to host all of your different domains and set up *redirects* on them. (Redirects are HTML code that automatically forwards links to a different page.) Instead, you only have to host two domains — your canonical site plus one other domain, and then "funnel" the other domains to it. You save money and effort and prevent duplicate content.

An IP funnel corrects the problem of multiple domains pointing to the same content. Figure 2-2 shows how you could set up an IP funnel to reroute many different domains to your canonical site domain.

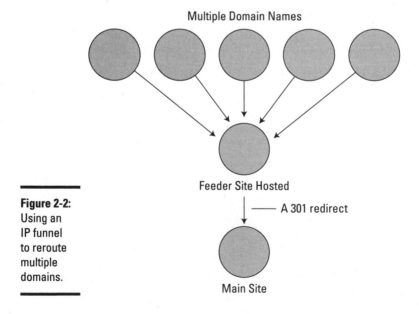

Multiple Domain Names

Feeder Site Hosted

A 301 redirect

Main Site

Figure 2-2:
Using an
IP funnel
to reroute
multiple
domains.

Most domain name registrars provide the ability to "point" or "forward" domains to another site. If you had six extraneous domains in addition to your main site domain, you would first choose one of the six to be your "feeder site" because it "feeds" all traffic to your canonical site. All the other five domains should point to the feeder site (not to your canonical site). These five extra domains do not need to be hosted on a server; you can just have all requests for those URLs forwarded automatically to your feeder site.

The feeder site (we'll call it `www.feeder.com`) should be hosted, but it doesn't need to have a visible user interface. The feeder site only needs to have two files:

```
www.feeder.com/index.htm
www.feeder.com/robots.txt
```

The index.htm file should have an optimized `Title` tag, `Meta` description tag and `Meta` keywords tag. It should also include a `Meta` refresh statement and a `Meta` robots `"noindex"` command.

The robots text file can be left blank. It just needs to exist so that when the search engine robots go looking for it, they aren't met with an error. For more on creating a robots text file, see the previous chapter.

The last thing you need to add is a 301 redirect command (server code that indicates where the site has permanently moved) to the feeder site. You want to redirect the feeder site domain to your main site so that any links are passed automatically. The feeder site can then correctly redirect traffic to your "real" site.

Choosing the Right Hosting Provider

Deciding where to host your Web site is very important. Pick a reliable host, and managing your site can be fairly headache-free. Choose a bad one, and you could have a nightmarish experience with unreturned calls, unanswered e-mails, and a Web site that's unavailable to visitors.

Unless you have your own server and other equipment in-house, and the technical know-how or staff to run them, you're going to need a Web-site hosting provider. *Hosting providers* are third-party companies that lease out Web space by month or by year, similar to office space. In addition to space on their servers, they offer varying degrees of additional services.

In this section, we explain the key things you should ask about when researching hosting providers. Keep in mind, however, that what works for your friend's site won't necessarily work for yours. Factors include the amount of traffic your site receives, how complex your site or application is, how much storage space you need, and so on. The best hosting provider is the one that meets your needs and provides the right balance between quality and value.

✦ **Customer service:** One of the most important elements of a good hosting provider is their level of service, which can range widely. How easy is it to contact them for support, and how quick and helpful is their response? You can get a feel for this by asking a few questions of different providers in advance. Don't let them intimidate you with technical-speak. They should be willing to answer your questions promptly and in an understandable way, or they aren't the people you want to work with.

✦ **Server:** The type of server software they use is critical. To ensure enough flexibility for SEO, make sure you go with either an Apache server or a Microsoft IIS server. (Chapter 1 of this minibook explains more about the servers.)

✦ **Dedicated versus shared IP:** If you have a small site that's just getting started, you might initially share an IP address with other sites. (Short for "Internet Protocol," an *IP address* is the numeric code that identifies the logical address of a server or a computer on the Web.) Having an IP that hosts only your Web site, however, is preferred for many SEO-related reasons. This is called a *dedicated IP*. Here are good things to find out from a prospective hosting provider:

  • If the IP will be shared, ask how many sites share it (the fewer, the better).

  • Ask if they offer dedicated IPs, and find out how you would get one.

✦ **Uptime:** *Uptime* means the percentage of time the site is up and running, not including scheduled maintenance periods. A guaranteed uptime of 99% is not uncommon, so make sure you're contractually covered.

✦ **Bandwidth:** The amount of bandwidth available to your site determines how much traffic your site can comfortably handle. *Bandwidth* refers to the flow of data transferring over an Internet connection. You can think of it like a pipe — the pipe's diameter determines how many gallons of water can flow through it at the same time. The bigger the pipe, the more water it can transfer. The higher the bandwidth, the greater the number of consecutive visitors your Web site can handle. You need more bandwidth if any of the following are true:

  • Your site is large (in number of pages).

  • Your site has a lot of traffic regularly at peak periods.

  • Your site serves many Flash and sound files, or has large images, audio, video, or other elements that require a lot of bandwidth to display.

Very large or application-intensive Web sites that need maximum connectivity should find a hosting provider that's physically located on what's known as the *Internet backbone*. This refers to the main hub connections of the Internet, which are primarily located in major cities around the world (Los Angeles, Denver, New York, and so on). A site right on a hub means that data can transfer to and from the site faster than if it had to travel through multiple spokes to reach the server.

✦ **Storage:** File storage space is cheap, and most hosting providers give out a generous amount even to the smallest sites. However, more storage space is needed if you plan to have a ton of image, audio, or video files on your site. If you're going to operate a *social media site* (a Web site enabling user participation and consisting of user-generated content) where people can upload their own videos, for an example, you want to be prepared with lots of storage space to hold them.

✦ **Server capacity:** This refers to the processing power of the server. You know how a new computer always seems to work faster than the old one did? That's because it has a much more powerful processor. Similarly, server capacity affects the performance speed and capacity of your Web site. If your site application requires a lot of processing power, ask about how they allocate server capacity and strongly consider requiring a dedicated IP.

✦ **Scalability:** *Scalability* means being able to expand your server resources as needed. If and when your Web site business grows, you want to be able to scale your server resources up to deliver the same or better site performance. You also may want to add storage space, bandwidth, or server capacity to your site at peak times, or all the time. Make sure you have a flexible hosting environment that is easy to adjust as your site needs change.

✦ **Clean IPs:** You don't want to move into a bad neighborhood, so you want to make sure your site isn't on a dirty *IP address* (the Internet Protocol numeric code that identifies the logical address of a server or a computer on the Web). Because you have no way to know in advance what IP address you'll get, make sure it's written into your service level agreement that you require a clean IP that's not *blacklisted* (listed on anti-spam databases).

When researching hosting providers, look up online reviews written by current or former customers. These can be very insightful. Just remember that each Web site's needs are different, so you have to take their comments with a grain of salt.

One last recommendation on choosing a hosting provider: Don't consider it a permanent arrangement. You hold the rights to the domain and the site assets, and you can host them wherever you think best. Be willing to move to a new hosting provider if your current provider isn't cutting it.

Understanding Subdomains

In the domain name system (also known as "DNS"), a *subdomain* is a dependent domain set up within the primary domain. Here's an example: The following code shows what the URL would look like if you set up a subdomain called `events` in your classic car customization business domain.

```
http://events.classiccarcustomization.com/
```

`Events` is the subdomain, `.classiccarcustomization` is the domain, and `.com` is the TLD.

Why people set up subdomains

Web sites often create subdomains in order to segregate sections of Web pages to create a virtual "site within a site." In the example in the previous section, an events subdomain could be used to hold information about classic car shows, car industry conventions, company-sponsored events, or other types of event-related information that you decided not to include within your main site navigation scheme.

Some social media sites automatically create a subdomain for each person who signs up (such as `myname.socialmediasite.com`). Similarly, some companies choose to create subdomains for their different employees. So you could have

```
http://bob.classiccarcustomization.com/
http://katie.classiccarcustomization.com/
http://susan.classiccarcustomization.com/
```

Other sites set up subdomains as a way of separating all of their Web site *content* into different categories, like this:

```
http://remodels.classiccarcustomization.com/
http://paint.classiccarcustomization.com/
http://parts.classiccarcustomization.com/
```

In other parts of this book, we recommend *siloing* your Web site, which basically means organizing your Web site content into a hierarchy of subject themes, with each silo focused on its own particular theme through keywords and relevant links. Although the subdomains shown here appear to be organized by subject theme (remodels, paint, parts), this is *not* siloing. (For more on siloing, see Book VI.) We don't recommend organizing the bulk of your site content by subdomains, for several reasons we discuss in the next section.

How search engines view subdomains

Search engines consider subdomains to be entirely separate sites. Subdomains endanger your search engine optimization because the search engines do not see the subdomain as part of your main site. They also don't see any connection between your various subdomains. By using subdomains, you effectively put up walls between your different sets of content. In essence, you are taking all the benefit of your inbound links and all of your well thought-out content and dividing them across several separate Web properties. Unless you have a lot of both, dividing them up is a really bad idea. But if you did it, you would need to optimize each subdomain for the search engines separately, if you wanted them to rank.

You benefit from using subdomains on your Web site only in the following cases:

✦ **Totally unrelated content:** If you wanted to start a side business selling bicycles, you wouldn't want to dilute your classic car customization Web site with pages on frame sizes, bicycle brands, and prices. You could register an entirely different domain for this, or you could handle this new business as a subdomain of your main Web site.

Blog (short for "Web log") sites provide another great example of subdomains. If you sign up for a blog account on WordPress.com (`www.wordpress.com`), for example, your blog would be assigned the `yourname.wordpress.com` subdomain. Your blog would contain your writing and thoughts and would have no relation to other people's blogs. Subdomains work well in this situation because each blog contains legitimately different content.

✦ **Large brands:** Huge companies with a highly branded name can successfully use subdomains to separate their content. Why? First, they have *tons* of pages about each division or product, enough so that each subdomain ranks well with the search engines on its own. Second, it benefits users to have the well-known brand name in every URL because it confirms that the pages legitimately belong to that company. Third, having multiple subdomains could yield multiple results on a search engine results page (SERP), if several come up for the same keyword.

Companies using subdomains include Google (`news.google.com`, `images.google.com`, `maps.google.com`, and so on) and National Geographic (`kids.nationalgeographic.com`, `video.nationalgeographic.com`, `animals.nationalgeographic.com`, and so on). Large education institutions (.edu sites) also use subdomains because each institution may only have one .edu domain name, leaving only subdomains to separate the different schools within it.

✦ **International sites:** Targeting different countries can be very effectively done through the use of subdomains. If you don't have the resources to buy `www.mybusiness.co.uk`, or if that domain is already taken (not all domains are available around the world), you can target the UK through `uk.mybusiness.com` instead. We discuss more about international SEO in Book IX.

✦ **Secure content:** If part of your Web site can only be accessed through a logon, it could be set up effectively as a subdomain. Search engines don't spider content that's behind a logon anyway, so having it in a separate subdomain doesn't matter to your SEO efforts.

Your site needs lots of subject-relevant content to reach the front pages of the search results. Most people struggle to have enough site content to support their keyword themes and get the rankings they're after. If you're like them, splitting up what content you have into separate subdomains is self-defeating. And if you're currently using subdomains as a way of organizing your site content, stop it. Use siloing instead. For more on siloing, see Book VI.

Chapter 3: Using Redirects for SEO

In This Chapter

✔ **Understanding when to use a redirect command**

✔ **Discriminating between the different types of redirects**

✔ **Understanding 301 and 302 redirects**

✔ **Knowing when to use Meta refreshes**

✔ **Considering JavaScript redirects**

✔ **Dovetailing your www and non-www domains properly**

*I*n your toolbox of search engine optimization (SEO) techniques, the redirect tool is an important one to master. *Redirects* are HTML or server commands that automatically forward incoming links to another page. With this tool, you can trim outdated pages off your site without losing the visitors who still go to those pages. You can also organize many *domains* (root names of Web site URLs) into one site, so that they won't be competing with each other. With redirects, you can avoid creating *duplicate content* (Web pages that search engines see as duplicates of each other) that could damage your rankings on search engine results pages (SERPs). And the best part is that redirects are not hard at all to learn.

This chapter covers the four main types of redirects. We explain what each type is for, although for SEO purposes, only one type of redirect is safe to use — a 301 redirect. Then in Chapter 4 of this minibook, you discover the "how tos" of placing 301 redirects in your Web site.

Discovering the Types of Redirects

There are several different types of redirects in the world of the Internet. These commands give you a way to redirect your site visitors from one *URL* (the Web address of a page, such as www.wiley.com) to another (like www.wiley.com/index.htm). Often, you need to use a redirect to reroute people linking to an old page to its replacement page, especially if your Web site undergoes reorganization so that files and directories have to be renamed and moved around. You also need to use redirects in the normal course of site maintenance, to help visitors coming to alternative *URLs* (such as the non-www version of your domain instead of the www version, and so on) to get to the URLs that contain the content they're looking for.

Short for "redirection status codes," the various redirects are defined by the World Wide Web Consortium (W3C), which is an organization that oversees Internet practices and creates standards that enable Web sites all over the world to work smoothly together as one giant network. Webmasters have a bunch of tricks they can use, but not all of them benefit you, your site, your users, or your search engine rankings. In the case of redirects, although the available redirect methods are intended to have different functions, only one is thoroughly search engine–friendly.

In this section, you find out about the four most common ways to handle automatically redirecting one URL to a different URL: 301 redirects, 302 redirects, JavaScript redirects, and `Meta` refreshes.

301 (permanent) redirects

The *301 redirect* is the preferred and most SEO-friendly form of redirect. Also known as a *permanent redirect*, the 301 informs a search engine that the page has been permanently moved to a new location. This is the cleanest redirect because there's no ambiguity — the search engines get a clear message that one page is history, and some other URL has now taken its place.

To put it in perspective, say your favorite barbeque restaurant closes without your knowledge. Fortunately for you, the next time you head over for their mouth-watering ribs, you see a sign in the window: "WE'VE MOVED TO NEW LOCATION: 123 Yummy Drive." This sign enables you to get back in the car and head to the restaurant's new location without too much inconvenience.

A 301 redirect is kind of like that "WE'VE MOVED" sign, but better. On the Web, visitors don't even have to realize you've moved. Your Web site automatically redirects them to the new URL and displays the new page.

If you've registered a *vanity URL* (an easy-to-remember domain that isn't your main business domain name), you should put a 301 redirect on it so that when users go to the vanity URL, they're taken to your real site instead. For example, people interested in a currently playing movie often type the movie title directly into their browser's address bar, so movie studios try to register those URLs in advance. For the 2008 movie *The Dark Knight*, if you typed in `www.thedarkknight.com`, you were automatically redirected to `http://thedarkknight.warnerbros.com/dvd/`, which was a sub–domain on the Warner Brothers studio site. That's because the studio wisely secured the movie title URL and then redirected it to the actual site using a 301, thereby capturing more Web site traffic.

For site maintenance, you could use 301 redirects when physically reorganizing your pages and directories. For instance, you might redirect a page with a ghastly long URL (such as `www.classiccarcustomization.com/extras/dashboard/gauges-chevrolet-impala/speed-or-tach/139348w9d.htm`) to a new and cleaner URL address (like `www.classic`

carcustomization.com/chevrolet/gauges/impala-tachometer. htm). You wouldn't want to keep the old page location active on your Web site, but there are *backlinks* (incoming links from other Web sites) to the old page that you don't want to break. So you can't bring in the wreaking ball and just demolish the page — you need to redirect the old URL to the new one instead. The right way to do this is to set up a 301 redirect from the old URL to the new one. Then users who click to come to the old page automatically find themselves looking at the new one; also, search engines get the message loud and clear.

When a search engine encounters a 301 redirect, it does three things:

✦ Drops the now defunct page from its *index* (database of Web pages from which the search engine pulls search results), so that that page won't be included in future search results.

✦ Includes the new page in the index, available for listing on search results pages.

✦ Transfers link equity from the old page to the new. (*Link equity* refers to the value of all incoming links to a page, which the search engines use to determine a Web page's authority, or expertise, in its subject.)

The 301 redirect is the SEO-recommended form of redirect because it reduces duplicate content within the search engine index. Duplicate content hurts your search engine rankings because search engines don't want to show their users results that are essentially the same. Therefore, if a search engine detects that two pages it has indexed are the same, it filters out the less-authoritative page, so that only one of the pages can appear in search engine results pages (SERPs). Because a search engine responds to a 301 by dropping the old page entirely from its index, the chance of having two pages in the index with the same content is nil. (See Chapter 4 of this minibook for details on implementing 301 redirects.)

302 (temporary) redirects

Another commonly used form of redirect is the 302. A *302 redirect* means "document found elsewhere" and it's meant for temporary relocations of a Web page. Search engines see the new page as only temporary and continue to crawl and index the original location instead.

Although the search engines claim to be able to interpret a 302 correctly, 302 redirects are known to cause duplicate content to be indexed. Because duplicate content can cause pages to be filtered from SERPs or be assigned to a supplemental index, for the sake of your SEO efforts, you should avoid using 302 redirects. (Note: We cover duplicate content in depth in Book V, Chapter 4.)

Remember, 301 and 302 redirects are server (not HTML) commands, whereas the following types of redirects are done within an HTML page.

Meta refreshes

A *Meta refresh* is a type of *Meta tag* (command located in the top or head section of a Web page's HTML code) that tells the page to refresh automatically after a given time interval. When you *refresh* a page (by clicking the browser's Refresh button, for example), it causes the page to reload and redisplay its contents. A `Meta` refresh command can be written in several ways:

✦ Refresh the page instantly (time delay = 0).

✦ Refresh the page after an interval (time delay = 1 or more seconds).

✦ Refresh the page repeatedly every *X* number of seconds.

✦ Refresh to another page (with or without a time delay).

Officially, search engines say that they handle `Meta` refreshes as follows:

✦ A `Meta` refresh with a time delay of zero (0) or one second (1) is treated like a 301 redirect.

✦ A `Meta` refresh with a time delay of two (2) or more seconds is treated like a 302 redirect.

However, we've observed that this isn't usually the case. The search engines sometimes follow the link (as they would with a 301 or 302), but sometimes they don't. Sometimes they index the new content, but sometimes they ignore it. The search engines don't handle `Meta` refreshes reliably, and that's one reason to avoid using them in your Web site.

Another reason to steer clear of `Meta` refreshes is that they look suspicious to the search engines. Because `Meta` refreshes can be used to show different content to a search engine than to a user, they have traditionally been used by *spam sites* (Web sites that intentionally deceive search engines about their real content). In one case, a site put up pages about baby blankets, but it was just a cover for a pornography site. The search engines didn't see the porn content because the `Meta` refreshes delayed the change. A grandmother searching for baby blankets discovered the truth and reported the site. The search engine's spam team went to work, and soon that site was banned from the index. (For more about spam, please see Book I, Chapter 6.)

Many sites use `Meta` refreshes for legitimate reasons, as well. For example, the *Los Angeles Times* (`www.latimes.com/`) uses a `Meta` refresh to refresh their front page every 600 seconds (10 minutes). They do this to make sure online readers always see the most up-to-date news because their stories change frequently. However, search engine spiders won't stay on the page for 10 minutes to read the new content. The spider only sees what's on the page at the outset.

With a typical site (less well known than the *L.A. Times*), you don't want the search engines to miss reading all of your rich content, so you can have the maximum chance of ranking in search results. Even worse, using a `Meta` refresh may get your site flagged as suspected spam. Search engines especially suspect sites that use a `Meta` refresh to fetch another page. Bottom line: if you need to redirect users and search engines to a new URL for a page, do it with a 301 redirect.

JavaScript redirects

The search engines have a hard time following and indexing your pages properly if you program a redirect using *JavaScript* (a scripting language used to add functionality to Web sites). JavaScript redirects give you the ability to customize the user experience, so the benefit is all on the usability end of the spectrum. (*Usability* refers to the user-friendliness of the site, which in this case runs counter to search engine-friendliness.) A JavaScript redirect is also not recommended from an SEO perspective. The problem is that search engines cannot execute JavaScript and therefore cannot follow the redirect to a new page.

With JavaScript, you can redirect users to particular versions of a page based on settings that can be detected by JavaScript. You can detect the user's browser type, Flash capability, cookies settings, and so forth. So you could deliver a page that has Flash animations to users that have the Flash plug-in installed, but show a non-Flash-enhanced page to others — in other words, personalize it somewhat. That's a useful application, but sites can also use JavaScript deceptively to create a "bait-and-switch" type of effect.

The search engines usually flag instances of JavaScript redirects for human review. Flagged sites are then dependent on the discretion of the human reviewer, who determines if the redirect benefits the user — in which case it's usually be allowed — or is a tactic for delivering a different page to a spider than a user — in which case the site could be penalized for spam (that is, thrown out of the index, or buried way down in the results page). And because the search engines continuously improve their spam-detection efforts, you want to make sure to keep your Web site practices in the safe harbor.

We recommend that you *never* implement JavaScript redirects, except for personalization. Even if you're not doing something wrong, you don't want to attract negative attention from the search engines. It's similar to driving when there's a police car present. You watch your speedometer to make sure you don't go over the speed limit even a little because that could catch the officer's attention. And if the police officer notices you, she might also notice that you're not wearing a seatbelt, or that your right taillight is out. You're better off just not attracting notice in the first place.

Reconciling Your WWW and Non-WWW URLs

How can you use redirects on a practical level? One common situation that's solved by a 301 redirect is how to reconcile your www and non-www domains.

If you're like most Web site owners today, you probably have two versions of your site URL, one with and one without the "www." in front of the domain name, such as

```
www.yourdomain.com
yourdomain.com
```

Having both versions is recommended because users have a tendency to type either of the above versions into their browser, and you want to receive all of that traffic. However, because these are treated as two different Web sites by search engines, you have to make it clear to them which one is the main, or *canonical*, site. Otherwise, you could end up competing against yourself for search engine rankings.

Unfortunately, many Web sites don't handle the dual-version URL issue correctly. They end up with pages from both the www and the non-www URL versions indexed by the search engines. This is a problem because if both the www and non-www versions of a URL are indexed, your pages look like duplicates in the index — this causes the search engines to filter some of your pages out of their search results. Similarly, if there are links pointing to both versions (either internal links on your own site or external links originating on other Web sites), your link equity is diluted because it's split between the two URLs. (*Link equity* refers to the value of all your incoming links, which search engines use to determine your page's authority and expertise on its subject matter.)

We always recommend that sites 301 redirect the non-www version of any URL on its site to the www version. Doing so prevents duplicate content from being indexed and also protects your link equity from being diluted.

It doesn't matter which way you go — you could point the www version to the non-www version just as effectively as you could point the non-www version to the URL starting with www. However, it's more usual to make your www version the main site.

To ensure that `www.yourdomain.com` is indexed as your canonical site, you need to do one of two things. The first and best way to make sure your site is indexed the way you want it to be is to set up a 301 redirect (permanent redirects, not any other kind) that points the entire `yourdomain.com` site to `www.yourdomain.com`. This ensures that any kind of spider or browser that comes to your site gets the version of the domain that you want them to see, with no mistakes. (Remember, you can find all the nitty-gritty details on doing this in Chapter 4.)

Specify your canonical pages

In February 2009, a rare collaboration by Google, Yahoo!, and Microsoft resulted in a new Head section tag called `link rel=canonical`. If you have a single Web site domain that has identical or nearly identical pages that have different URLs (such as pages with session ids or tracking codes), there's now a way you can specify which page you prefer to have indexed and treated as the original.

Identical but separate pages within a site can be the result of poor site design, but more often than not it's the result of a content management system (CMS) spitting out long URL strings full of parameters, categories, or session IDs. This causes search engines to find lots of different URLs that all contain the same page content. That kind of duplicate content is bad for your search engine optimization.

The big three search engines say that this new feature is not something that should take the place of proper redirects or any of the other best practices we cover for avoiding duplicate content (in Book V, Chapter 4, for example). However, if your site has duplicate content issues that you cannot solve in one of the preferred ways, you should use this to hint to the engines which page they should treat as the original.

You add `link rel=canonical` tags to your HTML pages to tell the search engines which of your pages to consider the canonical versions, and which ones to consider duplicates. You could do this for every instance of duplicate content on your site. Here's how:

Say that your preferred (canonical) page for Ford Mustang hubcaps is

```
http://www.classic
    cars.com/product.
    php?item=MustangHubcaps
```

But your CMS sometimes creates URLs like these for the same page:

```
http://www.classiccars.com/
    product.php?item=MustangHub
    caps&category=accessories
http://www.classiccars.com/
    product.php?item=MustangHub
    caps&trackingid=1234&session
    id=5678
```

You can now add the following tag inside the Head section of these duplicate content URLs, to tell the search engines where to find the canonical version of that page:

```
<link rel="canonical"
    href="http://www.classic
    cars.com/product.
    php?item=MustangHubcaps" />
```

Remember that this only works for pages *within* the same domain, but it includes subdomains. So it works for *yourdomain*.com and www.*yourdomain*.com, but you can't use this feature to clarify things between *your domain*.com and *otherdomain*.com.

For more info on using this tag, you can read about it in Google's blog post (`http://googlewebmaster central.blogspot.com/2009/02/ specify-your-canonical. html`); Yahoo!'s version (`http:// ysearchblog.com/2009/02/12/ fighting-duplication-adding- more-arrows-to-your-quiver/`); or Microsoft's announcement (`http:// blogs.msdn.com/webmaster/ archive/2009/02/12/partnering- to-help-solve-duplicate- content-issues.aspx`).

However, if you don't have the ability to

set up 301 redirects and you don't want to dump your Web host, you have another option. You can submit www.*yourdomain*.com to Google as your preferred domain. (This works for Google only, so you might still have issues with Yahoo! and Microsoft Live Search.) Google allows you to submit your preferred domain to them in their Webmaster Tools. This allows you to decide which versions of your URLs you want indexed, which can help prevent any potential problems from the non-www issue. Please see www.google.com/support/webmasters/bin/answer.py?answer=44231 for more information about this particular feature.

Chapter 4: Implementing 301 Redirects

In This Chapter

✔ Redirecting a page to a new URL

✔ Creating 301 redirects on an Apache server

✔ Implementing 301 redirects in Microsoft IIS

✔ Setting up 301 redirects in ISAPI_Rewrite

✔ Accomplishing 301 redirects using header inserts

✔ Moving a site to a new host

*R*edirects are HTML or server commands that automatically forward incoming links and users from one page's URL to another URL, which is an extremely useful Web site-maintenance technique.

Of the four types of redirects we covered in the previous chapter (301, 302, `Meta` Refresh, and JavaScript redirect), only the 301 redirect passes the test for search engine optimization (SEO) friendliness. In this chapter, we cover how to set up 301 redirects and show you some specific situations that call for them. Because a lot of this explanation involves step-by-step instructions, we give a set of instructions for each server. Your *server* is the software that runs your Web site. The server receives and "serves up" user requests to display pages or perform other site tasks.

If you aren't sure what type of server your site runs on, ask your Webmaster or your *hosting provider* (the service where your Web site is physically hosted).

Getting the Details on How 301 Redirects Work

The 301 redirect tells the search engine that the page at location A has permanently moved to location B. It says that one URL is forever replaced by another URL, like `www.shoe-site.com/oldpage.htm` has moved to `www.shoe-site.com/newpage.htm`, which is a very clear-cut, unambiguous message. The search engine responds by doing three things:

1. Dropping the now defunct page from its *index* (database of Web pages from which the search engine pulls search results).

   This ensures that the old page won't be included in search engine results pages (SERPs).

2. Including the new page in the index, so that it's available for searching.

3. Transferring the old page's link equity to the new URL.

   (*Link equity* refers to the value of all incoming links to a page, which the search engines use to determine a Web page's authority and expertise in its subject.)

In the next few pages, you find instructions for creating 301 redirects on the following types of servers:

✦ Apache server

✦ Microsoft IIS server

✦ ISAPI_Rewrite for the Microsoft IIS server

Don't forget to test. After you've put your redirect in place, be sure to test to make sure you did it properly. Just type the old URL into your browser's address bar and press Enter. If you've implemented your 301s correctly, you'll immediately see the new page (and the new page's URL in your address bar).

When setting up redirects, you must be careful. The server programs require a strict syntax to be followed, similar to a programming language. If you change a server configuration file (such as .htaccess) and your changes are just one character off, it can literally take your site offline until the mistake is corrected. Reading this book alone cannot prepare you to work at the server level. Make sure that whoever makes the types of modifications shown in this chapter really knows what they're doing.

Implementing a 301 Redirect in Apache .htaccess Files

Redirecting pages or sites on an Apache Web server is very easy. You do it by modifying a file on your Web site called the .htaccess file (note that the actual file name begins with a period.) The *.htaccess file* is a control file that allows server configuration changes on a per-directory basis. The file controls that directory and all of the subdirectories contained within it. Usually, this file is placed in the root folder of your Web site. It is very important that when you edit Apache files that your editor saves the file in UNIX format or errors may occur.

The .htaccess file should be set up by default, but if your root folder doesn't contain the file, have someone who understands how to build an .htaccess file create it. Be careful here. Some upload (FTP) programs hide the .htaccess. You don't want to overwrite an existing .htaccess with your update.

Here's an example of a .htaccess file for a site that moves from ASP to PHP and redirects the non-www version to www (note that where it says *mydomain*, you should put in your own domain):

```
# BEGIN
  <IfModule mod_rewrite.c>
  RewriteEngine On
  RewriteCond %{HTTP_HOST} !^www\.mydomain\.com$
  RewriteRule ^(.*) http://www.mydomain.com/$1 [R=301,L]
  RedirectMatch 301 (.*)\.asp$ http://www.mydomain.com$1.php
  </IfModule>
  # END
```

Before you start, you should make sure that you can access your .htaccess file. If you have access to your server so that you can upload and modify files, you should have no problem. (With the Apache server, modifying the .htaccess file does not require administrator-level access rights.) If you cannot access files in your Web folders, call your hosting provider and request this ability (or contact the person who can access these files for you).

To edit the .htaccess file to redirect page(s) on your Web site, you must first know the URL(s) of each Web page/site you want to redirect, and the URL(s) of the new page/site where each will be redirected to. Then follow these steps:

1. **Log on to your Web site. In the root Web folder, locate the file called .htaccess.**

If there is no .htaccess file present, you need to create one. Again, be careful that there really is no .htaccess present and that you aren't overwriting one.

.htaccess is a hidden file, so you need to enable your FTP program to view hidden files to be able to see it.

2. **Open the .htaccess file using a text editor such as Notepad.**

A code editor like Adobe Dreamweaver also handles the .htaccess file perfectly, because it opens it as text, but a simple text editor also does the job.

3. **Edit the file as needed, being careful to follow the exact syntax required. (See the examples in the following sections.)**

To add a 301 redirect to a specific page in Apache

Add a line to the .htaccess file that tells the server what to do. The two ways to do this follow, and they both accomplish the same thing. (Note: You would substitute your own file URLs and *domain name* (the root part of your site's URL) when using the examples given here.)

```
RedirectPermanent /old-file.html http://www.mydomain.com/
   new-file.html
```

or:

```
Redirect 301 /old-file.html http://www.mydomain.com/new-
   file.html
```

To 301 redirect an entire domain in Apache

To redirect an entire domain, you would add a line to the .htaccess file that gives the server your instructions. A redirection from one domain to another would be written like this:

```
RedirectPermanent / http://www.new-domain.com/
```

To break these down, each 301 redirect command contains three parts:

✦ The first part tells the server what to do, and you can type this in two ways, either `RedirectPermanent` or `Redirect 301`.

✦ The second part shows the old file's *relative path* (its file location in relation to the current directory where the .htaccess file is located). If your .htaccess file is in your root Web directory, you can use the file's URL without the domain name, such as `/old-file.html`.

✦ The third section is the *full path* to the new file. Starting with the `http://`, you want to include the complete URL (such as `http://www.mydomain.com/new-file.html`).

After you've inserted the commands to 301 to redirect your pages, you need to put a blank line at the end of the file. Your server reads the .htaccess file line by line, so you have to include an endline character at some point to let the server know you're finished.

Implementing a 301 Redirect on a Microsoft IIS Server

Whereas an Apache server is comparatively easy to deal with, IIS is much more complex. Our recommendation would be to consult with your ISP to validate all IIS changes before you make them live. If your Web site resides on a Microsoft IIS server, you must have administrator-level access rights in order to set up a 301 redirect. You can add greater flexibility to your IIS server by installing a plug-in called ISAPI_Rewrite. With this plug-in, you can access your Web files without needing administrator access rights to the server. (We recommend that you request the ISAPI_Rewrite for your IIS server because with it you can work with the files hands-on, rather than relying on a third-party to make the changes you need.)

To redirect page(s) on your Web site, you must first know the URL(s) of each Web page/site you want to redirect, and the URL(s) of the new page/site where each will be directed to. Then follow these steps depending on which version of IIS you're running.

To 301 redirect pages in IIS 5.0 and 6.0

To redirect pages in these versions of IIS, do the following:

1. **Start the Internet Services Manager (Start⇨Programs⇨Administrative Tools⇨Internet Information Services Manager) and select the Web site you want to redirect from.**

2. **Right-click on the file or folder you wish to redirect and choose Properties.**

3. **Click the Home Directory tab and select the option at the top labeled A Redirection to a URL.**

4. **Enter the full URL of the page/site you're redirecting to.**

5. **Make sure A Permanent Redirection for This Resource and The Exact URL Entered Above are selected.**

6. **Click Apply.**

You may also want to pass a *control variable* to the new URL (the one you're redirecting to), which is a code that communicates additional instructions to the server. Control variables can make your job a lot easier, giving you shortcuts for applying changes. Table 4-1 shows the various options.

**Book VII
Chapter 4**

Implementing 301
Redirects

	Table 4-1	**Control Variable Options for a Microsoft IIS Server (Version 5.0 or 6.0)**	
Variable	*Function Function*	*Example*	
$P	Passes parameters that were passed to the URL to the new URL	If the request contains parameters such as www.mydomain.com/mypage.asp?Param1=1, $P would represent all the values after the question mark in the URL (for example, $P would equal Param1=1).	
$Q	Passes the parameters including the question mark	This is identical to $P but includes the question mark (so $P would equal ?Param1=1).	
$S	Passes the matching suffix of the URL to the new URL	If the request is for www.mydomain.com/mydir/mypage.asp, $S represents /mypage.asp. If the request was for www.mydomain.com/mydir, the value of $S would be /mydir.	
$V	Removes the server name from the original request	If the request is for www.mydomain.com/mydir/mypage.asp, $V would contain everything after the server name (such as /mydir/mypage.asp).	
*	Wildcard symbol used to take the place of any character	If you want to redirect all requests for HTML pages to a single .asp page, you could do so using *;*.htm;myasp.asp.	

To 301 redirect an entire domain in IIS 5.0 and 6.0

When redirecting an entire domain, the control variable $V is the most useful. If you're preserving the directory structures and page names completely and only want to change the domain name, you can simply type the new URL (such as the one below) with the variable in the Redirect to text box:

```
http://www.new-domain.com$V
```

Putting the $V control variable at the end of the new site URL redirects all directories and pages from the old site to the new one, as long as they have not changed. For example, www.oldsite.com/directory1/page1.html would redirect to www.newsite.com/directory1/page1.html. For comparison, without the $V variable, you would only redirect the home page. When you have pages that rank well with the search engines in your site, it's especially helpful to redirect those pages using these variables as well.

How to move a site to a new host

Occasionally you may need to change hosting providers or move your site to a new IP address. Your domain name stays the same, but your new *IP address* (the numeric code that identifies the logical address where your site resides on the Web) must be communicated to the Internet at large. There can be a delay before all computers see your new location, because of the way DNS servers *cache* (store) domain information. (A *Domain Name System (DNS) server* is an authoritative database that publishes information about the various domains assigned to it, which the rest of the Internet can see.)

The following procedure helps to minimize the downtime and confusion your site may experience while your new DNS information is being propagated. Refer to the following figure and follow the path numbers as you read the corresponding numbered steps.

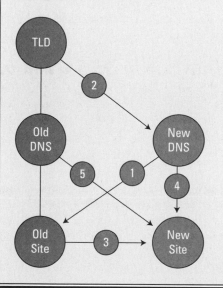

To move a site to a new hosting provider, do the following:

1. Modify the DNS on your new host to point to your existing (old host) site first. Don't skip this important first step.

2. Change the *TLD* (top level domain) information at your *domain registrar* (the company where you registered your domain name) to point to your new site DNS. Your old site should still show by either IP or domain name. This step starts propagating your new DNS information to DNS servers worldwide.

   Although the actual length of time varies depending on when each server next grabs its update, it's a safe bet that the whole process will take up to 72 hours to complete. Therefore, you shouldn't proceed with the next steps until waiting about four days.

3. Copy your existing site to your new site, and then validate that all files have transferred and that the links work.

4. After waiting the four days for your new DNS information to be propagated, point your new DNS to your new site.

5. Check to confirm that your old site's mailboxes have been emptied before you change any DNS information. After this DNS change occurs, you won't be able to retrieve your old mail.

6. After everything has been validated, point the old DNS to your new site. (This is for safety, just in case you run into a propagation problem.)

To implement a 301 redirect in IIS 7.0

This is how to implement a 301 redirect within a Microsoft IIS 7.0 server. Note that there are many cases where it would be more appropriate to *rewrite* a URL, which means changing just the displayed URL, rather than sending a user to a new page. (We talk about rewrites in the next chapter.)

You would set up a redirect in IIS 7.0 when you physically move files or directories, or when you need to relocate your physical site contents from one domain to another. In order to set up a 301 redirect on a Microsoft IIS server version 7.0, you must have administrator access to the Internet Information Services (IIS) Manager. In order for you to have this access, your site must use a *dedicated* server (meaning that yours is the only site on the server) and you must have administrator-level access rights.

If those preparation issues are taken care of, you're ready to set up your 301 redirect:

1. **Open the Internet Services Manager (Start⇨Programs⇨Administrative Tools⇨Internet Information Services (IIS) Manager).**

2. **In the left column, select the site, directory, or page that you want to redirect from.**

3. **Next, using the Features View in the main window, locate the icon labeled HTTP Redirect and double-click it.**

4. **Check the box labeled Redirect Requests to This Destination and type in the URL where you want to redirect to.**

    These examples show the proper syntax for different types of destinations:

    Redirecting to a single page:
    www.*mydomain*.com/*newpage*.htm

    Redirecting to a directory:
    www.*mydomain*.com/*newdirectory*

    Redirecting to a domain:
    www.*mydomain*.com/

5. **If you're keeping the directory structures and page names the same, make sure the two check boxes under Redirect Options remain unchecked:**

    Redirect All Requests to Exact Destination: You would only check this option if you wanted every file that's within the directory or domain you're redirecting from to be rerouted to a single page.

    Only Redirect Requests to Content in This Directory: You would check this option if you wanted to redirect only the files located in the selected directory, but not redirect any subdirectories.

6. **For the Status Code, choose Permanent (301).**

7. **From the menu in the right-hand column, choose Apply.**

Implementing a 301 redirect with ISAPI_Rewrite on an IIS server

The ISAPI_Rewrite plug-in can make your life much easier if your site runs on a Microsoft IIS server. It allows you to upload, download, and modify your Web site files yourself, without having to have administrator access to the server. It also lets you handle 301 redirects without having to get your hosting provider involved.

You can obtain ISAPI_Rewrite from a number of software vendors, but here are the ones we recommend you check out:

✦ **Helicon Tech:** The ISAPI_Rewrite plug-in from Helicon Tech (`www.isapi rewrite.com/`) is excellent; this is the one we usually use in-house. They have a free and a paid version. If you are on a shared hosting server, you need the paid version to apply the changes to only your site as the free version makes changes globally (to all sites on the Web server). This software works with IIS versions 5.0, 6.0, and 7.0.

✦ **Microsoft:** If you're using IIS version 7.0, which ships with Microsoft Server 2008, you can use the Helicon Tech tool or the Microsoft URL Rewrite Module, which can be downloaded and installed into IIS 7.0. The download is available in two versions, so download the appropriate one for your server, either 32-bit (`www.iis.net/downloads/default.aspx?tabid=34&g=6&i=1691`) or 64-bit (`www.iis.net/downloads/default.aspx?tabid=34&g=6&i=1692`). Two exciting features of this product are its ability to import Apache .htaccess files and convert them into the rule set for IIS, and its helpful interface for writing rules that's an improvement over simply editing configuration files.

Because there are different flavors of the ISAPI_Rewrite software, your actual code syntax may be different. You need to follow the specific rules for your software. However, for your reference, we give you two samples of redirects created in ISAPI_Rewrite in the next two sections.

To 301 redirect an old page to a new page in ISAPI_Rewrite

Follow these steps:

1. **Open the file named httpd.ini located at the root of your Web site.**

2. **Type the code into the file, following this example but substituting your own *oldpage* filename and *newpage* URL:**

```
RewriteRule /oldpage.htm http://www.mydomain.com/
    newpage.htm [I,O,RP,L]
```

To 301 redirect a non-www domain to the www domain in ISAPI_Rewrite

Follow these steps:

1. **Open the file named httpd.ini located at the root of the non-www version of your Web site (the site you're redirecting from).**

2. **Type the appropriate code into the file, following this example, which is for redirecting http://domain.com to www.domain.com (be sure to substitute your domain name):**

```
RewriteCond Host: ^mydomain\.com
RewriteRule (.*) http\://www\.mydomain\.com$1 [I,RP]
```

Using Header Inserts as an Alternate Way to Redirect a Page

If you're just skimming through this chapter because you don't have access to your server configuration files (the .htaccess file on Apache, or your Windows IIS Manager), fear not! We have another solution that enables you to redirect Web pages. It's a bit more tedious, but it works.

An alternative way to implement 301 redirects is by adding code directly into the page you want to redirect. Yes, it means opening and modifying each page individually, but sometimes that kind of granular control is a good thing — especially if you only need to redirect a few pages. Called a *header insert*, this method involves placing a small amount of server code into the HTML of each page you want to permanently redirect to another URL.

Most Web programming languages allow you to add a header insert on a page. Note that all of these languages are *server-side*, meaning that they're compiled or interpreted on the server into a page, and then the compiled version is sent back to the user's browser. This type of 301 redirect involves modifying the *response header* information on a page (extra information that's passed from the server to the browser, which helps the browser display the page properly but which is not visible to users). So you must insert the code at the very top of your page's HTML code (on line #1) for the 301 to work. This ensures that the server sees this code first before sending the page back to the user.

For your reference, we've compiled a list of the most common programming languages and given sample code for each. Note that the examples are case-sensitive, so you want to follow their use of uppercase and lowercase characters exactly. Based on which programming language your Web site uses, you can refer to the correct example in the upcoming sections to see a header insert that accomplishes a 301 redirect in your programming language.

PHP 301 redirect

The PHP scripting language is widely used for creating Web pages. (PHP originally stood for Personal Home Page, but it's grown a lot since its infancy in the mid-1990s.) Some attributes of PHP are

✦ Usually used with Apache Web servers, but can also work with IIS.

✦ Has really good community support and several plug-ins/frameworks that make it pretty easy to use.

✦ Is fairly fast.

Here's the sample 301 redirect code for PHP:

```
<?php
header("HTTP/1.1 301 Moved Permanently");
header("Location: http://www.mydomain.com/newpage.php");
exit();
?>
```

ASP 301 redirect

ASP stands for Active Server Pages, which is Microsoft's original server-side script environment. Developed to run with their Internet Information Server (IIS) version 3.0 Web server software, it's admittedly an old program, but many Web sites still use it. (Note that Microsoft is currently vending IIS version 7.0.) Some attributes of ASP include

✦ Works with IIS servers. With the advent of ASP.NET development, most ASP scripts are being upgraded to ASP.NET.

✦ Is backed by Microsoft, so the support is pretty good. There are a lot of good examples and scripts to use and customize.

✦ Is fairly fast.

Here is sample 301 redirect code for ASP:

```
<%
Response.Status = "301 Moved Permanently"
Response.AddHeader "Location", "http://www.mydomain.com/
    newpage.asp"
%>
```

ASP.NET 301 redirect

ASP.NET is a free Web site-building technology available from Microsoft. Some attributes of ASP .NET are

✦ Almost always used with IIS servers. This technology also works with Apache servers that have the MONO extension installed.

✦ Has great support from Microsoft.

✦ Overall, the speed is good. The initial request may take a little longer while the application puts everything together, but after that's done, it's fast.

The following sample 301 redirect code for ASP.NET must be inserted in the .aspx file:

```
<script runat="server">
private void Page_Load(object sender, System.EventArgs e)
{
Response.Status = "301 Moved Permanently";
Response.AddHeader("Location","http://www.mydomain.com/
    newpage.aspx");
}
</script>
```

JSP 301 redirect

JSP stands for JavaServer Pages, which is a Java-based Web development technology. Here are some attributes of JSP:

✦ Usually used on the Apache Tomcat Web server.

✦ Supported by Sun and an open source community. It has excellent documentation.

✦ The speed is good, with the initial request taking a little longer while the application puts everything together.

Here is some sample code for a 301 redirect on JSP:

```
<%
response.setStatus(301);
response.setHeader("Location","http://www.mydomain.com/
    newpage.jsp");
response.setHeader("Connection","close");
%>
```

ColdFusion 301 redirect

Now an Adobe product, ColdFusion is another programming language frequently used for Web pages. Some attributes of ColdFusion are

✦ Usually hosted through a Microsoft IIS Web server, but can also be run in Apache.

✦ Made and supported by Adobe. The documentation is adequate.

✦ The speed is okay, but not great.

ColdFusion 8 or later versions require 301 redirects to be written like this:

```
<cflocation url="http://www.mydomain.com/newpage.cfm"
    addToken="no" statusCode="301">
```

ColdFusion 7 or earlier versions require 301 redirects to be written like this:

```
<cfheader statuscode="301" statusnext="Moved Permanently">
<cfheader name="Location" value="http://www.mydomain.com/
    newpage.cfm">
```

CGI Perl 301 redirect

Some Web sites are built using CGI (Common Gateway Interface) scripting in the Perl programming language. Some attributes of this are

✦ Perl can be run on anything, but is usually run through an Apache Web server.

✦ Perl has been around for a very long time, which makes finding examples and documentation easy. There are a lot of modules that you can use to help with specific tasks.

✦ The speed isn't as good as some of the other, newer languages, but it still delivers fast enough Web responses.

Here is sample 301 redirect code for CGI Perl:

```
$q = new CGI;
print $q->redirect( -uri =>

 "http://www.mydomain.com/newpage.cgi", -nph => 1, -status =>
    301);
```

Ruby on Rails 301 redirect

This Web development tool is specifically designed for building database-backed Web applications. Attributes of Ruby on Rails include

✦ Fast application development, can run through the IIS and Apache Web servers, but requires a back-end server like Mongrel as well.

✦ Ruby on Rails is a newer language. The documentation and community support are good.

✦ The speed is not as good as some other scripting languages.

Here is sample 301 redirect code for Ruby on Rails:

```
headers["Status"] = "301 Moved Permanently"
redirect_to "http://www.mydomain.com/newpage/"
```

Chapter 5: Watching Your Backend: Content Management System Troubles

In This Chapter

✔ Meeting the content management system (CMS)

✔ Understanding why CMS-generated pages aren't search engine-friendly

✔ Rewriting URLs to eliminate dynamic URLs and session IDs

✔ Selecting a good CMS

✔ Making your CMS work with your search engine optimization (SEO) efforts

✔ Using Yahoo! Merchant Solutions effectively

*B*ehind every Web page viewed in a browser is a host of technologies and services working to make the star performers look good: the *backend*. Just as a Hollywood blockbuster has a crew of people supporting the actors, your Web site has servers, code, shopping carts, and, most importantly, your content management system that all must perform at their best to turn out a superior experience for your customers. A Web *content management system (CMS)* is a software program that helps simplify Web site creation. A CMS uses a database (such as your database of products, if you have a store), and publishes Web pages in an orderly, consistent fashion. It pulls information from your database and builds pages *dynamically*. This means the pages don't actually exist until someone asks for them. If you have 10,000 products, you don't want to build 10,000 individual pages by hand. Instead, you use a CMS to build them dynamically on the fly.

In this chapter, you discover the problems inherent in using a CMS to build your Web site. For all of their advantages, content management systems can sabotage your search engine optimization (SEO) efforts. You also discover some technical solutions that can help you overcome these CMS issues, such as rewriting URLs to have names that are more search engine-friendly. We also give you tips for picking a good CMS, if you must have one, and how to modify its settings to work better for SEO. Last, for those of you who use the Yahoo! Store module, we tackle how to optimize those product pages.

Avoiding SEO Problems Caused by Content Management Systems

Content management systems seem like a Web site owner's best friend. A CMS gets a Web site operational fast and keeps it running smoothly. It can manage data, image files, audio files, documents, and other types of content and put them together into Web pages. They create the pages based on *templates*, which are standard layouts that you design, so that your Web site has a consistent and cohesive look. Large sites managing thousands of items use them because the CMS keeps everything organized and systematic. Small sites benefit because with a CMS, they don't even have to know *HTML* (HyperText Markup Language, the predominant markup language used on the Web): The CMS can do the technical work for them.

There is a catch, however. With automation comes a loss of control. When an airline pilot puts his plane on autopilot, the computer takes over completely and flies the plane according to a set course, adjusting things like altitude and speed based on its preprogrammed settings. If the plane needs to land unexpectedly, the pilot first has to take it out of autopilot mode. Otherwise, the autopilot stubbornly keeps the plane on its predetermined course.

Similarly, a CMS can be pretty inflexible when it comes to allowing you to make changes. And in order to optimize your Web site for the search engines, you must be able to customize your pages down to the smallest detail.

Understanding why dynamically generated pages can be friend or foe

If you have a store with several thousand products for sale, you don't want to create a page for each item by hand. Instead, you're going to use a CMS to assemble Web pages with product descriptions, pictures, prices, and other content pulled directly out of your product database. These dynamic pages look unique to the end user, but behind the scenes, they're usually not.

For your pages to rank well in search engines, they must be unique. Search engines want to give their users a selection of relevant results. The search engine isn't doing a very good job if half of the first 10 search results all point to the same content. Instead, search engines try to give users a choice by offering results that each deal uniquely with the *keywords* (the word or phrase the user searched for). So the search engines are always on the lookout for *duplicate content* (Web pages containing some or all of the same text). When they identify duplicate content, they keep what they think is the most authoritative version and throw out the rest. Because of this, pages that are too similar run the risk of being excluded from Search Engine Results Pages (SERPs) altogether.

CMSs typically create all kinds of duplicate content problems. By default, they often build *non-targeted content*, or generic text that isn't customized for your various subject themes and keywords. You want to make sure *each and every* of your Web pages has *unique* text for all parts of your Web pages, including

✦ **Title tags:** The `Title` *tag* is part of the HTML code behind each Web page, and the search engines pay a lot of attention to it. The `Title` tag usually gets displayed as the bold heading in a SERP result, so it should specifically contain that page's keywords.

CMSs often put the same `Title` tag on every page. It might be the company name, the *domain name* (the root part of the Web site URL, such as `wiley.com`), or the company name plus a few keywords — but it's applied as one-size-fits-all.

✦ **Meta tags:** Your `Meta` description and `Meta` keywords HTML tags also need to be different on every page. The `Meta` description is often what shows in your SERP result as the two-line description. The `Meta` keywords tag needs to contain the keywords that are specific to that page. Out of the box, your CMS can't be trusted to build these `Meta` tags in an SEO-friendly way.

✦ **Headings:** Your `H#` heading tags are HTML-style codes applied to your page's headings and subheadings to make them stand out. The search engines look at these heading tags as clues to what a page's main points are. They need to be keyword-rich and unique.

CMSs often create heading tags that are generic (such as "Features Overview" or "More Details"), rather than specific and full of your targeted keywords.

Dealing with dynamic URLs and session IDs

Content management systems create pages that search engines may consider duplicates in another way, and that's through dynamic *URLs* (the Web address of a page, usually starting with `http://`).

CMSs build the URL string dynamically for every page request. Dynamic URLs created by a CMS often contain *variables* (characters that vary). When variables are added to the end of a URL, it forms a new URL. Search engines think each URL is a distinct page, which causes duplicate content issues when the same content shows up under many different URLs.

Here are two common types of variables that CMSs often add to URLs, but there are many others:

✦ **Session IDs:** Many CMSs add a session ID code to the end of URLs as a user travels through the site. The purpose is to track the user's *session* (the time period the user has been active on the Web site), but appending the session ID to the URL is a really bad way to pass it from page to page. It causes every view of every page to have a different URL.

✦ **Categories:** Products can be classified in many ways. For instance, a shoe store online could let users search by style, color, size, price, and so forth. Giving users many different paths to get to the same pair of shoes is good for your business and your users, but your CMS needs to handle it correctly. Often what happens instead is that the same product page ends up displaying under multiple URLs. For example, the two following URLs would both point to the same content, but the URLs differ because the CMS put the parameters for color and brand in a different order based on the user's selection path:

```
www.shoe-site.com/pumps.asp?color=red&brand=myers
www.shoe-site.com/pumps.asp?brand=myers&color=red
```

There are many good reasons not to like dynamic URLs:

✦ **They can cause duplicate content.** As we mentioned, you can end up with different URLs having the same page content because their parameters vary.

✦ **They aren't user-friendly.** Dynamic URLs usually include *query strings*, which are the parts of a URL that pass data to a page. Query strings aren't readable because they contain symbols (such as ?, &, and +) as well as codes, session IDs, and so on. They look messy, or worse, intimidating, to your human visitors.

✦ **They're long.** Dynamic URLs with query strings end up being really long and cumbersome. These URLs are impossible to remember and difficult to type. Studies have shown that long URLs on search results pages aren't clicked as often as shorter, understandable URLs, so your long URLs could actually be driving business away from your site.

✦ **Search engines don't like them.** To ensure that your site is easy to crawl and index, you should prefer *static URLs* (URLs that don't change). If a URL has a long string of parameters, the spider may just stop right there and not even crawl the page. (Note: The search engines continue to improve their techniques, and they may someday overcome this difficulty. However, making the search engine spider's job as easy as possible is always the safest course.)

✦ **They're bad for your SEO.** If the search engines don't crawl your page, it won't end up in their *index* (database of Web pages that search engines maintain), which means that searchers won't be able to find it.

The best condition for search engine optimization is to *have one static URL per unique page*. Where the page content remains unchanged, there should be no change to the URL. You don't want to put any variables directly into your URL strings except for ones that actually correspond with changed page content. You need unique content for every URL.

Now that we've made a case against the use of dynamic URLs, we want to explain how you can compensate for them on your Web site.

Here are some solutions for dynamic URLs:

✦ **Remove session IDs:** If your site passes session IDs through the URL string, you should correct your CMS or server application so that it no longer does this (using cookies or some other technology). If that's not possible, consider using "user agent sniffing" to detect search engine spiders or you can try the link `rel=canonical` tag discussed at the end of the previous chapter. When the page detects a search engine spider, the exact same content could be displayed, but in a parameter-free URL instead.

✦ **Control the parameter order:** Make sure your CMS allows for ordering logic. You need to specify the sequence of parameters in URLs. One product could fall into many different categories on your Web site, but no matter how the user navigates to find it, that unique product should have only one page at only one URL address.

✦ **Limit the number of parameters:** If possible, keep the number of parameters being passed to a minimum. If you can limit it to one parameter in a URL, the search engines should be able to spider your pages and users won't find them too intimidating. Here's a sample URL with one parameter:

> `http://www.yourdomain.com/product.cfm?product_id=xyz`

✦ **Rewrite the URLs:** If your CMS simply won't cooperate and insists on building URLs that are long and ugly, you can go over its head and rewrite the URLs at the *Web server* (the software application that runs your Web site, receiving each user request and "serving" back the requested pages to the user's browser) layer.

Rewriting URLs

At the server layer, you can rewrite those complex URLs as clean, concise, static-looking URLs. Rewriting doesn't change the name of a physical file on your Web server or create new directories that don't physically exist. But rewriting changes the page's URL on the *server layer* (the viewable layer, or how the URL appears to the user and to search engines) and is visible on the *presentation layer*. So for example, if you have a shoe Web site and your CMS spits out product pages with long, parameter-laden URLs like this:

```
http://www.shoe-site.com/product.cfm?product_id=1234&line=wom
    ens&style=pumps&color=navyblue&size=7
```

You could rewrite them to something simpler like this:

```
http://www.shoe-site.com/womens/pumps/productname.cfm
```

Notice how much more readable the rewritten URL is. This directory structure shown is just an example, but it illustrates how potentially you can have the domain name, directories, and the filename give information about the Web page. In this case, not only have you gotten rid of the ugly query string, but also the directories "women's" and "pumps" are short, understandable labels. Anyone seeing this URL has a good idea what the Web page contains before they even click to view it. Presenting a concise, informative URL like this to search engines can increase your Web page's ranking — you've basically got the makings of a keyword phrase right in the URL. Additionally, presenting this type of short, readable URL to users can also make them more likely to click to your page from a SERP, which increases traffic to your site.

The process of rewriting a URL is often called a *mod_rewrite*, which stands for module rewrite because that's what it was originally called on the Apache server. Today, that term is used generally to refer to any URL rewrite, regardless of which server brand is involved. A mod_rewrite basically involves two parts:

✦ **RewriteRule:** You specify what rule, or action, you want the server to apply.

✦ **RewriteCond:** You also set up the conditions for when and how the rule should be applied.

When you rewrite Web pages to new URLs, you also need to *redirect* the old URLs if they are already indexed with the search engines. (A *redirect* is an HTML command that automatically forwards incoming links to a different page.) One SEO rule of thumb is that whenever you remove a page that has been indexed, you must redirect it with a 301 (permanent) redirect to another page. That way, the search engines and any visitors linking to the old page are automatically sent somewhere new. You also don't lose the *link equity* (value of the incoming links, which the search engines count towards your page's authority) from whatever links may exist on external Web sites pointing to your old URLs. (We cover redirects in Chapters 3 and 4 of this minibook, if you want more information.)

You can do the redirect as part of a rewrite just as a failsafe measure, or you can find out for sure whether a particular page has been indexed first. On Google, you can do a search such as [site:*yourdomain*.com], replacing *yourdomain* with your actual domain (and removing the brackets). This search shows you every page Google has indexed from your domain.

You need someone trained to work with your server software to create mod_rewrites. If you're determined to try it out yourself, we've listed a few Web sites below that you can look at for reference, based on your server:

✦ **Apache server:** The Apache Web site has full documentation on how to do mod_rewrites (`http://httpd.apache.org/docs/2.0/mod/mod_rewrite.html`).

✦ **Microsoft IIS server version 6.0 or earlier:** You need to install an ISAPI_Rewrite plug-in in order to rewrite your URLs. We recommend the one from Helicon Tech (`www.isapirewrite.com/`). From the same site, you can access extensive documentation that includes lots of examples.

✦ **Microsoft IIS server version 7.0:** You can install the Microsoft URL Rewrite Module that can be downloaded and installed into IIS 7.0 (`www.iis.net/downloads/default.aspx?tabid=34&g=6&i=1691`).

✦ **Extras:** We like the well-organized and helpful cheat sheets provided by `www.addedbytes.com/`. You can click the Cheat Sheets link at the top to see what's available (mostly for Apache).

Choosing the Right Content Management System

Despite the disadvantages of content management systems for your SEO campaign, you might have a site that simply can't do without them. For large stores, social media sites, forums, and other sites that have a large amount of page content that changes frequently, a CMS that can produce a site dynamically is a practical necessity. The CMS's advantages in automatically managing all of that changing content outweigh its disadvantages.

You do need to find a CMS that won't *impede* your SEO efforts. The main thing you want to find is a customizable system. You need to be able to change anything and everything on a per-page basis and not have your hands tied. SEO requires a lot of tweaking as you monitor each page's performance, your competitors' pages, the user experience on your site, and so forth. You must be able to modify a `Title` tag here, a `Meta` keywords tag there.

Here are some things to look for when you're shopping for a CMS:

✦ **Customizable look and feel:** This isn't SEO really, but it's important nevertheless — you want to be able to choose a "look" for your site that fits your subject matter and appeals to your audience. We've already discussed minimizing bounce rates and increasing conversions. If the design turns off your target visitors, or it looks like a bunch of other sites, you're sabotaged from the start. Be sure that you can modify the HTML *templates* (page layouts) and *CSS styles* (formatting of fonts and so on, using Cascading Style Sheets) so that you can ensure an appropriate look and feel that's consistent throughout your site.

✦ **Ability to externalize CSS and JavaScript:** Look for the ability to set up external JS and CSS files. You need to externalize it to keep your code nice and tidy and keep your pages running fast. Plus, if your CSS is externalized, you have to make changes to only one file instead of hand-editing every single page each and every time you want to tweak the look of your site.

✦ **Customizable directory structure:** You want to be able to control how your files and directories are organized. Ideally, when you categorize your Web site into subject themes (which we call *siloing* your Web site), this is reflected in the physical file structure as well as in your internal linking scheme. Deciding how to categorize your Web site is an SEO activity, based on how people search and what brings in the most traffic. You don't want your CMS dictating, for example, that your files should be organized by brand and then by product type, if your SEO research tells you that you'll get more search traffic organizing by product type and then by brand. (For more on how to silo your site, see Book VI.)

✦ **Customizable page elements:** Your CMS must allow you to customize the `Title` tag, `Meta` description tag, `Meta` keywords tag, heading tags H#, link *anchor text*, image `Alt` attributes, and every other element on your pages. You need this flexibility for every page, whenever needed, as you see fit.

✦ **Customizable HTML output:** You need to be able to control the HTML output of pages on your site. How the HTML is structured matters because that's where the search engine spiders crawl. You want to control, for example, the order of tags in the head section (`Title` at the top, followed by description, keywords, and then any other `Meta` tags you need). You may also need to do *content stacking*, which moves large blocks of HTML coding down to the bottom of the page so that the spiders can get to your rich text content as soon as possible. You want to ensure the other SEO-friendly guidelines are followed, such as using an external .CSS file to control formatting, and an external .JS file to house JavaScript if that's used on your site.

✦ **Ability to include analytics tracking codes:** You need to know what is happening to your site, where your visitors are from and where they're going to, what their behavior is and follow each visitor through a conversion.

✦ **Customizable rules:** Your CMS should let you specify rules that can be applied across lots of pages at once, especially if you have a site with thousands of products. You don't want any factory presets spitting out the same `Title` tag on every page, for example. Instead, you should be able to write a rule for how each product page's `Title` tag should be created to ensure each tag is unique and SEO-friendly (for example, "Item Category Brand" or "Category Item") and the ability to change any element by hand if deemed necessary.

Which CMS is best for SEO?

We wish that we could come right out and tell you which CMS we recommend. But we can't. First of all, the CMS that's right for one site doesn't necessarily work for another. They have different features and capabilities, and you have to choose one based on what your site needs. Secondly, *no* CMS that we know of today is really geared for SEO. At this point in their development, SEO-friendliness is sort of off the features lists. As more and more potential customers demand SEO-compatible features in the future, we hope that changes.

A relatively new product called PixelSilk, however, promises to be fully-SEO friendly. It was designed with SEO in mind and is probably worth a look. (In the interests of full disclosure, we worked closely with the PixelSilk team during their product development.)

Customization is crucial for your search engine optimization. You *need* a CMS that allows for customization of every single element on your Web site. Period.

Customizing Your CMS for SEO

The shopping list we just laid out can help you pick out a good CMS if you plan to purchase one. Or, if you already have a Web site running on a CMS, the list should point out the strengths or weaknesses of that purchase. Better yet, if your site doesn't have lots of changing content, you can avoid the CMS issue altogether! But for those Web sites that need a content management system, this section gives you tips for making your CMS work for you.

The two main principles are

✦ Set up rules that make every page have the ability to exist with unique SEO elements.

✦ Customize these individual page elements as needed to optimize them against the competition for the search engines.

Creating rules for each of your important SEO elements is a key part of making a CMS work for you. You should be able to define how the CMS puts together the `Title` tags, `Meta` description and keywords tags, heading tags, hyperlink anchor text, image `Alt` attributes, and everything else on your pages.

For instance, if you have an e-commerce store, you have many fields in your database that pertain to each product, such as the product name, product ID, and product description. You've also done some categorization work and probably have each product assigned to a product category, style, type, size, color, flavor . . . you get the idea.

Often, manufacturers require that all retailers use their predefined product descriptions. You might be struggling with this very same problem because obviously it's hard to rank well for product searches if your page just duplicates the same text shown on countless other sites. Here's what we suggest you can do to make your product pages stand above the rest:

✦ In addition to the mandatory product description, include more descriptive text on the product page itself. How-to instructions, useful historical information, even just a paragraph about a hands-on viewpoint are all options for adding keyword-rich content.

✦ Make sure you fully optimize the other on-page factors and use these to help increase keyword effectiveness on the page.

✦ Make sure the image `Alt` attribute is unique and contains keywords.

✦ Customize the `Title`, `Meta` description, and `Meta` keywords tags on the page.

✦ Enable users to write product reviews on your site. This adds content about the product in the users' own words, which can potentially match more search queries.

Create rules that define how the `Title` tag, `Meta` description tag, and `Meta` keywords tag should be put together on each product page. These rules should produce tags that meet the best practice guidelines for SEO, including the proper length, capitalization, ordering, and so on. (You can find best practice details in Book V, Chapter 3.)

Also create rules that apply heading tags `H#` appropriately throughout your page. Headings should be hierarchical, with a `H1` at the top of the page and other heading tags (`H2`, `H3`, and so on) throughout the page. Search engines look at the heading tags to confirm that the keywords shown in the `Title` and `Meta` tags at the top are accurate, so make sure that they contain the page's main keywords and are unique to that page.

You should specify rules for every output element possible. You want to take advantage of the CMS's ability to automate your site, but control that efficiency. Make sure that your resulting site is search engine-friendly and user-friendly, full of pages that are each unique.

After you have rules set up for how the CMS should construct your pages, the second part is customization. You should be able to tweak individual pages, applying all of the SEO principles covered throughout this book as needed. Here are a few scenarios to consider.

✦ **Single page tweaking:** Your online shoe store might carry a shoe that's a hot seller in brick and mortar stores, but for some reason you aren't getting much traffic for it online. You might want to do some competitive research and keyword research, and then manually modify the keywords in the tags and body copy of that particular product page to see if you can improve sales through that page. (You could also consider creative marketing options to attract more business for that product, such as adding supporting pages with articles, video, images, reviews, links, and so on.)

✦ **Long-Tail keyword targeting:** If your tags and headings contain specific product information, this helps you rank well for *Long-Tail searches* (search queries that contain multiple specific terms, rather than generic words). For instance, someone who searches for a particular shoe with a specific search like [Rockport Navigation Point brown] tends to be a serious shopper ready to make a purchase. It's beneficial if your pages are optimized for long-tail searches, in that case, because the lower amount of traffic they generate is offset by the high potential for conversion. Make sure your CMS doesn't build only generic tags and headings.

✦ **Generic word targeting:** To balance out the previous scenario, you also may want to bring in more traffic to your site by optimizing for generic words and phrases. For instance, the pages on your shoe store site that have Rockports could also be optimized for the phrases [Rockport shoes] or [mens shoes] or [leather shoes]. In those cases, you want the ability to tweak certain things on the individual pages in order to rank for generic keywords as well, and capture more traffic to your site.

SEO is often a balancing act. The previous two bullet points illustrate this — these two scenarios explain why you want to optimize the same shoe product page simultaneously for specific (Long-Tail) keywords and for generic keywords. We can't stress enough the need to have full customization control over your Web site: Finding the right balance in a situation like this may take some trial and error. To practice effective SEO, you must be able to override the default output created by the CMS and modify individual pages as needed.

Optimizing Your Yahoo! Store

Yahoo! has a service called Yahoo! Merchant Solutions (`http://small business.yahoo.com/ecommerce/`) that many people use to set up an e-commerce site quickly. The platform provides an easy way for a small store to get up and running. It offers store owners design templates, a step-by-step wizard for inputting products, site hosting, and an e-commerce function that can accept credit card, debit card, and PayPal payments. It's like a proprietary content management system just for Yahoo! We're not endorsing the Yahoo! store here, but because many people use it, we felt it had a place in our book. If that includes you, read on: This section shows you how to get the most SEO value out of your Yahoo! store.

We're just scratching the surface here. If you really want to dive into the unique opportunity that Yahoo! stores represent, check out *Starting a Yahoo! Business For Dummies* by Rob Snell (published by Wiley).

The good news is that it *is* possible to make a Yahoo! store rank highly for certain keywords. The bad news is that it's going to be harder to do than if you operated your own site and used a customizable CMS. Your ability to optimize a Yahoo! store for the search engines is limited. You can modify some things, such as the look of the site, the domain name, and some of the important page elements (which we explain shortly). However, you can't tinker with the inner workings of your site, such as

✦ **Robots text (.txt) file:** You can't touch your *robots.txt* file, which instructs the search engine spiders which pages not to index and where to find your *site map* (file that lists the pages in your Web site, linked so that spiders can easily navigate). All Yahoo! stores have an identical robots.txt file.

✦ **JavaScript:** You can't modify the *JavaScript* (a programming language used to apply interactive features to your Web pages).

✦ **Control file:** You cannot directly modify the *.htaccess* file, which is the central file you use to configure commands for an Apache server. This means that you can't set up page-specific 301 redirects, which are the SEO-preferred method.

You can create `Meta` refreshes, which are not search engine-friendly but do accomplish a redirect by causing the page to reload and display a different URL.

✦ **Other:** You basically cannot make server-level modifications to your store site, and your ability to customize pages is also limited. Yahoo! has its own programming language (RTML), and this coupled with the limitations has driven many store owners to hire third-party design firms that specialize in customizing Yahoo! stores to do the customization for them.

An SEO checklist for Yahoo! stores

To optimize your Yahoo! store, you should approach it like any Web site optimization project. Go through this checklist of items we explained throughout this book:

✔ Know clearly what your site is about, who your target audience is, and what your site's goals are.

✔ Inventory your site and your off-site resources (such as printed material and so on) to see what kind of content you can add to enhance your site's subject relevance.

✔ Do keyword brainstorming and research to determine what words and phrases you want to optimize for.

✔ Do competitor research for those keywords, looking for opportunities to move your pages up in the search engine rankings.

✔ Silo your site by establishing clear subject themes between related pages through linking.

✔ Examine your pages (using tools) and then work to improve the on-page elements like text content, headings, and `Meta` tags, optimizing for your keywords.

✔ Make sure every page, heading, and tag is unique.

✔ Create a keyword-rich site map.

✔ Implement good navigation links throughout the site that pass link equity to the main pages you want to rank well and give users an easy way to move through the site.

✔ Consolidate different domains into one (such as the non-www and www versions of your domain) to avoid having duplicate content.

✔ Monitor, analyze, and continue to go through this checklist, refining and adjusting your site. (Remember, SEO is never finished.)

From an SEO perspective, the best way to use the Yahoo! platform is to integrate it with an existing site. For example, you could operate your online shoe store by building your own Web site with everything except the shopping cart pages. Users would browse and make selections within your site, and then you could programmatically pass them to your Yahoo! store pages for the checkout process. You could integrate the two parts of your site together almost seamlessly by giving them the same look and feel.

Yahoo! offers three packages to choose from: starter, standard, and professional (for details, check out `http://smallbusiness.yahoo.com/ecommerce/plans.php`). The three options vary widely in terms of the monthly and transaction fees. Your best option depends on your expected revenue and your business model; however, the standard and professional packages allow for more customization, analytics, reports, and other features that are helpful if you're trying to optimize the site.

Because it's operated by a search engine, a certain degree of search engine friendliness is already built into Yahoo! Merchant Solutions. One big SEO advantage is that Yahoo! stores are automatically included in the Yahoo! index, so they can come up in Yahoo! search results.

On a practical level, here are some Yahoo! store site elements you can control that are important for SEO:

✦ **Domain name:** By default, Yahoo! structures your store's domain like this: *storename*.`stores.yahoo.net`. If you want your store to rank in the search engines, you should use your own domain instead. Register a good domain name (see Chapter 2 of this minibook for some guidelines), and then use the Domain Redirect Setting in Yahoo! to permanently redirect all Yahoo!-generated URLs for your store to your domain name.

✦ `Title` **tags:** Yahoo! creates a `Title` tag for each page using your business name and the page name. Because the `Title` tag is a key indicator to the search engines of what your page is about, you probably need to customize what shows up in your `Title` tags so that they are each unique, of an appropriate length, and contain the keywords you're trying to rank for in the search engines. Yahoo! lets you edit your `Titles` individually (manually) using the Advanced Editor mode.

✦ `Meta` **tags:** Go to the Site Settings area of your Yahoo! account to see how your `Meta` description and `Meta` keywords tags are being built, modifying them as needed. You can also modify them for an individual page using the Page Settings link.

For guidelines on writing effective `Title`, `Meta` description, and `Meta` keywords tags that help your pages rank with the search engines, see Book IV, Chapter 3.

✦ **Site map:** Yahoo! automatically builds an XML site map page for you that's invisible to users, but available to the search engines. You also have the option to create your own, which they upload if it follows proper protocol. For tips on creating a site map, see Book VI, Chapter 3.

✦ **Custom 404 error page:** When a user tries to access a page that doesn't exist, your Yahoo! store handles the 404 server status (the error code that means the page is not found) by redirecting the user to your store's home page. This is not user-friendly or spider-friendly behavior, so you should create your own custom 404 error page and upload it. (For help building a custom 404 page, see Book VII, Chapter 1.)

You can read step-by-step instructions for making the changes we describe in the previous bullets when you search the Yahoo! Help system (go to `http://help.yahoo.com/l/us/yahoo/smallbusiness/store/`). Figure 5-1 shows the Search Help box you use to find articles you need.

Figure 5-1: Find detailed instructions for editing your Yahoo! store in their Help system.

Chapter 6: Solving SEO Roadblocks

In This Chapter

✓ Ensuring that search engines see your site

✓ Creating effective site maps

✓ Avoiding page hijacking from 302 redirects

✓ Handling SEO problems connected with secure sites

*Y*ou know the part of an instruction manual that's just labeled "Troubleshooting"? It's sort of a catchall for problems you might have that don't fit anywhere else in the manual, with tips for what you can do about them. This chapter is sort of like that troubleshooting section — a place for us to address miscellaneous problems you might run into and give some advice on how to resolve them.

You should look at your search engine optimization (SEO) project as an ongoing process. It's not a journey with a fixed end point. There's no "destination" that you can reach and then hang up your keyboard and mouse and declare, "Ahh . . . we've made it!" Even if you reach the number one spot on the search results, you can't relax; you must continually monitor and fine-tune your site to stay ahead of the competition.

Occasionally, you will hit roadblocks to your SEO progress. These shouldn't be confused with the time lag that normally occurs before results become apparent. Usually it takes an SEO project three to six months to see a Web site rise considerably in ranking and traffic, after you put the initial site optimization in place. Of course, results are always based on the keywords and condition of your site when the project starts. Your mileage is going to vary based on the competition. Sometimes it happens within a few weeks or even a few days, but that's very unusual — normally, results take several months. Some keywords actually take years to rank well.

However, you can run into obstacles with SEO. You might find out that a search engine doesn't have any of your pages in its *index* (database of Web pages that a search engine pulls results from). Or you might find your site plummeting down the search engine results for no apparent reason. Or you might have difficulties related to setting up a secure *server* (the software and hardware that runs a Web site) for parts of your Web site. In this chapter, you find out what to do when you run into these kinds of roadblocks.

Inviting Spiders to Your Site

You may have pages that are missing from one or more of the search engines, which causes lower or non-existent search engine rankings. If you suspect a specific page is missing, find out for sure by entering a long snippet of text from that page in a search query, enclosed in quotation marks like this: ["Here's a long snippet of text taken directly from the page"]. The quotation marks force the search engine to look for an exact match, so your page should come up in the results if it's in the index at all. (By the way, this is also a great way to find duplicate content from your site.)

You can also check to see how extensively the search engines have indexed your entire Web site in a single search. To check for this at Google, enter the search query [site:*yourdomain.com*], replacing *yourdomain.com* with your actual domain (and removing the brackets). To check in Yahoo!'s search index, use Site Explorer (`http://siteexplorer.search.yahoo.com`). Enter your domain (or a specific page's URL, if desired) into the uppermost box and click Explore URL. As shown in Figure 6-1, the initial view is the Pages tab, which shows you the total indexed page count and the beginning of the page results.

Total indexed page count

Figure 6-1:
Yahoo! Site Explorer reveals how many of your site pages are indexed.

If desired, you can page through the results, or click the Export First 1000 Results to TSV link to get the pages into a format you can re-sort and work with in a spreadsheet program such as Microsoft Excel.

If you discover important pages that haven't been indexed, you need to invite the spiders to your site. You want them to travel all of your internal links and index your site contents. What follows are several effective ways you can deliver an invitation to the search engine spiders:

- ✦ **External links:** Have a link to your missing page added to a Web page that gets crawled regularly. Make sure that the link's anchor text relates to your page's subject matter. Ideally, the anchor text should contain your page's keywords. Also, the linking page should relate to your page's topic in some way so the search engine's see it as a relevant site. After the link is in place, the next time the spiders come crawling, they follow that link right to your page. This sort of "natural discovery" process can be the quickest, most effective way to get a page noticed by the search engines.

- ✦ **Direct submission:** Each search engine provides a way for you to submit a URL, which then goes into a queue waiting for a spider to go check it out. It's not a fast or even reliable method to get your page noticed, but it won't hurt you to do it.

- ✦ **Internal links:** You should have at least two links pointing to every page in your Web site. This helps ensure that search engine spiders can find every page.

- ✦ **Site map:** You should have a *site map* (list of the pages in your site with keyword-rich links) for your users, but for the search engines, you want to create another site map in *XML* (eXtensible Markup Language) format. Make sure that your XML site map contains the URL links to the missing pages, as well as every other page you want indexed. When a search engine spider crawls your XML Sitemap, it follows the links and is more likely to thoroughly index your site.

**Book VII
Chapter 6**

**Solving SEO
Roadblocks**

The two versions of your site map provide direct links to your pages, which is helpful for users and important for spiders. Search engines use the XML site map file as a central hub for finding all of your pages. But the user's site map is also crawled by the search engines. If the site map provides valuable anchor text for each link (for example, "Frequently Asked Classic Car Questions" instead of "FAQs"), it gives search engines a better idea of what your pages are about. Google specifically states in their guidelines that every site should have a site map (www.google.com/support/webmasters/bin/answer.py?answer=35769#design).

Supplementing siloing with `rel="nofollow"`

The `rel="nofollow"` attribute may also help with *siloing* your site, which is a method of organizing the site into subject themes. Because the search engines look for the most relevant pages for any search query, you can strengthen your site's subject relevance by linking related pages together into themed silos. Each silo should have a main landing page and at least five supporting pages linked to it, all centered on a particular keyword theme. To reinforce your landing pages' relevance to certain keywords, you can apply a `rel="nofollow"` sparingly to only those cross-silo links that might be necessary for your users, but which would only confuse the spiders' understanding of what the page is about. (For more on siloing, see Book VI.)

There is a limit to the number of links you should have on the user-viewable site map. Small sites can place every page on their site map, but larger sites should not. Having more than 99 links on a page looks suspicious to a search engine because spammers have tried to deceive the search engines by setting up *link farms* for profit, which are just long lists of unrelated hyperlinks on a page. So just include the important pages, or split it into several site maps, one for each main subject category. (For more tips on creating an effective site map, see Book VI, Chapter 3.)

However, unlike a traditional site map, XML site maps don't have a 99 link limit. There are still some limitations, but the file(s) is meant to act as a "feed" directly to the search engines. For full details on how to create an XML site map, visit `sitemaps.org`, the official site map guideline site run by the search engines.

In addition to having the search engine spiders come crawl your site, which is the first goal, you also want to think about directing them where you want them to go within your site. For comparison, when people come over to your house, you don't just let them roam around and look anywhere they want to, right? You lead them around, showing them what you want them to see — probably skipping the disorganized garage and messy utility room.

With search engine spiders, you don't want them to see every page or follow every link either. The two reasons you want them to crawl around are

+ **Indexing:** You want the search engines to index your pages so they'll be found relevant to people's searches and returned in search results.

+ **Better ranking:** When the spiders follow your links, they pass *link equity* (the perceived-expertise value of all the inbound links pointing to a Web page, which is a search engine ranking factor) to your *landing pages* (the pages you've set up to be the most relevant for a primary keyword). Concentrating link equity on your landing pages makes those pages move higher up in the search engine rankings and bring in more traffic.

Some pages, like your Privacy Policy or Terms of Use, need to be in your global navigation but they don't need to rank well in the search engine's index. You don't want to rank for those pages, or to dilute the link equity being passed to your landing pages. Instead, you should "herd" the spiders where you want them to go. To keep spiders away from certain pages, here are a couple of techniques you should know:

✦ **Nofollow:** You can put a `rel="nofollow"` attribute on any link that you don't want the spiders to pass Link Equity to. Using this technique on links to unimportant pages, you could concentrate link equity onto your landing pages.

✦ **Robots text file (.txt) exclusion:** Be consistent. If you add `rel="no follow"` to a link to prevent spiders from crawling to your privacy policy page, for instance, do it everywhere. Put the `nofollow` attribute on every link to that page. Also instruct the spiders not to index the page by excluding it in your robots text file (a central file that gives instructions to spiders of where *not* to go, check out Book VII, Chapter 1 for more on editing your robots.txt file).

✦ **Meta Robots exclusion:** Another way to put up a "Do Not Enter" sign for search engines is with a `noindex` Meta robots tag on a specific page. (A *Meta robots tag* is an HTML command in the head section (top part) of a Web page's HTML code that gives instructions to search engine spiders whether to index the page and whether to follow its links.) This tag is not needed if you've excluded the page in your robots.txt file. But to put the exclusion directly into the page code, you could add a tag such as this:

```
<META NAME="ROBOTS" CONTENT="NOINDEX">
```

So far in this book, we've talked only about the search engine spiders. Those are the good spiders — the ones you want coming to your site. However, there are also bad spiders out there, ones that come only to harm you.

Spiders called *scrapers* come to steal your site content so that they can republish it on their own sites. Sometimes they grab entire pages, including the links back to your site and everything. One problem with scraping is that it creates *duplicate content* (the same or very similar text on two or more different pages) on the Web, which can cause your page to drop in ranking or even drop out of the search results if the search engines don't correctly figure out which page is the original. Another problem is that scraped content may end up ranking above your page/site and grab traffic that should have been yours. Scraping is a copyright violation, and it's also a crime punishable by law, if you choose to pursue that. Unfortunately, the more good text content you have on your site, the more likely you are to attract scrapers. So as your site expands and your SEO project raises your rankings, you're probably going to run into this issue.

Webmasters have tried to prevent site scraping in various ways. Some have gone so far as to build a *white list* (a list of approved sites or agents) that contains only the known good spiders, and then exclude all non-white listed spiders from entering their site. That extreme measure is not commonly done because it's difficult to maintain a current white list without potentially excluding legitimate traffic to your site.

A more typical defensive move is to "sniff" out a bad spider using a server-level process known as *user-agent sniffing*. This process identifies spiders coming to your site, kind of like a security guard at your front door. If you know who a bad spider is, you can detect their arrival and keep them out. Or, some Webmasters choose to do more than just block them; they redirect them to a page with massive quantities of data in hopes of crashing the bad spider's site. Block them or punish them, you choose, but unfortunately you can only do this *after* you've identified a spider as a scraper — not before you know who they are.

 To deter others from copying your content, we recommend that you display a copyright notice on your Web site *and* register for a federal copyright. For more suggestions on handling scrapers, see Book V, Chapter 4, in the section titled, "Scrapers."

Avoiding 302 Hijacks

Here's a scenario that we hope never happens to you. Your Web site is running smoothly and ranking well with the search engines for your keywords. One day, you find that your search engine traffic is dropping dramatically. Then you notice that your pages have disappeared from the search engine results pages.

This nightmare scenario could mean that your site was a victim of a 302 hijack. A *302* is a type of *redirect* (an HTML command that reroutes a user from one page to another automatically) used to indicate that one Web page has temporarily moved to another URL. The search engine retains the original page in its index and attributes the content and link equity of the new page to the original page.

An unethical way to use 302 redirects is called *302 hijacking*. This technique exploits the way search engines read 302 redirects in order to cause a Web page's traffic and SERP rankings to be drained away and given to some other page (the "hijacker"). The hijacker is basically stealing your Web site, rankings, and search traffic.

Here's how it works: The hijacker sets up a dummy page, often containing a scraped copy of your Web page's content, and 302 redirects it to your ranking page. The search engines see the 302 and think that the hijacker's page is the *real* version, but it's temporarily using your page's URL. So the 302 tricks the search engines into thinking that your ranking page is the temporary version of the hijacker's virtual page. The search engine therefore gives all of your link equity and rankings away to the hijacker's URL. Figure 6-2 shows how a hijacked page's listing might show in a SERP. Notice that the URL on the bottom line does not match the company name shown in the listing; clicking this link would take the user to some other page off the company's site.

A 302 hijacking can be devastating to a site, causing duplicate content penalties and loss of ranking. The search engines are aware of this issue and have all tried to put preventive measures in place. They have had some success combating this crime, but it still happens.

Be on the lookout for page hijacking by regularly searching for snippets of your page text (do a search using quotation marks to find an exact match) to identify copycat pages, but you know for certain that it's happening when you see someone else's URL showing up on your SERP listings. If you have this problem, contact the third-party site and ask them to cooperate with you to fix the situation. Page hijacking is often accidental (through improper use of 302 redirects), so you may be able to resolve it with the person easily. If you discover that their intentions are malicious, however, you should report the site to the search engines immediately for investigation. If you're ever in this situation, you need to contact the search engine directly. Unfortunately, there's not much you can do to fix it on your own — the search engines have to remedy the situation for you.

Hijacker's domain   Hijacked result

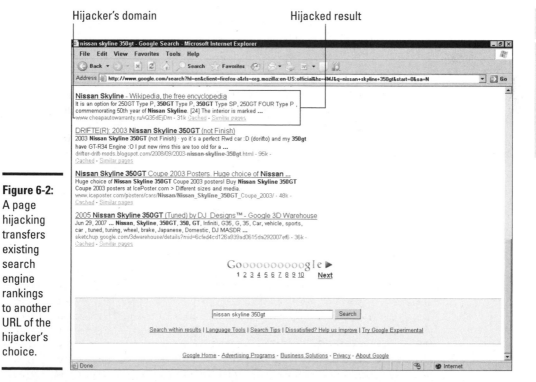

Figure 6-2:
A page hijacking transfers existing search engine rankings to another URL of the hijacker's choice.

Handling Secure Server Problems

You may have pages on your site where users provide sensitive data, such as a credit card number or other type of account information. The Internet solution for protecting sensitive information is to put those Web pages on a *secure server*. Technically, this means that the Web page is on a secure port on the server, where all data is *encrypted* (converted into a form that cannot be understood except by knowing one or more secret decryption keys). You can tell when you're looking at a Web page on a secure server because `http:` changes to `https:` in the URL address.

Secure servers can cause duplicate content problems if a site has both a secure and non-secure version of a Web page. Two versions of the same page end up competing against each other for search engine rankings, and the search engines pick which one to show in search results. Also, because people link to both versions of the page, neither page can rank well because they've split their link equity.

Here are some SEO-minded best practices for handling secure servers:

✦ **Don't make duplicates:** Many times, people just duplicate their entire Web site to make an `https` version. This is a very bad practice because it creates instant duplicate content. Never create two versions of your site, or of any page on your site. Even if you exclude your secure pages from being indexed, people link to them at some point and the search engines find the secure versions through those links.

✦ **Only secure the pages that need to be secure:** If the page doesn't receive sensitive account-type information from users, it doesn't need to be secured. This is easily handled with a rewrite rule; refer back to Chapter 4 of this minibook for more on redirects and rewrites.

✦ **Spiders *shouldn't* be allowed to crawl secure pages:** Search engines do index secure pages, if they can get to them. Banks usually have secure pages indexed because they often put their entire site on an `https`. Because of the nature of their business, it makes sense that banks want to give their users the utmost level of confidence by securing their whole site. However, the best practice is not to try to rank for pages on a secure server.

✦ **Access secure pages through a logon:** The cleanest way to handle secure pages is to put them behind a logon. Search engine spiders can't crawl pages that require a logon to access, so they definitely won't be indexed. You also raise the user-friendliness of your site by including a logon because users will clearly understand why they've moved into a secure server environment and feel more comfortable entering their account information there.

If your Web site has secure pages that violate these best practices, here's how to fix it:

1. **Identify which pages on your site need to be secure.**

   Secure only the pages where users need to enter account information.

2. **Make sure your secure pages are not duplicated.**

   Your secure pages should only have an `https://` version. Do not offer a non-secured duplicate version. All links to and from secure pages should be full path links; that is, they should begin `http://` or `https://`. Relative links to secure pages is just asking for trouble.

3. **Clean up duplicate pages using 301 redirects.**

   If you currently have secure pages that don't need to be secured, redirect them to the `http` version using a 301 permanent redirect. That way, any links going to the secure pages are automatically redirected to the right pages. The same goes for non-secure pages that should be secured, only vice versa.

Book VIII
Analyzing Results

The 5th Wave   By Rich Tennant

DATA MINING

Hold on Brad - I forgot the canary.

Contents at a Glance

Chapter 1: Employing Site Analytics 535

Discovering Web Analytics Basics 535
Measuring Your Success...538
Examining Analytics Packages 546
Getting Started: Log Files Analysis 551

Chapter 2: Tracking Behavior with Web Analytics 557

Measuring Web Site Usability 557
Tracking Conversions 562
Tracking the Success of Your SEO Project..568
Analyzing Rankings 569

Chapter 3: Mastering SEO Tools and Reports 571

Getting Started with A/B Testing..571
Discovering Page and Site Analysis Tools...584
Understanding Abandonment Rates 585
Measuring Traffic and Conversion from Organic Search 586
Using Link Analysis Tools..588

Chapter 1: Employing Site Analytics

In This Chapter

✔ Discovering Web analytics basics

✔ Measuring success

✔ Identifying what you're tracking

✔ Key performance indicators

✔ Examining analytics packages

✔ Analyzing log files

*W*eb analytics are two words that can strike terror into the heart of any unsuspecting practitioner of search engine optimization (SEO). You've been monitoring your pay per click (PPC) campaigns (advertising campaigns where you pay every time someone clicks on your link) and you are watching to see how well your pages rank within the search engines. So you should be able to do Web analytics, right?

Well, Web analytics can be a little more complicated than that. For a lot of people, Web analytics seems to consist of wild guessing and reading tea leaves. It can be pretty complex, but we walk you through it so it hopefully makes a little more sense. In this chapter, we give you a basic overview of Web analytics, before we dive into the nitty-gritty later on in this minibook. We go over how to measure your success in the search engines, identify what numbers you need to be tracking, point out key indicators to be watching when measuring your performance, and cover tools and software that help you with Web analytics and what a log file analysis is.

Discovering Web Analytics Basics

Web analytics is taking the information you have gleaned from all of your research and sitting down, looking at it, and figuring out what all of it means. Bear with us: This can get a little tricky because the terms are so similar. In order to figure out Web Analytics, you need to know the two different sets of numbers you are looking at — Web metrics numbers and Web analytics numbers.

Web metrics

Web metrics is the measurement of what's happening on the Internet itself. It's focusing on the number and types of people online, the number of broadband versus dial-up connections, advertisers, advertisements (shapes, sizes, level of annoyance) and all things related to the Internet as a whole. Web metrics is asking: How many Web sites are there? How many searches? How many e-mails? How many of those e-mails are spam? Does it make sense to promote items online for sale to certain countries or to seniors? How many people search at Google versus Yahoo! versus MSN?

There are four ways of tracking Web metrics data, and several kinds of companies that fall into a particular niche. These firms study the Internet as a whole. Think of them as Internet archeologists. They take all of the raw data they get and interpret it in their own way, using information from many, many sites and sources out there on the Internet:

✦ **People:** The first kind of company that tracks Web metrics data does so by using large panels of people whom the companies follow as they surf the Internet as part of their daily routine. These companies report which sites are the most popular and can have their panels check out your competitors and do a comparative analysis. These are companies like Nielsen Online (www.nielsen-online.com/) and comScore (www.comscore.com/).

✦ **Hits:** The second type of Web metrics firm checks out the hits on the ISPs (Internet service providers). These firms are watching the masses out there surfing on the Internet. They report on how these unidentified (and sometimes unwashed) users research cars, read the latest celebrity gossip, and watch news stories. Hitwise (www.hitwise.com/) is one such firm that tracks ISP hits.

✦ **Responsiveness:** A third type of Web metrics firm watches the responsiveness of popular Web sites. They track how well a popular entertainment site holds up during the Oscars or the Emmys or if sports sites can handle the traffic during the Super Bowl, and which ones run the fastest and which ones drown under the increased demand. Two firms who do this kind of Web metrics are Keynote Systems (www.keynote.com/) and Tealeaf (www.tealeaf.com/).

✦ **Commerce:** The final group tracks online commerce. They watch how much these commerce companies are spending on advertising, and what percentage the consumer is spending on the Internet. They also track the growth rate of companies as compared to their competition. One of the big tracking companies in this niche is eMarketer (www.emarketer.com/).

Web analytics

On a smaller but no less important scale is Web analytics, which concerns itself with the particulars of a single Web site, instead of the entire Web.

The people who do Web analytics are looking at how successful your site is in attracting the kind of visitors who bring you *conversions*. Visitors who convert do whatever your Web site is asking of them: make a purchase, sign up for a newsletter, watch your videos, and so on. Using Web analytics means looking beyond just finding out where you rank or how many people clicked over from the search engine listing and actually checking to see how many visitors came to your site and provided you a conversion.

Your first step with Web analytics should be to determine what your visitor does and what they should be doing when they arrive on your Web site. Where do they go on your site? Do your visitors drill down to the product information? Do they put things in their shopping carts? Are they less costly customers because they use the online customer care tools and services? Do they leave your site right away or do they stay a while?

Hopefully they're able to easily accomplish what they came to your Web site to do. But if you have a Web site, you need to be able to measure whether your Web site design and development are worth the effort you've put into it.

This site-level arena in Web analytics is governed by software for sale and systems for use that gather, crunch, and report on data from server logs, cookie data, JavaScript, e-commerce information, and so on.

Without Web analytics, search marketers would be obsessed only with achieving a high ranking. If they're a little more on the ball, they focus instead on generating as much traffic as they can. Unfortunately, high ranking and high traffic are only part of running a successful site. If you are getting high volumes of traffic but your visitors aren't doing what you want them to do (for instance, no one is asking for you to customize their classic cars), all that high traffic is just going to cost you money. Your server is now handling more non-converting traffic, your PPC campaigns are being clicked on with no return on investment, and even the time you spent on optimizing your site to rank organically is time that could have been spent making money. Traffic is only worth it if it provides return on investment (ROI).

REMEMBER

This is why targeted traffic is so important. *Targeted traffic* is traffic that is interested in your product or service and provides you conversions. Your success is determined not by the volume of visitors you receive, but the quality. First, however, you need to figure out what it is you want that targeted traffic to be doing. That's what we cover in the next section.

**Book VIII
Chapter 1**

**Employing Site
Analytics**

Measuring Your Success

The first thing you need to figure out before you get started with Web analytics is to figure out your goals for your site. Say you have a Web site that specializes in classic car customization services. The first thing you want to do is measure the amount of sales generated on your site. That's easy enough — but there are other activities that need recording as well. Other activities you can record include e-mail newsletter signups, file downloads, *RSS subscriptions* (news feeds that automatically show updates to a site that offers one), and user account creation.

There is no one-size-fits-all approach to measuring success. Goals differ based on what your Web site does and what you want users to do once they reach your site. For example, your custom car site would be tracking different user actions than a political site that wants people to sign up for a newsletter. Many advancements have been made in analytics, so if there's something you need to track, you can do it with an analytics program.

You're probably like most people building commercial sites: A Web site is a key component of your business, and you need to be making money from your site in order to be successful. The common adage is true: You have to spend money to make money; however, you need to be spending money in the right places or you might as well be setting the cash on fire. So, what is it that you want your Web site to do? This should be a fairly obvious question, but in order to accurately do Web analytics for your site, you need to know what it is that gets you conversions. It's extremely important to define your business objectives.

There are four basic classifications for commercial Web sites: e-commerce sites, content sites, lead generation sites and self-service sites. We've provided some basic goals for the four types of commercial Web sites. You can use this information in defining your own business objectives:

✦ **E-commerce sites:** The objective with e-commerce is to increase your sales and decrease your marketing expenses. Basic measures include sales, returns and allowances, sales per visitor, cost per visitor, and conversion rate. Advanced measures include inventory mix, trend reporting, satisfaction, and RFM (recency, frequency, monetary analysis).

✦ **Content sites:** The objective here is to increase your readership-level of interest and time the user spends on the site. The things you measure are visit length, page views, and number of subscriptions and cancelled subscriptions.

✦ **Lead-generation sites:** Here the objective is to increase and segment lead generation (things like newsletters). Basic measures include downloads, time spent on the site, newsletter opt-ins, reject rates on contact pages, and leads-to-close ratio.

✦ **Self-service sites:** Finally, the objective here is to increase customer satisfaction and decrease customer support inquiries. Basic measures include a decrease in visitor length or fewer calls to a call center, as these are measures of customer satisfaction.

With clearly defined objectives and a good analytics tool, measuring your Web site's success becomes a whole lot easier. Your objectives state what you want to do with your Web site or your marketing campaigns.

Identifying what you are tracking

In order to start analyzing whether your Web site is doing what it needs to be doing, you have to acquire a sample of data. This sample allows you to extract a baseline report of data on your users.

Types of data vary from site to site. A data sample from an e-commerce site reads differently than a sample from a political newsletter. For Web sites that are not impacted by *seasonal trends* (meaning they see a spike in business around a certain time of year), a three-month sample is a great baseline range to work with. After you've determined what your baseline sample is (if you have seasonal trends, take a sample from your busy and slow periods), start recording numerical and trended data for analysis.

As someone who is going to be doing Web analytics from a SEO perspective, you have to be looking at the information that makes your life easier in the long run. You can do that by focusing on the elements that are most relevant to search engine referrals — information such as

✦ Percentage of traffic from search

✦ Conversions (leads, sales, and subscriptions) from search

✦ Average time spent on site (or "visit duration")

✦ Share of search traffic (Google versus Yahoo! versus Live Search, and so on)

✦ Pages clicked on

The information that you use in your baseline should be unique to your business goals and ambitions.

It's also critical to separate your paid search results from your organic search results. Paid search results come from pay-per-click (PPC) programs, where you can buy an advertising link on Google or any of the other search engines and pay a sum every time a user clicks on your ad. You need to separate these two types of results because it can skew your data and throw off proper analysis. You have to understand how subtleties in an SEO program, like descriptions in a listing or movement in a *SERP* (search engine results page), can impact your traffic and productivity.

This is also true with all of your PPC paid search programs, when you need to calculate your return of investment (ROI) on specific engines, *keywords* (search terms), or ad campaigns. Many PPC programs include the ability to tag your pages and track visitors from click to purchase. For more on PPC analytics, please refer to Book X, Chapter 1.

With analytics, you can use different types of reports from any number of analytics packages as long as you know what to look for. But even without the analytics part, you need to think about a quality search experience. Regardless of how a user searches, you have to get them the information they want, while also trying to get them to perform your desired actions.

To help get you started, here are a few tips on items that you can track and measure:

✦ **Top search queries:** You would be surprised how many businesses lose out on those desired conversions simply because they're targeting the wrong keywords. This is why keyword research is so very necessary. Sometimes what you think would be a good keyword search term turns out to be quite the opposite. This is why it's so important to be thorough in keyword research. You can read more on how to properly research keywords in Book II. This can be a tricky thing to measure because it's a self-fulfilling prophecy. Targeting terms that already are bringing you traffic could mean missing out on a better term that would bring you even more traffic. Watch this metric, but don't put all your eggs in this basket.

✦ **Top landing pages:** A *landing page* is a page that someone uses to get onto your site. It might not always be your main page, but generally that would be the one you want to be your big landing page. When dealing with top landing pages, your concern should be the source of referrals. Because we're talking about search engine optimization, we recommend looking at search engine results. This is your first contact with a potential visitor, so make sure that elements of your landing page speak to the search terms and the type of user you want to bring to your site. Changes in page titles, listing descriptions, and URLs can have an impact on a user's desire to click on your page.

✦ **Top exit pages:** Something you also have to monitor are the exit pages. If users are consistently leaving your site on a common page, it's a good idea to figure out why. The process of *pathing* is reviewing the flow, page by page, that a user takes while visiting your site. If you begin to see that quality search referrals come into your site but are always leaving at a particular point, you need to work on the content or user experience you provide to keep those users from leaving. To figure out your exit pages, you need to perform a reverse path analysis to determine why so many people are leaving at this one particular page. If the top exit page is the Thanks for Ordering page, you have nothing to worry about. However, these situations are rare. The most common top exit page is usually your home page.

✦ **Bounce rate:** The *bounce rate* measures the percentage of people who leave your site right after entering a page, usually within seconds and without visiting any other page on the site. This stat goes hand-in-hand with measuring exit pages. If you have specific pages designated for SEO purposes, be sure to measure and track the bounce rate on a regular basis. You don't get desired conversions if no one wants to stay on your page. Maybe you're targeting the wrong people with that landing page — after all, just because you rank well for a particular keyword doesn't mean the page that ranks is saying the right things to the people who come to that page. You need to dig in deeper and figure out what the mismatch is. Are your images loading too slowly? Is the page layout confusing? Does the content of the page not meet the visitor's expectations?

Experimenting with Web analytics is key, especially because all sites and report suites differ. So find out as much as you can about your visitors and don't be afraid to experiment with your reports and theories. There is always more information to know, and like everything else in life, we often don't even know what we don't know. The only way to shed light on the activities going on with your site is to start investing in Web analytics.

Choosing key performance indicators

Key performance indicators help organizations achieve organizational goals through the definition and measurement of progress. Key performance indicators (KPIs) are the yardstick by which you measure your Web site's success. In order to properly do Web analytics, you need to know what your goals are in order to know what it is you need to be watching.

Your key performance indicators (KPIs) should be based on your overall business goals and the role your Web site plays in achieving those goals. KPIs should be specific to your company, not influenced by the industry averages or your competitors' KPIs, and they should be specific, significant, and measurable:

✦ **Organizational goals:** It is important to establish KPIs based on your own business goals rather than standard goals for your industry. For instance, a company whose goal is "to be most profitable" has different KPIs than a company who defines their goal as "to increase customer retention fifty percent." The first company has KPIs that relate to finance and profit and loss, whereas the second is focusing on customer satisfaction and response time.

✦ **Measurement purpose:** It's important to analyze KPIs over time, allowing you to make changes to improve Web site performance and then periodically reevaluate performance to verify your progress. So KPIs must be measurable. The goal "increase customer retention" is useless because there is no real goal; the goal of "increase customer retention by fifty percent" has a definite number that can be tracked.

✦ **Managerial consensus:** It is important to have all managers on the same page because personnel from different functions within your company help create the KPIs. If your KPIs truly reflect your organizational goals, all levels of your company have to get with the program. Encourage company unity and enthusiasm for the project, and make sure that everyone knows what the KPIs are. Everyone has to be on board, and they have to know what it is that they're doing. A crew can't steer a ship if one half of the crew thinks they're sailing to Zanzibar and the other half thinks they're supposed to be Saskatchewan pirates.

✦ **Goal continuity:** KPIs are *long-term* considerations designed to help with your strategic planning. Although it is important to have targeted goals, they should also lead to an overall success. Just because something is measurable does not mean that it is significant enough to be a key performance indicator. You must define your KPIs and weigh them the same way from year to year. It's not that you can't adjust your goals, but you should use the same unit to measure those goals. Like, your Web site goal should be to increase of the number of conversions the same amount year in and year out.

Although you should be creating very specific KPIs for your business, a few metrics qualify as regular key performance indicators all across the board. These include the KPIs for measuring reach, acquisition, conversions, and retention.

Measuring reach

Every business that promotes products and services needs to measure it's reach on an ongoing basis. *Reach* is how you reach your customers, basically. These following metrics are useful for understanding the effects of marketing programs designed to reach new customers:

✦ **Overall traffic volumes:** This tracks large spikes or dips in the requested page views.

✦ **Number of visits:** This indicates how well you reach and acquire your visitors.

✦ **Number of new visitors:** This number gives you the first part of two numbers needed to calculate ratios to determine quality of new visitors. Are they giving you your needed conversions? Conversions divided by the number of new visitors gives you the overall conversion rate. Obviously, higher is better.

✦ **Ratio of new to returning visitors:** Identifying changes in overall audience makeup. In general, it's cheaper to keep an old customer than bring in a new one. Are you retaining your customer base? Have you made changes that alienated your core demographic? Was your core demographic converting as well as the new demographic?

+ **Percentage of new visitors:** This helps track the changes in your traffic due to marketing reach and acquisition efforts.

+ **Visitor geographic data:** Here you identify your traffic spikes from unexpected locations. Where is your traffic coming from? This can give you information you can use to better reach your customers.

+ **Your top 5-10 error pages:** This metric helps you identify and resolve visitor experience problems.

+ **Impressions served:** The number of times the page loaded and a user viewed the content. You can use this metric to calculate your reach and the overall success of your marketing campaigns.

Acquisition

Measuring acquisition is easier than measuring reach. *Acquisition* is the measure of users that you bring to your site. The difference is that reach metrics depend on information from various sources, whereas acquisition metrics come from your own Web analytics data.

Acquisition measurement is focused on the number of visitors your Web site is acquiring and where they all come from. What follows are the metrics that can help gauge the success of your Web site and marketing initiatives in acquiring prospects and customers. The metrics you should be watching for acquisition are

+ **Percent of new visitors:** You can use this number to flag big changes in new visitor acquisition and their effect on overall Web traffic. You use this number in conjunction with your total conversions to help you determine if they are giving you conversions or just slowing down your servers?

+ **Average number of visits per visitor:** This stat can help you ensure that content consumption remains stable, which is an indirect measure of user experience.

+ **Average number of page views per visit:** This metric allows you to understand the changing nature of visitors attracted to your Web site. Do they peruse the whole site, or escape after one or two pages?

+ **Page *stick and slip* (time on page and bounce rates):** View big changes in stickiness (how long a user stays on a page) or slip (how quickly visitors leave a page) on your home page and key entry pages, including PPC campaign landing pages.

+ **Average pages viewed per visitor:** This is a short-term measure of how well you direct visitors beyond home page or landing page.

+ **Cost per visitor:** This is a rise/fall metric that shows fluctuation of visitor acquisition costs due to an increase or decrease in your marketing spending.

**Book VIII
Chapter 1**

Employing Site
Analytics

Response metrics

Response metrics are what your users are responding to on your Web site, be it an image or a newsletter or an email. These are the key items you need to be watching for:

✦ **Responses and respondents:** These are important indicators of campaign success.

✦ **Cost per acquisition or cost per click:** Measuring these keeps you within campaign budget.

✦ **Referring domains/URLs:** These help you watch your visitors based on needs and origin. Where are they coming from and what can you glean about their needs from the site they originated from?

✦ **Search engines:** Check and see who's coming in from the search engines to ensure that the money you spend on SEO and PPC is justified.

✦ **Search keywords and phrases:** Track what keywords are bringing visitors to your site. You can use this info from search queries to refine your marketing message and materials to include these keywords.

Note that the raw data for the preceding metrics is not useful by itself: Your most important metric is the relationship between your current and previous data measurements. As indicators of change, the preceding KPIs can alert you to the ever-changing quality and quantity of your visiting traffic, and this may call for additional research.

Conversions

Conversion metrics are among the most important indicators to measure and monitor. Conversion rates are easy to measure and can be improved by fine-tuning your Web site; every online business should watch these numbers and have Plan B ready in case key conversion rates suddenly plunge.

When you measure conversions, you are also looking at abandonment — the ones who got away. Maybe they intended to complete an action but were frustrated during the process and bailed out. Industry-neutral average conversion rates hover around 3 percent. This means only 3 out of 100 visitors across all industries complete an intended action.

What conversion rates should you measure? There are three basic processes that can be measured for conversion versus abandonment and each depends largely on what your ultimate goal for your site is.

✦ **Activities that lead to an acquisition or conversion:** The user makes a purchase or requests a service. This one is probably the easiest to measure because you know when it's done and you have the money in hand. You can see the actual impact in your bottom line.

✦ **Activities that lead to gathering important data:** The user fills out a form, signs up for a newsletter, or contacts you. You haven't actually made a sale yet but you have more information about that user and probably also their permission to continue the business relationship. This might be the end in itself, or just a step along your conversion process.

✦ **Activities that direct visitors to information that reduces your operational costs:** This one is trickier to measure because you'll have to track multiple data points — how often someone accesses your FAQ or Help section, how many calls to your customer support group you're receiving, how much those calls diminish after implementing a change aimed at giving greater support up front, or any other operational changes aimed at reducing overall cost.

Retention

Retention is how many customers you keep once they come to your Web site. Customer retention is important to Web sites for various reasons. For instance, research shows that keeping existing customers costs less than attracting new customers. Studies have shown that the cost for acquisition on a per-customer basis is much more than that of customer retention. Research also says there is a small chance of converting a prospect to first-time customer status, and a low percent chance of reacquiring a lost customer. So customer retention is key.

The following metrics and ratios can help tell you how you rate at customer retention:

✦ The number of returning visitors

✦ The average frequency of your returning visitors

✦ The ratio of returning visitors to all visitors

✦ The frequency of the visit

✦ How recent the visit was

✦ The activity of retained visitors

✦ The views of key pages and contents

✦ Your retained visitor conversion rate

✦ The customer retention rate

✦ The average frequency of return for retained visitors

Although some business models do not expect customers to make a second purchase right away (for example, auto, housing, or travel), very few Web sites are designed for a single visit from a visitor without a return. The KPIs listed here should be tracked regardless of your business model or industry:

✦ The ratio of daily to monthly returning visitors — a quick measure of the average frequency of return for all visitors.

✦ The percent of returning visitors and the frequency of those returns.

✦ The loyalty measurements for groups of returning visitors — it monitors big changes in visitor loyalty. How many are you losing?

✦ Your retained visitor conversion rate — this helps in determining Web site or campaign success.

✦ Your customer retention rate — which helps determine your Web site success.

Examining Analytics Packages

Analytics takes a long time, several in-depth volumes, and possibly a college course or two to really properly do on your own. Fortunately for you, several analytics packages out there do the number-crunching for you and make sense of all of the metrics you're watching out for. Analytics packages are governed by software for sale and systems for use that gather, crunch, and report data from server logs, cookie data, JavaScript, ecommerce information, and so on. We go over a few here in this section.

Google

Web analytics offerings range in price from free to, well, not even close to free. On the free side, the most well known is Google Analytics. Google Analytics (`http://analytics.google.com/`) is a tool for Web analytics. Google is putting everything they can think of in this tool in order to show you just how important it is for you to keep buying more keywords. Google Analytics also generates detailed statistics about the visitors to a Web site. The main highlight of this program is that it's aimed at marketers as opposed to Webmasters and technologists from which the industry of Web analytics originally grew, which means it's geared specifically towards business types, not tech types.

Google Analytics can track visitors from all referrers, including search engines, display advertising, pay-per-click networks, e-mail marketing, and even digital collateral such as links within PDF documents. Google Analytics also allows you to track your landing page quality and monitors your conversions. Remember, conversions don't always mean sales. This program can track whether users are viewing the page you want them to. Figure 1-1 shows you the overview from Google Analytics.

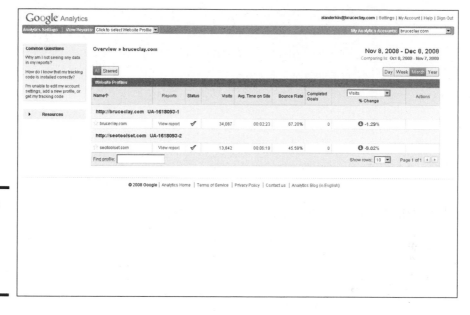

Figure 1-1:
Google
Analytics
is a free
analytics
program.

You can also use Google Analytics to determine which of your ads are performing (when used in conjunction with Google AdWords, Google's Pay-Per-Click advertising program, more on that in Book I). Google Analytics also provides shorthand information for the casual user and much more in-depth info for those who are a little more versed in Web analytics.

Google Analytics works through the Google Analytics Tracking Code (GATC). The GATC is a snippet of JavaScript code that the user adds onto every page of their Web site. This code acts as a beacon, collecting anonymous visitor data and sending it back to Google data collection servers for processing. Data processing takes place hourly, although it can be three to four hours before you can get your data back. The Google Analytics Dashboard (as seen in Figure 1-2) can give you information at a glance about traffic, site usage, and traffic sources, among many others.

The Google Analytics Tracking Code also sets first party cookies on each visitor's computer. *Cookies* are parcels of text that are used to track, authenticate, and maintain specific information about users. The cookies are used to store anonymous information such as whether the user has been to the site before (new or returning visitor), what the timestamp of the current visit is, and where the user came from.

Figure 1-2:
The dashboard for Google Analytics provides at-a-glance reporting on your site.

Google Analytics is very easy to install on your Web site. They provide HTML code snippets that you can copy and paste into your page through the Global element, which means that the code snippet applies to every page across your site, and you won't have to go in and add it by hand, unless you're using goal tracking or conversion tracking code.

Not to be outdone, both Yahoo! and MSN Live Search also have analytics packages. But as of writing, both of these programs are still in beta and might be a little buggy. But hey, they're also free.

Omniture Site Catalyst

So with the free packages out there, why would you pay for an analytics tool? After all, they can wind up being very expensive. Because there's more to running a Web site than attracting people through the search engines. Google Analytics is aimed primarily at users coming from search engines, but paid tools such as StatCounter and Omniture capture an enormous amount of information. Google provides you a lot of pre-formatted reports and can do a limited amount of custom reporting. But Google also won't report when a user downloads PDF files, JPEGs, or Flash files. And if you need to know about server error messages, you have to look them up on your own.

The more sophisticated the tool, the more sophisticated the analysis you get back. Here's an example of a detailed analysis: Say you want to know how those who bought from you found your site. Using an analytics package, that's pretty easy. But what if you want to compare users who bought over a period of several weeks against the path those users took through your site and the time of day they showed up? And then you wanted to see how many people came from the same source (banner ad, keyword, press release) but then dropped out and left your site? This is where the more sophisticated Web analysis comes in.

You would need a high-end analysis tool in order to perform these multidimensional queries. If you have a smaller Web site, knowing who showed up when from where and what they did would probably be enough data for you. But if you're a much larger company, you need these more sophisticated tools in order to help you find more prospective customers and figure out the competition better.

These paid Web analytics tools are worth every penny you spend on them. Which is good, because Omniture is pretty expensive. Be prepared to spend $1,500 or more for this monthly subscription service if you purchase it directly from Omniture. Installation is also expensive: Set-up fees are usually around $5,000. But it's worth it: Omniture is one of the best analytics packages out there. Figure 1-3 is the Omniture dashboard.

Omniture is both JavaScript and pixel-based and is good for large sites. It can do both A/B and multivariant testing. *A/B testing* is comparing one page with another, and *multivariant* is comparing multiple pages.

Omniture is also good because you can tie in outside data, like your marketing and your log file analysis (more on that in the next section) and get a more comprehensive report, whereas Google Analytics only covers online data.

One way to trim your costs is to buy Omniture through a reseller. Omniture costs a lot if you buy it directly from the company. They sell in "blocks" of page views per months. For example, the first block Omniture directly offers is 1–1,000,000 views; if your site only gets 8,000 views, you still have to pay the same amount as someone who gets 1,000,000 page views. A reseller, such as Bruce Clay, Inc, buys the blocks from Omniture and then sells out the individual page views. A reseller buys the 1,000,000 page view block, and then sells to four sites that each get 250,000 pages views for a lower rate. We sell ours at $98 per 100,000 page views a month. Thus, you get a break.

Figure 1-3:
The Omniture suite of analytics tools is among the best in the industry.

Others

StatCounter (www.statcounter.com) is another analytics package that is available as a free service. Like Google Analytics, it offers a stat counter that you can choose to have visible on your site or not. It also offers custom summary stats based on all your visitors and a detailed analysis of your last 500 page loads. Plus, it gives you the ability to manage multiple sites from one account.

Also using StatCounter, you can figure out

✦ What keywords visitors use to find your site

✦ Which are your most popular pages

✦ Which links are used to reach your site

✦ What countries your visitors come from

✦ How visitors navigate through your site

StatCounter is pretty good for a free service, but you're not going to get as much detailed information as you would get from one of the paid analytics packages.

WebTrends is another popular analytics company (available at www.web trends.com/.) It offers tools tailored specifically to your business model, like retail, travel, technology, and so on, and has programs for international Web sites as well, including Germany and France. Pricing is available upon request because they tailor specifically to your needs. Contact them via their Web site for more info.

ClickTracks (www.clicktracks.com) starts at about $299 dollars a month. ClickTracks promises fast statistics, a way to track user behavior, the ability to segment data (email, PPC campaigns, keywords, search engines, and so on), and an ability to watch your return of investment (ROI). This is software that runs on your desktop.

Getting Started: Log Files Analysis

Your Web site generates a lot of information. All you need to do is check out your server logs and you can see that. Your *server log* is something your server automatically creates of all the activity it performs. It's a record of everything that happens during a given time period, be it hours, days, or minutes. More than just recording page loads, the server load includes every image loaded, every script run, and so on. It is a moment by moment map of site activity that involves your server. So it should be really easy to just pull up your server logs and read who's coming into your site, what they did, and where they came from, right?

Well, no, not really. Figure 1-4 is what your server log looks like. It does not make for light afternoon reading.

It's filled with incredibly dense information because the computer is recording it in its own language, which isn't exactly readable for someone who doesn't speak serverese.

When a user connects to your server, the server records a line of data that looks a little like this:

```
72.173.901.16 - - [06/Oct/2008:19:46:42 -0800] "GET /
    Mustang67red.html HTTP:1.1" 200 22832 "-" "Mozilla/4.7
    (compatible; Firefox)"
```

The numbers on the left tell you who is asking for the file. A *reverse DNS lookup* (looking at what server the user is coming from) tells you that it's someone from www.mabelsmotors.com. This means someone came onto your site and looked up a file named Mustang67red.html. Time is calculated in the Greenwich Mean Time (GMT), in this case 19:46:42 (7:46 pm on the 12 hour clock), and the -0800 means the visitor is in the Pacific time zone. The request was from the 1.1. Hypertext Transport Protocol, and your server returned a 200, which meant it happily showed the file. A 404 or any other *error code* (message the server sends when something goes wrong) means that it could not find the file or something went awry on your site. Errors are usually found in a separate error log.

Then the log file shows us that the server sent back 22,832 bytes of data, and the hyphen in quotes ("-") lets us know the referral link. (The hyphen indicates that the Web site link was entered manually rather than clicked. A visitor coming from a link would have a referring URL in place of the hyphen.) The end line lets us know that the user is using the Netscape 4.7–compatible Firefox browser.

If your head is spinning, that's completely understandable. And here's what's worse: the preceding code is (comparatively) simple to understand and analyze. But a big Web site generates something in the neighborhood of more than 80 gigabytes of server logs *a day.* So it could get pretty tedious, extremely time-consuming, and definitely frustrating to try and do this all by yourself. Fortunately, that's why you have a computer.

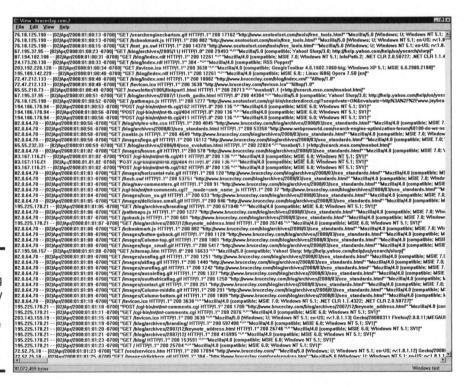

Figure 1-4:
A server log is extremely informative after you've learned to read it.

If you have a large site, you definitely want to host your log file analysis on a different server than the one you use to serve up the Web pages on your site. Major companies like Google have rooms and rooms full of servers because they serve millions and millions of pages a day, but they have entire server farms dedicated to log file analysis. Serving data is one thing; actually analyzing it is another bag of cookies altogether.

If you serve a million pages and each page is made up of ten files and each file is about 20 kilobytes, your server has to find, read, and send 200 gigabytes of data. To analyze the data, the software needs to categorize it, hold it in memory, compare it, and report on the findings. Sifting through a gigabyte of data is not something you want to do on the same machine that is serving those pages. The amount of work the machine has to do makes viewing your site incredibly slow, never mind making the server keel over and catch fire. So having a separate server (or servers) for your log file analysis is a good thing.

There's the human factor, as well. It takes much more than a few IT guys on entirely too much caffeine to do a log file analysis. You're going to need some tools to help you as well. But choosing the right one is a little tricky and there are some things you need to be thinking of when choosing a log file analysis tool:

✦ **What is the target audience for the software?** You need a log analysis tool that you can tailor specifically to your Web site's needs. Some tools are meant for large, robust sites that have to crunch huge numbers daily; others are made for only basic use. Some are very user friendly, and others expect a certain level of expertise on your part. You have to take into consideration your industry, your Web site's ins and outs, and your promotional campaign.

✦ **Flexibility:** The more powerful the tool, the more flexible it can be. Generic reports can be useful, but if you want to make your log file analysis really work for you, you need a tool that you can customize to your Web site's goals. It's not likely you'll be able to do this with a log file report.

✦ **Archiving:** Log file analysis becomes more successful over time, but storing the data can become unwieldy. You need a tool that offers file compression and archiving that shrinks the files and stores them for future use.

✦ **Output:** Some tools just spit out numbers. Others arrange them neatly into graphs. A really good tool allows you to manipulate the data much easier than a bad tool, in order to compare and contrast from outside sources.

✦ **Scalability:** The larger the site, the more likely it is that a low-end tool (or even a free one) is not going to cut it.

✦ **Speed:** The difference between getting your log reports right away versus getting them the next week depends on how powerful your machine is. But faster reporting gives you an edge, and the better tools use special indexing techniques to allow them to perform much faster.

Be aware that there is no such thing as an overnight success, no guarantees, and no instant gratification. Log file analysis, like all of SEO, is something that takes time and concentrated effort to do properly. Remember, the cheaper you want it, the cheaper you get it. High performance accurate tools that don't crash if there is too much data are worth what they cost you.

Log file analysis tools

There are several log file analysis programs out there (usually running a quick search on Google will turn up several), but here are a few so you know what to expect.

✦ **Weblog Expert (`http://weblogexpert.com/`):** From their Web site: "Weblog Expert will give you information about your site's visitors: activity statistics, accessed files, paths through the site, information about referring pages, search engines, browsers, operating systems, and more. The program produces easy-to-read HTML reports that include both text information (tables) and charts." There is a free demo version available, and commercial versions start at $74.95 and $124.95.

✦ **Sawmill (`www.sawmill.net/`):** Has three different versions available. Sawmill LITE is the cheapest of the bunch and does the basics of log file analysis. Sawmill Professional is the next step up and is highly customizable. Sawmill Advanced is the most expensive, and has the most gadgets, including multi-processors and e-commerce options. There is a trial version available, and the commercial versions run from $99 to $30,000. Enterprise versions for extremely large sites are also available.

✦ **123LogAnalyzer (`www.123loganalyzer.com/`):** 123LogAnalyzer can do reports by cities/states/countries, analyze `.zip` and `.gz` (Unix) compressed log files on the fly, and support logs from server farms (or load balanced servers) without having to upgrade license. There is a trial version available, and commercial versions run from $99 to $699.

Check out traffic numbers

Here is a list of things to look out for in your log files to make sure your numbers are correct. Not every visitor to your site is a human, and it's the humans you want the data on — not the robots:

✦ **Search engine spiders:** Search engines use programs commonly called spiders or robots that come to your site and "read" it to help the search engine to analyze your site. You can check and see if the robots.text file was requested (this is how you figure out if your site was spidered or not). When you recognize a spider, grab the IP address and let the analytics software know to ignore hits from that address. Most good log analyzers reverse IP lookup the IP address to find spiders and ignore them for you.

✦ **Masked IP addresses:** Not every IP address represents an individual user. Corporations, universities, and even users from AOL can show your server a single IP address when in fact many people have visited your site. Watch for high traffic from a single IP address to see if you have more visitors than your log file suggests.

✦ **Cookies:** Don't expect accurate visitor counts from cookies. Many people set their browsers not to accept cookies. Cookies also can't distinguish multiple users on the same computer (like a library or school computer). Log files, however, do not contain cookie info.

✦ **Busting caches:** Caching is what happens when there is a saved copy of your Web site. It throws off your analytics numbers because you can be accidentally working off of an old copy of your page. (JavaScript doesn't cache, so you do not have to worry about this if you are running JavaScript tags.) One way to solve this problem is to create a dynamic page. A *dynamic* page is a page that is built on the fly from the database using scripts. You can also set your server to prevent caching if you have enough bandwidth.

✦ **Know your audience:** Some sites only track users who are logging on from home or from work, those sites filter users coming in from libraries and schools using public terminals. In general, this means they require a login or a persistent cookie, which public terminals are not likely to allow.

Analytics is not just about gathering data. It's all about knowing what you want from your Web site and then being able to read the pile of data you've acquired in order to see whether those goals are being reached, and what else you need to be doing differently to get a higher rate of conversion.

Chapter 2: Tracking Behavior with Web Analytics

In This Chapter

✔ **Measuring Web site usability**

✔ **Getting a handle on conversion tracking**

✔ **Tracking the success of your SEO project**

✔ **Analyzing rankings**

*I*n order to properly do Web analytics, you need to gather your data. But Web analytics is not just about collecting data. It's about collecting your data in such a way that you can read and understand it, and you can use it to make the necessary changes to your Web site. In this chapter, you discover several ways to gather analytics data.

You have to measure your Web site's usability, in order to figure out whether your Web design works for your users and brings you those conversions. Next we talk about conversion tracking. Is your site getting the number of *conversions* you want? Conversion tracking helps you measure not just the final number of conversions, but where people drop off before they make the final conversion.

Tracking the success of your SEO project is monitoring your keywords and your search engine rankings, and whether they're at the place they need to be, and if your traffic is increasing due to those rankings. Finally, we discuss how to analyze your rankings by putting them in the context of your business. Do your rankings in the search engine mean anything to your ROI (return of investment)? Read on to find out!

Measuring Web Site Usability

One of the first things you should do is to gather data in order to measure your Web site's usability. This means going through your site and testing how your users see your site, measuring whether the users are interacting with your site the way you want them to. There's a few different ways to do this: by using personas, A/B and multivariate testing, and cookies and session IDs. We discuss all of these methods in the upcoming sections.

Personas

Personas are created in order to measure certain statistics for a Web site. To create a typical persona, you profile a user who fits the demographical information of your target audience, but you customize the profile to fit a real person.

Here are a couple of sample persons: Jill is a 20-something white female from New York. She's a professional with a fairly large disposable income. She reads through your Web site, and because your Web site is about classic car customization, she doesn't find anything of interest to her, so she clicks on through. Doug is in his mid-thirties, works for a real-estate firm, and has three cars of his own already. He wants to stop and take a look at your site, and quite possibly subscribe to your newsletter.

But here's the thing: Neither Jill or Doug are real. They're made-up people, or *personas*, created by marketing or usability firms in order to go through your Web site to see if your site is properly targeting its demographics. A persona can give you an idea whether your Web site is going to work for your target demographic. A firm often designs 7–10 different personas who are then used as a preliminary test market for your Web site. These are people from different age groups, socioeconomic backgrounds, and ethnicities, and they go through your site and allow you to gather data on whether your pages are working the way you want them to or if you're turning off the very people you want to entice. If your audience is the go-getter type like Jill, a long meandering trip to the conversion point is going to lose her early on. But rushing someone like Doug could make him uncomfortable and cause him to bail out, leaving a shopping cart full of goodies behind.

If your site sells shoes, a persona can help you more effectively target your market because you can keep track of whether Jill is going through your site and actually making a purchase as opposed to hitting your site and leaving immediately afterwards. We offer a lot more information about personas and creating them in Book V, Chapter 1.

A/B testing

One of the most commonly used tools for testing your Web site usability is *A/B testing*. It's like doing a science experiment. You test your old version of your Web site (A) with the new version (B) to see which one measures up better. A/B testing and multivariate testing are somewhat complex. This section and the next describe them so that you understand what they mean and how they can help. Afterwards, we describe options to implement testing.

The big advantage of A/B testing is that you can send half of your traffic to the page(s) with the proposed changes while sending the other half to the current page. That way, you can compare your current conversion rate for at least part of your site traffic in case some of the proposed changes aren't working.

But you can't run off and do a hack and slash job on the test page and expect to get any sort of meaningful data out of it. Here are some guidelines to help you get meaningful, measurable results, if you plan to run A/B tests on a Web site change or an e-mail campaign:

✦ **Change only one variable at a time.** It's harder to figure out what exactly is working for you if you've changed several variables on the site.

✦ **Learn the precise process for diverting traffic.** One of the problems in A/B testing is that some marketers don't understand how to divert traffic and don't get accurate traffic numbers.

✦ **Establish accurate measures of volume.** It's hard to do a comparison test if you don't know how many people you're testing.

✦ **Look for significant differences.** If you see a difference in the conversion rate for the B test, you need to ensure this difference is significant. A miniscule change to your goal is probably not going to be worth the effort, whereas a significant change is.

✦ **Take the time to do a null test.** A *null test* is a test you run on two A pages (pages you haven't made any changes to) in order to establish a baseline and make sure the traffic isn't coming in weird. This is to make sure that your have half your traffic going to one page and the other half is going to the other page, and that you have enough people going into the test.

✦ **Run your test long enough to ensure results are real.** You're not going to get an accurate amount of data if you run the test only for a day, or a week. Make sure you run it long enough to get enough data to do an accurate comparison, typically a month, or more. Remember, with Web analytics, the more time you take to do something right, the better your results are.

✦ **Run segmentation tests.** A *segmentation test* is testing the variables in your incoming traffic, like testing the demographics of your incoming traffic by asking them to answer a couple of questions. Really, you can test any variable as long as you set it up right. The more information you have on your different variables, the better you can target specific changes to your site to drive up your conversions.

We cover much more on the ins and outs of A/B testing in the next chapter.

Multivariate testing

A/B testing is about measuring big changes to your site. It's comparing the old site with the completely new version. *Multivariate testing* is about testing all of those smaller changes to your site, like the change of a certain font, or a button instead of an arrow. Typically, you test many small changes to the same page at once instead of two totally separate pages like in A/B testing.

Most of the testing tools involve copying and pasting a piece of JavaScript into the code of the pages that you are testing. The control code on the top of the HTML page tells you that someone is trying to load the page. The tracking script at the bottom of the code tells you that the visitor saw the page, and then you have another code on the conversion page (whatever page the user views after they have completed a conversion) that tells you they converted and what version of the page they were looking at. If you do a test, each version of the landing page has a unique sticker for you to identify it by. If you're doing the test with Google Analytics, after the test runs for a while, Google populates reports for you. Other programs work similarly.

Here are some quick guidelines to keep in mind when running your test:

✦ **Test a small number of variations.** The rule of thumb is less than 100 variables per combination of tested pages.

✦ **Test big changes.** If you can't see any difference between two variations in eight seconds, your visitors probably won't either and their reactions won't tell you anything. They can't react to what they don't notice.

✦ **If conversions are relatively rare in your business, consider testing for early indicators.** If you're selling a $100,000 software package, for example, you won't have a high number of sales to test. Instead, optimize for conversion indicators such as request info, view product details, and so on.

✦ **Don't jump to conclusions.** A two-week test is not enough time to gather your data. Run each test for at least one month, if not two.

Cookies

When we talk about cookies, we don't mean a tasty sugary snack. *Cookies* are little files that get saved in your browser to keep track of information on a particular site. A cookie is what enables you to automatically log onto your Facebook account regardless of whether you've closed your browser session or even logged off and powered down your computer.

Once upon a time, a server would send out Web pages when they were requested, but didn't record any data on who requested the page, where it went, or any other associated user behavior. Cookies were created to save this information. Cookies are used to enhance the browser experience, improve usability for customer interactions, increase purchase behavior, and improve commercial Web site performance by keeping track of what the user is doing.

Cookies are either first-party or third-party, depending on the type of Web site that sets them. A first-party cookie is set by the site that the user is visiting, such as `www.classicarcustomization.com`. A third-party cookie is set by a third-party site providing a service to the main Web site, like a Web analytics vendor.

A first-party cookie can contain personal information such as user name and a login ID so that the user can be recognized when they visit a site. If cookies did not store this data, Web sites would have to request it every time the user returns to the site.

A third-party cookie tracks a visitor's path through `www.classiccar customization.com` so it can identify which pages work and which don't, helping optimize for better site performance. The ad network cookies track user behavior across multiple sites, helping them classify user behavior. This helps in the targeting of ads to user segments. For instance, frequent visitors of sports sites are given sports-relevant ads. Although anonymous, this multi-site gathering of visitor information has also caused some controversy regarding privacy violations.

Deleting third-party cookies

Your browser gives you options for deleting cookies. This, and the advent of anti-spyware software, has resulted in the deletion of third-party cookies. Cookie rejection is also being enabled by new software mechanisms that block cookies from ever being set on users' computers.

This is a slight problem in that mass cookie deletion and rejection can make it appear that a Web site's new visitors are increasing while returning visitors are decreasing, which is a change in visitor behavior that is pretty unlikely.

Solving the cookie dilemma

To fix this skew, client-side Web analytics vendors have enabled their cookies to be set by their client's Web site, making them first-party cookies, which are less frequently deleted. Although this does not prevent all cookie-caused inaccuracies (users can still delete all cookies or use different computers), this can help.

An alternate solution suggested by Jupiter Research is to use Adobe Flash *Local Shared Objects* (LSOs) as a cookie replacement or backup. Similar to a cookie, an LSO is a text file that can be read only by the Web site creating it. There's an extra benefit to using LSOs: Browsers and anti-spyware programs can't delete them, and most users don't know how. Although this works for now, it won't be long before users figure out how to eliminate these as well.

The solution to the cookie dilemma may be to better describe the cookies because some users see cookies as adding to the browser experience whereas others see them as an invasion of their privacy. It's easy to get confused between first-party and third-party cookies — which is helpful and which is of questionable value? In the end, every user has to decide for herself whether to delete cookies based on the pros and cons.

Session IDs

Instead of using a cookie, you might be tempted to use a session ID. A session ID is a way of tracking a user when they come to your Web site. Generally, we recommend that you don't use session IDs because they are assigned no matter who the visitor is, including a search engine robot. This means that every time a session ID is used, the search engines see a new page, and duplicate content mucks with your rankings in the search engine. Additionally, a session ID is not very useful when it comes to measuring your Web site usability because a session ID only tracks that user for the duration of their visit to the site. A cookie remembers that user when they return, whereas a session ID doesn't.

Overall, it's much better to use cookies to track your visitors, if they have cookies enabled in their browser.

Tracking Conversions

Your Web site's objective is to make you money, not just sit out in cyberspace and look pretty. Each activity on your site should be subtly directing the visitor toward a conversion. A *conversion* is a term used by marketers to describe the final outcome of a site visit. As long as that visitor does what you want them to do, they've completed a conversion.

Before any further analysis can be done, you need to identify which processes on your Web site you want to measure, and how your Web analytics solution will help in the measurement.

As a rule of thumb, keep these three things in mind when deciding which processes to measure:

✦ **Contact:** Make sure visitors can contact you if they have difficulty with the process.

✦ **Collect:** Make sure you can collect the appropriate data when visitors complete the process so that you can retain the visitors in the future.

✦ **Competitors:** If visitors have difficulty on your site, find out whether they are able to complete a similar process on a competitor site.

Before going into the details of conversion metrics, it is important to note that you are dealing with two types of conversions, your *Web site conversions*, conversions gained from your Web site, and your *marketing campaign conversions,* which is a conversion of any kind in the brick and mortar world. Because this is a book dealing with the online aspect, we concentrate on the Web site conversions.

So what should you be tracking on your site? We've put together a list of things you should be looking for. Feel free to add to this list as needed; this is just a jumping-off point for you to get started.

Measuring marketing campaign effectiveness

The first thing you should look at are your marketing campaigns. It's important to measure the effect of marketing campaigns on your Web site traffic. The following metrics are specific to marketing campaigns aimed at driving traffic to your site.

✦ **Campaign conversion rate:** The effect of conversions from specific campaigns. Did the conversions rise due to the ads you placed on other Web sites? Or a grassroots viral marketing campaign, like "These Come from Trees"? ("These Come from Trees" was an effort by an environmental group asking its users to place "These Come from Trees" stickers in public restroom stalls in order to curb over-usage of paper products — towels, toilet paper, and so on. These stickers had the URL of the organization's Web site printed on them, where they provided more information and stickers.)

✦ **Cost-per-conversion:** Cost effectiveness for specific campaigns. You have a great idea for a marketing campaign, but giving away twenty dollar bills stamped with your Web address might cost more than the actual conversion you're aiming for. Make sure you can afford the campaign before you start it.

✦ **Campaign ROI (return on investment):** Cost effectiveness for specific campaigns. Is your campaign bringing in the conversions you need, or are you losing money?

✦ **Segment conversion rates:** Track conversion progress over time. Your conversions most likely won't change overnight. Watch them over a long period of time to make sure that your campaign is effectively working.

✦ **Percent of orders from new and repeat customers:** Determines the effectiveness of marketing or customer retention programs. You want to attract new customers, yes, but you also want them to turn into repeat customers.

✦ **New and repeat customer conversion rates:** Helps understand barriers to online purchases. One repeat customer is worth more than a new customer because not only do they mean future conversions, but they also cost less than new customers because you don't have to spend a whole lot to keep them.

✦ **Sales per visitor:** Measures marketing efficiency. How much is someone likely to buy? How little? Get an average so you can figure out how to budget your campaign more effectively.

Here are some key metrics you should track regardless of whether your site is e-commerce, research, or any other kind of Web site:

✦ The conversion rates for any process that makes or saves money or is critical to the customer experience.

✦ The campaign conversion rate for current campaigns or the most expensive campaigns, if you have a lot of them.

✦ The cost-per-conversion for the campaigns you selected to monitor.

✦ The segment conversion rates for key or critical group conversions.

Here are some specific metrics that e-commerce sites should be tracking:

✦ The site-wide conversion rate (all purchases to all visits or visitors)

✦ New and repeat site-wide customer conversion rates

✦ The percent of orders from new and returning customers

✦ The average order value, site-wide and for new and returning customers

✦ Sales per visitor (compare to site-wide conversion rate)

After you have decided which site-wide processes to measure and how to measure them, the following metrics can help you understand visitor success or failure. These are metrics that follow whether a customer stays, searches, and actually makes a conversion:

✦ **Home to purchase:** The abandonment rate for visitors going through the sales path.

✦ **Search to purchase:** The abandonment rate for visitors coming from a site search.

✦ **Special offer to purchase:** This is the effect of various merchandising and pricing options.

✦ **Lead generation:** The abandonment rate when personal data is requested.

Establishing site objectives or goals and all of the parts that make up these objectives (the who, how, where, what, and why) are essential when tracking the conversions on your site. One of these factors could contribute to the success of your campaign and just as easily derail it.

Building conversion funnels

After your site objectives are established, you can measure your progress through the use of a conversion funnel. In the previous chapter, we defined the four basic Web sites: e-commerce, content, lead-generation, and self-service. On an e-commerce site, a conversion is obviously a sale. For a content site, it might be the number of newsletter subscriptions. Lead genera-tion sites try to gather information for later contact. Self-service sites are tar-geted at solving a customer's problems, so the measure might be time spent on the site.

In the conversion funnel in Figure 2-1, each step in the sales process on the way to conversion is fraught with visitor drop-off. (Steps in the funnel differ based on the type of business and conversion that you're seeking.)

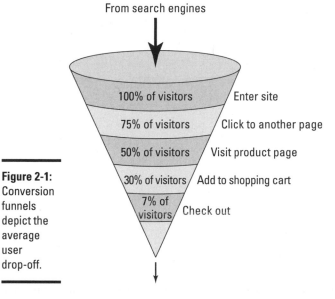

From search engines

100% of visitors — Enter site

75% of visitors — Click to another page

50% of visitors — Visit product page

30% of visitors — Add to shopping cart

7% of visitors — Check out

Figure 2-1:
Conversion funnels depict the average user drop-off.

Each block on the conversion funnel becomes smaller as we go down the sales (or conversion) path. This represents the amount of users you lose along the way to a conversion, for whatever reason.

The point of using a conversion funnel is to figure out where you are getting the most drop-off. In a perfect world, there would be no conversion funnels because all visitors to your site would perform your desired action and you would have a conversion column. But because this isn't a perfect world, your main goal is for the drop-off rate to be as low as possible.

It's a challenge to measure your Web site's conversion rate because there are a number of steps leading to that final action, and sometimes visitors are thwarted in their quest to complete an intended action. You can hope that you lost them just because their browser crashed, but sometimes they simply didn't find what they were looking for, or the site was too confus-ing, or it took too long for them to get to their objective, and so they left. Additionally, many sites measure only their final conversion rate. This does not give Webmasters the opportunity to improve their drop-off rates by analyzing the sales path and finding the bottlenecks in order to make the site improvements that result in higher conversions.

Don't measure your end result conversion rate without tracking the *path* that your customers take to conversion.

Preventing conversion funnel drop-off

In a typical conversion funnel, visitors drop off along the way to the final step that completes the sale or achieves the desired action. The good news is that when your *analytics program* (like Omniture or Google analytics, see Chapter 1 of this minibook for more info) tracks the micro steps required to reach the final conversion act, it reveals data that can be used to prevent drop-off. The analytics package you have does the work and the analysis so that you don't have to. Just be sure to implement the changes it recommends.

One of the things you can do is to eliminate all the unnecessary steps to visitor conversion to reduce the conversion funnel drop-off. The fewer steps needed for a visitor to convert, the greater the likelihood of a conversion. You should create an effective call-to-action for every step in the sales path. Your conversion rate reflects your ability to persuade visitors to complete their intended actions.

Analyzing your conversion funnel

Your conversion funnel is the path a user follows on your site on the way to a purchase. It's important to follow the conversion funnel closely and analyze where you're losing the most people by percentage. It's very unlikely that 100 percent of your visitors will continue on step by step, but you do want a high percentage of visitors to continue on.

Say you have an e-commerce site that gets 2,000 visitors per month, your site has a three-step sales path, and your average sale is $11 per item. If half of your site visitors enter the sales path, that means 1,000 prospects drop off at the first step. A 50 percent drop-off rate at the first step could be due to an impediment such as requiring site registration. If 40 percent of that total drops off at the second step, and 30 percent of that group completes the sale, you have $1,980 in sales at a 9 percent conversion rate because only 180 of the original 2,000 prospects made a purchase.

When people drop off, they have not found what they were looking for on your site. By identifying high abandonment pages, you can take a closer look to see what might be making visitors leave and test for ways that would make them want to stick around and continue on the conversion funnel. By properly analyzing this data, you can make sure you won't lose as many people along the conversion funnel. More people convert, which means more money for you.

Making site improvements

Using the math from the previous example, if you can improve the final step of the sales path by just 10 percent, it would bring you an additional $198 in sales, upping your conversion rate to 9.9 percent. However, if you can make improvements at the first step of the sales path, reducing your 50 percent drop-off rate to 25 percent, you can increase your sales by $5,940, resulting in a 36 percent conversion rate.

However, if you do not know what to measure and why, or haven't a clue of what indicators to evaluate in your analytics reports, you can't take the necessary actions to improve your site performance. So take the time to figure out the data to analyze based on your site objectives and then follow up on the data revealed through the use of your analytics software.

Simply picking out indicators that look good at first glance, like the increasing number of referrals from Google and Yahoo!, or the number of increased page views, might not help you improve site performance. It's not that these numbers are worthless, but they just might not be the right metrics to improve your site. Knowing the basic analytic principles ensures that you know what metrics to check for when making your business decisions.

So far in this chapter, we've talked about overall site objectives, but you also need to consider objectives for the individual pages within your site. That's what we discuss in the next section.

Assigning Web page objectives

Assign individual objectives to each page, especially the ones that require the user to perform an action. Every page should be designed to have a user perform an action, even if that action is something as simple as clicking over to the next page.

In order to effectively implement this, every page on your Web site that requires action should answer the following three questions:

✦ What action is required? These are things such as clicking to the next page, playing a video, or reading the text on the Web site.

✦ Who must take that action?

✦ What information does your visitor need to take the required action?

By answering these questions, you can define your objectives and apply good analytics solutions to test and optimize your pages for improved results. The same principles you used for site optimization can also work for page optimization.

Tracking the Success of Your SEO Project

Besides watching your conversions, you still need to keep an eye on the big picture: Is the time, effort, and money you are putting into your SEO project actually bringing you a return? You need to know whether the keywords you are using are actually working out for you. Are they affecting your rankings in the search engines? Have your rankings gone up, stayed the same, or actually gotten worse? And in particular, has your traffic increased as a result of search engine traffic?

Determining success relies on tracking your keywords more effectively. *Keywords* are the search terms that users put into the search engines, (we go over them in depth in Book II). When you are tracking keywords in order to see if they're working out for you, remember that it's not just the broad phrases you should be looking at, but also the smaller, more specific keywords and keyword phrases. *Keyword phrases* are groups of three or more keywords that users put into a query window, such as [classic car customization Poughkeepsie].

Using analytics, you can keep track of which keywords are working for you to gain more conversions and which ones are just not working out at all. You can keep track of how much you are spending on these particular keywords (through ad campaigns and whatnot, see Book II for more details) and if the ROI is really worth it.

Remember, if the keyword is not working out for you, don't be afraid to get rid of it and find a keyword that does.

SEO is much more nebulous when it comes to identifying and tracking the metrics. A good keyword might bring you more traffic, but if those users aren't giving you conversions, they're just using up server space and costing you time and money. That's why it's essential that you have relevant keywords and that you provide your users with the information or products you are advertising. For instance, if your keywords are [Classic car customization], your site should provide information on classic car customization.

There's also such a thing as too much information. The longer a person stays around your site, and the more they explore it, the more likely they are to provide you a conversion. So do provide them information, but don't do it all on one page. Spread it around your site, and make sure your users can have access to it.

Also keep in mind that SEO takes a while to fully work, so give it a decent amount of time before you really start to worry if you don't see a whole lot of change. It takes time for the changes to really take place, so be prepared to be patient, but it is truly worth it to put the time and the effort in.

Analyzing Rankings

Getting high rankings in a search engine is one thing. Say that you've achieved a coveted second or even first place spot on the first page of Google results for the keywords you wanted. However, getting to the top of the search engine results page means nothing if it doesn't help your conversion rate or your ROI. You're not doing SEO to get high rankings; you're doing SEO to get more conversions.

A high ranking in the search engine results page only increases your traffic, and that's great if the conversions you are looking for happen to be a high volume of traffic. But if your traffic volume doesn't provide you the conversions you need, and your bounce rate is pretty high, you need to figure out what's wrong with your site.

Analytics packages (such as those we talked about in the previous chapter) allow you to put these metrics next to one another, which you can then pair that data with a ranking monitor so that you can see the amount of your conversions next to how you are ranking.

You also need to be tracking the path your visitor took on the way to your site, so make sure that all of your visitors have a cookie. That way, you can know which users arrived from the search engines and which ones came from outside links, or from their own bookmarks. And if you know that, you can properly read the data coming in from the search engines. Also, be aware of seasonal trends in the search engines. Remember, some traffic is seasonal, especially around the holidays, so take that into consideration when you're watching your search engine rankings.

Chapter 3: Mastering SEO Tools and Reports

In This Chapter

✔ Getting started with A/B testing

✔ Getting to know page and site analysis tools

✔ Using link analysis tools

*I*n this chapter, we cover the nuts and bolts of A/B testing. We walk you through it step by step and hopefully demystify the process a little bit. We show you how to fix common conversion and usability problems, and introduce you to some page and site analysis tools. Finally, we discuss how to use link analysis tools.

Getting Started with A/B Testing

Say that you've gathered your data and done the proper analysis, and now you've decided that some things need to be changed on your Web site. Making major overhauls to your site requires A/B testing. *A/B testing* is testing the original version of the Web site (A) against the one you made the major changes to (B). The A/B test is a tool that tells you which changes have a better effect and to what degree.

We've discussed A/B testing in the previous chapters, but now we're going to go a little more in-depth and tell you how to actually *do* an A/B test. Before we get started, here are some cardinal rules you need to keep in mind for running an A/B test:

✦ **Change only one variable at a time, especially when A/B testing involves major changes to your site.** If you change more than one variable at a time, you can't determine which variable is responsible for the change and to what degree. Systematic testing helps you isolate important variables.

✦ **Divert enough traffic to your test page for a valid sample.** The object of traffic diversion is to redirect a percentage of visitors through the page you made all those changes to. Ideally, the percentage of traffic to be redirected can be easily changed without having to completely overhaul those pages.

✦ **Get a "visitors per page" count from your Web analytics tool.** This ensures that you actually get the percentage of traffic you're expecting moving through your site based on the number of changes tested. For instance, if you expect to run half through A and half through B, you should see nearly equal numbers of visitors to the first page in the process. If you are running a three-way test (testing A/B/C pages), you should aim for a distribution of 33/33/34 percent of visitors running through each path.

✦ **Look for significant differences.** If you see a difference in the conversion rate for the B test, you need to ensure this difference is significant (like more than .5 percent) so you can be certain it comes from the change you made to the B page. Smaller differences can be due to variations in your visitors or any other number of environmental factors. Keep running your test until all of the changes can be attributed to the exact step that was tweaked, or until you are certain there was no change.

✦ **Take the time to do a null test.** A *null test* is putting 50/50 traffic through two identical pages to be A/B tested. It's basically doing a control test for your science experiment. In this case, you replicate page A, calling this copy page B. Then without making any changes to page B, you test your analytics and conversions, which should be equal. A null test verifies that you get the same conversion and abandonment rates and that your measurement tools are set up correctly. If you are not getting close to the same rates for both pages (about .5 percent), something is wrong, and your data from the A/B test will be skewed. If this happens, check that you are sending visitors into the tests exactly the same way, and that you are running enough visitors through the test. Depending on your traffic volume, you need to attain a reasonable sample, and this can take time. You must run a null test to make sure the data you get back from the actual A/B test is accurate.

✦ **Run your test long enough to ensure results are real.** It takes time to gather good, solid data from an A/B test. For example, you may see trends in the first few hours that reverse themselves later. You need a representative sample before you can assume that B is better than A or that A is still better than B.

✦ **Run segmentation tests.** Segmenting (dividing into like groups) the subjects you are testing allows you to monitor their activities when they return to your site. This lets you target a group of visitors if it turns out that a good percentage of your B test visitors (presuming that A/B test results favored B over A) returned to the Web site within two months to make another purchase, especially if these were people who provided you with conversions.

The upside of A/B testing is that if your proposed changes don't work, not all of your visitors are subjected to the bad changes, only those whom you put through the B test. This is better than just making the change without testing and crossing your fingers. The downside is that A/B testing is a long, complicated process that takes knowledge, precision, and time.

Because conversions are critical to your business's success, start up a program of A/B split testing before making final site changes. Test two different versions of your page when you're testing things like changes on a call-to-action landing page, one at a time. Table 3-1 shows the hypothetical results of such a test.

Table 3-1	Sample Results of an A/B Test		
	Page A (Original)	*Page B*	*Page C*
Percent of traffic received	34%	33%	33%
New sales generated	200	220	150
Percentage of change	N/A	10%	-25%

Getting ready to run an A/B test

You can use any of several different tools to run an A/B test. Both Google Analytics and Omniture feature options for running A/B tests and *multivariate tests* (which are like an A/B test except that they test smaller details, like a different font color, instead of large changes, and you can test all variables at once with different permutations). In this section, we outline the broad steps you have to take before you run the test.

The first thing you need to do before running your test is to choose your test page. Not every single page needs to have an A/B test run on it: You probably don't care about conversions from your About Us page, for example. To be a good candidate for testing, the page needs to offer an action the user can take, like a purchase, download, or signing up for something. The action can be as simple as a link that you're wanting your users to click on — the point is that it has to be a measureable response.

For your first test, choose a landing page (the page that visitors first land on when they arrive at your Web site) that receives high volumes of traffic, like the top of a category or a PPC (pay per click) landing page. This lets you see meaningful results quickly.

The second step is choosing your conversion page. A *conversion page* is the page on which the action occurs that you want the user to take once they reach your Web site, be it the aforementioned purchase, download, or sign-up. If you have more than one conversion page, choose the one with the most traffic. You should use this page as the link from your test page.

For your first experiment, it's not important what the link does. When you're doing further, more in-depth testing, choose the conversion you wish to track in order to measure the success of your test page. Remember, these tests are to figure out whether they're successful from a user standpoint.

**Book VIII
Chapter 3**

**Mastering SEO
Tools and Reports**

The third step is to figure out which kind of test you want to run. The Website Optimizer, a free tool from Google that we cover later in the section, "Doing an A/B test with Website Optimizer," allows you to run an A/B or multivariate test. Depending on what kind of changes to your site you want to make, you can choose to either run the A/B test (for the big changes) or the multivariate test (for the small ones).

A/B tests compare the performance of two entirely different pages, which means trying out entirely different layouts, moving around sections of the page, or changing the overall look and feel of a page. A/B tests are simpler to run, and you can obtain results must faster.

Multivariate tests allow you to test content variations in different sections of your page simultaneously. So instead of tracking one or two big changes, you can test two different headlines, three different images, and two different product descriptions. Obtaining results from these kinds of tests take longer, but they're more flexible than A/B tests.

The fourth step is choosing the content you want to test, if you're running a multivariate test. For a multivariate test, for example, you might test the headline and an image to go with it, not a totally new page structure.

For an A/B test, you wouldn't need to choose the content you're testing because you're comparing two completely separate pages, as shown in Figure 3-1. (They don't necessarily have to be two separate pages — you can run an A/B test on just about anything, like which offer brings in more conversions: free phones or free kittens.)

The fifth step is creating the actual content variations you want to test. For a multivariate test, for example, you could try a heading in a new font and test out some new wording, and perhaps a different image as well (see Figure 3-2). Smaller changes like this should be tested with a multivariate test, not an A/B test, because you get better results.

For the A/B test, you need your test page A (your control page) and your test page B (the page with significant changes).

During the experiment, your visitors either see your control page (A) or your test page (B). This way, you can test whether the variations in the content or page lead to more conversions. Do people react differently with different images or text? Or does re-arranging your site differently lead to easier access for your users and more conversions for you?

The variations need to be *significantly* different than the original content. You're not going to see much change if your headline changes from "Welcome!" to "Come on in!," for example. Someone brand new to your page should be able to tell at a glance what's different about the page. Subtlety has no place in an A/B test.

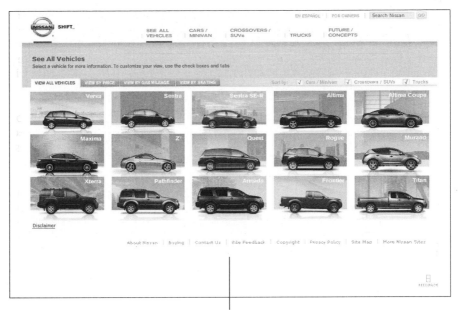

Page A-Original

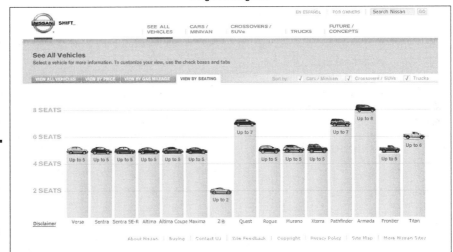

Page B-Test

Figure 3-1:
For an A/B test, you run version A against version B to see which performs better.

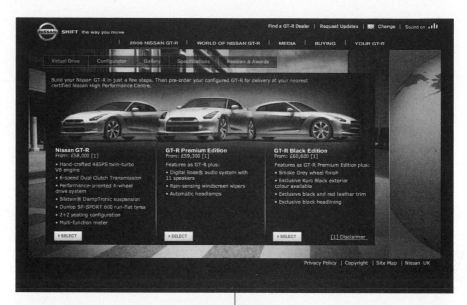

Page A-Original

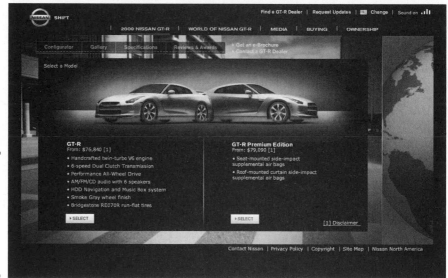

Figure 3-2:
Multivariate
tests use
multiple
variables on
the same
page.

Page B-Test

The last step is deciding how much traffic you want for your test. You are running this test on your actual Web site, so you might not want to lose a whole lot of your site traffic. You can actually choose to limit how many of your visitors see the new version of your page. But keep in mind that if you limit the amount of traffic to the test page, you're going to have to wait a lot longer to get any sort of meaningful results from this test. You need to run your test for at least a month to get any kind of decent results, and it may take even longer than that. Don't quit too soon and make a judgment based on early numbers.

Doing an A/B test with Website Optimizer

Website Optimizer is a free tool provided by Google (available at www.google.com/analytics/siteopt/splash?hl=en) that runs A/B and multivariate tests. After you sign in and agree to the user terms, you're all set and ready to go. We walk you through using this tool because it's quick, accurate, and free.

In order to start the A/B testing process, you need to do the following things:

1. **If you're using Website Optimizer within Google AdWords, sign in to your AdWords account and visit the Campaign Management tab, and then choose the Website Optimizer tab.**

If you're using Website Optimizer through the standalone site, just sign in there (see Figure 3-3). Click Get Started, and you're on your way.

After accepting the Google Analytics Terms of Service (if you haven't already), you reach the Experiment List page, which displays a summary of all your experiments.

**Book VIII
Chapter 3**

**Mastering SEO
Tools and Reports**

Figure 3-3:
Click the
Get started
button to
continue.

2. If this is your first experiment, your list is empty, like in Figure 3-4. Click Create Experiment, and you're on your way.

3. The next screen (Figure 3-5) asks you to choose between an A/B experiment and a multivariate experiment. For this example, we're doing an A/B test, so click the A/B experiment link.

4. On the next screen, review the checklist they provide, which is similar to the previous section in this chapter:

   1. Choose the page you would like to test.

   2. Create alternate versions of your test page.

   3. Identify your conversion page.

Check the box labeled I've Completed the Steps Above and I'm Ready to Start Setting Up My Experiment, and then click the Create button. You're off to step 1 of the testing process!

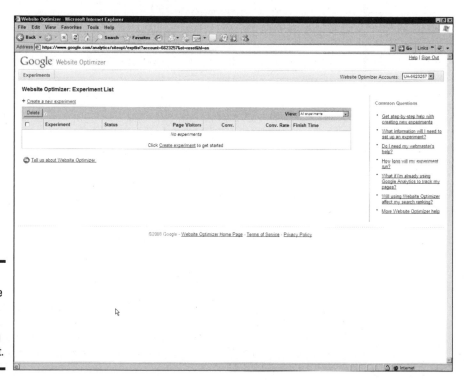

Figure 3-4:
Click Create Experiment to proceed with setting up your test.

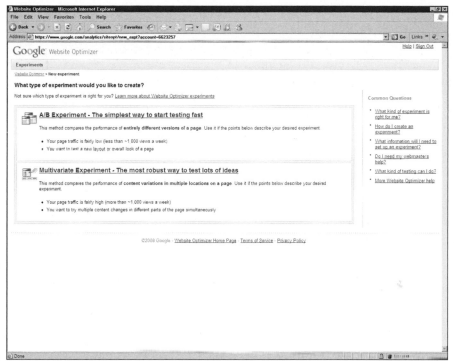

Step 1: Name your experiment and identify pages

In order to begin, you need to supply the Website Optimizer with some information, as shown in Figure 3-6:

1. **Enter a name in the Name Your Experiment box.**

   You can call it pretty much anything, from "Experiment 1" to "Experiment 92: Electric Boogaloo." The only thing you need to be able to do is distinguish one experiment from the other.

2. **Enter the URL of the test page that you picked out in the Identify the Pages You Want to Test box.**

   The URL you enter should not contain any information after the page's file name (such as index.htm or productpage.html). If you include query parameters, they are ignored. Enter any other URLs you have for each alternate page you have created. Remember, each alternate page you create has to be saved at a unique URL in order to be used in an A/B test.

3. Enter the URL of the conversion page in the Identify Your Conversion Page box.

Like the test page, it should not have any extra information after the page's filename.

After you have entered this information, Website Optimizer validates the URLs. If you leave either the test page or conversion page field blank, or if Website Optimizer got an error trying to access either page, it generates an error message.

Your pages must all be on the same domain.

After you have validated the URLs, you go back to the experiment work flow page. You can save your pages at any point in the process by clicking on the Save Progress and Finish Later link, as is shown in Figure 3-7. You will be taken back to the main page to see where you are in the process.

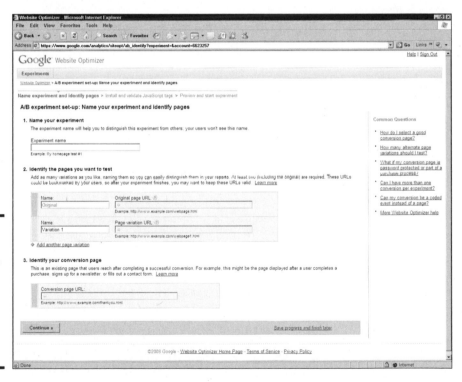

Figure 3-6: Enter the name of the campaign and the original, test, and conversion page URLs.

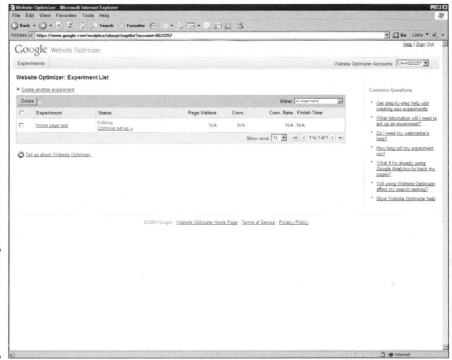

Figure 3-7:
The Website
Optimizer
with the
first step
complete.

Step 2: Install and validate JavaScript tags

The next step is installing the JavaScript HTML tags into your site's code. You have an option of doing it yourself, or letting someone else with a working knowledge of HTML do it for you. Website Optimizer provides the specific script to be installed, as well as detailed instructions available in their installation guide. This script also sets a *cookie* (a piece of text that allows a browser to remember a previous session) in your visitor's browsers, so you should ensure that your site's privacy policy covers the setting of cookies.

After you or your Web team has installed all the tags, you need to validate them. Website Optimizer provides a validation tool that examines your pages and verifies that the tags have been installed properly. If the validation tool detects any problems with the installation, you need to fix them before continuing. Website Optimizer won't let you go on to the next step without validating.

Website Optimizer has two methods of validating your pages:

✦ The first method requires you to provide the URLs for your test and conversion pages. If your pages are externally visible, Website Optimizer accesses them and notes any errors, as described previously.

✦ The second method is used if Website Optimizer can't access the pages on your live site. You would need to upload the HTML source files for your test and conversion pages. This is helpful if your pages are part of a purchase process, behind a login, or inaccessible for some other reason. All you need to do is save the HTML source of your pages and upload the files, and Web site Optimizer validates them.

After you've validated your pages for a second time, you are directed to preview your pages.

Step 3: Preview and start experiment

After you've tagged your pages and created your variations, relax: The hard part's over. All you need to do now is turn the experiment on. But be warned: After you start running the experiment, you can't change any of the variables, so make sure everything is as you want it to be before you start.

If you do find a problem, all you need to do is click the Back button to return to the Experiment Work Flow page, and click the Preview link. But if you change the page URLs at this point, you have to go through and re-install the code on the new pages and re-validate everything.

Step 3 is also where you get one last chance to preview the alternate page variations that are displayed to visitors during the experiment. If anything needs to be changed, click Back and Preview.

Ready, Set, Go!

After you click Start, you are sent back to the Experiment Work Flow page.

You also see an additional section on the page describing the progress of this experiment, including estimated duration and the number of impressions and conversions tracked during the experiment. Your test page starts showing different variations immediately, but a delay of about an hour takes place before your reports start displaying data. The progress and duration of the experiment depends on how much traffic goes through your test and conversion pages.

After you've got some significant data, the reports have preliminary results ready for you. Click View Report to see experiment results.

Viewing your results

Be sure to check that *impressions* (number of times the pages displayed) and conversions are being recorded soon after starting your experiment. If you're not getting any impressions or conversions, check the troubleshooting guide for some suggestions on what might be causing this error. Sometimes errors occur that don't show up until the experiment is actually running.

Hold off on checking your reports right away. Until a minimum amount of data has been collected, you get a message along the lines of Hold on There, Cowboy, We Don't Have a Complete Report Yet. (Well, okay, not literally, but you get the idea.) Check back in a day or two in order to see your results start coming in. With any A/B test, you want to wait long enough to gather enough data for it to be meaningful. When you have enough data, you can check your reports, which look something like Figure 3-8.

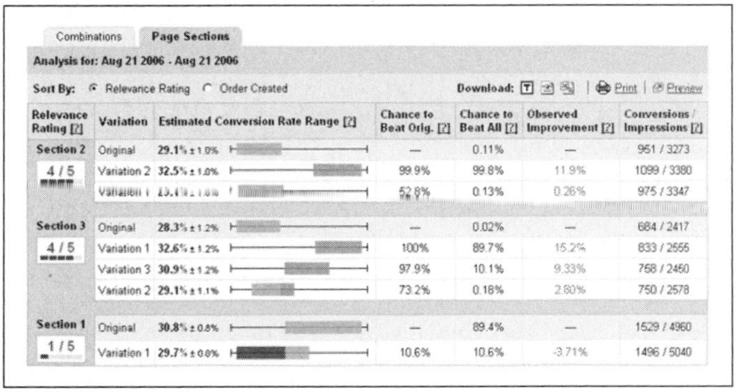

Combinations | Page Sections

Analysis for: Aug 21 2006 - Aug 21 2006

Sort By: Relevance Rating / Order Created — Download: Print | Preview

Relevance Rating [?]	Variation	Estimated Conversion Rate Range [?]	Chance to Beat Orig. [?]	Chance to Beat All [?]	Observed Improvement [?]	Conversions / Impressions [?]
Section 2	Original	29.1% ± 1.0%	—	0.11%	—	951 / 3273
4 / 5	Variation 2	32.5% ± 1.0%	99.9%	99.8%	11.9%	1099 / 3380
	Variation 1	[illegible]	52.8%	0.13%	0.26%	975 / 3347
Section 3	Original	28.3% ± 1.2%	—	0.02%	—	684 / 2417
4 / 5	Variation 1	32.6% ± 1.2%	100%	89.7%	15.2%	833 / 2555
	Variation 3	30.9% ± 1.2%	97.9%	10.1%	9.33%	768 / 2460
	Variation 2	29.1% ± 1.1%	73.2%	0.18%	2.80%	750 / 2578
Section 1	Original	30.8% ± 0.8%	—	89.4%	—	1529 / 4960
1 / 5	Variation 1	29.7% ± 0.8%	10.6%	10.6%	-3.71%	1496 / 5040

Figure 3-8: Page reports from Website Optimizer provide confidence scores.

The table looks pretty complicated, but Website Optimizer has a guide on how to read it at `www.google.com/support/websiteoptimizer/bin/answer.py?answer=55944`. Here's what they say, slightly paraphrased:

- **Estimated conversion rate range** provides the most immediate insight into overall performance. When the bar is green, a combination is performing better than the original. Yellow bars mean the result is still up in the air; they don't have enough data yet. Gray bars mean that a page is performing on the same level as the original. A red bar means that the combination isn't doing as well as the original.
- The **chance to beat original** column, immediately to the right, displays the probability that a combination will be more successful than the original version. The higher, the better the test page will do.

✦ **Improvement** displays the percent improvement over the original combination or variation. You can ignore this one until you have a lot of information. Low numbers will lead to unreliable data.

✦ **Conversions/visits** is the number of conversions and visits a particular combination generated.

They also have an option to learn the specific technical results at `www. google.com/support/websiteoptimizer/bin/answer.py?answer= 61146`. The explanation is pretty number-intensive, so tread at your own risk.

With enough time and data, the Optimizer identifies the winning variation. It's all a matter of how long you run the experiment and how similar the variations are. If you've run the experiment for a long time and still don't have a clear winner, your variations might be too similar to get correct data, so you may need to make some tweaks and run another experiment.

In order to stop the experiment at any time, click the Pause link on the Experiment page.

Discovering Page and Site Analysis Tools

When you run a pay-per-click (PPC) campaign, you spend money whenever potential clients click on your advertisement. Because you're spending money on that campaign, you want to know how much money or value you're getting back for that campaign. That's where PPC Conversion reports come in.

First, you need to know what you want your Web site visitors to do. This can be anything from purchasing products, to signing up for a newsletter, to just getting more traffic to your Web site. After you know what you are measuring, you can view how well you're doing in your Analytics software.

PPC Conversion reports tell you things like how many people are buying products. They can also be configured to tell you how much money you made from selling products to people who came from a PPC advertisement. For example, in Google Analytics, you can run an AdWords Campaigns report and find the information shown in Figure 3-9.

The report in the figure tells us how many Visits you had for a particular keyword, the number of times the ad was displayed (Impressions), the number of clicks that you received (Clicks), and how much those clicks cost you (Cost). With all of that information, the report determined your ad's *click-through rate* (CTR), how much your *cost per click* (CPC) was, and how much you made from that advertisement based on the *revenue per click* (RPC).

Figure 3-9:
Your
AdWords
campaigns
can be
a good
source of
information
about
your site.

Dimension: Keyword	Visits ↓	Impressions	Clicks	Cost	CTR	CPC	RPC
1. seo software	2	0	0	$0.00	0.00%	$0.00	$0.00
2. seo tool set	1	24	2	$4.15	8.33%	$2.08	$0.00
3. seotoolset	1	31	2	$0.48	6.45%	$0.24	$0.00

With these types of reports, you can analyze your spending and your revenue based on PPC ads. This information helps you decide which keywords, advertisements, and campaigns are working the best for you and which ones are not working so well. With this information, you can optimize your PPC campaigns by limiting your spending and maximizing your revenue based on the spending constraint.

Understanding Abandonment Rates

Abandonment rates can be broken up into two categories: how soon the visitor left your site, and what page they were on when they left your site. These both have different meanings, and it is important to understand what they mean.

When visitors leave your site, it's natural to want to know why. When a visitor leaves after visiting a lot of pages, or going through a process on your Web site, that is when you want to know which page they left from. If they leave the site on the first page of their visit, the visitor is probably not satisfied with your site at that time. Reasons for their exit could range from the site not answering a specific need of the user to a bad design that just makes the visitor want to leave. Another reason is that the visitor only came to your site for one thing, found it, and then left — this is often the case with a blog. The percentage of visitors who leave after only looking at one page is called the *bounce rate*.

An *exit page* is the last page the visitor was on before they left the site. Most users leave usually because they have not found what they were looking for or they find your site hard to use and think they can find a better alternative. It is important to note that in most cases, the exit page that has the most number of visitors leave is usually the page that contributes most to your bounce rate.

**Book VIII
Chapter 3**

**Mastering SEO
Tools and Reports**

Both types of reports can be found in almost every analytics suite. Figure 3-10 is an example of a bounce rate graph: It shows how often a visitor leaves after only viewing one page.

Figure 3-10:
Your bounce
rate can
help you
tune your
demographic
targeting.

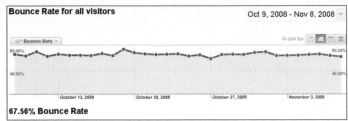

Figure 3-11 shows the top exit pages on your site (bottom half of the figure), so that you can see where people are most frequently abandoning your site. Locating these pages can help you strengthen the weak points in your conversion process.

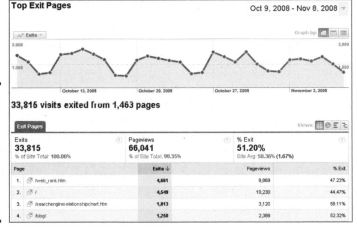

Figure 3-11:
Exit pages
may
indicate
weak points
in your
conversion
funnel.

Measuring Traffic and Conversion from Organic Search

Measuring how much of your traffic and conversion is from *organic* (non-paid) search is important because it tells you how much traffic and money you are getting for your SEO efforts. Every SEO campaign costs you time and money, so you want to know what you're getting back for it. Most analytics software packages come with an out-of-the-box report for getting traffic from organic search. Figure 3-12 is from Google Analytics.

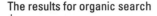
The results for organic search

The results for organic search

Figure 3-12:
This graph shows the number of visitors who came to the site via organic search and which pages they landed on most often.

Click maps

Click maps are reports that overlay your pages and tell you, on a per-page basis, which links visitors are clicking on to go to other pages on your site. Often, the most clicked-on links are bigger, have a richer color, or a note telling you how many clicks the link received.

These reports are helpful because they give you some insight on what visitors find interesting about your Web site. Using these reports, you can determine if a call-to-action is working, or if the visitors are reading and clicking on what you want them to on any specific landing page.

These reports are made by loading the current page, and then using an overlay with the link statistics on it. Each statistic is displayed where the link on the underlying page is. The example in Figure 3-13 is from Omniture. The picture receives the most amount of clicks, indicated by its darker color. Other links in this example also have click activity.

Pathing

Now that you know where visitors are coming from, whether the visitor converts, and which links they are clicking on, you can put it all together with pathing. *Pathing* tells you how a visitor navigated through your site to wind up at their final destination. This helps you determine if people are just searching through your site until they get something they are looking for, or if they are following a predetermined path that gets them to something you want them to get at.

The example in Figure 3-14 is from Omniture. In this graph, you can see the most popular paths taken on this site.

Highlights indicate popular links.

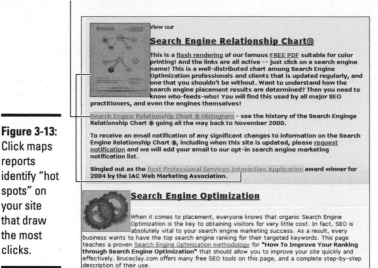

Figure 3-13: Click maps reports identify "hot spots" on your site that draw the most clicks.

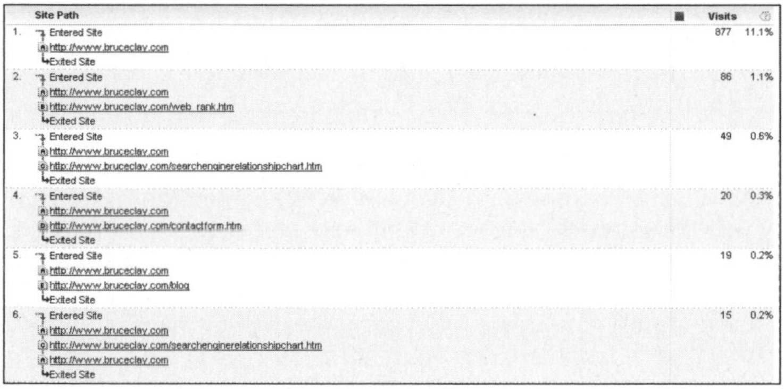

Figure 3-14: Pathing reports from Omniture allow you to track popular paths on your site.

Using Link Analysis Tools

Web sites earn a variety of inbound links. Some of these you get naturally, and some of them you might pay for. Either way, it's helpful to know if those links are sending worthwhile visitors to your site. You can measure that by finding your conversions from referring links.

First, you need to know some things about referring links. *Referring links* can span a lot of different types, including referrals from search engines, social media, and even your own site. Because of this, it may be a good idea to divide your referring links into different segments. You could divide your reports into links from Search Engines, Blogs, Paid Banner Ads, Internal

Blog, and more. By doing this, you have an easier time determining which initiatives are giving you the most return, instead of looking at them one link at a time.

Second, you need to determine what a conversion on your site is. This could be anything that you want your visitors to do. After you know what that is, you can set up your analytics software to report measurements on that metric. For example, say you're trying to find how many new visitors you're getting from our new profile on the social networking site Twitter (`www.twitter.com`). In this case, your conversion metric is a new visit and your referring link would be anything from `www.twitter.com`, including from subdomains such as `m.twitter.com`, which is the mobile version of the site.

Knowing these pieces of information, you can run a report that tells that you had 302 new visitors to your site in the last month from Twitter, as shown in Figure 3-15. You can also see that this represents only 1.27 percent% of your total visitors in the last month:

Now that you have this information, you can determine if your time managing and keeping up with your Twitter account is worth the additional exposure that you're getting. This is very useful to help decide whether a specific initiative is really paying off.

Figure 3-15: This report tells you that your traffic from Twitter. com and m.twitter. com was responsible for 1.27 percent of your total traffic.

New Visits	
302	
% of Site Total: 1.27%	
Source	New Visits ↓
1. twitter.com	300
2. m.twitter.com	2

Book IX
International SEO

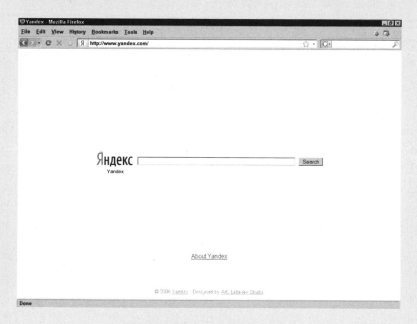

Yandex rules in Russian search.

Contents at a Glance

Chapter 1: Discovering International Search Engines 593

Understanding International Copyright Issues..593
Targeting International Users 595
Identifying Opportunities for Your International Site...........................600
Realizing How People Search 602

Chapter 2: Tailoring Your Marketing Message for Asia 609

Succeeding in Asia..609
Discovering Japan 612
Succeeding in China 613
Finding Out About South Korea...618
Operating in Russia 619

Chapter 3: Staking a Claim in Europe 621

Succeeding in the European Union 621
Knowing the Legal Issues in the EU...622
Working within the United Kingdom...623
Discovering France...625
Operating in Germany..627
Understanding the Netherlands 629

Chapter 4: Getting Started in Latin America 633

Succeeding in Latin America...633
Geotargeting with Google Webmaster Tools 635
Working in Mexico..635
Operating in Brazil...637
Discovering Argentina..638

Chapter 1: Discovering International Search Engines

In This Chapter

✔ Dealing with international copyright issues

✔ Targeting international audiences

✔ Identifying opportunities

✔ Quantifying how many people search

Throughout this book, we talk mainly about what to do to optimize for search engines here in the U.S., but what about the international market? What about Europe, Latin America, and Asia? This minibook covers what you would need to know about working on an international level.

In this chapter, you discover all the basics you need to know to start thinking globally. International copyright laws are different from domestic copyright issues, so you should definitely do some research before you jump right in. After you familiarize yourself with the law, you figure out how to actually target your international audiences. Cultures and languages vary across the globe, and if you don't properly adjust your market strategy for your international audiences, you risk failure.

You also need to be aware of the different opportunities there are in international search, and how many people out there are using search engines. Not to worry: We've got an overview all ready for you, so just read on.

Understanding International Copyright Issues

When doing business in other countries, you have to be aware of laws other than those of the United States. Unfortunately, to make things difficult on all of us, there is no such thing as a standard international copyright law. National laws, to no one's surprise, apply only to businesses operating within that country. Two countries can barely agree on pizza toppings, metaphorically speaking, let alone a standard international law. Instead, we have to contend with various international conventions, unions, and treaties.

Most nations in the world belong to some form of trade convention, treaty, or union. In case you're feeling daring (or suffering from insomnia), you can look up a list of all the various countries and the copyright treaties/conventions they belong to online at the U.S. government copyright site at www. copyright.gov/circs/circ38a.pdf.

The U.S. is a contracting party to the following treaties: the Berne Union, the Paris version of the Berne treaty, the North American Free Trade Agreement (NAFTA), the UCC, the Paris revision of the UCC, the WIPO Copyright Treaty, and the WIPO Performances and Phonograms Treaty. These treaties all have different levels of copyright protection and jurisdiction rules.

A copyright infringement case with international aspects is brought where the infringement took place. (This is when someone steals your stuff and passes it off as theirs or violates your copyright in any way.) This gets quite tricky when you throw in the whole "it happened on the Internet" part of the deal.

Courts all over the world have labored over this particular question, possibly in the same way that the general populace grapples with the chicken/egg conundrum. The kinds of questions these courts run into are something like this: Is the infringement location determined by the location of the server or the residence of the person committing the infringement? Does it depend on the residence of the copyright holder or the defendant? What about where the harm from the infringement occurred? It's a little like the riddle involving the goose, the fox, and the bag of grain. When someone tells you that international copyright issues are complicated, they're not lying.

But here are a couple of things that most courts all over the world agree on:

✦ The fact that you can view a Web site with *infringing content*, like a site that is illegally hosting a movie, in a particular country does not give that country jurisdiction unless you make a purchase, like buying a pirated DVD.

✦ The fact that the offending Web site is hosted on a server within a country does not give that country jurisdiction either.

It's becoming increasingly common that two or more countries have jurisdiction to hear the dispute. A good example is if the person with the offending Web site lives in Germany, and the copyright holder also lives in Germany, but the target market and the host server are both in Holland. The case can be brought to a court in either Germany or Holland because both countries have connections to the dispute.

What can also sometimes happen is that a court applies the laws of other countries. It's not something that judges like doing, but they will if the situation calls for it. Usually, this occurs because the parties in a contract agree to a specific forum. For example, a company in Germany and a company in

Thailand have both agreed to do business in Thailand, and they draw up a contract stating that any disputes are subject to German law and will be filed in Germany. If the Thai company exceeds the scope of the licensing agreement, the German company can file suit in Germany. If there was no contract in place, the German company might have to file the suit in Thailand and be subject to Thai law. If there is no contract in place, courts apply the law to the forum country, which is usually where the infringement takes place.

On an international level, the U.S. government became a member of the Berne Convention in 1989 and fully supports the Universal Copyright Convention. Under this convention, any work of an author who is a national of a convention country automatically receives protection in all countries that are also members, provided the work makes use of a proper copyright symbol (©). The degree of protection may vary, but some minimal protection is defined and guaranteed in that agreement. Jurisdiction for prosecuting violations lies exclusively with the federal government.

Targeting International Users

Say that you've decided to take your business to the international markets. You know that there is a market for classic car customization, and it will generate a whole lot more revenue for you and your company.

However, you have to think about certain challenges when you're gearing up to start working in the international markets. First of all, be aware of the different browsers other countries use. Not all of them use Internet Explorer or Mozilla Firefox, and when designing or tailoring your international Web site, you need to be aware of the constraints of whatever particular browser is popular in your target country or region. This is why good coding is so important. Remember to always test your Web pages in a validator like the one at the World Wide Web Consortium's Web site, www.w3c.org (more on validating your code can be found in Book IV, Chapter 3).

Another thing you need to be aware of is any difference in currency. It affects shipping rates and the prices of the goods you are trying to sell. For example, at the time of this writing, one Euro is the equivalent of 1.2933 United States dollars (USD), whereas one Japanese yen is the equivalent of .0100331 USD. But the exchange rates fluctuate continually. A good currency converter is available at XE (www.xe.com/ucc/).

The language barrier is a fairly tricky one to navigate as well. Some countries have multiple languages spoken by the populace. For example, in the Netherlands, there are two main languages spoken by the population, Dutch and Frisian, but most people speak English or German as well. Marketing in the correct language can be trickier than you'd think. Having local input is the best way to make sure you're getting it right.

Be especially aware of cultural dimensions within that language. Spanish is spoken in many different countries, but there are different variations, and what can be a completely innocent word in one country can be a very nasty slang term in another. For example, in the U.S., when you want to determine what is causing a problem, you'd say you're trying to get to the "root" of the problem. In Australia, "root" is slang for something very different and using it in a business meeting will probably get you accused of sexual harassment. It's equally important to understand the impact of culture on the language. In Japanese culture, four is an unlucky number, so if your company has "four" in the title, or in advertisements, you might want to make a couple of tweaks if you're going to expand into the Japanese business market. It's the same as being aware of the number 13 and its impact in America.

Some other issues to think about with language include

+ **Local terms:** This is especially important if you hope to do local business within that country. Your classic car customization site for Southern Germany could use a listing of dealerships in Bavaria, for instance.

+ **Spelling and grammar differences:** The Spanish spoken in Spain and the Spanish spoken in Central or South America all have some key differences when it comes to spelling and grammar. For one thing, in Spain, Spanish makes use of verb conjugations for the plural second person, "vosotros," whereas Spanish spoken in Mexico rarely uses it.

+ **Popular culture references:** Be aware of dating yourself. Keep up on the pop culture trends in that country if you have a business that would be related (such as one that sells clothing). For example, if a site from Bulgaria talked about a popular sitcom character named Steve Urkel, when the sitcom the character is from hasn't been on the air in the U.S. in many years, it would date the site.

+ **Translation issues:** You risk a big hit to your credibility if you're not careful translating your Web site content from its original language to a new one. For example, in Wales, a Web site that had been improperly translated for a school listed their staff as a "stave made out of wood" in Welsh. We suggest adding someone who is fluent in both languages (and preferably someone actually from that country) to your content building and marketing process.

+ **Vocal culture issues:** This becomes an issue with languages that have different sounds than English. For example, in Japanese, there is no "t" sound, the closest approximation is "tsu," so a word like "fruit" would sound like "fruits" when pronounced in Japanese.

✦ **Visual design:** Figure out a country's particular design aesthetic. Study the visual culture of the target country. In both Japan and Korea, to look professional, you would want your Web site to have lots of bright colors and a busy page full of words and links. Google's ultra-clean homepage doesn't play well to that audience, but Yahoo!'s busy portal does. In England, however, a super busy and bright page is considered completely unprofessional. Similarly, color is an important consideration. In China, white is the color of death, much as black is here in the U.S. — probably not the best choice for your wedding site. Use red instead to represent joy.

When you are doing keyword research, make sure to do it in the target language. Don't just copy/paste into an online translator to find keywords to try. You run the risk of missing out on nuances, subtleties, and all of the cultural references you could be using in keywords, and you may run afoul of many tricky conjugation rules.

In order to truly succeed in a different language, we recommend you get experts in each country on your team. Have a German classic car customization Web site? Hire someone from Germany who's an expert in classic cars. He can tell you about the different slang terms Germans use for cars, what kinds of cars are popular, and any of the cultural references you would miss if you relied on just yourself and a German dictionary.

When translating the Web site copy you already have, you should consider language issues and not try to translate your pages directly from one language to another. To get the best final result for your foreign-language Web site, follow this process:

1. **Break the original English down into main bullet points.**

2. **Have this translated by a professional into the second language.**

3. **Use that document to create your actual page copy for your target language.**

Hire a marketer who is native to the language and region so that you know she is getting the tone and slang right. Web marketer Ian McAerin refers to this process as the *Symantec Expression Equivalency Document* (SEED) process.

If all else fails, use the local rule of thumb. Use local terms, local keywords, and local structure in order to truly succeed in your foreign market. Words like *glocal* have started to be bandied about: *Glocal* is defined as localizing the global market.

The impact of languages and culture should not be underestimated. By understanding culture and languages, you can adapt better, succeed in your efforts to localize, and get more sales and respect. Showing an interest in communicating in the native language boosts interest in your company.

Domains and geolocating

Internationalization revolves around *domain* (where the site actually exists on the Web), language, culture, and geolocation issues. *Geolocation* is the identification of a Web page as belonging to or being relevant for a particular country. You also have to be aware of the country-code *top level domain,* which is the last part of an Internet domain name, as in the letters that follow the final dot of any domain name. A country-code top level domain (ccTLD) is a TLD that is specific to a particular country, such as .ca, .cn, .uk, .mx. Be aware that ccTLDs are in that country's language, so the ccTLD for Germany is actually .de, for *Deutschland.*

Creation and delegation of ccTLDs is performed by the Internet Assigned Numbers Authority, or IANA (www.iana.org/). A full, comprehensive list of ccTLDs is available at IANA's Web site at www.iana.org/domains/root/db/.

The rules for obtaining a ccTLD are different for each country because each country can administer its own registered ccTLD as it chooses. A little bit of research is always required. For example, in order to obtain a .de (Deutschland) ccTLD, you need to not only have your site hosted on a German server, but you have to be doing business in the country physically as well. In Norway, a company can only own 20 domains. For more information on how to obtain a ccTLD, go to www.iana.org/domains/root/cctld/.

Some countries have licensed their TLDs for worldwide commercial use. Tuvalu and the Federated States of Micronesia, small island countries in the South Pacific, have partnered with VeriSign and FSM Telecommunications respectively to license domain names using the .tv and .fm TLDs to interested parties. More information on country-code TLDs can be found in Book VII, Chapter 2.

Search engines do not like to display duplicate content. If you have multiple domains connected to a single page, they're only going to choose one domain to display. They choose which domain to display based on the *link equity* (however many links lead to your site and how much authority they pass) on the page, opting for the page with more links. If you want to be geolocated for a particular country and your site is .com, have your site map point to the ccTLD, but make links within the site .com.

Site architecture tips

In order to have your site accessible in the international market, there are some very simple architecture guidelines you can follow:

✦ **Have your site coded in** *UTF-8* **(Unicode).** This is a type of code that allows your site to be translated into languages from around the globe. It is backwardly compatible with ASCII and it encodes up to four-byte characters.

✦ **Don't translate your** *Meta tags and page titles* **(HTML coding for your site to define characteristics of your page) from English to the language you're working in.** Work in the language itself and make all your tags individually. Plan to adjust for plurals, prepositions, special characters, and so on. Like your Web page content, these are too important to just leave for a straight translation.

✦ **Adopt a global press release strategy.** There are many online press release portals for different languages. Sending out articles announcing news on your company or your products generates links and helps build your global presence.

✦ **Manage your 301s.** *301 redirects* send users from a URL that no longer exists to one that does automatically. This is the only type of redirect that is considered to be search engine friendly. The typical global site has hundreds of links going to Page Not Found errors. Domains around the globe are often incorrectly set up, and *meta-refreshes* (having the page automatically reload) are often present, which are not SEO-recommended methods for handling page redirects.

✦ **Make sure your URLs contain** *keywords* **(words that are used in searches) you want to rank for in that country.** Just like optimization in the U.S., keywords in the URL help users identify your site as relevant and promote recognition.

✦ **Use and source local links.** This also enhances your credibility to your international users.

✦ **Use experts for keyword research.** What do you do if there's no direct translation for a word? Employ someone fluent in that language to help you with the translation issues.

✦ **Use ccTLDs.** These are the domains that relate to a particular country and are more likely to inspire trust in your site.

✦ **Have lots of content on your Web site that reads well to your target audience.** Use good, clean copy and make sure you're using the right character sets.

Identifying Opportunities for Your International Site

When expanding into the international market, you have three options when it comes to your site architecture: one site, multiple sites, or a combination of the two. With one site, you take advantage of subdomains (smaller domains linked to bigger domains) and subdirectories pointing to pages in different languages or geared towards specific countries. Multiple sites require you to build an individual site for every country with a local cc.TLD, preferably hosted in the country.

Each of these three options have their pros and cons. It's up to you to do the research and figure out what's best for your company in your target markets. However, you can understand the differences by reading the details we cover in the following sections.

Single sites

Having a single site and targeting using subdomains (such as `uk.myglobal site.com`, `fr.myglobalsite.com`, `jp.myglobalsite.com`, and so on) provides you with several benefits. It's easy to set up. You only have to keep track of one server and one domain, and you can keep all of your files in one place.

All of the *incoming links* (links from outside sources) and all of your Web traffic point to one domain, rather than being split between two or more sites. Although lots of traffic doesn't necessarily mean a high conversion rate, it sure doesn't hurt.

In addition, if you use a single site, you will have more pages in the search engine's *index,* which is the search engine's database of Web pages that they periodically search to offer up to users for search queries. Grouping by language prevents duplicate content. Remember, search engines remove a site from their search results if they think it is duplicate content.

On the other hand, here are some disadvantages of a single site approach:

If your home page is in the "wrong" language, it can be confusing for your international users. To avoid this problem, you would need to create an entry page that allows a user to select what language they want to view the site in. These pages tend to be text-light, however, and not good for search engines.

Another disadvantage can be a home page that ranks highly in only one language. Having your site pop up high in the rankings for German is great, but what if you also want to do business in the English-speaking world and you're nowhere near the top 100 search results? You have to spend the same amount of effort on each section of your site, which can be time-consuming.

If you were to group by country, you are risking duplicate content. Although it's okay to have different pages in different languages, if you have separate pages for each Spanish-speaking country but don't provide unique content, the search engines read repeat pages as duplicate content and don't count them.

If you do decide you want to maintain a single site, you can do some of the following:

✦ Specify the target country for each subdomain in Google Webmaster Tools. To set a geographic target, do the following:

1. Sign into Google Webmaster Tools with your Google account.

2. Click the URL for the site you want.

3. Click Settings.

4. Under Geographic Target, select the geographic region you want to target.

✦ Redirect country-specific domains to the appropriate subdomain or subdirectory.

✦ Internal and external links should be language-appropriate and use the country-specific domains.

Multiple sites

Having multiple sites means you set up a separate domain for each country. Expanding to new countries is technically easy. You can add sites one at a time as needed, without impacting any of your current Web sites. Domains with local ccTLDs usually rank well in multiple country-specific search engines.

Certain countries require you to host your site on one of their servers in order to qualify for a ccTLD. But even if it's not a requirement, it's a good practice because search engines do try to match your server location to your physical location. Hosting the site in the same country means that you have a home-team advantage.

But here are some of the disadvantages of a multiple site approach:

The most obvious disadvantage is that maintenance is harder. Having more sites equals having more sites to update, more servers to troubleshoot, and more domains to keep registered. Additionally, you wind up putting in more time to your SEO. Multiple sites mean multiple SEO efforts. Dividing your time and resources could cause it to take longer for your main .com site to rise in the rankings.

With multiple sites, you're forced to target countries instead of languages. There are many Spanish-speaking countries in the world, for example, and maintaining a site focused on each and every country can get costly and time-consuming.

Some tips for this approach include

✦ Target the country in Google Webmaster tools.

✦ Make sure that external links have appropriate anchor text and link to the right country-specific domains.

The blended approach

If you have an international site on the .com top level domain, you can use a blended approach, which is a combination of single and multiple sites. This approach might be the most realistic for worldwide presence. With it, you can start with a .com site and build country-specific sites as needed. It can be costly to create, maintain, and update, however, because every site needs to be kept up-to-date and in step with all the others.

Here are some tips for implementing the blended approach:

✦ Specify countries in Google Webmaster Tools, but your international site — the one that serves any interest — should be left without a specific target country.

✦ Link your multiple country sites carefully and logically. External links should be logical. Keep the globally applicable content on the international site and country-specific information on country specific sites.

You can use IP sniffing to automatically detect a user's location and serve up a translation in the local language to direct them to the proper site. If you do that, always let them know that they are leaving the current domain and going to a new domain.

Realizing How People Search

In this section, we introduce you to how the rest of the world searches by discussing several internationally popular search engines. First up is Google, as shown in Figure 1-1. This figure shows the French, Japanese, and Brazilian versions of the site.

Google is available pretty much everywhere. Here's a small sampling of the languages Google is available in: Afrikaans, Amharic, Basque, Bihari, Chinese, Dutch, Finnish, Hindi, Kazakh, Malay, Norwegian, Quechua, Slovak, Tagalog, Twi, Urdu, Yiddish, and Zulu. This is only a sample, but our point is that Google's available pretty much across the globe.

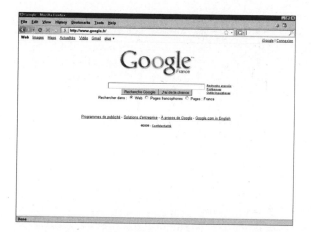

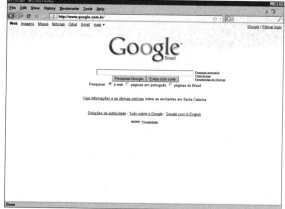

Figure 1-1:
Google
has a site
for many
international
markets as
well as the
flagship
.com
address.

As for the other U.S. players, Yahoo! (`www.yahoo.com`) seems to be losing market share in most places worldwide and Microsoft Live Search (`www.live.com`) is gaining. Ask.com (`www.ask.com`) is a relatively minor player. One extremely important thing to note here is that YouTube (`www.youtube.com`) actually gets more searches per month than Yahoo! does. Video content is key even on an international scale.

Even search engines local to the target country are mostly backfilled (supplemented when there is insufficient inventory in the local engine's index) by Google's search index and paid ads. AltaVista (`www.altavista.com`) is still alive in Europe.

Not every country out there is using Yahoo! or Google. Hold on tight: We're going to take a whirlwind tour around the global to look at some of the most important search engine brands outside the U.S.

Baidu (`www.baidu.com`, shown in Figure 1-2) is the leading Chinese search engine for Web sites, audio files, and images. Baidu has an index of more than 740 million Web pages, 80 million images, and 10 million multimedia files, and attracts 5.5 million visitors annually.

Yandex (`www.yandex.com`, shown in Figure 1-3) is a Russian search engine and the largest Russian Web portal. Yandex was launched in 1997. Its name comes from *Yet Another iNDEXer* (Yandex).

Figure 1-2:
Baidu leads
search in
China.

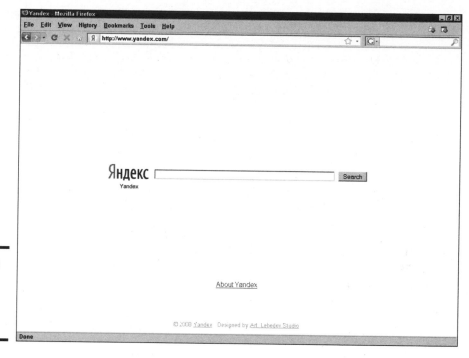

Figure 1-3:
Yandex
rules in
Russian
search.

Seznam (www.seznam.cz, Figure 1-4) is a Czech search engine with a customizable home page and other features such as e-mail, maps, and a company database.

Naver (www.naver.com, Figure 1-5) is the most popular search portal in South Korea. Naver was launched in June 1999, the first portal in Korea that used its own proprietary search engine. Naver received two billion queries in August 2007, accounting for more than 70 percent of all search queries in Korea, and making it the fifth most-used search engine in the world, following Google, Yahoo!, Baidu, and Microsoft Live Search.

Najdi.si (www.najdi.si, Figure 1-6) is a Slovenian search engine and Web portal created by Interseek. It's the most visited Web site in Slovenia.

These are just a sampling of the search engines across the world. So where do you want to advertise? Simple answer: on all of them. You always want to be where your customers are looking for you. However, if that's too broad and a little daunting, narrow your target market by demographic or search engine. Start out small and then expand as time goes on (depending on your success in the international markets, of course).

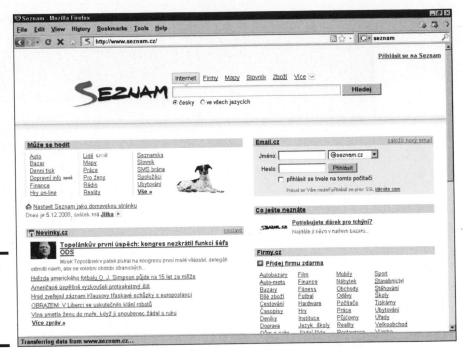

Figure 1-4:
Seznam
is a Czech
search
engine.

Figure 1-5:
Naver is
the most
popular
search
portal in
South
Korea.

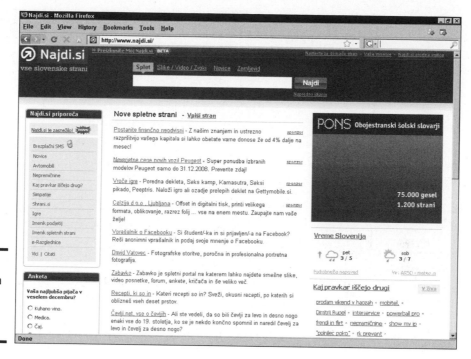

Figure 1-6:
Nadji.si is a
Slovenian
search
engine.

It's time for a small, shameless plug: With the free SEOToolSet toolbar (available for Internet Explorer and Firefox), as well as the new version of the SEOToolSet from Bruce Clay, Inc., you can do three things for international search that make your international campaigns easier to manage:

✦ **You can use it for local searches through a proxy server.** This means that if you are in California and want to see what the Google local search results for London, England look like, you can see what someone in London would see.

✦ **Search in different languages.** The toolbar is available to do searches in more than 20 different languages, and growing all the time. Doing local research is key to succeeding internationally.

✦ **Search in multiple engines, including country-specific engines like the ones we discussed previously.** We think it's a great tool, and not just because we built it. You can download the toolbar from SEOToolSet (www.seotoolset.com). For more about the capabilities of the toolbar, check out Book III, Chapter 2.

Chapter 2: Tailoring Your Marketing Message for Asia

In This Chapter

✔ Succeeding in Asia

✔ Discovering Japan

✔ Succeeding in China

✔ Finding out about South Korea

✔ Operating in Russia

The first stop on our world tour on online marketing in the international venue is the Asia region, which includes Japan, China, South Korea, and much of Russia. In the previous chapter, we briefly touch on the search engines popular in this region, along with a few tips and tricks for operating a Web site in those countries. In this chapter, we go into more depth on operating online in Asia. You discover tips on how to succeed in the targeted country, the demographics of the region, and any other hints we think would we useful to you along the way.

Succeeding in Asia

Starting up a site or expanding your Web site into the Asian region can be a little daunting. Asian culture can be very different from Western culture, with nuances that can harm you and your company if you miss them, and that's not even considering the language barrier. Not to worry, though. We've put together a step-by-step getting started guide for building or translating your site to work in the Asian markets.

It's important to note that one chapter in a book is not enough to make you an expert in SEO for the Asian market. In fact, the most important message you should take away from this chapter is that there is no shortcut or substitute for research and local know-how.

Assessing your site's chances

Your first step is simple: Assess the usability of your translated site — is it going to work for your target country? What works in the U.S. might not work in Asia. If you want to work in any country other than your own, you should be hiring some people who are native speakers from the local markets. This doesn't have to be an expensive proposition. You might find some international students at your local college campus who want to earn a little money by looking over your translated site and pointing out anything you have missed. Look around and see who's available to you and get them to tell you everything they can about your new target market.

Just as you would analyze the market back home, you want to consider the viability of your niche when marketing in Asia. The trick here is that you're dealing with an entirely new culture. You need to find out what's popular before you can start selling it, after all. So maybe there's not a huge market for custom classic cars in Asia, but maybe you have a side operation that sells all sorts of classic car memorabilia, including fuzzy dice. Through your research, you discover that, in Asia, they can't get enough fuzzy dice. You're in business!

Sizing up the competition and sounding out the market

After you have your market, it's time to analyze your competition. Having figured out that there is a large market for fuzzy dice in Asia, you need to sit down and study how your competition is doing in the foreign market. Check out other sites that sell fuzzy dice, especially if they're local companies. This is where someone who speaks the language or knows the culture would come in very handy. All the tips and tricks from Book III are going to come in especially handy here. Follow the same step-by-step procedure to gather and analyze information.

You'll have an easier time gathering information using the proper tools. There are a lot of SEO toolbars out there. We obviously recommend the SEOToolSet toolbar from Bruce Clay, Inc. (www.seotoolset.com). You can adjust the toolbar so that you can view it in more than 20 different languages, including Japanese. You can also use it to do a local search in the area you are targeting so that you see the same results that someone doing a local search sees. It's a free tool, and it'll help you a lot in your research.

After you've sorted out your competition, you need to broaden your research to the entire Asian market in order to plan your strategy and tactics. How does marketing work there? Who is online and how are they searching? A quick search turns up these stats:

✦ China has 162 million online users — 45 percent female, 54 percent male, and overwhelmingly in the 18–24 age group.

✦ In Japan, 69.9 percent of the population is online, which represents 89.1 million people. Women 20–35 years old have 80 percent of the purchasing power.

✦ South Korea has an incredible Internet infrastructure, and most of the population is online, many with broadband access. (North Korea's stats are largely unknown.)

Determining your plan of attack

After you've determined your suitability, competition, and strategy, you can move on to the actual implementation. Your next step is the planning phase: Here's where you create your Asian marketing plan.

If you have an *e-commerce site* (any Web site that sells a particular product or service, like fuzzy dice), you need to start with Japan, and then expand into South Korea and China. However, if you're *branding* (establishing your name and associating it with your business, like Nike or Xerox), you need to start with China and then move into South Korea and then Japan.

Sound strange? It's really not. China is notorious for knock-off brands, so you should be starting there immediately if you want to expand your brand. In Japan, they tend to copy technology faster and tend to be conscious about brand, so you need to establish yourself as the authority product and then work on your brand so that you're recognized as the only brand to have.

Next, you need to know the search engines you'll be using. Google is used almost everywhere in the world, but certain search engines are actually more popular in a particular country or region. You need to know which search engines are the most prevalent in your target market, and look at getting *indexed* (getting your site into the search engine's database) as soon as you can. The search engine statistics look something like this:

✦ In Japan, Yahoo! has 43 percent of the online market share, although Google is gaining on them every month.

✦ In China, it's all about Baidu (www.baidu.com), which is the major Chinese search engine and the fourth most-used search engine in the world.

✦ In South Korea, Naver (www.naver.com, a popular Korean search engine) and Yahoo! together have 80 to 85 percent of the Internet search market. Google has only 1.5 percent market share.

Use localized keywords (search terms), advertising copy, and landing pages (the page a user arrives on when they first visit your site). Do not use an unnatural mix of English and the local languages. Think of how funny but untrustworthy misspelled signs or menus are. You might think a store offering "Creem donuts" is hilarious, but you probably wouldn't make a purchase from them. The same is true when English speakers attempt to do business in other languages.

Building trust and face-to-face interaction are a *huge* part of selling yourself in the Asian market. Putting a face on your brand is very important, and you need to be selling yourself as much as your product. Be prepared to log some frequent flyer miles. Meeting with clients, vendors, and others you do business with face-to-face helps to establish trust.

You should also be monitoring your local competition. You're the foreigner, so you are starting at a disadvantage. Be looking for an edge: something that separates you from the local competition, but at the same isn't too foreign or untrustworthy.

In this chapter, we cover things that you should generally be aware of as you move into the Asian market. But each country has its own quirks and legal issues, so you need to do your research.

A man named Jianfei Zhu monitors all Chinese, Japanese, and Korean algorithms for spam. He has a blog at `googlechinawebmaster.com`. It's in Chinese, but you can use Google Translate (which should be available on the link to his site through Google) or another service to translate it. It might be worth it for you to check it out if you're curious about search engine spam.

Discovering Japan

After the United States, Japan has the second largest economy in the world. This is even after the prolonged recession in the 1990s, and with the current one occurring as we write this book. Japan also has open markets that actively encourage foreign investment. This means that expanding into the Japanese market might be slightly easier than operating in other Asian countries.

The most demanding shoppers in the world live in Japan. There is a huge market for brand name services and goods, and the Japanese are very big on brand names as status symbols. Louis Vuitton, Vivienne Westwood, and others do a healthy share of business based on their brand names alone.

Japan also leads other countries in terms of personal savings. The largest public savings purse is 14 trillion Japanese yen in total, which translates to about $90,000 in U.S. currency for every citizen of Japan. The online business world in Japan is also expanding. The country's online ad spending increased 30 percent in 2007 and 2008.

The Japanese are aware that the language of business on the Internet is English, but to really do business with the Japanese, you have to be able to communicate in Japanese. The Japanese design aesthetic is also different from the western one. Check out this music site from Japan in Figure 2-1.

This is a professional Web site in Japan. People in Japan are much more likely to trust a Web site that looks like this, as opposed to one that looks much simpler.

Figure 2-1:
A typical
Japanese
Web site
tends to
have lots of
images and
movement.

To establish a Web presence, get a `.jp` domain (the space your site occupies on the web, like a `.com`, or a `.net`, or in this case, `co.jp`, `or.jp`, or `ne.jp`). Hosting your site on a server actually physically located in Japan is a good idea as well. Be sure to include your contact info on your Web site, like a number someone can call and receive information. Be sure that the person in charge of this phone line speaks Japanese and is able to answer any question.

As with starting a business in any foreign market, we recommend getting a person on the ground. Hire someone familiar with Japanese language and customs, and if at all possible, someone who actually lives in Japan. A local resident can help you navigate the differences between the Western world and Japan and help you achieve greater success in the long run.

Succeeding in China

China is a new frontier when it comes to the business world. It's also a tricky one to navigate. Not only do you have the language barrier and the cultural issues to work through, but you also have more extensive and stringent government regulations to deal with. However, China's economy is booming, and if you are willing to take the steps, now is a good time to get in the front door.

Searchers in China are very different than users in the United States or elsewhere. Twelve of the top 100 Chinese Web site domains include numbers. Why? Because there are 13,500 Chinese standardized characters. That means if you were designing a keyboard to have one key per character, there would be more than 13,000 keys! This is why so many businesses have adopted the number platform.

You also definitely need to get a Web site domain within China's ccTLD (country code Top Level Domain) of `.cn` (or `.com.cn`, if you can). You also need to host your site in China to avoid gateway issues.

If you're getting started in search marketing (PPC or SEO) in China, start with Google through their interface. Although they are not the dominant search engine in China, they're a good place to start your optimization campaign. The rules are familiar, and you can get your campaign up and running without too many hurdles.

The home page for Google China (Figure 2-2) is very different from the one here in the United States: As soon as you start typing, the search box drops down to offer a guided search (a search suggestion). Again, this is because the language has so many characters. It helps users to find information a lot more quickly.

Figure 2-2:
Google's
home page
in China.

Two products that Google is currently testing in the Chinese market are

✦ **Popular Searches:** This tool breaks down popular searches by category, allowing users to click to navigate to the search results page. Instead of having to type in [this week's biggest music performers], Popular Searches just displays "Justin Timberlake" or whoever is big at the time. This would be a good way to do keyword research.

✦ **Website Directory:** This is a list of Web sites based on categories and services. It's algorithm-based, which means that it isn't just a static list.

A site that might be worth checking out is Tom.com (`www.tom.com`), which is one of the top 10 Web sites in China (see Figure 2-3). It has tons of links on the page without a search box above the fold. Users come here as a destination site, not to search.

Because people often use *guided search* (where the search engine makes suggestions on your queries, much like Google or Yahoo! Suggests) in China, search engine optimization is a little easier because search marketers know off the bat what queries searchers are using. Also, you can use Google China's Popular Searches function.

Figure 2-3:
Tom.com is
one of the
Top 10 sites
in China.

Baidu (www.baidu.com, China's top search engine and their answer to Google or Yahoo!) has a minimum implementation fee of $3,000–5,000 U.S. and funds must be prepaid by wire. Additionally, they have only Chinese-speaking support, and they subject all sites to a tough validation process.

Analytics-wise, Baidu and Yahoo! provide no impression results. But Google Analytics is available in China. On Baidu, the paid listings are mixed in with the *organic*, (which means search engine results that pop up in a normal search of the index) and studies suggest that the users don't know the difference. *Long-Tail search queries* (keywords, or search queries, made up of several words or a phrase) don't really exist in China because users don't do as many searches as we do. They rely more on guided search.

Here are some key observations on Baidu:

✦ It's the most popular search engine for lifestyle searches, but not for business. Google trumps Baidu in business searches.

✦ Baidu's results are overwhelmingly influenced by paid advertising campaigns.

✦ Baidu has its greatest reach with young lifestyle-centric searchers.

✦ Display advertising that charges by the page view, called CPM (which stands for *cost per mille*; that is, cost per each thousand impressions, *mille* being French for 1,000) advertising, is most popular with Baidu.

Being a foreigner in China can be both a disadvantage and an advantage. Although there is always going to be the natural tendency to push back against the unfamiliar, in China, you have something of an advantage if you're an expert. When you come in to speak, if you have any kind of credentials, you're treated like a rock star. Additionally, by being a foreigner, you can get away with not knowing the customs at first. Be warned, however, that your grace period ends quickly, and you should be ready to adapt to Chinese culture.

There are a few challenges in the Chinese market that, while not unique to the country, are certainly worth knowing ahead of time:

✦ **Budgets for local companies are small.** If you're a search marketer, you'll find that you're dealing with less capital than you might have expected.

✦ **Clients are very particular about their contacts in your company.** Have a point person who is extremely knowledgeable in the culture and can handle your business dealings in the local markets.

Business is very relationship-based in China. Good relationships are absolutely critical to success. You have to be introduced to the right people at the right places. Many Westerners underestimate exactly how important it is to have good contacts. It's true everywhere, but especially in China: It's about who you know, how well you know them, and who you work with.

Your employees make or break a deal in the long run. Most of the advertising in the Chinese market is branding. It's not about trying to convert. If you do decide to tap into the Chinese market, make sure you're willing to be flexible and do things their way.

When looking at hiring people abroad (and this includes all countries), be sure to check the following things:

✦ Check the credentials for the people you're meeting.

✦ Confirm they are doing the work themselves and they're not outsourcing it.

✦ Establish goals and document them in contracts.

✦ Do periodic checks of the quality of the ads and the effectiveness of campaigns.

You should pick your teams based on their effectiveness. Offer incentives for employees to maintain loyalty. As with any business, a happy employee is an efficient and loyal employee. Pick your partners well and do a lot of research on their capabilities.

In China, most users are still accessing the Internet via desktop computers (96 percent), although access via mobile devices is becoming trendy at 27 percent of mobile users and growing. The growth in search from cell phones is due to increased interest in the Internet and the availability of 3G handsets and connectivity.

What does all this mean to the outside world? There are a lot of opportunities to market to the Chinese if you do it on their terms and within their comfort level. The key to succeeding in China is relationships, patience, diligence, and an open mind. The truth is that most people in China still don't trust the Internet. E-commerce is still very much in its infancy in China, and online marketing is mostly still for branding. Keep this in mind as you expand into the Chinese market.

Finding Out about South Korea

When we say Korea, we're talking about South Korea. North Korea is a cipher to pretty much all marketers, and we're going to ignore them entirely. You should too.

South Korea has an incredible infrastructure and much (70.7 percent) of their population is online and searching. Nearly half of that number has broadband access. You can use Flash and lots of images without fear. In fact, that's an advantage to you in Korea. The population tends to prefer very busy-looking professional sites (lots of color and text), so a Korean page can look a little something like Figure 2-4. Because of this push for color and content, Google's clean designs do very poorly in Korea.

Operating in South Korea is a lot like operating in Japan and China. They prefer face-to-face interaction, and your success is a matter of establishing trust and accessibility. Get a `.co.kr` domain for your Korean site and get started optimizing.

Figure 2-4: The typical Korean Web site uses lots of images to engage users.

You absolutely must do local link building. Work on making connections, gaining trust and links, and getting the local search engines to recognize those things. International links are fine, but local links carry more weight in the long run. Remember, relevancy is always key and local is more relevant than non-local.

Naver (www.naver.com) is Korea's biggest search engine. It currently commands a 77 percent share of all searches in South Korea. The other contenders are Daum (www.daum.net) with 10.8 percent, Yahoo! with 4.4 percent, and Google with an itty-bitty 1.7 percent of Korean Web searches.

When Naver was first launched, its founders discovered a real dearth of pages in Korean on the Internet. So Naver decided to create content and databases, so that when you would search in Korean, you would be able to find quality content. Naver set up Knowledge Search in 2002, enabling Koreans to help each other in a type of real-time question-and-answer platform. On average, 44,000 questions are posted each day, with about 110,000 returned answers. The tool allows users to ask just about any question, such as requests for recipes or how to subscribe to international magazines via the Internet, and get answers from other users. This tool was used by Yahoo! as the inspiration for Yahoo! Answers.

Operating in Russia

We include Russia in the marketing for Asian strategy for reasons of geography as well as strategy. Expanding to the Russian market is a lot like expanding into the Chinese market. In order to have a fully successful venture, you're going to need a person on the ground in Russia.

This means you need someone who not only knows the language and culture, but also who actually lives and works there, to provide you a brick-and-mortar foothold in the country. Having someone who is based in Russia can also help in dealing with any legal or local bureaucratic issues that could spring up.

About 23 percent of Russia's population is online, which is about 32.7 million people. Of those, only about 2.9 million had broadband access in September 2007. Consider the design limitations for your site when dealing with an audience running at dial-up speeds. Fancy technologies and enormous pages are going to be hindrances rather than a help.

The largest search engine in Russia is called Yandex (www.yandex.com, Figure 2-5).

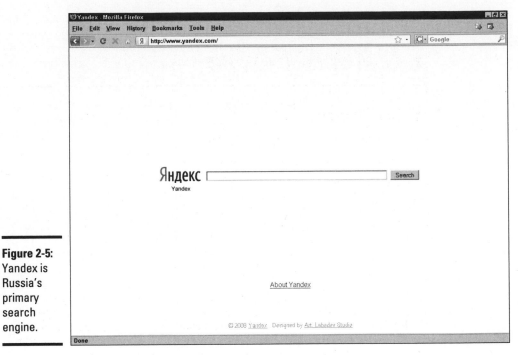

Figure 2-5:
Yandex is
Russia's
primary
search
engine.

Yandex was launched in 1997. The net income of the company in 2004 constituted $7 million U.S. In June 2006, the weekly revenue of the Yandex.Direct context ads system exceeded $1 million U.S., and it's still growing.

The closest competitors of Yandex in the Russian market are Rambler (`www. rambler.com`) and Mail.RU (`www.mail.ru`). Services like Google and Yahoo! are also used by Russian users and have Russian interfaces. Google creates about 21–27 percent of search engine-generated traffic to Russian sites, and Yandex has around 44 percent. One of Yandex's largest advantages is recognition of Russian inflection in search queries.

As with all of the other countries we mention in this chapter, it's best to have a domain within the country's ccTLD and someone physically located on the brick and mortar side who lives and works in Russia to give you valuable credibility. You must do cultural research to pin down the right tone for your Russian audience.

Chapter 3: Staking a Claim in Europe

In This Chapter

✔ **Succeeding in the European Union**

✔ **Knowing the legal issues in the EU**

✔ **Working in the United Kingdom**

✔ **Discovering France**

✔ **Operating in Germany**

✔ **Understanding the Netherlands**

A cross the pond from the United States lies the European Union (EU). When we talk about the EU, we're referring to the group of countries that actually belong to the EU and thus are subject to certain laws and regulations, and all the countries that are actually located within Europe itself.

Succeeding in the EU isn't as simple as copying and pasting your Web site into German or French and then hoping the traffic comes to you. You have to consider legal and cultural differences, along with the technical issues that come from running a Web site in another country. In this chapter, we talk about how to succeed in the European Union, some legal issues you should be aware of, and some specific facts about doing business in the United Kingdom, France, Germany, and the Netherlands that should give you a little more insight into the search markets in the European Union.

Succeeding in the European Union

You might think that getting started with the European Union would be pretty easy. It's actually not. For one thing, you have to remember that Europe is made up of lots of different countries with their own languages and customs and their own markets for searchengines. You can't make up one Web site for the whole EU, and then call it a day.

First you need to figure out what countries you want to target. This is important in terms of tailoring your marketing campaign. Each country has its own language, culture, and social mores that you need to use when doing your keyword research. For example, in the United States, personal telephones are called *cell phones*, so when a user does a search, they most likely enter keywords such as [cellphone], [cell phone], [cellular phones], and the like. But in the United Kingdom, personal telephones are referred to as *mobiles*. So a U.K. user would, for the exact same product, use keywords like [mobiles], [mobile telephone], and so on.

You also have to contend with the technical difficulties associated with obtaining and using a proper country code *top level domain* (the letters that follow the final dot of any domain name, for example, .com or .net). A country-code top level domain, or ccTLD, is a TLD that is specific to a certain country. The United States has .us and the United Kingdom has .uk. Users within a specific country are much more likely to trust a Web site that's within their own country's ccTLD than one with a foreign ccTLD.

European users are also much more likely to trust a foreign Web site if it includes links to sites within their country, especially local links.

You can also use the free SEMToolBar from Bruce Clay, Inc. to help with your international SEO. It has tools built-in to enable you to do a local search in the area you are targeting, so that you can see search results as someone would see them in Germany, even if you're sitting pretty in Denver. The toolbar supports 20 different languages, including French and German, so it's useful for your entire team, no matter where they're based. The search is re-routed using a proxy through a local IP address, so the search engine thinks you are located in the country you are searching for.

Knowing the Legal Issues in the EU

As a marketer to the EU, you benefit somewhat from the fact that standardized trade policies have been agreed on by all the member countries. However, one thing we have to stress is that the European Union is made up of many different countries, each with its own languages and laws.

For example, France is constantly suing Google over *pay per click* or *PPC ads* (paid advertising that appears in the search results, for which advertisers pay a fee every time their ad is clicked). In the United States, you can bid on a trademarked keyword and win it if you put up enough money (and the keyword relevant to your company). In France, this is not the case, and there have been several lawsuits over this issue. All of the high courts in France (the Court of Nanterre, the Court of Paris, and the Court of Appeals of Versailles) have found that bidding on a copyrighted trademark is a copyright infringement.

However, according to the Cour d'Appel de Paris, the French courts have no jurisdiction if the ads in question lead only to Web sites owned by companies established outside of France and appear only on google.co.uk, google.de, and google.ca, but not google.fr (decision of June 6, 2007,

Google Inc. and Google France versus Axa et al, CRI 2007, 155 ff). This means that if you have an ad for a trademarked keyword, you can use it as long as you are not a French company and it doesn't appear on the French version of Google.

Another fun legal issue comes to us from Belgium. Several Belgian newspapers sued Google News for displaying and storing their content. A company called Copiepresse claimed that Google violated Belgian law by keeping archived versions of stories in its search cache and using headlines and excerpts within the Google News service. Google claimed that their activities fell under "fair use" laws, but a Brussels court did not agree.

Because the legal system varies from country to country, you might want to hire a lawyer within the country you wish to be working in. You need someone who can help you with the ins and outs of that country's legal system.

Working within the United Kingdom

It's tempting to think that optimizing for the U.K. is going to be easy because you're at least working in the same language. "Aha!" you think, "The United Kingdom is a lot like America because English is the primary language of both." True — except that they're really not speaking the same language at all. English in the U.K. has a lot of spelling conventions that an American spelling checker reads as misspelled (the "u" in words like *colour* and *favourable*, an "s" instead of "z" in words like *customisation*, and so on). British English is not exactly like American English, and you need to be well aware of that. There is no faster way to shoot down your credibility than forgetting cultural mores and language differences when working in another country.

It's not just spelling that's different. U.K. English often uses different words for everyday objects (a *cell phone* in the U.S. is called a *mobile* in the U.K., for instance), different slang terms, and the same word mean totally different things. These differences can be subtle, but they stick out like a sore thumb to a native. Blogs like Separated by a Common Language (`http://separatedbyacommonlanguage.blogspot.com/`) are good resources for pinpointing the diversions between British and American usage.

In the U.K., Google is the predominant search engine, even more so than in the U.S., but there are some key differences:

✦ Google paid some outside agencies in the U.K. to bring people to AdWords (Google's PPC program). This created two types of PPC agencies in the U.K. — the optimizers (the ones that add value) and the discounters (agencies that relied on how much you could spend). Google has since stopped this practice.

+ The U.K. has something called the Financial Services Authority (or FSA). It's a body that regulates financial matters and financial companies like banks. Be aware that all it takes to cause you grief is an e-mail to the FSA.

+ In the U.K., people use different currencies because they are members of the EU, so you'll see euros and British pounds. Multi-currency transactions are difficult to manage and track.

With Google, you get two sets of search results. *Organic results* are the links that naturally match a user's search, and *pay per click* (PPC) results are the ads paid for by the advertising companies. When surveyed, more than 80 percent of U.K. respondents said that the left side (organic) results offered the best results. Only 6 percent in 2007, and 4.66 percent in 2008, answered that the paid search results gave the best results.

So how much do U.K. firms spend on search? Nine percent of U.K. firms are spending more than £1 million U.K. annually on paid search. One in six U.K. companies spend more than £50,000 U.K. on search.

Compared to Internet users globally, U.K. users are quite confident online. They're not scared to give their credit card information to a brand they recognize. They're also a little more search engine-savvy than a typical American user.

Certain Internet issues are also of concern to the U.K. public:

+ The U.K. has concerns about child safety issues, especially when it comes to online predators. There are growing calls to adopt a U.S.-like Amber Alert system, where automatic calls are sent out looking for missing children.

+ Social networking sites can create problems at work, undermining employee relationships through gossip and also as a recruitment issue. People in the U.K. use social networking sites as much as Americans do. Unfortunately, this can be a bit of a problem for companies doing research on potential employees and finding, say, evidence of a potential employee doing questionable things on his MySpace profile.

You need to be aware of two laws when you expand into the U.K. market. The first is the *John Doe law*. The term comes from an 18th-century law. This particular law lets court proceedings go ahead even when the identity of the person is unknown. What it can mean for online marketing is that after a court order has been obtained, it is possible for a plaintiff to go to the *ISPs* (Internet service provider) or even the search engines to prevent the defendant from entering sensitive information on a blog or Web site.

The second law is known as the *Spartacus Order.* The person responsible for anonymous activities must come forward and make himself known to the court or they could be found in contempt of court — a whole extra set of charges that the offending party may want to avoid. This means that if someone files suit against you, even if they don't know who you are (using the John Doe law), and you fail to come forward, you are actually in danger of contempt of court. For online activities, where it's not uncommon for the person behind a Web site to be unknown and untrackable, this is another level of trouble.

Discovering France

In France, more than 30 million people are connected via the Internet. But the digital economy makes up only 6 percent of the GNP (gross national product) in France, as opposed to 14 percent in the United States. More than thirty-seven percent of the population uses search engines several times a week, whereas almost 50 percent uses them several times a month. Most users between 45 and 54 say they don't look past the first page of results, and women are less likely to go to the second page than men.

The search engine market in France looks something like this: Google is the biggest with 87 percent, and then Microsoft Live Search with 3 percent, Yahoo! with 3 percent, Voila (www.voila.fr, a French search engine, see Figure 3-1) is at 2 percent, with the rest of the pack making up the remaining 5 percent.

Figure 3-1:
Voila.fr is a French search engine.

There are a couple of ways to use Google in France. You can use the French version of Google (www.google.fr/), or you can use the English version (www.google.com/) and ask for your results in French. Most people in France, not surprisingly, use the French version of Google. Many of the most visited sites within France are French-specific Web sites such as Orange (www.orange.fr), Free (www.free.fr/), PagesJaune (www.pagesjaunes.fr/), and Copains d'Avant (http://copainsdavant.linternaute.com/). In 2008, French businesses planned to invest 29 percent of their resources in search marketing (22 percent was invested in 2007).

The top searched-for subject categories in France aren't much different than in the U.S.: entertainment, computers, and business. French searchers look for entertainment more than the U.S. markets do, however. The top search terms include YouTube, *jeux* (games), and *meteo* (weather). This can be useful to you in terms of figuring out which keywords you want to target while working in France; however, remember that France is very strict about copyrighted keywords. You cannot use a copyrighted keyword that you do not own in any way. Although U.S. legislators have split on the issue, in France, nearly every case has gone the copyright holder's way. Copyrighted keywords cannot be used in metadata or to trigger paid search ads.

Seasons differ between countries. In the States, the Christmas season officially begins the Friday after Thanksgiving. In other countries, the Christmas season can begin even earlier because there's not another holiday in the way. Travel is also different in France (where people typically have five weeks of paid vacation), so holiday-related search words are in high use. You need to adjust your marketing strategy to take advantage of these differences.

Online social networks are booming in France, and the traffic is proportionately huge compared to the U.S. Skyrock (http://fr.skyrock.com), a French social networking site that's a lot like MySpace, is the big social media site (see Figure 3-2), and Copains d'Avant (http://copainsdavant.linternaute.com/) is like Classmates.com for France, popular for reconnecting with old schoolmates and friends.

Cell phones aren't used a lot for search in France. Fewer than three percent of mobile phone users said they've used a phone to find information via search engines.

Here are some special French search engine issues you should keep in mind:

✦ You can submit your site/URL to most of the French search engines, but generally only if you have French language content.

✦ If you put an accent on the word, it may change the meaning of the word. If you ignore accentuation, the French word for *diaper* is the same for *making love*.

✦ Many French search engines try to analyze the word environment to try and understand the meaning of a word, even without accents, but it isn't perfect.

Figure 3-2:
Skyrock is
a popular
social
networking
site for
France.

Operating in Germany

Germany is a country of 82.3 million people. Of that number, 53 million people are online and the equivalent of $49 billion dollars was spent online in 2007. As of this writing, Germany's GDP (gross domestic product) per capita is about $31,400. It's a pretty healthy economy.

The search engine landscape in Germany looks a little like this: `Google. de` has 95–98 percent market share. Yahoo! and Ask.com are there too, but Microsoft Live Search is barely on the chart. If you are going to operate in Germany, it's probably best to concentrate on `Google.de`.

Local search, which is a search that is specifically targeted to businesses within the searcher's local area, is almost nonexistent in Germany. It's still in the starting stages, but it is growing.

In Germany, there are 11 million `.de` domains. If you're thinking about going into Germany, you need to get a `.de` domain. Don't use a *subdomain* (a dependent domain set up within the primary domain, such as `de.classicar customization.com`); it will not have as much success as a country specific top-level domain.

To obtain a .de, you need to have a branch of your company physically operating in Germany, which means you need a local contact. The server that will be hosting your .de Web site must also physically reside in Germany. Remember when we said that the rules are different for every country? This is a good example.

Credit cards are just becoming popular in Germany. Not a whole lot of purchases are made with credit cards. (Many Germans are leery of giving out personal information over the Internet.) So make sure that they have an alternative way to pay in Germany if you are running an *e-commerce* (online retail) business.

Germans are also known to spend a lot of time researching. This is something to keep in mind if you're running a *research site* (a Web site geared for providing information) as opposed to an e-commerce site; you might do well there.

If you are running an e-commerce site in Germany, there are some steps you can take to ensure that the process is as easy as possible for both you and your German users:

✦ Put on your landing page that you can ship worldwide and make it clear that it's easy for you to do so. A *landing page* is the page where a user arrives on your Web site. (See Book IV, Chapter 4 and Book X, Chapter 1 for more information on landing pages.)

✦ Have a German bank account so that transferring money for purchases is as easy and hassle-free as possible.

✦ Have a German phone number where people can call and request more information if they need to. This is why having a physical location in Germany really helps, and not just in terms of obtaining a .de ccTLD.

In the German social networking arena, local companies are very strong, much stronger than the U.S. companies like Facebook or MySpace. As of the writing of this book, Facebook has just launched in Germany. Important German social networking sites include studiVZ (www.studivz.net), which is a networking site for students and university students that is similar to Facebook. Another important social networking site is Yigg (www.yigg.de), as shown in Figure 3-3. Yigg is similar to the U.S.'s Digg.com. It's a site where German users can vote on a particular news story. The more popular a news story becomes, the more likely it is that it will appear on the front page of the site.

The German language is much different than English. There are some common phrases, but for the most part, if you don't speak German, you're probably not going to understand it. There are also special characters in the German language that people in the U.S. aren't used to. You want to keep all of this in mind when doing keyword research.

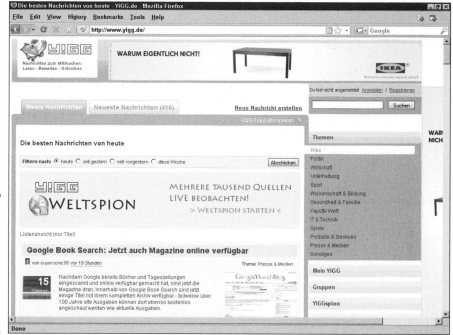

Figure 3-3:
Yigg is
Germany's
answer to
social news
networking
sites
like Digg.

Understanding the Netherlands

In the Netherlands, about 87.8 percent of the population is online, which is the second-highest number of users online in the world and 16 percent more than the U.S. The Dutch also spend about $6 billion online, which makes them the fourth largest market in Europe.

However, that being said, the Dutch search engine market is actually fairly small, although highly competitive. The Dutch search engine usage is as follows: Google commands 93 percent of the market, Vindex.nl (a Dutch search engine shown in Figure 3-4) is at 2 percent, and Ilse.nl (another Dutch search engine) commands 1 percent of the market. Interestingly, Ilse carries Google ads.

When researching your keywords, be aware that Dutch is spoken by 15 million people in the Netherlands, which is the vast majority of the population. About a million speak Flemish, which refers to dialects of Dutch. Be aware that the paid search campaign you're running in one language won't work in the other. That being said, English is taught in all Dutch schools, and most of the population of the Netherlands is fluent in English.

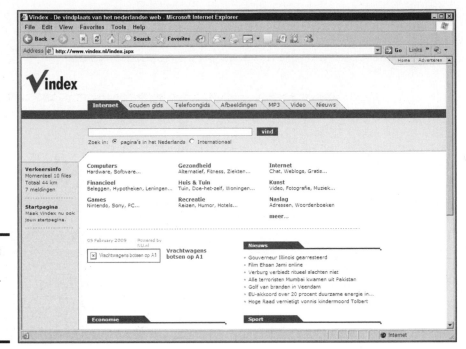

Figure 3-4:
Vindex.nl
is a Dutch-
language
search
engine.

Stemming (the difference between the ending of a word that makes it sin-gular or plural) is one of the anomalies in the Dutch market. For example, a single tree in Dutch is *boom*, while more than one tree is *bomen*. This means for Dutch keywords, you would have to target both "boom" and "bomen." As for all keyword research in languages not your own, we recommend that you employ someone who is fluent in your target language and preferably an actual resident of that country.

As for local search, the Netherlands has Marktplaats (`www.marktplaats.nl`, see Figure 3-5), which is their biggest online marketplace site. It's where a lot of the local search queries go.

Spam (sneaky or deceptive ways of fooling the search engines into giving a Web page higher rankings) is unfortunately pretty common in the Netherlands. If some shady operator does a bit of no-frills spam and some aggressive link buying, they rank pretty highly. People still do link farms too, so be wary when requesting links to your site. You can spot link farms a lot sooner than you could in the U.S. because there are only about two million Dutch Web sites out there.

Don't be tempted by those link farms, however. Remember that honesty is the best policy, and it's best to be operating aboveboard from the start. That way, when the Netherlands starts to clear out the spam in their search engines, you're in the clear and way ahead of the game.

Figure 3-5:
Marktplaats
is Holland's
online
marketplace.

Chapter 4: Getting Started in Latin America

In This Chapter

✔ Succeeding in Latin America

✔ Using Google Webmaster Tools for geotargeting

✔ Making your Web site work in Mexico

✔ Operating in Brazil

✔ Discovering Argentina

*L*atin America is the final stop on our search engine optimization (SEO) world tour. Latin America includes Mexico and both Central and South America. Keep in mind, as with the European Union and the Asian region, that the Latin American region is made up of many different countries, all with different cultures, economies, and languages. Many countries in Latin America have Spanish as their dominant language, but not all. In South America, the biggest country, Brazil, speaks Portuguese.

As always, you need to do research before you launch an online business in a particular country. Hiring someone with knowledge of the local language, customs, and legal ins and outs is also an invaluable asset to your company if you are looking to expand into the Latin American region. In this chapter, you find out a bit about operating in Latin America and discover some stats on a few countries in the area. Latin America is a pretty big place, so realize that we're giving you only a peek into the region.

Succeeding in Latin America

Latin America is another up-and-comer in the search engine optimization industry, with a population that's hungry for everything the Web has to offer. Latin American countries have a total of 53 million Internet users. Whereas the global average of hours per month spent online is 25 hours, the average in Latin America is higher, at 29 hours per month.

The amount of money spent online in Latin America is growing fast, both in terms of consumer spending and advertising. In 2006, online advertising in Mexico accounted for $80 million, Argentina $50 million, and Brazil $180 million (all in U.S. dollars). E-commerce purchases in Brazil reached $114 billion in 2006, which represents 82 percent growth compared to 2005.

In Latin America, language matters. Results differ by including accents or using the English or Spanish language versions of Google. When you're researching *keywords*, have someone help you who's from the country you are actually targeting, and not just a generic Spanish speaker. The language has subtle variations due to both regions and culture, and what might be a perfectly innocent word in one region might be an offensive slang term in another. For example, in Mexico, the term *cajeta* means a caramel dessert topping. In Colombia, it's slang for a bodybuilder, like meathead in English. In Costa Rica, it means a form of low-quality marijuana. But in Argentina, it refers to female private parts. Definitely *not* a mistake that you want to make! These are just some examples of regional differences. Obviously, you should take great care.

If you are going to be translating your site into Spanish to target Latin American users, do have a way of getting your products to your customers! Learn from the mistakes of Best Buy Español. In November 2007, this leading North American retailer translated its site into Spanish in order to target Spanish-speaking customers. Best Buy Español was then immediately *indexed* (included in the search engine's database of Web sites, which they pull from when a user does searches) and got huge numbers of people visiting their sites. The problem was that they were showing up in the search engines in Spain and Latin America as well as in the U.S., but they didn't have the ability to ship to those places! If you are going to translate your Web site just for the U.S. Spanish-speaking population, be aware that you will probably draw traffic from these other countries. If you do, have a way to ship to them! There's nothing wrong with people wanting to buy things from you. Just make sure that you can provide what it is you are selling.

Also, do be aware that not all Latin American countries speak Spanish. Several countries, such as Brazil, use Brazilian Portuguese (distinct from that spoken in Portugal) as their primary language. Other countries still have a large native population that speaks their own diverse languages and dialects. Argentina, for instance, has a large German-speaking population and a large English-speaking population as well. This is something to look for when you do your research, and keep in mind when you target your keywords and create a version of your site to run in those countries.

The SEM ToolBar from Bruce Clay, Inc. can help you do your keyword research and local optimization. Not only can you use it in 20 different languages, including Spanish, but you can also use it to view local search results from international sites. You can see what a Brazilian user would see, without ever having to leave the country. It's a free tool and available for Internet Explorer or Firefox. We think it's pretty cool, but try it out and decide for yourself.

As with expanding into any foreign market, it's also best to hire a legal expert working in the country or region you are targeting. They help you work out any legal issues, commerce headaches, or trade and tariff rules you need to understand to do business in that country.

Geotargeting with Google Webmaster Tools

Google's Webmaster Tools, which is a tool Google provides in order to help you build your site, has an option to help you associate a Web site with a particular country in order to enhance that Web site's presence in the particular country's local search results. A *local search* is a search geared specifically towards a user's physical address, usually via the location of the server they are using.

In geotargeting, Google looks at a couple of signals to determine where a site is located or what particular region it belongs to:

✦ The server location of the Web site.

✦ The top level domain (TLD). A *domain* is the root part of a Web site address, such as `wiley.com`. The *TLD* is the part that identifies where the Web site is registered on the World Wide Web, and is marked by `.com`, `.net`, or other. In the case of international domains, the TLDs (known as country code TLDs, or *ccTLD* for short) identify the country where the domain was registered, such as `.us`, `.uk`, `.co.jp`, and so forth.

With the Webmaster Tools, you can do geotargeting even if your site is hosted in Colorado. If your Web site aims specifically for business in Argentina, you can use the tools to have your site appear in local searches for Argentina by setting it to that country in the Tools.

For more information on geotargeting using Google Webmaster Central, go to the Google Webmaster Tools site at `www.google.com/webmasters/tools`.

Working in Mexico

Mexico has approximately 25 million Internet users, and there is an increasing demand for broadband Internet services. By 2007, the vast majority (78 percent) of personal computer Internet access was via broadband. There are approximately 7.6 million Internet hosts in Mexico, which means they rank eighth in the world. People online in Mexico have fast connections, which enables them to do online search much more effectively. Telmex is *de facto* the only company providing DSL connectivity in Mexico. They used to be owned by the government and had a complete monopoly. Although that's no longer the case and the company is now privately owned, they still have near total control.

Mexico is a signing member of 12 separate trade treaties, the most important one being the North American Free Trade Agreement, or NAFTA. NAFTA is a trilateral trade bloc between Canada, the United States, and Mexico. This means that these three countries have agreed to eliminate tariffs, quotas, and preferences on most goods and services between them. Whatever your political views on NAFTA, it does make commerce between the United States and Mexico slightly easier if you are looking to create an e-commerce site that targets Mexico, as opposed to other Latin American countries.

As for the search engines, Google, Yahoo!, and Microsoft Live Search have versions for Mexico users: `google.com.mx`, `yahoo.com.mx`, and `msn.com.mx`. In fact, Google has a version for almost every Latin American country, including `google.com.ar` (Argentina), `google.com.co` (Colombia), `google.com.pe` (Peru), `google.com.ec` (Ecuador), `google.cl` (Chile), and so on.

For keyword research, you would be wise to add someone to your staff who both speaks Spanish and is actually from Mexico. This person can help with translating your Web site, pointing out cultural differences a simple translator tool might miss, and helping you effectively target your market.

You might also want to dip a toe into the YouTube (`www.youtube.com`) pool. Mexico and Brazil are the biggest consumers of YouTube in the world, and you have plenty of opportunity to connect with your users there. YouTube Mexico (`mx.youtube.com`) serves videos targeted at the Spanish-speaking market (Figure 4-1).

Figure 4-1: Mexico and Brazil are the biggest consumers of YouTube in the world.

To take advantage of YouTube's popularity to help promote your Web site, upload a few Spanish-language videos there, providing links back to your own site in the sidebar, and see where it takes you. This can be a very effective tool in marketing your brand and reaching a completely new audience.

Operating in Brazil

Brazil has the largest Internet population of any country in Latin America, with a total of 33 million users at last count. But this is a country of 186 million people, so less than 20 percent of Brazil's population is online. But, in recent years, the increased number of fixed telephone lines, cell phones, broadband access, and economic stability has afforded more Brazilians the opportunity to be online.

There is a high Internet usage among the upper and middle class in Brazil. Even with only 20 percent of the population online, a large number of people with purchasing power are online.

The Brazilian Internet Steering Committee has a survey about Internet usage in Brazil online. The full survey is available at www.cetic.br/publicacoes/index.htm, in both English and Portuguese. The survey reports that 75 percent of online users actively use search engines. The main searched-for categories include entertainment, jobs, health, and travel. This is a useful survey to look up when you're starting to figure out your keywords.

Brazil is also one of the nine countries where Google has launched a local version of YouTube. As we mentioned in the Mexico section, uploading a few videos to this video-sharing site with links back to your Web pages can get you attention and bring you more traffic.

Orkut (www.orkut.com) (Figure 4-2) is the most popular social media site in Brazil. It's run by Google, and the majority of users are from Brazil. The initial target market for Orkut was the United States, but the majority of its users are in Brazil and India.

As of May 2008, 53.86 percent of Orkut's users are from Brazil. Using social media helps you be where your potential customers are, develop relationships, and promote brand awareness for your site, so it might be worth checking out. Search-engine wise, Google is still the most popular. Yahoo! and MSN are up-and-comers.

Here are some other things to keep in mind while operating in Brazil:

✦ Do not just translate your ads into Portuguese. Take into account localisms and slang.

✦ Provide multiple payment systems, using both credit cards and *Boleto*, which is a local bank invoicing system.

✦ If you are running an e-commerce site, be aware of high taxes and duties that Brazil requires. Hire someone well-versed in Brazilian commerce legal issues to help you out.

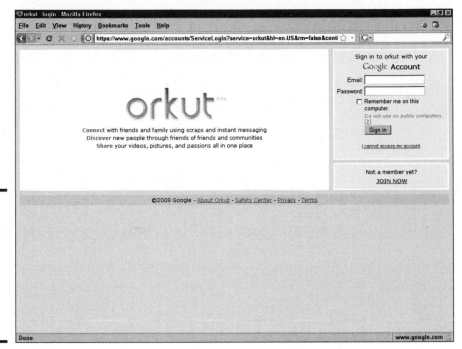

Figure 4-2:
Social media targeting in Brazil should always include Orkut.

Discovering Argentina

Argentina is another Spanish-speaking Latin American country with a large online population. The number of Internet users in the country has been estimated at 16 million in 2007. As of 2008, among the seven million PCs registered in Argentina, the number of residential and business computers connected to Internet totaled about 3.3 million, 92 percent of which were connected via broadband access to the Internet. Those without access to a PC at home make usage of Internet cafes called *locutorios*, so even those who don't own computers may still have online access.

The most popular search engines in Argentina are Google at `google.com.ar` and Yahoo! at `yahoo.com.ar`, with Microsoft Live Search not really registering on the radar.

Google also powers the following Argentinean search engines: Ubbi at `www.buscador.clarin.com`, Terra at `www.terra.com.ar`, and Uol at `www.terra.com.ar`.

Google also powers Grippo (`www.grippo.com.ar`), an Argentinean directory of Web sites, as shown in Figure 4-3.

There are also regional differences in language in Argentina. Argentinean Spanish is closer in pronunciation to Italian, and they have a very distinct accent because of it. Italian is the second-most spoken language in Argentina, followed by German. In Argentinean Spanish, they also incorporate the usage of the pronoun "vos," instead of "tu," which is the informal "you." Only a few other Spanish-speaking countries use "vos," including El Salvador and Honduras.

As we *always* recommend, if you're going to go international and target specific countries, do hire someone from that country who can help you out with the language and cultural differences. Having someone who knows the ins and outs of the language and culture on your side makes expanding into the international market a whole lot smoother for everyone involved.

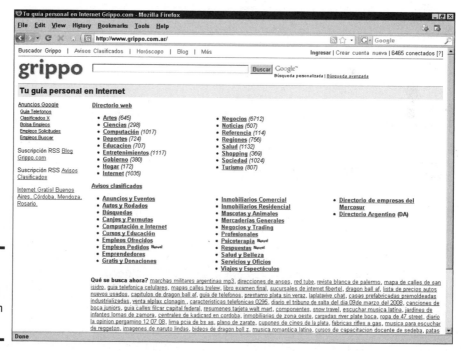

Figure 4-3:
Grippo is a directory of Argentinean Web sites.

Book X
Search Marketing

Contents at a Glance

Chapter 1: Discovering Paid Search Marketing...................643

Harnessing the Value of Paid Search 644
Making SEO and Pay Per Click Work Together.......................658
Supplementing Traffic with PPC 662
Making Smart Use of Geotargeting..663
Starting Your Seasonal Campaigns 664

Chapter 2: Using SEO to Build Your Brand 669

Selecting Keywords for Branding Purposes............................670
Using Keywords to Connect with People 670
How to Build Your Brand Through Search 672
Using Engagement Objects to Promote Your Brand..............676
Building a Community..677

Chapter 3: Identifying and Reporting Spam...................691

How to Identify Spam and What to Do About It......................691
How to Report Spam to the Major Search Engines 696
Reporting Paid Links 700
Reducing the Impact of Click Fraud 704

Chapter 1: Discovering Paid Search Marketing

In This Chapter

↳ **Understanding the value of paid search**

↳ **Integrating SEO and PPC**

↳ **Getting more market coverage with SEO and PPC**

↳ **Building your brand through PPC**

↳ **Increasing your traffic with PPC**

↳ **Running seasonal campaigns for maximum return on investment**

Paid search marketing (placing ads on a search engine results page, or SERP) and search engine optimization (SEO) are two different things, but they can work together, hand in hand. SEO focuses on moving your Web pages up in the *organic search results*, which are the Web pages that the search engine finds most naturally relevant to a user's search terms. The goal of SEO is to make your Web pages appear on the search results pages for certain search terms, so you can attract the right kind of people to your site. But there's another, quicker way to get your listing on a search results page: You can buy an ad.

In this chapter, you discover how to use paid search ads to your advantage. You find out how to use them as a shortcut to get placed in the search engines. You also discover how they can assist your SEO efforts by letting you test *keywords* (the search terms your Web page is most relevant to) on a trial basis. It takes time and effort to make a Web page support a certain keyword strongly enough that the search engines recognize that page and bring it up in the rankings. Paid search marketing lets you "try out" a keyword first to make sure it's worth the work.

In this chapter, we use a different convention for discussing keywords and searches. Because paid search has its own syntax, the practice of delineating keyword phrases in square brackets won't work here. Therefore, we switch, for just this one chapter, to using braces like this: {keyword} instead of square brackets like this: [keyword]. We make the change because in Google AdWords, inputting a keyword in square bracket means that you're looking for an exact match (much like using quotation marks in Google's regular search.) Why is it different? Who knows? The mind of Google works in mysterious ways.

Harnessing the Value of Paid Search

The most common business model for search engine ads is *pay per click* (PPC), in which advertisers pay the search engine each time someone clicks their ad. Clicking a PPC ad takes the user to a particular page on the advertiser's Web site selected by the advertiser (unlike organic listings, where the search engines choose the page they think is most appropriate). PPC ads appear at the top or side of a SERP and are labeled as Paid Listings, Sponsored Links, Sponsored Listings, or Featured Listings. Figure 1-1 shows Google's SERP for the search query {Mustang hubcaps}, which includes PPC ads (they use the term Sponsored Links) both above and to the right of the organic results. In terms of page layout, Google AdWords alternates between the top one, two, or three advertisers appearing above the organic listings, only one top advertiser appearing above the organic listings, and all paid advertising on the right column. This is a random cycle and an advertiser cannot specify in which layout they would like to have their ads appear.

Pay per click ads

Figure 1-1:
Google PPC ads show as Sponsored Links above or next to the organic results.

You should consider using paid search advertising in addition to your SEO activities as part of your overall search marketing strategy. For example, if you would like to attract more muscle car business to your classic car customization Web site, you could use PPC ads as a testing ground for different keyword phrases. You could set one up for {muscle car customization}, another for {hot rod customization}, another for {pony car customization}, and so forth. Then you could track what kind of traffic you received for each keyword/ad combination and compare the results. Remember, it's not just numbers you're after — you want to know which keywords bring in people who are truly interested in what your Web site has to offer and actually end up converting. Conversion data is key to PPC advertising — without knowing how well you convert visitors to customers, you have no way to measure if your PPC campaign is generating a positive return on investment (ROI). Conversion data is key because it tells you who is converting versus who is clicking through. Click-through data only tells you who is coming to your site and not what is giving you money.

PPC ads give you a relatively quick and easy way to experiment so that you can apply the lessons learned to your main Web site optimization, too. Here are some reasons to use PPC ads:

✦ **Immediate results:** PPC ads give you a way to get your Web page on the front page of SERPs almost instantly. You may or may not get traffic through your ad, but either way, you have instant feedback.

✦ **Qualified visitors:** Because your ad only appears when users enter a specific search query of your choosing, people clicking your ad should already want what you have to offer. This should make them highly qualified traffic to your site.

✦ **Keyword research:** PPC makes a great keyword testing ground. With PPC ads, you can try out different keywords to see which ones attract the most visitors and make the best "bait" for the kind of traffic you want. You're interested in data, and PPC gives you data quickly that you can analyze.

✦ **Conversion testing:** You can test what kind of traffic a keyword and ad bring to your site by paying particular attention to their *conversion rate* (the percentage of site visitors who actually buy, sign up, subscribe, register, or do whatever action your site wants people to do). You don't just want hordes of visitors; you want people who give you conversions. The flexibility of PPC lets you change ads at will, so it's an easy way to test the market.

All of the major search engines give you reports and ways to track your ad's effectiveness. To do PPC properly, you must *tag* your pages (insert HTML programming code provided by the search engine) to track everyone who comes to your site through a PPC ad, from clicking the ad to landing on your site and all the way to exiting. This detail helps you analyze the effectiveness of each PPC ad. It also helps you find weaknesses in your Web site. For instance, you can track users through your site's *conversion funnel* (the path users follow to accomplish a conversion on your site). If you find that very few visitors can get past a particular page and on to the next step, it may be that your signposts to take action on that page are unclear, or that some other improvement is needed. (Find much more on tracking conversions in Book VIII, Chapter 2.)

Third-party PPC analytics tools are available that can help you measure and analyze your paid search ads. If you're running campaigns on multiple search engines, it might be a good idea to invest in a software package like this because it can track activity from *all* of your ad campaigns and identify for every conversion the search engine ad where it originated. Google AdWords provides much of this data on its own, or you can install one of many analytics products that we cover in Book VII.

No matter which tool you use, the important thing is to set up analytics on your site and track how effective your PPC ads are after users get to your site. Know what your metric is for conversion and revenue: Is it a purchase, a sign-up, a subscription, or something else, and how much average revenue do you generate per conversion? Watch what your visitors do once they arrive at your site. PPC pairs very well with analytics because everything can be tracked and quantified in terms of dollars spent and dollars earned. Analyze your data and make sure your return on investment (ROI) makes sense. If you're spending $200 in PPC ads to bring in $100 of sales, that doesn't add up. With PPC, you can find and adjust for problems like this quickly if you're really watching your analytics.

Who shouldn't do PPC

Like any advertising campaign, PPC takes money. If your Web site sells products with very low markup or a narrow profit margin, or if you're a non-profit organization, PPC might not be for you. You must be able to track dollars spent and dollars earned to justify and manage a PPC campaign. If you can't put a monetary value on your conversions, how will you know what your return on investment is? PPC makes the most sense for online businesses that have products or services for sale. Then you can track the extra visitors brought in by your PPC ad, see how many of them converted, and count the dollars earned.

The only exception to this is Web sites that generate income from traffic. If you have a Web site that gets paid X dollars for each visitor (or a set number of visitors) and you spend Y dollars in PPC advertising to get those visitors there, make sure that $X>Y$.

You can also use your analytics to compare different keywords that you're thinking about optimizing your Web site for. ROI may only provide part of the picture; also look at data like how many people go beyond the *landing page* (the initial page the ad link brings a visitor to) into your site for each keyword, by looking at bounce rate and average page views.

Through the use of a *cookie* (small file stored on the user's computer), your analytics package can also track how many times a user returns to your site, and what those return visits lead to. These factors can be just as important as an initial-visit conversion rate when determining which keywords to optimize your Web site for long-term. You can use your PPC ads as a fertile testing soil for the data you need to make educated keyword decisions for your organic SEO.

If you decide that PPC ads are worth a try, the next decision you need to make is what keywords to advertise on. Keywords in a PPC campaign are just as important as in an SEO campaign. Making sure you're bidding on keywords that people are searching for is critical to your PPC success. Bidding on the wrong keywords leads to frustration and wastes your hard-earned time and money.

To help choose the right keywords for your PPC ads, some research is in order. The same keyword-selection principles we've described elsewhere (particularly in Book II) will help you here, such as knowing your target audience, brainstorming a keyword list, researching top-ranked sites for those keywords, and analyzing your competitors' sites to see how they're attracting searchers. The keyword research and log file analytic tools mentioned in Books II and VIII are available to let you see exactly what terms were used by the searcher. These are great resources for finding Long Tail keywords that may lead to conversions and for helping you to understand what terms your audience might be using.

You should also run your proposed PPC keywords through the Google AdWords Keyword tool (go to `https://adwords.google.com/` and click Get Keyword Ideas). Figure 1-2 shows the Google Keyword tool. You can edit this by clicking the Edit link if you need to target a new location.

If you already have a PPC campaign up and running, you have the choice to generate additional keyword ideas by using Existing Keyword, which populates a list with the terms that you are using and allows you to choose one of the terms to find similar terms that you may be missing.

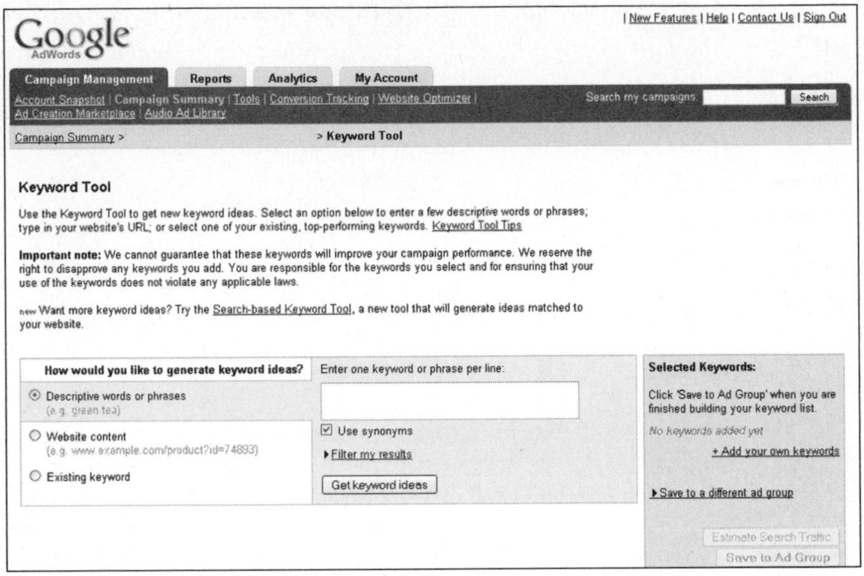

Figure 1-2:
The Google
AdWords
Keyword
tool lets you
evaluate
keywords
for PPC.

If you select the Website Content radio button under How Would You Like to Generate Keyword Ideas?, the Keyword tool scans your Web site for what Google feels are relevant terms. This is a great tool to find keywords that naturally have a higher *Quality Score* (QS), which Google uses to set the bid price of a keyword based on the quality and relevance of the landing page, because the relevance is already determined by Google. You still have to be sure that the term is a marketable term with your audience, however.

When you click the Get Keyword Ideas button, Google displays a long list of related and synonymous keywords for your consideration, complete with statistics. As shown in Figure 1-3, the list shows you approximately how often each keyword is searched and some month-by-month data. Using the pull-down menu, you can choose to view other columns such as how much advertiser competition there is for each suggested keyword. Clicking on the descriptive phrases button brings up a box for you to enter all of your keywords or new keyword ideas.

Don't make the mistake of choosing the highest volume keywords just because you think they'll bring in the most traffic. High volume keywords are broad and general and tend to attract visitors that are only researching and not ready to purchase. This means you are using your advertising budget on researchers instead of purchasers. These keywords may be hot for searching, but advertising on them can burn you if you're not careful, especially because you're paying for every click. It's better to select transaction-based keyword phrases that you know will convert at the start, even if they aren't searched for very often.

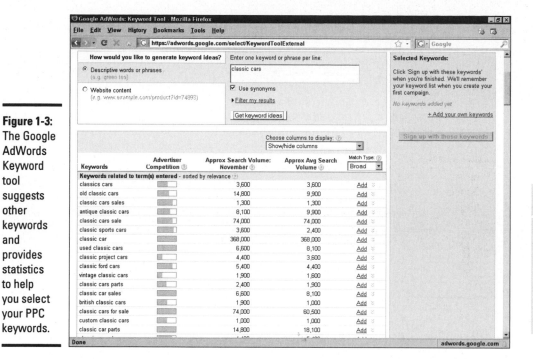

Figure 1-3:
The Google
AdWords
Keyword
tool
suggests
other
keywords
and
provides
statistics
to help
you select
your PPC
keywords.

Also be aware that the list of related and suggested keywords Google shows you (like the one in Figure 1-3) is the same list your competitors see for the same keywords. You might find that those keywords have a low ROI because the PPC price is steep and the clicks are already spread too thinly. Run searches to find out who's already bidding on those keyword phrases and how many competing ads there are. Keep thinking outside the main keyword list, looking for creative ways to bring in more traffic with a high conversion rate. Try to find good, conversion-producing keywords that your competitors haven't thought of yet. This is also a good place to start building your negative keyword list. A *negative keyword list* is made up of the words that you do not want your ads to show up for. If you see terms on the generated list that make no sense to you or are definitely *not* terms you want associated with your product, add them to your negative keyword list.

After you've determined the keywords you want to bid on, you need to decide which type of keyword matching to use. For example, if your targeted keyword is {customize a car}, do you want your ad to appear only when that exact phrase is searched? Or do you want it to be a bit looser? You can fine-tune your keyword matching to target your ad to the right users.

When you place your PPC ads, you can choose between the following match types. Most vendors offer similar match types to those offered by Google; we've noted differences in the following list where they exist:

+ **Broad match:** Broad match allows your ad to show up for your keyword phrase along with plural or singular forms, synonyms, and other relevant variations. So your ad may show up for all of the following queries: {customize a car}, {custom car}, {car customizing}, {auto customization}, {customize a vehicle}, {customizing an old car}, and so on.

  Broad is Google's default match type, but that doesn't mean it's the best choice. You could spend your entire PPC budget quickly with broad match turned on if you didn't put filters in place because it causes your ad to display more often, but not necessarily to the right people. (Note: In Yahoo!, broad match is called Advanced Match Type.)

  To keep a broad match from bringing in unqualified traffic, you should also put filters in place that exclude inapplicable words from a user's query. See the bullet labeled "Negative (or excluded) keywords" later in this list.

+ **Phrase match:** In Google, a phrase match type causes the ad to appear whenever a user's query includes your keyword phrase and possibly other terms that appear before or after your keywords (but not in between). For instance, if your keyword is {Ford Mustang}, Google could display your ad for {1984 Ford Mustang} as well. Microsoft adCenter offers the same Phrase Match ability. (Yahoo! does not offer an equivalent to phrase match.)

+ **Exact match:** Exact match is the most restrictive match type. Your ad can only appear to users who type in the exact keyword phrase, with no additions or changes. As we mentioned, in Google AdWords, you mark an exact match by putting the keywords in square brackets. (Yahoo! calls this Standard Match and it includes exact matches to your keywords plus singular/plural variations and common misspellings.)

+ **Negative (or excluded) keywords:** The search engines give you a way to narrow your search traffic by also excluding words that someone might type. Because you don't want to pay for clicks from people who clearly aren't interested in what you're offering, use this feature for keywords with multiple meanings. In Google, you'd use *negative keywords* to remove irrelevant words. In Yahoo!, you'd use their Excluded Words feature to accomplish the same thing. For example, if a keyword is {Mustang}, you could exclude searches that also contain the word {horses}. In this example, an advertiser must be careful in considering whether this may exclude persons searching on the term {Mustang horse power} if it is important to them. In this case, you would use {horses} as a negative term, but allow {horse}. Sometimes it can become Catch-22 situation. Be sure to think of all the possible queries that might contain your keywords plus all the other words that wouldn't pertain to your site at all and block those extra words.

If you are just starting a PPC campaign, Broad match or Phrase match are probably better places to start as they allow you more visibility and allow you to capture more keyword phrases leading to possible new search terms.

With Exact match, you get results only if your audience searches for exactly what you use, giving you no extra keyword data to work with. We recommend starting with Phrase match. You can always A/B test against Broad and Exact matches to find what converts best. For more on A/B testing, see Book VIII, Chapter 3.

Another decision you need to make is what search engine to place your PPC ads on. Which search engine will provide the most effective market for you? Google is an obvious first choice because they command more than 60 percent of all Internet searches. However, remember that you're after *qualified* traffic — the searchers who want what your site offers enough to click your ad, arrive at your site, and then convert. Here is some information to help you select your PPC vendor of choice:

✦ **Google AdWords (`http://adwords.google.com/`):** Google AdWords gives your ad the biggest potential viewing audience because Google has the largest percentage of search traffic. Besides appearing on all searches powered by Google, your ad will also show up on searches run through AOL, Ask.com, EarthLink, and NYTimes.com. Beyond that, Google's Content Network option enables your ad to go even further, including to searches run in other countries. Be warned, however, that the Content Network should be used for branding only and is usually not a good producer of conversions in most cases. Many users have developed "banner blindness" and aren't likely to click on ads appearing on a Web site, so you should take advantage of that to instill name recognition through repetition instead.

✦ **Yahoo! Search Marketing (`http://searchmarketing.yahoo.com`):** With the second largest total search market share, Yahoo! is another good option for mass ad appeal, especially if you know that your audience fits the Yahoo! user demographic. (The typical Yahoo! user is older than the average Google user, as an example.)

✦ **Microsoft adCenter (`https://adcenter.microsoft.com/`):** Microsoft Live Search ranks third in total number of Internet searches. Although it has a smaller share of the market, Microsoft's paid search product, adCenter, is worth checking out. adCenter is currently the only search engine to allow ad targeting by *demographics* (user data such as gender, age, and so on). Because of this capability, studies have shown that a well-targeted ad has a much higher ROI on Microsoft adCenter than on Google AdWords or Yahoo! Search Marketing.

✦ **Others:** If your industry has a specialized search engine, the traffic it attracts could provide a rich concentration of people interested in your Web site. You need to know who that search engine is reaching to make sure it's worth your investment. But if the demographics fit your Web site, you could mine that traffic with a PPC ad and watch your conversion rate grow.

When you sign up for a PPC ad campaign, either in Google or other engines, you can control many variables. The primary items you're asked to specify are

✦ **Keywords:** You select the keywords (search terms) that cause your ad to display. The engines also let you group your keywords to make them easier for you to manage. Organize your various PPC keywords in a way that makes the most sense for how you want to budget your advertising dollars.

✦ **Daily budget:** To help you control your ad campaign's costs, you can set a maximum total amount you're willing to spend per day. The search engine keeps track of how many times your ads are clicked and stops displaying your ads when the budget is reached.

✦ **Delivery method:** This is something that is specific to Google only. Make sure your campaign settings are set correctly. The defaults in Google AdWords are designed to be the most profitable for Google. Using the default delivery method means that Google shows the ads as quickly as possible. For example, say that out of 100,000 possible impressions, your budget only allows you 1,000 click-throughs a day. If you have a high click-through rate, you exhaust your budget early in the day and your ad doesn't show in the evening. You can set the delivery method in Google AdWords to appear throughout the day based upon your budget. This means you can choose to run your ads later in the day and in the evening. Two of the advantages of running later in the day is that your competition may run out of click-throughs and not show up during those hours, and the cost-per-click is less expensive because of less competition. For more control over your spending, you can set your delivery method to Standard to spread your ads over the hours you are advertising. With Accelerated delivery, your budget is used earlier in the day, and you are left without ad presence for the rest of the day.

✦ **Maximum cost per click (CPC):** You set the maximum cost that can be charged per click for each keyword you bid on. Here's where the competition heats up because different people bidding on the same keyword can be awarded better placement or more *impressions* (times the ad appears in search results to users) partially based on who had the highest CPC bid. With highly competitive keywords, it's not uncommon for advertisers to check and adjust their CPCs multiple times a day.

✦ **The ad itself:** You specify the ad title (the top line, which displays in a larger font), descriptive text (which shows in the middle two lines), and the URLs. When you create an ad, you have two URLs to consider: a display URL (which is what is displayed with the ad) and a destination URL (which is the actual URL used to link to the landing page). The display URL can be as simple as the home page to your ad (such as `www.classic carcustomization.com`) or may include keywords even if it's not a real URL (`www.classiccarcustomization.com/Mustang`). If you do use a fake URL, be sure to use a 301 redirect to transfer it to the real landing page. The display URL can be a great tool in increasing conversion as it helps attract attention. A typical PPC ad is shown in Figure 1-4.

Figure 1-4:
A typical
PPC ad on
Google.

> **Classic Cars**
> Browse **Classic Cars** For Sale
> Online with AutoTrader Classics.
> AutoTrader**Classic**s.com

You can give the search engine a single ad, but remember that PPC is
your testing ground. You can provide two (or more) ad versions for each
keyword. So you might have two versions of your PPC ad for the keyword
phrase {customize a car}:

```
Customize your car
Restore your vehicle with our
classic car customization services.
www.classiccarcustomization.com

Customize a classic car
Restore your car to mint condition
with expert customization services.
www.classiccarcustomization.com
```

When you provide several versions of an ad, the search engine rotates them.
If you use the Optimize setting, Google automatically compares the effectiveness of each ad version by the number of *click-throughs* (people clicking the
ad and going to your site) as well as the *bounce rate* (percentage of users
who click the ad but then click right back to the results page, obviously not
finding what they were after). Then they start automatically favoring the
"most effective" (as defined by Google based on click-throughs) version, displaying that ad more frequently to maximize your campaign. Although that
sounds good, remember that the search engine's definition of "most effective" and yours may not be the same.

Google is interested in click-throughs because that's what makes *them*
money. But you're more interested in conversions because that's what
makes *you* money. For this reason, we suggest you use the Rotate setting
instead of Optimize and run no more than two versions of an ad at a time.
The Rotate setting forces Google to give your two ads equal time. This lets
you do a true A/B test to get clear conversion data, and then control which
ad is shown more, based on your own site results. (Book VIII covers testing
in more detail, if you want to find out more.)

Writing and testing the ad

Your ad itself needs to contain a *call to action*, which is an instruction written with an *imperative* (or command form) verb such as *buy*, *sell*, *trade*,
grow, *expand*, or as in our sample ads shown previously, *restore*. Your call
to action should lead the user to do something by including a brief benefit
statement, if possible. So in the previous example, the phrase "Restore your

car to mint condition" contains both an imperative phrase — "Restore your car" — that tells the user to do something, as well as a compelling reason why to do it — to bring your car "to mint condition."

In writing and testing ads, sometimes a one-word change can make a signifi-cant difference in *clickthrough rate* (CTR) and conversions. For instance, the phrases "bargain prices" and "discount prices" can actually have different effects on different consumers. Just because one phrase works for a specific group of keywords does not mean it will work for all your keyword groups. Test for each group and use the results for each group separately. You may end up using "bargain" for some keyword groups and "discount" for others.

Here's another trick you can use to help your ad stand out — use your key-words in your ad. You want to do this because the search engines automati-cally **bold** the user's keywords on the search results page. Hence, your ad is more eye-catching.

Preparing the landing page

When writing your PPC ads, never lose sight of the landing page where users end up when they click. Your ad sets up a particular expectation in the user's mind — make sure that your landing page lives up to it by giving them what you advertised. If the ad is about restoring your car to mint condition, the landing page should focus on that in the title and text. Also include your keyword phrase on the page.

Every PPC landing page must be customized for the keyword and theme, so you generally need a different landing page for each keyword group. Finding out what needs customizing is all part of why you are running the A/B test. Even if you are promoting complementary products, do not use the same landing page for different groups of products. Instead, send prospects to individually designed landing pages.

Pictures can be worth a thousand words. Consider using engagement objects such as graphics or other engaging *rich media* (pictures, video, audio, and so on) to grab the user's attention and help sell your product or service. For example, your landing page for "Restore your car to mint condi-tion" could show before-and-after photos of an old jalopy transformed to a gleaming beauty.

Most importantly, you want your landing page to contain a clear call to action that instructs the prospective customer to do exactly what you want them to do. If you want them to call you for a quote, list your phone number and provide instructions several times ("Call us Monday–Friday from 8:00 to 5:00 PST at 1 (800) 555-0100"). Repeat the phone number in bold text in your page content. The call to action and the action itself (like the button that must be clicked to proceed) should appear "above the fold" in the immedi-ately viewable window (as opposed to below the fold, which would require scrolling the window to view) as well as other strategic places.

Test your landing pages until you find a clear winner. When testing, you can send an identical ad to each landing page and compare the conversion rates for each page. Limit testing to two or three pages at one time for a specific keyword group. Other A/B comparisons can include copy length, layout, image size, call to action, and pricing. Remember that PPC gives you an ideal testing ground, so don't be afraid to tweak everything and track all the results until you find your winning combinations.

Again, just because a landing page is more successful for *one* group of key-words does not mean that it is the right landing page for your *entire* PPC campaign. Each group of keywords needs to have its own testing and results for that group. You may end up with a different landing page that is most successful for each of your keyword groups.

**Book X
Chapter 1**

**Discovering Paid
Search Marketing**

Figuring out ad pricing

To help you determine what your maximum CPC bid should be, the search engines give you an estimator tool. Figure 1-5 shows Yahoo's estimator tool, which can be found at `http://sem.smallbusiness.yahoo.com/searchenginemarketing/marketingcost.php`. Enter the keyword in the first box and use the slider to set your proposed budget in the second box; click the Calculate button.

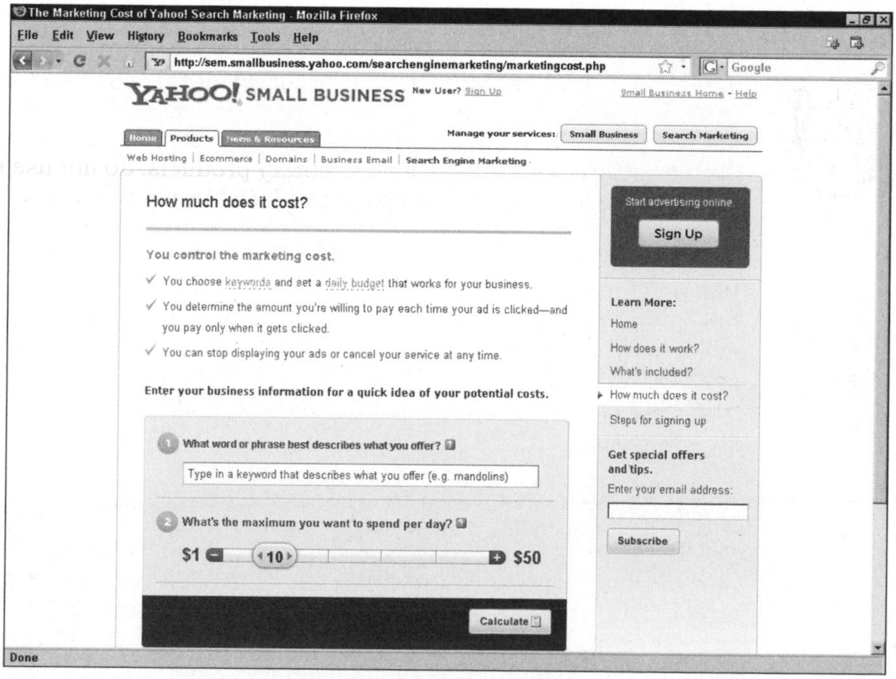

Figure 1-5:
Yahoo! estimates your number of impressions, click-throughs, and a recommended maximum CPC based on your keyword and budget.

Figure 1-6 shows Google's version of the same tool, which lets you compare multiple keywords at once. You can access this tool even without an AdWords account at `https://adwords.google.com/select/ TrafficEstimatorSandbox`. (Once you have a Google AdWords account, you can run this report from inside your account.) Be aware: The estimated CPC is based on system-wide use of the keyword. The CPC might actually be much lower based on geographic targeting. In rare cases, it might actually be more. Google does not give figures based on specific geographic targeting.

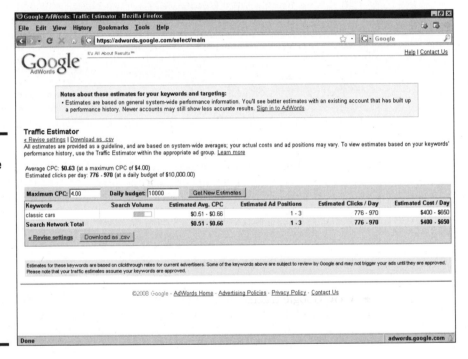

Figure 1-6: The Google AdWords Traffic Estimator computes an estimated CPC and daily cost for each keyword you enter.

When you set up a PPC ad, you don't need to commit to the search engine's recommended maximum bid amount. You might want to start with it to get a benchmark, but then change your bid on a regular basis to find out what amount brings you the best results in terms of traffic and conversions. The key behind PPC is to *test, test, test*.

Keep in mind that the search engine's recommended bid spans a 24-hour day, which may be wrong for your ad. A feature called *day parting* allows you to specify when during the day your ad is shown. Google calls this feature Ad Scheduling. For example, if your target audience is preteens, you probably won't get much activity (that is, searches on your keyword and click-throughs) on weekdays when students are in school, compared to the after-school hours each weekday.

If you keep your ad displaying 24 hours a day, your ad might rank well in the off hours, but during the heavy search times when your competitors show their ads, yours may drop off the SERP altogether. In that case, you're better off using day parting to restrict your ad to peak search times and possibly raising your maximum bid to be more competitive if this is a good converting time. Also, one factor that consistently affects how much you pay is the keyword's competitiveness. The more people are competing for the same keyword, the higher the price is just to get in the game.

It's important to remember to use analytics data to compute your *return on investment* (ROI) for each keyword. If a keyword makes you a certain amount of profit, your total cost including your PPC ad fee cannot be more than that profit or you're going to end up losing money.

You can't control precisely where your PPC ad shows up on a SERP. There's a ranking system involved in PPC. In the old days, it was simple: The highest bidder got the top spot. Today, all the major search engines use a formula to determine which PPC ads to display and in what order, and maximum CPC is only one of the factors.

Google has developed a formula for assessing a PPC ad's relevance to a user's query, which they call the keyword's Quality Score. According to Google AdWords Help (`http://adwords.google.com/support`), *Quality Score* is "a dynamic variable calculated for each of your keywords." Each time a user searches for keywords that have PPC ads, Google calculates the Quality Scores afresh and uses those scores plus the ads' maximum CPC bids to determine each ad's SERP position. Quality Score is an algorithm that takes into account many factors, including

✦ **CTR:** Google tracks the ad's historical *click-through ratio* (CTR) (percentage of clicks per ad impressions, or *CTR*) for that keyword and the matched ad. This is a *big* quality factor for Google because they make money on your ad only if people click it.

  To raise your CTR, make your ads as compelling as possible for your target audience. You should also consider using *geotargeting* (specifying the geographic area where your ad will display) or day parting to narrow your ad's exposure, but only if doing so increases your CTR without negatively impacting your bottom line.

✦ **Account history:** The combined CTR of all the ads and keywords in your PPC campaign plays a role.

  You can improve this factor by watching your account and eliminating ads that historically have very few click-throughs. One exception to this rule is an ad with a low CTR but a really high conversion rate. You'd want to keep that ad in place because it translates into a very nice ROI (that is, low cost per conversion).

Book X
Chapter 1

Discovering Paid
Search Marketing

✦ **Relevance:** Google evaluates how relevant the ads it displays are to the searcher. They compare the search query to the keyword and the ad and look at how relevant the keyword is to the ad text, as well as to the rest of the ads in your *ad group* (one or more ads that target a set of keywords, which you group). Google also compares the relevance to the landing page (that is, does the keyword appear on the landing page text in a relevant manner?).

To maximize the relevance of your ads, make sure that you choose keywords that are relevant to your site (actually used on your site) and also use them in your ads. Beyond that, you can boost your relevance quotient by creating ad groups of related terms, categorizing them by product type, brand, or some other method that helps you match ads and keywords with landing pages.

✦ **Landing page and site quality:** Google gives higher ranking to sites they decide are better quality in terms of original content, navigability, and so forth. Applying your best Webmaster practices and fleshing out your site with lots of good content helps you with this.

Your Quality Score affects where your ad is positioned in the Sponsored Links search results, as well as how much you pay for your PPC ads on Google. As Google says, "The higher a keyword's Quality Score, the lower its cost-per-clicks (CPCs) and the better its ad position," compared to competitors with the same bid. Google wants to place the most useful links in front of their users, so it makes sense that they wouldn't let advertisers simply buy their way to the top. The better your ad performs, the higher your Quality Score is.

Making SEO and Pay Per Click Work Together

Web site owners may work on SEO to rank organically *or* they may purchase ads, but they often don't do both at the same time. The fact is, it's not an either/or proposition. PPC ads can work in conjunction with SEO to complement and strengthen your search marketing plan.

Remember that with SEO, ranking is not the end goal — what you're really after is traffic to your site that leads to conversions. And PPC provides another way to lay out a welcome mat that brings many new visitors to your site. At this point, it's a good idea to evaluate your home front. You need to make sure your Web site is prepared to receive those visitors.

As we mentioned in the last section, pay careful attention to your landing pages. They provide the first impression of your site for everyone who clicks one of your ads. Each landing page needs to look appropriately clean and professional (for your subject and industry). Every industry is different, so make sure you adhere to your industry's standards. What might look professional in one company might be inappropriate for another. More importantly, your landing page needs to meet the visitor's expectations because that person is going to decide in about two seconds whether your Web page has what they're looking for. Put yourself in the user's shoes, and make sure that the page delivers what the user is after, based on the search query and your ad text.

Your landing page must also get your user to convert with clearly marked instructions that make it easy to follow whatever action is desired on your site. Make sure that your call to action appears "above the fold." You would be surprised how many people still do not understand the concept of scrolling down a page or how to use a menu. People are much more likely to convert if the page they land on gives them exactly what they hoped to find *and* lays out a simple way to accomplish what they want to do.

Of equal importance is your *site navigability* (link structure for moving around the site). Make it very easy for users to get around your site after they arrive at your landing page. Sometimes a site may look nice, but it doesn't contain a clear path to guide users where they need to go. In particular, you want your visitors to be able to get to the conversion point easily, whether that's your checkout process, sign-up form, or some other type of conversion page.

For searchers who are just in the information-gathering stage, it's equally important for the landing page to provide links to related pages where they can read about your subjects in more detail. You can keep those searchers on your site by helping them gather the information they need at this stage and hopefully move them to the next step that could potentially lead to conversion. The easier you make it for your users to cross the finish line from anywhere in your site, the better.

Complete market coverage with SEO and PPC

You can think of the search engine results pages (SERPs) as real estate. You want your Web page to be in the Page One neighborhood, where there are 10 main "lots" for organic results. The organic results are not for sale, but in the margins above and to the side of those 10 lots, space is available that *is* for sale.

For your main keywords, you want your Web page to show up in the results. If you can claim one of the top 10 organic spots, great! If you can show up in the margins with a PPC ad, that's good, too. If you can do *both*, you're taking up lots of visible real estate on the page — and denying that much real estate to your competitors at the same time.

But there are other reasons to want to show up in both places. Studies show that when your ad appears *with* your organic listing on the same page, the click-through rate skyrockets. What's surprising is that people are far more likely to click your organic listing if they see your ad on the page as well.

You can also target different types of users with the two different types of listings, based on their intent. You can classify these types of intent-based searches as follows:

✦ **Information-based search:** People looking for information are doing research. They may still be early in the purchase process and just educating themselves. Or they could be gathering information for an academic purpose or other types of research. These queries tend to be broad and more generic, like {muscle cars} or {classic Mustangs}.

✦ **Transaction-based search:** Searchers who are shopping or are ready to buy perform transactional searches. These searches tend to use more specific queries, such as {customizing a 1950 Ford Mustang} or {prices for classic Ford Mustangs}.

Ideally, you want your Web site — and your SERP listings — to appeal to *both* types of intent-based searchers. The most obvious reason is to bring in more traffic. But keep in mind that consumers move through these two stages in a cycle. Today's informational searcher becomes tomorrow's more educated buyer. You want to serve their needs at both points.

Information-based searchers tend to choose organic listings almost exclusively. People doing a transactional search, however, are likely to click paid listings. So your PPC ad with its marketing-friendly copy can attract these ready-to-buy consumers, whereas your organic listing appeals to the researchers in the crowd. By having both types of listings on the SERP, you're attracting both types of searchers.

Google AdWords tracks clicks that come through a clicked ad with a 30-day cookie so today's informational searcher can still be tracked and identified by the original PPC query when they later convert with a PPC ad for up to 30 days. A *cookie* is a flag saying the visitor was at that site before, searching on a specific keyword. The cookie remembers what that search term is.

SEO and PPC have many things in common. With your SEO campaign, you're trying to optimize your pages around certain keywords so that when people search for those keywords, the search engines find your page among the most authoritative. With a PPC campaign, you're advertising so that when people search for certain keywords, they think your ad is perfect for their needs. What's the common theme? A need for good keywords.

Before you start optimizing a page around the keyword phrase, for example, {antique car restoration}, you could give the keyword a test run using a PPC ad. You need at least a month to gather benchmark data and up to two months if you don't have any PPC history. After a benchmark has been set, you can usually make a decision on A/B testing within a few days if enough data or impressions are produced. Right off the bat, however, it's very hard to make an assessment with just a few days of data because you just won't have enough traffic. The only way you can make an assessment after a few days is if you have a high volume of traffic for that test. If you don't have a lot of data, you'll have to wait until you get more. Statistically valid sample sizes are commonly around 10,000 impressions, although you may see clear patterns of behavior with far fewer counts. Intuition and experience play large roles here. Running an A/B test on your PPC campaigns gives you lots of data, such as:

✦ **Number of impressions:** You find out how many times your ad showed up on a search results page. This gives some indication of how often the keyword is searched and how competitive it is.

✦ **Number of click-throughs:** You know how many people searching on that keyword were interested enough to come to your site.

✦ **Bounce rate:** You find out the percentage of visitors who arrived at your landing page and decided it wasn't for them. A bounce rate of less than 50 percent is good. If it's as high as 70 percent or more, you probably need to change the landing page. It needs to be more focused on what those searchers want, more engaging, or both.

✦ **Conversions:** You find out what those visitors did once they got to your site. If many of them reached conversion (by making a purchase, and so on), your site is doing a good job. However, if your Web site takes users through a three-step conversion process from landing page to qualifying page and then to the check-out, and you find out that you're losing 95 percent of the people at the second step, you know you have to make some changes on your site to improve your *conversion funnel* (the process users go through to make a purchase or other type of conversion).

✦ **Cost per conversion:** For a bottom-line analysis, you can find out what your total ad costs were per conversion you received. If you spent more money than you made, that's not going to be a good ad for you to continue as is, but it doesn't necessarily mean that the keyword isn't worth optimizing for.

If you didn't get very much traffic at all, it may be because the keyword phrase is not a good one for your site. Here's where you need to use some discernment, though. Just because a keyword doesn't get click-throughs on a PPC ad doesn't mean it wouldn't generate traffic if you had an organic result. It could be that the keyword is geared for information-based searching, for example. In that case, people would be more likely to click an organic listing than a PPC ad.

Always remember to look at your conversions. If you have a poor CTR but get conversions on the few visitors you do get with the ad, it's a good PPC keyword. However, low or no PPC traffic could also mean the keyword or the ad is a dud. Do several A/B tests with alternate ads to see if the ad or the keyword is the problem. To maximize your time and energy, start by focusing on those keywords that have proven successful in both PPC and organic SEO, and let them work synergistically to bring you more traffic.

Reinforcing your brand with PPC

Paid search ads can bring in traffic, but they can give you another benefit as well — reinforcing your brand.

Your *brand* is a name or trademark that identifies your company, product, or service. Local businesses pay for brand advertising all the time. The neighborhood Little League field displays banners of local real estate agents or dry cleaners who've sponsored them. High school drama groups and bands hand out programs that contain scanned business cards and logos of local business people who've paid for the privilege. These are all examples of advertising for the purpose of brand lift. A parent watching a tee ball game or a choir concert isn't likely to pick up the phone and make a call to that business right then, but the ad in the program or out on the field creates an impression that can lead to a future call.

Similarly, just showing up on a search results page can give your brand some needed visibility. This is especially true if you're trying to break into a business with established competitors. You want your name to show up somewhere, anywhere, on the primary search engine results for your main keywords. PPC gives you a way to shortcut that process by paying to be there.

When people run a search, they quickly scan the first results page and usually decide what to click within the first five seconds. Eye-tracking studies have found that most people see the first few organic listings and the first few PPC ads during those brief seconds (for more about this, see Book I, Chapter 3). When your brand appears either in the title, description or URL of a PPC ad, it has the ability to create an impression in the user's mind linking your brand to their search topic.

As we discussed in the previous section, your organic listing gets clicked much more often when people see your PPC ad on the same page. This is due to increased brand recognition. People feel more comfortable trusting a vendor who seems to have a higher visibility. If you're showing up twice, you must be better, or so the logic goes.

Consider buying PPC ads for your own brand name if it's a keyword that's searched for. Your site gains visibility and you gain relevant traffic.

Supplementing Traffic with PPC

Some Web sites simply must appear in the search engines in order to get their businesses off the ground. But for competitive keywords, moving up in the organic rankings can take months. If you *must* appear for a keyword, taking out PPC ads is your answer.

But while your PPC ads are running, don't stop optimizing your site for natural SEO, either. Let your search engine rankings continue to rise while your PPC ads are humming along bringing in business. While you're working on SEO, your PPC ads can help your cash flow.

When you've made it to the top of the Google heap and your organic search listing can stand on its own, you still should keep doing PPC. As long as you're making money, don't give up your ads.

One reason for continuing with PPC has to do with search engine real estate. If you've earned *two* top positions on the SERP, one for your organic listing and one for your PPC ad, why give up a spot that could get taken over by a competitor? It makes more sense to keep both results in place and cover more real estate on the SERP. As we explained earlier in this chapter, the two different types of listings attract different types of searchers, so they work together well to bring in more total traffic to your site.

A study done in 2005 by eMarketer revealed that more than 60 percent of people didn't really understand the difference between the organic and paid results on a SERP. Internet searchers are getting savvier as time goes on, but a lot of people still don't understand why some links show up in the right column versus the left. What attracts people to click one or the other probably has more to do with how they're worded. That explains why the marketing-driven wording of a PPC ad pulls more transactional searchers, whereas the informational searcher tends to click the organic listings.

**Book X
Chapter 1**

**Discovering Paid
Search Marketing**

Making Smart Use of Geotargeting

Geotargeting provides another way to use PPC ads to increase traffic. If you have a local business like a bakery or a dry cleaner, the idea of advertising on a nationwide search engine where you could get billed for clicks from anywhere could send you running for cover. But what if you could limit your ad to display only to people in your town? By using geotargeting, you can capture local search traffic and searches on mobile devices such as smart phones within your area. So if your business is local, geotargeting lets you run a PPC campaign that makes sense.

All of the major search engines let you specify a city and state where you'd like your PPC ad to display. Google also allows a PPC ad to be linked to their Google Maps and searches done within Google Maps. With Google, you can pinpoint a custom area by plotting points on a map or even specifying how far something is from your store location, like a two to three mile radius around a pizza shop for deliveries, as shown in Figure 1-7.

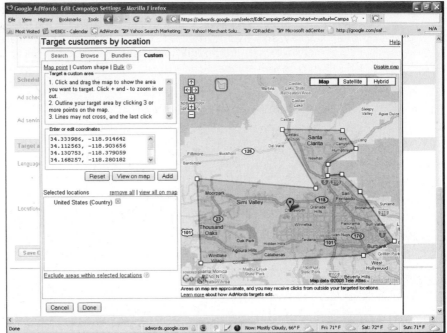

Figure 1-7:
Google
AdWords
geotargeting
lets you
control
where your
ad displays.

You may have other marketing reasons to use geotargeting, as well. For your classic car customization business, you could place PPC ads in a city that has a big car show, advertising a show-themed discount for new customers. Or if you discover that a particular part of the country has a high interest in 1950s muscle cars, you can mine that market with some geotargeted PPC ads for those keywords. You can also geotarget using keywords alone: for example, {Los Angeles muscle cars} allows you to hit people using that search term, as well as people in Los Angeles searching on {muscle cars}.

Starting Your Seasonal Campaigns

PPC's flexibility makes it the perfect way to handle short-term or seasonal advertising on the Web. For example, if you want to offer an April spring-cleaning sale on hubcap polishing through your classic car customization Web site, SEO wouldn't be the way to drum up business for it. SEO is a relatively slow process that moves your Web pages up in the search engine rankings over time, usually taking several months. However, PPC is incredibly flexible. You could put PPC ads up quickly and possibly drum up a lot of extra traffic during your sale.

If your Web site sells products that are seasonal, use PPC ads to supplement your traffic. Businesses typically spend more advertising money during peak times anyway, so why not use some for paid search ads? By applying a few principles we explain in the following sections, you can make sure that your PPC money is well spent.

Principle #1: Start your seasonal campaign in advance

Timing may not be everything in advertising, but it plays a huge part. With seasonal PPC campaigns, the best practice is to start early. If you run a seasonal business, your true buying season doesn't line up with the holidays on the calendar. For Halloween sales, you might need to be selling by the end of summer for retail sales, and early spring if you're a wholesaler marketing spooky wares to stores. (*Retail* refers to selling to consumers. *Wholesale* involves selling in quantity to retail businesses, for resale.) Similarly, retail stores set up Christmas displays two or three months in advance, so the Christmas wholesale buying season begins well before that.

The bottom line is this: You want your ads to be there when the shopping season begins. Have your PPC ads show up early before the ads crowd in from competitors with less forethought than you. Be one of the first ads to appear for a seasonal item, and you increase your chances of click-throughs and conversions from those early shoppers. Starting early also gives you time to tailor your ad and to A/B test landing pages.

Principle #2: Adjust your spending levels as the buying season progresses

When you first start your seasonal campaign, you don't need to spend a lot of money. Keep your maximum CPC bid on the low side and set a low daily budget amount. Remember, the competition hasn't heated up yet, and neither has the search traffic for your keywords. However, searching *has* begun, so this is a great time to do some testing.

Test several versions of ads and different keywords to find those perfect matches that convert well, while it's still early in the season. Then you can choose the best-performing ads and have those running during the peak sales time.

As the buying season heats up, watch your PPC analytics closely and adjust your spending levels as needed, making sure that there is sufficient budget to last for the entire season. Consider using day parting if necessary to have maximum exposure during peak conversion hours each day (which are different for each situation). You want to maintain your placements as much as possible as more and more competitors' ads enter the scene. However, never outbid at the expense of your bottom line. You don't want to pay $5 per click for a keyword if it pushes your ROI into the red.

If your season is tied to a holiday like Christmas or Halloween, chances are that sales will continue to build steeply up until a few days before the holiday, or whenever your cutoff date is for shipping products in time for customers to receive them by the holiday. At that point, you should disable the PPC ads you've been running because you don't want to attract frantic last-minute shoppers who would come to your Web site only to find that you can't deliver their gift or costume in time. Don't pay for clicks that can't convert!

If you still have sufficient stock leftover for an after-holiday stock reduction sale, you can put up new PPC ads in the days after the holiday. For an after-Christmas sale, for example, you might want to stay up late on December 25th so you can log on to your PPC account and activate the after-Christmas sale ads at midnight. Currently, Google AdWords does not have the capability of switching ads on a schedule, so it has to be done manually.

You want to monitor your PPC analytics closely over the days following the holiday, too. When you see conversions start to fall off, you can stop the ads.

Principle #3: Use some of the same keywords your site already ranks for

Keyword selection doesn't need to be different for your seasonal campaign. It's better to advertise using the same keywords you've already optimized your site for, and just let your ad wording draw in the seasonal business. For one thing, your Quality Score benefits if your ad text and keywords match keywords used in your Web page because that increases your relevance to the user's search query. Plus, you can get the advantage of more coverage on the search results page.

You can use your usual keywords for PPC ads even if you already rank for them organically (through SEO). For keywords that you haven't ranked for yet, taking out a PPC ad can bring in valuable traffic that you never get any other way. For your high-ranking keywords, you have just as much reason to use PPC. If the search results page shows *both* your organic listing talking about your product and another result advertising a sale on that product, imagine how effectively you can bring in the traffic. Figure 1-8 shows what it looks like to someone interested in classic Ford Mustangs if both your organic listing and your PPC ad show up in Google.

Note: This figure was mocked up to reflect a possible search result for our fictional car customization site.

Figure 1-8:
A PPC ad
supplements
your traffic
even for
keywords
you already
rank for.

Remember, you can use keywords in the display URL even though that particular URL may not really exist, as long as the base domain matches your "destination" domain. Placing the keyword in a display URL gives you an additional place to get bolded terms in your ad and shows relevance to the searcher as well.

Chapter 2: Using SEO to Build Your Brand

In This Chapter

✔ Selecting keywords that help build your brand

✔ Using search to maximize brand awareness

✔ Distributing press releases effectively on the Web

✔ Increasing your chances of showing up through blended search

✔ Creating engagement objects

✔ Building an online community

✔ Using social bookmarking to promote your brand

Traditional marketing just isn't enough to build a *brand name* (company or product name) these days. You can't just have a good product and decent service, take out a yellow pages ad, print some business cards, and set up shop. Your marketing plan now needs to be bigger, more engaged, and more interactive. To build a successful brand name, you need to be where people will see you, hear what others say about you, and join in the conversation — and that's on the Web. A good marketing plan today needs to consider that "word of mouth" has gone digital, and somehow tap into that online buzz.

Search engine optimization (SEO) gives you the skills you need to make sure your Web site can be seen where people search. That's crucial because the majority of people coming to any Web site get there through a search engine. But to really grow your brand, you have to stretch beyond pure SEO and do some broader Internet marketing, which means to delve deeper into understanding your target audience and interacting with them. In this chapter, we discuss how you can associate your brand with other things that your target audience is interested in. We also cover how you can give your audience a voice and form a "community" online that supports your business goals. These are the branding activities that help you thrive in the world of Internet marketing.

In this chapter, you discover how to do online brand building from A to Z. We begin with the meat-and-potatoes of SEO, keyword selection, but approach it from a brand-building perspective. Then we move into creating press releases, videos, images, and other objects that help engage the audience members you need to attract. Last but not least, we take you into the brave new world of *social media* (Internet sites that enable people to share and discuss information and build relationships, like Facebook, Twitter, or Digg). You find out how you can use blogging and the many available social media outlets to monitor and manage your reputation and build a community at the same time.

Selecting Keywords for Branding Purposes

If the goal of branding is to make your name known and respected, the first step in Internet branding is to make your name visible in the search engines. To get started, for each of your notable brand names (your company name, your product name, and possibly your own name, if you're trying to become an authority in your industry), run some name searches and see whether your Web site ranks for your brand in the search engines.

If your company name is a unique brand, like Nike or Bruce Clay, Inc. or John Wiley & Sons, Inc., you definitely want your own Web site to come up in searches for your brand. However, you may have chosen a brand name containing *keywords* (the terms people search for) instead. Examples are *Classic Car Customization* and *RunningShoes.com*. If you have a brand name like that, you'll be competing against lots of other sites to rank for your brand because those are their keywords, too. It takes time and a lot of SEO know-how to get your brand to the top of the search engine results pages (SERPs). However, moving your brand up in the search results should be a goal for any company that wants to build a long-term clientele. The payoff comes when past customers or people who've heard about you through word-of-mouth go looking for you by name in a search engine and can find your site.

Using Keywords to Connect with People

There's a lot more to branding than just showing up in search results for your name. You can also do branding by using the Internet to connect with prospects and then raising their awareness of your brand, as we discuss throughout this chapter.

Selecting the right keywords is the foundation of search engine optimization. You need to know what keywords best describe what your Web site has to offer. Then you can optimize your Web site's *on-page factors* (the HTML tags and the visible content on the Web page) to be about those keywords. In turn, search engines find your pages among the most relevant to users' searches for those terms, and voilá — you rank well in search results, attract lots of people to your site, and get the *conversions* that you're ultimately after.

In addition, there's another whole approach to keyword selection that's geared to branding, not ecommerce. Rather than trying to find keywords that convert immediately, this approach concentrates on finding keywords that connect with the people you're trying to target. This is how you start building *brand awareness*, a sense of who your company is before your potential customers even know that they'd be interested in you.

Say, for example, that you have a business customizing classic cars. For SEO, your Web site is optimized around keywords that correspond to the *content*, which is the actual meat of your site. You have pages and pages of articles, pictures, and more about customizing classic cars, and sprinkled strategically throughout this content are your keywords. Now focus on the people who're reading your content. Looking at your current customer list, who is your target audience? What do you know about them *besides* the fact that they like classic cars?

Discover keywords that represent your visitors' shared qualities or interests. Find out what else your target audience has in common, besides being interested in your product or service. Look at demographics like age, gender, lifestyle, location, education, beliefs, and occupation. Also think about attitudes they may have in common — for instance, if they all tend to be bargain hunters who won't purchase something unless it's a "good deal," that affects the kinds of offers you make in ads and on your site. If you've created *personas* (imaginary models of typical customers) to help you evaluate your Web site user experience, the same research will help you come up with things your target audience has in common. (For more on personas, see Book V, Chapter 1.)

For your classic car customization Web site, as you look at your current customer list, you may start to notice some patterns. For example, you might discover that nearly all of your visitors are between the ages of about 40 and 60. This helps you identify keywords that represent what your audience has in common. After you have those keywords in mind, you can use them to research where those people might congregate on the Web. You could look for a forum or social media site that's made up mostly of baby boomers. Or think about other hobbies baby boomers participate in: Are they wine tasters? Classic rock concertgoers? Motorcycle enthusiasts?

After you identify a list of your target audience's other interests, start brainstorming how you can make your brand more visible to them. If it's wine-tasting they're into, you could send a letter or e-mail to a wine-tasting Web site suggesting that they link back to your site because many of your wine-tasting customers are also interested in customizing classic cars. Alternatively, you could offer an article for the other Web site to post on their site about customizing classic cars; it would give them free original content, and your only condition would be that they link back to you. Or you could suggest a joint project such as a wine-tasting booth at the next local car show, and then issue a joint press release to publicize it.

TIP

Your brand is boosted in people's minds every time they see your brand mentioned somewhere else. Start looking for places where you can show up *outside* your own Web site, where your desired prospects will see you. The more exposure you get, the better your brand.

How to Build Your Brand Through Search

You have a great opportunity to increase your brand's online presence through the many different search avenues available today. Once upon a time, there was only your Web site to represent your company online. Like a solitary island in a sea, you just had to hope searchers would know enough about your company to notice the blip of your Web site on their radar. Today, you can use search marketing to connect your Web site to the world. Through SEO, you can enable your site to show up when people search for your keywords. But there's also much more you can do to make your brand visible.

The goal is to increase awareness of your company, to make your brand something people recognize and even talk about, and the big win is to have your brand searched for. Search marketing gives you lots of channels to accomplish this, from search engines to social networking to video sharing to press releases to blogs to news to *wikis* (information sites containing all user-generated content, such as Wikipedia, www.wikipedia.org) to bulletin boards . . . and the list goes on. When you make your brand name show up in many of these, it builds an online presence that raises your brand. You can think of it as *halo media* — a variety of media channels that surround your company like a halo, giving it presence and making your brand known, as shown in Figure 2-1.

Figure 2-1: Halo media happens when your brand is visible through many online channels, not just your own Web site.

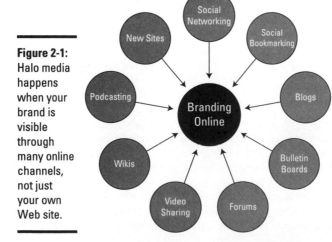

The flip side of using search to build your brand has to do with managing your brand's reputation. It's all well and good to get your name out there, but what happens when someone misrepresents you or posts something awful about your company? And when the buzz about your company starts to turn negative, it can turn into a firestorm fast. Once again, search comes to your aid! You can monitor the online conversation and decide when to jump in and do some damage control.

In the remainder of this chapter, we cover the practical steps you can take to create halo media around your brand. We begin the discussion with press releases, and then move on to discuss videos and other engagement objects and tips for diving into the world of social media. Throughout the chapter, you build the skills you need to manage your brand and make it thrive in the online world.

Writing press releases

Distributing Internet press releases is an effective and not-too-costly way to increase public awareness of your company. To do this, write and send your press release to a third-party distribution company such as PRWeb (www.prweb.com) or one of the others we mention later in this section. That company publishes it on their site, and pushes it to other news sites that may pick it up and republish all or a part of it, so for a short time, your news continues to circulate on the Web and get exposure. For the long term, the distribution company archives the press release on their Web site, and you should also archive your press releases in a News or Press section of your site.

When writing press releases (as with any content), keep in mind your keywords. Use your keywords throughout the text, and especially use them within the first 200 words on each page because that's the part the search engines count more heavily when calculating a page's relevance to a user's search. Don't repeat the keywords over and over again — that's called *keyword stuffing* and should be avoided — but use them within the natural flow of your writing.

Also include links to your site in your press release. This ensures that you not only acquire an *inbound link* (hyperlink on an external site that takes users to your site), but also that it is from a page with relevant content and optimized *anchor text* (the link text that can be clicked). The links would ideally go to the home page and high-priority *landing pages* (the pages where users arrive at your site because they're the ones most focused on particular keywords) for your most profitable and most searched services. Be sure to use a top keyword as the anchor text rather than using a URL.

To keep buzz circulating about your company, distribute press releases regularly — at least once every two to three months, but more frequently if possible. Our schedule is semi-monthly based on announcement-worthy content, so your mileage may vary. Your press release should announce some achievement or event about your company, so always be thinking of good topics that could be publicized. An effective press release should contain factual information that doesn't sound too much like marketing copy. (It's a good idea to put opinion-type statements like "Our super-fantastic new buffing tool is going to revolutionize the car customization industry!" into quotes.)

Newsworthy ideas for press releases include

✦ New service or product being launched

✦ Special deal announcement

✦ News about the Web site or company in general

✦ Employee promotion or new hire (especially of a company executive or notable person)

✦ Contest being offered through your Web site

✦ Launch of a cool interactive feature on your Web site

✦ Award given to your company

✦ Other significant event or announcement

We recommend you check out the following press release distribution services. Compare their coverage, options, and prices to find the one that suits you best. Also, different services feed different news outlets, so if there's a particular news outlet that you definitely want your news appearing in, that could be a deciding factor:

✦ **PRWeb (www.prweb.com):** Besides being a very reliable distribution service, they offer helpful tips on how to write an effective press release (see www.prweb.com/pressreleasetips.php).

✦ **Marketwire (www.marketwire.com):** Marketwire news stories pop up nicely to the top of Google search results and elsewhere, so they're another good one to consider.

✦ **PR Newswire (www.prnewswire.com):** This is one of the biggest press release operations in the U.S., so it's another good choice.

Optimizing for blended search

All the major search engines can display a mix of different types of results in the SERPs, a technique known as *blended search*. (Google calls it Universal Search, but it's the same concept.)

Before the advent of blended search, when you went to a search engine and looked for something, your search results only contained Web page links.

You had to choose Images in order to search for photos, News if you wanted to find news articles, Video if you were looking for videos, and so forth. With blended search, your results may contain these types of links in addition to Web site listings, all presented together in a single SERP.

You can run a search for a specific well-known person or thing to see blended search in action. For instance, if you search on Google for [1969 ford mustang], you get back a variety of different images, Web pages, and video results all blended together, as shown in Figure 2-2.

**Book X
Chapter 2**

**Using SEO to
Build Your Brand**

Figure 2-2:
Blended search gives users various types of results mixed together.

What does blended search mean to you as a Web site owner? It means that you can't afford to have a Web site full of text alone anymore. A Web site that includes videos, images, and other types of media has more chances to be shown in search results than a text-only site does. In fact, sites that include videos and other media elements now outrank those that do not, all other factors being equal.

You might wonder why a site with a video should outrank a site without one. We know that Google and the other search engines' goal is to present the most relevant content based on a user's search query. That in itself doesn't explain it. However, they also want people to like using their search engine and to be satisfied with the Web sites they go to. The search engines want the experience of searching to be as engaging as possible. A SERP with a mix of photos, videos, news articles, and book links increases user engagement. In addition, users are better satisfied with the results if the sites themselves are more engaging. By making the entire experience more satisfying, blended search is a win-win for the search engines and for searchers.

Using Engagement Objects to Promote Your Brand

The lesson of blended search is clear: enhance your Web site with engagement objects, and you will be rewarded for it. *Engagement objects(™)* are non-text elements such as images, videos, audio, games, and applications that help engage your Web site visitors' interest. When people first come to a Web site, they tend to decide whether to stay or leave within the first two to five seconds.

Say someone is searching for [classic Mustang colors] and finds your classic car customization Web site. If they see just a headline and several paragraphs of information, they probably head for the Back button. To grab their interest, your page needs photos of Mustangs, hopefully showing the various paint colors. You might also have a video link showing how to prep a classic car for repainting. Or you could have an interactive wheel created in Flash that shows all the manufacturer's color choices for the model year that's selected. The more engaging you make the landing page, the more likely it is to satisfy your visitor. And, all other things being equal, the more likely Google and other search engines are to list your landing page among their top search results.

Engagement objects are expected to play more and more heavily in search ranking as time goes on. The search engines have been working hard to "read" non-text content and understand what it's about. They're getting better at converting the various types of non-text-based files into words that they can *index* (include in the search engine's database of Web page content for search results). Google in particular made great strides in 2008, beginning to convert the soundtracks from video and audio files into text. Search engines can now read non-moving text created in Adobe Flash, as well (Flash is a software program used to create animated and interactive objects for Web sites). As search engine technology advances, you can expect engagement objects to continue to gain importance as a ranking factor.

You can consider including several different types of engagement objects to optimize your Web site for blended search. We've listed the most common ones below, with some notes:

✦ **Images:** Search engines scan Web sites to find large photos, diagrams, illustrations, or other types of image files. To help the search engine understand what your image is about, include a brief description in the surrounding text, in the image's `alt` *attribute* (HTML description), and in the file name.

✦ **Video:** Embed your video right in your Web page for maximum benefit (so people can visit and possibly link directly to your site).

✦ **Audio:** Include audio files embedded in your pages and be sure to explain what they're about in the surrounding text. Also, don't annoy your users — be sure to set the default audio file to "off."

✦ **Flash:** It's against SEO best practices to create your whole Web site in Flash because the search engines can't index moving text or images. However, you can make your Web site more interactive by including Flash objects, and the search engines can now index non-moving text created in Flash. Consider using Flash to build useful or entertaining animated elements (or *widgets*) for your site that engage your visitors, and be sure to describe them well in the surrounding text.

✦ **News articles:** If your press release gets picked up by a news organization, it could become a news result. Plus, archiving your press releases on your site gives you more content and possibly search traffic if people go looking for the information later.

✦ **Blog posts:** Search engines scan blogs that are updated regularly, especially if many people contribute to them. Recent posts to a blog sometimes come up in related search results, so an active blog on your Web site can increase traffic. (More on blogging in the section, "Blogging to build community," later in this chapter.)

✦ **Games:** Games are a great way to build user loyalty and increase engagement. High score tables, badges of achievement, and bragging rights are all ways to keep a user excited about your game and your brand.

✦ **Interactive applications:** This is sort of an "everything else" category. Financial calculators, AJAX apps that let someone design their own car, fun quizzes, and anything else that you could put on your page that a user can engage with and respond to all make great content for fixing the message of your brand in people's minds.

**Book X
Chapter 2**

**Using SEO to
Build Your Brand**

Building a Community

We've already talked about the need to target your specific audience, and that comes into play when building a community, too. Who are the people your brand appeals to? What other products, services, sports, hobbies, and things interest them, besides your brand? When you can identify their other common interests, you can work to associate your brand with them. If your car-customizing enthusiasts also tend to be into wine-tasting, you can research to find where wine tasters hang out online. Wherever it is, you want to be there, too! As your target audience starts to see your brand and your voice popping up around in the Internet, not just when you're selling to them but particularly when you're just part of the conversation, they find out who you are and start to trust you. They begin to feel like you're one of them. That's community building.

To build a community online, you need to use blogs and the various types of social media sites. Think of these sites as channels for communication — channels that go in both directions. You can get your message out to your prospects and develop a voice in your industry, but you can also listen. Probably never before has there been more opportunity to hear what people think about your products, your services, your ideas, and your company. Social media provides that channel. So use social media first and foremost as a way to research what people like and don't like about your brand and your industry. Approached with a willing ear and an open mind, these online conversations can give you an unlimited flow of ideas for improving your business.

Being who you are online

Before diving into the various places you can be social online, take a moment to think about who you want to be when you get there. Most importantly, you want to be genuine online. Don't claim to be someone you're not, or you'll get burned. The Internet population at large doesn't take kindly to imposters, and when the discovery is made, your brand could be damaged permanently.

The perils of posing as someone else

An infamous example of a company getting caught misrepresenting themselves online is Wal-Mart. In mid-2006, a blog called *Wal-Marting Across America* featured the travels of two "regular people" driving across the country, independently interviewing Wal-Mart employees. When it was discovered that the two people were actually being supported by Wal-Mart and that the blog had been concocted by Wal-Mart's PR firm, bloggers across the Internet retaliated with angry posts. Both Wal-Mart and its PR firm were seriously embarrassed by the flap.

You need to be transparent about your identity online. Many CEOs and other company executives now write blogs online, such as Tony Hsieh, CEO of Zappos, Bill Marriott, chairman and CEO of Marriott International, and Jonathan Schwartz, CEO of Sun Microsystems. Writing as themselves is the key, and allows them a platform where they can spread a message but also become a real person that customers can get to know. You don't want to *claim* to be the CEO if you're really writing the blog as a freelancer in another state.

Some companies choose to set up an alias to blog under, which is fine, as long as you make it clear that it's an alias. The *Chicago Tribune*, for instance, has set up Colonel Tribune as their social media ambassador. "He" has a profile in lots of social media sites, where he posts interesting bits of news with links back to *Tribune* articles and blogs, as well as other sites. His picture is an illustration rather than a photo (see Figure 2-3), which helps to prevent any confusion.

Figure 2-3:
The *Chicago Tribune's* Colonel Tribune doesn't claim to be someone he's not.

Whoever you choose to be in the social media realm, make sure you do it authentically. After all, you're trying to build customer and industry relationships that will last. You're trying to create trust. You have the opportunity to become a voice. You first need to know who you are and be true to that.

Blogging to build community

Blogging is arguably the oldest and most mature type of social media on the Web. It also can be important for your company Web site and SEO efforts. The search engines have a *vertical engine* (specialized search that finds one type of result only) devoted just to blogs, and blog posts are now being linked in blended search results when they closely match a search query.

Adding a blog to your company Web site has many benefits beyond possible search results. First of all, it's a great way to add content to your site that's fresh and original. It also invites visitors to have a conversation with you, which builds valuable relationships with your target audience. Through your blog posts, you can express your ideas and let your personality come through. You can start conversations, guide them, and establish yourself as a leader. When people post comments to your blog, you get user-generated content that other people trust and want to read. You get feedback that can help you see opportunities and put out fires. With an active blog on your site, you have a community in the making.

If you're just starting a blog, you might check out the various blog software programs available either for free or for purchase/license. Blog software is a specialized type of *content management system* (software that automates Web page production) designed just for maintaining a blog, such as WordPress (http://wordpress.org/) and Movable Type (www.movable type.com/). There are a wide variety of choices out there, though. We suggest you consult with your Webmaster and research to find the best option for your site.

For a corporate blog, you should consider hosting your blog on your domain (for example, you find our blog at www.bruceclay.com/blog/), but if you're just blogging as yourself, a hosted blog at a site like Blogger (www.blogger.com) could be just fine. (Alternatively, if you're a really big company, you can *buy* the hosting company and put all of your official blogs there. That's what Google did. Their official blog is http://googleblog.blogspot.com/. However, most of us don't have that option.)

You can use some tips and tricks to help you use blogging effectively to build an online community. Here are some blogging dos and don'ts:

✦ **Do** write in your blog regularly and often. Set a minimum goal of one new post per week, but write more frequently as ideas come to you.

✦ **Do** write in a conversational tone that's informative and entertaining to read.

- ✦ **Don't** use much profanity or vulgarity in your writing. You'll want to write appropriately for your target audience, but keep it a cut above to encourage readers to feel comfortable in your space.

- ✦ **Do** take the time to run your posts through a spelling checker (by putting them in a word processor if your blog software doesn't offer this feature) and proofread them before posting them. Keeping typos and mistakes to a minimum helps you look professional and makes people take your comments more seriously.

- ✦ **Do** include links to other people's blog posts and articles, and let the anchor text be meaningful words, not just a URL. Things you read on other blogs within your industry can be great topic starters, so feel free to summarize in your own words, and then rebut or expand on their posts in your own blog (including a link to the original post). This is another way to form industry connections and build community.

- ✦ **Don't** be afraid to raise controversial topics related to your industry. Stating a contrary opinion can generate lots of interest and comments. People are more likely to talk about what you wrote in other social media sites as well, and even if they disagree with you, they often link back to your site.

- ✦ **Do** use your blog to show you care about your industry. Talk about issues and develop a strong industry voice. This generates respect for you as a thought leader, but you also may find yourself helping to steer your industry.

- ✦ **Do** encourage conversation by approving people's comments promptly (but not the ones that are obviously spam). Also, write your own comments in reply when appropriate.

- ✦ **Do** comment on other people's blogs, too, especially other thought leaders in your industry. You can use your brand name with a link back to your blog or home page as your signature line, but other than that, be careful not to be overtly selling/pushing anything. Done with tact, posting on other people's blogs can help build community and a name for yourself within the industry.

Try to avoid responding to unfounded attacks. Many people try to engage others on the Internet for the wrong reasons. Lowering yourself to their level is seldom a good move: That way lies madness.

Here's one more idea for you: be on the lookout for other people's blogs that are popular with your target audience. When you find one that's highly read, get in touch with the blogger and let him or her know about your company and product. If you can encourage the blogger to give your product a try, you can suggest that they review it in their blog and give an independent opinion. People are highly influenced by a trusted reviewer's opinion, so this could generate a lot of traffic and help boost your brand.

Using other social media to build community

The good news is, you have lots of ways to talk to people online. The bad news is, there are *lots* of ways to talk to people online! Because your time is probably limited, it's important to figure out which Web sites and methods most effectively help you connect with your target audience on the Web. We give you some tips throughout this section on how to go about making that decision.

The important thing is to be where people are talking about your company and products — or, if your business isn't very well known yet, to be involved in related conversations where you can help to make it known. Social media sites give you a way to do that.

Being connected through social media can also help you deal with a public relations crisis. If a customer slams you online, it can become a PR nightmare. Although it might be tempting to think of the offending customer as evil and clearly attacking you, try to think of it as an opportunity to demonstrate your care and interest, resolve the issue, and then thank them. Try to turn a problem into a positive statement that you are care about their comments.

There are a few ways social media can help you deal with bad publicity:

✦ You hear about the complaint quickly, while it's still a small flare-up, because you're monitoring conversations about your brand name.

✦ You can analyze the complaint and determine its validity (or lack thereof). Self-analysis before jumping into a crisis is always wise.

✦ You can contact the person directly to resolve the issue, if you choose. You might turn a disgruntled customer into a loyal one through your fast response and excellent customer service.

✦ You can publicly post an explanation and apology, if appropriate. But do not attack the attacker! They are your clients, or should be.

✦ You can monitor and "control" the conversation, as needed.

✦ You can enlist the help of your *brand evangelists* (people who've supported your brand online in the past) to stick up for you, if you decide a response would be better coming from an impartial source.

✦ You can use social media profile to help push down the offending sites in the search engine results pages so they do not get as many views from potential customers.

According to a September 2008 study conducted by Opinion Research Corporation for Cone, Inc., 60 percent of Americans use social media, and nearly 60 percent of those people interact with companies on social media Web sites. The survey (www.coneinc.com/content1182) found that 93 percent of social media users believe that companies should have a presence in social media — and the majority said they "feel both a stronger connection with and better served by companies that interact with them in a social media environment." So there's a real opportunity for business owners here. With so many people "talking" online, you can't really afford to be out of the conversation. And the rewards of building a brand community and managing your reputation online make it worth the effort.

Connecting to your audience with social networking

Social networking involves "meeting" people online through a Web site designed for this. Popular social networking sites in the U.S. include MySpace (www.myspace.com), Facebook (www.facebook.com), LinkedIn (www.linkedin.com), Xanga (www.xanga.com), and Twitter (www.twitter.com), although the list is very long and constantly evolving.

To participate in a social networking site, people first set up their *profile* page, which contains a variety of basic or trivial information about themselves such as name, age, favorite books, favorite music, or whatever they choose to enter, as well as photos and links and a customizable background. Some sites (such as Facebook) have a way for a business to set up a business profile instead of a personal one and assign more than one person to have access.

Before jumping into a social networking site for your brand, do a little homework first. Research the demographics of the various social networking sites. About.com provides a short list of the top social networking sites (http://webtrends.about.com/od/socialnetworking/a/social_network.htm). and provides a few facts about each, including the geographic region where it's most popular, and some basic facts about each site's focus and purpose. We also suggest the direct approach — talk to your current customers and ask them where they "hang out" on the Web. You're looking for the social media sites that are the most popular with the people you're trying to reach.

After your profile is set up, you can connect with other users by request. On MySpace or Facebook, you send a "friend request"; on Twitter, you choose to "follow" another user. Another good method is to invite people to "Join our community" by including links on the bottom of e-mails and e-newsletters you send out. You could include links to your profile pages on various social networking sites, giving the person a choice. If they also have a profile on that site, they can easily request you as a friend/follower.

After a request is made, the recipient can either approve or deny it, so you have some measure of control over who you network with. Facebook allows you to build your network even faster by suggesting friends-of-friends that you might know. So after you start to build your network, use the technology to help it grow. You can also use search functions to find people talking about issues that matter to you (that is, your keywords). These let you dive right into the middle of conversations where you want to have a voice.

How you choose to interact with your network depends a lot on your strategic goals. Maybe you're trying to

✦ Build closer relationships with your best customers.

✦ Generate awareness about your brand and products.

✦ Build trust with potential customers.

✦ Find people for a long-term focus group.

✦ Gather ideas for new products and services.

✦ Locate disgruntled customers and put out fires.

✦ Assist with Customer Service inquiries or general information

You could have any number of different objectives for getting involved in social networking, so make sure you're starting off with your goal clearly in mind so that your time and efforts are well spent.

As an example, the cable television company Comcast has successfully improved their customer service and company image through Twitter. They set up a profile named "ComcastCares" and assigned an employee to do nothing but monitor Twitter for any mention of their company. Figure 2-4 shows its profile page on Twitter.

Figure 2-4:
Through
a Twitter
profile,
Comcast
reaches
out to its
customers.

How to stay on top of your keywords in Twitter

Using the search function at `search. twitter.com`, you can search for a specific keyword or phrase in Twitter to find all the recent entries. Then you can subscribe to a feed for that query to be proactive. Every time someone types that keyword into Twitter, you are automatically notified through an RSS feed (a type of automatic syndication of Web content, which you can read in any number of feed readers that are available for free, such as the Google Reader). A couple of services (TweetBeep at `www.tweetbeep.com` and Twilert at `www.twilert.com`) e-mail you when your keyword is mentioned on Twitter. This is how the ComcastCares guy knows instantly whenever someone gripes about Comcast, and it's also how you can stay on top of your keywords and meet people talking about what's important to you online.

When someone types a complaint or other comment about Comcast in Twitter, the ComcastCares person responds immediately through Twitter and helps the user resolve the issue (putting the person in touch with a technician, if necessary). But he's also a real person who enters unprompted comments, so that the other people on Twitter get to "know" him and build a sense of community with him. It must be working: At last count, the ComcastCares guy had 5,394 people following him.

Spreading the word with social bookmarking

Social media sites can help you generate interest in your brand and specifically in your Web site. Links from blog pages, social media sites, wikis, or forums only help your link equity for a short time and should not be relied on in the long term. However, many of those people who find your site through such a referral may end up liking what they see and bookmarking it or linking to it themselves. Plus, you're bringing in more traffic and building more awareness of your brand.

You can harness the power of social bookmarking to help get your word out. *Social bookmarking* lets users recommend a Web page to others through a social bookmarking site. There, they can also write a review, comment on it, start a discussion about it, and so on. Say someone reads your article "Making a Chrome Bumper Shine without Elbow Grease" and loves it. The reader can recommend it by bookmarking it to a site such as Digg (`www. digg.com`), Delicious (`www.delicious.com`), StumbleUpon (`www.stumble upon.com`), reddit (`www.reddit.com`), Yahoo! Bookmarks (`bookmarks. yahoo.com`), Google Bookmarks (`www.google.com/bookmarks/`), or any number of others. If it's the first time someone has bookmarked this particular article, it gets linked there, and people searching for your topic on that social bookmarking site find it. If the article was already bookmarked by another user, the reader's bookmark results in another vote for the article.

By counting the number of reader recommendations (both positive and negative), the social bookmarking sites can naturally rank articles based on how popular they are with their readers.

Your goal is to get others to see something on your site and then post about it elsewhere. Make it easy for your readers to share your articles with the rest of the world. Beneath each of your articles, you can offer *chiclets*, which are small icons or links that let the reader recommend it to a social book-marking site. Figure 2-5 shows a typical set of chiclets on a Web page.

Figure 2-5:
Readers can share or promote an article by clicking their favorite chiclet.

Chiclets

You can add chiclets to your Web pages rather easily via freeware available on the Internet. In the next section, we cover two options you can try, but there are probably many others. What's nice is that they let you pick and choose which social networking sites' chiclets you want to offer for those who want to channel the conversation (although we don't see any problem with being all-inclusive and offering every chiclet available).

Keotag

This free tool makes a Webmaster's job of adding chiclet code easy. We like it because you can edit the code when you paste it into your Web site and alter the titles slightly for each service so that your headlines appeal to their different audiences. Their list of available services, however, is limited. Figure 2-6 shows the tool you'd use to create your social bookmark links and the instructions follow.

Figure 2-6:
Keotag offers a good free tool for building chiclet code fast.

Here's how to create chiclets for an article using Keotag:

1. **Go to Keotag's Social Bookmark Links Generator at `www.keotag.com/sociable.php`.**

2. **Enter your article's URL — which must be unique — and a brief title for your article in the appropriate boxes.**

   Make it relevant to the text content and use keywords if possible.

3. **Click to select the check boxes of the various social networking services you'd like chiclets for.**

4. **Copy the auto-generated HTML code and paste it directly into your Web page or blog, right below your article.**

ShareThis

Many sites use this handy tool, which puts a single ShareThis icon under your article. If a user clicks it, a box opens up with lots of choices. Users can share the article on a social media site, post it to their own blog or profile, or send it by e-mail, as shown in Figure 2-7.

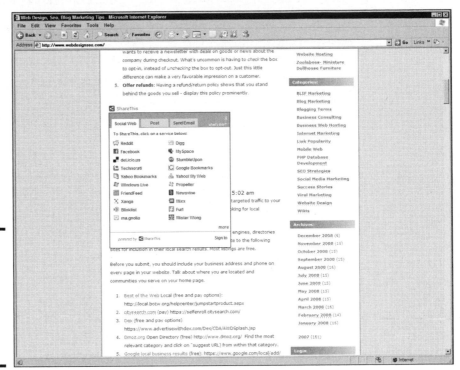

Figure 2-7: The ShareThis interface gives users more ways to use your articles.

Here's how to create a ShareThis interface for your Web site:

1. **Go to the ShareThis site at `http://sharethis.com/getbutton`.**

2. **From the Pick Your Platform drop-down list, choose the blog software that you use to build your site — either WordPress, Blogger, or TypePad. If you don't use any of those platforms, choose ShareThis Button for Other Websites.**

3. **Under Customize Your Widget, you can do just that. Select the appropriate check boxes and radio buttons to make your ShareThis widget look the way you want it to.**

If you select "Custom," for example, you can pick and choose exactly which social Web services you want to offer from a list of 39. You can even modify the colors of your widget to make it blend in better with your Web site.

4. **Click the Get ShareThis Code button.**

5. **Complete the registration form that pops up, including your name, e-mail address, your blog or site domain, and a password, and then click Create Account. You are now a registered "publisher" with ShareThis, which means that whenever you want to modify your ShareThis in the future, you can sign back in and get new code.**

6. **Paste the HTML code that ShareThis provides into your Web page beneath your articles.**

Chapter 3: Identifying and Reporting Spam

In This Chapter

✔ Knowing spam when you see it

✔ Avoiding spam on your own Web site

✔ Reporting spam violations to the search engines

✔ Recognizing paid links

✔ Reporting paid links for the search engines to investigate

✔ Understanding click fraud

When you hear the word *spam*, it might make you think of the many unwanted e-mails littering your inbox. Or maybe the first thing that comes to mind is cans of processed meat. (Mmmmmm, processed meat . . .) But in the world of search engine optimization (SEO), *spam* is any deceptive tactic used on a Web site to fool the search engines about what that site is about.

In this chapter, we recap the different types of spam polluting the Internet. Although we describe the different forms of spam in-depth in Book I, Chapter 6, in this chapter, we explain what you can do to clean it up if you find it on your own site, and what choices you have if you find it on someone else's. This chapter contains specific instructions for reporting spam to all the major search engines, which could be good reference for you in the future. You also find out about a type of fraud that affects paid search advertisers, and how you can guard against this in your *pay-per-click (PPC)* campaigns (search engine ads that display on search results pages, and that you pay for only when users click your ads).

How to Identify Spam and What to Do About It

You need to know spam when you see it for a few reasons:

✦ You can prevent your own Web site from inadvertently doing anything the search engines consider spam.

✦ When you're looking for good candidates among third-party sites that you could ask to link to your Web site, you can stay away from those with shady practices so your site doesn't get tainted by association.

✦ If you can recognize when someone else (such as your competitor) uses spam, you can distance yourself from them and even report them, if you choose. Knowledge is power, after all.

If you've ever done a search for car parts and clicked a result that took you to a page filled instead with a list of random *hyperlinks* (words or phrases a user can click to jump to another Web page) — or which sold something else entirely, like condominiums in the Bermuda Triangle — you've seen search engine spam. Chances are you blamed the search engine for this mistake. But the truth is that the search engine thought that the Web page it gave you *really was* about car parts. How did the search engine go so wrong? It was probably fooled by spam.

Spam takes many forms. We recap the most common kinds of spam briefly, and then get to what we really want to cover here — what you can do about each one.

Hidden text or links

When text or hyperlinks on a page are invisible to users but can be read by a search engine, that's considered spam. Spammers hide text or links from site visitors by using the same font color as the background color (such as white text on a white background), by positioning the text outside the visible page, or by layering an image or other element on top of the content, thus hiding it from site visitors. Here's what you should do when you run across hidden links:

✦ **On your own site:** Make sure you don't have any hidden text or hyperlinks on your pages. Drag your cursor over your pages or press Ctrl+A to select all of the page content to make sure it doesn't contain hidden white-on-white elements. You also should make sure your photos and other large elements aren't covering vestiges of older versions of your page.

✦ **On other sites:** If you detect lots of hidden text or hyperlinks on another site that's ranking decently in the search engines, it's a sure bet the search engines haven't discovered it yet. Search engines crack down hard on this type of deliberate spam, and may even ban offending sites from the search engine's *index* (the database of Web page information that the search engine maintains).

You could report a site using hidden text or links to the search engines as spam. (We give reporting instructions in the section titled "How to Report Spam to the Major Search Engines" later in this chapter.)

Doorway pages

A *doorway page* is a Web page created solely for search engine spiders, usually filled with text content that makes it rank high for a certain *keyword* (a word or phrase that users may enter in a search). There is no intention of letting users see the doorway page, however. When someone clicks to go there from a search results page, the Web site automatically redirects the user to another page that may be about a totally different subject. Here's what you should do when you suspect that you've found doorway pages:

+ **On your own site:** You want your pages to focus clearly on their various subjects and keywords and not deceive the search engines or the users. If you have any doorway pages on your site, get rid of them. If the pages are landing pages for PPC, use a `Meta` robots tag to specify `NOINDEX`, or use a 301 redirect to redirect them elsewhere.

+ **On other sites:** You can make a spam report to the search engines to report doorway pages, if you find them. The search engines hate giving their users misleading results, so they will gladly investigate. It's your option.

Frames

Webmasters may use *frames* (an HTML technique for combining multiple documents within a single browser window) as a page layout tool, although today it's thought of as an outdated technique. However, a spammer may use frames to hide content from the search engines because search engines read each frame as a separate HTML document. So users might see a page about car parts *and* other things that appear in additional frames, whereas the search engine thinks the whole page is about car parts. How do you go about solving the frames problem? Here's how:

+ **On your own site:** Because you want search engines to be able to digest all your Web content easily, be careful using frames. In fact, if your Web site is primarily constructed with frames, we suggest you ask your Webmaster to redesign it. Frames could hurt your SEO because not all of your content is indexed properly.

+ **On other sites:** If you think a competing site is using frames for intentional spam and you don't want them to get away with it, you can submit a spam report.

Deceptive redirection

Deceptive redirection is a type of coded command (usually a `Meta` *refresh*, which instructs a user's browser to automatically refresh the current Web page after a given time interval) that takes the user to a different location than what was intended via the link that was clicked. Spammers create a page with content that ranks for a certain keyword, yet when you access that *URL* (Web address), you get redirected to an entirely different site that has nothing to do with your search. This technique is often used by pornography and gambling sites to grab unwitting visitors. In order to combat deceptive redirects, take these actions:

✦ **On your own site:** Avoid using `Meta` refreshes on your site. The search engines may flag your site for a spam investigation if they find you using them because they're highly suspicious. When you need to redirect an old page to a new page, the only safe way is to use a *301 permanent redirect* (a type of server command that automatically reroutes an incoming link to a different URL). (Note: Book VII, Chapter 3 is all about redirects, if you want to know more.)

✦ **On other sites:** When you find a search engine result taking you to a completely different site maliciously, you have the option to report it as spam to the search engine. Depending on the situation, you may be performing a public service. The fewer sneaky sites out there, the better.

Cloaking

Through a process of IP delivery called *cloaking*, a Web site detects who's requesting to see a page and may show a different version to a search engine spider than to all other users. So the spider sees and indexes content that isn't what you would see if you went to that URL. If the purpose of cloaking is to deceive search engines (which is the very definition of spam), there is a severe penalty. It's no wonder the search engines hate it. Although not all forms of IP delivery are evil, deceptive cloaking is always wrong. Cloaking can be handled in a couple of ways, depending on if it's your site or another site:

✦ **On your own site:** Don't do it without consulting an ethical professional, and even then be cautious. If you have pages that detect the search engine spiders and change the page content as a result, you're operating in dangerous waters that could get your site banished from the search engines.

✦ **On other sites:** If you suspect that a competitor is using cloaking to gain an undeserved ranking in the search engines, you can compare their Web page to the version of the page that the search engine last *cached* (stored in their index). Do a search that you know will include that Web page in the results set, and click the Cached link under the URL. This shows you the Web page as it last looked to the search engine. If you see entirely different content when you go to their live site, you're probably looking at cloaking.

Cloaking can definitely be reported as spam.

Unrelated keywords

Spam also includes deliberately using keywords that are not related to the image, video, or other content that is supposed to be described, in the hopes of increasing traffic. Cleaning up a mess made by unrelated keywords is pretty simple — just follow these guidelines:

✦ **On your own site:** Make sure your page content is cohesive, with text, images, videos, and so on all focused on the same subject and keywords. An image's *Alt attribute* (brief description of the image included in the HTML) should accurately describe the image; each page's *Meta data* (HTML tags the spiders read that are supposed to describe the page) needs to contain keywords that are also used in the page text users see, and so forth. You rank better in the search engines with focused content anyway, so this is good advice all around.

Including keywords that have high traffic (query) counts but are not part of that page's content sometimes hurts your rankings, and never helps them. Avoid using keywords that do not relate to your content, and be sure that all words that are displayed on the page contribute to your SEO project.

✦ **On other sites:** You can view the page source code to see what's going on in another site's HTML. If you see *Alt* attributes or *Meta* data that's full of unrelated keywords, they may just be remnants of older versions of the page that never got cleaned up. But if it looks like they're doing it intentionally (there's no hard and fast rule here, so just go with your gut), it can be reported to the search engines for their investigation.

Keyword stuffing

Here's an example of keyword stuffing: "Customize your custom car customized with our car customization customizing cars service!" This text is so full of keywords that it no longer sounds like natural English. If you read something like that on a site, you know the Web site is trying to increase its relevance to those keywords by repeating them, hoping that search engines will rank them higher in the search results. Keyword stuffing can also happen sneakily, away from the user's view, by overusing words in the *Meta* data or in image *alt* attributes. How should you correct a keyword stuffed page? Here's how?

✦ **On your own site:** There's an art to using enough keywords, but not too many, so that search engines know what your pages are relevant for without thinking they're spam. To get the proper *keyword distribution* (the way keywords are spread throughout a page) and *keyword prominence* (the keywords are common to the content, more so than the other words but not enough to be spam), you can do competitor research to figure out what's "normal" for your keywords and follow our recommended guidelines. (Read up on this important technique in Book V, Chapter 3.)

✦ **On other sites:** If you find another site keyword stuffing, you can report it as spam.

Link farms

A *link farm* is a group of unrelated Web sites that each have hyperlinks to all the other sites in the group. This is spam because it's a fabricated collection of links connecting pages for the purpose of inflating rankings. Link farms are designed deliberately to increase their *link equity*, which is the combined value of all the links pointing to a page that is part of search engines' ranking *algorithms* (formulas for determining which Web pages are the most relevant to a user's search query). Search engines try to identify link farms and filter those links out of their calculations, and may even pull these sites from the index in order to keep them from affecting search results.

There is no way for a site owner to verify that link equity is being passed. High PageRank pages that link to your page may actually *not* be passing link equity if the search engines consider it link spam or the site to be part of a link farm. To avoid link farms with your own site and deal with them in your industry, you can do the following:

✦ **On your own site:** You want to encourage links from quality testimonial grade Web sites and avoid links coming to your site from unethical sites, such as sites involved in link farms or other types of spam. They can seriously harm your search engine rankings by association. Now, you can't actively stop someone from linking to you. However, you can avoid requesting links from these sites, and if you have been linked to by a link farm, you can send them a note asking them to please remove the link. The best links come from sites that strongly relate to your industry or to what your Web page is about and that operate ethically.

✦ **On other sites:** The search engines generally do a good job combating link farms, but if you find that another site participating in a link farm is still ranking, you can report the site(s) as spam. Never, ever link back to a link farm page. As a willing participant, you are subject to a penalty.

How to Report Spam to the Major Search Engines

Fighting spam is a top priority for the search engines. Google alone has a squadron of PhDs who do nothing but identify and combat spammers and their techniques. Fighting spam is important to Google because their business depends on presenting reliable, relevant results when you search. This is why their spam filters are getting better all the time.

The major search engines have posted "quality guidelines" to spell out what Webmasters should and shouldn't do — stuff like avoiding hidden text or hidden links, not loading pages with irrelevant keywords, and so forth. The search engines also encourage people to submit a spam report about sites that violate their quality guidelines and cross the line into spam. You should report spam when you see it. Eliminating search engine spam makes the world of SEO a fairer place, and searchers around the world get better results.

Google

Google has two ways to submit a spam report:

✦ Registered Webmaster Tools users can submit an authenticated spam report form at `www.google.com/webmasters/tools/spamreport?pli=1`. Google promises to investigate every spam report submitted by a registered Webmaster Tools user.

✦ Anyone can fill out an unauthenticated spam report form located at `www.google.com/contact/spamreport.html`. Google says they assess every unauthenticated report in terms of its potential impact, and investigate "a large fraction" of these reports, as well.

Figure 3-1 shows the easy-to-complete spam report form that's available to Webmaster Tools users.

**Book X
Chapter 3**

**Identifying and
Reporting Spam**

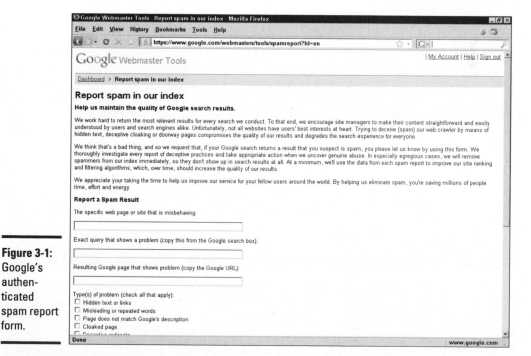

Figure 3-1:
Google's authenticated spam report form.

Yahoo!

If you detect search engine spam in Yahoo! search results, there's a form you can use to report it to them (`http://help.yahoo.com/l/us/yahoo/ search/spam_abuse.html`), as shown in Figure 3-2.

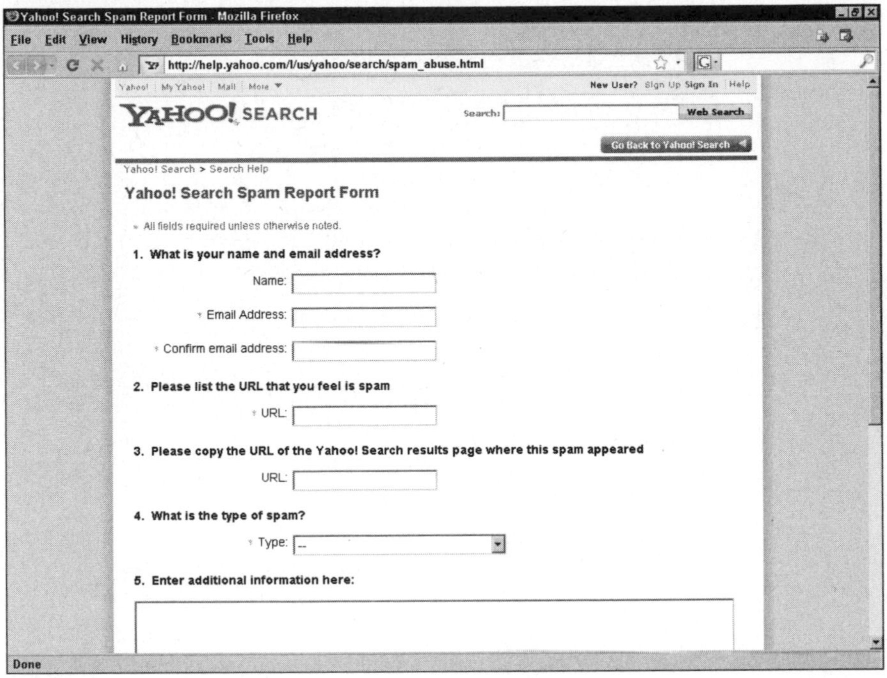

Figure 3-2:
Yahoo!'s spam report form.

Microsoft Live Search

Microsoft Live Search doesn't have a spam report form at a specific URL, but there is a way to report spam nonetheless. Figure 3-3 shows the form you use — we outline a few steps you need to take next.

Here's the drill for reporting spam to Live Search:

1. **On Live Search (www.msn.com), run a search that brings back the offending Web page in the results set.**

2. **Scroll down to the lower-right corner of the page and click Feedback.**

   You can see the form in Figure 3-3.

3. **Choose Found Spam from the Type of Feedback drop-down list box.**

4. **Type in any details you feel are needed in the Please Type Your Feedback Here text box.**

5. **Specify the spammy Web page by entering its URL in the If You Found Spam or Expected a Specific Website in the Search Results but It Wasn't There, enter the Web Address (URL) Here box.**

6. **Click Submit.**

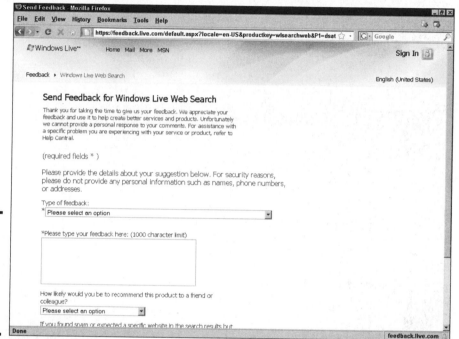

Book X Chapter 3

Identifying and Reporting Spam

Figure 3-3: You can report spam using the Feedback form in Live Search.

Ask.com

If you want to report an inappropriate search result in Ask.com (www.ask.com), you can use their generic form for reporting a site issue, which is shown in Figure 3-4.

To report spam to Ask:

1. **Go to http://asksupport.custhelp.com/ and click the Report Site Issue tab.**

2. **Enter your e-mail address (required) and then select an option from the Topic drop-down list (we suggest Web Search Results if you're reporting spam).**

3. **Enter details in the Message field. Because Ask.com's form is rather generic, they give you a few guidelines for what you should include in the Message text box. Tell them the following:**

- The exact key words or phrases you used to get the search results in question.

- The exact Ask.com Search channel you are using, either Web, Images, News, or other.

- The URL of the page where you see the inappropriate result.

4. **Click the Continue button, then click Submit.**

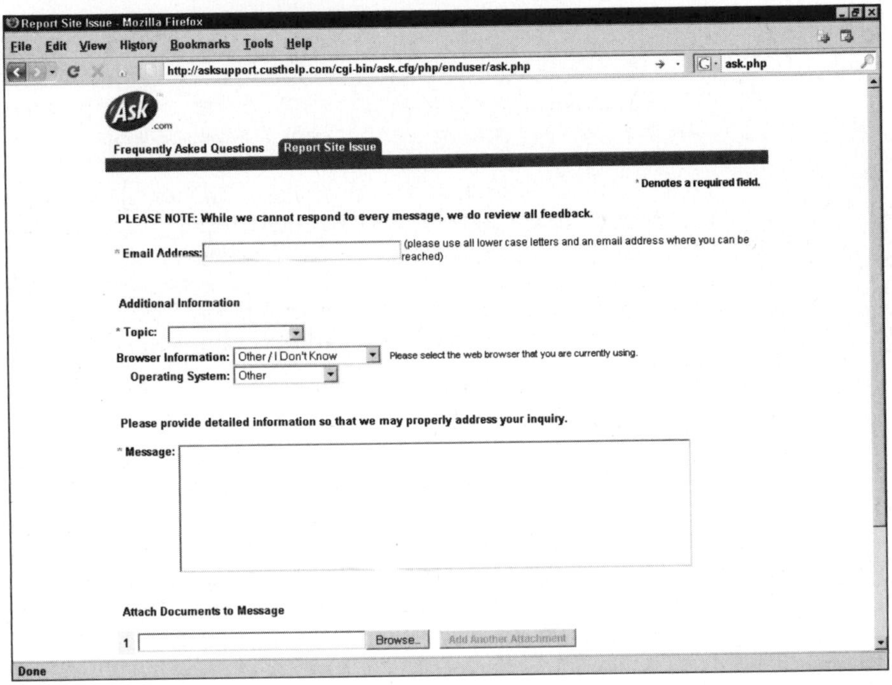

Figure 3-4:
The Report Site Issue form lets you report spam to Ask.com.

Reporting Paid Links

Remember that the search engines pay a lot of attention to links when determining a Web page's popularity and authority. They look at both the quantity and quality of inbound links to the page and calculate the page's *link equity* (the value of all inbound links to the page). Link equity plays a big part in the search engines' ranking algorithms. Because a lot of inbound links show that a site has "authority" on its subject, it's a pretty good measure of a page's value to users. Link equity plays a particularly large role in Google's algorithms.

When Webmasters try to cheat the system by buying and selling links, it violates Google's quality guidelines. If sites can artificially raise their PageRank score by buying links, their site may get a higher ranking in search results than it deserves, which compromises the integrity of Google's ranking algorithm. Thus we have Google's declared war against paid links. Google works hard to detect and devalue paid links and the pages where they're found. In fact, if Google finds just one paid link on a Web page that appears deceptive, it's likely to ignore *all* the links on that page. The bottom line is that buying links is not a smart way to increase your Google PageRank score.

What if you suspect that one of your competitors has purchased links and is ranking higher because of it? You can report them to Google for investigation. We explain how later in this section. First, however, you need to make sure that the competitor really *is* abusing the system.

Book X
Chapter 3

Identifying and
Reporting Spam

Reporting paid links is different than reporting spam. It isn't as clear-cut a decision, for one thing. Some people in the Internet marketing industry say you should not report paid links at all — they feel that buying and selling links are a natural part of Internet commerce, and there shouldn't be anything unethical about paid links. Others argue that because it violates search engine guidelines and manipulates the ranking algorithms, paid links are wrong.

The different search engines view paid links differently, too. Although none of the major search engines *want* Webmasters to buy links for the purpose of increasing their rankings, only Google has been adamant about it, even providing a form for reporting paid links. In interviews, reps for Yahoo! and Microsoft Live Search have explained that they're much more interested in how valuable a link is to users than whether it was paid or unpaid. They don't encourage paid links, but they call them a "gray area" and don't share Google's hard-line policy against them.

Keep in mind that *your* links could be reported to Google, as well. That's not a deciding factor if you don't have paid links, but if you have any questionable ones, it might make you think twice about reporting someone else. You can see whether anyone's reported your Web site to Google through your Webmaster Tools account. Google courteously notifies you about any violations that have been reported or found on your site. In fact, if you don't already have a Webmaster Tools account, as soon as you do sign up, you see any previous reports or violations, as well.

Before you decide to report a link that you believe is paid, first confirm that the link is set up to pass link equity. In other words, you want to see whether the site is really trying to get away with something. Otherwise, you could be reporting someone who's not breaking the rules.

Not all paid links are bad

When they're done for advertising purposes, rather than to manipulate the search engines, Google says paid links are no problem. For instance, lots of sites sell space for *banner ads* (graphic ads displayed usually above or in the side margins of a Web site that can be clicked), and that's a normal part of commerce on the Web.

The important thing is that you're not trying to deceive anyone. According to Google (`www.google.com/support/ webmasters/bin/answer.py?hl= en&answer=66736`), you just need to make sure that links purchased for advertising

are designated as such. You can do this in two ways:

- ✔ Add a `rel="nofollow"` attribute to the hyperlink. This is a bit of HTML code that you can insert to tell the search engine spiders not to follow or count the link.

- ✔ Redirect the links to an intermediate page that is blocked from search engines within the site's robots text (.txt) file. (A robots text file is a file located at the root of a Web site that contains instructions for search engine spiders. More information on robots.txt files can be found in Book VII, Chapter 1.)

You can look at the Web page's source code by choosing Source or Page Source from your browser's View menu. Find the hyperlink (an A tag) for the paid link and see if it includes a `rel="nofollow"` attribute. If it does, everything's above-board — the Web site is not trying to pass link equity through that link.

To see `nofollow` links more easily, you can install a free plug-in for the Mozilla Firefox browser called Search Status (currently in version 1.27). (The Firefox browser itself is available free at `http://www.mozilla.com/ en-US/firefox/`.) As you look at any Web page, links with a `nofollow` attribute automatically show up highlighted in pink. This is only one of many useful SEO features that this plug-in offers, by the way. Here's how you can get and use Search Status:

1. **In Mozilla Firefox, go to `www.quirk.biz/searchstatus/`.**

2. **Click the big Download Search Status button, and then scroll down a bit and click the Firefox icon. Complete the installation procedure.**

   After it's installed, you see some new icons in the lower-right corner of your browser window.

3. **Right-click on the Quirk icon to open the context menu for options and select Highlight Nofollow Links.**

If the suspicious link doesn't have a `nofollow` attribute, it may be reportable as a paid link. However, the Web site might be blocking a search engine spider from following the link in a couple of other ways, and thereby complying with Google's guidelines:

✦ **Robots text file exclusion:** Look at the Web site's robots text (.txt) file and see if that page or the page's *directory* (the folder where the file is saved) has been blocked to search engine spiders. If it has, it's in compliance with Google guidelines.

✦ **Meta robots exclusion:** Another way the site might have blocked search engines is with a `noindex` or `nofollow` Meta robots tag on the specific page. (A *Meta robots tag* is an HTML command in the *head section* (top part) of a Web page's HTML code that gives instructions to search engine spiders whether to index the page and whether to follow its links.) This tag is not needed if they've excluded the page in their robots text file. But if it's used, you see it near the top of the page beginning with this code:

```
<META NAME="ROBOTS" CONTENT=
```

Book X
Chapter 3

After you've satisfied yourself that the paid link is indeed shady (in other words, that it's trying to pass link equity), you can report it to Google, if you choose.

To report paid links to Google, go to www.google.com/webmasters/tools/paidlinks. Be sure to sign in to your Google account. Then complete the form and click Submit. You can see Google's form in Figure 3-5.

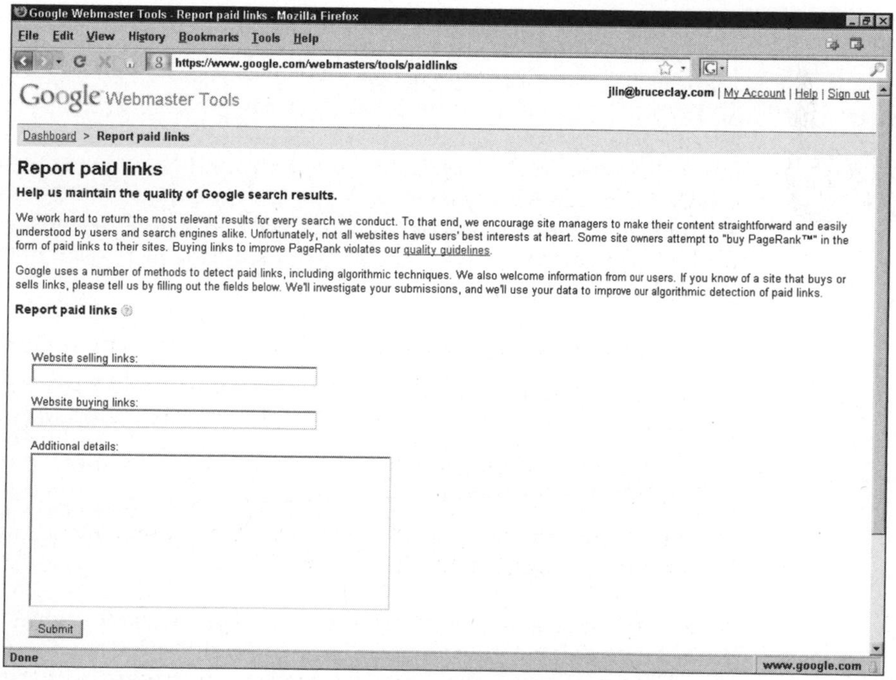

Figure 3-5: Google provides a simple form to report paid links.

Reducing the Impact of Click Fraud

Here's a scenario you don't want to be in: You've set up a PPC campaign with several ads for your classic car customization Web site that show up in Google when people search for your PPC keywords. Since the ads are pay per click, you've set a daily budget of, say, $200, which means that Google keeps track of how many times people click your ads and stops displaying them when your maximum $200 daily spending limit has been reached.

Now your competitor, Devilish Devin's Custom Auto, wants your ad campaign to fail and his ads to grab all the traffic. So Devilish Devin (who's obviously unethical) hires some people to do nothing but search for your keywords over and over and click your ads each time they come up. None of these are converting customers, of course, but their clicks add up. Within a short time, your daily budget is reached, and now your ads won't display for the rest of the day.

What we've just described is called *click fraud*. The search engines want to protect their advertisers from click fraud, so they examine clicks and credit back the invalid ones to the advertiser's account. They have lots of filters to detect invalid activity — they look for patterns such as many clicks coming from the same IP address, repetitive or duplicate clicking, and the time of the clicks. Because they've been pretty successful monitoring and detecting click fraud, it's far less of a problem today than it was even two or three years ago. However, the problem now is that even though the search engines will credit back the money into your account, you're still missing out on all of those people that would have seen your ad.

All of the major search engines give you reports and ways to track your PPC ads' effectiveness. You tag your pages with code provided by the search engine, and track everyone who comes to your site through a PPC ad — from clicking the ad to landing on your site and all the way to exiting. This detail gives you a way to analyze clicks on your ads. You can watch for click fraud using these analytics, too.

Here are warning signs to look for that may indicate you're the victim of click fraud:

✦ Unusual peaks in *impressions* (number of times your ad shows on a search results page)

✦ Unusual peaks in the number of clicks

✦ No increase in the number of conversions during peaks in impressions or clicks

+ Drop in the number of *page views* (how many pages were visited per visitor) during peaks in impressions or clicks

+ Higher *bounce rate* (number of people clicking your ad and then quickly going back to the search results page) during peaks in impressions or clicks

When you detect a pattern that may indicate click fraud, you should report your findings to Google AdWords, Yahoo! Search Marketing, or to whichever search engine is running your PPC ads. It's possible that they've already identified the same behavior and credited your account for those clicks. However, if they haven't, they can analyze their data to determine if it is indeed fraud, and will usually credit your account if they find that it is.

It's worth the extra effort to watch for unusual patterns in your PPC analytics. Even if you're only getting a few more clicks than your average at a certain regular time of day, you might notice that you're not seeing any accompanying increase in conversions, which could be due to malicious intent. You might not think that there is any click fraud involved, but if each of those clicks costs more than $20, the cost can add up quickly. It can even deplete your daily ad campaign budget. A little diligence to protect yourself from click fraud pays off.

Appendix: The Value of Training

In This Appendix

✔ **Making the most of industry conferences**

✔ **Choosing a conference: small or big**

✔ **Getting the most out of conference networking**

✔ **Picking the right training courses**

✔ **Finding professional training**

✔ **Doing it yourself**

Throughout this book, we walk you through the basics (and the not-so-basics) of search engine optimization (SEO). However, there are plenty of opportunities out there for taking your SEO education even further. One of the best ways you can do this is through training.

You can go about achieving further training in one of several ways. You can attend Internet marketing industry conferences like Search Engine Strategies, Search Marketing Expo, PubCon, or ad:tech. You can sign up for individual training courses, attend a training session, or have someone come out to help train you and your staff. There are courses for those who are seriously invested in SEO, and options for people who are just beginning to dabble. If you're wondering what to do in order to get further SEO training, not to worry; we've got you covered in this appendix.

Making the Most of Industry Conferences

In 1999, the first Search Engine Strategy (SES) show was launched to give search marketers a crash course in search engine optimization and getting listed in the search engines. It was a fairly small and intimate gathering. But as Internet marketing and search engine optimization became viable tactics, this conference began to grow, with other large search conferences springing up as well.

These conferences offered introductory sessions on a broad range of topics and let search marketers pick the sessions they thought were most important. These days, search marketers have lots of choices when it comes to which search marketing conference to attend. No matter what, the first rule is bring a *lot* of business cards with you. You won't be sorry!

First off, you have the mainstays such as

✦ **Search Engine Strategies (SES):** This one happens all over the place, including San Jose, New York, Chicago, London, and other cities. SES is purely about Internet marketing, and, of the larger conventions, it's the one most specialized towards search marketing. Specialized content can be found at SES's smaller shows like SES Latino. More information can be found at their Web site, www.searchenginestrategies.com/.

✦ **Search Marketing Expo (SMX):** SMX is similar to SES, but still fairly new, so it's one of the smaller shows. This is a show geared towards search engine marketing and boasts a host of both major conferences (SMX East in New York and SMX West in Santa Clara, CA, among others) as well as smaller niche conferences targeted at specific topics (Local, Social Media, and so on). Their Web site is www.searchmarketingexpo.com/.

✦ **WebmasterWorld PubCon:** PubCon is a large conference designed to meet the needs of Webmasters. Topics tend to be in a wider range than SES or SMX, but it's still a niche show. This is where you go to find more information on the running of a Web site. The real gold of PubCon is PubCon Classic, a networking event held on the last day where all the real value is found. More information on these guys can be found at www.pubcon.com/.

✦ **ad:tech:** This large show also has conferences worldwide, with shows in New York, San Francisco, Chicago, London, Shanghai, Sydney, Hamburg, Paris, and Singapore. Their draw includes company executives from many major corporations. ad:tech is about Internet marketing as a whole, so it goes beyond just search engines or social networks. They incorporate a little bit of everything and focus on branding, marketing, and promotion. Search engine–specific marketing is definitely in the minority here and that little bit usually focuses on the PPC side of things when it's discussed at all. The conference often has no sessions discussing SEO specifically. More information can be found at www.ad-tech.com/.

Besides those stalwarts are some new, smaller niche shows. These shows allow search marketers to network with a targeted group of their peers and dive into topics on a much more advanced level. Some of the more popular niche shows and educational opportunities include

✦ **SEMpdx:** These Portland-based mini-conferences happen fairly often. These guys are also geared towards search engine marketing specifically. If you're in the Pacific Northwest, they might be worth checking out (www.sempdx.org/).

✦ **Small Business Marketing Unleashed:** Unlike a lot of conferences, where a panel is four speakers that all go over the same topic, SBMU gives the stage to one expert who explains her topic to a small audience. This conference covers online marketing (`http://unleashed.smallbusiness answers.com/2008/columbus/index.php`).

✦ **Elite Retreat:** A very small convention of about 35, this event happens once a year. When they say "elite," they mean it. They focus on one-on-one techniques and on search engine marketing. More information, costs, and scheduling can be found at their Web site (`www.elite retreat.info/`).

Smaller, focused events might be the way to go if you're considering SEO as a career. They give you more opportunity for networking than the larger shows, but *all* of the shows strive to provide education and knowledge transfer.

Small versus large conferences

One advantage of a large conference is that there's something for everyone. They offer so many panels and sessions and information tracks that the hardest part can be choosing which session to attend. If you are just starting out in SEO, attend a big conference so you can get exposure to a wide variety of disciplines. Internet marketing comes from discovering how to combine several disciplines for maximum efficiency. The more tools you have in your toolbox, the better: When all you have in your toolbox is a hammer, every problem looks like a nail. Search engine marketers can learn from Google, whereas the social media marketers can go hang out with the people from Digg. On-demand marketers can go to TiVo. Brand managers know which ad networks are going to pay off big. A marketer should be able to find a way to use all of these elements in order to make their whole media campaign a success. Large conferences afford you the opportunity to sample each of the disciplines and add more ammo to your search marketing arsenal.

Keep in mind that there's more to Internet marketing than search engine optimization. At one conference, for example, attendees choose from panels on pay per click, Web analytics, and mobile marketing, in addition to search engine optimization. Even traditional media like television and print have panel discussions devoted to them, especially in terms of digital advertising.

At a large conference, instead of 15 speakers, you have the chance to hear 50. Speakers at big conferences are guaranteed to expose you to new thoughts and ideas that have probably never occurred to you before. These conferences afford you the opportunity to incorporate the best parts of their teachings into your new strategy.

But if you're looking to establish real connections, you want to pay close attention to the small conference circuit. When you're in a room with 1,000 people, it's hard to actually talk to anyone. You're left looking up at the speakers on the stage, which, although informative, isn't exactly an optimal environment for learning, sharing, or networking.

At the smaller shows, it's different. The small group setting creates an environment where attendees aren't afraid to start up a conversation with the speaker. The benefit of smaller shows is that everyone is able to meet up at a central location after the sessions have ended and take part in the understanding that comes with sharing war stories with your peers and partaking in meaningful conversation. You can really find out what those around you do for a living, where they work, what their specialty is, what they hope to get out of the show, and more. Networking is about establishing relationships, and that's always best done in an intimate setting.

Another thing about smaller shows is that they give you a unique opportunity to get up close and personal with the speakers. In smaller shows, you get direct access to panelists during the sessions, lots of time to ask questions, and ample opportunity to hunt someone down during lunch or after hours for a quick chat. This is a key advantage for search marketers, especially those looking to expand their repertoire of SEO knowledge. What's also great about one-on-one time with the speakers is that they remember you later, so they might be willing to lend you a hand down the road. At a large conference, getting face time with your favorite speaker can be nearly impossible.

These smaller shows are also very topic-centric, focusing on smaller, niche aspects of search engine optimization and search engine marketing. Topic-centric shows help to spice up the speaker pool and ensure that attendees are always seeing something they have never seen before. For that reason, you want to carefully read a show's description before deciding to attend to make sure it lines up with what you're hoping to learn.

But although you might see the rising new voices at a niche conference, for the big names in SEO, you might want to lean toward the big conferences. Big conferences can afford to bring in the big-name panelists. Not only do you recognize the names of the speakers, but all the big companies know that they'll find an audience there. They know that at a big conference, they have the opportunity to reach thousands of people, which makes it worth their while to participate.

In the final balance, big or small, going to conferences can be a valuable investment of time and money for you and your company. Whether you're just starting out in SEO, needing help with your Web site, or looking for new ideas as an SEO veteran, you're bound to get something out of your conference experience.

Networking effectively at conferences

SEO industry conferences are generally considered a must if you want to get anywhere with your brand and your site, mostly for conference networking. Networking is how you get clients, make contacts, and expand your sphere of influence. However, if you're a first-timer or somewhat introverted, it could be a little like your first day at a new school when you were a kid. The only difference is that, unlike back in grade school, you just spent a considerable amount of money to feel horribly uncomfortable.

At a conference, you have lots of opportunities to make new connections. In your day-to-day existence, chances are you won't run into anything like the variety of people that show up for a large conference. Marketers, C-level execs, reporters, and programmers — they all come to the big conferences to meet and greet.

You can't just hang around on the edges of things during conference time. That kind of thing hurts not only your personal brand, but the brand of your company as well. So when you're attending a conference, you have to put on your game face and master the tricks of making connections with ease.

Strategy 1: Show up prepared

One of the most effective ways to calm pre-show nerves is to show up prepared. Optimize your schedule by taking a look at the conference agenda a few days prior to the show and marking down everything you want to attend. Take care to check who's speaking at which sessions, and consider whether you can benefit from a meet-and-greet. Create a list of everything you want to do and everyone you want to meet while you're at the conference. This helps keep you on track in the midst of all the craziness and serves as motivation to get everything on your list covered.

Conferences are something of an endurance test, especially if you've never been to one before. Be prepared for the inevitable head explosion that hits near the end of the first day. This is why keeping a conference "scorecard" listing the names of all of the people you want to meet goes a long way in making sure you leave that conference feeling like you've accomplished something.

If there are certain people you want to meet, research them so you have something to talk to them about. Knowing your industry experts and what they specialize in (and what buttons to push) is always a good plan. Striking up a conversation is often as easy as knowing what to talk about.

Strategy 2: Start branding yourself before you get there

It's a lot easier to introduce yourself face-to-face when you have an established brand you can lean on. A few weeks before conference time, start reaching out on the social networks and let people know you'll be there. Use

Twitter. Join that conference's Event page on Facebook. If there is no official Event page on Facebook, create one. Make plans to meet up with people beforehand. Who can help you promote your company and your goals the most? Find out who they are before you go. These are the folks you want to score some face time with.

Use the lead-up time to start talking about the projects you're working on and generate some buzz. If you're going to be releasing a new blogging widget, plan the release date around the conference. Have something you can plug or a lead-in to a conversation. It's always best to have something to say before you start a cold conversation.

Strategy 3: Use the buddy system

One of the best ways to network and work a room is to attach yourself to someone who is an extrovert. Extroverts love meeting new people and love to walk you around and introduce you to everyone they know. It's perfect: You get to meet everyone in the room without ever having to actually introduce yourself. And if you've already established a brand for yourself beforehand, folks are excited to meet you and immediately bring you into the conversation.

Do beware when using the buddy system, though. Sticking with an extrovert is different than simply huddling in a corner with another nervous soul. Unless you have been surgically attached to the friend that dared come with you, you do not have to stand by their side the entire night. As comforting and warm and fuzzy as it feels, you want to avoid this at all costs. Doing so is a great way to ensure that you only speak to each other or to those you both know without ever meeting anyone new. The whole idea of networking is to get yourself out there and meet people who you think can help you out, and vice versa. Step outside the box and take a chance on someone new.

Strategy 4: Have a gimmick

Regulars in the search engine optimization community have seen all kinds of unique attention-grabbing attempts on the conference grounds including distinctive clothing — bright yellow shoes for one marketer, bright orange suits for another — and various forms of pretexts for getting photos (here, try on my silly hat so I can take a picture of you). These are all attention-getting gimmicks at conferences. Think of it as in-person link bait. It's all about grabbing people and striking up a conversation. Having a gimmick makes it easier for you to approach people and harder for them to ignore you.

If you were attending a networking event and a smiling face approached you and asked you to pose for a photo holding a potato, you'd do it, right? And after you agree, you open up the door for that person to hold a conversation with you and explain why you need to randomly have your photograph taken with a tuber. You'll also definitely remember them when you spot them walking around the conference hall. That's the power of having a gimmick.

However, do be careful when using the gimmick technique: There's a fine line between being funny and being annoying. Opt for something quirky and unobtrusive like a T-shirt for something that promotes a cause benefitting someone other than yourself, like a charity. Above all, keep in mind that if you think it might be offensive and obnoxious, it probably is, so don't do it.

Strategy 5: Don't use a gimmick

As effective as the gimmicks above can be, people sometimes grow tired of them. Your best bet is to be genuine and yourself. Sometimes a firm hand shake and a warm smile is all you need to forge a real connection with someone.

The worst thing you can do is leave a conference with regrets. Meeting people and sharing work and life war stories are too valuable to pass up. When you meet someone at a conference, it's safe to say you have similar interests and are involved in the same industry. Strike up a conversation with that as your jumping-off point. When it comes to conference networking, there's no room for shyness. Be confident and willing to bust out of your shell.

Picking the Right Training Courses

A wide variety of training options are available for search engine optimization. But in picking the right courses for you, what should you be looking for? Ask yourself what you think you and your company need from the training. Is it enough to just learn the basics or should there be more to it than that? Should these classes convey search engine philosophy as well as techniques for optimization? Should these classes be setting standards and testing the knowledge you gain during them?

Well, yes. These are some of the things you should be able to take away from a good training course:

+ **Fundamentals:** Any course that you take should give you a good grounding in the history and understanding of search engine optimization. It should discuss terminology, ranking factors, and all the components that make up a search engine-friendly Web page. You should leave the class with a clear understanding of the basic methods of SEO.

+ **Philosophy:** Any course you take should be upfront about its approach to search engine optimization. The reasoning behind the course's methods should be clearly defined.

✦ **Ethics:** Any course should have a stated commitment to ethical (*white hat*) SEO. Both the industry and individuals benefit the most from ethics and good conduct, and these courses should require the same from their students.

✦ **Something to hang on your wall:** This might seem frivolous, but having something physical to take away from any course is about more than just a pretty piece of paper. Certification from a respected authority serves as a reinforcement of the values and techniques reported in the class.

Beyond just making you better at SEO, better training courses raise the bar for all players. If you learn (and pass on) good solid techniques that adhere to ethical standards, everyone benefits. Where once few courses were available, a wide variety of choices is now available, and the hard part is finding the best one.

So which is the right training course for you? There are three basic options out there. Remote training, in-person destination training, and on-site training. We cover all three in the upcoming sections.

Training remotely

Remote training is usually done over the phone, online, by e-mail, or through video lessons. Remote training is the most convenient of your training options, allowing you to do it from your home or office. It's also one of the cheapest methods. The price on this kind of training varies wildly and runs from $250 to $3,000 per package, depending on the method, difficulty level, and length of the program. A few high-quality advanced search engine optimization courses are offered through remote training. But most of the programs available remotely are best for beginners who need to learn the most basic SEO methodology and techniques.

Remote training works via video and online programs. These have the added benefit of allowing students to move at their own pace. Be aware that students can't receive lessons faster than the program schedule dictates, so those trainees that are a little more advanced than their peers might get a little impatient with the pace of the courses. Attendees also have limited opportunities to ask questions of instructors. To alleviate this problem, some of these remote programs host private discussion groups. With remote training, you also have less chance to personalize the training to your own Web site's needs as compared to in-person and on-site SEO training courses.

One remote location training service is the SEMPO Institute, located at www. sempoinstitute.com/:

✦ **Subject matter:** Several basic and advanced search engine marketing training courses includes Insider's Guide to SEM, Advanced SEO, and Advanced Search Advertising.

✦ **Method:** Online, self-paced courses, lessons, resources, and quizzes help students reinforce the information as it's taught. Certification is awarded after completion of either advanced course.

✦ **Cost:** $399 Insider's Guide; $1,399 Advanced SEO; $1,399 Advanced Search Advertising. Discounts are available for SEMPO members, students, and military.

✦ **Other info:** Insider's Guide topics include identifying keywords, writing Web content, avoiding roadblocks, setting up and managing PPC programs, and ethics issues. Advanced SEO focuses on ranking organically, site review, Web site structure, site maps, design, tools and analysis, reporting, tracking, analytics, and brand reputation. Advanced Search Advertising teaches search advertising and auction media models, writing effective ad copy, bidding strategy, tracking ROI metrics, differences among PPC programs of major search engines, click fraud and proper use, and integrating PPC into advertising and branding campaigns.

Another remote training course is through Internet Marketing Ninjas at www. Internetmarketingninjas.com/:

✦ **Subject matter:** Getting links from relevant, quality sites, integrating traditional media and online marketing for maximum rewards, effective site structure, and other advanced search engine optimization issues.

✦ **Method:** A dozen 30-minute videos over one year.

✦ **Cost:** $2,995.

✦ **Other info:** Membership includes extra Web content, a free pass to a live SEO Ninjas training class, and bonus videos throughout the year. Included analytics tools and a set of bonus SEO tools allow you to analyze your site against your competitors' sites. Lessons cover advanced topics.

Training around the country

For those who want face-to-face basic and advanced search engine marketing (SEM) and SEO training courses, several are available across the U.S. These courses usually cost anywhere from $750 to $2,000 per person, depending on their length and comprehensiveness. These courses are relatively cost-efficient, after you factor in travel expenses.

Location-based training provides opportunities to ask questions specific to your Web site, making it an opportunity for practical learning. In-person training addresses those who learn by visual and audio aids, as well as by application, as opposed to those who learn purely through visual means. Many courses include lab time for attendees to use SEO tools, sometimes included with the training package, on their own domain with the instructor available for help or suggestions.

Some places that offer training courses around the country are

SEOToolSet Training from Bruce Clay, Inc. (www.bruceclay.com):

✦ **Subject matter:** Basic and advanced search engine optimization training course includes ample time for questions and answers, plus lab time to practice the techniques you learn on your own site.

✦ **Method:** Three-day basic course offered every month and one and a half-day advanced certification course offered every other month.

✦ **Cost:** $1,795 SEOToolSet Training; $1,195 Advanced Certification Course (prerequisite: SEOToolSet Training).

✦ **Location:** Simi Valley, California and New York, New York.

✦ **Other info:** Designed for marketing and Web design staff, the face-to-face training covers standard SEO practices and ethics issues, plus certification for those who complete the advanced course. Subscription to the SEOToolSet of diagnostic tools is included with the course.

Another option is High Rankings (www.highrankings.com/seo-classes ?gclid=CIKV9NC70ZECFQc-gwod6lcqaQ):

✦ **Subject matter:** Topics covered include keyword research, site architecture, copywriting, Title tags, Meta descriptions, links, publicity, social media, and measuring success with analytics.

✦ **Method:** One-day SEO training course.

✦ **Cost:** $749.

✦ **Location:** Framingham, Massachusetts.

✦ **Other info:** Classes are limited to six students and are offered monthly. This course is geared toward new SEOs, Internet marketing managers, entrepreneurs, copywriters, and Web designers. Through this personalized training course, you can create an organic, site-specific SEO strategy.

Training on-site

On-site SEO training is the most expensive of all training methods, but it's also the most personalized method. On-site SEO training can be specifically tailored to your site and your company's SEO and search engine marketing needs. On-site training can usually run you $150 to $500 an hour, with minimum time or minimum participant requirements. In order to get the most out of on-site training, come up with a list of expectations for your SEO campaign before consulting with several of these training companies to see what type of topics they cover. On-site training is the most useful for companies planning on training many employees and performing all of their SEO in-house. Most on-site training programs are tailored to a specific project, provide a syllabus of topics that are relevant to your objectives, and offer follow-up consultation.

Some of the companies that offer on-site training include

SEOToolSet Training from Bruce Clay, Inc. (www.bruceclay.com):

✦ **Subject matter:** Basic and advanced search engine optimization training course includes ample time for questions and answers.

✦ **Method:** Three day concentrated program combining standard and advanced training.

✦ **Cost:** $2000 per student on average.

✦ **Other info:** Designed for marketing and Web design staff, training covers standard SEO practices and ethics issues. Subscription to the SEOToolSet of diagnostic tools is included with the course. On-site SEO and SEM training is also available for companies that want to train 24 or more employees.

DISC (www.2disc.com/on_site_training.html):

✦ **Subject matter:** Discover your company's optimum ROI, benefits of PPC campaigns, how to write content, how to interpret analysis and reports, how to optimize your CMS, and how to conduct keyword research, in a personalized, company-specific manner.

✦ **Method:** DISC evaluates your team, delivers training materials, performs a one- or two-day workshop at your location, and provides follow-up questions and answers.

✦ **Cost:** Packages range from $12,300 to $15,500, plus travel expenses.

✦ **Other info:** On-site and conference-style training afford companies the ability to have many employees trained at the same time, in a comfortable environment, focusing on techniques personalized for your specific project. You receive detailed training materials with step-by-step guidelines for performing essential SEO procedures. Packages are tailored to your company's needs. Phone and e-mail training is also available.

Beanstalk Search Engine Positioning, Inc. (www.beanstalk-inc.com/services/training.htm):

✦ **Subject matter:** Site structure, site and page optimization, advanced link-building techniques, statistical analysis and personalized, company-specific issues are addressed.

✦ **Method:** On-site, over-the-phone, and conference training available.

- ✦ **Cost:** Starts at $500/hour, plus $100/hour preparation costs.
- ✦ **Other info:** This training is intended for companies that want to improve their in-house SEO program. On-site and conference-style SEO training afford companies the ability to have many employees trained at the same time, in a comfortable environment, learning techniques personalized for your specific project.

From basic to advanced lessons offered at your desk or at your door, SEO training comes in all shapes, sizes, and price tags. It's important to realize how training can be helpful and then to choose the training method that best fits your needs.

Training for Professionals

When we talk about *professionals*, we mean people who already know more than a beginner's course of SEO and want to expand their general knowledge and expertise. This section is for people who take SEO very seriously and want to be on par with the experts in the field. In general, these are people making a living at providing SEO as a service.

Attending conventions

If you're a business person just getting your arms around search, in the big spender category, or are looking for a way to immerse yourself into the search engine optimization field, the bigger, more general trade shows may work for you. These are the giant conventions like ad:tech or PubCon. But at some point, you will want more than just the broad topics these conventions cover. You eventually reach a point where you need to become a true expert in your craft. At that point, you must start networking with those who can help you meet your goals. When you get to that level, you find that the smaller, niche shows provide far more value. They're more approachable and provide a far better networking and educational environment.

Broad Internet marketing training may have had value when the industry was less competitive, but in order to compete today as an SEO, you have to know your stuff inside and out. In other words, you have to go beyond the introductory courses offered at the large shows. This is another area where small, topic-focused shows thrive because they strip away that introductory-level material and get into the meat of the issues. Larger shows like ad:tech and SES simply can't do this because they're forced to cater to a beginner audience.

If you're looking to build your industry knowledge and expertise, seek out the small shows that emphasize the aspects that you want to dive into. Maybe you want to advance your branding techniques, or dive further into networking via social media. The smaller shows are the ones that are going to really benefit you.

The sessions at the smaller, niche conferences are taught by the field experts. They are there to teach you real-life tactics, strategies, and methodologies so that you can go back and use what you have learned. Not only does this help you build your own set of SEO tools, but it also sets you up on your way to becoming experts in a specialized field. This makes you invaluable in your home office and in the industry as well. You can gain fame by making yourself a noted expert in a singular field. As the industry matures, it's less about knowing a little bit about everything and more about becoming a specialist.

At these shows, you get speakers who can deliver success stories and anecdotes of failure, who can test a theory because they weren't constrained by budgets, and who are willing to tell you what happened because they're not afraid that it'll be revealing something. Learning from those who have gone before is a time-honored way to increase your knowledge and gain inspiration.

Getting advanced training

Another way to further your advanced SEO knowledge is to attend advanced training courses. Both SEMPO and we here at Bruce Clay, Inc. offer advanced training courses. With advanced training, you go beyond the basics of search engine optimization (like finding out what a `Meta` tag is, for example) and really delve deep into the ins and outs of doing search engine optimization for you and your company. With advanced training, you find out more about how to read your competition and analyze your site, which means you can tell whether or not the changes you made to your site are actually working. This involves knowing what converts, and what ranks, and what draws in traffic. Seeing the complete picture is a must if you want to continue to work in search engine optimization.

You can find out more about advanced training courses at

✦ Bruce Clay, Inc.: `www.seotoolset.com/training/courses.html`

✦ SEMPO: `www.sempoinstitute.com/`

Following trusted authorities

If you are looking to specialize in SEO, start following trusted authorities in the SEO field. Authorities can be individuals, companies, or Web sites, but what they have in common is that they're respected and they typically deliver solid, reliable information.

Several news stream sites out there are geared towards search engine optimization. These Web sites keep up with the latest SEO news and statistics, and are always a bastion of good helpful information. (And sometimes some not-so-helpful information, so be discerning.) Some good sites to start with are

✦ **Search Engine Land (`http://searchengineland.com/`):** A great resource, Search Engine Land is a search marketing industry news site. Here you can learn the latest news out of Google, Yahoo!, and Microsoft Live Search, among others. It's run by the same company that runs SMX, which is one of the larger SEO conferences, and therefore it's a pretty trustworthy site.

✦ **Sphinn (`www.sphinn.com`):** This is the Internet marketing social news site — the Internet marketing version of Digg. If you see an SEO story that you feel is newsworthy, you can click on the Sphinn chiclet and vote it up.

✦ **Google Reader (`www.google.com/reader`):** This is an important tool that helps you keep up with all the latest SEO news (and all your other subscription feeds). This allows you to read RSS feeds you've subscribed to, including those related to Internet marketing, all in one convenient place.

✦ **Search Engine Roundtable (`www.seroundtable.com/`):** This is a forum-based news site. This site will bring you all the latest news from the forums, so they catch stuff that other news sites might miss.

Performing experiments

By "performing experiments," we don't mean you get to play Mr. Mad Scientist with your company's Web site. For one thing, randomly changing things here and there on the site can lead to a decrease in the site's rankings, a drop in conversions, and the loss of your job. But it is important to learn how to test the changes you make to the site in order for you to gain rankings, traffic, and your ultimate goal, more conversions.

Learning SEO requires doing SEO because it's often a matter of trial and error. It's challenging because the environment constantly changes (both competitors and search engine algorithms alike). Proper SEO takes time, diligence, and patience. Getting accurate test results is a matter of months, not hours or days. You have to be willing to work and have the patience to watch your experiments to make sure that things are going the way you want them to.

On the flip side, you also can't be afraid to continue to tweak things if your tests aren't getting you the results that you want. Run several tests instead of just one or two. Change one thing at a time. And if you get bad results, don't be afraid to change it back!

If you can't experiment on your own site, consider building another site up just for the purposes of testing. Tinkering, playing, and all-around messing with your site is the only way of really being sure you know that what you're doing works. Take chances and see if they pay off. Like gambling, don't bet what you can't afford to lose, but make sure that you're investing enough to make it all pay off in the end.

Getting Things Done for Do-It-Yourselfers

We've covered what to do if you want to wade into the professional world of search engine optimization. But what do you do if you're a do-it-yourselfer just trying to make your Web site succeed? Say you have your own classic car customization Web site and you and your brother *are* the company. Because your brother can't use a computer to save his life, the burden of running and maintaining your company's Web site falls on you. So what can you do in terms of optimizing your own Web site? A few things, actually.

Training

Most training courses out there are aimed at the beginners. Take some time out or make an investment in some basic training for search engine optimization. They're worth the time and effort, so go do some research into what's right for you. We listed plenty of beginner training options earlier in this appendix. Focus on the ones that offer face time with a real expert and offer some kind of tangible metric for success.

Testing, testing, testing!

Like we said in the section about professional SEO, testing is one of the most important things you should do. Test your site to make sure anything you've done to it, from tweaking your keywords to adding more Engagement Objects, is actually working the way you want it to.

This might seem like common sense, but some people think that they can just make changes across the board and see returns immediately. Your site is one of a million sites, and being a top ranked site takes time and effort, neither of which allow immediate results. Unfortunately, SEO is a process that requires time and fine-tuning, so if you've added new keywords to your site, watch them! Study your rankings and your server logs to see if traffic has gone up since you made the changes. Check and see if this increased traffic has equaled conversions for you, or if the extra site visitors simply arrived at your front page and then immediately clicked the Back button to navigate away.

Drawing traffic to your site is just one part of the process. You have to make money. If no one is coming to your site and asking you to customize a classic car for them, you need to do further tweaking to your site.

Networking

Another important thing you can do is network. Start engaging other people who know and work in SEO. Hang around the forums that discuss SEO and start checking these people out on Twitter. Don't be afraid to ask for help or guidance if you're not quite sure what you're doing. But be aware that some advice should be taken with a grain of salt. Always be sure to test out the advice you get before accepting it as the gospel truth.

Go to conferences. Budget and take some time off to attend one of the larger SEO trade shows like SES, SMX, PubCon, or ad:tech. These are good places to get your feet wet and get a little bit of networking in. Make a list of things you feel you need help on and then reorder your schedule so that you can attend. Don't be afraid to talk to people; no one was born an expert in search engine optimization. They all once started out where you are. Ask questions if you're lost and take plenty of notes! You can always learn stuff, and you should do your best sponge impersonation and soak up as much information as you can.

Be discerning about the information that you gather. SEO is not an exact science, so you get conflicting reports on what to do and what not to do.

Also, start looking at newsletters from reputable sources. Ask around and do your research to find these sources. You can start with free newsletters from these places:

✦ *SEO Newsletter* Bruce Clay, Inc.: `www.bruceclay.com/web_news letter.htm`

✦ *Web Marketing Today:* `www.wilsonweb.com/wmt/`

✦ *MarketingSherpa:* `www.marketingsherpa.com/newsletters.html`

✦ *Big Mouth Media Newsletter:* `www.bigmouthmedia.com/contact_ bigmouthmedia/subscribe/`

✦ Grok.com: `www.grokdotcom.com/`

✦ *SearchCap:* `http://searchengineland.com/searchcap-news letter-begins-friday-search-month-open-for-signups-9961.php`

Knowing when to call in the experts

Unfortunately, almost inevitably in the course of your SEM campaign, you will run into problems with your SEO that are beyond your scope of training and expertise. Find a mentor: someone who can help you out and guide you through the tricky world of search engine optimization. Make sure that they're someone you can trust, and that they're a respected authority in their own right. Meeting someone like this is why it's important for you to start checking out search marketing forums and Twitter feeds and attending conferences.

Don't be afraid to ask for assistance. Call in a professional consultant if you need help. But remember: You must at least be familiar with the technical side of your Web site and your SEO; that way, you can tell if your consultant is taking you for a ride or giving you good advice.

Index

A

A1-Webmarks, 442
A/B testing
  content selections, 574
  conversion page, 573
  difference identification, 572
  length suggestions, 572
  link selections, 573
  multivariate versus, 573–576
  null tests, 572
  pay per click (PPC) ads, 661
  pre-test preparations, 573–577
  results viewing, 583–584
  rules, 571–572
  segmentation tests, 572
  site usability, 558–559
  test page selections, 573
  traffic diversion, 571
  variables, 571
  visitors per page, 572
  Website Optimizer, 577–584
abandonment rates, 585–586
About Us link, 222
absolute links, 254–255
account history, 657
acquisition, 543–544
acronyms, 320
Active Server Pages (ASP), 301, 505
ad groups, 658
Ad Scheduling, 656
ad:tech, 708
adCenter, 32, 62–64
Adobe Dreamweaver, 204–205
Adobe Flash MX, 262–268
advanced search operators, 66–71, 374–375
advanced training courses, 719
advertising, 10–11, 27, 109–115
advertising links, 431–432
AdWords Campaigns, 584–585
AdWords Keyword tool, 647–649
age of audience, 10–11, 295
Alexa, link evaluation, 401
algorithmic immunity, 138
algorithms, 23, 30, 32
allin, 67–68
allintitle, 67–68
alltheweb, search engine relationship, 18–21
Alt attribute, 16, 53, 183, 255–256, 313–315
AltaVista, 18–21, 61
Amazon, 14
America Online (AOL), 31, 59, 298
Americans with Disabilities Act (ADA), 314
analytics, 299. See also Web analytics
analytics tracking codes, 516, 518
anchor text
  call to action, 238
  external links, 383
  landing pages, 122, 183
  link factor, 391
  link naming, 288–289
  links, 168, 222, 253–255
  synonyms, 289
  virtual siloing, 381
anti-spyware, 561
AOL search, 18–21, 33
Apache servers
  filenames, 208
  404 error page, 466
.htaccess file, 496–498
  mod_rewrites, 514
  open-source Web server, 452
  redirects, 496–498
Apache Software Foundation, 452
AppWeb, Web server, 453
architecture, 26, 154–156, 599
archives, 35–36, 70, 351, 553
Argentina, 638–639
article pages, 408, 411–414
articles, 398–399, 473, 686–687
Asian market, 609–620
Ask Jeeves. See Ask.com
Ask.com
  Google AdWords affiliation, 31, 59
  married women, 33
  search attributes, 33
  search engine relationship charts, 18–21
  spam reports, 76, 699–700
  target audience, 11
ASP (Active Server Pages), 301, 505
ASP.NET, 506
Associated Content, 441
asterisk (*), wildcards, 459
astro-turfing, 445
Asynchronous JavaScript and XML (AJAX), 385, 391
audio, 187, 216, 229–230, 677
author credits, 362–363
autosnippets, 245

B

background music, 210
backgrounds, 321

backlinks
  category structure, 281
  competitor analysis,
    168–169
  incoming links, 30
  indexed backlink search,
    188
  link equity, 187–188
  results page ranking
    factor, 173
  SEMToolBar analysis, 176
  301 redirect command
    use, 489
  unpaid requests, 393–396
  virtual siloing, 381
  Yahoo! analysis, 174
BackRub. *See* Google
bad neighborhoods,
  424–425
Baidu, 604, 611, 616
bandwidth, 104, 482–483
banner ads, paid links, 702
Barracuda, server, 453
barter, 387, 391
Bazaarvoice, 322
BBedit, 262–268
Beanstalk Search Engine
  Positioning, Inc.,
  717–718
behavioral search, 48–51,
  35, 225
Belgium, legal issues, 623
beliefs, audience, 296
benchmarks, 197
Bibsonomy, 441–442
bid amounts, 655–656
Big Mouth Media Newsletter,
  722
black hat, techniques, 81
blended search, 33, 43–46,
  185, 227, 674–676
Blendtec, 386, 399
BlinkList, 442
block quotes, 362–363
blog posts, 677
Blogger, 55
BloggingZoom, 441
Blogoria, 442

blogs
  advanced searches, 70–71
  astro-turfing, 445
  community building,
    680–681
  content development, 312
  dos/don'ts, 680–681
  Jianfei Zhu, 612
  link building, 435–437
  microblogs, 441
  misrepresentation,
    678–680
  RSS feeds, 55, 401–402
  Separated by a Common
    Language, 623
  subdomains, 485
  target audience, 681
  trolling, 437
  unfounded attack
    response, 681
  User Generated Content
    (UGC), 323
  vertical search engines, 55
  Wal-Marting Across
    America, 678
`Body` tag, 183
boldface formatting, 251
BookmarkTracker, 442
bounce rates, 26, 104, 541,
  543, 585–586, 705
brainstorming sessions,
  88–89, 144, 309–310, 328
brand awarenesss, 671
brand building
  blended searches, 674–676
  blogs, 680–681
  communities, 677–689
  competitor analysis,
    151–152
  engagement objects,
    676–677
  halo media, 672
  keyword selections, 670
  misrepresentation,
    678–680
  pay per click (PPC),
    111–112
  people connection
    keywords, 670–672

  press releases, 673–674
  reputation management,
    673
  search avenues, 672–676
  social bookmarking,
    685–689
  social networking,
    683–685
  wikis, 672
brand evangelists, 682
brand names, 243–245,
  442–445, 472, 485,
  611–612
brand reinforcement, 662
Brazil, 637–638
Brazilian Internet Steering
  Committee, 637
broad match, 650
browsers, 42, 156, 162–164,
  175–177, 321
BuddyMarks, 442
bulleted lists, 319, 376
business listings, 358–359

C

cache, 173, 184–185, 555
call to action, 653–654
Canada, 476
canonical pages, 493
Cascading Style Sheet (CSS)
  clean/simple code,
    203–205, 216–217
  CSS Validation Service,
    259, 261
  `Div` tag positioning,
    272–273
  duplicate content, 346–347
  externalizing, 268
  source code best
    practices, 164
  text/image formatting, 163
case studies, 303
categorized phrases, 103,
  118–121
category classifications,
  512
category links, 222
C-block, IP addresses, 392

cease and desist order, 360
CGI Perl, 507
channels, YouTube, 15
Check Server tool, 454–457
Cherokee, Web server, 453
Chicago Tribune, Colonel
    Tribune, 679
chiclets, 438, 686–687
child pornography, IP
    blacklists, 468–469
China, 610–611, 613–617
chip speed, 458
Chrome, 339–340
cite attribute, 362–363
clarity, keyword, 103
clean IPs, 483
click fraud, 704–705
click maps, 587–588
click-through rate, 31–32,
    61, 97, 112–113, 397, 654
click-through ratio, 657
ClickTracks, 551
ClickTrends, 372
client niche, 93
ClipClip, 441
cloaking, 79, 167, 457, 694
clueless newbies, 353
CNN, Yahoo!, 61
ColdFusion, 507
Collarity, 35, 226
Colonel Tribune, 679
colors, readability, 321
columns, 157–158
Comcast, 684–685
ComcastCares, 684–685
comments, User Generated
    Content (UGC), 323
commerce, 536
Common Gateway Interface
    (CGI), 507
communities, 678–689
Compete, 152, 401
competitors
    Asian market, 610, 612
    business, 147–148
    content, 309–311
    content analysis, 190–192
    conversions, 148–149
    identifying, 143–145

industry research, 92–93
link analysis, 168–169,
    187–192
link discovery, 393–396
Page Analyzer tool,
    156–161
real versus imagined,
    145–147, 151–152
research categories, 154
Site Checker analysis,
    164–167
traffic versus conversion,
    149–151
Web site size, 169–170
comScore, 31, 152, 301, 536
Connectedy, 442
Consumer Review Network,
    Yahoo!, 61
Contact Us, 222–223
content management
    system (CMS), 211–212,
    334, 350–351, 510–522
content syndication,
    348–349
contents. *See also*
    duplicate content;
    stolen content
A/B testing, 574
acronyms, avoiding, 320
audience reading level,
    319–320
backgrounds, 321
blended searches, 43–46
brainstorming, 309–310
bullets, 319
call to action, 325–326
clarifying words, 331–332
code limits, 163
colors, 321
competitive analysis
    tools, 340
competitor research,
    154–156, 190–192,
    309–311
copyright filing, 360–361
customer feedback, 310,
    312
developing with
    keywords, 329–334

duplicate content, 245
dynamic tone, 299–300, 334
Engagement Objects, 25
fair use doctrine, 362
five pages per theme, 308
font selections, 321
font substitutions, 321
frequently asked
    questions (FAQs), 312
hidden text/links, 76–77
HTML code optimization,
    334–338
HTML stacking, 271–273
images, 313–315
infringing contents,
    594–595
integrating other site
    contents, 361–362
intentional spam, 351–354
international markets, 599
landing pages, 121–122,
    183–185
length suggestions,
    250–251
link bait, 330, 398
link magnets, 224, 386
local search optimization,
    356–359
margins, 320–321
Meta tag/keyword
    matching, 200–201
min words per page, 308
nicknames, 332
non-targeted, 511
noun conventions, 319
offline materials, 310–312
paragraph breaks, 319
print style sheets, 321
problem solving, 253
pronoun suggestions, 319
proofreading, 318
ranking weight, 250
reader education, 253
reader engagement, 252
refreshing, 333–334
region-specific, 357
relevancy, 331
research site keywords,
    196

contents *(continued)*
research words, 252
rich text content, 219–220
search engine results
factor, 25
siloing, 190–192
social media, 403–404
spell checking, 318
stop words, 333
styles, 301
synonyms, 251, 332–333
target audience, 252
text formatting, 251
theme resources, 251
URL parameters, 190–191
user engagement, 323–325
User Generated Content
(UGC), 321–323
videos, 315–318
Web site, 538
white space, 320–321
writing styles, 330–331
yours versus competitors
analysis, 170–171
conventions, 718–719
conversion funnels, 233,
564–566, 573, 646
conversion pages, 573
conversion rate, 98, 645
conversions
call to action, 238–239,
325–326
competitive measure,
148–149
high versus high traffic
search, 71–73
lead generation, 564
marketing campaigns,
563–564
purchase metrics, 564
target audience goal, 14
traffic versus, 149–151
user dropoff, 238–239
Web analytics, 539,
544–545, 562
Web site versus marketing
campaign, 562
cookies, 35, 347, 547, 555,
560–561, 647

Cool Savings, 61
Copains d'Avant, French
Web site, 626
copyrights, 223, 352,
360–362, 528, 593–595
Copyscape, 339, 353–354
coRank, 441
cost per click (CPC), 58–59,
652
country code top level
domain (ccTLD), 430,
475–476, 598–599, 622
Creative Commons license,
Flickr, 440
CSS content positioning, 77
CSS Validation Service, 259,
261
cultural awareness, 596,
610, 621–622
Current, 441
customer conversions, 563
customer service, 303, 312,
482

D

daily budget, 652, 704
databases. *See* content
management system
(CMS)
day parting, 31, 656–657
deceptive redirection,
spam, 78–79, 693–694
dedicated IP address, 468,
482
Delicious, 392, 399, 404, 685
delivery methods, 652
demographics. *See also*
target audience
customer surveys, 297–299
results personalization
element, 50
social networking site
research, 683
target audience, 11–12
DexKnows.com, 35
Digg, social news site, 392,
399, 404, 437–438, 441,
685

Diigo, 442
direct submissions, 525
direct type-in traffic, 479
directories
address conventions, 278
category structure,
276–281
indexes versus, 27
link acquisition, 392
local search, 358–359
Open Directory Project, 32
people-compiled, 27
relative links, 254–255,
283–284
directory structure, 231,
378–379, 515–516
directory-relative links, 379
disambiguation, 41
DISC, on-site training, 717
distribution, keywords,
130–133
Div tag, 272–273
DNSstuff, 469
Doctype, 163, 258
Dogpile.com, 36–37
domain name registrar,
474–475
Domain Name System
(DNS) servers, 501
domain names
auctions, 475
brand names, 472
concatenated words,
472–473
country-code TLDs,
475–476
direct type-in traffic, 479
feeder sites, 481
generic TLDs, 477–478
geolocating, 598
hosting providers,
481–483
hyphen (-) character,
472–473
ICANN management, 475
industry identification,
472
IP funnels, 480–481
length suggestions, 472

licensing period, 474
longevity, 473
misspelling registration, 479
part-of-speech articles, 473
placeholder sites, 472, 474–475
purchasing pre-registered, 472, 474–475
query modifier, 66
registration process, 474–475
reregistering, 474
restrictive name, 473
selection, 471–473
subdomains, 484–486
301 redirect command, 481, 488–489
underscore (_) character, 473
vanity domains, 478–479
variation registering, 478
WWW/non-WWW redirect reconciliation, 492, 494
Yahoo! Merchant Solutions, 521
domain referrals, 544
Domain.com, 474
doorway pages, 77–78, 693
double dots (..) characters, 254
duplicate content. *See also* contents
archives, 351
CMS duplication, 350–351
content management system (CMS), 510–513
content syndication, 348–349
different domain, 345–346
dynamic pages, 347–348, 512
intentional spam, 351–354
localization, 349
mirrors, 349–350
multiple URLs, 342–343
outside-your-domain, 342
own site, 344–345

printer-friendly pages, 346–347
ranking impact, 341
research resources, 343–344
scraper concern, 527
secure servers, 530
session IDs, 347–348
302 (temporary) redirect command issue, 489
within-your-domain, 342
dynamic pages, 211–212, 347–348, 510–513

E

eBay, 14
e-commerce sites
Asian markets, 611–612
keyword guidelines, 196
marketing campaign metrics, 564
Web metrics data, 536
Web site classification, 538
Yahoo! Shopping templates, 54
education (.edu) sites, 296, 392, 429–430
elephant words, 106
Elite Retreat, conferences, 709
e-mail, 359, 386, 395–397
eMarketer, 536
encryption, 530
engagement objects, 25, 185–187, 206, 227–230, 654, 676–677
Enquiro Research, Golden Triangle, 41–46
entertainment, 14–15
error pages, 543
estimators, 655–656
European Union, 621–631
exact match, 650–651
exchange rates, 595
Excite, Yahoo!, 61
exit pages, 540, 585–586
external content, 361–362

external CSS file, 163, 203–205, 216–217
external links. *See also* links
advertising links, 431–432
anchor text, 383
category structure, 281
complementary subject relevance, 426–427
expert relevance, 427–428
inbound link, 421–422
incestuous links, 423
link farms, 424
outbound links, 430
quality testimonial links, 428–429
reciprocal links, 422–423
spider invitations, 525
virtual siloing, 383

F

Facebook, 392, 404, 440, 683
fair use doctrine, 362
fast track, Yahoo! Search Marketing sign-up, 29, 61
Featured Listings, 644
federal copyrights. *See* copyrights
Federated States of Micronesia, 476, 598
feedback, 297–299, 310, 312, 323
feeder sites, 481
Feedreader, 402
file formats, 316–317
file paths, 254–255, 283–284
file references, 254–255, 283–284
file storage, 483
files
asset organization, 206
case conventions, 208
compression rates, 228
.htaccess, 496–498, 520
image naming, 313–314
interactive, 227–230

files *(continued)*
Local Shared Objects (LSOs), 561
naming, 206–208, 313
robots text, 519
robots text file, 458–461
update procedures, 231
filters, 37
Findlaw.com, 34
first-party cookies, 560–561
Flash
cross linking, 385
engagement objects, 187, 677
links, avoiding, 391
Local Shared Objects (LSOs), 561
robot detection, 208–209
Scalable Inman Flash Replacement (iSFR), 262–268
site navigation, 286–288
splash pages, 18, 209
supported video format, 316–317
user navigation, 270
Flesch-Kincaid, 319–320
Flickr, photo-sharing site, 440–441
flow charts, 376
folders, 280–281, 378–379
font tags, 164
fonts, 261–268, 321
footer navigation, 222–224
forms, 297–299, 697–700
forums, 323, 443
404 error logs, 467
404 error page, 464–467, 522
frames, 221, 270–271, 693
France, 622–623, 625–627
Free, French Web site, 626
frequently asked questions (FAQs), 312
Froogle. *See* Google Product Search
Furl, 399, 442

G

games, 398, 677
Gawker Media Network, 423
gender, audience, 10–11, 295
generic TLDs, 477–478
geographic search, 356
geographics, 543
geolocation, 598
geotargeting, 34–35, 49–50, 61, 657, 553–554
Germany, 476, 627–629
glocal, 597
Go Daddy, 474
Go2Net, Yahoo!, 61
goal continuity, 542
goals
algorithmic immunity, 138
clean code, 256–257
customers, 294–295
organizational, 541
site design, 236–237
social networking, 684
traffic versus rankings, 47
Web analytics, 538
Golden Triangle, 41–46
Google
Ad Scheduling, 656–657
AdSense, 59
advanced search operators, 66–68, 374–375
autosnippets, 245
backlink analysis, 168–169
blog search, 70–71, 312
Chrome browser, 339–340
click-through ratio (CTR), 657
day-parting, 31
duplicate content research resource, 343
Googlebot, 22
inbound link search, 422
indexed backlink search, 188
international searches, 602–603

IP blacklist search, 469
landing pages, 27, 184–185
local search, 358–359
misspelled domain names, 479
news archive search, 70
Open Directory Project (ODP), 463
opting out of results, 50–51
paid link reports, 700–703
PPC ad relevance formula, 657
PPC estimator tool, 656
Quality Score, 657–658
removing indexed content, 460
search attributes, 30–32
search engines, 9, 18–21
site map, 525
site quality, 433–434
Sitemap Protocol 0.9, 418
spam reports, 76, 432, 697
subdomains, 485
supported languages, 602
synonym resource, 332–333, 339
target audience, 11
tilde (~) character, 91, 339
Universal Search, 185
vertical search engines, 34–35
Web site analysis, 170, 172–173
Website Optimizer, 577–584
Zeitgeist, 94
Google AdWords
cost-per-click fees, 58–59
Google Keyword Tool, 373
keyword tracker, 95–96
paid results, 29, 31–32, 58–60
pay per click (PPC) ads, 647–651
Google Alert, 54
Google Analytics, 299, 372, 546–548, 584–587, 616

Google Analytics Tracking Code (GATC), 547
Google Blog Search, 55
Google Bookmarks, 685
Google China, 614–615
Google Directory, 32
Google Docs, 105
Google Jumpstart, 59
Google Keyword Tool, 373
Google Local, 34–35, 56–57
Google PageRank, 30, 32, 135–136, 390–391, 429
Google Product Search, 14
Google Reader, 402, 720
Google Trends, 94
Google Webmaster Guidelines, 433–434
Google Webmaster Tools, 470, 635
Googlebot, 22, 28
GoTo!. *See* Yahoo! Search Marketing (YSM)
government (.gov) sites, 429–430
Grippo, Argentina, 639
Grok.com, training, 722

H

hackers, 468–469
halo media, 672
header inserts, 504–508
headers, 221–222, 242–247, 493
Heading tags, 98–99, 164, 182, 201–203, 248–250, 335–336, 344, 511
Health Ranker, 442
Helicon Tech, 453, 503
hidden text/links, 76–78, 432, 692
high conversion keywords, 106–107
High Rankings, 716
high traffic keywords, 104–106
hijacking, 528–529
hits, Web metrics data, 536

Hitwise, 152, 401, 536
Home page, 222
home to purchase metrics, 564
horizontal silo, 192
hosting providers, 483, 501
HowStuffWorks, 31, 59
how-to guides, 398
.htaccess file, 496–498, 520
HTML
  absolute links, 254–255, 283–284
  body section constructs, 248–256
  clean/simple code, 203–205, 216–217, 256–257
  content management system (CMS), 516
  content stacking, 271–273
  CSS Validation Service, 259, 261
  head section constructs, 242–247
  header inserts, 504–508
  Link Checker, 259–260
  link rel=canonical tag, 493
  markup, 204
  Markup Validation Service, 258–260
  on-page factors, 670
  optimization tools, 334–338
  relative links, 254–255, 283–284
  Scalable Inman Flash Replacement (sIFR), 261–268
  SEO-compliant site, 16–17
  site maps, 415–417
  source code, 156, 162–164
  WC3 compliant code, 257–261
  widgets, 445–447
HTML Kit, 262–268
HTML/CSS editors, 262–268

http://, links, 254, 283–284
https://, secure servers, 530
humorous material, 398
hyperlinks. *See also* links
  keyword phrases, 99
  link farms, 80
  landing pages, 121–122, 183
hyphen (-), 207, 313, 472–473

I

IceWarp, Web server, 453
iframes, cross linking, 385
image formatting, 163
image maps, 269
images
  advanced searches, 69
  Alt attribute, 16, 53, 255–256, 313–315
  asset organization, 206
  body section construct, 255–256
  descriptive text placement, 313
  engagement objects, 186, 677
  file size, 314–315
  filenames, 313–314
  results page layout, 40–41
  site design, 216
  site navigation, 284–285
  vertical rankings, 53
impressions served, 543
inbound links, 345, 392, 421–422, 673
incestuous links, 423
income, audience, 10–11
indexed content, 460
indexed pages, 170
indexes versus directories, 27
indexing, data, 23
industries, competition research, 92–93

industry conferences, 707–713
industry identification, 472
industry-specific vertical search engines, 34
information-based search, 660
InfoSpace, Yahoo!, 61
infringing contents, 594–595
inline quotes, 362–363
interactive applications, 677
interactive files, 227–230
internal links. *See also* links
  category structure, 281
  duplicate content, 345
  equity optimization, 407–408
  link equity factor, 222
  siloing structure, 383–384
  spider invitations, 525
  subject theme structure, 405–407
internal site search engines, 35–36
international search engines, 693–595, 602–607, 611, 625, 629–630, 639. *See also* search engines
international sites, 486
international users, 595–607
Internet Assigned Numbers Authority (IANA), 598
Internet backbone, 483
Internet Corporation for Assigned Names and Numbers (ICANN), 475
Internet Explorer, 175–177, 298
Internet Protocol (IP) address, 452
Internet Server Application Program Interface (ISAPI_Rewrite), 453
Internet Service Provider (ISP), 359

IP addresses
  C-block, 392
  cloaking spam, 79
  dedicated IP address, 468
  hosting providers, 482
  IP blacklists, 468–469
  log file analysis, 555
  server diagnostics, 468–470
  server monitoring, 454
  virtual IP address, 468
IP blacklists, 468–469
IP delivery, cloaking, 694
IP funnels, 480–481
ISAPI_Rewrite, 453, 503–504, 514–515
italicized text, 251, 363
IWON!, search engine relationship, 18–21

J

Japan, 610–613
JavaScript
  clean/simple code, 203–205, 216–217
  content management system (CMS), 515
  cross linking, 385
  deceptive redirection, 79
  external JS file, 163
  externalizing, 268
  Google Analytics Tracking Code, 547
  hiding links, 431
  links, avoiding, 391
  multivariate testing, 560
  navigation, 270
  redirects, 491
  site navigation, 285–286
  source code, 164
  spider trap, 241
  Yahoo! Merchant Solutions, 520
JavaServer Pages (JSP), 506
John Doe Law, UK, 624
Jumptags.com, 442
Jupiter Research, 561
jurisdictions, 594–595

K

Keotag, chiclet tool, 687
key performance indicators (KPIs), 541–542
Keynote Systems, 536
Keyword Activity, 339
keyword density, 139, 156–161, 180–185
Keyword Discovery, 95, 105, 339, 373
keyword phrases
  advanced searches, 68–69
  click-through rate, 97
  conversion rate, 98
  detailed descriptive words, 98
  everyday language, 98
  heading placement, 98–99
  hypertext links, 99
  international users, 597
  Page Analyzer statistics, 137–139
  pay per click (PPC), 113, 645
  ranking factors, 308–309
  selection criteria, 97–99
  stop words, 99
  stuffing, 99
  theme consolidation, 124–127
  theme identification, 370–372
  title placement, 98
keyword rankings, 16–18
keyword research, 645, 647–649
keyword searches, 685
keyword stuffing, 79–80, 99, 695–696
keyword variables, 652
keywords
  anchor text, 122
  Asian market, 611
  audience appropriate, 103
  brainstorming, 88–89
  brand awareness, 671

brand building, 111–112, 670

categorized, 103

clarifying words, 103, 331–332

click-through rate analysis, 112–113

client niche, 93

competition research, 92–93, 154–156, 340

content, 329–334

density, 130–133

distribution, 130–133

doorway pages, 693

dynamic content, 334

e-commerce site, 196

elephant words, 106

European Union, 621–622

evaluation tools, 95–96

frequency, 130–133

`Heading` tag, 201–203

high conversion, 106–107

high traffic, 104–106

HTML code, 334–338

international markets, 599

keyword stuffing, 247

landing pages, 121, 281–283

list building, 327–329

Long Tail concept, 72–73, 113

`Meta` tag, 200–201, 247

metadata, 52

minimum bid price, 27

multi-page analyzer, 139

negative keyword list, 649–650

nicknames, 332

Page Analyzer, 134–139

people connection, 670–672

performance, 133–134

ranking monitor, 197–200

refreshing contents, 333–334

relevance, 103, 331

research tools, 196, 372–373

search engine, 117–118

search query element, 12

seasonal trends, 93–95

SEMToolBar, 175

SEO code of conduct, 81

site design, 197–201

site themes, 88–91

source code, 163

stop words, 333

subject evaluation, 329

subject outlines, 89–90

subject themes, 118–120

synonyms, 251, 332–333

target audience, 12

targeted, 103

themes, 99–103

unrelated, 695

updating, 134

Web analytics, 544

writing styles, 330–331

kirtsy, 441

Knight Ridder, Yahoo!, 61

L

landing pages

A/B testing, 573

anchor text, 122

construction, 180–185

depth of content, 121–122

keyword evaluation, 329

minimum bid, 27

pay per click (PPC) ads, 654–658

selection criteria, 281–283

siloing structure, 408, 410–411

subject categories, 121

supporting page, 308

Web analytics data, 540

language barriers, 595–596, 623, 626, 628–630, 634

Latin America, 633–639

lawsuits, 360

Lawyers.com, 34

lead generation, 538, 564

leading slash (/), 254–255, 283–284

lifestyle, audience, 296

Link Analysis Report, 394–395

link bait, 330, 386, 398–399

link buying, 189, 387

Link Checker, 259–260, 395

link equity, 187–188, 222, 497–408, 428–430

link farms, 80, 382, 391, 400, 424, 432, 630–631, 696

link magnets, 174, 224, 386, 396, 398–399

Link Popularity Check, 174

`link rel=canonical` tag, 493

link requests, 386

Link Sleuth, 259

LinkaGogo, 441–442

LinkedIn, 441, 683

links. *See also* external links; hyperlinks; internal links

A/B testing, 573

About Us, 222

absolute, 254–255, 283–284, 379–380

acquisition, 389–393

advanced search operators, 66

advertising, 431–432

anchor text, 168, 222, 253–255, 391

author credits, 363

backlinks, 30, 168–169, 281

bad neighborhoods, 424–425

blogs, 435–437

broken link discovery tools, 395

buying for ranking, 400

category-specific, 222, 224

chiclets, 438, 686–687

click maps, 587–588

community building, 442–445

competition discovery, 393–396

links *(continued)*
competitor analysis, 154–156, 168–169, 187–192
Contact Us, 222–223
content spam, 76–77
copyright information, 223
cross-linking, 384–385
directory-relative, 379
duplicate content, 345
equity formatting, 391
ethical site relationships, 382
external, 281, 383
footer navigation, 223–224
gradual acquisition, 393
Home page, 222
horizontal silo, 192
inbound, 392
incestuous, 400, 423
internal, 222, 281
IP address ranges, 392
irrelevant site solicitation, 400
keyword phrases, 99
link bait, 397–399
Link Checker, 259–260
link farms, 424
link magnets, 397–399
longevity factor, 392
naming, 288–289
natural acquisition, 382
navigation, 220–224
outbound, 430
PageRank, 390–391
paid, 396–397, 400–401, 700–703
press releases, 402–403, 673
privacy policy, 223
purchase, 382
quality testimonial, 428–429
ranking relevancy, 382
reciprocal, 387, 391, 422–423
referring links, 588–589
rel="nofollow" attribute, 192, 282, 431
relative, 254–255, 283–284,

379–380
research, 389–393
root-relative, 379
RSS feeds, 401–402
run of site, 400
search verticals, 39–40
siloing structure, 17, 122–124
social media, 392, 440–442
social networking, 438–440
social news, 437–438
solicitation, 393–397
spam, 399–400
sponsored, 27
stability factor, 392
Tab Separated Values (TSV), 188
terms of use, 223
theme-specific, 222
top-level country domains, 392
unethical site damage, 390
unique content, 392
unpaid backlink, 393–396
update procedures, 232
videos, 52
Was this helpful?, 323
Web rings, 424–425
widgets, 445–447
W3 A to Z, 258
Xenu's Link Sleuth, 259
lise.nl, Netherlands, 629
lists, 251, 327–329
local links, 599
local search engines, 34–35, 56–58, 358–359
Local Shared Objects (LSOs), 561
local terms, 596
Local.com, 35
localization, 349
locutorios, Argentina, 638
log files, 457–458, 467, 551–555
logons, 486, 530
Long Tail queries, 72–73, 113, 321, 331, 518
Los Angeles Times, Meta refresh, 490

LYCOS, 18–21
Lynx, 173

M

Mail.RU, Russia, 620
managerial consensus, 542
maps, 71, 356
margins, content, 320–321
market research, 92–93. *See also* research
marketing campaigns, 563–564
Marketing Ninjas, 715
MarketingSerpa, 722
Marketleap, 170
Marketwire, 674
Marktplaats, Netherlands, 630–631
Markup Validation Service, 258–259
markup, 204
married women, 33
marital status, 296
masked IP addresses, 555
maximum bid price, 31–32
measurement purpose, 541
MemeStreams, 442
mentors, training, 723
meta refresh commands, 78–79
Meta tags
content management system (CMS), 511, 516, 518
content optimization, 335
deceptive redirection, 693–694
header descriptions, 245–246
keyword stuffing, 247
keyword to content matching, 200–201
keywords, 247
landing page analysis, 182
Page Analyzer display, 136–137
refresh redirects, 490–491

source code, 163
spider blocking, 461–463, 527
Yahoo! Merchant Solutions, 521
Metacafe, 316, 318
Metacrawler.com, 36–37
metadata, 16–17, 52
meta refreshes, 599
metasearch engines, 36–37
Mexico, 635–637
microblogs, Twitter, 441
Micronesia, 476, 598
Microsoft AdCenter, 651
Microsoft Excel, 104–106, 156–161
Microsoft Internet Information Services (IIS)
administrator-rights, 452–453
dedicated server, 452
404 error page, 466–467
ISAPI_Rewrite plug-in, 453, 503–504
mod_rewrites, 514–515
proprietary Web server, 452–453
301 (permanent) redirect command, 499–504
version 7.0, 502
versions 5.0/6.0, 499–500
Windows Server 2008, 452
Microsoft Live Search
adCenter, 32, 62–64
advanced search operators, 67–68, 374–375
blog search, 71
cached page analysis, 174
duplicate content research resource, 344
paid link reports, 700–703
paid results, 62–64
removing indexed content, 460
search attributes, 32

search descriptions, 463
search engine, 9, 18–21
spam reports, 76, 698–699
target audience, 11
URL difference analysis, 174
Web site analysis, 174
Microsoft Visio, 376
Microsoft Word, 319–320
minimum bid price, 27
mirrors, 349–350
Mister Wong, 441–442
mod_rewrite, 514–515
Moniker, 474–475
Montenegro, 476
Moveable Type, 55, 680
Mozilla Firefox, 175–177, 192, 298, 339, 702
MSN Local, 57–58
MSN Search. *See* Microsoft Live Search
MSNbot, Microsoft Live Search spider, 28
Multi-Page Analyzer, 139, 340, 373
multivariate testing, 559–560, 573–576
music, 210, 229
MX Lookup, 469
MyBlogLog, 441
MyLinkVault, 441–442
MySpace, 404, 440, 683
MyStuff, 442
myVmarks, 442

N

Najdi.si, Slovenian search engine, 605, 607
Namecheap, 474
National Geographic, 485
Naver, South Korea, 605–606, 611, 619
negative feedback, 323

negative keyword list, 649–650
Neilsen Online, 536
Netherlands, 629–631
Netscape search, 18–21
Network Solutions, 474
networking, 711–713, 722
news, 54, 69–71
news aggregators, 401–402
News Archive Search, 70
news articles, 677
News Interactive, 31, 59
news results, 40–41
news wire services, 54
NewsIsFree, 402
newsletters, 722
niche markets, 93
nicknames, keywords, 332
9rules, 441
noindex Meta robots tag, 527
non-clickable links, 77
non-targeted content, 511
Notepad, 204, 262–269
NowPublic, 442
null tests, 559, 572

O

occupation, audience, 296
off-beat material, 398
offline materials, 310–312
Omniture, 299, 372, 548–550
123LogAnalyzer, 554
online archives, 35–36
online predators, 624
online quizzes, 446
Open Directory Project (ODP), 32, 463
open source, 13
operators, 66–71, 374–375
Opinion Research Corporation for Cone, Inc., 682
Orange, French, 626
order percentages, 563

organic results
  behavioral search, 49
  overlapping w/pay per
    click (PPC), 114–115
  results page, 40–41
  search engine, 28–32
  visual clues, 20, 22, 27
  Web analytics, 539
organic searches, 586–588
Organization Chart, 376
organizational goals, 541
Orkut, Brazil, 637–638
outbound links, 430
outlines, 89–90, 375–377
output, 553
Overture. *See* Yahoo!
  Search Marketing
  (YSM)
OYAX, 442

P

Page Analyzer
  competitive analysis, 340
  competitor research,
    156–161
  content optimization,
    336–338
  Flesch-Kincaid, 319–320
  frequently used words,
    336–337
  head section analysis, 336
  keywords, 134–139,
    156–161, 336–338, 373
  landing page analysis,
    180–185
  reading level, 337
page consolidation, 345
page count, 40–41
page stick and slip, 543
page views, 543, 705
PageRank, 30, 32, 176,
    390–391, 429
PagesJaune, 626
pagination, 40–41
paid links, 387, 396–397,
    400–401, 431–432,
    700–703

Paid Listings, 644
paid results, 20, 22, 27–32,
    49, 58–64, 538–540
paid search marketing. *See*
    pay per click (PPC) ads
paragraph breaks, 319
parameters, URL, 190–191
part-of-speech articles, 473
pathing, Web analytics, 540,
    587–588
pay per click (PPC) ads
  A/B testing, 661
  account history, 657
  ad groups, 658
  ad placements, 644
  ad specifications, 652–653
  avoiding, 646
  bid amounts, 655–656
  bidding process, 109
  brand building, 111–112
  brand reinforcement, 662
  call to action, 653–654
  click fraud, 704–705
  clickthrough rate (CTR),
    654, 657
  conversion funnel, 646
  conversion reports,
    584–585
  conversion testing, 645
  cookies, 647
  cost per click (CPC), 652
  daily budget, 652
  day parting, 656–657
  delivery methods, 652
  engagement objects, 654
  estimator tools, 655–656
  European Union, 622–623
  geotargeting, 657, 663–664
  immediate results, 645
  information-based search,
    660
  keyword click-through
    rate analysis, 112–113
  keyword phrase testing,
    645
  keyword research, 645,
    647–649
  keyword variables, 652

  landing pages, 654–656,
    658
  market coverage, 659–661
  match types, 649–650
  negative keyword lists,
    649
  overlapping w/natural
    keyword rankings,
    114–115
  pricing guidelines,
    655–658
  qualified visitors, 645
  Quality Score, 657–658
  ranking systems, 657
  relevance, 658
  return on investment
    (ROI), 645–646
  search engines, 10–11,
    644, 651, 664–667
  site analysis, 110–113
  site navigability, 659
  supplemental traffic,
    662–663
  theme identification, 370,
    372
  transaction-based search,
    660
  user targeting, 660
  writing/testing, 653–654
period (.) character, 207,
    313
Perl programming language,
    507
permanent redirect. *See* 301
    (permanent) redirect
    command
permissions, 362
Personal Home Page (PHP)
    scripting language, 505
personal information,
    560–561
personas, 301–306, 558
persuasion, 324
photographs, 216
phrase match, 650
physical address, 223, 357
physical silos 123
PixelSilk, 211, 526

placeholder sites, 472, 474–475
PlanMaker, 105
plug-ins
  ISAPI_Rewrite, 453, 503, 514–515
  Search Status, 192, 702
  SEMToolBar, 175–177
podcasts, 206, 229
police reports, 360
polls, Web 2.0 widget, 446–447
PostOnFire, 441
PPC Conversion reports, 584–585
PR Newswire, 674
presentation layer, 513
press releases, 348–349, 399, 402–403, 599, 673–674
printer-friendly pages, 346–347
printing, 321
Privacy Policy, 223, 527
product demos, 228
product evaluations, 303
profiles, 683
prominence, keyword, 130–133
pronouns, 324
proofreading, contents, 318
proxy searches, 176
PRWeb, 402, 673
public domain, Creative Commons license, 440

Q

Q tag, 362–363
quality links, 426–428
Quality Score, 61, 657–658
queries
  advanced operators, 66–71, 374–375
  autosnippets, 245
  landing page keywords, 281–283
  Long Tail, 321, 331
  Web analytics data, 540
query strings, 512
QuestionPro, 297
QuickTime, 316
quizzes, Web 2.0 widget, 446
quotation marks ("), 362
quotes, integrating site contents, 362–363

R

Radio UserLand, 402
Rambler, Russian, 620
ranking monitors, 197–200
rankings
  anchor text, 253–255
  behavioral search, 48–51
  bounce rate, 26, 104
  competitor research categories, 154–156
  content weight, 250
  current market, 18
  duplicate content, 341
  ethical site, 382
  images, 53
  keywords, 308–309
  link equity, 187–188
  link relevancy, 382
  Meta tag keywords, 247
  news, 54
  PageRank, 429
  pay per click (PPC) ads, 114–115, 657
  results page factors, 172–173
  search engine fluctuation factors, 171–172
  SEO-compliant site, 16–17
  SERP (search engine results page), 10
  shopping, 54
  site consistency, 18
  subject themes, 17, 368–370
  Title tag, 243–245
  traffic versus, 47

vertical search engines, 52–55
videos, 52
  Web analytics, 569
ratios, 545–546
RawSugar, 442
RDF Site Summary. *See* RSS feeds
reach measurements, 542–543
Really Simple Syndication feeds. *See* RSS feeds
Realtor.com, 34
reciprocal links, 387, 391, 422–423
recordings, site design, 216
Red Hat, 453
Reddit, 399, 404, 437–438, 685
redirection technology, 81
redirects
  duplicate content, 345
  header inserts, 504–508
  IP funnels, 480–481
  JavaScript, 491
  Meta tag refresh, 490–491
  redirection status codes, 487–488
  testing, 496
  301 (permanent) redirect command, 481, 488–489, 495–508
  302 (temporary), 489, 528–529
  update procedures, 232
  WWW/non-WWW reconciliation, 492, 494
referring links, 588–589
region-specific content, 357
Register, 474
rel="nofollow" attribute, 192, 282, 431, 526–527, 702
Related searches, 40–41
relative links, 254–255
relevance, 26, 103–104, 658
repeated text, 344

research. *See also* market research
competitor categories, 154–156
competitor's size analysis, 169–170
content words, 252
customer interviews, 297–299
duplicate content resources, 343–344
industry, 92–93
keyword research tools, 372–373
link analysis, 168–169
links, 389–393
Page Analyzer, 156–161
pay per click (PPC) ads, 645, 647–649
search engine use, 13
Site Checker, 164–167
site design element, 216
social networking site, 683
research sites, 196
resolutions, 42, 315, 317–318
response metrics, 544
response time, 26
results pages
architecture factors, 26
behavioral search impact, 48–51
blended searches, 43–46
bounce rate, 26, 104
browser resolutions, 42
by location, 49–50
content factors, 25
demographics, 50
Golden Triangle, 41–46
high ranking factors, 172–173
layout elements, 39–41
organic results, 27
placement rankings, 10
popularity factors, 26
response time factor, 26
spam, 48
sponsored links, 27
traffic versus rankings, 47
Web history, 50

retention metrics, 545–546
return on investment (ROI), 563–646
reverse DNS lookup, 551–552
reviews, 321–323
RewriteCond, 514
RewriteRule, 514
rich media, 654
Rich Site Summary. *See* RSS feeds
rich text content, 219–220
robots
blocking, 458–463
Flash animation, 208–209
Robots Exclusion Protocol (REP), 458–461
Robots Exclusion Protocol (REP), 458–461
robots text file, 164–165, 458–461, 519, 527
Roost.com, 34
root-relative links, 379
RSS feeds, 54–55, 348–349, 401–402
Ruby on Rails, 508
rules, 516, 571–572, 594
Russia, 619–620

S

sales per visitor, 563
sans serif fonts, 321
Sawmill, 554
scalability, 483, 554
Scalable Inman Flash Replacement (iSFR), 248, 262–268
scrapers, 352–353, 527–528
Search box, 39–40, 224–226
Search Engine Land, 720
search engine optimization (SEO), 11
Search Engine Optimization/KSP, 95
Search Engine Relationship Chart, 386
search engine results page (SERP). *See* results pages

Search Engine Roundtable, 720
Search Engine Strategies (SES), 708
search engines. *See also* international search engines
advanced search operators, 66–71, 374–375
AOL, 33
Asian market, 611
Ask.com, 33
behavioral, 35
click fraud, 704–705
depth of content, 121–122
development, 9
directories versus indexes, 27
duplicate content research, 343–344
dynamic URL treatment, 512
Google, 28, 30–32
indexing, 23
industry-specific, 34
internal site, 35–36
JavaScript, 491
keyword id, 117–118
link rel=canonical tag, 493
local search, 34–35, 55–58, 356–359
Meta refresh, 490–491
metasearch engines, 36–37
Microsoft Live Search, 28, 32
notability versus accuracy of information, 13
opting out of personalization, 50–51
organic results, 20, 22, 27
paid link reports, 700–703
paid results, 20, 22, 27
PPC (pay per click), 10–11, 109–115, 644
ranking fluctuation factors, 171–172

relationship charts, 18–21
removing indexed
    content, 460
research resource, 13
search by percentage
    rankings, 31
SEO (search engine
    optimization), 11
SEO code of conduct, 81
SEO Code of Ethics, 82–83
SERP (search engine
    results page), 10
shopping resource, 13–14
shopping sites, 14
spam avoidance, 48
spam reports, 696–700
spider blocking, 458–463
spider invitations,
    524–528
spidering, 22, 25
sponsored links, 27
static URL preference, 512
stolen content report, 359
subdomain treatment,
    485–486
synonym trigger, 91, 339
target audience, 10–12
301 redirect, 489, 495–496
302 redirect, 489
vertical, 34–35
vertical rankings, 52–55
Web analytics, 544
Yahoo!, 28–30
search history, 35, 50
Search Marketing Expo
    (SMX), 708
Search Status, 192, 702
Search Submit Pro (SSP),
    29–30
search to purchase metrics,
    564
search traffic, 539
search verticals, 39–40
SearchCap, training, 722
searches. *See also* queries
  advanced operators,
    66–71, 374–375
  blended, 674–676
  blogs, 312

brand building avenues,
    672–676
geographic search terms,
    356
Google China, 614–615
high traffic versus high
    conversion, 71–73
inbound links, 422
indexed backlinks, 188
information-based, 660
international users,
    602–607
IP blacklist, 469
keyword element, 12
landing page keywords,
    281–283
local search, 356–359
logical local search, 356
map searches, 356
SEMToolBar, 176
synonym trigger, 91, 339
transaction-based, 660
Web analytics data, 540
seasonal campaigns,
    664–667
seasonal trends, 93–95
secure contents, 486
secure servers, 530–532
segmentation tests, 559, 572
self service, 29, 61, 539
SEMpdx, 708
SEMPO Institute, 714–715,
    719
SEMToolBar, 173, 175–177,
    189, 607
sensory words, 324
SEO code of conduct, 81
SEO Code of Ethics, 82–83
SEO Newsletter, 722
SeoDigger, 372
SEOToolSet
  advanced training,
    716–719
  keyword tools, 95, 105
  Link Analysis Report,
    394–395
  ranking monitor, 198–200
  SEMToolBar integration,
    177

serif fonts, 321
server capacity, 483
server layer, 513
server logs, 299, 551–555
servers
  Apache HTTP, 452
  AppWeb, 453
  Barracuda, 453
  Cherokee, 453
  chip speed, 458
  cloaking, 457
  dedicated IP address, 468
  diagnostics tools, 454–457
  404 error pages, 464–467
  hosting providers,
    481–483
  IceWarp, 453
  improper redirect, 453
  IP address, 454, 468–470
  IP blacklists, 468–469
  logs, 457–458
  Microsoft IIS, 452–453
  performance, 457–458
  processing speeds,
    453–454
  Red Hat, 453
  response time factors, 26
  robots text file, 164–165
  script errors, 453
  secure server, 530–532
  Site Checker analysis,
    164–167
  spider blocking, 458–463
  status codes, 165–167,
    455–457
  Sun Java System, 453
  301 redirect, 488–489
  302 redirect, 489
  virtual IP address, 468
  Yaws, 453
server-side scripts, 298
ServiceMagic.com, 34
session Ids, 347–348, 511,
    513, 562
Seznam, Czech, 605–606
shadow page/domains,
    78–79
shared IP addresses, 482
ShareThis, 688–689

shopping, 13–14, 54
Shopping.com, 14
side navigation, 221, 224
siloing
    absolute versus relative
        links, 379–389
    article pages, 408, 411–414
    category structure, 276–281
    content, 190–192
    creating, 408–414
    directory structure,
        378–379
    horizontal silo, 192
    index page, 410–411
    internal linking structure,
        383–384
    landing pages, 282–283,
        408, 410–411
    link naming conventions,
        288–289
    maintenance items,
        414–415
    physical versus virtual,
        123, 381
    rel="nofollow"
        attribute, 526–527
    site maps, 415–417
    subject themes, 17, 122–
        124, 377–385, 405–407
    subpages, 408, 411–414
similarities, 144
Site Checker, 164–167
site design
    asset organization,
        205–206
    background music, 210
    benchmarking, 197
    call to action, 238–239,
        325–326
    category structure,
        276–281
    clean/simple source code,
        203–205, 216–217
    content styles, 301
    content types, 196–197
    dynamic tone, 299–300
    dynamic Web sites,
        211–212
    embedding files, 227–230

engagement objects,
    226–230
expansion allowance,
    230–231
file naming, 206–208, 313
footer navigation, 222–224
frames, 270–271
Heading tag, 201–203
keyword selections,
    197–201
KISS concepts, 208–211
Meta tag/keyword
    matching, 200–201
navigation, 220–224,
    269–271
page goals, 236–237
preplanning, 215–216
procedure checklist,
    212–213
ranking monitors, 197–200
research elements, 216
rich text content, 219–220
Scalable Inman Flash
    Replacement (sIFR),
    261–268
Search box, 224–226
side navigation, 221, 224
spider-friendly code,
    216–217
styles, 218–219
target audience, 301–306
themes, 218–219
top navigation, 221–222
updates, 231–232
usability/conversion
    balancing, 232–239
Site Explorer, 66
site maintenance, 488–489
site maps, 223, 344, 405,
    415–417, 522, 525–526
site navigability, 659
site usability, 557–562
Sitemap Protocol, 418–420
sites
    advanced search operator,
        66
    IP blacklists, 468–469
Skyrock, French, 626–627
Slashdot, tech reviews, 350

slogans, 344
Slurp, Yahoo! spider, 28
Small Business Marketing
    Unleashed, 709
Smart Solutions, PixelSilk,
    211
social bookmarking sites,
    685–689
social media sites
    bad publicity, 682
    community building,
        682–683
    content submissions,
        403–404
    link building, 440–442
    site interest generation, 392
    subdomains, 484–486
social networking sites
    brand building, 683–685
    community building,
        442–445
    link building, 438–440
    profiles, 683
    U.K. concerns, 624
social news sites, 437–438
sounds, 229
source code
    clean/simple, 203–205,
        216–217
    CSS Validation Service,
        259, 261
    doc type declarations, 258
    externalizing, 268
    Link Checker, 259–260
    Markup Validation
        Service, 258–260
    on-page optimization, 241
    optimization tools,
        334–338
    spider-friendly design,
        216–217
    viewing, 156, 162–164
    W3C compliant, 257–261
source links, 599
South Korea, 610, 618–619
spaces, file naming, 207, 313
spam
    Asian market, 612
    avoiding, 48

bad neighborhoods, 424–425
black hat techniques, 81
call to action, 326
cloaking, 79, 694
clueless newbies, 353
CSS positioning, 77, 273
deceptive redirection, 78–79, 693–694
described, 75–76
doorway pages, 77–78, 693
frames, 693
Google reports, 432
hidden text/links, 76–78, 432, 692
incestuous links, 423
IP blacklists, 468–469
keywords, 79–80, 695–696
link farms, 80, 424, 432, 696
link solicitation, 399–400
Meta tag, 490–491
meta refresh, 78–79
multi-hyphenated domain names, 473
Netherlands, 630
non-clickable links, 77
Page Analyzer, 137
paid link reports, 700–703
purchased links, 382
recognition signs, 691–692
reporting, 76
scrapers, 352–353
search engine reports, 696–700
SEO code of conduct, 81
SEO Code of Ethics, 82–83
stolen content, 353–354
unrelated keywords, 79, 695
white text/links, 77–78, 432
spamdexing. *See* spam
Spartacus Order, UK, 624–625
special offer to purchase metrics, 564
speeches, 228–229
speeds, 554

spelling checkers, 318
spelling/grammar, 596
Sphinn, 720
spider traps, 241
spidering, data, 22, 25
spiders
  blocking, 458–463
  coding practices, 216–217
  doorway pages, 693
  Flash animation, 208–209
  indexing, 526
  log file analysis, 555
  Meta tag exclusion, 527
  ranking factors, 526–527
  rel="nofollow" attribute, 526–527
  response time factors, 26
  robots text file exclusion, 527
  scrapers, 527–528
  search engines, 28–32
  secure server, 530
  site invitations, 524–528
  user-agent sniffing, 528
  white lists, 527–528
splash pages, 18, 209
sponsored links, 27, 40–41, 644
Sponsored Listings, 644
spreadsheets, 104–106, 156–161
Spurl, 442
StatCounter, 550
static URL, 512
status codes, 165–167, 455–457
stock market tickers, 447
stolen content, 353–354, 359–360. *See also* contents
stop words, 99, 184, 333
storage, 483
studiVZ, German, 628
StumbleUpon, 399, 404, 437–438, 685
style sheets, 163, 259, 261, 321, 346–347

styles, 218–219, 301
subdomains, 484–486, 600–601
subject outlines, 89–90
subject themes. *See also* themes
  category, 118–120
  depth of content, 121–122
  internal link structure, 405–407
  keyword rankings, 17
  keyword research tools, 372–373
  landing pages, 121
  link building, 385–387
  outlining, 375–377
  pay-per-click (PPC) programs, 370, 372
  ranking factors, 368–370
  siloing, 377–385, 405–407
  sub-theme identification, 367–375
  tracked keyword, 370, 372
  Web analytics, 370, 372
subjects, 104–107
submissions, 525
subpages, 408, 411–414
success rates, 144
suggestions, 41
summaries, 362
Sun Microsystems, 453
SuperPages.com, 35
surveys, 297–299, 637
Symantec Expression Equivalency Document (SEED) process, 597
syndication, 348–349
synonym search, 91, 339
synonyms, 251, 289, 332–333

T

Tab Separated Values (TSV) links, 188
Table tag, 271–272

tactics, 144
target audience. *See also*
    demographics
  age, 295
  behavioral search, 48–51
  beliefs, 296
  blog identification, 681
  client niche keywords, 93
  content matching, 252
  content styles, 301
  conversions, 14
  current customer data
    analysis, 295–296
  customer interviews,
    297–299
  day-parting, 31
  demographics, 11–12
  dynamic tone, 299–300
  education, 296
  entertainment interest,
    14–15
  European Union, 621–622
  gender, 295
  geotargeting, 49–50
  goal recognition, 294–295
  income level, 10–11
  international users,
    595–599
  lifestyle, 296
  location, 296
  log file analysis, 553, 555
  married women, 33
  marital status, 296
  occupation, 296
  personas, 301–306
  reading level, 319–320
  research-oriented users,
    13
  shoppers, 13–14
  site design, 218–219
  surveys, 297–299
  Web history, 50
targeted phrases, 103
Tealeaf, Web metrics, 536
Technorati, 441
templates, 211–212, 349,
    510
Tencent, 31, 59

terms of use link, 223
Terms of Use, 527
Terra, Argentina, 639
testimonial links, 428–429
testing, 721–722
text, 52–53, 299–300
text based navigation, 270
text editors, 204, 262–268
text formatting, 163, 251
text links, 220–224
TextEdit, 262–268
themes. *See also* subject
    themes
  consolidating, 124–127
  content resources, 251
  keyword brainstorming
    sessions, 88–89
  keyword rankings, 17
  reinforcing, 99–103
  site design, 218–219
  site planning, 88
  subject identification,
    367–375
  subject outlines, 89–90
  supporting page, 308
theme-specific links, 222
301 (permanent) redirect
    command
  Apache servers, 496–498
  duplicate content, 345
  feeder sites, 481
  header inserts, 504–508
  international markets, 599
  Microsoft IIS servers,
    499–504
  search engine treatment,
    489, 495–496
  testing, 496
  use guidelines, 488–489
302 (temporary) redirect
    command, 489, 528–529
thesaurus, 332
third-party cookies,
    560–561
tilde (~) character, 91, 339
time on page, 543
time search took, 40–41

`Title` tag
  brand placement, 111
  character limitations, 244
  CMS concerns, 511
  content management
    system (CMS), 516, 518
  content optimization, 335
  duplicate content, 344
  head section construct,
    242–245
  keyword phrase, 98
  keyword-rich, 244–245
  landing page, 182
  Page Analyzer, 136–137
  uniqueness, 244
  Yahoo! Merchant
    Solutions, 521
titles, 137–138, 163, 182
Tom.com, China, 615
T-Online, 31, 59
Top 10 lists, link bait, 398
top level domains, 392,
    429–430, 475–478,
    598, 622
top navigation, 221–222
Top Trends report, 94
tours, 228
tracked keyword, 370–372
tracking data, 539–541
traffic, 47, 71–73, 113,
    149–151, 479, 539, 542
training courses, 713–718,
    723
transaction-based search,
    660
translations, 596–597
treaties, copyright, 594
Trellian, 373
TrueLocal.com, 35
trusted authorities, 720
tutorials, 262–268
Tuvalu, 476, 598
TweetBeeps, 685
Twilert, 685
Twitter, 392, 393, 441,
    443–444, 683, 685

U

U.S. Copyright Office, 361
Ubbi, Argentina, 639
underscore (_) character, 207, 313, 473
uniform resource locator (URL), 173, 190–191, 278, 313–314, 342–343, 511, 513–514
United Kingdom, 476, 623–625
United States, 476
Universal Copyright Convention, 361, 595
Universal Search, 185
UNIX/LINUX servers, 204
unrelated keywords, 79, 695
Uol, Argentina, 639
updates, 18, 231–232
uptime, providers, 482
urlset tags, 419
usability, 233–235, 609–610
user forums, 323
User Generated Content (UGC), 321–323
user search history, 35, 50
user testing, 303
User-Agent HTTP header, 79
user-agent sniffing, 528
UTF-8 (Unicode), 599

V

vanity domains, 478–479, 488
verbs, 323–326
vertical search engines, 34–35
videos
  advanced searches, 69
  asset organization, 206
  compression rates, 228
  descriptive text, 52–53, 315
  directory paths, 315–317
  embedding, 228, 316–317
  engagement objects, 186–187, 228, 677
  file size, 315, 317
  interviews, 228
  keywords, 52
  length, 315, 318
  links, 52, 398–399
  placement, 315–316
  playback, 315
  posting to video-sharing sites, 316, 318
  product demos, 228
  quality concerns, 315, 317–318
  rankings, 52
  site design, 215
  speeches, 228
  supported formats, 316–317
  tours, 228
  YouTube, 15
View Text mode, 173
Vindex.nl, Netherlands, 629–630
viral marketing, 386
virtual IP address, 468
virtual silos, 124, 484–486
vision-impaired users, 314
visitors, 539, 542–543, 585–588
visual design, 597
vocal culture, 596
Voila, France, 625

W

Wal-Marting Across America, 678
Was this helpful? link, 323
Web analytics
  A/B testing, 558–559, 571–584
  abandonment rates, 585–586
  acquisition metrics, 543–544
  bounce data, 541
  click maps, 587–588
  ClickTracks, 551
  conversion funnels, 564–566
  conversion metrics, 544–545
  conversion tracking, 562–567
  cookies, 560–561
  exit pages, 540
  goal setting, 538
  Google Analytics, 546–548
  home to purchase metrics, 564
  key performance indicators (KPIs), 541–542
  landing pages, 540
  lead generation, 564
  log files, 551–555
  marketing, 563–564
  multivariate testing, 559–560, 573
  null tests, 559, 572
  Omniture Site Catalyst, 548–550
  pathing, 540, 587–588
  personas, 558
  rankings, 569
  reach measurements, 542–543
  referring links, 588–589
  response metrics, 544
  retention metrics, 545–546
  search queries, 540
  search to purchase metrics, 564
  segmentation tests, 559, 572
  SEO project tracking, 568
  session IDs, 562
  site classifications, 538–539
  site usability, 557–562
  site-level data, 537
  special offer to purchase metrics, 564
  StatCounter, 550

Web Analytics *(continued)*
  theme identification, 370, 372
  tracking data, 539–541
  Web analytics, 566
  Web metrics numbers, 536
  Web page objectives, 567
  WebTrends, 551
Web Analytics Association, 299
Web history, 50
Web log. *See* blogs
Web Marketing Today, 722
Web metrics, 536
Web Page Analyzer, 458
Web pages
  competitor, 154–156
  doorway pages, 77–78
  engagement objects, 185–187
  landing page, 180–185
  link bait, 330
  link equity, 187–188
  link rel=canonical tag, 493
  Meta tag, 490–491
  mirroring, 349–350
  objective assignments, 567
  on-page, 241
  printing, 321
  source code, 156, 162–164
  W3C compliant, 257–261
Web rings, 424–425
Web servers. *See* servers
Web site consistency, 18
Web site design. *See* site design
Web sites
  A1-Webmarks, 442
  ad:tech, 708
  adCenter, 62
  addedbytes.com cheat sheets, 515
  Alexa, 401
  algorithmic immunity, 138
  Ask.com, 76
  Associated Content, 441

bad neighborhoods, 424–425
Baidu, 611
Bazaarvoice, 322
Beanstalk Search Engine Positioning, Inc., 717
Bibsonomy, 441
Big Mouth Media Newsletter, 722
Blendtec, 228
BlinkList, 442
BloggingZoom, 441
Blogoria, 442
BookmarkTracker, 442
Brazilian Internet Steering Committee, 637
Bruce Clay's Search Engine Relationship Chart, 20
BuddyMarks, 442
canonical page, 492–493
Check Server tool, 454
Chrome, 339
ClickTracks, 372, 551
ClipClip, 441
CNN, 319
Collarity, 35
Compete, 152
comScore, 401
Connectedy, 442
content siloing, 190–192
Copains d'Avant, 626
Copyscape, 339
coRank, 441
Creative Commons license, 440
Current, 441
Delicious, 399
Digg, 399
Diigo, 442
DISC, 717
DNSstuff, 469
Domain.com, 474
Elite Retreat, 709
eMarketer, 536
Engagement Objects, 25
Enquiro Research, 42
ethical relationships, 382

Facebook, 404
Feedreader, 402
Flickr, 440
Free, 626
Furl, 399
Gawker, 400
Gawker Media Network, 423
Go Daddy, 474
Google AdWords, 58
Google Alert, 54
Google Analytics, 299
Google Bookmarks, 685
Google blog search, 312
Google Keyword Tool, 373
Google Local, 56
Google News Archive, 70
Google Reader, 402
Google site search, 226
Google spam reports, 76, 432
Google Trends, 94
Google Webmaster Guidelines, 173, 433–434
Google Webmaster Tools, 470
Google Zeitgeist, 94
Grippo, 639
Grok.com, 722
Health Ranker, 442
Helicon Tech, 453
High Rankings, 716
Hitwise, 152
hosting providers, 481–483
IANA (Internet Assigned Numbers Authority), 598
ICANN (Internet Corporation for Assigned Names and Numbers), 475
IP checker tools, 469
Jumptags.com, 442
Keotag, 687
Keynote Systems, 536
Keyword Activity, 339

Keyword Discovery, 95, 105, 339, 373
kirtsy, 441
Link Checker, 395
Link Popularity Check, 174
LinkaGoGo, 441
LinkedIn, 441, 683
Los Angeles Times, 490
Mail.RU, 620
Marketing Ninjas, 715
MarketingSerpa, 722
Marketleap, 170
Marketwire, 674
Marktplaats, 630
MemeStreams, 442
Metacafe, 316
Metacrawler, 37
Microsoft, 503
Microsoft adCenter, 651
Microsoft blog search, 71
Microsoft Live Search, 76
Mister Wong, 441
Moniker, 474
Movable Type, 680
Mozilla Firefox, 339
MSN Local, 57
MX Lookup, 469
MyBlogLog, 441
MyLinkVault, 441
MySpace, 404, 440, 683
MyStuff, 442
myVmarks, 442
Najdi.si, 605
Namecheap, 474
National Geographic, 485
Naver, 605
Neilsen Online, 536
Network Solutions, 474
NewsIsFree, 402
9rules, 441
NowPublic, 442
Omniture, 299, 372
123LogAnalyzer, 554
Open Directory Project (ODP), 463
Opinion Research Corporation for Cone,

Inc., 682
Orange, 626
Orkut, 637
OYAX, 442
Page Analyzer, 135
PagesJaune, 626
PostOnFire, 441
PR Newswire, 674
PRWeb, 402, 673
QuestionPro, 297
Radio UserLand, 402
Rambler, 620
RawSugar, 442
Reddit, 399, 685
Register, 474
Sawmill, 554
Scalable Inman Flash Replacement (iSFR), 262
Search Engine Land, 720
Search Engine Optimization/KSP, 95
Search Engine Relationship Chart, 386
search engine result factors, 25–26
Search Engine Roundtable, 720
Search Engine Strategies (SES), 708
Search Marketing Expo (SMX), 708
Search Status, 192, 702
SearchCap, 722
SEMpdx, 708
SEMPO Institute, 714–715
SEMToolBar, 173
SEO (search engine optimization), 11
SEO Code of Ethics, 82
SEO Newsletter, 722
SEO-compliant, 16–17
SeoDigger, 372
SEOToolSet, 95, 105
SEOToolSet Training, 716
Separated by a Common Language blog, 623
server status codes, 455

Seznam, 605
ShareThis, 688
siloing structure, 17, 122–124
Site Explorer
Sitemap Protocol, 418
Skyrock, 626
Slashdot, 350
Small Business Marketing Unleashed, 709
Sphinn, 720
spider invitations, 524–528
Spurl, 442
StatCounter, 550
studiVZ, 628
StumbleUpon, 399, 685
Tealeaf, 536
Technorati, 441
Terra, 639
Tom.com, 615
TweetBeep, 685
Twilert, 685
Twitter, 399, 441, 683
U.S. Copyright Office, 361
U.S. government copyrights, 594
Ubbi, 639
Uol, 639
UsabilityEffect, 237
Vindex.nl
Voila, 625
Web Analytics Association, 299
Web Marketing Today, 722
Web Trends, 372
Weblog Expert, 554
WebmasterWorld PubCon, 708
Website Optimizer, 577
WebTrends, 551
WHOIS Lookup, 359
Whois.net, 474
Wikipedia, 672
WordPress, 485, 680
Wordtracker, 95, 105, 339
W3C (World Wide Web Consortium), 165, 258

Web sites *(continued)*
Xanga, 683
XE, 595
Xenu's Link Sleuth, 259
Yahoo! blog search, 71
Yahoo! Bookmarks, 685
Yahoo! Help system, 522
Yahoo! Local, 57
Yahoo! Merchant
 Solutions, 519
Yahoo! Search Marketing,
 60, 651
Yahoo! Shopping, 54
Yahoo! spam reporting, 76
Yahoo's Top Trends
 report, 94
Yandex, 604
Yattle, 442
Yelp, 322
Yigg, 628
YouTube, 52, 316, 399, 439
YouTube Mexico, 636
Zappos, 444
Web Trends, 372
Web 2.0, 445–447
Weblog Expert, 554
Webmasters, 393–397
WebmasterWorld PubCon,
 708
WebMD, medical search
 engine, 34
Website Optimizer, 577–584
WebTrends, 551
white hat, 80
white lists, 527–528
white space, 320–321
white text/links on a white
 background, 77–78
WHOIS Lookup, 359
Whois.net, 474–475
widgets, 445–447, 677,
 688–689
Wikipedia, 13, 672
wikis, 672

Windows Media, 316
Windows Server 2008, 452
WordPress, 55, 211, 485, 680
Wordtracker, 95, 105, 339
World Wide Web
 Consortium (W3C)
code standards, 257–261
CSS Validation Service,
 259, 261
Link Checker, 259–260
Markup Validation
 Service, 258–260
redirection status codes,
 488
server status codes,
 165–167, 455–457
World Wide Web, non-
 WWW domain redirect
 reconciliation, 492, 494
writing tone, 299–300
written materials, 215,
 310–312

Xanga, 683
XE, currency converter, 595
Xenu's Link Sleuth, 259
XML site maps, 405,
 418–420, 525–526

y

Yahoo!
 advanced search, 66–68,
 374–375
 Asian market, 611
 backlink, 168–169, 174, 188
 blog search, 71
 cached page analysis, 174
 click-throughs, 61
 duplicate content, 344
 inbound link search, 422

international searches, 604
paid link reports, 700–703
PPC estimator tool, 655
removing indexed
 content, 460
search attributes, 28–30
search engine, 9, 18–21
Search Submit Pro (SSP)
 Trusted Feed, 29–30
Site Explorer, 66
spam reports, 76, 698
Top Trends report, 94
URL difference, 174
Web site analysis, 174
Yahoo! Bookmarks, 685
Yahoo! Directory, 30, 463
Yahoo! Local, 34–35, 57
Yahoo! Merchant Solutions,
 519–522
Yahoo! Search Marketing
 (YSM), 29, 60–62, 651
Yahoo! Search Technology,
 11, 30
Yahoo! Shopping, 14, 54
Yandex (Yet Another
 iNDEXer), Russian,
 604–605, 619–620
Yattle, 442
Yaws, Web server, 453
YellowBook.com, 35
YellowPages.com, 35
Yelp, online reviews, 322
Yigg, German, 628–629
YouTube, 15, 52, 316–318,
 399, 439
YouTube Mexico, 636–637

Z

Zappos, 444
Zeitgeist, Google, 94
Zhu, Jianfei, spam, 612
Zillow.com, 34
ZIP codes, 34–35